Proximity

PHAENOMENOLOGICA

COLLECTION FONDÉE PAR H.L. VAN BREDA ET PUBLIÉE
SOUS LE PATRONAGE DES CENTRES D'ARCHIVES-HUSSERL

87

Proximity
Levinas, Blanchot, Bataille and Communication

JOSEPH LIBERTSON

Proximity
Levinas, Blanchot, Bataille and
Communication

1982

MARTINUS NIJHOFF PUBLISHERS
THE HAGUE/BOSTON/LONDON

Distributors:

for the United States and Canada

Kluwer Boston, Inc.
190 Old Derby Street
Hingham, MA 02043
USA

for all other countries

Kluwer Academic Publishers Group
Distribution Center
P.O. Box 322
3300 AH Dordrecht
The Netherlands

Library of Congress Cataloging in Publication Data

Libertson, Joseph.
    Proximity, Levinas, Blanchot, Bataille, and
communication.

    (Phaenomenologica ; 87)
    Includes bibliographical references.
    1. Communication--Philosophy. 2. Levinas,
Emmanuel. 3. Blanchot, Maurice. 4. Bataille,
Georges, 1897-1962. I. Title. II. Series.
P90.L43   001.51'01   81-18999
ISBN 90-247-2506-2   AACR2

ISBN 90 247 2506 2 (this volume)
ISBN 90 247 2339 6 (series)

PRINTED IN THE NETHERLANDS

CONTENTS

INTRODUCTION

The problematic reality of an alterity implicit in the concept of communication has been a consistent attestation in formal discourse. The rapport of thought to this alterity has been consistently described as a radical inadequation. By virtue of the communicational economy which produces discontinuity and relation, illumination and the possibility of consciousness, an opacity haunts the familiarity of comprehension. Consciousness' spontaneity is limited by the difference or discontinuity of the exterior thing, of the exterior subject or intersubjective other, and of the generality of existence in its excess over comprehension's closure. An element implicit in difference or discontinuity escapes the power of comprehension, and even the possibility of manifestation. Within the system of tendencies and predications which characterizes formal discourse, however, this escape of alterity is most often understood as an escape which proceeds from its own substantiality: the unknowable in-itself of things, of subjects, and of generality. Alterity escapes the power of comprehension, on the basis of its power to escape this power. That which escapes the effectivity of consciousness, escapes on the basis of its own effectivity. For this reason, the rapport of inadequation described by the escape may function in formal discourse as a correlation. The inadequation of comprehension and exteriority may function as the vicissitude of a larger adequation. The latent principles of this adequation are power and totalization. When the difference of exteriority is subordinated to its in-itself, this in-itself may function as an autonomy whose escape is an action limiting comprehension. The anti-intellectualism of modern philosophy has correctly pointed out the reduction of alterity implicit in this configuration. The alterity which escapes totalization or comprehension on the basis of its autonomy and its power to escape, is an alterity designed in the image of the Same. Its escape describes a higher power, in a universe exhausted by the notion of power. The totality which governs the inadequation of Same and Other tends to function, in philosophy and religion, precisely as the totality of this correlation: a totality defined as a higher power and a higher truth. Thus this totality or generality of communication itself describes the image of comprehension's autonomy and spontaneity. Since inadequation is a function of a larger correlation, the distinction of Same and Other is lost. The alterity of the Other is reduced.

1

The ambivalence which attests a dissymetry or inadequation in order to subsume this inadequation within a larger adequation or correlation, is a perennial and uneliminable moment of the economy of thought. But this moment does not exhaust this economy. The proposition of an escaping alterity which frustrates certainty while leaving intact the inadequate but familiar dimension of comprehension, is not the only experience of thought. The self-critical attestation of alterity's excess indicates another fundamental experience, which characterized the rooting of philosophy and science in myth and religion prior to the modern era, and which characterizes the most virulent anti-intellectualism of modern thought. This is the experience of alterity's excess as a communicational moment which affects or changes thought. Myth, magic, religion, the history of art and literature, and the informal discourse of the everyday have traditionally attested an escape of alterity which is also an alteration of thought, and which therefore concerns or weighs upon subjectivity in a communicational moment which is not yet or no longer comprehension. This altering incumbence of exteriority remains subordinate, in formal discourse and in what is called "common sense", to the proposition of a higher or "other" power which compromises the complacency of thought. The great anti-intellectualists of modern thought, including Nietzsche, Proust and Freud, have sought to give formal meaning to consciousness' experience of an incumbence of alterity in a dimension outside manifestation — this experience being irreducible to the correlation of Same and Other as power and superior power which has characterized the West's thinking of communication. The common denominator which links these thinkers and which produces the provocative or controversial aspect of their texts, is their refusal to characterize alterity as a power or effectivity, and their concomitant tendency to thematize subjectivity itself as a radical passivity or heteronomy: not a dependence upon another power, but a pure passivity in a reality without power. The modern philosophy of communication, particularly in psychoanalysis and in the philosophy of difference, attests the approach of a powerless element over which consciousness nevertheless has no power — an element which changes and concerns thought on the basis of its very passivity and inactuality. This element is an alteration without being an effectivity, and its immemorial approach to interiority defines the latter as a preoriginary alteration. Formal discourse, through this provocative, unequal, and often ambivalent attestation, has rejoined a perennial current of human curiosity to which the exigencies of certainty in the modern era have been essentially allergic, but to which the fascinated movements of informal discourse have always been attracted: the problem of subjectivity as passivity, in the approach of a concerning exterior.

The purpose of the present study is to document an involvement which links three of the most compelling texts in the twentieth century's meditation of communication, and to describe the logical universe in which this involvement has meaning. These are the theoretical texts of Georges Bataille, Maurice Blanchot, and Emmanuel Levinas. The anomaly which haunts these disparate and exceptionally private texts is the following: each of these thinkers has the capacity and the inclination to speak in the voices of the other two thinkers. This inclination is perceptible not only in the occasional thematic or lexical congruences which link these texts, but also at the most solitary level of their definitions and predications. Underneath the thematic disparity which distinguishes Bataille's world of excess, irony and violence, Blanchot's economy of impersonality and nocturnal dispersion, and the Levinasian universe of gravity, dissymetry and responsibility, a single configuration of communication insists. By virtue of this subterranean and largely unacknowledged congruence, the texts of these three thinkers describe a common inspiration. This inspiration occasionally results in direct invocations of names or concepts, as in the massive textual interference surrounding each thinker's discovery of the *il y a* — the "weakness' of the negative — during the 1940's;* or in the detour of Levinasian dissymetry which haunts Blanchot's *L'Entretien infini.*** These invocations do not, however, exhaust the sense of this inspiration. It is possible to perceive at the heart of the Levinasion *éthique* the configuration of "transgression", in its Bataillian definition, as well as Blanchot's concepts of "inspiration" and "essential solitude" — not as comparable or similar thematic tendencies, but as necessary and sufficient predicates to which oblique reference is made in the Levinasian text itself. The *éthique* is the destiny and the precise context of Bataillian transgression — and *vice versa*. Blanchotian impersonality is the precise communicational configuration which articulates the meaning of Levinasian substitution or assignation — and *vice versa*. And transgression is the precise context of impersonality and of inspiration — as Blanchot attests by placing Orpheus' transgression at the logical and thematic center of *L'Espace littéraire*. Bataille, Blanchot and Levinas are among the most private and independent of twentieth-century thinkers. Their respective indifference to the prevailing intellectual currents of their time, and the resulting marginality and lack of influence which characterize their texts, are most palpable. Yet, within this very privacy and marginality, each of these thinkers remains involved with the other two.

This involvement concerns the themes of proximity and the approach. In titles such as "Approach of the literary space", "The Book to Come", "Language and Proximity", "Sensibility and Proximity", and in the series of terms which includes *approche, proche, prochain,* etc., Blanchot and Levinas invoke the notion of a communicational alterity whose inaccessibility is also its incumbence or weight. The factor in communication which escapes totalization and recedes into indefinition or ambiguity, approaches as it escapes. Its distance is a contact, its inaccessibility is an involvement. It is "near" or "close" to the subjectivity created by communication — without this subjectivity being "near" or "close" to this inaccessible element. This approach or proximity does not appear in a physical universe of relation and correlation, but rather insists in a communi-

---

* Cf. below, Chapter 4, "Negativity and *Il y a* in Proximity".
** Cf. below, Chapter 6, *"Parole* and *Entretien".*

cational universe of irrectitude, dissymmetry, and contamination. The Other in communication is "near" — not relatively, but absolutely. Its approach is the element and the intensity of separation or differentiation in the "general" economy of inspiration and heteronomy which is described by Bataille, Blanchot, and Levinas.

This general economy produces the differentiation and discontinuity which make possible multiplicity and relation within being. But it cannot produce totalization or correlation. The negative, in this economy, is "weakened" or contaminated by the movements of a communication which forecloses the limits and intervals constitutive of autonomy and determination. Contamination, inextrication, and alteration are the necessary and sufficient predicates of closure and rapport in such a dimension. The unicity produced by communication is the paradoxical density or intensity of an involvement with exteriority. Closure is a difference: a heteronomous intrication with exterior elements, and with the radical exteriority of a communicational factor which is irreducible to the proposition of closure. And closure is a proximity: a pre-originary involvement and an uneliminable rapport with this Other of closure which has collaborated in the latter's constitution. The alterity which escapes totalization, in the "weakness" of the negative, alters the unicity which attests or experiences this escape. Such an alterity does not merely frustrate comprehension in an epistemological universe. It creates subjectivity in a universe of inspiration. As it escapes comprehension, it concerns and changes subjectivity. It does so because its powerlessness and unsubstantiality participate in the economy of alteration which is subjectivity itself. Its immemorial approach is the element of interiority's conation. The proximal terms which articulate this dispossessing investment of closure by the exterior include: solitude, impersonality, *glissement,* metamorphosis, substitution, and *écart.* These terms describe a lack of self-coincidence which implies closure's involvement with an incumbent exteriority.

When the negation which would consecrate autonomy and relation is weakened, closure becomes a radical heteronomy, and relation becomes an uneliminable, contaminating rapport. The three basic predicates of this heteronomous unicity are excess, incompletion, and the fragmentary remainder. Closure's intensity or density results from the excess of its investment by exteriority. By virtue of the force or incumbence of the alterity which collaborates in its conation, closure is excessively closed. Its turgidity is a spasm toward the exterior. In Levinas' words, its conation is an "inside-out" without an "inside". The force of its closing proceeds from the Other. Unicity is thus a desire and an exigency: the intense excess of a closure which veers toward the exterior by virtue of its immemorial involvement with the latter. In its essential solitude, unicity always approaches the Other — but this movement is a function of the Other's own approach. The proximal terms which describe this movement of excess in individuation include: transgression, *parole, dépense,* exigency, inspiration, desire, responsibility, assignation, plethora, and *pour l'autre.*

The excess of unicity is also its incompletion. No negative or dialectical interval grounds unicity as a self-coincidence which might subsequently enter into relations with exterior elements. Instead, the excess of communication produces unicity as a primordial susceptibility to the exterior itself. This radical passivity of inextrication, this involvement in an uneliminable rapport, is the subjectivity of closure, and signifies the possibility of relation in general: the effect upon closure of an exterior being. The proximal terms which describe this irreducible passivity of closure in an economy of inextrication include: exposition, experience, subjectivity, incompletion, *psychisme*, fascination, *oubli*, nudity.

Where negation and contradiction do not operate, closure is essentially *au dehors*: within the exterior, and not in a locus or position with relation to the latter. The excess and incompletion of closure produce a remainder or *reste* — a fragmentary element of unicity which remains outside. Unicity in proximity is an ex-centric heteronomy whose center of gravity is always outside itself. Yet closure or interiority is not a mere dispersion. It is an extraordinarily or exccess-ively dense unicity which is forced precisely by the gravity of exteriority. This heteronomy of closure is not a determination, not a dependence upon an exterior autonomy or upon an alterity which would itself have the form or function of an autonomy. The exterior itself is a passivity and a subjectivity which can neither limit nor destroy interiority, but which always alters the latter. The proximal terms which describe this uneliminable remainder and this ex-centricity of closure which is "outside" itself include: *parole,* fragment, trace, *il y a, sens, oeuvre, errance,* error. The general economy is a dimension whose differences, in their failure to produce totalization and correlation, produce an incessant and uneliminable noise and disturbance: the indefinite movement of the fragment within the exterior, and the forcing of closure itself "into" the exterior, as a function of its very unicity. Interiority in proximity has, in Proust's phrase, a "rendezvous with itself", outside itself — outside everything. This rendezvous, and the radical dispossession it implies, are the latent investment of interiority's very familiarity. This familiarity, in Bataille's "profane world" of prohibitions, in Levinasian *jouissance* and sensation, and in the "world" or "day" in Blanchot, can be the supporting intimacy it is, only by virtue of the Other's participation in this intimacy. And this participation implies the exterior destiny of interiority, in transgression, in recurrence, in the night. Closure's familiarity is a function of the Other's approach.

The only solitude of interiority in the absence of negation and correlation is its investment by the exterior. This investment is an inspiration: a dispossessing force which also supports and excessively fulfills. Closure's immemorial involve-ment with alterity is an excess which inclines or forces closure outward: *au dehors, pour l'autre,* toward the Other. The difference that is unicity is also a non-indifference: a congruence of vulnerability and desire which defines unicity as a paradoxical "exigency of the Other." From within, from without, alterity invests and dispossesses interiority. The "sense" of inspiration, the problematic "direction" of irrectitude and heteronomy in the general economy, is a univocal or dissymetrical "one-way" of difference: toward the Other, into the exterior. When illumination and comprehension enter the general economy as possibilities conditioned by communication, their "meaning" or truth will be a regional function of the *sens* of proximal alteration: a *sens* which is always the *sens unique* or dissymetry of communication without correlation. The proximal terms which articulate the force and univocity of inspiration in the general economy include: exigency, impression, inspiration, *essoufflement,* signification, *hauteur, courbure, dépense,* desire.

The inaccessible Other with which unicity remains involved, as a function of its latent birth in proximity, is an unsubstantial and powerless element over which unicity has no power. The Other is not a totality which might be correlated with closure; nor is it an effectivity which might determine or limit closure. It is a passivity which concerns, alters and dispossesses closure, because it invests the latter. Since alterity is neither a powerful substantiality nor a negativity, it can neither destroy nor disperse unicity. Yet it is an indefinition which grips interiority, a weakness which compels, an inexistence which seizes. Its approach is the paradoxical incumbence of an instance which will never arrive, but which cannot be stopped. Its names in the text of proximity include: image, *visage,* trace, neutrality, *il y a,* illeity, infinite, *Autrui,* Someone, the non-concerning, the non-violent, the *autrement qu'être,* the inessential, the inactual.

The subjectivity of differentiation in the general economy is the heteronomy of closure. This heteronomy results from the passivity of the economy as a whole, in its inability to produce negation, totalization, and power. Bataille, Blanchot, and Levinas invoke the same name for this general passivity: "impossibility". There is no power in the economy of communication. Consequently, there is no spontaneity and no manifestation. Receptivity in this dimension is not comprehension, but alteration and passivity. Exteriority is an inactuality toward which proximal interiority cannot be indifferent and from which no distance can be taken. In a universe of "impossibility", the principle underlying receptivity is not the spontaneity of comprehension, but rather an "inability to close the eyes", an "inability not to understand", an "inability to stop moving": the rapport of interiority with an inaccessibility of which it "cannot let go." The proximal terms which describe this heteronomous receptivity in an economy without power include: *non-savoir,* dissimulation, experience, fascination, obsession, *psychisme,* the "idea" of infinity.

The time of the Other's approach is a temporality of communication, in which all intervals are involvements and in which all discontinuity is alteration. This is a time of repetition and proximity, without spontaneity, punctuality, adequation or ekstasis. The temporal differentiations of proximity produce subjectivity as a function of their inefficiency and weakness: the lapsing, collapsing, contaminating communications which alter temporal intervals. In this proximal time, the Other's concerning escape produces an immemorial or irrecuperable past which was never present; and the Other's approach produces an imminent, compelling, eternally futural future which will never become present. The Other's altering and uneliminable incumbence produces the present as the pure passage of an element without punctuality or actuality, and as the immobile, distended incessance of a "present which does not pass". Time is a function of the Other's proximity, and is therefore a dimension of inadequation, inaccessibility, and inextrication. In time as in space, we cannot see the Other — nor can we avoid seeing the Other. Alterity is, in Blanchot's words, "an impossibility which makes itself a seeing." The proximal terms which describe the repetitive time of communication include: trace, impression, recurrence, *à venir*, imminence, event, *attente, espacement*, dephasing, lapse, senescence, *diachronie*, delay, *nouvelle origine*.

The concept of proximity in the texts of Bataille, Blanchot, and Levinas describes a theory of separation and of communication. The enigma of a closure which has the capacity or inclination to be affected by the exterior, animates this theory. Such a capacity cannot be deduced from principles such as corre-lation, determination, relation, or non-contradiction, because these principles articulate this very enigma. They describe an economy exhausted by the principles of autonomy and power, in which correlation proceeds from the absolute solitude of its elements, and in which an essentially untroubled identity enters into the rectitude and reciprocity of relations with other identities. For the philosophers of proximity, from Hegel, Nietzsche, Freud and Proust to Bataille, Blanchot and Levinas, such relations are unthinkable without the proposition of a primordial alteration of closure which would make possible these relations. Only an altering rapport of Same with Other can make possible the multiplicity and the relations which structure the Same. Without this altering rapport, the concept of relation is a contradiction in terms, and the Same assumes not only the aspect of immobility or reification, but also the aspect of undiffer-entiation or dispersion. Only a heteronomy implicit in differentiation itself can make possible a generality of existents which might include movement, rapport, action, or manifestation. Such a generality, in its very definition as a totality, must itself be involved in a communication with an element irreducible to totalization — an Other outside the totality — in order that it be what it in fact is: a plurality and a communication. The exigency which animates the philosophy of proximity is the thematization of a separation or interiority which is a unicity without being a totality. This thematization requires the proposition of an alterity which does not merely escape the power of mobilization implicit in the concept of comprehension, but which changes subjectivity as a function of its very alterity. Thus the Other, in its very transcendence, remains "here below", remains in a rapport with interiority. And thus the Other's transcendence or alterity is not a power to escape, to disperse, to destroy — is not an effectivity modelled after the image of the Same itself — but is a powerlessness which alters. The Other's retreat inspires or invests the desire which pursues it, in the dissymetry of communication. This desire is a positive ontological event, in which the eventualities of comprehension, action, and relation are produced. Although the Same's internal relations will describe a situation of homogeneity and undifferentiation, in the immobility of correlation, these relations repose upon the subterranean economy of desire and inspiration. And when the Same imagines an alterity which escapes the power of comprehension, on the basis of its superior power and superior truth, this image will conceal the insistence of an alterity which changes the Same by virtue of its immemorial excess — an inaccessibility with which the Same remains involved. This involvement is a compromising contamination in which nothing remains the same. Metamorphosis, alteration and desire are the latent principles of the Same's violent spontaneity. These principles describe what Levinas calls a "non-allergic" rapport of Same and Other which underlies their perennial allergy, and which is inadequate to the predications of formal discourse, in its persistent commitment to the alternative of totalization and destruction or dispersion. The Other's approach cannot change the world, although it is the world's alteration. This approach does not appear in a universe of action. Yet it cannot be stopped, since it appears in a universe without power. It is an approach, and only an approach, but its inactuality implies an ontological event more basic than any encounter within the actual. It is in the approach and the proximity of the Other that the Same can be what it is: not a mere totality, but a violent and ambivalent economy of communications.

SEPARATION AND THE GENERAL ECONOMY

DISCONTINUITY IN BATAILLE

The exuberant thematic and conceptual diversity of Georges Bataille's thought is informed by several common denominators. Perhaps the most important of these is the concept of a differentiation which produces excess. The figure of closure or unicity in Bataille's text has two basic predicates: its inadequation to identity or self-coincidence and, correlative to this inadequation, its density or excessive force. The "general economy" of differentiation and individuation meditated by Bataille, is an economy whose principle is not totalization, but communication. The intensity of closure as an economic instance is, on one hand, the disturbance produced by its excess over its own integrity (a movement Bataille will eventually name *transgression*), and on the other hand a fundamental vulnerability with regard to the exteriority with which closure is essentially intricated (and this contamination or inextrication will be the principle of what Bataille will call *expérience*). The interval of separation produced by the general economy is not negativity. The "weakness" or "failure" of the negative, in Bataille, is the principle of closure's excess and vulnerability. The conation of interiority or closure, in the general economy, is a paradoxical spasm "toward the outside": a simultaneous explosion toward and invasion by the exterior. This dual dispossession is not, however, a simple destruction or dispersion of interiority. It is rather the economic investment of unicity itself, in its excessive and incomplete closure. The contamination which inclines interiority toward the exterior is the production of interiority by communication in Bataille. This contamination is also the production of subjectivity as a properly economic instance which appears in being on the basis of differentiation, rather than as a moment of manifestation, in a philosophical inspiration. The description of this communicationally defined subjectivity is the basic tendency of Bataille's discursive practice.

In his early essays in *La Critique Sociale, Documents* and *Acéphale,*[1] Bataille tended to observe and privilege the excessive or heterogeneous aspect of certain objects or contexts, in an inspiration similar to that of surrealism. The phenomenality of these objects, in his eyes, exceeded their capacity of assimilation by a logic of non-contradiction whose principle of coherence was the notion of utility. "La Notion de dépense" (1933)[2] was a critique of the logical primacy of utility, and an enumeration of comportments ("luxury, funeral processions, wars, religious ceremonies, the construction of extravagant

9

monuments, games, spectacles, arts, perverse sexual activity"[3]) whose purpose or animating principle could not be properly thematized by such a logic. For Bataille, each of these comportments implies a loss or *dépense* which cannot be subordinated to the notion of a subsidiary or underlying profit. Their rejection as irrationality, or their recuperation as culturally valid or valuable comportments, by prevailing philosophical and scientific systems, constitutes a reaction to the irreducibility of the loss they imply. The excessive or heterogeneous aspect of these and other phenomena was thematized in Bataille's early texts in a repeated hesitation with regard to their rapport with subjectivity. In "Le Gros orteil" (1929),[4] the toe is said to have a "hideously cadaverous and simultaneously shrill and prideful aspect," although its "form" "is not, however, specifically monstrous: in this it is different from other parts of the body, for example the inside of a wide-open mouth."[5] Excess is neither a "merely subjective" impression nor an objectively situable predicate. In "La Structure psychologique du fascisme" (1933–4),[6] this ambiguity of excess is clearly situated for the first time within an articulation of utility and the economy of subjectivity. Here Bataille draws the outlines of a "homogeneous" world, governed by the implicit values of utility and conservation, and organized by the systematic interdependence or "commensurability" of its elements. Identity, in this dimension, is a function of utility, and determination is a function of conservation ("the conservation of goods on one hand – ... the reproduction and conservation of human lives on the other"[7]). Bataille defines the heterogeneous as "incommensurable" to the systematic assignment of value which is homogeneity, and names *dépense* as the principle of this incommensurability ("the *heterogeneous* world includes the collective results of *unproductive* loss [*dépense*] .... This is to say: all that the *homogeneous* society rejects either as waste or as a superior transcendental value."[8]). Within this context, Bataille's hesitation regarding the manifest aspect of heterogeneity and homogeneity repeats his earlier difficulties. Homogeneity is defined as a "commensurability of elements and a consciousness of this commensurability,"[9] and heterogeneity is defined as an "affective" aspect of objects which is nevertheless not simply "subjective" ("the action of objects of erotic activity is manifestly founded in their objective nature"; "it is possible to speak of the violent and excessive nature of a decomposing cadaver"[10]). This hesitation leads to a problematic of reification, in which homogeneity is defined as an incomplete reduction of the heterogeneity of phenomena, by the "science" of the homogeneous society. Heterogeneity is an irreducibility to utility which is integral to manifestation in general, but which is always reduced by the movement of an intentionality for which conservation is a necessity.

The object of science is to found the *homogeneity* of phenomena; it is, in a certain sense, one of the eminent functions of *homogeneity*. Thus, the *heterogeneous* elements which are excluded [by homogeneity] are also excluded from the field of scientific attention: in its very principle, science cannot know *heterogeneous* elements as such.[11]

Science is a reduction of heterogeneity, and thus an inability to thematize the latter directly. Therefore, in a cultural sense, "it is all the more easy to understand that incursions made in the *heterogeneous* domain have not yet been sufficiently coordinated to result in the simple revelation of its positive and clearly defined existence."[12]

The hidden or reified aspect of heterogeneity, its association with affectivity and the unconscious,[13] its irreducibility to the economic values of the homogeneous society, and its incommensurability to a logic of conservation of human life, are the derivative moments of Bataille's demonstration. His early contact with phenomenology, Marxism, psychoanalysis and, perhaps most importantly, Nietzsche, informs the exuberance of "La Structure psychologique du fascisme". At the same time, the concept of *dépense,* the positing of homogeneous and heterogeneous "worlds" or ontological dimensions ("science" being defined as a "function" of the former dimension), and the compression of both homogeneous and heterogeneous aspects in the phenomenality of *any* object, point to the discursivity of the mature Bataille. The last of these strategies is most notably articulated in the notion of the capitalist God, which is simultaneously an affective moral imperative and an "introjection" of this imperative which reduces its violence to the values of utility;[14] and in the figure of the fascist leader, who is simultaneously a "transcendent object of collective affectivity" and a symbol of "duty, discipline, and accomplished order."[15] These and other examples lead Bataille to posit homogeneity as more than a simple reification. Homogeneity is a reduction of the heterogeneous, but in the form of a contamination and an intensity: "The *heterogeneous* mode explicitly undergoes a profound contamination [*altération*], which results in the production of an intense *homogeneity* without the fundamental *heterogeneity* being reduced."[16] The opposition of homogeneity and heterogeneity, and the implicit duality of cognition and affect which accompanies it in Bataille's essay, are supplanted by the notions of contamination and intensity, which are basic principles for any thematization of subjectivity or phenomenality. From this perspective, the inevitability of reification, and the exceptional aspect of heterogeneity, are no longer ultimate in Bataille's thinking. The most radical aspect of Bataille's Nietzschian inspiration is his grounding of homogeneity and heterogeneity, beyond a denunciation of the former and a privileging of the latter, in a larger element which exceeds and conditions their opposition.

"The reality of *heterogeneous* elements is not of the same order as that of *homogeneous* elements. *Homogeneous* reality presents itself with the abstract and neutral aspect of strictly defined and identified objects (. . .). *Heterogeneous* reality is that of force and shock."[17] Heterogeneity is a force in being, whose irreducibility to manifestation is also its production and conditioning of manifestation. Homogeneity is the heterogeneous *altéré* — contaminated — and is also the *altération,* the becoming-other and contamination, of homogeneity itself as closure. That which reduces heterogeneity is itself an instance forced or produced by heterogeneity. Alterity is not "that which is reduced" or "that which is invisible", but is the economy of interiority. Escape and reification are no longer the coordinates of its insistence in being. Alterity contaminates. It is the production and alteration of the Same. The closure which characterizes the homogeneous "world" is integral to the function of subjectivity, in a sense Bataille will ground and explain later in his career. But it is heterogeneity that "forces us to think", and that participates in our reduction of it. Heterogeneity is not understandable as affect, since homogeneity itself proceeds from a "reaction" to the heterogeneous which is not understandable as intentionality or cognition. The definition of cognition in the homogeneous dimension as a "reduction of heterogeneity" (a rapport with heterogeneity which makes possible this reduction) indicates an economy of subjectivity for which the duality of reason and passion is no longer pertinent. Although the Bataille of "La Structure psychologique du fascisme" is not yet able to render explicit the implications of his concepts, his reader perceives in heterogeneity the beginnings of a stable Bataillian conceptualization which subordinates the possibility of manifestation to the priority of differentiation. In the definition of heterogeneity, a differentiation which produces not identity or closure, but force and contamination, also produces subjectivity as a passivity or susceptibility to this force. The implicit obsession with conservation and utility which governs what Bataille calls "current practice",[18] cannot be situated with regard to a prior definition of consciousness, but indicates a closure consequent to differentiation which will no longer be a given, but an effort or exigency. The involvement of this exigency with the heterogeneity it reduces, and with the intensity of this reduction, indicates a priority of differentiation over negativity, and the production of the homogeneous as a properly differential unicity. The importance of "La Structure psychologique du fascisme" among Bataille's early essays is its communicational definition of closure, and its implication of a subjectivity which is produced in the movement of this communication. Closure is not an integrity, but an excess, i.e. a density or intensity which is an irreducible involvement with exteriority. The dualities which prepare this moment, whether invented by Bataille or derived from his readings, lose their dialectical aspect in the contaminated moment they produce. The integrity of opposition, and the synthetic homogeneity which normally accompanies it, are supplanted in Bataille by a suspended moment of contamination which is not a resolution, but an intensity.

*

As mentioned above, the discursive tendency of the early Bataille is to draw attention to a heterogeneous instance which defies totalization, and to privilege this defiance over the relatively submissive or servile "world" of totalization. "La Structure psychologique du fascisme" is already an adjustment of this dualistic tendency, and is followed by a series of unequally explicitated statements of the same basic configuration. It is with the publication of *L'Expérience intérieure* (1943), and with the *Somme athéologique* in its entirety

(*Le Coupable*, 1944, *Sur Nietzsche*, 1945), that the subject of differentiation assumes a dominance equal to that of manifestation in Bataille's text. Bataille's later discursive studies, including most importantly *La Part maudite* (1949) and *L'Erotisme* (1957), are books about differentiation which devote far less attention to manifestation than did the aphoristic texts of the 1940's. There is a moment in *L'Expérience intérieure* at which Bataille's reader may perceive the effect of this displacement of emphasis upon the concept of heterogeneity. At this moment, the heterogeneous as escape and alterity is supplanted by heterogeneity as a synonym for discontinuity or closure:

From one simple particle to another, there is no difference in nature, nor is there is a difference between this one and that one. There is *some of* this which is produced here or there, each time in the form of a unity, but this unity does not endure in itself. Rhythms, waves, and simple particles are perhaps merely the multiple movements of a homogeneous element; they possess only a fleeting unity and do not disrupt the homogeneity of the whole.

Only the groups composed of numerous simple particles have this heterogeneous character which differentiates me from you and isolates our differences in the rest of the universe. What one calls a "being" is never simple, and if it has a durable unity, it only possesses this unity imperfectly: the latter is disturbed by its profound interior division, it remains poorly closed, at certain points vulnerable to the exterior.[19]

In this quotation, the meanings of homogeneity and heterogeneity have been reversed. Heterogeneity defines the particularity or separation of a differentiated entity, and homogeneity defines an "element" irreducible to particularity in general. The priority of this element in a differentiation which produces not "unity" but incompletion, is the priority of difference itself as the principle of individuation. In this context, identity becomes "movement", "fleeting unity": a fugitive ontological instance without the positivity of determination. The "interior division" which haunts closure, is already the interior difference of a communicational unicity. The phrase "vulnerable to the exterior" describes the subjectivity or susceptibility to exteriority which is inherent in a differential economy. The priority of differentiation over identity, of incompletion over integrity, and of subjectivity over spontaneity, are the axes of Bataille's discovery of the *économie générale*. The *Somme athéologique*, in its totality, is an attempt to adequate this configuration and its implications to the exigencies of discursive communication; hence its concern with terms such as *savoir, non-savoir, méditation,* etc. *La Part maudite* and *L'Erotisme* are articulations of a differentially defined subjectivity with its manifold possibilities and comportments, including that of discursivity. In these most fundamental of Bataille's later texts, manifestation is no longer the primary context of communication. Differentiation has become the principle of a larger dimension, whose ontological positivity is problematic, and of which manifestation (along with its correlate, totalization) is merely a region.

In *L'Erotisme,* the figure of a differentiated and communicationally or "economically" defined unicity has the name "discontinuity".

> Reproduction brings into play [*met en jeu*] discontinuous beings.
> Beings which reproduce themselves are distinct from one another and beings reproduced are distinct from their progenitors. Each being is distinct from all the others. Its birth, its death and the events of its life may have an interest for the others, but only this being is directly interested. It alone is born. It alone dies. Between one being and another, there is an abyss, there is a discontinuity.
> This abyss is situated, for example, between you who listen to me and myself who speaks to you. We try to communicate, but no communication between us can suppress a primary difference. If you die, it is not I who dies. We are, you and I, discontinuous beings.[20]

Discontinuity is the purely formal designation of a distinction which is not yet negativity or determination, but the non-coincidence of a "primary difference". Its production in differentiation is the context of *L'Erotisme*'s concern with reproduction in its involvement with death. "Reproduction leads to the discontinuity of beings, but it brings into play [*met en jeu*] their continuity, which is to say that it is intimately linked with death."[21] The notion of "continuity" describes, in Bataille's terms, an excess of the concept of life over the distinct or discontinuous beings which are its incarnations. This excess may be empirically perceived at the moments of scissiparity, fecundation, and death, where life is a passage from discontinuity to continuity to discontinuity, in an essentially instantaneous temporality. The dividing of cells or organisms, their unification, and their decomposition in death describe "an *instant* of continuity."[22] Each of these instances implies death, since division, unification and decomposition describe a disappearance of the discontinuous being which loses itself in these processes — without, however, a loss from the point of view of the conservation of matter and energy. The ambiguity of death is its annihilation of separation in which, however, nothing is lost. The irreducibility of death to negation is a basic principle of *L'Erotisme,* derived from the lengthy meditation of "particles" and "compositions" which structures much of the *Somme athéologique.* The only incarnation of continuity is discontinuity. But discontinuity proceeds from, and tends toward, a differentiation which is irreducible to the closure it invests. The term "continuity" describes this excess of differentiation over discontinuity. It is not a negativity, and its only positivity is its instantaneous and essentially fugitive insistence in the economy of life. But it conditions the closure of its incarnations, whose fugitive or limited life spans themselves describe a "passage" in being. "The new being is itself discontinuous, but it carries in itself the passage to continuity, the fusion — mortal for each one — of two distinct beings."[23]

The only determination of discontinuity in the general economy of life is the *mise en jeu* (the placing "in play") of discontinuity, i.e. its inextrication from differentiation, its involvement with death, and its continual contamination as a function of its closure. "Life is always a product of the decomposition of life. It is a tributary in the first place of death, which leaves space [for life]; then of decomposition [*corruption*], which follows death, and places in circulation those substances necessary for the incessant appearance of new beings."[24] The economy of life is a 'rotting", a "fermentation",[25] an insistence of differentiation in the integrity of discontinuity. Continuity and death are the forms of this insistence as the production and density of the living being. In reproduction and death, nothing is lost. Life is "transferred" "to the impersonality of life."[26] Yet, from the perspective of the individual, this transfer is a loss or *dépense* which both produces and destroys its interiority. "If growth occurs to the profit of a being or an ensemble which exceeds us, it is no longer a growth, but a gift [*don*]. For him who gives it, the gift is the *loss* [*perte*] of his possession."[27] The violence that affects the individual in reproduction and death suggests an irreducibility of the general economy of life to the principles of conservation and integrity. Violence and loss exist within this economy. "Sexuality differs from the miserly growth of possession: if, considered from the point of view of the species, it appears as a growth, it is nonetheless the prodigality [*luxe*] of the individuals."[28] Reproduction is a generosity and a loss. It is, either immediately or "à longue échéance"[29] (on a deferred basis), the disappearance of the progenitor. The general economy is a dimension of exuberance, decomposition, and loss; a priority of "impersonality" in the constitution of interiority. Since loss is the principle of the economy – a principle irreducible to negativity, and thus to a dialectical or other foundation of the integrity of living beings – it is not possible to thematize the generality of the economy as a conservation. Nor is it possible to conceive the economy itself as a true positivity – and this is its fundamentally differential aspect. The general economy is not a dimension which produces totalizations, and is not itself a totality. If its sum of matter and energy is "constant", its production of interiority describes an ontological dimension which is irreducible to this constancy.

The concept of loss or *dépense,* and the violence or *luxe* which is its correlate, cannot have pertinence for an ontology which grounds identity in negativity and non-contradiction. For such an ontology, the economy of the negative grounds the positivity of a totalization which is always essentially conserved. In spite of its figuring of violence in philosophy, the negative is a conservative principle which describes a situation in which nothing is lost. The concept of loss is possible only in a differential or communicational economy, in which the condition for unicity is the permanent dispossession of an involvement with exteriority. On one hand, the general economy discovers loss in its attention to the "point of view" of the individual; and on the other hand, it discovers loss in the basic configuration of an individuation which is not guaranteed by negativity, but rather is "forced" by an intrication with alterity, in the form of continuity and death. The term "discontinuity" describes differentiation in its investment of interiority; the terms "continuity" and "death" describe differentiation in its excess over the possibility of an integral interiority.

As mentioned above, the most stable predicate of differentiation in Bataille's thought is excess. In "La Structure psychologique du fascisme", the investment of homogeneity by heterogeneity is an intensity, i.e. an excess of the homogeneous with regard to itself. In *L'Expérience intérieure,* the closure of the separate or isolated being is defined as an interior economy which both produces and exceeds the form of closure:

> What you are is produced by the activity which links the manifold elements that compose you, by the intense communication among these elements. It is contagions of energy, of movement, of heat, or of transferred elements, that constitute the interior life of your organic being.[30]

The closure or conation which is survival, in its opposition to death, is more fundamentally a region of the general economy. Its only unicity is the intensity of the exchanges, deaths, and decompositions which compose it. The opposition to continuity or differentiation which is survival, is itself an economy, and thus an excess over its own closure. "There is a horrible excess of the movement which animates us," writes Bataille in *L'Erotisme.*[31] The movement which seeks to create self-coincidence and self-sufficiency out of differentiation, is animated or produced by differentiation. The sense of the *économie générale* is its thematization of an economy which conditions closure, and of a closure whose density is not a conservation, but the permanence of loss:

> It is to the *particular* living being, or to limited ensembles of living beings, that the problem of necessity is posed. But man is not only the separate being who competes with the living world or with other men for his share of resources. The general movement of exudation (of dilapidation) of living matter animates him, and he cannot arrest it; indeed, at the summit, his sovereignty in the living world identifies him with this movement; it dedicates him, in a privileged way, to the glorious operation, to useless consumption [*consommation inutile*].[32]

Beyond its considerable implications for political economy, the notion of loss in the *économie générale* is a discovery of differentiation and excess in the constitution of subjectivity, in particular, and separation, in general. The existential and epistemological implications of this configuration are the context of Bataille's later discursive texts. The irreducibility of closure to identity and determination is also the irreducibility of its comportments to conservation.

On a most basic level, it is the discontinuous in the general economy that has a fugitive, passing aspect, and the continuous or differential, that has the paradoxical permanence and stability of its irreducible excess over totalization. Separation, by virtue of its economic constitution, is in a sense an illusion. "Only the instability of the liaisons (this banal fact: however intimate a link may be, separation is easy, and may multiply and prolong itself) permits the illusion of the isolated being, withdrawn into itself [*replié sur soi-même*] and possessing the power to exist without exchange."[33] Separation is defined necessarily and sufficiently as a communication. Therefore, the interpretation of unicity as identity to self is impossible. The possibility of reproduction, in which discontinuity approaches and engenders alterity as a function of its own closure, attests the absurdity of this interpretation. "Fecundation – fusion – would be inconceivable if the apparent discontinuity of the simplest animate beings were not an illusion [*leurre*]."[34] However, this "interpretation" of discontinuity as integrity is survival itself: the exigent subsistence and self-conservation of that which always exceeds by its loss the possibility of this subsistence. Conservation is an irreducible detour in the economy, although it is not the principle or "truth" of the economy. This is the sense of the most fundamental figure of excess in Bataille's thought: the exigency of closure. The intensity or conation of the surviving being proceeds from its intrication with the general economy. This is its animation. The force which opposes continuity (communication and differentiation in their excess over closure) is animated by continuity. The opposition is always what Bataille will call a "more profound accord". The struggle to survive is animated by death, although not by death as a negativity which grounds the positive. It is animated by death as difference and communication: the other of integrity which invests all interiority as contamination. The "power" with which interiority maintains itself in its separation is actually the radical passivity of its investment by continuity. This passivity is not the result of determination, since the economy produces no integral terms which might enter into causal relation with each other. The passivity of closure is the absence of power in the economy as a whole. Therefore, the exigent closure of discontinuity is always a desire, i.e. the intensity of a closure which can never become an integrity, or the movement of a closure which is always an intrication with the exterior. Conation in the general economy, to paraphrase Emmanuel Levinas, is always "in reverse" or "inside out". Interiority is always an "introjection" of the exterior or, more precisely, a dispersion or exteriorization of the interior. The duality "outside/inside" is essentially exceeded by the notion of discontinuity, which is at the same time a dispersal and a unicity produced by dispersal. The economy produces no identity or integrity, but is an "economy" nonetheless. It produces a differential unicity which is far more intense and "over determined" than the simple non-contradiction of an identity to self.

The closure or conservation of discontinuity is the permanence of its loss or *dépense*. Discontinuity is always excessively closed, by virtue of the inherence of the exterior to its conation – and never closed enough, by virtue of the essential incompletion which is its rapport (not its relation) with the economy that invests it. Separation "contains more than it can contain", and condenses toward the outside. These three principles – loss as the animation of conservation, passivity as the investment of power, desire as the intensity of closure — define the density of a communicational unicity in Bataille. This unicity is always an exigency, i.e. a conation invested by exteriority, a retreat from alterity in which alterity collaborates. There are four fundamental Bataillian terms which describe this intensely incomplete closure. In the first place, closure is a *glissement,* a slipping or sliding between two modes of being, continuity and discontinuity, interiority and exteriority: "where you try to seize your intemporal substance, you encounter only a *glissement,* only the imperfectly coordinated play of your perishable elements."[35] When Bataille's demonstrations, in any context, approach their point of greatest density, the term *glissement* tends to intervene, often without definition. It describes the contamination of both location and quiddity which is consequent to a priority of difference over totalization. On one hand the *glissement* suggests the ambiguity or undecidability of difference in individuation. On the other hand, it describes the alteration — the contamination and becoming-other — of the Same in the general economy. In the second place, closure is not a given, not a determined state, but an exigency or effort: "It is not as a unitary thing [*chose définie*] that man confronts nature (. . .). It is an effort toward autonomy [*effort d'autonomie*]."[36] The economic production of closure is on one hand its condensation or conation as a retreat from the continuity that threatens it, and on the other hand the inherence and force of this continuity in the animation of the movement of closure. In the third place, by virtue of this intrication of interior and exterior, the excessive density of closure is always an incompletion or *inachèvement*:

To the extent that beings seem to be complete, they remain isolated, closed upon themselves. But the wound [*blessure*] of incompletion [*inachèvement*] opens them. Through what one may call incompletion, animal nudity, wound, diverse separate beings *communicate,* come to life losing themselves [*se perdant*] in a *communication* from one to the other.[37]

Inachèvement is the breach haunting a closure which, from the point of view of identity and determination, is entirely and adequately closed. Thus, it is the principle of desire: the condensation "outward", the "conation in reverse" of interiority. It is also the principle of subjectivity in the general economy: an aptitude to be affected by exteriority which must be grounded in a fundamental inadequacy and inadequation of closure. Subjectivity in Bataille, as in Blanchot and Levinas, proceeds from differentiation itself, defined as a creation of discontinuous entities which are essentially non-indifferent to, and therefore vulnerable or subjected to, the economy from which they are differentiated. As will be discussed below, incompletion is also the basic Bataillian principle of proximity: a conation of the interior or of closure which brings alterity close and closer. Autonomy in proximity always describes an approach of the Other in an indefinite future — an approach whose incumbence or urgency proceeds from the pre-originarity of its intrication with interiority. In Bataille, this pre-originary approach will take the form of death, sexuality, *non-savoir,* and the principle of these terms, transgression. (To approach the limit in transgression is to be approached by the limit, in an incumbence analogous to that of death. Transgression is a passivity.) In the fourth place, and perhaps most importantly, closure in Bataille is an *impossibility*: "the savage *impossibility* I am, which can neither avoid its limits nor hold to them."[38] Impossibility describes the irreducibility of closure to identity, non-contradiction and determination. Discontinuity is a dispersion which is a unicity. Its closure is its involvement with differentiation, and thus the impossibility of its closure. Although it is differentiated, it is not determined. It cannot enter into a relation with other "terms" in the economy, because there are no "terms" in the economy. Closure is thus an inadequation and a permanent inequality or dissymetry. It is invested by alterity — the Other of closure — and essentially inclined toward, or non-indifferent to, this alterity. There can be no reciprocity among the terms of the economy, because they do not condition "each other", but are conditioned by an instance which forecloses their self-coincidence. Alterity invests each term from an exteriority which is always "within", and inclines or forces interiority in an irreversible sense or direction: *au dehors,* "outside". The alterity which invests closure never approaches the latter as to a center of gravity, and never inclines it toward an Other which would itself be a center. Instead, closure in the general economy is essentially excentric: animated by an outside which is already inside, and inclined toward an indeterminate exteriority whose very indefinition is its proximity to interiority. The impossibility of closure is also the impossibility of relation. At the same time, impossibility is an absence of negation in a differential economy. Interiority is not guaranteed by negation in a founded non-coincidence with exteriority. Instead, it is fundamentally involved or intricated with exteriority by differentiation. And this absence of negation is also an absence of power in the economy, as the etymology of "impossibility" indicates. Discontinuity is a heteronomy, although not in the sense of a determined identity. As closure, it is animated by the other of closure: continuity. Therefore, the "power" with which it condenses and conserves itself, particularly in survival, proceeds from the Other (from which nothing can proceed as from a cause or identity). Underneath every power in the economy, a more fundamental passivity may be perceived: not a passivity which results from determination by a superior power, but a passivity which results from an absence of power in differentiation. This radical passivity will structure each important thematic moment in Bataille, including transgression, *non-savoir,* and literary communication, and will contaminate the apparently voluntaristic dualities which describe the manifold "possibilities" of Bataillian sovereignty. In a larger sense, the passivity of closure in differentiation will condition the many predicates of subjectivity in proximity, and will define the inadequation of this instance to both dialectical and ontological descriptions. The real in proximity is a dimension without spontaneity, without power, without freedom, and without determination.

The four basic notions *glissement, effort d'autonomie, inachèvement, impossibilité*, describe a closure whose economy is communication rather than determination. This closure, in its interiority, is involved with and turned toward the exterior — not in the sense of an illumination or disclosedness which would be correlative of its status as an interval within being, or a negativity whose being is "always in question". The lack of self-coincidence of a phenomenologically defined subjectivity proceeds from its destiny in manifestation, and its spontaneity which is correlative of negation. In Bataille, these possibilities are not presupposed, and are conditioned by a communication which is an inextrication essentially inadequate to manifestation. Subjectivity in proximity is never able to assume a distance from exteriority which would be adequate to manifestation or phenomenality. There are no intentional "objects" in the general economy. The susceptibility to the -exterior which defines subjectivity is precisely the impossibility of such a transcendence on the part of consciousness. The "too much" of Bataillian excess ("All that is . . . is too much."[39]) is the "too close" of exteriority: its excess over the possibility of phenomenality. As the present study will have frequent occasion to point out, the philosophy of proximity always tends to discover its definitions in differentiation rather than in the categories of manifestation. In Bataille, Blanchot, and Levinas, consciousness is always derived from subjectivity, which is produced by differentiation, and which is inadequate to any definition of consciousness as interval, illumination, or totalization. Although in their discursive techniques these thinkers share a debt to phenomenology, their common tendency is a meditation of difference and communication which is foreign to the aims of phenomenology, and perhaps of philosophy in general.

"The *interior experience* of man is given in the instant at which, breaking the chrysalis, he is conscious that he himself tears himself asunder rather than to oppose his resistance to the exterior," writes Bataille in *L'Erotisme*.[40] The intensity of discontinuity's closure proceeds from the constraint or pressure, in a differential sense, of its intrication with alterity. This is why closure, for all separation in the general economy, is essentially an *expérience*, i.e. a subjectivity or susceptibility to the exterior which is the interior difference or incompletion of closure. The *dehors* begins within closure. The Other approaches from within. Subjectivity is a breach or *fêlure* within totalization. This breach affects both moments of the opposition between separation and communication (between prohibition and transgression, *savoir* and *non-savoir*, the profane and the sacred, etc.) which structures Bataille's text. This ubiquity of incompletion is apparent in the following formulation:

In human life. . . sexual violence open a wound. Rarely does the wound close by itself: it is necessary to close it. Indeed, without a constant attention, founded by anguish, it cannot remain closed. The elementary anguish associated with sexual violence is significative of death.[41]

The involvement of sexuality with death — with communication in its excess over closure — suggests a breach or "wound" within closure. The "attention" or anguish which maintains the necessary closure of this wound, is not a production or modality of integrity, but an effort to reduce that which is permanent and irreducible: the breach which conditions closure. Attention, anguish and necessity are terms which themselves describe this opening and this lack of integrity. The only opposition to incompletion is incompletion itself. The force of closure is an economic force, which involves the Other. Subjectivity's vigilance — the entire dimension of *savoir* — is an exigency to prevent this already open wound from opening. In another sense, consciousness' attention is this very wound, considered in its exigency as distinct from its vulnerability. Like Swann, alone in his carriage in pursuit of Odette, Bataillian subjectivity senses that it is not alone, that its integrity is compromised, and that this breach must be surveyed with care and attention, like a disease. Unlike Heideggerian *Sorge,* which is grounded in spontaneity, freedom and manifestation, the attention and anguish meditated by Bataille proceed from the impossibility of these intervals which describe *Dasein* in its suspension between authenticity and inauthenticity. On the other hand, the proximity of a *dehors,* and its hyperbole in the breach, describe a violence which may be the ultimate resonance of facticity and *Geworfenheit* in Heidegger: a proximity to existence which exceeds and conditions the possibility of manifestation.

"Erotic activity does not always openly have this pernicious [*néfaste*] aspect, it is not always this *fêlure* [cracking, splitting]; but profoundly, secretly, this *fêlure,* being the distinctive feature of human sensuality, is the principle [*ressort,* mainspring, animation] of pleasure."[42] The coincidence of sensibility and sensuality in the breach attests a priority of incompletion in the constitution of all forms of experience. Subjectivity, defined as the modality of closure in differentiation, is the principle of cognition ("attention"), sensation, anguish, desire, etc. Pleasure and reality principles, in their essential intrication, describe the fundamental ambivalence of desire in proximity: a tendency to repulse the exterior which is always already an approach of and to the exterior. The production or maintenance of interiority requires a distancing of the outside; but the outside always collaborates in this distancing. Closure as desire — the exigency of the Other (in the ambiguity of this phrase) — is always closure as breach. When the Other recedes, it approaches, from within. Pleasure is both the concupiscence of communication — a fulfilling immersion within a differential element which produces and supports interiority — and the permanent incompletion or lack of integrity which is correlative to this communication. It is this fundamental incompletion, and the increasing momentum of a desire which nourishes itself from its own fulfillment, that produces the common misconception of pleasure and desire as aspects of need. Pleasure is the absence of the possibility of completion. It is the inextricable simultaneity of excess and lack in the exigency of closure. It has only one modality and one temporality: it increases. The more closure completes itself (and closure itself is the tension of a "more and more" which is excess in being), the more it is *inachevée,* i.e. contaminated and altered by the proximity of alterity. The involvement of pleasure with pain, of repulsion with attraction, and of desire with death, is closure's irreducible rapport with the other of closure. Freud's difficulty in *Beyond the Pleasure Principle* is his tendency to pose reality and pleasure principles, repetition and the death instinct in configurations of opposition, and his reluctance to point out and explain their inextrication from, or communication with each other — a communication required by the logic of differentiation which is their condition. Pleasure is a form of knowledge; knowledge is an Eros; the reality principle is imaginary or "phantastic", in its irreducibility to manifestation; the death instinct is not a return to inanimation, but a tendency toward the same differentiation which produces and exceeds life. Bataille was never to write an important text on psychoanalysis, but in his own meditation of closure and *dépense,* he understood and repeated the radicality of the Freudian concepts.

Every Bataillian opposition hides a communication. Prohibition is already transgression, the profane is already the sacred, reification is already an inscription of excess. Separation, most generally, is already communication in Bataille. The ipseity of *L'Expérience intérieure* which "wants to become All", wants to become a totality, also wants to "lose itself" in the exigency of closure.[43] Totalization, in a communicational economy, would be an abolition of interiority as well as exteriority, since the only closure in such an economy is the differential unicity of communication. To recoil from the economy, in survival or conation, is to recoil into the economy. As Blanchot says so well of death, "se dissimuler à elle, c'est d'une certaine manière se dissimuler en elle." "To hide from it is in a sense to hide in it."[44] Closure's exigency is a double impossibility: to place the exterior at an adequate distance, or to engulf the exterior within a totalization. It is the participation of the exterior in both these exigencies that defines their impossibility, and also their problematic actuality or effective reality, as the economy of interiority. The two ambitions of Western culture — to totalize the Other in comprehension, to engulf the Other in communion — are impossible exigencies. A fundamental characteristic of this culture is its assumption of these exigencies as possibilities. The radicality of a Nietzsche, a Bataille, a Freud, is the tendency to ground and condition these exigencies in a communicational concept of closure.

On a thematic level, Bataille's opposition of separation or isolation on one hand, and communication or "violence" on the other, tends to describe and value negatively a closed, "profane" world whose complacency is interrupted by an upsurge of transgressive communication which "cannot be stopped", and which is privileged for its escape from profane constraints. The excellence of transgression, in this context, is its radical dispossession and absolute alterity with regard to the world of identity and utility. This alterity has the implicit predicate of independence from a world of servile concepts and comportments. The absolutely other cannot be known by this world, but only reified, recuperated or domesticated. Its superiority is its escape. It is this presentation of transgression that motivates the many misunderstandings of Bataille, from early rejections of his "mysticism" to later, approving interpretations of his discovery of an absolute alterity beyond constraint or totalization. Bataille's invitation of such interpretations is manifest in statements such as the following:

> Let us say immediately that violence, and death which signifies it, have a double meaning: on one hand horror, linked with the attachment to life, keeps us at a distance; on the other hand a solemn and simultaneously terrifying element fascinates us, introducing a sovereign excitement [*trouble*].[45]

Subjectivity "tries to obey" the constraints of its world of utility, but "succumbs" to a violent movement which is "irreducible to reason."[46] Thus, transgression cannot be stopped. The opposition to it is not powerful enough to arrest its explosion. This thematization of transgression is unfaithful to Bataille's concepts, for two basic reasons. In the first place, transgression does not escape constraint, but invests a closure which is already a *dépense,* already more or other than a constraint. Transgression's escape from totalization is its production of an interiority which is itself not a totalization. Closure, produced by communication, is always itself a transgression in Bataille. For this reason transgression, defined as a comportment, always "fails" to escape or to destroy closure. Its definition as the excess of communication is also its definition as the investment of interiority, separation, and limits. In the second place, the inevitability of transgression, the fact that it "cannot be stopped", is not its approach as a destruction, but its pre-originarity in the constitution of closure. It is true that transgression cannot be stopped: not because it is an absolute alterity which will destroy constraint, but because it is an Other of closure which participates in the differentiation of closure. Considered in itself as such an alterity, transgression can never appear in its positivity as a transcending moment. Its incumbence is rather its economic insistence in the intensity of closure. Thus, the fact that it cannot be stopped is also the fact that it will never arrive, or will never "take place" as a positivity. Its incumbence is its approach, and the indefinition and insubstantiality which distinguish the notion of approach from that of possibility.

Transgression insists, but never exists. This insistence is, to paraphrase Maurice Blanchot, its "domination": the domination or approach of that which has no power. The familiar reading which characterizes Bataille as the thinker of the absolutely other, an alterity more radical than that which is dreamed by Western metaphysics, is in reality a reduction of Bataillian alterity to destructive negativity, and a reduction of Bataillian closure to constraint. It is also a reduction of the differential communication meditated by Bataille to a dialectical communication governed by the notions of power, constraint, and the privilege of transcendent violence which eliminates constraint. The effectivity of transgression in this reading is its substantiality and positivity, which are unwittingly modelled on the efficiency and positivity of closure itself. It is not accidental that an enthusiasm for absolute alterity should reproduce in spite of itself the concepts which delineate the servility of closure. The absolutely other — that which escapes, can never be known, and exceeds the constraints of the "here below" — is Western culture's perennial eschatology and perennial optimism. An absolute alterity conceived itself as an independence and as the principle of an elimination of constraint, is an image of alterity as liberation. The West's anthropocentrism is its conception of alterity as a power, an independence or freedom, and an effectivity — that is, as the very image of identity to self. The overman is more man than man, the eternal return more Same than Same, in the context of a power beyond power — such are the concepts of alterity in philosophy's recuperation of Nietzsche, which is both more false and more inescapable than the recuperation of Bataille. Alterity in Bataille, as in Nietzsche, is always "here below". It has no independence and no effectivity. It does not destroy, but it invests. Its principle is not negativity, but communication. Its domination is its lack of power. The urgency of its approach is its indefinite futurity. A basic tendency of the philosophy of proximity, from Nietzsche and Proust to Blanchot and Levinas, is its lack of interest in the absolutely other, which is always modelled on the image of totalization, and its interest in the powerless Other which invests and contaminates totalization itself. In the quotation above, Bataille writes that violence "fascinates" us in spite of our "horror" of it. He will always stipulate, implicitly or explicitly, that fascination is the principle of a communicationally defined cognition, and that horror is always a resonance of desire's ambivalence. Subjectivity does not "try to obey" the laws of conservation, and then "succumb" to absolute dispossesion. Instead, conservation is an exigency whose impossibility (whose force) is dispossession itself. As will be discussed below, interiority is an ontological instance which "must" conserve itself and "must" transgress, and is never "able" to conserve itself or to transgress. Subjectivity is this "must", this exigency in being, which results from the general economy's failure to invest closure as integrity. Every Batallian opposition, as mentioned above, hides a communication. Every Bataillian desire hides an ambivalence. Transgression is not a resolution of this dilemma: it is this dilemma itself. An interiority which always transgresses interiority in the moment called "impossibility", is an interiority defined as *expérience*.

The incompletion which defines closure in its production by differentiation is simultaneously an excess and a lack. Excess is a disturbance of the immobility of determination in the dimension of totalization. The insistence of the general economy within and on the margins of this dimension, produces a fugitive displacement and dissymmetry which Bataille had perceived as the "intensity" of homogeneity. This movement proceeds from the dispossession which conditions closure in the economy. It has two basic predicates, whose apparently opposite movement indicates a single sense or orientation in being. The first of these predicates, as mentioned above, is nudity or vulnerability. "Through what one may call incompletion, animal nudity, wound, diverse separate beings *communicate,* come to life losing themselves in a *communication* from one to the other". Closure is an incompletion, and thus is always haunted by a breach which is its susceptibility to exteriority. Considered as an integral surface, closure is a nudity which can never be covered. Nudity is the excess and the susceptibility — the subjectivity — of closure. It is at the same time a hyperbole or concupiscence of the surface, in its very integrity, which concerns the exterior, and an insufficiency of this surface which implies an approach of exteriority.* In this dual sense, nudity repeats the modality of the breach. The latter indicates on one hand a susceptibility to alterity which already penetrates, and the dispossession of an interiority which escapes its own closure and disperse itself, leaving a permanent remainder or *reste* outside itself. On one hand, alterity approaches from within, and on the other hand, interiority's excess and remainder describe the breathless movement of its conation toward the outside or "inside out". The Other participates or collaborates in both these movements. They describe an inextrication which is the proximity of alterity, i.e. its incumbence which is correlative of its economic involvement with closure. "*Others* in sexuality ceaselessly offer a possibility of continuity, *others* ceaselessly menace, and propose a tear [*accroc*] in the seamless gown [*robe sans couture*] of individual discontinuity."[47] The proximity of the Other, in its indefinition and futurity, is already its contact with and inherence to interiority. Exteriority escapes, and cannot be seized, because it is inactual or insubstantial; but in this escape, it intrudes. This is its proximity.

When alterity invests the presence of a constituted intersubjective other, the excess of this other, in its involvement with interiority, is called a *pléthore.* It is not the other's interiority or particularity that concerns subjectivity in sexuality, but rather the Other of interiority, as it conditions the presence of this other person. "It is, it seems, less the similitude than the *plethora* of the *other* that plays a role in the approach [*rapprochement*]. The violence of the one proposes itself to the violence of the other: on each side there is an internal movement which obliges one to be *outside oneself* [*obligeant d'être hors de soi*] (outside individual discontinuity)."[48] Although, as will be discussed below, Bataille's panoramic view of the intersubjective presence is essentially misleading, he correctly describes an incumbence of the Other which obliges or weighs upon interiority. This force of alterity does not proceed from the interiority of another person who is his own center of gravity, but from the impersonal Other which is the Other of closure. It obliges or forces interiority from within. The plethora is neither the other person nor the self. It is the excess of differentiation or communication over the possibility of closure. It forces closure outside itself, because it is already the "outside", the *au dehors,* of closure in its proximal definition. For this reason, the concept of an

---

* The extremity of this structure will be called *souillure*: a contaminating contact of nudity with alterity. Cf. below, Chapter 5.

intersubjective presence does not describe "the one" and "the other", but rather an involvement of Same and Other: closure and the Other of closure. It describes not a reciprocity, but a single direction, sense, or orientation in being: *au dehors,* from the inside out, toward the Other. From the outside, the Other forces interiority — from the inside. This is the plethora, the excess, of the Same: what Levinas will call its *pour l'autre.* Again, Bataille's concept of differentiation recalls Proust's intersubjective economy. When the narrator approaches Albertine's face as toward a point in space, the face becomes fragmented. But from this fragmented or essentially indefinite exteriority, which is not her interiority, Albertine involves the narrator, in the same impersonal sense that something, some instance, "amalgamated itself" to Swann in the solitude of his carriage. Albertine is the fugitive, but she is also, in the repeated metaphor of illness, an instance which concerns the narrator from within. Her absence resembles a mortal wound, because she escapes from within. In proximity, one must imagine the approach to Albertine's face as more than the movement of the narrator's curiosity or need. It is this movement, and the frustration of this desire for totalization, but it is also the force of the exigency. The plethora of the other is already our approach to it. When we approach, it escapes into indefinition. But our approach is already its approach, its incumbence and its force. The intentionality of the narrator's gaze is already the radical passivity of a movement which proceeds from the Other. That the other person might, from his own point of view, desire me in this moment, is of no consequence for the intersubjective presence. The movement is univocal: from Same toward Other (the impersonal Other of closure). Proust underlines this essential univocity or dissymetry of communication by staging each love relationship in the *Recherche* as a non-reciprocity.

Differentiation in Bataille produces an interiority which is an involvement with the Other, a vulnerability to the incumbence of the Other, and therefore a subjectivity or *expérience.* Subjectivity is the modality of the differential economy, to the extent that this economy produces incompletion. As does Hegel, Bataille situates subjectivity within the objective, but in an opposite sense. In Hegel, the presence of the concept in the real is a negativity which introduces and guarantees totalization. In Bataille, subjectivity is consequent to the impossibility of totalization. It proceeds not from negation but from incompletion. It is a collapsing, a passivity, a heteronomy in being. For this reason, the subjectivity of the economy is irreducible to consciousness and manifestation — although, as differentiation, it will condition the regional possibility of manifestation in the "world" of *savoir.* Subjectivity is not consciousness, but it is the *expérience* — the subjectivity — of closure, the *expérience du dedans* or *expérience intérieure* which describes inanimate as well as animate entities. "I accord even to the inert particle, beneath the animalcule, this existence *for self* [*pour soi*], which I prefer to call the experience of the inside [*expérience du dedans*], the interior experience...

This elementary feeling [*sentiment*] is not consciousness of self."[49] "Of the continuity of being, I will say only that for me it is not *knowable* [*connaissable*], but in aleatory forms, always partially contestable, the *experience* of it is given to us."[50] The *expérience* is not an intentional or transitive relation to exteriority, but is rather a susceptibility or subjection to the exterior which is correlative of incompletion. It is an involvement with the Other, and not an illumination or totalization of the Other. In his predominantly derivative philosophical terms, Bataille is rarely able to clearly situate the economy of subject and object in proximity, in the manner of Blanchot or Levinas. Yet his early hesitation with regard to subject and object, affect and cognition, is entirely transcended in his later theoretical texts. The priority of differential subjectivity or incompletion over intentionality is a constant in these texts, and is often expressed in terms which will appear in Blanchot and Levinas with greater precision. One such term is *obsession*. Another is *passion*. These terms, in their everyday sense, describe a rapport with exteriority which is an involvement rather than a phenomenal interval. In an economic sense, they describe differentiation as proximity: an approach to the Other which is also an intrication with the Other. The general economy is a passion, an obsession, a subjectivity. It creates fragments or remainders which are non-indifferent to the reality from which they are differentiated. Passion or obsession is the modality of differentiation which conditions the possibility of a cognitive or intentional relation. Bataille writes: "Being, most often, seems to be given to man outside the movements of passion. I will say, on the contrary, that we must never represent being outside these movements."[51] This formulation does not privilege affect or sensibility as a reduced but more immediate form of knowledge. It indicates the priority of a communicational rapport with alterity in any thematization of experience. In addition, it describes the priority of desire in any communicational model of subjectivity, whether it be that of psychoanalysis, the philosophy of difference, or the philosophy of proximity. The susceptibility of interiority to the Other in differentiation is always desire, because closure itself is desire, in its economic definition as the "exigency of the Other". Desire is the economic principle of differentiation, and the condition for any notion of phenomenality. Again, the centrality of Proust in the philosophy of communication is palpable. In Proust, as in Nietzsche and Freud, the unconditioned term of cognition has no privilege. The lover is always the "last to know" what everyone knows about the beloved: his homosexuality or his promiscuity. (This reality will be revealed when it has become "indifferent" to the lover, i.e. when he no longer loves.) But the blindness of desire, which pursues the escaping other, is the only "truth", in a Proustian sense, of the other. When Swann has finally extricated himself from Odette, and laments the waste of his time on a woman who was "not his type", the narrator's irony is at its extreme. This return to the quotidian verities of Habit is precisely the extrication of subjectivity from the fundamental "truth" of communication: a truth which can never be known, but only desired in the exigency of a *recherche*.* As Gilles Deleuze writes so well of Proust, the signs are not to be interpreted, but to be chosen. The other is not a phenomenon, but an instance which involves subjectivity, in desire. The truth of Habit is desire in its exhaustion by utility, and is the passage of time in the blind repetition of the habitual. Love and Habit are both grounded in desire. The difference is in how one loses one's time. The everyday truths about individuals are themselves produced by desire, in the parochial blindness of Combray, the Guermantes, or the narrator himself. Habit is the *habiter* of desire, its organization of reality as a familiarity adjusted to subjectivity's solitude. Love is desire in its involvement with the Other and its interruption of solitude. Both desires are the permanence of loss. Their difference does not describe a privilege of truth over error, but a priority of desire over its tendency in Habit to mimic the form of Truth. When Swann realizes that he is not alone in his carriage, and that a new world of pain and vigilance is opening for him, he has the sense that his life has become more "interesting". This is perhaps the only sense of Proust's valorization of desire over Habit: it is not an authenticity, not a truth, but an involvement more fundamental than that of truth. The pain of the other's escape, and the frustration of pursuit and abandonment, are desire's excess over the semblance of truth in Habit. This excess is more "interesting", more fundamental, than our adjustment of a familiar reality to our desire in the quotidian. Subjectivity's common denominator, in Proust as in Bataille, is its transgression of interiority — its radical heteronomy — even though this transgression may be mobilized to invest utility or the world of Habit. Bataille's intuition of this affinity is the principle of his excellent writings on Proust.[52]

Discontinuity in Bataille is an inextrication or incompletion which is the investment of interiority by communication.

It is the plethora that begins a *glissement* in which (a) being divides, but it divides at that very moment, at the moment of the *glissement,* at the critical moment at which these beings, which will presently be opposed to one another, are not yet opposed. The crisis of separation [*crise séparatrice*] proceeds from the plethora: it is not yet separation, it is ambiguity.[53]

Separation produces a plethora: the difference and non-indifference of the same in communication. Separation in the general economy, irreducible to mediation, manifestation, or totalization, produces closure as the subjectivity of an involvement with the Other. The fugitive, passing existence of closure — its fundamental mortality — is this involvement, for which the term *glissement,* and its complement, *mise en jeu,* are the basic predicates.

* The only properly "intellectual" moment of a Proustian character's life is the love affair in which the possible actions and associations of the beloved, in an indefinite past and future of repetition, become the object of a painful research.

It is the crisis of (the) being: (the) being has the interior experience of being in the crisis which puts it to the test [*met à l'épreuve*], it is the *mise en jeu* of (the) being in a passage from continuity to discontinuity, or from discontinuity to continuity.[54]

Closure in Bataille is a *mise en jeu* or *glissement:* an intrication with alterity which is closure's irreducibility to closure itself. This is closure as the impossible, in a reality without negation and without power.

On a most basic level, the phrase "not manifestation, not totalization, but communication" describes the general economy. The phrase "not negation, but desire" describes the economy's principle of differentiation. Closure is an exigency, forced by the Other. Bataille's intuition of proximity proceeds from his thinking of differentiation in its production of the following concepts: (1) a closure which is excessively closed and not closed enough, by virtue of its economic constitution; (2) a radical passivity in being, which is a direct product of differentiation, and is called subjectivity or *expérience;* (3) the non-indifference of this passivity toward the economy from which it is differentiated, and the non-reciprocity or dissymmetry of communication which results from this non-indifference (the *pour l'autre* or conation "inside out" of interiority); (4) the movement or disturbance which haunts the immobility of determined Being by virtue of the excess inscribed in it by differentiation (called transgression in the generality of Bataille's system, and called *parole* in the communication of Bataille, Blanchot and Levinas). Bataille's originality does not lie in his thematization of an instance outside totalization and outside manifestation. Such a thematization of an absolutely other which escapes, and whose economy is exhausted by the fact that it escapes into the independence of absolution, is a constant in Western thought. It is the principle of consciousness' doubt before its object, and of the self-criticism of philosophy in the ambivalence of idealism and realism. As Levinas will show in convincing detail, this self-criticism is itself an intuition of proximity which must reduce the latter in the interest of manifestation. The originality of Bataille, and his communication with Nietzsche, Proust, Freud, and most fundamentally Blanchot and Levinas, is his discovery of an alterity outside the totality but within the general economy, which approaches as it escapes. As mentioned above, the Other in proximity is essentially "here below". Its escape from identity and determination is its investment of a passivity in being which is called subjectivity. The insistence of the Other in the economy of interiority describes a reality without power, in which the exigency of totalization and the frustration of this exigency are not the ultimate dimension. The notion of "impossibility" in Bataille, Blanchot, and Levinas, describes a rapport with an instance in being which has no power, and yet weighs upon or is incumbent upon subjectivity. This incumbence is the extrication of alterity from its anthropomorphic image as the efficiency of escape and the power of a hyperbolic violence beyond determination. When subjectivity finds itself to be involved with or concerned by an instance which exceeds its spontaneity, without, however, having the power to limit or determine subjectivity, the approach of the Other becomes the principle of experience, and proximity becomes the economy of Being.

SEPARATION AND COGITO IN LEVINAS

Bataille, Blanchot, and Levinas, as mentioned above, share an important debt to phenomenology, in spite of their consistent tendency to thematize the general economy in terms other than those of manifestation. This debt to phenomenology, particularly in its Hegelian inspiration, takes the form of a strategic fidelity to the latter's situation of subjectivity within the economy of the real. For Hegel and his descendants, subjectivity is a moment, an instance or, in Levinas' words, an "event" in being which is involved in the differentiation of the existent — rather than a constituted consciousness posed in isolation from a real defined as an objective totality. Within the largely intellectualist context of the Hegelian concepts, the real does not function as a totality which would resist, on the basis of its being "in itself", the comprehension of consciousness, and thus frustrate certainty. Instead, the real functions as a subjective or spiritual totality which knows or comprehends itself in a dimension more fundamental than certainty — in spite of the adjustments or refinements of this self-consciousness which form the bulk of the *Phenomenology*. The subject's doubt before the opacity of the object may be situated, in Hegel's eyes, as a preliminary dialectical moment which is, in spite of its indefinite recurrence at the successive levels of the dialectic, secondary to the more fundamental communication of subject and object which is itself to be thought in a dimension beyond doubt and uncertainty.*

Hegel's preliminary aim is a reduction of the *a priori* subject-object dualism which motivates philosophy in its perennial oscillation between an idealism and a realism which are complementary. His more basic aim is the well-known metaphysical situation of a real which may be immediately conceived in the terms of totalization and comprehension. One common denominator within the Hegelian genealogy of the concept of consciousness is the dignity or importance of a consciousness which is thought as an authentic economic

---

* The insufficiency of consciousness at each moment of the dialectic is the "fixity" of its "auto-position" which tends to view the exterior as the immediacy of an objective or phenomenal presence. Consciousness repeatedly fails to perceive its own "experience", which is a dialectical "communication" with exteriority in the process of differentiation. The duality of consciousness' experience and its insufficient view of this experience is the animation of the dialectic. Although the ultimate Hegelian definitions of this experience are thematically organized in terms of comprehension and totalization, the basic duality of experience, communication, or differentiation, on one hand, and consciousness' naive and "interested" attitude toward this experience, on the other, describes an essentially communicational moment in Hegel which radically exceeds the intellectualist or "idealist" stratum of his thought. This moment, to which the philosophers of proximity are not sensitive in their discussions of Hegel, is the true locus of their debt to his concepts. It informs a series of properly differential definitions which punctuate the *Phenomenology* in its totality, and reaches its hyperbole in the chapter entitled "Force and Understanding.[55] (Cf. below, Chapter 4)

moment within the real, rather than as an essentially limited approach to objects whose exteriority always exceeds its transitivity. Consciousness is manifestation: a fundamental moment, rooted in differentiation, by which the real itself becomes phenomenal. The vicissitudes of this common denominator are well known. They include the idealism of Hegelian metaphysics, the primacy of the subjective in phenomenology, the irreducibility of freedom in Sartre, the essentiality of comprehension in Heidegger, etc. The contribution of Levinas (and, on a less explicit level, of Blanchot and Bataille) to this tradition takes the form of the following question: if subjectivity's receptivity, grounded in its involvement in a process of differentiation, implies predicates irreducible to the notion of consciousness as illumination, spontaneity, intentionality, etc., and if subjectivity must be thought as a moment in the economy of being, what adjustments to philosophy's concept of the real as an objective totality are required by this economy? If differentiation is not negation, and if the subjectivity of differentiation is not the phenomenological consciousness of negation and totalization, is it not necessary to situate the possibility of totalization within a larger element: a general economy for which totalization is not the ultimate principle?

In Bataille and Blanchot, the term *expérience* appears in the general economy on the basis of differentiation's irreducibility to negation, and interiority's irreducibility to totalization. The *expérience du dedans* in Bataille is discoverable in consciousness, in the one-called animalcule, and in the inert particle, because this experience proceeds from the communicational insufficiency of closure. Bataille's economic definition of interiority as an exigency, a density, and a vulnerability, is his grounding of subjectivity as a predicate of differentiation in the economy. In Blanchot, terms such as *errance, exigence, parole, inspiration,* and *expérience* itself, articulate the heteronomy and subjectivity of an "essential solitude" whose communicational economy parallels that of closure in Bataille. For both thinkers, subjectivity is a product of differentiation. Those ontological factors which exist for subjectivity (such as the notion of loss or *dépense* in Bataille, and irreality or the image in Blanchot) have an effectivity or positivity on this basis alone, but derive their more fundamental positivity from their own origin in differentiation. *Dépense* and the image are not perceptual or intentional factors which derive from the "point of view" of interiority in the economy; they are, in themselves, products of differentiation or moments of the economy. (When "each thing recedes into its image"[56] in Blanchot, this becoming-absent and becoming-other is not a perceptual or intentional moment, but is an instance of the properly differential investment of closure in the economy. Cf. below, Chapter 5.) Differentiation, which is not negation, produces subjectivity, although not as an illuminating interval correlative to a closure guaranteed by the negative. Subjectivity is a heteronomy, not a spontaneity. It is grounded by an absence of intervals, rather than by the existence of intervals. At this level, the extent and the limit of the Hegelian inspiration in Bataille and Blanchot is clear. Both thinkers appropriate the phenomenological procedure which situates intentionality within a real which must henceforth be termed spiritual or subjective. But their meditation of subjectivity in terms of differentiation and communication leads to the notion that since subjectivity or *expérience* is not intentionality, then the general economy may not be conceived in the terms of manifestation. Since closure is not identity, the general economy may not itself be conceived as a totality, or as a production of totalities. Rather, it must be defined in the terms of differentiation and communication — terms which include *dissimulation, parole, exigence, attente,* etc.

Levinas' thinking of interiority within the economy of being operates at the same level as that of Bataille and Blanchot. Although the "professionally" philosophical context of his thought constrains him always to situate his concepts with regard to manifestation and totalization, Levinas' interest in subjectivity and its situation within being centers on differentiation rather than illumination. The subjectivity of sensation and the passive synthesis in *En découvrant l'existence* and in *Autrement qu'être,* the subjectivity of *jouissance* in *Totalité et infini,* and the subjectivity of the *cogito* throughout Levinas, is an instance irreducible to manifestation which defines the real as an economy irreducible to manifestation: an economy which includes moments "outside the totality". For Levinas as for Blanchot, totalization may be said to exist within the real, but it exists on the foundation of an instance irreducible to it: proximity. Proximity is the "other than to be" or *autrement qu'être* which deploys itself in, insists in, or invests, Being: "qui, certes, s'entend dans l'être."[57] Proximity is the "irreality" of which, in Blanchot, "reality" is "merely the negation".[58]

The debt to Hegel in Bataille, Blanchot and Levinas is an important one, and is, perhaps for this reason, rarely acknowledged. Without the fundamental procedure which allows subjectivity to take a place in, and condition, the economy of the real, it would not be possible to describe the real, on the basis of a meditation upon subjectivity, as an economy which is not exhausted by the concept of totalization. On a most general level, then, it may be said that Hegelian manifestation has descendants which include intentionality in Husserl, comprehension in Heidegger, the primacy of the concrete, the subjective and the spontaneous in phenomenology — and, in a separate and less public dimension, the notion of proximity and the general economy as a communication irreducible to any of these surrounding concepts.*

* To this Hegelian genealogy, whose roots in ancient philosphy have been convincingly described by Heidegger, must be added a most secretive and problematic communication with the philosophy of difference. For example, the complex series of terms which articulate difference and subjectivity (e.g. *Idée, problème, apprendre, question, soutirer, contracter, intensité*) in Gilles Deleuze's *Différence et répétition* (Paris: P.U.F., 1968), describes an economic production of heteronomy and therefore of subjectivity whose involvement with Hegelian mediation is most intimate. As do the philosophers of proximity, however, Deleuze and the philosophers of difference ground subjectivity in a contamination of totalization, rather than in its efficiency. As mentioned above, this tendency itself is discoverable in Hegel, who must himself be assigned a place in the philosophy of difference.

Along with the One beyond being in Plato's *Parmenides,* the problematic of constitution and passive synthesis in Husserl, and a few other central pre-occupations, Descartes' *cogito* has been a lifelong meditation for Levinas. The most penetrating expression of this meditation is to be found in *Totalité et infini,* and its context is the notion of interiority and economy. A basic and most stable moment in Levinas, which does not harmonize thematically with the subordination of interiority to communication in Bataille and Blanchot, is an insistence on the definition of *separation* in the real. Separation for Levinas is a "point of departure" without which the radical alterity of communication cannot be thought.

The alterity, the radical heterogeneity of the Other, is only possible if the Other is other with regard to a term whose essence is to remain at the point of departure, to serve as the beginning [*entrée*] of the relation, to be the Same, not relatively, but absolutely. *A term can remain absolutely at the point of departure only as a Self* [*Moi*].[59] *

The absolute alterity sought by Levinas throughout his career in phenomenology cannot be articulated with a subjectivity whose unicity is dissolved in the universalizing correlations of Hegelian totalization. Nor can it be articulated with the subjectivity of traditional humanism, whose exceptional status is subordinated to a logic of totalization and communion which is not fundamentally different from the logic of correlation. In both cases, interiority is essentially reduced by a system that transcends it: the totality. Alterity, for Levinas, cannot be an instance dialectically reducible to totalization. Nor can it be the principle of a dimension defined as simple undifferentiation or dispersion. Alterity must be defined relative to a Same, and this Same must be, in its way, authentically autonomous or Separate. It cannot be determined by an Other which, by virtue of this power to determine, would itself have the form of a totality. This dual proposition — the refusal of an adequate, classically defined interiority, and the insistence upon a separation which would be yet more radical than the unitary self-coincidence of an identity — is one example of Levinas' problematic status within the culture of his time, a culture concerned essentially with its need to re-establish a humanist subject or to abolish such a subject once and for all.

Separation is basic to the production of alterity within the economy of being.

* The term *Moi* (as opposed to the *moi* of unicity in election) refers to interiority in its lack of correlation to an alterity which is "in a different concept": the Other of closure. Although the *Moi* of the *cogito,* of *jouissance,* of egoism and atheism, has not yet been subjected to the approach of the Other in recurrence (as will be the *moi* of irreplaceable unicity), this *Moi* must also be thematized as a "point of departure" which cannot be correlated to alterity. It is this initial moment of separation's interiority that Levinas describes in his reading of the Cartesian *cogito.* In later demonstrations, the Self (*Moi*) of totalization and correlation will be opposed to the Me (*moi*) of non-interchangeable unicity.

But separation is only possible as an escape from the universal and from dialectical reduction — that is, as an escape from the totality. Long before the critical experience of substitution, recurrence, and the idea of the infinite — that is, within the very moment of its initial "egoism" — separation must be, in its own constitution, an *autrement qu'être,* an instance outside totalization. Since the adequate and adequating self-coincidence of identity to self is nothing more than an aptitude of interiority to be subsumed by the impersonality of comprehension and correlation, the unicity of separation must consist, paradoxically, of a structure irreducible to closure. This structure will already be a communication and a proximity, whose density corresponds to the subsequent density or "gravity" of election and irreplaceability. Thus, paradoxically, the only true separation in Levinas is the radical heteronomy of an involvement with alterity. For this reason, it may be said that while Levinas' insistence upon interiority as point of departure appears thematically to contradict the tendencies of Bataille and Blanchot, his more fundamental identification of separation with communication describes the same concept of proximity that is to be found in the texts of these thinkers.

In sensation, as will be discussed in a later chapter, the ambiguous constitution of a subjectivity defined as the *sentant-senti,* the intrication of interior and exterior, allows the predication of separation to such a subjectivity. In the case of the *cogito,* a similar lack of autonomy founding separation is discovered. Strategically accepting the economic notion of subjectivity as an illumination within being, Levinas thinks the *cogito* as a contradictory configuration in which a secondary moment, consciousness, renders manifest the primary moment — the real — which constituted it. The effect, consciousness, renders manifest and thus "conditions" the manifestation of the cause or condition, the real. Since differentiation and temporalization are subordinated to manifestation in ontology, the *cogito* which manifests its condition becomes the condition of its condition. The effect behaves as though it preceded its cause, the effect assumes and constitutes its cause.

Even its cause, anterior to it, is yet to come [*à venir*]. The cause of a being is thought or known by its effect *as though* it were posterior to its effect. We speak lightly of the possibility of this "as though" which would indicate an illusion. Now, this illusion is not gratuitous, but constitutes a positive event. The posteriority of the anterior — an absurd logical inversion — could only be produced, one would say, by memory or by thought. But the "unbelievable" phenomenon of memory or of thought, must indeed be interpreted as a revolution in being. Thus theoretical thought already — but by virtue of a deeper structure which subtends it, *psychisme* [separation as a subjectivity grounded in heteronomy] — articulates separation. Not reflected by thought but produced by it. The *After* or the *Effect* here conditions the *Before* or the *Cause:* the Before *appears* and is simply assumed [*accueilli,* welcomed, received].[60]

In this quotation, as in so many moments of Levinas' text, it is important to note his characteristic anti-intellectualism. Theoretical thought in the *cogito* "articulates" separation, in spite of and because of its very intellectualism. Philosophy, desiring to found a *cogito* adequate to the objective real, describes a *cogito* of separation. And in this *cogito* as described by philosophy, separation is not thought or discovered, but produced. Thus the *cogito,* though it be defined as manifestation, is a moment of separation entirely irreducible to the latter. How this *cogito* might interpret its own separation — true or false, certain or uncertain — is of no interest to Levinas. In a sense, the *cogito* as manifestation is of no interest to him, except insofar as the logic of manifestation attests or "articulates" separation itself.

The *cogito,* in its entirety, is an "illusion", the illusion that the effect may precede, found and condition its cause. This illusion, this "invraisemblance" which interrupts the repose of an undifferentiated plenitude, is separation in being: a separation whose movement may here be called "consciousness" or "subjectivity". The "as though" of the *cogito* is quite precisely the modality of manifestation (the becoming-subjective of being in differentiation) as the *cogito* produces the latter. Following the phenomenological situation of consciousness discussed above, it is necessary to define this preceding of cause by effect, this reversal of historical time, as an authentic ontological moment whose paradoxical but irreducible modality, within the existent, is a *comme si* or "as though". The effective reality of the *comme si,* the appearance of the conditional tense in common time and of the conditional mode in being, is the *cogito*. Thus Levinas, in his implicit, strategic dialogue with Hegel, gives foundation and reality to the intuition of another celebrated reader of Hegel, the Mallarmé of the *Coup de dés.*

The *cogito,* even in its conditionality and "invraisemblance", effectively reverses the cause-effect progression, and thus, in its putative function as manifestation, confounds the historical time correlative of manifestation. In other words, manifestation in its own awakening, reverses the univocity of its own movement. Three temporalities are to be noted here. In the first place, the *cogito* reverses the historical time it inaugurates. In the second place, the *cogito* introduces into temporalization the conditional mode of the "as though" (i.e. the real which is essentially inactual). And in the third place, the *cogito* as effect conditioning cause must preexist itself and thus "pronounce," in the words of Blanchot, "its own *Fiat lux*." These three temporal paradoxes attest the priority of a proximal differentiation which is not made explicit by Levinas in his reading of Descartes, but which informs and organizes the entire Levinasian text. Manifestation is a moment or modality of proximity: a moment of differentiation in the general economy. Differentiation produces moments or effects whose only closure or quiddity is their intrication with each other. The general economy produces discontinuity or unicity without producing totalization. The proximity of economic singularities is a rapport which precedes (and which will condition) the possibility of identity and of the relations into which a constituted identity may enter. This rapport is both more fundamental and less "actual" than causality, relation, or non-contradiction. The moment of manifestation, which for philosophy is also the primary moment of totalization, is economically informed and conditioned by the movement of difference and proximity. It is for this reason that the *cogito*'s economy is paradoxical, from the point of view of totalization, but not from the point of view of proximity. The reversal of cause and effect, in this context, attests a discontinuity in the real, and a rapport of exteriority with subjectivity, which precedes the causal relation of totalities, and may indeed, from the perspective of causality, assume the form of a reversal. The linear univocity of causality is less the result of a linear concept of temporality than it is the univocity of a communication in which totalization must always precede relation. The involvement of proximal entities precedes and forecloses totalization. Yet this involvement or inextrication is the movement of a differentiation which is the very possibility of totalization, i.e. of discontinuity within being. The rapport of subjectivity and exteriority is a separation, but not a relation between totalities, and for this reason is essentially irreducible to determination. From this perspective, it is possible for the effect to influence and thus to condition its cause, in a sense which is not itself that of causality.

Effect and Cause, After and Before, communicate in a moment of differentiation which is not yet totalization, and which will never be exhausted by its regional mobilization or "catalysis", the totality. In this primary moment, differentiation produces communications or rapports whose economy is not negation, not non-contradiction, but difference. And differentiation is also temporalization: a production of temporal discontinuities whose rapport is itself differential and proximal. Philosophy calls this inextrication or involvement over temporal intervals "repetition". Within the movement of a communicational temporalization, it is possible for a differential entity to "pre-exist" its entry into being, to persist after its annihilation, and to insist in the general economy at indefinite temporal intervals. This is because the unicity of the differential entity is produced not by the complementarity of negation, non-contradiction and totalization, but by the communicational heteronomy of difference and proximity. The temporal "moment" of repetition is inadequate to the notions of punctuality, anteriority and posteriority, because its differential rapport with other moments is not a negation. Thus difference produces an "unbelievable" involvement of Effect and Cause, and repetition produces an "unbelievable" intrication of After and Before. These involvements result from the irreducibility of communication to totalization and relation. Their "invraisemblance", their "illusory" character results from the basic irreducibility of communication to manifestation. The cornerstones of manifestation are negation and its complement, totalization, which consecrate and guarantee the interval of phenomenality between subject and object (or the interval within being in which phenomenology situates consciousness' spontaneity). Since differentiation produces rapports prior to, and in excess of, the possibility of totalization, these rapports must always assume the predicate of illusion, inactuality, or inexistence, from the perspective of manifestation.

Just as the simulacrum is the form of unicity in a differential dimension, the Blanchotian *inactuel* or *irréel*, and Levinas' *autrement qu'être*, designate the effective reality of that which is nevertheless not "actual": proximity.

The illusory, conditional, or fantastic effect produced by the *cogito* results from its production in differentiaton. The appearance of subjectivity in being is made possible by the fundamental heteronomy — the passivity and alteration — of a communicational closure. It is this heteronomous communication that confounds the logic of totalization and negation. Because subjectivity is a communication, subjectivity is an "invraisemblance" or, in Bataille's words, an impossibility. Levinas' fascination with the *cogito* results from the fact that this impossibility which exceeds its own punctuality* and actuality, functions in philosophy as the very inauguration and guarantee of those ontological dimensions which are exceeded by its economy: manifestation, causality, and the progressive temporality of totalization. At the same time, as Levinas notes in a Hegelian inspiration, there is a basic difference between the *cogito*'s experience of separation and its interpretation of this experience. The *cogito*'s aptitude to assume a reality which preceded its conation is a communicational moment, grounded in the economy's irreducibility to totalization, and in the radical dispossession which is correlative of this irreducibility. Yet the sense of this heteronomous communication, for the *cogito* itself, is its own spontaneity and autonomy. Articulating by its awakening the communicational moment of separation in being, the *cogito* mobilizes this moment as a power and an independence from exteriority. Separation is not dispersion, but discontinuity. The *cogito*'s "egoism" or "atheism", in Levinas' words, is its tendency to interpret this discontinuity as totalization or identity, and to inaugurate by this "catalysis" of identity an important though not exhaustive region of the general economy: the totality. This tendency is the desire by which closure is forced or invested as an economic exigency. The sense of totalization for Levinas, as for Bataille and Nietzsche (and, at intervals, for Hegel as well), is a communicational intensity of incompletion which assumes the predicates and functions of a constituted integrity. The totality is a region or dimension of the general economy of communication, whose overwhelming and totalitarian spontaneity is invested precisely by the intensity of this communication.

By its reversal of time and causality, and by its articulation of the inactual, the *cogito* produces an escape from totalization, or attests a separation in being whose principle is not negation. The primary vicissitude of this economic

---

* In Levinas as in Blanchot, the indefinite futurity of the *à venir* or "yet to come" is correlative of the anteriority or "always already" which haunts punctuality in repetition. In the passage quoted above, Levinas writes: "Through time, in fact, being is not *yet*; which does not confuse it with nothingness [*néant*], but maintains it at a distance from itself. It is not in a single moment [*d'un seul coup*, all at once]. Even its cause, anterior to it, is yet to come."[61] The *cogito* as separation unites the "not yet", the "already", and the "as though", by virtue of its communicational excess over both punctuality and actuality.

moment may be totalization itself, defined as a "catalysis" of identity and determination in being; but what is important to Levinas is that, by virtue of the *cogito*'s paradoxical insistence within the real, the real itself resists totalization. "The original role of *psychisme* does not consist, in fact, in merely reflecting [*refléter*] being. It is already a *manner* of being [*manière d'être,* a mode or moment of being], a resistance to the totality. Thought or *psychisme* opens the dimension required by this manner."[62]

The subtlety of Levinas in his discussion of the *cogito* consists in his strategic acceptance of the logic of manifestation in order to derive and found an instance within the real which is an effective escape from totalization. It is only the principle of manifestation itself, as interval and illumination, that permits the conclusion that the *cogito* conditions its cause, pre-exists itself and reverses time. Levinas desires to show that the problematic of manifestation, in spite of itself, articulates an instance which escapes its own concept of the general economy. By virtue of the *cogito*'s existence (by virtue of separation itself as a moment of differentiation), the totality may no longer be conceived as the sole model for the economy; manifestation as spontaneity may no longer be conceived as the sole model for illumination and temporalization; causality may no longer be conceived as the principle of relation in an economy differentiated by proximity. On one hand, Levinas is concerned to show that theoretical thought moves in spite of itself toward the *autrement qu'être* and then toward the *éthique.* His consistent aim is to demonstrate that the *autrement qu'être* and the *éthique* are conditions for *any* concept of manifestation, experience, or critical thought. On the other hand, in answer to the implicit objection "Why speak of manifestation and causality at all, if these factors are not pertinent to the economy?", it must be said, following the generality of Levinas' definitions, that manifestation, causality and the totality are not simply inexistent factors. Levinas, like Blanchot, will always attest the effective reality of negativity, totalization, etc., even as he insists upon the latent economy of these ontological moments. Without denying their existence, he will contest their primacy and irreducibility. Just as negation is conceived in Blanchot as an effect or product of dissimulation (an economic factor irreducible to manifestation), manifestation in Levinas is an authentic moment whose overwhelming supremacy in Western thought reflects its positive ontological status. This factor, however, does not exhaust the sense of the economy. There is a reality "outside the totality". And it can be shown that this "other" reality, the "other" of the actual and causal, conditions the totality itself. The *cogito,* cornerstone of totalization, is a basic example of Levinas' discursive strategies as well as his own view of the economy.

*

The *cogito*'s awakening within an element that precedes it describes a rooting of consciousness within an economy rather than an *a priori* opposition of these terms. Because of the paradoxical predicates of this awakening, Levinas refuses to accord it the status of a simple manifestation, and refuses to equate its intrication with alterity to Hegel's notion of a consciousness dialectically rooted in being. There are two basic axes of this refusal to reduce the *cogito* to a function of illumination. Their common denominator is the ambiguity of the *cogito*'s constitution with regard to alterity, and the concomitant impossibility of defining this constitution in dialectical terms. On one hand, the *cogito*, like the exigency in Bataille, is an "interiority outside", a communication with exteriority whose modality is not negation, but proximity. As such, it is already other than an intentionality whose distance from exteriority would constitute its adequation to and totalization of this exteriority. On the basis of this ambiguous proximity to alterity, Levinas refuses to conceive an originary rapport with exteriority in terms of utility or manipulation, and derives the term *jouissance* to describe a more fundamental intrication. The lengthy sections of *Totalité et infini* which present this argument must certainly be understood as refusals of the Heideggerian characterizations of *Dasein;* but more fundamentally, they should be understood as refusals of Hegel's subordination of proximity to negation and manifestation, as it informs not only Heidegger's text but also that of Husserl and of phenomenology in general. The central regularity of Levinas' reading of phenomenology is his approval and appropriation of the concept of ambiguous constitution, as it is implied by intentionality, sensation, the *Urimpression,* the impersonality of *Dasein,* etc., and his refusal of phenomenology's reduction of this moment to noesis, comprehension, manifestation, etc. *Jouissance,** a rapport irreducible to intentionality which must condition intentionality, is the central expression in *Totalité et infini* of this critical procedure.[63] *Jouissance* and the *vivre de* . . . are not relations of a constituted intentionality to a real defined by Levinas as an *élément;* they are instead the very constitution of subjectivity as an intrication prior to, and conditioning, any notion of consciousness. It is for this reason that *jouissance* concerns an "element" rather than a differentiated existent, and that *jouissance* is not yet a "care" (a transcendence and intentionality), not yet a manipulation, but an insouciant happiness, enjoyment, and properly orgastic joy (a fulfillment which overflows and dispossesses): the

---

* The predicates of *jouissance* are based on its description of a communicational moment irreducible to consciousness, in which subjectivity's rapport with exteriority is not negation, but a proximal investment and a radical heteronomy. Thus, the predicate of "enjoyment" describes this fulfilling or nourishing investment by a supportive "element". The predicate of "joy" describes a pre-intentional or pre-objectal moment of insouciance, not yet definable as the concern or *Sorge* of a consciousness involved with its objects. The predicate of "orgasm" describes an excessive economic investment of subjectivity by an exteriority which overflows interiority's closure. The common denominator of these predicates is their description of a subjectivity of differentiation which is always both an excessive "fulfillment" by exteriority and a radical dispossession — the coincidence of these factors being required by the inadequation of the economy to closure as integrity. The heteronomy of *jouissance,* its subjection to exteriority, is for Levinas its "subjectivity".

enjoyment of a pure interiority supported and indeed created by the plenitude and excess of the real. This Levinasian interiority, whose involvement with the economy is an insouciance destined to become the vigilance and insomnia of intentionality, is also Bataillian interiority: a *dépense* destined to take itself for a conservation.

Intentionality is rooted in a moment which exceeds intentionality itself.

I bathe in and am nourished by the world I constitute. It is an aliment and a "milieu". The intentionality which envisages [*vise*] the exterior, changes its sense [*change de sens,* changes meanings, direction or orientation] in its very aim [*visée,* orientation, inclination], becoming interior to the exteriority it constitutes, comes, in a way, from the point toward which it goes, recognizing itself as past in its future, lives on [*vit de*] what it thinks.[64]

No negation or adequate differentiation allows intentionality, at this moment, the function of illumination accorded it by philosophy. The alterity it envisages, animates or invests the movement which envisages. The Other invests the eye which considers the Other. This intrication with alterity makes of intentionality a true "interiority outside". *Jouissance* is the modality of this ambiguity, rather than a characterization, in the Heideggerian manner, of an originary relation to objects.

If the pure interiority of this "egoism" of *jouissance* is always "not yet intentionality", the question becomes: what factor gives to interiority its critical, intentional destiny? The answer to this question, elaborated separately for *jouissance* and for the *cogito,* is that the fundamental dispossession of an investment or animation by alterity is the principle of this critical or properly "theoretical" moment of consciousness. In the case of *jouissance,* Levinas points out that the plenitude or concupiscence of subjectivity's primordial experience is also the contamination of interiority's closure by the inherence and proximity of the exterior. The Other which bathes and supports, also intrudes upon and escapes from a closure which is not a totality. The rapport of interior and exterior is not a communion, but a proximity. It is for this reason that *jouissance* is subject or subjected to alterity's approach, in the form of the *il y a* of being beyond negation (cf. below).[65] This subjection is the very subjectivity of *jouissance.* "The perfidious element gives itself while escaping."[66] Exteriority supports and fulfills while it dispossesses. The *il y a* is the pre-originary or proximal "future" of *jouissance:* the vigilance which haunts this moment of insouciance. The *il y a* is a reality beyond negation and without objects, of which one cannot be conscious (as a transcending intentionality), and of which one cannot but be conscious (as a subjection to a proximity which approaches by virtue of its investment of interiority).

In the case of the *cogito,* Levinas again derives the notion of a critical or theoretical moment of consciousness from the proposition of subjectivity's investment by alterity. In his reading of Descartes, Levinas interprets the doubt which prepares the *cogito* as a strategy of negation which reaches deeper and deeper levels, none of which may itself resist negation. The sense of this movement is the ontological sense and positivity of negation itself. "Doubt regarding objects implies the evidence of the exercise of doubt itself."[67] Negation is the modality of a "breaking of participation" by which the egoistic or atheistic subject tends to assert its own separation as an autonomy. But the ultimate sense of this negation is an "abyss" a context beyond the correlation of affirmation and negation, which Levinas describes by a term derived in earlier books: *il y a*. *Il y a* is that moment in being at which negation ceases to exert its totalizing power. *Il y a* is the limit of negation — being beyond negation (cf. below, Chapter 5). It is at this moment that the negations of an apparently constituted intentionality lead to the appearance of the *cogito*: an affirmation in the midst of absence, an affirmation where there is no negation. This affirmation could never appear in the midst of intentionality's doubt, because it does not arise within the context of consciousness' activity as negation. Instead, it proceeds from alterity to invest or condition consciousness. "The self in negativity, manifesting itself by doubt, breaks its participation [in being], but does not find in the *cogito* alone a terminus [*arrêt*]. It is not Me [*Moi*, the self of the *cogito*] — it is the Other that can say yes. Affirmation comes from it. It is at the beginning of [the] experience."[68] Interiority is subjectivity: the capacity or aptitude to be affected by exteriority. In a more radical Levinasian sense, interiority is the aptitude of exteriority to weigh upon or be incumbent upon a point in being which becomes, by virtue of this gravity, an interiority or *Moi*. Subjectivity is not intentionality — the ability to take a distance from, and illuminate, the exterior. Rather, it is an affirmation (i.e. the intensive movement of an economy without negation), coming from alterity to the subject, which may create the effect of illumination. It is a proximity which, like dissimulation in Blanchot, "tends to become negation" or creates the effect of negation. In either case, it is a contact with alterity, irreducible to negation and manifestation, that conditions the possibility of these concepts. This contact with alterity, this event or *manière* in being, is the *cogito* or, more generally, the concept of interiority in Levinas.

In certain sections of his text, Levinas will state that interiority in its egoism can have no truly critical or theoretical dimension until its spontaneity is placed in question by the approach of *Autrui* (i.e. Others: the other person or subject, as invested by the Other of closure). At other junctures, such as the discussion of the *cogito* and the problematic of sensation, he will derive and define interiority itself as an involvement with alterity or an affirmation proceeding from alterity. The reason for this ambiguity or inequality is that *Autrui* is not the Other person or Other subject in his integrity, defined as the center of his own universe. *Autrui* is not "transcendent" in Levinas, as in Sartre. Instead, *Autrui* is the form, or the differentiation, of alterity itself, defined as Being in its irreducibility to totalization and manifestation. Alterity is Being in its proximity which precedes and conditions its phenomenality. In the context of *récurrence* Levinas will say that the Other invests my freedom, or that I "come back to myself through the Other". In considering the entire problematic of inspiration, substitution, and recurrence in Levinas, it is important to note the inseparability of *Autrui* from alterity in a more general sense. Any contact with, or inspiration from, *Autrui*, is traceable to the more basic definition of interiority itself as an intrication with alterity, as in the *cogito*. Conversely, the seemingly impersonal inherence of alterity in the interiority of the *cogito*, of sensation, or of *jouissance*, is already the implicit approach of the Other as *Autrui*. This preorginary approach is the sense of a fundamental Levinasian assertion: "le sensible est déjà dit" (the sensible is already spoken).[69] The aptitude to receive an impression in sensation is already *récurrence*, already a receiving of and answering to the Other of Levinasian "responsibility". Alterity is always intersubjective, in spite of its impersonality. In intersubjectivity, in sensation, in *jouissance*, in the *cogito*, the impersonal Other of closure invests and weighs upon interiority. It is for this reason that Levinas admires Descartes' argument that the certainty of the *cogito* is placed in consciousness by alterity, in the form of God. Cartesian certainty is not the predicate of interiority, but of alterity in its affirmation. The idea of the infinite is "mise en nous": placed in us. The dual status of alterity — its impersonality and its intersubjectivity — informs a statement like the following, in which Levinas' two tendencies are joined:

Descartes seeks certainty and stops at the first change of level in this vertiginous descent. The fact is that he possesses the idea of the infinite [the communication of interiority with exteriority, the Other], and can measure in advance the return of affirmation from behind negation. But to possess the idea of the infinite is already to have received [*accueilli*] *Autrui*.[70]

Autrui in Levinas, as in Bataille and Blanchot, is always an affirmation, an impersonality, before it may be a person, another subject. Thus *Autrui* arises from the *il y a* of Being beyond negation, the *autrement qu'être* of Being beyond totalization, before the drama of substitution and responsibility may take place. In other words, the *cogito* and interiority are already a recurrence "à partir de l'autre", proceeding from the Other, already an implicit intersubjectivity, in the very solitude of their "egoism". The *cogito* in Levinas, like the exigency in Bataille, and essential solitude in Blanchot, describes a subjectivity which is always already an intersubjectivity, in the basic moment of its *expérience*.

ESSENTIAL SOLITUDE IN BLANCHOT

Levinas' concern with the *cogito* results from his insistence upon the derivation of separation within the economy of being. Levinasian alterity must be articulated with a Same, a *Moi* or interiority, in a rapport which is not that of correlation. Though it be invested by alterity as a radical heteronomy, this Same must retain its separation, its interiority, and its "quant à soi". The rapport with alterity is not a simple explosion or dispersion of interiority, but an investment and a proximity. It is by virtue of this communicational rapport that Levinas will often say that alterity does not "limit" the Same. Alterity is not a superior power, not a destruction, not a substantiality. Its powerlessness and lack of positivity are precisely its alterity. Subjectivity's rapport with the Other is not an encounter of two powers or totalities. It is rather the rapport of the totality, the Same, with an Other of totalization which invests totalization. In this encounter, interiority is neither destroyed nor transcended by an ethical drama which exceeds its egoism. Subjectivity, in the proximity of the Other, always "knows what is happening to it." It is precisely this irreducibility of unicity, however heteronomous its investment or its economy may be, that permits the paradoxical and indefinite approach of an Other which cannot itself assume the predicates of a totality.

Maurice Blanchot's meditation of subjectivity follows a similar direction to that of Levinas. However, Blanchot does not share Levinas' concern with the definition of an irreducible economic closure which must function as a "point of departure" in the rapport with alterity. For this reason, there is no explicit Blanchotian equivalent of Levinas' *Moi* whose very separation is an escape from totalization, in the *cogito,* in sensation, or in *jouissance.* The economy of interiority and alterity in Blanchot is elaborated at the moment of the Other's approach, rather than at the moment of separation. Blanchot's discovery of this economy takes place at the second, more dramatic moment of Levinas' demonstration: the moment of recurrence. For this reason, the figure of a classically defined ipseity or intentionality in Blanchot takes the form of a purely strategic initiality. Rather than to thematize a *cogito* in economic terms, in the manner of Bataille or Levinas, Blanchot posits a self-coincident and self-present intentionality whose spontaneity constitutes an approach to exteriority. This approach will take the characteristic form of a univocal movement or trajectory which is interrupted by the complex moment of an involvement with alterity. This moment will always have the temporal aspect of an "event" which supervenes to subjectivity, although the economy of its appearance escapes both the concept of a linear time and the concept of a punctual event. The rapport of alterity with the Same, in Blanchot as in Levinas, is a pre-originary economic intrication and investment. For this reason, the approach to alterity is a movement whose latent temporality is that of alterity itself. It is alterity that directs or conditions this approach. Thus the punctuality of the Other's approach will involve aspects of a proximal temporality which exceeds the possibilities of presence and punctuality. The Other's appearance will unite the "always already", the *à venir* or "yet to come", and the inactuality of this temporality, in a moment which is both compelling and monotonous, both urgent and, in Blanchot's phrase, "non-concerning". It will be, not an appearance, but a proximity and an approach.

Subjectivity's approach to the exterior or *Dehors* in Blanchot will describe the following progression: intentionality, conceived as a linear trajectory, will be interrupted at an indeterminate "point" by an instance in the real which throws this intentional movement back to a point prior to its initiation. This new point, called by Blanchot a *nouvelle origine* or "new origin", has introduced interiority to a dimension without trajectory or linearity. Subjectivity, at this point, is still characterized by its intentional movement, whose tendency toward subject-object distinction, immediacy and totalization is seen by Blanchot as an irreducible detour in its constitution. At the secondary point of the *nouvelle origine,* however, an intrication or involvement with alterity (the Other of closure) places subjectivity in a dimension for which this spontaneous movement is not a possibility. There is "no place", no space, no interval, in this dimension, for the displacement implicit in intentionality's distance from the exterior. The intentional self is now in a moment of proximity which does not allow it to deploy its initiative ontologically, Phenomenal being, conditioned by the adequate and adequating negativity which is consciousness' element, has taken the new form of an intrusive and suffocating proximity which disarms the ekstases of manifestation. No adequation of the irreducible transitivity of consciousness to this dimension of proximity is possible. Intentionality, whose new origin is no longer an "ex-istence" which might illuminate and act upon a phenomenal reality, becomes the insistent, fragmentary movement of a trajectory without direction or destination: a pure initiative in a universe inadequate to initiative. Blanchot calls this hesitant, exigent, and repetitive movement *Indecision.*

There are two fundamental implications of the moment of indecision in Blanchot's text. In the first place, the putative linearity and spontaneity of consciousness' movement have implicitly reached their "destination": a problematic contact with the exterior or *Dehors;* and it is this contact or involvement that plunges subjectivity into its *nouvelle origine.* On the other hand, the accomplishment of an intentional movement which seeks to enter into a phenomenal or objective relation with exteriority, remains out of reach. "No longer a consciousness produced in negation, but a subjectivity produced by communication": such is the *nouvelle origine* for Blanchot. Consciousness, in its movement toward a *Dehors* conceived as an object or subject-object correlation, has crossed an implicit point at which its own interiority has become a contact, intrication, or involvement with a *Dehors* whose very exteriority is the fact that it cannot become an object. This contact is not the "thrownness", facticity, or primordial proximity to being which phenomenology attests, in its Hegelian inspiration, and which is always correlated in phenomenology to a distance or interval by which subjectivity's relation to the exterior may assume the predicates of a comprehension. Instead, it is an absence of interval, a "weakness" of the negative, and a proximity of the *Dehors* in excess over the possibility of phenomenality.

The second basic sense of indecision as *nouvelle origine* produced in subjectivity's approach to the exterior is the very pre-originarity of this moment. Alterity insists in the constitution of intentionality's initial transitivity, and thus conditions the movement which putatively precedes its punctual appearance. The new origin of intentionality is indecision. The overall trajectory of the intentional act which encounters a proximate *Dehors* is precisely the trajectory of the movement called indecision: an exigent beginning or initiative which finds itself, in a problematic and indefinite punctuality, to be involved with a reality beyond decision. This undecided movement, the "always already" of subjectivity, is also, according to the temporality of the new origin, the being of subjectivity as repetition.

Thus, the moment strategically conceived by Blanchot as an event within the actual, designates a more fundamental moment whose insistence within being takes the economic form of a repetition, and describes an effective reality which is not actual or phenomenal. Blanchot will derive and define this temporality of repetition and inactuality, on the basis of an "impossibility of initiative" or "impossibility of decision", in many contexts. At the same time, he will consistently describe a subjectivity which discovers its new origin in a moment of apprehension or encounter — a description inaugurated in the famous opening pages of *Thomas l'obscur*. At this moment of apprehension, which is not an apperception and is not properly understandable as the act of a consciousness, subjectivity will discover the proximity which forecloses its transitive movement, in an event of terrifying proportions, and will be thrown into the dimension which combines this transitivity and its other: indecision. The notion of indecision as commonly understood, with its sense of beginning, interruption and repetition, describes this subjectivity whose intentional directionality is not abolished, but remains to insist repetitively as a moment or detour in being which, in Blanchot's words, "va de-ci, de-là."

Orpheus will break the gods' injunction "from his first step toward the shadows."[71] The animal which digs its burrow will render inevitable and imminent the approach of the other beast, from the first moment of its excavation. The creative writer will enter the realm of the incessant and interminable, from his first confident initiative in the production of the *oeuvre*. Blanchot's writing offers many examples of the interrupted approach and its contaminated, repetitive result. In every case, the temporality of repetition underlies that linear and progressive time which is proper to subjectivity's initiative, and eventually appears to contaminate this linearity. (Linear time has an effective reality within the general economy. It is, to paraphrase Blanchot, "one way time has of accomplishing itself." Like the totality in Levinas or the profane world in Bataille, however, it is not the only dimension of being, and is invested by another instance.) In every case, the urgency and passivity of this interruption attest a latent investment of subjectivity's exigent activity by the alterity which is eventually to disarm it. Intentionality's arrival at a critical "point", its crossing of an implicit line or barrier, in the complex punctuality of the *nouvelle origine,* describes Blanchot's sense of interiority's very conation as a transgression, and his profound affinity with Bataille, at every moment of the latter's text.

The confusion of a consciousness which finds itself in a dimension inappropriate to its voluntaristic, objectifying intentionality, and which, in the absence of any adequating alternative, "va de-ci, de-là," is Blanchot's only rendering of the *cogito*'s classical awakening. The pure initiality of the intentional movement which is interrupted by this awakening concerns Blanchot only as a tendency or irreducible *conatus* of a consciousness which is immediately conditioned by the pre-originary awakening of indecision. Thus, the *cogito* in Blanchot appears immediately at the point of what Levinas will call *récurrence*. Consciousness comes back to itself already and always already intricated with alterity. This return to self proceeds from the Other. Alterity collaborates in the creation of interiority. "A" comes back to "A", in the principle of identity, already involved in an assignation with the Other. The economic exigency which is closure's conation in Blanchot resembles survival in Bataille and the egoism of the *Moi* in Levinas. This exigency describes an entity which can only be defined by its absolute intrication with the economy, but whose principle of self-coincidence is its basic tendency to abolish that intrication. Yet the principle or force of this exigency is precisely the intrusion of the exterior, and the economic investment of the individual.

SOLITUDE

The intrication of interiority with a *Dehors* whose economy constitutes interiority in its new origin as an "impossibility" (an instance appearing in a reality without negativity and without power), takes the paradoxical name "solitude" in Blanchot. "Essential solitude", in Blanchot's terms, is a moment within the real which proceeds from the defection of what Blanchot calls "solitude in the world". The latter expression refers to a consciousness defined phenomenologically as an illuminating interval in being whose involvement with negativity makes possible interiority and the subject-object correlation. The predicates of this consciousness, meaningful to Blanchot individually and in their interdependence, include work, decision and temporalization.

We deny [*nions*] being — or, to illustrate this by a particular case, we transform nature — and, in this negation which is work and which is time, beings accomplish themselves and men stand erect in the freedom of the "I am". That which makes me myself [*me fait moi,* a self] is this decision to be insofar as separated from being, to be *without* being [*sans être*], to be that which owes nothing to being, which takes its power from the refusal to be [*refus d'être*]. . . . [72]

The possibility of decision and refusal is correlative to the basic phenomenological definition of action, manifestation, and temporalization as modalities of a differentiation whose principle is negativity. Consciousness' situation in an ontological interval adequate to totalization is the principle of its spontaneity. This phenomenological context is invoked by Blanchot at many points in his discourse, and is always granted the dignity of an irreducible moment within existence. The Blanchotian refusal of phenomenology, not only in the 1950's and 1960's, when the "philosophy of existence" was most influential in Europe, but later on as well, most generally takes the form of the assertion that negativity is not the only moment of differentiation within the general economy. On occasion, however, in essays such as "La littérature et le droit à la mort",[73] "La solitude essentielle et la solitude dans le monde",[74] and "Le grand refus",[75] Blanchot will describe his notion of a general economy in which the negative has no differentiating function, but appears as a form or effect of another instance which is itself entirely irreducible to negation. These essays are important to the Blanchotian corpus, because they designate communication as an economy which conditions or produces negativity as a regional and even illusory instance, rather than to insist upon the margins of a phenomenologically defined "world of activity". The stipulation that a certain "world" is organized by the spontaneity of decision and action, is clearly important to Blanchot. But the basic direction of his concepts is incompatible with such a model of existence, and the appearance in his text of direct refusals of the phenomenological concepts underlines this incompatibility. The "world" of the negative in Blanchot, like the profane world in Bataille, and the totality in Levinas, is a regional dimension invested and contaminated by impossibility or dissimulation, by transgression, or by the *autrement qu'être*. It is for this reason that the "world" of the actual and effective will never be "entirely the world",[76] and will never entirely foreclose the fugitive upsurges of proximity which haunt it.

An interiority rooted in negativity is the principle of the common concept of solitude. "It happens that this magisterial possibility of being free from being, separated *from* being, becomes also a separation *of* beings...."[77] This separation, in spite of its gravity and its importance on an empirical level, is a notion which "conceals the essential."[78] For this "solitude in the world" is not solitude. It is rather the solitary or opaque aspect of a subjectivity absorbed by totalization and correlation, in a universe of manifestation. The closure produced by the negative in totalization has only a superficial experience of solitude, because its larger permeability is its rooting in totalization and in a manifestation which knows no true exteriority. Interiority in this dimension is dissolved in its manifold adequations to the exterior. It is not alone, because it encounters no alterity. Its unicity is secondary to, and reduced by, its function as the axis and the principle of correlation. For Blanchot as for Levinas, interiority acquires a unicity only when it enters a rapport with an exteriority which is "not in the same concept." Unitl this moment, interiority is not true separation, but only a moment of the totality.

Essential solitude or separation is, for Blanchot as well as Levinas, a moment indefinable by a classical ontology of identity and non-contradiction. It is in fact the defection and contamination of such an identity. Speaking of the rapport with alterity, Levinas says: "My freedom does not have the last word. I am not alone." Proximity in philosophy is indeed a meditation upon subjectivity which subverts the solitary meditation of the intentional self. True separation is produced by the approach of the exterior whose incumbence dismantles the principles of identity's adequate closure. At the same time, the proximity which conditions essential solitude interrupts the impersonal system of correlations by which subjectivity is absorbed in philosophy, and permits the description of an interiority whose inadequation to this system may be understood as a more fundamental "solitude", outside the totality. Philosophy tends to think subjectivity within the alternative of totalization and destruction, or of manifestation and undifferentiation, as though in the absence of totalization, ipseity were unthinkable. The philosophers of proximity are concerned with a subjectivity whose separation results from its lack of totalization, its escape from the totality, and tend to ground this separation in a radical heteronomy (a rapport with alterity) which is not the reduced heteronomy of determination. It is this description of separation in terms of proximity that allows us to discover a common denominator between Blanchotian impersonality and Levinasian election or irreplaceability which is more than a formal homology, and which illuminates the concentrated violence of interiority in both thinkers.*

Of essential solitude Blanchot writes: "When I am alone, I am not alone." Solitude is not the formal interiority guaranteed by a system for each of its terms. It is rather the paradoxical interiority produced by a communication prior to relation or determination. It is a unicity whose contraction or condensation is always already an economic process, an involvement with alterity. This unicity will be "impersonal" by virtue of its inadequation to the linguistic and ontological system in which the "person" is absorbed. But this impersonality will be a unicity whose intensity is more intimate and perhaps more "personal" than that of ipseity in philosophy. Impersonality in Blanchot is not only a refusal of the unproblematized integrity of the humanist subject. It is, more fundamentally, a refusal of the abstraction and interchangeability which foreclose the separation of this subject. The communicational unicity which is true separation, as distinct from simple integrity, takes the name *Quelqu'un*, Someone.

---

* As will be discussed below (cf. Chapter 6), the accusative *se* of election in Levinas, as well as the proximal rapport of subjectivity with *illéité* in the trace of the Other, describe the precise locus of Blanchotian impersonality in Levinas' thinking, although Blanchot is curiously unable to perceive this relationship in his ambivalent readings of Levinas. For both thinkers, the defection of the "personal" self of philosophy attests the approach of alterity. But this approach defines a new interiority whose impersonality is also a unicity unknown in philosophy's totalizations of subjectivity. The progression from identity to impersonality to a non-interchangeable unicity which is not identity, but the true separation of proximity, is common to Blanchot and Levinas.

When I am alone, I am not alone, but, in this present, I already come back to myself in the form of Someone [*Quelqu'un*]. Someone is there, where I am alone. The fact of being alone means that I belong to the dead time [*temps mort*] which is not my time, nor yours, nor common time, but the time of Someone. Someone is that which is still present, when there is no one [*personne*].[79]

Essential solitude follows the economy and the temporality of the Blanchotian *cogito*. I come back to myself, with a new origin: Someone. Solitude is subjectivity seized at a moment prior to its integration in the totality as a self-coincident, self-identical "person". The figure of this subjectivity, not yet absorbed into the Self/Other correlation, is Someone. Solitude is a belonging to a "time" which is no longer the element of the person, i.e. the element of decision, initiative, intentionality, manifestation, and the condition of these possibilities, totalization. Yet the dead time of solitude is the time of a unicity. Without totalization, there is not nothing, not dispersion or undifferentiation: there is Someone. Here the personal self, like the consciousness of the *cogito*, finds itself thrown into a time which is not linear but communicational and repetitive. The instants within this new duration — which is the *nouvelle origine* of all duration — are defined economically through their communication with each other. As a consequence, no beginning or ending, no punctual present — moments which would be free of their intrication with surrounding moments in the economy — is possible. The singular moment of presence becomes, in this time, a repetition: a moment which precedes and follows itself, a "present which does not pass," the strange punctuality of an involvement with or proximity to other moments. This repetitive aspect of "dead time" corresponds to the communicational aspect of Someone: not Self or Other, but a third instance which, in its irreducibility to ipseity, has aspects of both (as well as aspects of the ostensibly non-conscious objective existent; cf. below, Chapter 5). Within dead time, there is unicity without totalization. This unicity is a communication and a proximity. The dead time of repetition is the time of the general economy. Upon its foundation, common time and the catalysis of identity in being — the undeniable and in many ways admirable concentration of communication in the totalitarian moment of identity and non-contradiction — will be established. The "person" will appear upon the foundation of Someone, impersonality, and communication, and this foundation will be forgotten, until the fugitive moment of the *nouvelle origine,* on the margins of the dimension of Identity and Possibility — in a detour such as literature or suicide. As mentioned above, the *nouvelle origine* is not the *cogito* of philosophy, but is the apprehension of a subjectivity which is not a consciousness. For this reason, both the "forgetting" of communication by ipseity and the "apprehension" of the new origin may be compared to repression, and may perhaps be the condition of repression — to the extent that psychoanalysis describes an irreducibility of both the repressed and its return to the notion of manifestation. (This description of a loss and a retention which are both inadequate to manifestation or comprehension is psychoanalysis' discovery of what Blanchot will call *oubli:* the proximity and dispossession upon which consciousness' retentions are founded.) Similarly, common time will make its appearance upon the foundation of dead time. Linear duration will be a modality or moment of the complex duration of repetition and indecision.

"Someone is that which is still present, when there is no one." The common denominator linking Blanchot's complex terms is negativity in its weakness or default in the context of proximity. *Quelqu'un* is produced not by the negativity which separates and totalizes in a universe of identity, but by the contamination of this negativity in communication. For this reason, *Quelqu'un* escapes the dualities by which philosophy, in its dependence upon the negative, tends to pose the moment of communication. Someone is neither you nor me, neither the you nor the Me, neither Self nor Other. It is rather a subjective instance which is a unicity, but not a totality. *Quelqu'un* is subjectivity's insistence in being, grounded in the heteronomy of communication, before the catalysis which reduces unicity to identity and communication to the totality. *Quelqu'un* is a unicity invested by, and involved with, the Other of closure — an Other which will often be situated by Blanchot "between" the You and Me, Self and Other, Person and Person. It is this Other that grounds the *entretien* — the possibility of intersubjectivity — and in itself it stands "between" or *se tient entre.* When this Other invests the communicational interiority of separation, this interiority becomes a closure both more intense and less adequate than identity. This excessive and incomplete closure, the hyperbolic intimacy of an impersonality, is Someone. Its appearance is predicated upon the failure of two negations: the negation which distinguishes Self and Other, on one hand, and on the other hand, the negation which distinguishes Someone from No one. The ambiguity of the French word *personne* in its isolation ("person", "no one") is sometimes accented in Blanchot's text in order to describe the fugitive aspect of Someone.

Someone appears where negation does not operate — where communication produces unicity. Thus, where I am alone, I am not alone. I am not in the solitude of integrity or identity, because the noise or disturbance of irreducible communication (called *il y a* in Levinas and the "presence of absence", among many other terms, in Blanchot) surrounds me. It surrounds, approaches, and intrudes upon me, because it invests me. It is the element and the forgotten familiarity of consciousness. At the same time, where I am alone, I am not there. The becoming-other and becoming-absent of subjectivity are irreducible predicates of its heteronomous investment by alterity. *Quelqu'un* is a unicity without presence, punctuality or substantiality — but not without reality. Where I am alone, I am not there, but *Quelqu'un* is there. Where I am alone, No one is there. No person, no subject, no positive presence produced by the action of the negative, is there. But *personne* — the fugitive instance whose indefinite, problematic "presence" proceeds from negation's weakness — is there: "person", "no one". In other words, the *impersonnel* is there:

Where I am alone, I am not there, there is no one [*personne*], but the impersonal [*impersonnel*] is there: the exterior [*dehors*] as that which forecloses [*prévient,* anticipates and prevents], precedes, dissolves all possibility of a personal rapport.[80]

The impersonal is a dimension within the real for which negativity is not the organizing economic principle. Effects of differentiation, in this dimension, are produced by communication and proximity. The personal self, with its intramundane "solitude", its ostensible noncoincidence with its surroundings, its freedom, initiative and intentionality, is one of these effects. The person is one of the effects of impersonality. Its apparent independence from the communication which conditions it is a basic element of the astonishing world of activity and totalization, and is interrupted only by the occasional, isolated, anomalous moment of the *nouvelle origine.* *

Communication in Blanchot, as in Bataille and Levinas, is thematized by an interpretation of differentiation within the real in terms other than those of negativity. Within this context, "La solitude essentielle et la solitude dans le monde" is one of Blanchot's most important essays. Here, Blanchot clearly describes his notion of an alternative to the phenomenological concepts for which he habitually expresses respect and consideration. This consideration remains an important part of his exposition.

Men affirm themselves by the power not to be [*le pouvoir de ne pas être*] : thus they act, they speak, they comprehend, always as other than they are and escape being by a defiance, a risk, a struggle which extends to death and which is history. This is what Hegel showed. "With death the life of the spirit begins." When death becomes power, man begins, and this beginning says that, in order that there be a world, in order that there be beings, it is necessary that being lack [*que l'être manque:* that being be lacking, be missing].[81]

At this point, having delineated in Hegelian terms the dimension of activity and manifestation, grounded in negation, whose effective though regional reality is a constant in his thinking, Blanchot undertakes a radical and extraordinarily condensed critique of the very notion of negativity:

What does this mean?

When being lacks, when nothingness [*néant*] becomes power, man is fully historical. But when being lacks, does being lack? When being lacks, does this

---

* As mentioned above, the *nouvelle origine* has complex appearances within the actual, such as literary creation and suicide. These appearances are a serious concern in Blanchot and particularly in Bataille. As will be discussed below (cf. Chapter 4), the "actual" dimension in Western culture tends to invoke the *nouvelle origine* in various contexts, in the characteristic form of the anomalous, monstrous, or the violently passive.

mean that this lack owes nothing to being or rather is it not being which is at the bottom [au fond] of the absence of being, what there is still of being when there is nothing? When being lacks, being is yet merely profoundly dissimulated [dissimulé]. For him who approaches [s'approche de] this lack, as it is present in "essential solitude", what comes to him is the being that the absence of being renders present, no longer a dissimulated being, but being [defined] as dissimulated: dissimulation itself.[82]

Here Blanchot does not thematize essential solitude as a dimension on the margins of a world regulated by negativity and its complements, power and manifestation. Instead, he conditions the very possibility of negativity and its effects by a more fundamental instance which is irreducible to them: être or being, defined as a reality which is essentially inadequate to negation, and consequently to manifestation. In the same sense that the personal self of phenomenology and of philosophy in general is defined as an "effect" of impersonality and of the Quelqu'un, the very postulate of negativity in the existent is an "effect" of dissimulation. Manifestation, phenomenality, and comprehension are effects of dissimulation, in the same sense that identity and non-contradiction are effects of communication and proximity. On one level, the appearance of a manque or lack in being is indeed an illusion which masks a persistence of being within or behind the manque. At the same time, however, the manque has its own problematic, regional positivity. It is an effect in being which is produced by a primary ontological moment called Dissimulation. The manque does not hide or dissimulate being: it is a product of dissimulation in being. Its positivity — the positivity of its very illusion or irreality — proceeds from dissimulation. The choice of the word "dissimulation" for this principle in being is appropriate, in the sense of the most general proposition: "Not manifestation, not mediation, not negation, but dissimulation organizes the real and makes it an economy." Dissimulation is an instance or factor which differentiates being as a communication, and not as a manifestation. The weakness of the negative in dissimulation is the impossibility of totalization in the general economy. Totalization, negation, and manifestation may appear in being as effects of dissimulation, in the "catalysis" invoked by Levinas; but their economy, their latent constitution, is dissimulation. Blanchot may continue to speak of a "world" of totalization on whose margins the strange effects of communication insist. But henceforth communication, for all its inactuality and heteronomy, must be understood as the "larger element" of whose economy the totality, the effective, the positive, the manifest, are merely effects. Dissimulation is Blanchot's general economy and his autrement qu'être.

It is significant that Blanchot includes Heidegger in his paraphrase of phenomenologically defined subjectivity: "I am he who is not, he who has seceded, the separate [le séparé], or, as it is said, he in whom being is placed in question."[83] Although the notion of dissimulation is central to Heidegger's thinking, Blanchot will always perceive negativity and manifestation as principles underlying the articulations of pre-comprehension, comprehension and authenticity in the universe of *Dasein*. In Blanchot's eyes, the Heideggerian "invitation" to think dissimulation[84] as a modality of the *Sein/Seiendes* duality is essentially compromised by what he will later call

the providential fact that being and the comprehension of being go together, being being that which illuminates itself [*s'éclaire*], opens itself and chooses as its destiny the *étant* [beings: Being understood as actuality] which makes of itself an opening [*ouverture*] and an illumination [*clarté*].[85]

For Blanchot, dissimulation in Heidegger is a vicissitude of manifestation, an event subsumed by the logic of comprehension in which it is posed.* Dissimulation for Blanchot describes a universe *without* manifestation in the philosophical sense. Death in its phenomenological sense as the hyperbole of the negative is replaced in this universe by what Blanchot will call *la mort sans vérité*, "death without truth". Manifestation, in this reality, does not have the positivity which is correlative to negation. Instead, it has the problematic, communicational positivity of an effect produced by dissimulation. It is a moment of the inactual. Death's excess over discontinuity is a moment of dissimulation's excess over totalization. Thus, it consecrates no truth. The general economy, for Blanchot, is inadequate to the notion of truth. Its positive principle of differentiation is not negativity but communication. Its positive mode of "appearance" is dissimulation. Here, more resolutely than in any text other than "Le grand refus", the concepts ancillary to negativity are denied any privilege. No interval in the real which would be adequate to a philosophical subjectivity or intentionality is proposed. The self-evident and overpowering "positivity" of mediation, power, and comprehension, in the real, are effects of an instance entirely irreducible to their own spontaneity. This fundamental positivity of dissimulation which can take numerous forms or invest numerous realities is expressed in the following terms:

In the tranquillity of everyday life, dissimulation dissimulates itself. In action, veritable action, that which is the work of history, dissimulation tends to become negation (the negative is our task and this task is a task of truth). But in what I call essential solitude, dissimulation tends to appear [*apparaître*].[86]

---

* It is for this reason that the strategy of the "step backward", the "jump" out of representational thinking into a dimension "where we are already admitted," the *Ent-Fernung* which creates an interval through which Being may "present itself to us" in a foreclosing of proximity, remain authentic possibilities for Heidegger. As will be discussed below (cf. Chapter 4), these and other definitions are the reason and perhaps the justification for the refusal of Heidegger by the philosophers of proximity, although many of the themes and concepts of proximity are discoverable in Heidegger's text.

Dissimulation, in the everyday, dissimulates its own movement or insistence, in a Heideggerian moment. More importantly, in action, dissimulation tends to become, or invests, negation. In essential solitude, dissimulation tends to appear *as* dissimulation, that is, as a reality outside manifestation. As mentioned above, this "appearance" will not be a phenomenality, but will be a communication, in the *nouvelle origine* of the *cogito*. Dissimulation can produce what is called phenomenality, action, truth, even illusion; but dissimulation itself is not reducible to truth, action, or even reality, which, as Blanchot will say, "is nothing but the negation of irreality."

The theme of the *cogito* in Blanchot may be properly stated, on a most general level, by the proposition: "In essential solitude, dissimulation tends to appear." The general economy meditated by Blanchot is governed by a complex principle of differentiation which is not negativity, although it may produce a *manque* or lack as one of its effects, and although it certainly produces those discontinuities which are familiar to us in the empirical existent. The intentional "self" produced by this differentiation is not a self but a solitude – that is, a moment at which subjectivity appears in the economy, as a result of the heteronomy of communication, and in a complex form which has aspects of intersubjectivity and even of the inanimate. This subjectivity is essentially inadequate to the empirical possibility of ipseity and identity, and thus has the name "impersonality" or "Someone". Similarly, the economic moment at which an *apparaître* or appearance becomes possible within this universe, is essentially irreducible to the models of manifestation based on the notion of negativity, and so has the name "dissimulation". In the moment of essential solitude, then, an instance which is not consciousness comes into contact with an appearance which is not a phenomenon or manifestation. These two moments will have many predicates in Blanchot, including fascination, interruption, the image, proximity, and most notably *parole*. Their definitions as impersonality and dissimulation indicate their irreducibility to the complementary notions of consciousness or intentionality and manifestation or phenomenality.

Solitude and dissimulation are indices of the basic anti-intellectualism which links Blanchot to Levinas and Bataille. The approach of alterity in solitude, like the exigency in Bataille and like recurrence and desire in Levinas, is not a revelation and is not to be understood as a philosophical or pre-philosophical truth or knowledge. Desire, indecision and the exigency, which concentrate themselves in the Bataillian-Blanchotian term *expérience,* are the general economy's only equivalent to the moments of totalization in philosophy, and their predicates are not those of totalization. The *cogito* in proximity is not a philosophical moment. If, within the economy of proximity, a *savoir,* an ontology, or a historical truth appears to contaminate the unicity of a *non-savoir,* an *autrement qu'être* or a dissimulation, this event will not be reduced ideologically by Bataille, Blanchot or Levinas, but will be meditated as a moment which has its own problematic positivity. The insistence of these thinkers upon situating the exigency of totalization within a larger economy which is not itself a totality or a production of totalities, is their solidarity with that tradition of anti-intellectualism which includes Nietzsche, Proust, and aspects of Freud, Husserl and Heidegger.

*

Essential solitude in Blanchot is a solitude belonging to No one. By comparison with the notion of a personal or identical self, this solitude may be thought quite literally as an anonymity or impersonality. It is a time and place without person. "When I am alone, I am not there." It is also a time without solitude: "When I am alone, I am not alone." Yet the subjectivity of solitude, of recurrence, of indecision and of impersonality, remains a unicity, in spite of its heteronomous constitution. The essential link between Bataille and Blanchot, with their apparent annihilation of a traditionally defined interiority, and Levinas, in his insistence on the irreplaceable unicity of the *cogito* and of the *moi* in recurrence, is the fact that the general economy produces interiority, even though its modality may be that of the impossible exigency. Closure, whether it take the form of totalization or ipseity, is not a "possibility" in the dimension of proximity. But, as Blanchot points out, "possibility is not the only dimension of our existence." The unicity of subjectivity is an important aspect of its constitution, and an important "effect" produced by communication within the economy. The thematization of this fugitive, metamorphosed unicity is a basic element in the thinking of proximity in the texts of all three thinkers.

FROM DECISION TO THE EXIGENCY

PROHIBITION AND TRANSGRESSION

An intentional subject conceived ontologically as the exigency of a problematic closure is not defined, in Bataille's text, as an originary receptivity which would be neutral or mechanical. Instead, intentionality itself is defined as the inescapable priority of a form of closure. This closure is the *interdit* or prohibition. Its primacy in the context of cognition or intentionality is the primacy of the *effort d'autonomie* as a basic predicate of ipseity. The *interdit* is a contamination of the notion of a receptivity defined as an originary comprehension — however limited or approximate — which would be founded and conditioned by an adequate breach between subject and object. Bataille's invocation of the *interdit* as an integral moment of the cognitive function of discontinuity, and the resulting definition of cognition as a "contaminated" receptivity, are designations of subjectivity as a moment or comportment for which the predicate "comprehension" is simultaneously excessive and insufficient — as is the predicate "integrity" for the moment of closure. The empirical reference for this notion of contamination in Bataille's text is the universality of prohibitions regarding death and sexuality in human societies, and a complementary devotion of the human community to work and to a logic of utility which would be solidary with the comportment of work. For Bataille, an institutionalized blindness to that aspect of life which transcends or exceeds survival is the condition for the unicity of a logic of utility which commands the "profane" world of work. Inspired by the Heideggerian meditation of utility in *Being and Time*, and more deeply, by Nietzche's perception of survival as a cornerstone of philosophy, Bataille posits as a condition for the manipulative protention of tool manufacture and use, the abolition of the affective protention that would envisage a cadaver. As a condition for the identity to self of a tool or person, conceived in terms of utility and of a "series of causes and effects" informed by utility,[1] he posits a proscription of sexuality and death conceived as problematic revelations of life transcending identity to self.

Speaking in an empirical context of decomposition and of the custom of burying bodies, Bataille points out an extraordinary status of the cadaver among objects. The cadaver is an upsetting phenomenon, because it reveals the "destiny" of discontinuity. But more than this, the cadaver is an apparition which is already less, or other than, a phenomenal reality, because its strange persistence, denoting the absence of the human being, reveals not only negativity but the other of negativity: the remainder or *reste* of proximity.

56

A cadaver is not *nothing*, but this object, this cadaver is marked in its appearance [*dès l'abord*, in the approach to it] by the sign *nothing*. For us who survive, this cadaver, whose future prudence [*prudence prochaine*] menaces us, does not respond in itself to any expectation [*attente*] similar to that which we had during the lifetime of this man laid out before us, but to a fear: thus this object is less than *nothing*, worse than *nothing* [*moins que* rien, *pire que* rien].[2]

The horrors of decomposition in Bataille, along with the manifold sacrificial excesses which accompany these corruptions and communications, are all secondary to and conditioned by this basic phrase *"pire que rien"*, toward which Bataille's entire system gravitates. The cadaver, as Blanchot writes in his extraordinarily dense and disturbing "Deux versions de l'imaginaire",[3] incarnates "the formless weight of being which is present in absence."[4] This excess or remainder within negativity is more than a predicate of one uncanny object: it is a modality of the general economy itself, "death without truth", negation without annihilation, concentrated in a singular apparition. The cadaver changes the space of its apparition, and indeed makes of space itself a dimension of proximity beyond phenomenality:

To remain [*demeurer*] is not accessible to him who dies. The departed, one says, is no longer of this world, he has left it behind him, but behind is precisely this cadaver which is not itself of this world, though it is here, which is rather behind [*derrière*] the world, that which the living person (and not the departed) has left behind him and which now affirms, from here on, the possibility of a world behind the world [*arrière-mode*], of an indefinite, indeterminate, indifferent subsistence, of which one knows only that human reality, when it ends, reconstitutes the presence and the proximity.[5]

The cadaver is the proximity of a subsistence beyond absence which is the modality of the general economy itself. Its presence, far more importantly than the spectacle of its decomposition, defines the economy as a dimension irreducible to the discretion of the here and now, of presence and absence, identity and non-contradiction. The persistence of the cadaver which is "not of this world" describes a presence of the inactual, a presence of absence, as a fundamental possibility of presence itself in the economy. This presence is not yet, and will never be, a simple phenomenality, but is the incumbence or "weight" of a communication: the approach of alterity. The uncertainty of the cadaver's "prudence prochaine", in Bataille's apt phrase, is the imminence of proximity rather than the simple protention of future annihilation.

Phenomenality or manifestation, in Bataille's general economy, proceeds from the burial of the cadaver — from the prohibition regarding death. The *interdit* is Bataille's articulation of the Levinasian *diastase* or catalysis by which proximity and the *autrement qu'être*, in their density or gravity, give rise to the intense closure of identity. Bataille's ethnological discussions always reveal an economic or ontological dimension. In the case of prohibition, the burying of bodies assumes the significance of an introduction of limited negativity where death has become the contaminated persistence of proximity.

A necessary primacy of utility in the world of survival is conditioned by a banishment of that which exceeds the logic of utility — until the day of the *fête*. On this day, that which was prohibited is permitted and even demanded. Animal or human sacrifices, ritual destructions of goods, and other "dilapidations" become the object of a bizarre, positive sanction which Bataille thematizes as the upsurge of an exigency of loss, a *dépense* whose name is transgression. At the ontological level which subtends the exuberance of Bataille's invocation of empirical data, a subtle and progressive application of conditions and articulations to the problem of subjectivity is pursued. The principal context of this strategy is the moment of imposition of the prohibition. Bataille transports the logic of the exigency in discontinuity to the context of prohibition, and employs the notion of ambivalence which is central to the exigency as a "motivation" for prohibition. This thematization in terms of ambivalence takes the form of a manipulation of the notions of "reason" and "affect" as they inform the moment of prohibition. The *interdit,* which inaugurates reason by banishing a form of "affect" introduced by death and sexuality, is defined as itself the result of an "affective" moment. A reduction of the "violence" represented by death and sexuality will not be defined as the proprietary act of a previously defined "reason", an adequate receptivity which would feel its clarity threatened from without. "Violence" will rather be reduced by "violence" itself, conceived as affect:

But the prohibitions, upon which the world of reason reposes, are not, on this basis, rational. In the beginning, a calm opposition to violence would not have sufficed to divide [*trancher entre*] the two worlds: if the opposition had not itself in some way participated in violence... reason alone could not have defined with enough authority the limits of the *glissement*. Only unreasoned horror and fear could subsist in the face of measureless explosions [*déchaînements*, destructions of limits or constraints]. Such is the nature of the *taboo*, which makes possible a world of calm and reason, but it itself, in its principle, a trembling [*tremblement*].[6]

The "participation in violence" of the intentionality which imposes the *interdit* is not the contamination of a constituted "reason" by "affect". Rather, it is the priority of the basic Bataillian category "excess" in the elaboration of *any* thematization of intentionality or cognition. Receptivity — subjectivity — implies prohibition, for Bataille. Notions such as "horreur" and "effroi", considered as moments of an exigency of closure before they might be defined as "emotions", insert the violence of the *glissement* and the *effort d'autonomie* into the economy of the concept "reason". In this way, "reason" is defined as an exigency, even as the terms of its definition appear to presuppose it as an adequate receptivity. Intentionality, conditioned by a prohibition whose predicate is violence, will have no component which would escape the priority of this violence. Cognition will be conditioned by the same problematic closure which defines subjectivity as a discontinuity.

"Horreur" or "effroi", conceived as moments of the exigency's intensity, have the Bataillian predicate "excess" and the complementary condition "closure". As motivations of the act that reduces what Bataille calls a *glissement*, they must also be defined as a *glissement*: the excessive violence of an exigency of closure, or of an economically defined closure upon which alterity may weigh or be incumbent. The movement which reduces violence is itself violence. The *interdit* is a closure whose condition is excess: a closure forced by excess. Intentionality, conceived as an opening within closure, is itself immediately conditioned by closure in the form of prohibition. Intentionality is prohibition. But it is prohibition as *glissement*. It is in this context that the *interdit's* function as a barrier is conditioned by its definition as a "tremblement".

The second moment of Bataille's meditation on prohibition consists of an application of the exigency's ambivalence to the moment of prohibition, in the form of desire. "The prohibition observed without fear no longer has the counterpart of desire which is its profound meaning."[7] Desire is the modality of the exigency, and is always ambivalent, since the exigency is an economic tendency toward closure whose animation is excess, i.e. the inherence of the economy. The object of "horror" consists of a presence correlative to a breach in closure. "I can tell myself that repugnance, that horror is the principle of my desire, that it is to the extent that its object opens in me a breach [*vide*] not less profound than death that it arouses [*émeut*, animates] this desire which at first is made of its opposite, horror."[8] The ambivalence of horror and desire is not an affective reaction to an object: it is rather the primary ambivalence of closure itself, and is the very possibility of the object. Here Bataille's thinking recalls Levinas' assertion that desire and the idea of the infinite precede and condition even the most basic intentional relations. The world of manifestation, totalization, or utility, must constitute itself upon the ground of a more fundamental desire which may, however, appear to be merely an exceptional moment. Phenomenality is an effect or vicissitude of desire, the more basic principle of differentiation within the economy.

In the first place, the *interdit* is not rational but "participates" in the violence it proscribes. In the second place, this violence of prohibition is ambivalent. The third moment of Bataille's thinking of prohibition consists of the notion that prohibition, on the basis of its modality as an exigency, is always in concealed solidarity with the transgression it outlaws. "The refusal does not signify rupture, it announces on the contrary a more profound accord."[9]

The concept *dépense*, when applied to the problematic of prohibition and transgression, will differentiate a violent exigency toward survival or integrity from another exigency whose increased momentum inclines an intentional subject toward loss. The axis of this differentiation will be this momentum or this "excess of excess' which momentarily exceeds the basic mobilization of violence in the direction of closure. More fundamental than the opposition of these two moments, however, is their solidarity as exigencies. It is this solidarity that defines the *interdit* as "an invitation at the same time as an obstacle,"[10] and that defines the sacred world, with its coincidence of the pure and the impure, and its exigency of abandon, as a production of the *interdit*: "the prohibition renders divine [*divinise*] that to which it outlaws access."[11] Bataille's formula: "the prohibition is there to be violated"[12] must not be understood as a declaration of the metaphysical priority of abandon over limits, but as one index of an ontological dimension for which obstacles and their destruction are not ultimate predicates. Writing of this context, Denis Hollier has correctly stated that "the imposition of the prohibition is in a sense already a transgression."[13]

Prior to the proximity of transgression in the profane world of work and utility, there is an immediate irony to the notion of work itself, in its irreducibility to a Hegelian context of negativity. Writing on Bataille, Blanchot describes this problem in an ironically Hegelian formula:

Everything happens, in truth, as though man had a capacity to die which far exceeds, and perhaps infinitely exceeds, that which is required to enter into death and, out of this excess of dying [*excès de mourir*], he has been able [*su*] to admirably make a power; by this power, denying [*niant*, negating] nature, he has constructed the world, he has gone to work, has become a producer, an auto-producer.[14]

As Blanchot implies, it is no longer death, with its definition as negativity, that renders possible the world of action and transformation. Instead, it is precisely Bataillian excess, immediately foreclosing the discretion and univocity of death as negation, that founds a world of work whose destiny is not totalization but transgression. Work itself, the paradoxical mobilization of excess and proximity in the direction of causality and identity, is an irony in Bataille – as will be, in their way, transgression and the sacrifice. The exigency of work and reason, paradoxically presenting itself as the non-violence of a profane knowledge, is in truth an *inachèvement* or incompletion contaminating the totality of the profane world. Its inability to equal the totalizations of a negativity is precisely its exceeding of negativity – an excess which has simultaneously the form of an irreducible remainder or *reste* ("this excess of dying"), and the form of a gap or breach within the absolute closure of a totality, which Blanchot calls desire: "the desire of the man without desire, the dissatisfaction of the man who is "completely" ["*en tout*"] satisfied, a pure lack [*défaut*], where there is however an accomplishment of being [*accomplissement d'être*]."[15] A desire which cannot be assuaged because it does not arise from a lack or need is the sign of a closure which is never closed enough: a closure which is an excess.

It is true, as Blanchot states, that desire will lead to "a surplus of nothingness," "a portion [*part*] of dying" that subjectivity "cannot invest in activity": "another exigency, not to produce but to waste [*dépenser*]."[16] But this exigency will not signal a destruction of closure or the abolition of limits. The mode of being of a subjectivity defined as an exigency will not be transformed by the momentum of its own excess. Rather, it will be led, in Bataille's words, to the "extreme of the possible" or to a "last degree of tension." This limit-case of the tense communication which is subjectivity, this "last degree" of a unicity conceived as excess, will be transgression.

*

The *interdit*, as described above, is the modality of manifestation and negation in the general economy. It is a contamination of cognition which is at the same time the very condition for cognitive "clarity". The burying of the cadaver is the exemplary instance of the reduction of the *arrière-monde* of proximity, and a subsequent interpretation of communicational exteriority by subjectivity as a phenomenal exteriority. The imposition of the prohibition is not a punctual or historical moment, not an ancestral tradition or inheritance, but is rather a basic moment of temporalization in the general economy. The "not yet" of death, and the causal future of the manipulated object are the very constitution of a progressive, historical time governing the profane world. Bataille calls this time the "primat de l'avenir" or primacy of the future: a time of utility and survival, whose univocity is based on the proscription of death in its indefinite approach. Prohibition reduces the proximity of time – the "prudence prochaine" of the cadaver, its inactuality, the approach of death – and produces a totalized duration in which the future is assumed by subjectivity's initiative. Bataille will always oppose this futural element of discontinuity's subsistence to a "present" moment of violence, irreducible to the protention of conservation. The "presence" of this moment, in his text, will always describe the radical passivity of a subjectivity and a differentiation whose context is neither manifestation nor spontaneity – in spite of the "independence" from conservation and the apparent spontaneity of the present in the transgressive acts Bataille discusses. Prohibition produces temporal ekstases grounded in negation and appropriated to intentionality's initiative. But its production of these intervals is economically informed and conditioned by its own constitution in proximity: the excess and heteronomy of discontinuity. Like Blanchot's world of decision and initiative, grounded in the economy of indecision, and Levinas' time of egoism and freedom, grounded in the proximal time of *jouissance* and the *cogito*, the profane world is a totalization produced by totalization's Other. This is its regionality, its egoism, and also its dignity, as the moment of Separation in the general economy.

As the axis of a closure which banishes violence from the "world of things", the prohibition is an exigency which is animated by that very violence. It prepares, calls for, invites, and even participates in a violence which it simultaneously renders inaccessible. It forbids that which it creates: the sacred world. Nevertheless, as the violence of the exigency gains momentum, an event occurs which apparently ruptures the solidity of the profane world through a violent abandonment of all its prescriptions and prohibitions. At this moment the *interdit* is *violated*. Bataille's text concentrates its attention upon the modality and conditions of possibility of this violation. If the perpetual closure of the *effort d'autonomie* defines the very unicity of the self, and if the primacy of the *interdit* conditions the very capacity of intentionality of a conscious self, how may an exigency toward loss accomplish the violation of an *interdit*? How may a discontinuity transgress?

The answer to this question lies in a Bataillian procedure which problematizes the notions of power and accomplishment through its basic *mise en jeu* of their complement, the notion of integrity as a correlate of negation. Within this context, the "problem of possibility" will be the background for a transgression which 'exceeds without destroying" a profane world of prohibitions.

Transgression exceeds [*excède*] without destroying a *profane* world, of which it is the complement. Human society is not only the world of work. Simultaneously – or successively – the *profane* world and the *sacred* world compose it, which are its two complementary forms. The *profane* world is that of prohibitions. The *sacred* world opens itself to limited [*limitées*] transgressions.[17]

The coincidence of simultaneity and succession in Bataille's formulation refers to a fundamental solidarity of prohibition and transgression which underlies their apparent alternation in a temporal perspective. This solidarity is the movement of the *glissement*, through which prohibition and transgression, or the profane and sacred worlds, condition and contaminate each other. The mode of succession is added to that of simultaneity according to the basic movement of *dépense*. Violence moves toward greater violence; the experience of limits moves toward its own limit.* Transgression, in Bataille's words, is "limited" because it is not a violence which would destroy closure. It is not negativity. It is rather a violence which exceeds closure while paradoxically remaining trapped within its limit. Transgression is the "complement" of closure, and not its elimination. This is because the limit is not an entity whose mode of being would be transgression's "other". On the contrary, the modality "excess within containment" defines both these concepts. Their coincidence in the constitution of a subjectivity conceived as an exigency is not that of a contradiction or mediation, but rather that of a *glissement*. This coincidence is stipulated by Bataille in many ways. He will declare, for instance, that the violation of an *interdit* is not an act that abolishes the primacy of reason or of the future,[18] or that transgression is not a return to animality, considered as a comportment unencumbered by reason.[19] In a highly charged aphorism, he writes, "the obstacle overturned, the

---

* This contaminated temporality is proximal time. Prohibition is already its destiny, transgression. Transgression is always already prohibition, the "flouted prohibition" which "survives transgression." Proximal time and repetition in Bataille produce a particular form of succession, which is that of the increase of violence and the imminence of destruction, which is also an imminence of totalization itself. Cf. below.

flouted [*bafoué*] prohibition survives transgression."[20] The sense of these stipulations, and of the many others articulated by Bataille, is that transgression requires prohibition not simply as the historical imposition of a barrier to be destroyed, but as the contemporaneous imposition of a barrier whose violation is not a destruction. Humanity, in Bataille's text, is neither an originary animality upon which prohibitions would be superimposed, nor an originary receptivity which would be contaminated by the intervention of limits. Humanity is itself a limit, although it is a limit in the form of a exigency.

These stipulations inform Bataille's most enthusiastic description of transgression, which is that of the sacrifice. Within this context, Bataille interprets the ritual destruction of goods, animals, or human beings as a *mise en jeu* of discontinuity whose ontological sense as "sacrifice" must be derived from its latent economy as a *glissement* and an impossibility. Bataille recognizes the sacrifice as a direct, total destruction of the discontinuity of a victim, in the context of a sacred ritual. But rather than to thematize this event as a destruction of isolation, he sees it as a liberation for the victim alone, and concentrates his attention upon the ceremonial function of the sacrificers.

The victim alone, in fact, will entirely take leave of the order of the real [*order réel*], in that he alone is taken all the way by the movement of the *fête*. The sacrificer is divine with reticence only [*n'est divin qu'avec réticences*]. The future is heavily reserved [*lourdement réservé*] in him, the future is his weight as a thing [*sa pesanteur de chose*, his belonging to the profane world of "things"].[21]

Only for the victim does death bring an end to the mode of being which was its life. For the sacrificers, the ritual is an exigency that is brought by the victim's death to an ultimate tension and violence, but not to a resolution. The sacrifice destroys the unicity of a victim, but it cannot destroy discontinuity itself, as the incarnation and the economy of life. This irreducibility of the discontinuous as a remainder defying the destructive negativity of the sacrifice is also the irreducibility of the "real", the "world of things", and the "primacy of the future" as factors contaminating the totality of the sacred world. In a most fundamental sense, this is the irony of the sacrifice, which cannot accomplish what it nevertheless accomplishes so overwhelmingly. And the irony of the sacrifice is Bataillian irony in its most characteristic form. The familiar clash of rapt subjectivity with the insolence of utter "folie" or "démesure" in Bataille's fiction, is not only the baffling of melancholy control by excess; it is more basically the irony of an abandon which cannot abandon. The sacrifice, and transgression in general, is a moment which is not what it is — destruction, abandon — and this is its irony.

Concomitant to the sacrifice's ambiguity of accomplishment is its ambiguity of intention. Bataille conceives the problem of an intentionality and a free will which would sacrifice, in terms of the exigency. In his empirical demonstrations, this conception will have the effect of a contamination and a *mise en jeu*. Thus, the sacrificer "is divine with reticence only". He is "divine", not in spite of his reticence or hesitancy, but because of it. The sacrifice is an event "made of a mixture* of anguish and frenzy,"[22] not because its violence triumphs over the hesitations of a unicity seeking to maintain itself, but because the unicity of subjectivity *is* an irreducible *mélange*: an excess and a closure. For this reason, Bataille repeatedly refuses to accord a univocal primacy to the term "destruction", calling such a configuration an "absence of rigor"[23] or a "blind violence which is reduced to explosion [*déchaînement*]."[24] "He who abandons himself to this movement is no longer human. . . ."[25] The "rigor" of the sacrifice is precisely its status as a contamination: a bringing into proximity, at the "extreme of the possible", of an exigency toward closure and an exigency toward abandon. Transgression is the limit-case of this *glissement* which is Bataillian interiority.

The sector of Bataille's text which describes the sacrifice as an exigency of abandon contains a repeated contradiction; indeed, Bataille's reasoning, like that of many influential thinkers, may be said in this context to proceed and to inspire itself by contradiction. For instance, the transgression of a "reasonable being" is described as the act of a subject "who tried to obey, but succumbs to the movement in himself which he cannot reduce to reason."[26] However, a succumbing to this movement "is no longer human" or "reduces itself to explosion." The twofold problem which structures such contradictions is the ambiguous intention of the sacrifice, and its ambiguous accomplishment. Bataille's contradictions, which will take the form in Blanchot and Levinas of condensed, carefully wrought paradoxes, are a necessary consequence in the elaboration of a movement which "succumbs without being able to succumb" or which "abandons without being able to abandon." The movement of the *mise en jeu* is an exigency whose modality escapes any logic of power, spontaneity, or accomplishment. In other words, it exceeds a logic of possibility. "The savage *impossibility* I am, which can neither avoid its limits nor hold to them," is a mode of being which always "must" and never "is able". This contradiction is the very ontology of this mode of being. Thus, the sacrifice is not the experience of the destruction of ipseity as closure, but rather the experience of the impossibility of such a destruction. Impossibility — the real without power — is transgression's ontological dimension. Transgression does not exist in the profane world. Rather, it insists in the *arrière-monde* of impossibility as a permanent and irreducible dimension of subjectivity's appearance in the general economy. Like proximity in general, transgression is real without being actual.

The *fête* is the ritual sacrifice of that which cannot be sacrificed. This is its precise ontological description. The sacrifice is a *dépense*, an *écart* or gap, a loss in the constitution of interiority, and not a negativity which would destroy

---

* The French word *mélange* means "contamination" as well as "mixture", as in the expression *sans mélange*, "unalloyed".

interiority. The most compelling and precise description of transgression's impossibility was written by Maurice Blanchot, in a footnote to his reading of Bataillian *expérience*:

> The prohibition marks the point where power ends. Transgression is not an act of which, under certain conditions, the power and mastery of certain men would yet be capable. It designates that which is radically out of reach [*hors de portée*]: the attainment of the inaccessible, the crossing [*franchissement*] of the uncrossable [barrier]. It appears in man when, in him, power ceases to be the ultimate dimension.[27] *

"The multitude of living beings is passive in this movement," writes Bataille. "At the extremity, nevertheless, we resolutely desire that which places our life in danger."[28] Bataille's contradictions, in their interplay, describe a dimension beyond identity and negativity, whose principle of determination is not causality or power, but proximity. Its discursive elaboration requires a *mise en jeu* of the categories of accomplishment and possibility, considered as the axes of a "logic of utility" whose primacy is inextricable from the exigency of knowledge itself, and is therefore ineluctable. (Cf. below, Chapter 4.) Such a *mise en jeu* must itself be a transgression which sacrifices that which cannot be sacrificed. And this is Bataille's own sense of thought as the rapport of *savoir* and *non-savoir*.

The basic object of transgression, through its many incarnations in Bataille's text, is that closure which always conditions subjectivity itself, whatever the context of its definition. A transgression envisaging utility, Good, a "profane language", the "integrity of the body", or "knowledge", will always be the exigency of escape from a closure which will itself be revealed as an exigency. Thus, transgression will always have, in the terms of accomplishment, the status of a "failure" for Bataille. The sacrifice, desiring the glorious destruction of utility through integrity, becomes the spectacle of integrity's ineluctable persistence in the contamination of *la part maudite*.* Crime, envisaging *le Bien* or

---

* Transgression is an effectively real economic moment whose context is inactuality and impossibility. The "experience" of transgression, and subjectivity's "access" to the inactual in a general sense, is desire. Bataille describes this experience in a comment on love which underlines his profound affinity with Baudelaire and Proust: "Its essence is the substitution of a marvellous continuity between two beings for their persistent discontinuity. But this continuity is sensible above all in anguish, to the extent that it is inaccessible, to the extent that it is a search [*recherche*] in powerlessness [*impuissance*] and trembling."[29] There is an access to the "anywhere out of the world" or to the absolute *ailleurs* of the voyage, there is an intimacy with the fugitive object of love. But the principle of these communications is not power. It is desire and impossibility. (Cf. above, Chapter 1; below, Chapter 3.)

* "La part maudite", an expression whose resonances in French defy translation, means "the accursed lot" or "accursed part". In Bataille's thought, this expression designates a remainder which is not eliminated by negativity and which has the "obscene" capacity to approach and contaminate the dimension of negation — whether this dimension take the form of discontinuity or of destruction. The sacrificial victim is one explicit incarnation of the *part maudite*, whose communications with the various zones of Bataille's system tend to define this term as the very figure of proximity in Bataille.

Good, finds itself to be always insufficiently criminal, always a "rationalized" violence. Creative writing assaults the limits of a "profane language" only to find its explosive movement trapped in a problematic structure of reification. Communication in erotism, desiring a penetration of the body's integrity, encounters a surface whose "nudity", whose "blessure" or wound is the very modality of its impenetrable closure. Penetration will become the more contaminated contact called *souillure*. *Non-savoir*, tending to abolish or escape the servility of a profane "knowledge", becomes a new reification which will itself be defined as a *glissement*. In these and other contexts, a closure which is always excessively closed and yet insufficiently closed will define transgression as the "privileged failure"* of an assault on a stubborn limit whose resistance is the fact that its *own* predicate is transgression. The context of this transgression which assaults transgression is the universe of the impossible: an authentic ontological dimension of the general economy. The differentiations and movements which characterize this dimension are not thinkable, ultimately, in terms of limits and their destruction. They must be described in the terms of a reality without power, in which every limit is already a breach, and in which contamination replaces the negativity of destruction. This reality is the general economy of proximity.**

* Maurice Blanchot's formulation of the exigency, quoted above, continues: "another exigency, no longer to produce, but to waste, no longer to succeed, but to fail. . . .".[30] Failure, in Bataille and Blanchot, is one paradoxical access of transgression or *expérience* to a dimension outside the world of possibility, accomplishment, and totalization. In addition, the notion of failure attests the radical passivity which is correlative to a rapport with the Other. As will be discussed below (cf. Chapter 7), this passivity of proximity is a basic communication of Bataillian-Blanchotian *expérience* with Levinas' *éthique* – a moment at which, in Levinas' words, "my freedom no longer has the last word" because "I am not alone." Cf. "Baudelaire" in *La Littérature et le mal*, "Le regard d'Orphée" in *L'Espace littéraire*.

** The irreducibility of proximity in transgression to the metaphor of limits and their destruction is demonstrated in an excellent essay on Bataille by Michel Foucault entitled "Préface à la transgression" (*Critique* 195–6, août-septembre 1963, pp. 751–69). Following a general discussion which stresses the ineluctability of limits in transgression, Foucault proposes a problematic series of formulas to describe the transgressive rupture of a limit. Initially he imagines a passage over a limit which disappears at the moment of passage:

> Such an experience, in which the death of God explodes, discovers as its secret and its illumination [*lumière*], its own finitude, the unlimited reign of the Limit, the emptiness of this crossing [*franchissement*] where it fails [*défaille*] and defects [*fait défaut*]. In this sense the interior experience is entirely an experience of the impossible (the impossible being that which is experienced and which constitutes the experience).[31]

The limit disappears at the moment of passage, demonstrating the inadequacy of this movement as access to the limit's "beyond". The limit is not at the point of rupture. The impossible is the rupture of a limit which is always elsewhere. Or, it is the rupture of a limit which incessantly reconstructs itself behind the subject of transgression, to exercise its totalitarian influence from another place:

The play [*jeu*] of limits and transgression seems to be governed by a simple obstinacy: transgression crosses and does not cease to cross a line which, behind it, immediately [*aussitôt*] closes again [*se referme*] in a virtually immemorial vacancy [*une vague de peu de mémoire*], receding once again to the horizon of the uncrossable [*infranchissable*].[32]

The movement of a rupture which does not rupture, in spite of its trajectory and efficiency, is the paradoxical transitivity of the impossible. And this is precisely the movement of closure in Bataille's text: the closure which contains more than it can contain. On the other hand, since Bataille's categories seem to foreclose even the possibility of a momentary rupture, the movement of transgression may perhaps be better described by a spiral, in which the limit displaces itself to accompany the movement of rupture in whatever direction:

> Transgression is therefore not to the limit as black is to white, the exterior to the interior, the excluded to the protected space of the dwelling. It is linked to the limit rather according to a spiral-like rapport [*en vrille*] which cannot be terminated by any simple rupture [*effraction*].[33]

The limit is the *infranchissable*. The impossible is that movement which pursues, and whose very being is to pursue, the limit in its perpetual, receding displacement. At the same time, however, there is in Bataille's thought a movement from violence to greater violence: an excess of excess, a *dépense* whose momentum differentiates transgression from prohibition and leads from the possible to the "extremity of the possible." Within the spiral, this movement of increased proximity to the limit must be described by a temporality of imminence:

> Transgression carries the limit to the limit of its being; it leads the latter to awaken to its imminent disappearance, to discover itself in that which it excludes (rather, to recognize itself there [in the excluded] for the first time), to experience [*éprouver*] its positive truth in the movement of its loss [*perte*]. And yet, in this movement of pure violence, toward what does transgression explode [*se déchaîne*], if not toward that which constrains it [*l'enchaîne*], toward the limit and that which is enclosed by it?[34]

In spite of his excellent anticipations of the Bataillian *aussitôt* of repetition (the limit is "already" behind transgression and always nevertheless *à venir*, always *en deçà* and *au-delà* in a proximal temporality), of imminence as the modality of the future in proximity, and of Blanchotian *oubli* as a constituent of the *expérience*, Michel Foucault's descriptions of transgression in terms of limits are undeniably cumbersome. This is because transgression occurs in an economy whose differentiations are not limits. The negativity of the destructive breach is replaced, in transgression, by an *écart* or breach which is precisely the failure of negativity to guarantee the limit of interiority. The metaphor of a destructive crossing and an ineluctable limit — both these concepts being grounded in negation — is inadequate to the contamination which is transgression. The breach which contaminates unicity, and the remainder which is left outside unicity by this breach, are the very constitution of "impossible" interiority in proximity. Prohibition is thus always the imminence of transgression; transgression always leaves behind it the unelimable *reste* or remainder of the prohibition. The only ontology of these ostensible opposites is their proximity, as Foucault states in resolving the difficulty of his metaphor:

> But does the limit have true existence outside the gesture which gloriously crosses and denies it? What would it be, afterward, and what could it be, beforehand? And does not transgression exhaust all that it is in the instant at which it crosses the limit, being nowhere else but in this point of time? Now, this point, this strange chiasma [*croisement*] of beings which, outside it, do not exist, but exchange in it all that they are, is it not also everything that, on all sides, exceeds [*déborde*] it?[35]

The impossibility of transgression as an accomplishment, the ambiguity of its intention and the ambivalent hesitancy of its problematic *déchaînement* or explosion, are not conditions which reduce this experience to simple undifferentiation or heteronomy. Bataillian violence is concentrated in the "must" of the exigency, as it insists in a temporality of proximity. Transgressions's unicity, like that of subjectivity, is a communication. Its punctuality is a repetition, but is not less dense or compelling for this fact. Transgression must take place: its escape from the dimension of possibility is this "must". Transgression cannot be stopped. Its failure to accomplish itself as a synthesizing resolution to the contamination of the *glissement* does not lessen, but indeed aggravates the imperiousness of its approach. Considered as the limit-case or extremity of a *glissement*, transgression is an ultimate proximity of two modes of being — closure and destruction -- whose abolition of each other, whose respective entry into being as totalities, is imminent. The failure of this mutual abolition to take place — the failure of transgression itself to "take place" in a world of totality and negativity — is not the resolution of this immenence in a *détente* of autonomy or heteronomy. Instead, the insistence of transgression in a dimension without totalization is precisely this imminence. For this reason, transgression — the incessant disturbance found in an economy whose elements exceed their own closure, and the suspended intensity of a dimension in which no unicity has yet accomplished its imminent totalization — may be understood as a basic context of Blanchot's *attente**** in being. This *attente* is an economic correlate of impersonality in Blanchot, defined as unicity's irreducibility to totalization. The affinity with Bataille which is described by these concepts informs the creativity of the following formulation, in which the ambivalence and contaminated temporality of transgression, and its proximal rapport with prohibition, are rendered with a strikingly appropriate density:

If man did not already belong in some way to this detour which he uses most often in order to turn away from it [*s'en détourner*], how could he start down this path which is soon lacking [*fait défaut*], with an eye to [*en vue de*] that which escapes all vision [*vue*], advancing as though backward [*à reculons*] toward a point at which he only knows he will not arrive in person [*en personne*]. . . .[36]

Transgression is not an intentional movement of subjectivity toward a "point". It is rather the passivity with which interiority, in an economy without power, exceeds its own closure, its locus and its punctuality. Subjectivity enters the "detour" of transgression "as though backward" because this detour, this excess of impersonality, is the latent element of subjectivity's own unicity. Like

---

* The concept of *attente* describes an "awaiting", an attention, an intensity, an imminence, and an irreducible "not yet" which weighs upon all punctuality in the general economy, as a function of the heteronomy and incompletion which define subjectivity in proximity.

Blanchot's Thomas, whose forward motion is animated solely by his desire not to move, Bataillian subjectivity transgresses through the very force of its exigency toward closure.

In Blanchot's thematic universe, the priority of proximity over negation will take the form of an ultimate urgency and danger whose paradoxical modality is the neutrality and monotony of the "non-concerning". In Bataille, the same moment will become a "last degree of tension" or the "extremity of the possible": imminent freedom from limits, imminent violence, imminent death, and the irony of a total destruction which nevertheless produces an insistent remainder: *la part maudite*. This urgency and irony, in an imminence conceived as duration without end, are the manifestation of subjectivity's "must" — the *glissement* — at its extremity. And this extremity is the ontological condition of closure itself, which, from the beginning, is an exigency about to accomplish itself. Transgression is the spasm of a closure which is excessively closed and not closed enough. For this reason, transgression's excess is also the principle of interiority's incompletion, and therefore of its receptivity. Transgression will be, in Bataille's thought, the basic economic model for the global term *expérience*.

DEATH AND INDECISION

The mortality of separation or interiority in the general economy is the involvement with alterity or exteriority which results from its communicational constitution. As Bataille often points out, individuation involves death: in transgression, and in *dépense*, which is the economy of closure. The "petite mort" of sexuality is, for Bataille, an attestation by common sense of this latent economy. The physical fact, and even the eventuality of death, are less significant moments in the general economy than subjectivity's rapport with a generality of death in the "decomposition", "fermentation", or essential excess of closure itself. Equated with differentiation or individuation in its excess over interiority, death may be understood as a principle of the general economy. But it is the principle of a differentiation which contaminates, and not the principle of a negativity which assures totalization and power. The scandalous aspect of the cadaver is not the annihilation of individuality it suggests, but the persistence of being over negation which is attested by it. The cadaver is a *reste* or remainder, and a spectacle of decomposition: the uneliminable exuberance of communication, and subjectivity's inability, even in disappearance, to "take a distance" from the economy of being. The persistence of the uneliminable is what Bataille calls *la part maudite*: the "less than nothing, worse than nothing" of communication. Death is the irony of that which annihilates without annihilating. It is negation and negation's cruel inefficiency.

From his earliest essays, Bataille's theme was contamination as a function of excess. For this reason, the domination of Hegel in the culture of Bataille's formation was not an obstacle to the development of the latter's concepts. In

"La Notion de dépense" and "La Structure psychologique du fascisme", the influence of Freud, Nietzsche and Marx is far more palpable than that of Hegel. In his later theoretical texts, Bataille mimics the procedures of Hegelian dialectics while consistently foreclosing the possibility of a synthetic moment which would arrest the contamination of the *glissement*. Although Bataille incoherently equates transgression with the *Aufhebung* in a footnote of *L'Erotisme*,[37] although he returns consistently to the figure of Hegel in his discussions of *non-savoir*, and although the concepts of phenomenology often intervene in his demonstrations (as they do in nearly all French theoretical texts of the twentieth century), it may nevertheless be said that Bataille is able to take Hegel lightly. This attitude is in one sense a function of Bataille's insouciant eclecticism, and is in another sense an indication of his superiority. As his reader knows, these two senses are inextricable. Bataille's incoherence, from the point of view of "professional" theory, is a function of his originality.

In Blanchot, the rapport with Hegel is more serious. The concepts of French phenomenology, in their persistent appeal to Hegel, are an important element in Blanchot's early essays. *Faux pas* (1943), *La part du feu* (1949), and *Lautréamont et Sade* (1949) are documents of Blanchot's involvement with these concepts. The exploration of a new element in *Thomas l'obscur* (1941), *Aminadab* (1942), and *L'Arrêt de mort* (1948) did not arrest this involvement during the 1940's. It is for this reason that "La littérature et le droit à la mort" (1948)[38] is an essential text in Blanchot's career as a thinker. The thematization of the *il y a* in this essay (developed, as will be discussed below, in a proximity to the concepts and the name of Emmanuel Levinas), which is Blanchot's most significant extrication of his thinking from that of Hegel, takes place in a discussion of literature and death. The congruence of these concepts will structure *L'Espace littéraire* in its totality. In both texts, it is Blanchot's description of death as an economic or communicational instance that informs his rejection of Hegel.

Literature's discovery of an instance beyond negation or prior to manifestation is the subject of "La littérature et le droit à la mort". In the first half of this essay, Blanchot analyzes the negation produced by the literary word in its fictional distance from the real, and insists upon the frailty of this negation when compared to that of action. Art cannot compete with action in the terms of action, not only by virtue of its irresponsible fictionality, but also by virtue of the inefficiency of its negations. Literature does not change the world, as does an action rooted in the negative. Instead, it reveals the paradoxical and contaminated subsistence of a world underneath negation. On one hand, this world is the presence of fiction itself, and on the other it is the disturbing materiality of the literary word, which preoccupies the creative writer. The word is not the thing, and its enunciation places the thing at a distance; but this enunciation leaves a remainder: the word itself, and the fiction it produces. Literature discovers a presence of absence, "the stubborness of that which subsists when all is erased and the hebetude of that which appears when there is nothing."[39] Blanchot's strategic accreditation of action in a Hegelian sense as the possibility of truth and authenticity will be a constant in his theoretical texts. In "La Littérature et le droit à la mort", as elsewhere, Blanchot accepts the notion of literature as an anomalous, inauthentic instance on the margins of the "real" world of totalization and negation. Its exceptional and somewhat guilty status results from its mobilization of negativity which results in an arresting of negation in the presence of absence. Here, a comparison with death intervenes. Literature discovers "the existence which remains [demeure] underneath existence, like an inexorable affirmation, without beginning and without end, death as the impossibility of dying."[40] The remainder produced by literary negation is a fiction and a word which do not have the "authentic" signification of totalization, but which are a "signification in general,"[41] a sense in being without totalization: "sense [sens*], detached from its conditions, separated from its moments, wandering [errant] like an empty power, with which one can do nothing, a power without power, a simple inability [impuissance] to cease to be."[42] This "inability to cease to be" of fiction and of the literary word is like the mourir or dying which contaminates the negativity of death:

But to die is to rupture the world; it is to lose man, to annihilate [anéantir] being; it is therefore also to lose death, to lose that which, in it and for me, made it death. As long as I live, I am a mortal man, but, when I die, ceasing to be a man, I cease also to be mortal, I am no longer capable of dying, and the death which approaches [s'annonce] horrifies me, because I see it for what it is: no longer death, but the impossibility of dying.[43]**

In this sentence, in the reference to the il y a and Levinas' De l'existence à l'existant which precedes it,[44] and in the second half of "La Littérature et le droit à la mort" which is informed by it, Blanchot in a single moment extricates

---

* The French word sens indicates first a sense, movement, or orientation, and then "meaning", "signification", etc. As do many French philosophers, Blanchot mobilizes this ambiguity in his invocations of sens (cf. especially the last pages of "Les deux versions de l'imaginaire" in L'Espace littéraire). As the present quotation shows, sens may indicate a properly economic dissymmetry or disturbance which is not yet "meaning" and which will invest the possibility of meaning. As will be discussed below, the primary sens which appears in the economy of proximity will be the pour l'autre or "toward the Other" of the Same, i.e. the heteronomy and subjectivity of interiority.

** In Totalité et infini (pp. 27–8), Levinas conceives the mourir, in a Blanchotian inspiration, as an interruption of historical time, an irreducibility to negation, power, and possibility (p. 27), and a function of separation. Levinas argues for a positivity and irreducibility of subjectivity's "anguish before death", in the same sense that Blanchot enthusiastically invokes an irreducibility of decision and initiative within the passivity of death's approach. For both thinkers, the irreducible detour of closure in the economy is not a mere constraint, but a positive ontological event, invested by communication. It is important to note that the dispossession stressed by Blanchot, and the closure of the Same as "point of departure" in Levinas, describe the same basic moment: Separation.

his discursive thought from that of Hegel and introduces the basic concepts of his maturity. When death ceases to be a possibility, the real becomes an impossibility: a dimension without negation and without power. Existence becomes proximity: an element without adequate and adequating intervals, structured only by communication. Death is no longer the hyperbole of power in negation, but is the limit of negation's power. In a primary moment, death is a communication which is irreducible to disappearance, as is revealed in the suspended moment of dying. In a secondary moment, death is an event which cannot be mobilized. It no longer invests power, but is the Other of power: the excess of communication over negation. The man who dies becomes immortal: not as the triumph of his individuality over negation, but as the dispersed persistence of a communication which lacks the power to disappear. Mortality is not the capacity to die, but the incapacity either to disappear or to enter existence as an integrity. The mortality of separation is its immortality. To die is to lose death as negation, and to encounter death as communication. It is in this sense, as mentioned above, that the punctuality of death is not its primary importance in proximity. Mortality is a function of differentiation as it invests and exceeds the discontinuity of separation. Separation cannot but die, and yet it cannot die. Separation is, as Blanchot will write on Bataille, fourteen years after "La Littérature et le droit à la mort" but in the same spirit and the same terms, "the endless becoming of a death impossible to die."[45] The terrifying aspect of death, its dispossession, is the only reality of discontinuity. The reassuring aspect of both death and identity to self — a distance with regard to the real — is foreclosed by this permanence of dispossession. The impossibility of identity in the *glissement* of separation, is the impossibility of death as disappearance. Death is not the economy of totalization and destruction, but is the economy of contamination.

Death's failure to invest totalization through negation is also its failure to produce and guarantee truth. The ontological intervals which produce phenomenality and identity to self, relation and determination, by virtue of their foundation in negativity, are contaminated by what Blanchot calls the *faiblesse du négatif* or "weakness of the negative"[46] in proximity. Death is the hyperbole or extremity of this weakness, rather than of negation. The term "weakness" is appropriate, because contamination introduces a reality without totalization which is necessarily a reality without power. "Impossibility" is the economic term in Blanchot, Bataille, and Levinas, that designates proximity's displacement of existence and effectivity. The notion of "death without truth" is a motif around which many of Blanchot's definitions gravitate, in his novels as well as his theoretical texts. Often, as in *L'Espace littéraire*,[47] he will speak of a "double death" or of "two deaths" — a death which grounds totalization in the "world", and a death without truth in a reality which is not yet the "world" (the totality). In the context of this characteristic deference to a totalization which effectively exists, Blanchot's reader must be attentive to the fact that, for all its dominance and efficiency, totalization is a region of a general ecomomy which exceeds it, haunts its margins, and in a larger sense conditions it from within. Proximity produces the differentiations which are mobilized, in the "world", as totalities. Death "without truth" is the principle of these differentiations, and the "death" which founds totalization is conditioned by death without truth, as negation is conditioned by communication.

Death is not in the same concept as totalization. It is for this reason that, in spite of its compelling imminence, death is not "sure", not a certainty. "That which makes me disappear from the world cannot find its guarantee [in the world], and is thus, in a sense, without guarantee, is not sure.'[48] In its inadequation to the possibility of truth as totalization, death is a function or principle of the central Blanchotian concept *dissimulation*: the essentially non-manifest communication which, in the "world", tends to become negation, and in the "other night" or in essential solitude, tends to appear:

If men in general do not think about death, hide before it, this is doubtless in order to flee it and to hide [*se dissimuler*] from it, but this evasion is possible only because death itself is a perpetual flight before death [*fuite devant la mort*], because it is the depth of dissimulation. Thus to hide [*se dissimuler*] from it is in a way to hide [*se dissimuler*] in it.[49]

In Blanchot as in Bataille, interiority is animated by communication, whose excess over interiority is death. The regionality of totalization is the fact that closure itself is a function of dissimulation. Death is not an annihilation from which we cannot escape; it is rather the principle of a communication which describes both our dispossession in physical death, and our dispossession in survival. The difference between these two dispossessions is that the first is a radical passivity which exceeds closure and articulates the multiplicity or pluralism of life's "decomposition", and the second is a passivity which tends to concentrate itself in the exigency of power, truth, and identity: the dimension of possibility. For Blanchot, Bataille, and Levinas, as for Proust's narrator in the moment of involuntary memory, the difference between survival and death is less significant than the common denominator of these terms: the definition of closure as a passivity, involved with the exterior. Dissimulation is the name of this common denominator. One of its functions is the uncertainty of death; another is the possibility of truth.

The only ontology of death is the fact that it approaches. Death has no positivity. It annihilates without annihilating. It alters, in decomposition, that which it had already altered or contaminated, in survival. In this sense, its punctuality as an ultimate moment of destruction is an illusion: the irony of death. *Thomas l'obscur* and *L'Arrêt de mort* are Blanchot's most elaborate presentations of this irony. In a most Bataillian aphorism, Blanchot writes, "Why death? Because it is the extreme."[50] Death is the extremity of closure in communication, and not its destruction. Death always approaches, and only approaches. But it approaches as a pre-originarity. It invests the interiority to which it is imminent and immanent. In Cocteau's *Thomas l'imposteur*, the wounded protagonist must "play dead" in order to save his life — but it is too late. He is already dead. The irony and theatricality of this moment are characteristic of Blanchot's "death without truth". As subjectivity prepares for death's negation, it is already invested by death's dispossession. When annihilation supervenes, it is weakened and inefficient. Subjectivity cannot but die, and yet cannot die. Its mortality is its immortality: the impossibility of taking leave of the real. Death is a primary figure of the Other in proximity. Its approach is its only reality, but this economic or communicational approach is infinitely more compelling and intimate than a merely actual event: "the substance of absence, the depth of the emptiness [*la profondeur du vide*] which is created when one dies, an eternal exterior [*dehors*], the space formed by my death and whose approach [*approche*] alone, however, makes me die."[51] The inevitability of death, the fact that it cannot be stopped, is the fact that it will not and cannot arrive or "take place". In a fundamental Blanchotian configuration, the inconsistency and irreality of death — its *insaisissabilité* — is its involvement with interiority, and thus its compelling intimacy — its *indessaisissabilité*. To flee it is to flee into it. To approach it resolutely, in the inspiration of Hegel and Heidegger, is to be approached by it. "Even when I decide to go to it, by a virile and ideal [*idéale*] resolution, is it not [death] still that comes to me, and when I think I seize it, [death] that seizes me, that dispossesses [*dessaisit*] me, delivers me [*me livre*] to the unseizable [*insaisissable*]?"[52] Death escapes as it approaches, and invests the intentional movement which would escape or approach it. Every resolution or resoluteness in proximity, including the extremity of transgression, conceals a passivity: the passivity of invested or animated power.

Death is always a futurity and an approach. Subjectivity's exigency is to mobilize this approach as its own approach to death, and to render death punctual and present. On the other hand, death is the hyperbole of a reality without power, and subjectivity's exigency is to subordinate this reality to its own power and decision. Finally, death is the dimension of dispossession, and subjectivity's exigency is to subordinate the indefinition of death to the form of identity. These are the three coördinates of Blanchot's meditation of suicide and literature in "La mort possible".[53] They describe an attitude or comportment toward death in its approach. To render this approach punctual or present (so that it may be experienced), to make of it a power (so that it may be overpowered), and to render it personal (so that it may be appropriated), are the aims of a subjectivity which approaches death. Considered in its pre-originarity, as the form of communication, death animates these three attitudes as modalities of survival itself. As Bataille shows, survival is a mobilization of the "unavailable" as identity, power, and presence. Suicide is not the willful destruction of separation, but rather its extremity. The paradox of suicide is the only "possible" attitude toward death. "A strange enterprise, contradictory, an effort to act where immense passivity reigns, an exigency that wishes to maintain rules, imposes measure and fixes a goal in a movement which escapes all aims [visée] and all decision."[54] As mentioned earlier, Bataille, Blanchot and Levinas share a debt to phenomenology's situation of subjectivity within the economy of manifestation. Death directs our approach to death. Its being includes our access to it, in the manner of the intentional object. The irony of this access, in proximity is its foreclosing of all the basic possibilities embraced by phenomenology. Death has no phenomenality, and directs or animates the resoluteness which is contaminated and dismantled by the approach to it. In its lack of truth, it orders our search for its truth.

An involvement or contact with physical death is a triple contamination. In the first place, death does not and cannot arrive as a presence. There is a dephasing in the punctuality of suicide. The hand that pulls the trigger is already, and yet is not, the same hand that drops the gun. Action here becomes metamorphosis. One is always, like Cocteau's impostor, "not yet" dead and "already" dead. The approach and the pre-originarity of death — its indefinition and its immemoriality — subsist in its fugitive punctuality. Death is inadequate to presence. In the second place, the resoluteness which approaches death is infected by the passivity of its investment by death. "It is thus an *extreme passivity* that we still perceive in voluntary death, the fact that action here is only the mask of a fascinated dispossession."[55] "He who wants to die, does not die, loses the will to die, enters into the nocturnal fascination where he dies in a passion without will."[56]

From this, the haunting repetition [hantise ressassante] of suicidal gestures. He who, by maladroitness, has failed [manqué, missed, botched] his death, is like a ghost who comes back only to continue to aim at [tirer sur*] its own disappearance; he can only kill himself again and forever. This repetition has the frivolity of the eternal and the weightiness of the imaginary.[57]

The approach to death is a resoluteness which becomes indecision, fascination, *ressassement*, passion — and the common denominator of these terms, passivity. The approach to death is always the approach of death: a movement invested by its other. The punctuality of death which pre-exists and succeeds itself — its "already" and its "not yet" — is its constitution as repetition, and its investment of the movement which approaches it as repetition. In the third place, death as communication and dispossession is the "essential solitude" of death — that is, its impersonality. "Do I die myself, or do I die always other, so that I would have to say that, strictly speaking, *I* do not die?"[58] Death is the

---

* The expression *tirer sur* means "to shoot at", "to pull at", and to "incline toward" or "verge on". Blanchot is accentuating the ambiguity of a repetitive gesture which tries to die, or aims at death, while being already involved with death, already less than alive, already therefore passive in the suicidal spasm of action and resolve.

extremity of the essential solitude — the alteration — of interiority. "One" dies, because "one" is the true ontology of separation. Death is inadequate to identity, as is life.

Suicide in Blanchot's presentation may appear to be an inauthentic approach to death. It tends to domesticate death, to remove its futurity and indefinition, to subordinate it to identity and power. It "takes one death for another,"[59] mistaking proximity for negation. Blanchot's reader, and particularly the reader of the 1950's, is invited to interpret "La mort possible" as a condemnation of suicide in the manner of a Camus. But where might one locate an authenticity in death or in the approach to death? There is no alternative to the paradox of suicide, that is, to the mobilization of the unavailable, to the passivity of resolution. Passivity cannot be assumed. Blanchot does not disapprove the contradiction or the futility of suicide. His comparison of suicide to literary creation (cf. below) is based on the irreducibility of both these comportments to the context of authenticity grounded in totalization and accomplishment. Death is the inauthentic, *par excellence*. The opacity of Blanchot's theoretical text, in 1955 as in 1980, is its mimicry of phenomenological procedures and existential themes, and its description of a reality which is as incomprehensible to phenomenology as it is to the formalisms which succeeded phenomenology. On one hand, death has no truth and no authenticity; on the other hand, death is not a simple dispersion, the vanishing of the subject, but is a dispossession which invests the possibility of truth, power, and identity within the totality. Blanchot's text describes an impossibility of thinking subjectivity in its subordination to spontaneity and authenticity, and also an impossibility of thinking subjectivity in its subordination to the impersonality of signification. Where the humanist subject suffered the anguish of his freedom, and where the formalist subject disappears (or assumes an ontological insignificance which approximates disappearance) in the freeplay of signs or structures, the subject in proximity persists as an indecision, a fascination, and a passivity which are produced by differentiation itself, and which are uneliminable. The common denominator of the two traditions in which *L'Espace littéraire* appears in its furtive marginality, is their subordination of communication to manifestation: a direct and unselfconscious subordination, in phenomenology's obsession with interiority, and a more ambivalent subordination in the formalisms' confidence in minimal unities, oppositions, and the pertinence of structural models. To the former tradition, the expression "essential solitude" must seem pertinent and yet insufficient (given Blanchot's insistence on passivity); to the latter, the expression "impersonality" must have the same attraction and deception (given Blanchot's insistence on the multiple remainders which contaminate dispersion, including subjectivity itself). To the reader who is conscious of their historical circumstances, Blanchot's theoretical publications present an extraordinarily perverse aspect of accessibility and mystery. Like the *oeuvre* he meditates, Blanchot's text assures its marginality. It does not belong to the world.

Death is the extremity of impossibility in the general economy. Because it is irreducible to negation and totalization, its only reality is its approach. This approach animates and conditions any intentional approach to death on the part of subjectivity. At the same time, death's inability to "take place" as a positivity and a punctuality is its inability to destroy or eliminate either separation or the comportments of separation. It invests and contaminates these comportments, but it cannot disperse or eliminate them, because it is a principle of their differentiation and their exigency. It is for this reason that the term *fascination* implies an element of intentionality, that *ressassement* implies an element of free will, and that indecision implies a persistence of decision in a dimension of passivity. Communication does not annihilate separation, but rather invests separation as a contamination. The inappropriate voluntarism of suicide is the only comportment "appropriate" to the alterity (the inappropriation) of death. It is this inadequation, and the spasmodic effort of the exigency to reduce inadequation, that links suicide to literary creation. The *oeuvre* is not the same instance as death, but the artist is linked to it in the same sense that the suicide is involved with death. "Both desire firmly, but, to what they want, they are united by an exigency which exceeds [*ignore*, does not know, is irreducible to] their will."[60] The term *exigence*, as discussed earlier, describes the production of interiority by differentiation. The exigency is the excess which produces and exceeds interiority as an *effort d'autonomie*. The creation of an *oeuvre* is, like suicide, an involvement with passivity and a desire or exigency to master this involvement: to render the *oeuvre* present, to subordinate it to the decision and initiative of writing, and to appropriate it to the identity of its author. In a most general sense, the exigency of writing — a dispossession in the form of a mastery — is the basic exigency of proximity, and always implies death and the mobilization of death. In this sense, every writer writes "in order to be able to die,"[61] in order to subordinate death to possibility. But, as Bataille says so well of Proust, the economic basis of creation is rather a "putting to death of the author by his *oeuvre*."[62] It is the passivity of alterity's approach — the approach of an alterity which itself has no power — that produces the virility of creation. In the general economy, the word "passivity" means death: alterity as the economy of the interior, the animation of conation. In this context, Blanchot points out the secret insouciance, the blithe carelessness, of the writer's anguished approach to his work, in a formulation which points to the essence of Bataillian transgression: "Voluntary death is a refusal to see the other death, the one which cannot be seized, which one never attains; it is a sort of sovereign negligence. The *oeuvre,* in a way, would wish to install itself in this negligence and abide [*séjourner*] there."[63] The exigency exceeds its own voluntaristic mobilization, by virtue of its latent passivity, and at the same time exceeds the density of its communicational investment by the carelessness with which it pursues its goal. This is the irony of transgression, the insouciance hidden within its solemnity and resolve — an irony close to that of Kafka. Like so many of Kafka's protagonists, the writer does not perceive the impossibility of what he is doing, does not see the mountains he displaces in placing his first words on paper. And when he does sense the improbability of his work, he goes back to work — *se remet à l'oeuvre* — still without realizing, in spite of his anguish, the time of repetition he has thus entered. This improbability — the congruence of the possible and the impossible in the simplest act of subjectivity — is the irony of closure's transgression, that is, the *expérience* of closure. The carelessness of anguish, consequent to the exigency's passivity, is a constant motif in the fiction of both Bataille and Blanchot, and is a principle of both authors' irony: the irony of impossibility.

"He who abides [*séjourne*] close to negation," writes Blanchot of the suicide, "cannot make use of it. He who belongs to it, in this belonging can no longer leave himself [*se quitter*], because he belongs to the neutrality of absence in which he is already no longer himself."[64] In proximity, the *neutre* (the other of distinction and opposition) underlies what appears to be the negative. Impossibility underlies the apparent duality of being and nothingness, actuality and potentiality. The impossibility of the phrase *séjourner auprès* or *demeurer auprès* is often stipulated by Blanchot in the context of the writer's rapport with the *oeuvre*. The proximity of the *oeuvre*, like that of death in suicide and that of communication in separation, is not a discretion, but an involvement. As discussed earlier (Chapter 1), a fundamental modality of the Blanchotian *cogito* is its approach to an alterity which forecloses all approach to it. In its escape from subjectivity's approach to it, the Other approaches subjectivity. The intentionality of approach becomes the spasm of an indecision which "va de-ci, de-là," which has lost its sense of direction, because the Other approaches from within and without, at the same time. Indecision is the *nouvelle origine* of initiative in the approach to the Other, as is fascination for perception, and essential solitude for identity. These terms, and the many others which describe subjectivity in Blanchot's text, define separation as a metamorphosis, i.e. an economic instance which is essentially intricated with alterity, and which, on the basis of this intrication, is denied the immobility or equilibrium of determination. Interiority is an alteration. Subjectivity moves and speaks, in proximity. The general economy is the scene of a disturbance and of a murmur or noise: the *parole* and the *errance* of a radical passivity or heteronomy in being. Discontinuity always transgresses discontinuity, toward the Other (*pour l'autre*): this is its closure and its subjectivity. The movement of excess which is the alteration of interiority in its very conation, may appear, in the "world", as an initiative or decision. In the violence of the "other night", it may appear as the dispersed hebetude of fascination or indecision. It is the inextrication of these tendencies or modalities of dissimulation that structures Blanchot's thought. Subjectivity is an absolute heteronomy, but the heteronomy of differentiation produces separation. Closure is an excess. The replacement of negativity by proximity, i.e. the difference and non-indifference of communication, defines separation as both a contamination and the hyperbolic intensity or density of this contamination. Separation is both more dense than identity (since it is excessively closed) and less adequate (since it is not closed enough).

This density which forces interiority outside itself, toward the Other, is simultaneously its mortality and its indecision. The approach to death and the approach of death are one movement and are the singular moment of differentiation in the general economy: the *pour l'autre* of separation.

ERRANCE

Subjectivity in the general economy is a unicity whose compression or density is produced by its intrication with alterity. In Bataille, such a subjectivity is a *dépense* or excess in the basic moment of its closure. In Levinas, interiority is a *récurrence*, involved already with an alterity which collaborates in its conation. In Blanchot, subjectivity is the vertigo and the strangeness of the *nouvelle origine*: an apparent vicissitude of consciousness' spontaneity which reveals the latent insistence of the radical passivity of closure. For all three thinkers, subjectivity is involved in a pre-originary economy with the *dehors* or exterior, understood as an Other of closure which invests closure. Subjectivity in *dépense*, in *récurrence* or in the *nouvelle origine* is always an "interiority outside": a rapport with alterity which precedes the spontaneity and decision with which a consciousness would confront the exterior. In the economy of communication, the exterior is a proximity before it may assume the form of a phenomenal or objective existent. Interiority itself is a product of this proximity, this incumbence, gravity, or pressure, before it may assume the form of a discontinuity. When the subjectivity of proximity goes resolutely to encounter the *dehors*, it moves unwittingly toward the scene of its latent constitution and its new origin. This is subjectivity's transgression and its *expérience*: an apparently anomalous interruption of consciousness' transitivity and a disarming of its spontaneity which are the ultimate axes of the *cogito* of proximity.

In Blanchot's text, proximity is often thematized as a place rather than as a moment or event. There are two basic forms of this Blanchotian sense of place in communication. On one hand, proximity is an exteriority which approaches and conditions interiority in the form of an intrusion, a suffocating claustration. This is the night: the context of the Burrow and of Orpheus' transgression.* On the other hand, proximity may take the form of an indefinite exteriority with which interiority is intricated, in a dispersion no less claustrated than the intimacy of the night, although its context is the agoraphobia of indefinite space and unlimited movement. This is the desert: the context of the prophetic word, the symbolic experience, and of *errance*.

As discussed in earlier sections of this study, heteronomy in the general economy is never a situation of undifferentiation. Heteronomy is rather the modality by which exteriority creates an instance of infinite density combined

---

* See below, "The Burrow and the Other Night"; see also Chapter 3, "Silence and Orpheus".

with infinite dispersion: a unicity without totalization. It is Levinas who insists most explicitly on this coincidence of heteronomy and unicity in this concept of separation. If the general economy may be said to have a differential or informational aspect, then its differences must be said to exert a paradoxical pressure which produces the extraordinarily intense *glissement* of interiority. The communicational factor by which a differential singularity escapes totalization — characterized by the philosophy of difference in terms which describe secondarity, referral, contamination, etc. — must be thought in proximity as the excess and the vulnerability of a closure which is invested by the exterior. Closure is a dense congruence of communications and a result of what Hegel correctly termed the "force" of communication. As Levinas says so well, closure is a "gravity" in being. Unicity in the general economy will always be produced, and given its cohesion and turgidity, by the same movement which forecloses the possibility of identity. Separation is the impossibility of totalization, considered as a positive unicity.

The desert in Blanchot is a realization of the predicates of subjectivity in proximity, to the extent that this subjectivity is *au dehors*, "on the outside," "in the exterior." Blanchot introduces the desert through the experience of the symbol, conceived as a communication which does not refer to a unitary signified, but rather transports subjectivity to a dimension outside the familiar context of signification. For Blanchot, the symbol does not exist as a unit of signification.[65] Instead, the symbolic experience exists as a dimension outside comprehension. "The symbol signifies nothing, expresses nothing. It renders present only — in rendering us present to it — a reality which escapes all other access [*saisie*] and seems to appear there, prodigiously near [*proche*] and prodigiously far away [*lointaine*], like a foreign [*étrangère*] presence."[66] The symbol is a change of place, a transport to a place in which infinite distance is infinite proximity. Indeed, the symbolic experience is what Blanchot often calls an *attrait sur place* or "attraction in place" — that is, not the ekstasis of a beyond, but an experience which changes familiar space into this other dimension, which "exposes" us to the "approach of another space."[67] Similarly, the prophetic word changes the dimension of its resonance. "When the *parole* [word*] becomes prophetic, it is not the future that is given, it is the present that is taken away [*retiré*] along with all possibility of a firm, stable and durable presence."[68] The desert is the space or dimension of exteriority produced by the transport or transformation — more precisely, the alteration — of symbolism and prophecy.

* The *parole* in Blanchot is a most private and problematic term which never means "word" or "spoken word", but indicates the primary disturbance created in the general economy by the excess of closure. When the spoken or written word becomes communication — when the intramundane situation of intersubjectivity becomes involved with the "arrière-monde" of proximity — the word becomes the *parole*. See below, esp. Chapters 5–7.

In the desert, there is no interiority which would not already be an inherence of exteriority; no space which would not already be "the approach of another space" or, in another repeated formulation, the "vertigo of *espacement*";* no time or punctuality which would not already be a repetition. These are the basic predicates of proximity as they inform the idea of a space or location; intrusion and dispersion, alteration, and repetition. Their common denominator is a displacement of negativity and non-contradiction by communication, and the resulting production of a dense and intense, although dispersed and dispossessed, unicity. As in all contexts of proximity, the failure of totalization is not the epistemological principle of a limit placed on understanding, but is more fundamentally an economic principle engendering a multiplicity of conditions affecting interiority. One of these conditions is the displacement produced by excess. In a formula which is closely related to Bataillian *expérience*, Blanchot describes the extremity of the artist's experience as "this excess which, within him, leads him outside himself and perhaps outside everything [*hors de tout*]."[69] The desert is one form of this *dehors* or exterior, rendered proximate by the excess of closure, and "into which" art, the symbol, or the prophetic word may transport us.

"The desert is this exterior [*dehors*] in which one cannot remain [*demeurer*, abide, reside], since to be there is always to be outside [*au-dehors*, on the outside, i.e. in a dimension inadequate to interiority]."[70] In the desert, interiority has no initial moment of self-coincidence which would precede its entry into relation with the exterior. Impossibility, the logical dimension of closure's unicity in proximity, is here an "impossibility of being for a first time [*impossibilité d'être une première fois*]."[71] This impossibility of initiality and self-coincidence is also the impossibility of the verb *demeurer*: the maintenance or endurance of the Same. The conditioning of interiority by a pre-originary *dehors* or "outside" functions analogously to the contamination of totalization: it produces necessary comportments, exigencies, and the vicissitudes of a radical passivity. Thus, in the desert, where there is no *demeurer*, interiority cannot stop moving. Subjectivity is always and essentially *en marche*, in movement, without the possibility of an arresting of this movement. The incessance of displacement is correlative to what Blanchot calls "dispersion",[72] the basic fact of an intrication with exteriority. Subjectivity is inclined or forced outward by the

---

* The word *espacement* ("spacing"), used by Blanchot as early as 1953 and later appropriated by the philosophy of difference, describes the economy of space and time, and their aproximity in communication. Space in *espacement* is a field of intervals without totalization or negation. It is a production of discontinuities which have not yet accomplished, and will never accomplish, their entry into being as totalities. As a dimension, space has not yet accomplished, and will never accomplish, its distinction from time. Space is a "spacing", a production of space, in a time of repetition without accomplishment. In *espacement*, the discontinuity of spatial and temporal intervals, and of space and time as dimensions, is not a negation but a proximity. The form of closure in this situation is alteration: the becoming-other of heteronomy. Seized at this suspended moment, space and time are themselves heteronomous alterations.

very process of its closure. Levinas will speak of a subject's "impossibility of arresting his forward movement [*marche en avant*]"[73] in the intersubjective context of responsibility and the *visage*. The thematic difference between the Levinasian *éthique* and Blanchot's desert masks a profound logical solidarity. In both contexts, subjectivity's displacement is passive and is inadequate to the notion of intentionality. Interiority moves toward the outside because interiority is already outside. This is its *pour l'autre* or "toward the Other": its excess and its vulnerability to the exterior.*

On one hand, dispersion is the condition of a passive movement in the desert. On the other hand, this movement is conditioned by the absence, in the space of proximity, of the possibility of a *lieu* or locus. Every location, in this dimension, is already a communication with other locations, and with an indeterminate *ailleurs* or "elsewhere" which is the Other of locus and point: the Other of closure in space. Thus, to be here or *ici* in the desert is already to be *ailleurs*. "Here" is essentially a communication with, and a proximity or approach to, "there". And this approach is not an approximation, but a dispossession. "There" is not another location but the Other of location itself, as it conditions any location in proximity. To be here is to be torn from here, and always already approaching the indeterminacy of the *ailleurs*, an "elsewhere" that can never be another "here".** Movement in the desert is a failure of interiority's non-coincidence with the exterior, and a correlative failure of location to extricate itself from an inherence of the *ailleurs*. This situation is exile, in the radicality of that concept: the fundamental impossibility of a dwelling or *demeure*. But it is also *errance* or wandering, in the radicality of this concept: the impossibility of even a momentary arrest of movement. In the desert, "the same is given in the vertigo of splitting [*dédoublement*]." Every "here" is already an "elsewhere", an indefinite *ailleurs* whose inadequation to common space gives it the basic aspect of a "nowhere": "here has melted into nowhere

---

* In the desert, one moves toward the outside, toward the Other (*pour l'autre*) in order to encounter the dimension of oneself which is already outside, already involved with the Other. In the Burrow, subjectivity will sense the approach of an Other which will again have aspects of subjectivity itself. See below, "The Burrow and the Other Night".

** The *ailleurs* of proximity's dispossession is a basic element of Baudelaire's meditation of subjectivity, particularly in Bataille's illumination of this meditation (see below, Chapter 3). On one hand, the *ailleurs* which is not another "here" is for Baudelaire the "anywhere out of the world", the principle of the voyage, an effectively real dimension whose only access is the dispossession and impossibility of desire. The *ailleurs* cannot be totalized and cannot be attained. Its impossibility is its necessary and sufficient condition. On the other hand, its effectivity is its approach to and intrusion upon a passive subjectivity, as in *Le Gouffre*: "all I can see out the windows is infinity." To be torn from the familiarity of the interior is correlative to the impossibility of attaining the absolute exteriority of the *ailleurs*. These two aspects are not terms of a dialectic, but proceed from a single concept: the passivity of closure in a dimension without totalization. The *ailleurs* in Baudelaire is perhaps best described by Blanchot's definition of "impossibility": it cannot be experienced (the only rapport with it is desire), and it cannot but be experienced (it invests and contaminates interiority as would a poison). The inability either to remain "here" or to escape "here" is one Baudelairian intuition of impossibility.

[*nulle part*] ."[74] Blanchot's reader is familiar with this expanding indeterminacy, combined with an intensified proximity, through the other mode of "doubling" called *personne. Personne* is simultaneously the Same, the Other, No one, and, in the Burrow, the possibility of the Other as Double.

Errance, the impossibility of immobility, is also and essentially *erreur*: a movement with three basic predicates. On one hand, "the locus of wandering [*égarement*, being lost] does not know the straight line; one never goes from one point to the other in it; one does not leave here to go there."[75] *Errance* is a movement inadequate to the concept of destination (a totalized locus), a bewildered wandering which "va de-ci, de-là." In the second place, if the effect or simulacrum of a destination insists in this dimension, then the approach to such a point must always be a detour. Linearity, grounded in the totalization of the point, is no longer a possibility. "He who wishes to advance must go out of his way [*se détourner*], this creates a curious crablike walk."[76] In the third place, the approach to a destination in the desert is, like transgression in Bataille, a relation to an instance whose only being is its approach — an instance "that one only seizes where one goes beyond it."[77] Movement here corresponds to the navigation toward the sirens in *Le Livre à venir* (see below, Chapter 3). One may drop anchor too soon, or too late. The destination is not a locality, but an approach. Finally, as travelers in the desert know, the destination has a paradoxical ability to retain its distance in spite of the mathematical certainty of reduced distance. This is the inadequation of the destination to an approach conceived in terms of attainment or accomplishment. One may have what Blanchot calls elsewhere an "always more initial rapport"[78] with the destination — one must, in fact, have such a rapport — but this proximity will never become arrival.

This "more initial rapport" is not only an increased proximity to that which paradoxically retains its distance (the distance of its alterity). It is also the proximal time of a pre-originarity. For the desert, like the *oeuvre* (and the desert is one of the principal notions which designate the approach to the *oeuvre* in Blanchot), is the context of what Blanchot calls a "time without decision". Repetition in the desert is correlative to that essential passivity through which "initiative" and "decision" are withdrawn from intentionality. Passivity and repetition are aspects of "impossibility" in an economy without totalization. "It is the time in which nothing begins, in which initiative is not possible, in which before affirmation there is already the return of affirmation."[79] The absence of initiative, in both Bataille and Blanchot, is that impossibility which is not negation and is therefore "no longer privation, but affirmation."[80] In the desert, as everywhere in proximity, subjectivity is already involved with that alterity which remains inaccessible. The Other's escape from totalization is not a negation. This is why the Other approaches, and why subjectivity cannot but approach the Other. "Rather than a purely negative mode, it is on the contrary a time without negation, without decision."[81] The desert is simultaneously a conditioning of the principle of identity by the inherence of the *dehors* and the *ailleurs*, a conditioning of intentionality by passivity rather than determination (and therefore a withdrawal of "free will" by a process far more radical than simple determinism), and a contamination of the temporal ekstases by the proximal time of repetition.

The locus of wandering [*égarement*] does not know the straight line; one never goes from one point to the other in it; one does not leave here to go there; no point of departure and no beginning to the walk. Before having begun, already one begins again [*recommence*] ; before having accomplished, one repeats [*ressasse*], and this sort of absurdity consisting in returning without ever having left, or in beginning by beginning again, is the secret of the "bad" eternity, corresponding to the "bad" infinite, which both harbor perhaps the meaning of becoming [*devenir*].[82]

The instance which wanders the desert is, to paraphrase Blanchot's reading of Nietzsche, "not the Same, but the eternal return of the Same" -- which is no longer a Same at all. The *détour* of the desert which proceeds from the failure of negation and totalization in space, is correlative to the *retour* of repetition, which proceeds from the same failure in time. Moreover, the space/time distinction is itself an impossibility in the desert, considered as "the vertigo of *espacement*." "The desert is not yet time, nor space, but a space without location [*lieu*] and a time without origination [*engendrement*, engendering]."[83] Space in *escapement* is always the "approach of another space." Presence is the irrecuperable past and future of the return, in the time of repetition and in the space to which I return before I have left. The "vertigo of *espacement*" is the *hic et nunc* of proximity: a contamination of both punctuality and locality by the communications of a general economy whose principle, it must be stressed, is not simple dispersion, but the strange compression of a unicity without integrity. The concept of indecision with its *nouvelle origine*, understood as an impossibility of intentional action upon exteriority, combined with an impossibility of initiative defined as repetition, is central to the elaboration of *errance* in the desert. The larger context of this economic moment, and perhaps the central expression of Blanchot's Nietzschian inspiration, is described by a statement in *L'Espace littéraire* which should be read in its most global sense: "that which is first is not the beginning [*commencement*] but the beginning again [*recommencement*] , and being is precisely the impossibility of being for a first time."[84]

As mentioned above, there is no immobility in the desert. Location is the defection of the *lieu* or locus, and this defection engenders an indecisive moment toward the outside and toward the Other.* Indecision indicates on one hand the

---

* The problematic passivity and irreducibility to totalization which describe communication are suggested by critics of referentiality in the notion of "intransitivity". This concept describes communication's lack of relation to a totalized exterior. However, it also tends to invoke an independence of communication with regard to a governing or terminal signified, and this independence cannot be discovered in the radical heteronomy of proximal communication, which is yet more "dependent" upon the exterior than the concept of referentiality or representation would imply. It is perhaps for this reason that the critique of referentiality tends to invoke for communication, particularly in literature, the predicate of "auto-referentiality", whose independence and transitivity are not thinkable within a proximal economy. See below, Chapter 3.

inadequation of this movement to the concept of destination, and on the other hand its inadequation to the concept of decision and initiation. Subjectivity is always already moving, in the desert. Motion is a passivity and a repetition. Before deciding to move, one would already have begun to move. Like the *parole errante*[85] which speaks before it speaks and perseveres after it falls silent, subjectivity always moves in the desert before it has started to move, and always moves when it has stopped moving, in the moment called *ressassement*. Movement, in this context, is less the exigency which makes Thomas walk when his decision is to remain immobile[86] than it is the fundamental communication which places subjectivity's center of gravity outside itself. The heteronomy of closure — its inclination, vulnerability, and spasmodic movement "toward the Other", is the principle of the general economy. *Errance* is a character of the place itself, as well as a predicament of the nomad or exile. Where totalization fails in the general economy, the immobility of determination is disturbed by a continual, spasmodic displacement: the excess of closure. This excess is also the insufficiency of the exterior which cannot constitute itself as a totality in opposition to interiority. Blanchot sometimes designates this imcompletion of the exterior as a surplus of place or *hypertopie* which interiority must continually move outside itself to fill.[87] This movement, described by the philosophy of difference in the concept of supplementarity, must be incessant and repetitive, because the economy which engenders it cannot produce totalization. Interiority cannot abide or *demeurer*, because the place of its conation inclines it and forces it outside itself, as a function of its closure. This is the "attraction in place" exerted by the proximal exterior upon interiority.

Errance is the form and the comportment of interiority in a proximity defined as a space. The repetition correlative to wandering is, to paraphrase Blanchot, "the way time has of accomplishing itself" in proximity. Finally, *errance* is *erreur*. No direction in the desert is the right direction. Every trajectory is a detour, and finally an indecision. Movement in the desert is always an *égarement*, a "losing one's way", and a *désoeuvrement* or vertiginous passivity and confusion.* There are two conditions of the concept of *erreur*. In the first place, as described above, the only possibility of destination in the desert is the approach. The destination is "that which is only seized when one is already beyond it." The impossibility of accomplishment in this dimension is concomitant to the impossibility of location. Secondly, and perhaps more importantly, the desert is a place of differentiation and proximity rather than of manifestation and accomplishment in the form of truth. There is no "right way" in the desert because its "time without decision" and "space without location" describe a universe without negation, without presence, without accomplishment, and without power: a universe inadequate to manifestation. The only phenomenality in this dimension is the mirage: the spectacle of a location out of

---

* The term *désoeuvrement*, which indicates an inadequation to the *oeuvre* or "accomplishment" in being, as well as passivity or confusion, will eventually assume a global economic sense in Blanchot (see esp. *L'Entretien infini*) and will function as an equivalent to the notion of impossibility.

its location, "in the middle of nowhere," the spectacle of subjectivity's inherence in the exterior, and above all the proximity of the image, which can neither be seized nor let go, and whose only intentional access is Blanchotian *fascination*. The desert, like the night in Blanchot, is a world without power and without truth. Yet the dissimulations of the desert may be the only possibility of a truth or authenticity outside totalization, as Blanchot suggests in his discussion of the Diaspora and in the following comment on Orpheus' transgression: "as though renouncing failure were much more grave than renouncing success, as though what we call the insignificant, the inessential, error [*erreur*] , could, to him who accepts its risk and gives himself to it without reserve, reveal itself as the source of all authenticity."[88]

The dispersion of the desert is the unicity of interiority. Specifically, it is this unicity *au dehors*, conceived and expressed in the predicates of extension and infinite space. The thematic contexts of proximity in Blanchot's text are of an extraordinary richness and complexity, and may contradict each other entirely on a thematic level. Thus proximity may be the "other night", more dense than the "night of day", and elsewhere a blinding illumination. It may be a suffocating intrusion or the emptiness of endless spaces; the inconsistency of the *insaisissable* which cannot be attained, and the terror of the *indessaisissable* which cannot be let go. These contradictions on the thematic level are informed by that other dimension which may be termed "economic", in which every Blanchotian utterance is a description of the constitution of subjectivity in proximity. At this level, each of Blanchot's themes will describe through the organization of its predicates the fundamental moments of proximity, such as passivity, ambivalence, heteronomy, displacement, etc. *Errance* and the desert are regions of Blanchot's thematic economy which propose more explicitly then most other regions the notion of a subjectivity "in the exterior", *au dehors*.

DESIRE AND THE HUNGER WHICH NOURISHES ITSELF

The force or intensity with which closure produces or encloses itself in the general economy — the force of closure's conation — proceeds from the exterior. It is for this reason that the hyperbolic density or turgidity of closure is also its heteronomy, its vulnerability to exteriority. The Bataillian term *inachèvement* describes an incompletion which neither supervenes to subjectivity nor appears as a temporary lack, defined in terms of negativity. This incompletion, instead, is absolutely integral to the "completion" or unicity of discontinuity. It functions as the economic process of closure in a dimension without negativity. And the economic character of this *effort d'autonomie* or "effort toward (and of) autonomy" as a moment of differentiation and individuation must be stressed. Discontinuity is not a constituted entity which would strive to enclose or protect itself. Prior to this configuration, discontinuity is an economy which creates an exigency of closure. The gravity or pressure of the exterior produces an intensity called interiority. A closure constituted by differentiation rather than negation is, in and by virtue of its very density, an extreme dispersion and heteronomy. From the perspective of identity and non-contradiction, the interiority of proximity is not a closure at all, since it is not a totality. It is this "escape from the totality" or from the overall context of unity, that Levinas defines as separation itself.

Desire, in its derivation as a concept in proximity, is a gap or *écart*, an irreducible lack in the constitution of a closure which cannot coincide with itself. Initially, desire is the pure incompletion of closure. This incompletion is not an equilibrium, but is a density and an intensity: the pressure of the exterior in its investment and dispossession of interiority. Closure is a spasm and a paroxysm, forced by the outside. It is Bataille's Nietzschian inspiration, combined with his penetration in the thinking of extremity and impossibility ("which can neither avoid its limits nor hold to them") that allows him to think discontinuity as an exigency, and the exigency as desire. An important aspect of Bataille's genius is his sustained view of the economy in its generality, and his resulting definition of an *expérience du dedans* which is an interiority without being a totality. The interplay of these two basic moments permits Bataille to thematize a universe analogous to that of difference or information, and to perceive within the circulation of the differential or informational trace the fugitive presence of the exigency: a lack of totalization which is not a mere dispersion. Bataillian closure is the unicity of a dispossession, the spasmodic contraction or condensation of a dispersion. There are two basic and simultaneous moments of this unicity's *inachèvement* or incompletion. The first is its lack, which Bataille calls a *fêlure*, *blessure*, or *plaie*: the "rip in the seamless gown of individual discontinuity."[89] The second moment is the remainder or *reste* which is produced by closure's irreducible excess, and which insists paradoxically in the *dehors* or exterior in a moment analogous to that of the differential trace. These two moments define the basic sense of the concept *dépense*. *Dépense* is an invasion and dispersal of interiority, understood as the process which grounds and conditions interiority as an irreducible unicity. Closure is a most tenuous and fugitive moment of radical heteronomy which is nevertheless irreducible and inescapable. It is the economy of the general economy. While it cannot achieve totalization and comprehension, its density is sufficient to produce opacity. Between "you" and "me", writes Bataille, nothing can reduce a "primary difference": our discontinuity. The economy of proximity, in Bataille as in Proust, produces an intersubjective rapport which is as opaque as the alterity of Sartrian phenomenology, and as intimate as the unconscious heteronomy of psychoanalysis. A function of Albertine's escape as the "fugitive" is the fact that her movements concern the narrator "inside" or "in his heart". Her escape is also her involvement with him. Because her being is not a totalization, she can be neither possessed nor excluded. In proximity, subjectivity is involved with an instance that remains inaccessible. *Dépense* is an invasion and dispersal of interiority, although not as an abberration, and not, in

Levinas' words, as a "violence". *Dépense* is rather the extremity or the plethora of interiority as closure. It is interiority's "element" or familiarity, before it may become the violence of loss.

In a most straightforward passage of *L'Erotisme* which bluntly and programmatically contests philosophy's models of comprehension, Bataille writes:

Being, most often, seems to be given to man outside the movements of passion. I will say, on the contrary, that we must never represent being outside these movements.[90]

Bataille's implication is that what he calls *passion* plays a more fundamental role in subjectivity's involvement with being than any concept based upon manifestation or comprehension. More profoundly, the problematic of discontinuity and *dépense* describes a general economy whose differentiations are themselves to be understood as passions: an existent whose economy is not totalization, not dispersion, but desire. At this most general level of Bataille's thinking, the proximity of Levinas and Blanchot to his text is at its most extreme. The notion that desire is the modality of closure's escape from the operations of negativity, and that on this basis desire must be defined as an economic principle more basic than negation, links the works of Bataille, Blanchot, and Levinas in an intimate communication which cuts across otherwise important differences in vocabulary and context.

The paradox of desire, from the point of view of identity and non-contradiction, is that it is an excess and a lack which proceed from a unicity that is nevertheless absolutely self-sufficient. As has been so often attested by psychoanalysis, identity knows only need, which may be satisfied by the economy of causality and determination. Need is the modality of a subjectivity which is already essentially *comblée* or fulfilled. It is the vicissitude of a totality. Desire is, from this point of view, a paradoxical failure of totalization where totalization is hyperbolically complete. It is this minimal failure, this uneliminable involvement with the outside, as a problematic function of totalization's very completion. In his essay on Bataillian *expérience*, Blanchot defines desire as an "excess", an "infinitesimal interstice" within totalization, which engenders what he calls "the desire of the man without desire, the dissatisfaction of the man who is 'completely' satisfied [*'en tout'*], a pure lack [*défaut*], where there is however an accomplishment of being."[91] Desire is an Other of totalization which conditions, in the general economy, the possibility of totalization.

Desire is a movement consequent to that ontological structure by which negation, accomplishment, unity and power are revealed in their secondarity and their regionality by the general economy. This multiple problematic illuminates the solidarity of desire with radical passivity, and is familiar to Bataille's reader under the name of impossibility. The "impossible" in Bataille describes a universe without power — although not without differentiation. In *L'Entretien infini*, where Bataillian and Levinasian inspirations are more numerous than in previous books, Blanchot writes (in an essay on Simone Weil): "desire is precisely this rapport with impossibility, (. . .) impossibility which becomes [*se fait*] a rapport, *separation* itself."[92] Blanchot specifies, in a most Bataillian phrase, that by impossibility he does not mean absurdity or intolerability, in an existential context — "negative determinations which proceed from [*relèvent de*] possibility."[93] Impossibility is not a privation but, as the Blanchot of *L'Espace Littéraire* writes, an "affirmation": an excessive investment of interiority by an economy without negation. Impossibility, affirmation, and desire are terms which refer, in their subtle displacements of emphasis and context, to a common denominator: the exigency in its irreducibility to negation and totalization. In Blanchot's phrase, whose involvement with the philosophy of Levinas is most intense, this exigency is the constitution of separation in being. Separation and the possibility of the rapport are productions of impossibility.

"The Other is not the negation of the Same as Hegel would have it. The fundamental fact of an ontological scission into Same and Other, is a non-allergic rapport of Same and Other."[94] Thus Levinas explains a separation in being which is not a negation and not a moment of totalization. The rapport of interiority and exteriority is not an adequate or dialectical distinction or opposition. It is not the "allergy" with which totalities enter into relation and correlation. It is rather a discontinuity or difference, and most basically a rapport or involvement. This *non-allergie*, as Levinas often explains, is neither the independence and reciprocity of ethics, a "peace through reason", nor the immobility of comprehension described by the "laisser être" or "letting Being be" of Heidegger's later texts. On the contrary, the instance which receives the names *non-allergie*, *non-indifférence*, *bonté*, etc. is a heteronomous involvement with alterity which corresponds, in spite of Levinas' refusal to qualify it as "violence",* to the most disturbing incarnations of menace and violence in Western mythology. This involvement with the Other which precedes the Same's coincidence with itself is Desire, described variously by Levinas (in a Bataillian congruence of excess and insufficiency) as "an insufficiency without possible satisfaction,"[95] "the astonishing fact of containing more than it is possible to contain,"[96] and most importantly, "an exigency coming from the other, beyond

---

* The term "violence" in Levinas means the "allergy" and totalitarian closure produced by negation and correlation within an economy of comprehension and totalization. The "non-violence" of heteronomy in the *éthique* corresponds both logically and thematically to those situations of passivity, involvement, etc. which are proscribed by the dimension of totalization, and which describe a more fundamental mode of violence whose elaboration organizes the texts of Bataille and Blanchot, and links these texts to that of Levinas in terms such as the *il y a*, impossibility, etc. Cf. below, Chapters 4 and 7.

the activity of my powers, to open a 'deficit' without limits, in which the *Soi** expends itself [*se dépense*] without reckoning [*sans compter*], freely." [97]

It is Levinas who most consistently points out that subjectivity does not desire a constituted other from the point of view of its self-coincidence, but is already involved with the Other in the process of its conation, and desires as a modality of this involvement. Thus the force of desire "comes from the other." "To pose being as Desire and as *bonté*** is not to isolate beforehand a self which would then tend toward a beyond. It is to affirm that to grasp oneself from the interior — to produce oneself as a self [*moi*] — is to grasp oneself by the same gesture which is already turned toward the exterior. . . ." [98] Desire is not a vicissitude of closure, but its principle. In the context of sensation, Levinas defines subjectivity's incarnation as a pre-originary "denucleation", a "non-coincidence of the self with itself", a *blessure* or "wound" in the Bataillian sense of this word. The miracle of desire for Levinas is subjectivity's capacity to be "concerned" with alterity in the very moment of its self-sufficient egoism:

a disquiet, an in-somnia, beyond the *retrouvailles* [the "findings" or concrete surroundings discovered by the *cogito* in its awakening] of the present — a pain which disarms the self [*moi*] or, in a vertigo draws it like an abyss, preventing it, posed in itself and for itself, from "assuming" the other which wounds [*blesse*] it, in an intentional movement [;] so that, in this vulnerability, the reversal of the *other inspiring* the *same* is produced. . . . [99]

The conation of interiority is a contraction "away from" the surrounding economy which cannot but describe an excessive movement "into" this economy. The repulsion of the exterior, as in Bataillian survival, is an attraction

---

* *Soi* means the "self" at the impersonal moment of the accusative *se*, i.e. the self intricated economically with alterity, and involved thematically in an obligation or responsibility toward the proximal "Autrui". As noted earlier (Chapter 1), *Soi* is the economic moment which succeeds the *Moi* (self) of ipseity and leads to the *moi* (me) of non-interchangeable unicity. The accusative case of the *Soi* describes the incumbence of an alterity which concerns or involves interiority and may therefore be said, in a sense, to envisage interiority — although this alterity is not another consciousness, not another centre of reference or *Moi*, as in phenomenology. (Although the orthographic distinction *Moi/moi* is sometimes declared explicitly by Levinas, as in *Humanisme de l'autre homme* (p. 99), its usage within his text is not consistent, as citations in the present study indicate.)

** *Bonté* or "goodness" in Levinas means the heteronomous investment by which subjectivity is economically inclined toward alterity. The *dépense* — the excess and vulnerability — which characterizes interiority's involvement with an incumbent Other, has the thematic predicate of generosity, in Levinas as in Bataille. As will be discussed below, this *pour l'autre* or "toward the Other" of interiority's conation — the foundation of the Levinasian *éthique* — may not be thought as the result of a transcendent value or obligation to which subjectivity sacrifices itself, as in ethics or in a philosophy of right. It is rather an economic principle of separation itself, and therefore of subjectivity's "egoism", and may function as the "source of unpunished crimes."

to and of the exterior. To turn away from the economy is to turn into the economy. Conation is the desire of the exterior: always a conation "inside out", a conation "in reverse". This essential ambivalence of desire whose non-dialectical basis has been psychoanalysis' consistent meditation, is also, as discussed earlier (Chapter 1), a principle of Western culture's most stable tendency: to totalize the Other at an adequate distance, and to engulf the Other in a communion. As Levinas implies, this ambivalence transcends the philosophical distinctions regarding subjectivity. It produces a congruence of sensation, pleasure and pain, attraction and repulsion, which must be thought not only as the economy of passion but also as the production of cognition and receptivity as possibilities. Desire, the force and the insufficiency of closure, is the principle of subjectivity.

In sensation and *psychisme*, the animation of identity is "the Other in me" — just as, following the negations of the *cogito*, it is the Other who can say "Yes". Desire "opens" subjectivity. This heteronomy is not only the egoism and *jouissance* of ipseity, but also the disquiet and preoccupation which proceeds from the approach of alterity. Levinas' text, like that of Bataille, oscillates between its description of alterity's pre-originary conditioning of subjectivity on one hand, and on the other hand its description of the compelling imminence of an encounter with alterity. Sensation, on one hand, and recurrence, on the other, are the axes of this oscillation in Levinas. And within the context of sensation itself, as will be discussed below (Chapter 5), the constitution of subjectivity's "complacency" by alterity is first the pleasure of pure interiority in an element which supports (the pleasure of the *cogito* and of *jouissance*), and then "aussitôt" — "already" — the disquieting inherence of alterity as a "wound", in an exterior which invades. From the point of view of discursive exposition, it would not be possible to reduce this oscillation, because alterity's intrication with subjectivity is both a pre-originarity and a destiny or imminence. It is a *nouvelle origine*: an immemorial event in an irrecuperable past (a past which was never present, a past "entièrement révolu") as well as the indefinite future of an approach. In the temporality of proximity, it is possible for the Other to be involved with me in a time prior to the awakening of my intentionality, and yet to await me in a time too intimate and too distant to be protended. And it is possible for both these times to weigh upon the present of intentionality with an imperious urgency more commanding than presence itself. What the organization of Levinas' discourse may not clarify sufficiently is that the time of subjectivity's involvement with alterity is a time of repetition and of proximity. Thus, recurrence and substitution, which appear to concern a constituted intersubjective other, are already at work in the context of sensation and the *cogito*, where subjectivity's constitution involves an apparently less differentiated alterity. In *Autrement qu'être...* Levinas occasionally links these seemingly disparate moments, as in the following passage from a section entitled "Sensibilité et psychisme": "In the context of responsibility, the *psychisme* [interiority*] of the soul [âme] is the other in me; the sickness of identity —

* See above, Chapter 1.

accused [*accusée**] and *soi,* the same for the other, the same by [*par,* by, through] the other."[100] The drama of responsibility and substitution begins with, or precedes, the primary context of sensation itself, and does not await the approach of a constituted other. This is the basic meaning of the proposition, "the sensible is already spoken."[101]

Concomitant to the paradox of desire which proceeds from a subjectivity which, in a universe of non-contradiction, would be "satisfaite en tout" or "completely satisfied", is the paradox of desire's bottomless and expanding "satisfaction". Since desire is not a lack or insufficiency in totalization which may be comprehended as a negativity, but is rather an incompletion consequent to a failure or weakness of negativity (a breach within unity and a remainder in the exterior), it does not insist within an economy of totalization, accomplishment or satisfaction. Desire tends to incorporate the exterior; but the movement which would satisfy desire — an increased inherence of exteriority — must necessarily become an excess added to excess. Incorporation cannot mean totalization. An increased intrication with alterity can only mean an increased excess of interiority's dispersion or involvement with the exterior: an increased intensity of its *pour l'autre,* its inclination "toward the Other". Like the *hypertopie* of Blanchot's desert, and like the supplementarity and intensity meditated by the philosophy of difference, desire knows no terminus and no satisfaction. *Inachèvement* or incompletion is the permanent animation and dispossession of unicity in a communicational economy. The movement which would reduce desire necessarily becomes a movement which increases desire. "True Desire'" writes Levinas, "is that which the Desired does not fulfill, but deepens [*creuse,* digs, hollows]."[102] Desire is an "increasing of exigencies [*accroissement d'exigences*]'",[103] in Levinas' very pertinent phrase, which "nourishes itself from its hunger."[104] Like *dépense,* desire is not thinkable in terms of a resolution of tension, and can only gain momentum. In a sense, it knows no diastole: its entire economy is the spasmodic, contracting *dépense* of its investment by alterity and its dispossession. The alternation of day and night in Blanchot, of prohibition and transgression in Bataille, and of egoism and the *éthique* in Levinas, is the rhythm of a single movement: the *pour l'autre* of subjectivity which contracts or condenses "toward the exterior". As Blanchot writes in *L'Entretien infini,* the object of desire is not something which "fait défaut" or is "lacking",[105] but is alterity as such, in its proximity. In this context, it must be stressed that desire in proximity cannot be understood as a movement arising within an ipseity, or as an exigency which has an "object". Prior to these possibilities, desire must be defined as a "passion of alterity", in the ambiguity of this expression. Interiority desires alterity; but it is differentiation within the exterior that produces both

---

* The word *accusée* refers to the accusative case of the rapport with alterity (cf. above). The adjective *accusée* also means "high-lighted", "accentuated". The hyperbole or intensity of identity's closure is its latent economic involvement with the Other.

interiority as closure and the Other of closure which is alterity. And the sense of alterity as "differentiation without totalization" — the Same's irreducibility to identity — is Desire itself. The economy desires. Alterity is desire. Both the transitivity of desire and its apparent origin within interiority are secondary to the economic, "impersonal" movement of desire as the force and the excess of closure.

Desire is the excess of closure over the possibility of closure itself as totalization. This excess inclines closure toward the Other, and produces the economic possibility of the Other's incumbence and approach. The multiple predicates of desire are basic to the conceptual and thematic organization of the texts of Bataille. Blanchot and Levinas. Thus, in the first place, desire is an incompletion which defines interiority as an involvement with, and a vulnerability to the exterior. Subjectivity is "preoccupied" by an alterity which has no power and is not a substantiality. In the second place, desire is an excess which not only inclines subjectivity toward the exterior, but also situates it within the exterior. In *errance,* in transgression, and in the *éthique,* subjectivity moves toward an exteriority in which an element of subjectivity is already posed. Within the exterior, the subject of proximity has a "rendezvous", in the words of Proust's narrator, "with itself." In the third place, desire is interiority's *dépense.* The hyperbole and excess of closure — its familiarity, the concupiscence of its egoism — is already its dispossession and the sacrifice implied by its paroxysm *pour l'autre*, toward the Other. This sacrifice will define the "idea of the infinite" for Levinas: a conation outward and a non-indifference toward exteriority which proceeds from differentiation itself. Levinas formulates a *cogito* of responsibility which may be read more generally as a *cogito* of desire in proximity: "I did not know I was so rich, but I no longer have the right to keep anything."[106] A sacrifice which proceeds from the untroubled plenitude of interiority describes the excess of a closure which "contains more than it is possible to contain" — a closure whose self-sufficiency is always already the exigency of loss. The absolute simultaneity of closure and loss in desire is basic to any reading of Bataille's text, in which accumulation, prohibition, etc. are always *aussitôt,* "immediately", the pre-originarity and imminence of loss. It is for this reason that Blanchot's description of transgression and the *expérience* as "another exigency, no longer to produce, but to waste"[107] must be considered to be misleading. Bataille's system is not the dialectic of two tendencies, but the elaboration of a single, contaminated exigency for which there is no dialectic. The exigency is a plenitude which is an insufficiency; an enclosure which is a pouring outward; a prohibition which is a transgression. In the fourth place, desire is an ambivalence. The discontinuity produced by differentiation is an irreducible detour in the general economy. Closure's exigency is a tendency to totalize the Other by eliminating its own involvement with the Other — and thus to eliminate alterity, by introducing an adequate interval between interiority and exteriority, (and) or by engulfing the Other within a communion which will be a totality. Desire — the force of an economy without totalization — is the animation of these inseparable tendencies, and their impossibility. Subjectivity's contraction "away from" the economy is always a contraction "toward" or "into" the economy. The only adequate or "possible" access to alterity is desire — and desire is the intensity of the impossible. In the fifth place, desire, in an economy without negativity, is a gap or *écart* in individuation which cannot be closed, and a resulting intensity of excess and insufficiency which can only be increased by its fulfillment. Subjectivity, in its very closure, is an "increase of exigencies", the permanence of excess in a world where, in Bataille's words, "all that is, is too much." The satisfaction of desire is its increase. "The more I fulfill my responsibility," writes Levinas, "the more I am responsible."[108] Desire is the "more and more" of a closure which cannot be conceived as an equilibrium within a system, but must be conceived as the intensity of a dispossession. In the sixth place, desire is the pre-originarity of a *nouvelle origine*: an apparent vicissitude of interiority which already collaborated in the production of interiority. Subjectivity is already involved with the inaccessible. That which I now go to encounter, in the *éthique*, in the Burrow, in transgression, I have already met — although I will never meet it in the "face to face" of a presence. Desire is the only principle of an introubled interiority which might then become involved with alterity. Before desiring, one already desires.

*

The general economy is a dimension of differentiation without the discretion of negativity. It is a heteronomous economy which produces separation. This separation, in Blanchot's words, proceeds from impossibility: a reality without power and without accomplishment. Interiority in the economy is an exigency whose conation is always "outward" or "in reverse", whose difference is a non-indifference — the non-indifference of the "Same by the Other", the Same *pour l'autre* which may never be absorbed by the totality and which must always, in Levinas' paraphrase of Plato, "desert its post" as a function of remaining at its post. The intensity of closure is the *attrait sur place* or "attraction in place" invoked by Blanchot. Thus, the differentiations of the general economy take the form of passions, obsessions, responsibilities, etc. whose common denominator is desire. The economy of proximity is desire, conceived as the paroxysm of a fugitive unicity *au dehors*, "on the outside".

There is, as discussed above, an ambivalence of the exigency, whose modality is a simultaneous tendency toward excessive closure and incorporation, and a pre-originary movement of loss, consequent to the heteronomy of closure itself. Closure's density is a dispossession. In anticipation of Levinasian non-reciprocity, it should be stressed that the dual valence of desire — an inspiration from exteriority and an excess returning to exteriority — must not be understood as the reciprocity of a substance or information received from and returned to the outside. Were this the case, the economy would simply be the universal of philosophy, in which determinations link totalities in their immobility. There is, instead, a *sens unique*, a non-reciprocal "one way" to the movement of difference or of "information" in the economy. The investing movement of inspiration or animation does not approach subjectivity in the same way, or along the same line, by which subjectivity approaches exteriority. Separation is a conation which is always already *au rebours du conatus*, "in reverse", "inside out" − a unicity which is already a heteronomy and a non-indifference. The autonomy by which an interiority might receive, in the immobility of its position, the determinations of a causal exteriority, is foreclosed by this very non-indifference. There is alterity in the general economy because this economy involves a radical exteriority: an Other of closure, an Other of the interior, which is not another closure, not another totality. The rapport of interiority with this Other cannot be a reciprocity. The Other is "not in the same concept," in Levinas' words. It has no power, no effective reality, and yet it concerns interiority. It is inaccessible, but subjectivity is involved with it. The Other invests the interiority it escapes. This investment proceeds "from within" as well as "from outside". Interiority is a "gravity", an intensity of heteronomy within the economy. It may be inspired or invested by exteriority, but it can never "receive" this inspiration. Its center of gravity is outside itself. There is only one direction or inclination within the economy of proximity. This is the *sens unique* of difference which is non-indifference, and the *pour l'autre* by which interiority's conation must always be "inside out": toward the Other. This single direction produced by interiority's heteronomous investment is the principle of what Levinas will call a *sens* (direction, inclination, dissymmetry, signification) in being: a possibility of manifestation and comprehension which is grounded in the heteronomy of subjectivity. In his meditations of intersubjectivity, Levinas will discover as a result of differentiation's *sens unique* a "curving" of space by which the Other's rapport with or approach to the Same is essentially different from the Same's rapport or approach to the Other. Levinasian intersubjectivity is not a rapport of two totalities, but a rapport of the totality with its Other. This rapport is essentially dissymmetrical. Separation or interiority is the impossibility of reversing this *sens unique* of animation and non-indifference − a reversal which would allow subjectivity to affect alterity, to receive the excess of desire, to be the object of desire: in other words, to become an identity to self, the interiority of philosophy. Thus, the ambivalence of the exigency is not exhausted by the notions of attraction and repulsion. Attraction and repulsion are conditioned by a more fundamental heteronomy whose *sens* is not reversible. In proximity, my center of gravity is essentially outside myself, and this subjection by which I am always "turned toward" the *dehors, pour l'autre*, is separation in its irreducibility to autonomy. The differential intensity of proximity can move toward me in animation, and away from me in *dépense* and desire − without ever moving toward me as the univocity of a determination. Interiority must always, and can never, "desert its post", is always *en marche*, always inclined outside itself by the *attrait sur place*, always forced into movement by the heteronomy of its conation. Nothing returns to subjectivity. It is inclined and dispersed in one direction only: *au dehors, pour l'autre*. It is incapable of constituting itself as either an origin or a terminus in the rapport with alterity. This incapacity is its subjectivity: the subjection implied by an intimacy or involvement with the inaccessible — an Other that is not another Same. This involvement describes interiority's aptitude — nearly always reduced in philosophy — to be affected by exteriority. Levinas' virtually solitary ambition as a thinker will be to discover and to thematize this subjectivity and the dissymetry which is its principle, in a situation from which his culture has always sought to banish alterity: the intersubjective rapport.

THE BURROW AND THE OTHER NIGHT

The basic irony which structures the bulk of Kafka's *The Burrow* is that every underground dwelling designed as a refuge from other animals must have an entrance at the surface. The anxiety of Kafka's protagonist becomes a vigilant watching of the burrow's entrance — often from outside the burrow itself. Prior to the appearance of a muffled noise which wakes the sleeping protagonist and is the subject of the story's conclusion, this irony of the entrance is the problem which motivates his meditation upon the burrow's safety and concomitant vulnerability. It is noteworthy that Blanchot's reading of *The Burrow* includes no mention of this dilemma of the entrance. Blanchot treats the problem of the burrow as though there were no entrance, no irony of the troublesome and irreducible imperfection of the burrow's closure. The barely perceptible noise which comes to signify the approach of another animal is interpreted by Blanchot, in the terms of proximity,* as a necessary consequence of the very invulnerability of the burrow. Danger does not proceed from the entrance, which represents the relation of interiority to an exterior which is the element of survival. Instead, danger arises from the depth of the burrow, and from the very efficiency of its retreat from the confusion of the exterior. Blanchot does not read *The Burrow* for the irony of a breach overlooked by the animals's "best laid plans"; instead, he meditates an approach which is correlative to the animal's industry and to the intimacy of the burrow. This approach is not an irony. It is not, strictly speaking, unexpected. Its insistence is somehow integral to the gravity of the excavation, somehow implied by the unspoken purposes of the animal's industry. The creation of the burrow is more than a complacency. The approach of the other beast is more than a frustration of complacency.

The thematization of the burrow appears within Blanchot's discussion of night and the "other night". Night, in the strategic context of this demonstration, is an obscurity whose relation to the illumination of the day is

* Proximity is not only the conceptual framework of Blanchot's section entitled "Le dehors, la nuit", but also its most consistent lexical regularity, in terms such as *proche*, *approche*, *s'approcher*. To an important degree, the same may be said of *L'Espace littéraire*, whose second chapter is entitled "Approche de l'espace littéraire". As will be discussed below, the literary dimension is not a space, but the "approach of another space."

dialectical. Night is the other of the day which is subsumed by the larger problematic of illumination and productivity. Night is always "la nuit du jour", "the night of day": an instance subordinated to illumination and providing the day with its differentiation. Night functions as a "limit"[109] of day which may have the forbidding predicates of alterity by virtue of this limiting status, but which also is conserved and appropriated by the dialectic of illumination. Day becomes "the whole of day and night",[110] the mobilization of differentiation as illumination. There is a sentence within this discussion which confuses Blanchot's reader, because it anticipates a development which will appear several paragraphs later. Since day subsumes night dialectically, Blanchot states: "The more the day extends itself [s'étend], with the proud aim [souci] of becoming universal, the more the nocturnal element risks receding into the light itself" — and he adds: "the more that which illuminates [éclaire] us is nocturnal, is the uncertainty and excess [démesure] of night."[111] The difficulty of this second proposition is its anticipatory definition of what Blanchot will call the "other night" — the "heart of the night" whose alterity is its irreducibility to day and to the dialectic of day. Night is the dialectical other of day, but the other night is proximity: a dimension of differentiation and communication in which limits and their participation in the universality of activity and accomplishment are not ultimate.

It is only during the day, writes Blanchot, that one may dream of the other night, of "knowing" it, of "seizing" it. In the night, the approach of the other night is not accessible to this dialectical model of desire, and will take the form of proximity as danger. At the end of his discussion of the burrow, Blanchot will conclude:

It is thus necessary to turn away from the first night. this at least is possible, it is necessary to live in the day and work for the day. Yes, this is necessary. But to work for the day is to find, in the end, the night, and then to make of the night the product [oeuvre] of the day, to make of it a work [travail], an abode [séjour], to construct the burrow, and to open the night to the other night.[112]

The interplay of these propositions which bracket Blanchot's discussion of the burrow, describes three forms of the relation between day and the other night. In the first place, the day's activity leads to night, and the night's activity encounters the other night, as though "in spite of itself". In the second place, the exuberance of the day, which respects night as an alterity, nevertheless dreams of the other night as a yet more radical obscurity which might also be possessed. In the third place, as day in its supremacy domesticates the night by its dialectical communication with the latter, there is a risk that illumination itself might become the démesure or excess of the nocturnal. "The more that which illuminates us is nocturnal, is the uncertainty and excess of night." While the first two of these relations maintain the opposition between the certainty of day and the danger of the other night, the third indicates a nocturnal risk inherent to illumination itself. The overall tendency of Blanchot's demonstration is a commentary on Hegelian dialectics, particularly in the context of the appropriation of death as negativity. The other night is the form of an alterity which cannot be appropriated or superceded, and thus frustrates the dialectical communion of day and night. The other night is inaccessible and irreducible. Yet, within the perspective of its inaccessibility, the other night may invest the day. Unlike the night, the other night is not a limit. Thus, it cannot consecrate - the day's accomplishments, but it may introduce into illumination the "excess" of the nocturnal. This third proposition, which enunciates a contamination of the substantial and accomplished by an excess with which it is secretly involved, is not understandable within the discursive universe of contradiction and the *Aufhebung*. It describes an alterity without substantiality and without power, whose incumbence or force derives from the very frailty with which it "recedes into the light." The other night is not the day's "opposite", and cannot limit or destroy the positivity of the day, in the manner of a negation. Yet the other night can "alter" the day. It is a communicational factor irreducible to negation, and proceeding from the "weakness" of negation in the dialectic, which invests the Same in general as an alteration: a contamination and a becoming-other. The relation of day to the "first night" is a dialectic of positivity and negativity within a universe exhausted by totalization and the vicissitudes of totalization — that is, within the Same. The rapport of day with the other night is the Same's rapport with its Other: an alterity which is not another Same.*

The other night is the Other of the duality of day and night. Prior to the arrival of the "first night" or "night of day", the accomplishment and comprehension correlative to illumination are already involved with the excess and passivity of the other night — a nocturnality which cannot be superceded because it is neither the negation nor the limit of the day, but its alteration and its latent heteronomy. Alterity is the excess of the day's very totalization, and the concomitant insufficiency of that totalization. Underneath the accomplishments of day — underneath negation — there is communication. The principle of this communication which can neither be eliminated nor totalized is the other night, defined as an Other of closure which invests closure. Thus, on one hand, day and other night are suspended in a "dialectic" without synthesis, as are closure and excess in Bataille. On the other hand, as Blanchot first thematizes in "La littérature et le droit à la mort", this irreducibility of communication

---

* As will be discussed below (Chapter 4), the Hegel of "Force and Understanding", through his meditation of alteration and interior difference (*Unterschied*) in the constitution of interiority, states many of the communicational themes associated with the philosophies of difference and proximity. Although his subordination of alteration to negation and the *Aufhebung* reduces the explicit impact of these communicational concepts, they remain a compelling detour in the movement of the *Phenomenology*. With the possible exception of the Bataille of *L'Expérience intérieure*, it must be said that the philosophers of proximity are not sensitive to Hegel's descriptions of alteration and heteronomy, and share with modern philosophy in general the image of Hegel as the philosopher of totalization.

produces a *nouvelle origine* of both day and night. Night is no longer a limit, but an "impossibility", and day is no longer manifestation but a "fatality".[113] The "whole of night and day," with its principle of negation, has given way to the *il y a* of reality beyond negation. Totalization has become impossibility: a reality without power or accomplishment. Illumination is no longer comprehension as action, but comprehension as impossibility, as described in a formulation in "La littérature et le droit à la mort" which is rarely repeated in Blanchot's later work: "The harassment of that which one cannot prevent oneself from understanding [*comprendre*], and the suffocating persistence [*hantise*] of a reason without principle, without beginning, which one cannot justify [*rendre raison*]."[114] In this "strange impersonal light", consciousness becomes an "inability [*impuissance*] to lose consciousness," a "blind vigilance" which Blanchot defines communicationally as "the only expression [*traduction*] of the obsession of existence, if the latter is the very impossibility of taking leave [*sortir*] of existence."[115] Consciousness is no longer grounded in the negativity of distinction and determination, but in the passivity and "impossibility" of an economy without negation. This impossibility is the latent nocturnality of the day.

Blanchot's definition of consciousness as an impersonal "spontaneity"[116] which is nevertheless a radical passivity, in the striking notion of the "inability not to understand", is a description of the other night as a destiny which weighs upon and conditions illumination in its very spontaneity. This proximal inherence of the other night transforms manifestation into illumination as the "obsession of existence" — that is, the economy of proximity. Such a transformation is only possible as pre-originarity, in a proximal temporality. On one hand, the other night is incumbent upon the day, from its very position in the future as the day's destiny. On the other hand, the other night is the "always already" of the day — an instance which conditions or collaborates in the day's industry and comprehension. One might paraphrase Blanchot in this context by saying that the day consists in a comprehension complacent in its apparent spontaneity, a comprehension which delays the apprehension of the passivity that constitutes it. Day is a general economy of obsession which takes obsession's illumination, for a "time", as the spontaneity of manifestation. However, in the same sense that prohibition is a preparation of and a producing of transgression, the day is already the approach of its *nouvelle origine*, the other night.

The approach of alterity proceeds from within. It does not supervene to a complacency, but follows an "invitation", in the words of Bataille. The complacency of closure in proximity is always haunted by a gravity or solemnity which is the weight of closure's excessive density, in the proximity of the Other. Closure is a heteronomy: a point of gravity in the economy. Prohibition in Bataille, sensation and *jouissance* in Levinas, and the day in Blanchot are situations whose predicates always include not only the frivolity and irresponsibility of untroubled activity, but also the intensity and fascination of a rapport with the proximal Other. Closure is always the blitheness and insouciance of its own excess, as well as the gravity of its heteronomy. It shares the fundamental ambivalence of transgression, because transgression is the hyperbole of closure — of excess and density — rather than its opposite. The most general sense of manifestation in proximity is the insouciance and complaisance of a subjectivity whose illuminating function is already conditioned by the priority of the economic factor which defines subjectivity: its capacity for subjection or passivity, its paradoxical aptitude for the *accueil* or "welcoming" of the Other: the reception of the given.

It is in the sense of the proximity of other night to day that *The Burrow* in Blanchot must be read. The animal which flees the surface world, excavating the depths, mimes the constructions of day: "One builds [*édifie*] in the manner of the day, but underground, and that which is erected plunges downward, that which stands up [*se dresse*] sinks down [*s'abîme*]."[117] But the intimacy and the solitude sought by the proprietor of the burrow will become — like all intimacy and all solitude in Blanchot — the other intimacy of proximity. The production of the burrow is the production of this proximity.

The more the burrow seems solidly closed to the exterior [*dehors*], the greater is the peril that one may be shut inside it [*enfermé*] with the exterior, that one may be left [*livré*] to this peril without escape, and when all foreign menace seems removed from this perfectly closed intimacy, then it is intimacy that becomes a menacing strangeness, then the essence of danger introduces itself.[118]

The barely perceptible noise which becomes the terror of the approach, does not begin. It wakes the protagonist from his sleep. The essence of this noise is its lack of beginning. It "may have been there before," "may have been there all along." And this is the sense of the story's final sentence: "all remained unchanged." The approach of the other beast is a shock and an imminence, but it is an immemorial imminence, and thus more intimate, more familiar than the impact of an immediate or substantial exteriority. The concept which structures *The Burrow's* profundity is this congruence of the unexpected and unknowable with a paradoxical but essential implication that one "always knew this was going to happen." Just as Orpheus' transgression and loss of Eurydice are implicit in his first steps toward the shadows, the other beast's approach begins with the first moment of the burrow's excavation. It is important to perceive within the industry of the animal's digging, an uneliminable element of the passivity which is its final attitude in the terror of the approach. It is this hidden element of passivity that Blanchot will meditate in the context of writing as *préhension persécutrice* or "involuntary prehension". (See below.) A hand holding a pen is "sick" and writes involuntarily and continuously. The other hand reaches to arrest this involuntary movement. But the passivity of writing is in the play of the two hands together. The "unaffected" hand cannot but intervene, and its intervention, which introduces differentiation into the movement of the pen held by the "sick" hand is not a limit imposed on passivity, but passivity itself, as it conditions all spontaneity. Indecision may be obscured by activity, but not eliminated. Indecision is the animation of action. The governing principle of "involuntary prehension", as of the burrow, is that interiority is always a transgression of interiority, and the passivity of an "entrapment with the exterior." In other words, interiority is always a proximity.

As mentioned earlier, Blanchot, Bataille and Levinas are so concerned with the thinking of the economy in terms of differentiation and communication that they are nearly indifferent to the very proposition of manifestation. Nevertheless, there is in Blanchot's notion of *oubli** a configuration which recalls the drama of the burrow. *Oubli* is not the forgetting of what was once known. Like repression − and in a sense which may define the economic possibility of repression − it is the immemorial inherence in subjectivity of an instance which penetrated its closure without ever becoming phenomenal or "conscious". *Oubli* is the presence within consciousness of an inaccessible instance which can never become an object. The object of *oubli* can never be "recalled" − not because it was never conscious or was subject to the function of an agency or instance within the psychic organism, but because it is essentially inadequate to the possibility of phenomenality itself. The object of *oubli* is the "phenomenon" in proximity: an instance whose communication with interiority precedes and exceeds the negative intervals requisite for the appearance of the intentional object. At the same time, *oubli* conditions intentionality. As Blanchot so often says, the reality of manifestation "reposes on the edifice of *oubli*." This is because any definition of manifestation requires the notion of a contact or proximity to the existent, and the notion of a receptivity correlative to this proximity. *Oubli*, with its complements *passion*, *obsession*, desire, etc., is the form of this conditioning communication. When consciousness is posed in an economy whose principle is not manifestation, but dissimulation (i.e. differentiation without totalization), consciousness becomes the heteronmous subjectivity of *oubli*, which may receive and retain, but which cannot totalize. Thus manifestation as spontaneity and accomplishment, like the light of day, reposes on the passivity of illumination, the "blind vigilance" of a light that is nocturnal. Intentionality is conditioned by the proximity of a paradoxical instance which is simultaneously unknowable − the alterity of night − and which "cannot but be understood"** − the passivity of illumination as obsession. The congruence of these impossibilities is what Blanchot calls the "obsession of existence": an impersonal and heteronomous economy without power. The temporality of this dimension, like that of the desert, is repetitive and proximal.

The existent which I now go to encounter, in the spontaneity of manifestation, I have already met in another dimension. This is one sense of the

---

* "Forgetting", "forgetfulness". The word *oubli* in Blanchot cannot be properly translated, since its manifold, overdetermined meanings all exceed the context of manifestation in which the notion of "forgetting" is normally defined.

** The most explicit statement of this heteronomous economy of subjectivity within the philosophy of difference is to be found in Gilles Deleuze's *Différence et répétition* (P.U.F., 1968). Difference, as Deleuze states many times, "cannot be thought and cannot but be thought." (See below, Chapters 4 and 7.)

temporality of imminence. The force of this immemorial encounter is integral to the approach of the exterior. The future, in *oubli*, may bear down upon me with this force of repetition, instead of approaching me with the ordered temporality of history. Its imminence must always be a surprise, an insistence for which subjectivity, like Kafka's *He*, can never be prepared. This surprise is its basic inadequation to intentionality defined as manifestation. At the same time, its insistence may bypass punctuality, and the presence of its arrival may already be immemorial, as in Foucault's thematization of transgression as a "virtually immemorial vacancy." But part of the residue created by the insufficiency of negativity in *oubli* is a contaminated awareness which creates the "sinking feeling" of surprise and recognition at the imminence of the approach: the mysterious sense that one "always knew this was going to happen." Such is the paradox of *oubli*: the approach of the future is not a protention, but an imminence and a surprise. Yet, in the "obsession of existence", one may "always have known" what one can never "know". One may forget — one must forget — what one has never known. Through repetition, there may be nothing new under the sun, yet through the same repetition, as attested by Nietzsche and Proust, the truly new becomes a possibility. Blanchot writes, "*oubli* is the depth of its memory [*la profondeur de son souvenir*]."[119] Repression, in proximity, is less an attribute or aspect of the psychic organism than it is a rapport with that dimension of reality which is essentially inadequate to memory and intentionality.

It is because of this "other rapport", outside negation and outside possibility, that the approach of alterity in the burrow, and the elsewhere in Blanchot, has a paradoxical thematic predicate. The "essence of danger" is "not at all terrifying", not al all "extraordinary".[120] Although danger is entirely "new", in the sense that it cannot be anticipated and one cannot prepare for its arrival, it is not entirely unexpected. At the same time, although the approach of danger cannot be stopped, and cannot be fought or even assumed in the virility of resoluteness, this greatest possible violence in Blanchot is already the strange monotony of the *non-concernant*. Violence is already impersonal, and does not "concern me", because the rapport with the Other is not an encounter of two powerful substantialities, but is both the defection and the immemorial constitution of the "me" — the Same — in proximity. Interiority itself is this transgression: the approach of an Other which is infinitely compelling, since it is the principle of interiority's heteronomy, and yet powerless and repetitive, since it is not itself a totality. It cannot destroy, but it will alter the Same. It will produce the Same as an alteration.*

* The violence of the *non-concernant* in Blanchot, which entirely invades "me" but does not concern or limit the personal "Me" of philosophy, is a precise equivalent of what Levinas calls a "non-allergy" of Same and Other which is not "violent". For both thinkers, there is a violence inherent in totalization and correlation (called by Levinas the "allergy of beings"), and another rapport, communicational and proximal, which is the intensity and dispossession of an interiority involved with the Other. As mentioned earlier, however, this heteronomy of communication underlies those forms of violence which are most disturbing to the Western imagination: forms whose principle is passivity. (See below, Chapter 4.)

Just as we perceive a spasmodic and indecisive industry of preparation in the increasing passivity of the protagonist's awaiting of the other beast, so we must perceive in the apparently complacent activity which constructed the burrow, something of this passivity and this indecision. The interiority which places alterity at a distance, in Blanchot as in Bataille, is also the collaboration of alterity in the exigency, and is thus the passivity of an *accueil* or reception. To recoil from the economy is to recoil into the economy.

Inevitably, the other beast never arrives. Blanchot treats with near-derision the claim that *The Burrow* is unfinished, and was to have included the description of a decisive combat.[121] The essence of the other beast — whose original appearance was immemorial, in a scratching noise which awakened the protagonist — is the approach. "There can be no decisive combat: no decision in such a combat and no combat either, but only the awaiting [*attente*], the approach, the suspicion, the vicissitudes of an ever more menacing menace, but infinite, but undecided, entirely contained in its very indecision."[122] The approach in proximity can gain momentum — like desire, like *dépense*, it cannot but gain momentum, its incumbence is its imminence — but its momentum is one with its unsubstantiality and its "indecision". Like death, it is never "sure". Immemorial and yet to come — *l'attente, l'oubli* — the approach is the intimacy of the indefinite, the incumbence of the inaccessible, and this is its violence. Alterity has no power, but power is not the principle of what Blanchot calls its "domination".

To dig the burrow is to go to meet the other beast — to approach the Other. Proximity is interiority "in the exterior" as well as a pre-originary "outside inside". Thus, while the other beast is paradoxically "known" to the protagonist in *oubli*, it is also true that the protagonist's being is not exhausted by the proposition of his solitude in the burrow. "Where I am alone, I am not alone." It is perhaps for this reason that Kafka places him at repeated moments outside the burrow, close to the throng of animal traffic past the hidden entrance. Interiority must oversee itself from the exterior — from the perspective of its involvement with alterity. The other beast is "known" in another way as well. If it were to arrive — which it cannot (this impossibility is, to paraphrase Blanchot, both its "privation" and its "domination", since its approach is more compelling than any arrival) — it would look like the protagonist. It would in fact be the protagonist, but the protagonist "become other".

What the beast senses [*present*] in the distance, this monstrous thing which comes eternally to meet it, which works eternally at [this approach], is itself, and if it could ever find itself in [the] presence [of the other], what it would meet would be its own absence, would be itself, but itself become the other, which it would not recognize, which it would not meet. The *other* night is always other, and he who knows it [*l'entend**] becomes the other, he who

---

* "Hears", "understands". The English "knows", in its sense of involvement and intimacy, approximates Blanchot's notion of a familiarity which is not a comprehension.

approaches it becomes estranged [*s'éloigne*] from himself, is no longer he who approaches it, but he who turns away [*s'en détourne*] from it, who goes now here, now there [*va de-ci, de-là*].[123]

The Other is not identical with me, does not resemble me, but has my aspect or is my alteration, in the strategic proposition of its arrival or manifestation. Closure's excess is simultaneously a breach which renders interiority subject or vulnerable to the approach of alterity, and an incompletion which leaves an uneliminable remainder within the exterior. This remainder is the principle of alterity's strange familiarity. Subjectivity knows or "recognizes" that which is entirely unfamiliar, because subjectivity's originary dispossession is its intimacy with the exterior. The disturbing and yet familiar aspect of the approach is this immemorial conditioning of interiority by an alterity whose unexpected insertion into subjectivity's reality, awakening it from its sleep in a new *cogito*, is not only the urgency of danger and the repetition of the *non-concernant*, but also a modality of subjectivity's "rendezvous with itself" in proximity. This *cogito* which comes to itself already involved with the Other has the same fundamental economy, in spite of terminological differences, as the subjectivity described by Freud in his *Das Unheimliche*. The "uncanny", with its paradoxical predicates, its irreducible congruence of familiarity and alteration, and its tendency toward the theme of the double, describes a proximal exteriority and a subjectivity whose receptivity is not understandable in terms of manifestation. Proximity is the dimension in which the uncanny may assume an economic meaning beyond its anomalous and exceptional status. The double is one form of a constituted or "phenomenal" alterity in proximity.

Interiority in proximity is always a transgression of interiority, a "too much" of closure which produces its vulnerability to the exterior. In Blanchot and Levinas, this transgression tends to take the form of a strategically linear temporality, in the drama of indecision, of recurrence, or of the burrow. Such a temporality, in spite of its destiny of repetition, describes a momentum and an urgency which are designated by the theme of the approach. The temporality of proximity, with its coincidence of repetition, imminence, and pre-originarity, is a time in which the indefinite may compel and weigh upon subjectivity, not in spite of, but because of its lack of presence. This gravity of an exteriority which is without power and substantiality is one basic sense of communication as proximity, and is the principle of the Levinasian *éthique*: a relation without correlation in which one term may "weigh upon" another.[124] For the philosophy of proximity in general, the Same is a closure whose insufficiency or incompletion produces an impending encounter with alterity. But the Other collaborates in the excess and insufficiency that define closure as the turgid density of the exigency — a density by which communication invests the possibilities of power and accomplishment. This collaboration of the Other is the secret nocturnality of the day, and the latent passivity of the resolute industry which digs the burrow. One may flee the Other in the burrow or approach the Other in the desert, but both these activities are moments of one basic "sense" in the general economy: the .approach of the Other. Interiority is involved with the inaccessible. To seek it is to fail to attain it. To flee it is to know its approach. But in any context, subjectivity cannot but receive the Other. It is this secret passivity, incarnated in the animal's spasmodic digging, that makes of the burrow perhaps the most basic figure of proximity in Blanchot.

PRÉHENSION PERSÉCUTRICE AND THE ARRESTING HAND

Blanchot and Bataille have in common an interest in certain exceptional situations whose predicates describe fundamental aspects of communication. These situations may tend toward the universal, and may organize significant sectors of each thinker's discourse (as for example the sacrifice in Bataille and the public domain of actuality and curiosity in Blanchot), or they may tend toward the extraordinary, and may be elaborated briefly or parenthetically. Certain of the latter instances may have, in spite of their momentary appearance, a basic significance within the text of their author. *La préhension persécutrice* or "involuntary prehension" is such an instance in Blanchot. In spite of its apparently anomalous status in an empirical context, the notion of an involuntary prehension is basic to Blanchot's concept of literary creativity and perhaps even of prehension and of the voluntary in general.

"It happens," writes Blanchot, "that a man who holds a pencil, even if he wishes strongly to let it go, his hand does not let it go: on the contrary, it squeezes it, far from opening. The other hand intervenes with more success, but one sees what we might call the sick hand trace a slow movement and try to recapture the object which moves away."[125] In the initial moment of Blanchot's text, literary "mastery" is given as the intervention of the "unaffected" hand which removes the pencil from the "sick" hand, or stops the involuntary movement. "Mastery is always the attribute of the other hand, the one that does not write, capable of intervening when necessary, of seizing the pencil and keeping it away. Mastery thus consists in the power to stop writing, to interrupt that which is being written [*ce qui s'écrit*: also "that which writes itself"], returning to the instant its rights and its decisive* cutting edge."[126] The overall significance of this interruption of continuity brought about by the other hand is a matter of considerable difficulty in Blanchot's subsequent discussions. (See below, Chapter 3.) Within the context of the basic description of involuntary

---

* The word *décisif* is rooted in the duality of "decision" and "indecision" which structures the opening sections of *L'Espace littéraire*. It indicates power and initiative, as opposed to indecision, fascination and passivity. In addition, it indicates the *dé-cision* of negativity which produces ontological intervals between totalities, as opposed to the alterations implied by heteronomy, and to the repetition produced by indefinitely communicating temporal moments. Hence *décision* produces the "instant", i.e. the discontinuous product of an adequate temporal interval.

prehension, however, the pertinence of the "unaffected" hand is its interruption or arresting of a movement which cannot be stopped. For this context, literary activity may require an intervention or arresting, but the moment of involuntary prehension will be irreducible, and basic to writing itself. The unaffected hand-must arrest a movement which remains continuous: a movement which may be interrupted but cannot be altered. It is this irreducibility of the non-voluntary or pre-voluntary, with its implicit predicates, that concerns Blanchot.

Involuntary prehension is not an anomaly or an accident in writing. Or, if it is anomalous, then literary writing is conditioned by this extraordinary moment. The hand that cannot stop writing points to a dimension within the real for which the familiar predicates of the notion of "writing" are not determining, and which nevertheless is the dimension in which the familiar concept of creative writing must be thought. As is the case with many of Blanchot's definitions, involuntary prehension may be misunderstood to be rooted in traditional notions of inspiration and creativity. The axis of this misunderstanding, and in fact the overall context of Blanchot's demonstration, is the concept of power as it relates to creativity. Inspiration is traditionally defined as an instance irreducible to the personality and ambitions of the writer, and to this extent is a concept which interests Blanchot. But inspiration is also defined as a higher power which operates through the subjectivity of the writer, and tends to be correlated to the concept of subjectivity as a superior but undifferentiated comprehension or power. Blanchot's definitions are not accessible to such a logic. However, the ambiguity of this "power outside power", this comprehension irreducible to comprehension, in spite of its appropriation to a subjectivity defined as the mysterious depth of a pre-comprehension, is tradition's intuition of a dimension for which power and comprehension are not ultimate principles. It is toward this dimension that Blanchot's discussion tends.

Involuntary prehension is one index of a most fundamental Blanchotian moment: the notion of a reality without power. This reality, whose dimensions are suggested by the burrow and the desert, and whose mode of manifestation is suggested by indecision and *erreur*, is not without differentiation. But the principle of its differentiations is not negativity, and the basis of the relations or rapports which organize it is not power, the perennial complement of negativity. This differentiation is rather a form of difference or communication, and its effects are not entities capable of determining each other in a universe of non-contradiction. The principle of closure is its involvement with an Other of closure, an instance grounded in the weakness of negation and totalization, which produces unicity as a radical heteronomy. The continuous movement of the "sick" hand, without beginning, ending, or decision, is the pure impersonality of its involvement with the Other (which appears thematically as the *murmure, affirmation*, or the *parole* which "still speaks when all has been said"), and it may be arrested, but not eliminated, by the intervention of the other hand. This uneliminable movement is the behavior of an interiority whose differentiation from exteriority is precisely its intrication with that exteriority.

The sick had is not "my" hand. It is the very form of my proximity to an exterior which is not the other of my interiority, but rather the other of interiority in general. The separation of subjectivity from the inanimateness of exteriority is precisely the impossibility of that separation, and is concomitantly the animation of the *dehors*, the appearance of the *dehors* as animate and even subjective.* The "sick" hand is at the same time my intentionality which has become other or exterior — the hand is not "my" hand — and the exterior whose proximity to me constitutes an appropriation of aspects of my very subjectivity. Like the forests of symbols in Baudelaire's "Correspondances", the intentional or subjective moment of the real, produced by me, is able to contemplate me from the outside. Subjectivity is essentially inadequate to the interiority which is its incarnation. Interiority exists within the real, but not as an integrity. Instead, interiority exists as an essentially ambiguous exigency toward differentiation, a movement of an outside inward or of an inside outward — the creation of an interiority "on the outside" — and the form of this exigency is precisely the non-voluntary movement of "my" hand, no longer mine, in the exterior.

The movement of the *préhension persécutrice* is not the intervention in consciousness of another power, psychic or otherwise, which would determine the hand's behavior from beyond intentionality. Instead, the movement is understandable as a manifestation of the Other of power itself; and the modality of its intervention is not determination, but communication. The movement of the hand, *au dehors*, is not causally determined "from inside" or "from outside", but is, in its automatic, ambiguous animation, the very moment in being at which proximity becomes the exigency of an "inside". The problematic independence of the hand is a moment of indetermination, but this indetermination is not to be understood as a power or self-determination. The uncertain "slowness" of the hand which seeks to close itself around the pencil which has been taken away, is of particular interest to Blanchot because of its manifest irreducibility to any notion of power. It is a radically passive — although undetermined — movement. "What is strange is the slowness of this movement. The hand moves in a virtually inhuman time, which is not that of viable action. . . ."[127] The movement of the hand is inappropriate to the notion of action, either autonomous or heteronomous. Its "passivity" is precisely the defection within being of a differentiation that could take the form of negativity and thus allow action to become a possibility.

The writer seems to be master of his pen, he can become capable of a great mastery over words, over what he wants to make them express. But this mastery

---

* It is also a tendency of the interior toward an inanimate, "objective" state. The movement of the hand is simultaneously automatic or dead, and independent or animate. Thus the sick hand is not only independent, but is already an animation of the inanimate, twice removed from intentionality.

only succeeds in placing him, in maintaining him, in contact with the fundamental passivity in which the word [*mot*], now only its appearance and the shadow of a word, can never be mastered or even seized, remains the inaccessible [*insaisissable*], the *indessaisissable* [which cannot be let go], the undecided movement of fascination.[128]

A fundamental character of radical passivity, as it is thought by both Blanchot and Levinas, is the coincidence of the *insaisissable* and the *indessaisissable*. The refusal of the object to accomplish its exteriority to intentionality and its concomitant self-coincidence withdraws the possibility of "objectivity" from its insistence in the real. And this lack of objective status is an *insaisissabilité*, either in the form of a non-totalized, non-integral word, "the shadow of a word," or of a pencil that cannot be seized by an intentional hand. At the same time, the inability of the object to become self-coincident and intentional is its communicational intrication with a subjectivity which itself fails to become an interiority, and this intrication is an *indessaisissabilité*, either in the form of a problematic consciousness which cannot take a phenomenal or dialectical distance from the words it would manipulate, or of a hand which cannot let go of a pencil or a phantom pencil. The escape from totalization which gives the object its evanescent, ethereal character as a "shadow", is simultaneously an intrication or intimacy with subjectivity whose hyperbolic proximity is most dense and most urgent. The proximal thing approaches as it escapes. Its distance is a contact. This simultaneity of the extremely compelling or urgent and the inconsistent, indefinite or *non-concernant*, is perhaps the most stable and recurrent figure in Maurice Blanchot's creative writing, be it discursive or narrative, and must be thought as a differential intrication which has become the pressure of an exigency and a proximity. The logic of difference, which tends to thematize an escape from totalization, must also thematize, in proximity, an economic pressure which is the intensity of the exigency. "This hand experiences, at certain moments, a great need to seize: it must take the pencil, it is necessary, it is an order, an imperious exigency."[129] The paroxysm of a hand which "must" seize the pencil is also the inhuman "slowness" of the unguided, automatic fingers which close indecisively, even langorously around an imaginary object. The hand's movement is not an action, and this is its strangeness. It is a pure exigency, outside the universe of action and determination, and as such it is both more and less decisive or compelling than an action. The pencil is "the inaccessible that I cannot stop attaining;"[130] it is the object defined as proximity.

The "virtually inhuman time" in which the hand tends to grasp the pencil, and in which the writer has his fugitive contact with the *oeuvre*, is a time whose moments are themselves defined in terms of their proximity to each other. The basic configuration of this duration, in which no instant may be extricated from its contact with surrounding instants, is repetition. Called variously by Blanchot "dead time", "absent time", the "incessant and interminable", or a "present which does not pass", this is a temporality whose differentiations are not negations.

Absence of time is not a purely negative mode. It is the time in which nothing begins, in which initiative is not possible, in which, before affirmation, there is already the return of affirmation. Rather than a purely negative mode, it is on the contrary a time without negation, without decision, when here is truly nowhere, when each thing recedes into its image and the "I" that we are recognizes itself sinking into the neutrality of a faceless "He".[131]

"Absence of time" is the temporality of communication, i.e. the time implied by the possibility of subjectivity's involvement with the exterior. Action, in this temporality, is foreclosed on one hand by the defection of negativity in the form of determination, and on the other hand by the temporal and ontological impossibility of beginning, spontaneity, and "initiative". The word *décision* is the index of this concomitant weakening of power and negation. In absent or dead time, subjectivity is not rooted in an opening of intervals or ekstases, but rather (as Levinas describes in detail in his readings of Husserl*) in a lapsing and collapsing of heteronomous temporal moments whose involvement compromises their integrity. This temporality is inadequate to illumination, and is characterized by the persistence of the absent, where the negative can no longer found disappearance. It is for this reason that "fascination" is the receptivity which appears in this dimension: a receptivity grounded in an inextrication from the exterior. The term, common to Bataille and Blanchot in their Nietzschian inspiration, which describes the intensity of this economy without negation, is *affirmation*. In a temporality whose effects or moments communicate indefinitely, it is possible to coherently define this term as "not affirmation, but the return of affirmation." Absent or dead time in Blanchot is a dimension in which existence is replaced by the insistence of moments and objects whose appearance is not a presence and whose punctuality is essentially repetitive. "What is present is inactual," writes Blanchot, and this statement is both ontological and temporal.[132] The inactuality of the instant in the temporality of communication is its proximity to other instants which, in other contexts, will have the paradoxical power to influence or exert pressure upon it, and which, in any context, transform it into a repetition. "That which is present is inactual; that which is present presents nothing, re-presents itself, belongs already and always to the return."[133] The inactuality of the object, in communication, is its radical "distance" from intentional subjectivity, produced by its inadequation to totalization, and a concomitant "proximity" which results from the fact that this inadequation itself is an intrication with subjectivity prior to the possibility of intentionality. Thus the object becomes its own image or "shadow": its lack of self-coincidence is its lack of phenomenal distance from subjectivity. The imaginary in Blanchot is this configuration of intimate proximity and infinite

* See below, Chapter 5

distance, based on a communicational situation of subjectivity in the real, and is not understandable in terms of traditional definitions of imagination.

The return of affirmation and of the image in a time without "decision" or "initiative" is correlative, as in the passage quoted above, to an inactuality of position or locus – "when here is truly nowhere" – and of an inactuality of the impersonal subject. "The 'I' that we are recognizes itself sinking into the neutrality of a faceless 'He'." Affirmation, the image, fascination, impersonality, the heteronomy of essential solitude and *errance,* and the dispossession of *préhension persécutrice* are concepts whose common denominator is the weakness of the negative and the failure of power and determination. As mentioned earlier, there is a problematic relation of this configuration to the general context of totalization and activity to which Blanchot characteristically attributes an undeniable existence within the real. This relation is elaborated both within the deeply private terms of essential solitude, and within the empirical context of literature in its historicity and its public domain. On the level of involuntary prehension and the literary word to which it is analogous, this relation to totalization takes the basic form of a remainder, an essentially fragmentary *reste* which has not been eliminated by an otherwise adequate and adequating negativity.

That which is written [*s'écrit*: also "writes itself"] delivers him who must write to an affirmation over which he has no authority, which is itself without consistency, which affirms nothing, which is not the repose, the dignity of silence, for it is that which still speaks when all [*tout*] has been said, that which does not precede the *parole**, for it prevents it rather from being a *parole* which begins, as it withdraws from it the right and the power to be interrupted [*s'interrompre*].[134]

Like the senseless excess of involuntary prehension, literature is the prolixity of a word which persists in the silent interval guaranteed the world of representation by negativity. The uncontrollable aspect of the literary word is its involvement with an excess contaminating the boundaries of a totalized world of comprehension. Blanchot is always willing to attribute to this world the totalizations it claims for itself and to recognize in its dialectical movement the completeness of a comprehension which becomes ever more actual. He insists, however, on the notion of an uneliminable remainder, a tiny excess, on the margins of this universe; and this is the implicit critique of totalization which is articulated in the context of dissimulation. The uselessness of this excess, its lack

---

* The *parole* is the excess which results from communication's irreducibility to negation and totalization. This excess always remains when "all" has been said, i.e. when totalization is complete. The *parole* is not a word, nor is it an instance produced exclusively by a constituted subjectivity in communication. More generally, it is the excess of closure in the general economy. But the intersubjective or literary word (*mot* or *parole*) will be involved with the *parole*, and will take its empirical consistency from its rapport with this excess and heteronomy of closure.

of truth, importance, or "seriousness" in the terms of action, are notions which Blanchot always accredits, both on the basic level of the word's "unavailability" or inaccessibility and on the empirical level. "Art cannot compete with action in terms of action," Blanchot writes in perhaps the most important programmatic statement of *L'Espace littéraire*.[135] There is no real irony in these negative stipulations, on one hand because Blanchot recognizes in totalization and history a real dimension of the general economy, and on the other hand because he has no interest in making claims of truth, authenticity or even importance for literature or art. His interest is in the strangeness of the marginal object which can lack truth. Like Bataille and Levinas, he welcomes the proposition of the frailty, uselessness, and even frivolity of this powerless instance which "speaks when all has been said." The contaminated remainder, and the heteronomous world in which it can insist, are the principles not only of the literary space, but also of transgression and the *éthique*. The common denominator of these three dimensions, particularly in Western culture, is that they are "serious" without being entirely "serious". They are serious, either as disturbances or as privileged domains, but they are not as serious as action. Contamination is their element. They are irreducible to action.

The fundamental relation of the creative writer to the subject of involuntary prehension is his involvement with a word that, escaping totalization, also escapes the context of mastery, intentionality and activity. The word cannot be initiated by the interiority of an intentional self. Its production is the very failure of the exigency to create an intentional interiority. Its lack of initiation is its essentially repetitive insistence within the real. It always precedes itself — "before the *parole*, the *parole* again" — and its presence is always an evanescent heteronomy. Its inadequation to decision and initiative, based on its inadequation to negativity, implies a continuity which refuses interruption and differentiation. The *parole* cannot be transformed by action, but it will transform action into indecision. At the same time, through the *parole* we do not attain a universe without differentiation and without the constraint of closure. The heteronomous unicity of closure in proximity is not a liberation, but is perhaps more opaque and stubborn than the constraining self-coincidence of identity. It is this rapport of communication and discontinuity that Blanchot, in a meditation close to that of Bataille, will attempt to thematize through the concept of silence. (See below, Chapter 3.)

Involuntary prehension is the anomalous appearance, within the empirical world of illumination and comprehension, of another space and another time. Underneath its anomaly, Blanchot perceives proximity as the "approach of another space", the approach of an *espace autre*, and the languorous hebetude of proximity's "dead" time. Involuntary prehension is notable for its presentation of the exigency "in action" within a dimension which proscribes it: the totality. The movement of the "sick" hand is uncanny and "virtually inhuman" because, in a world for which all movement must be action, this movement is not an action. The eccentricity and strangeness of involuntary prehension will also be the strangeness of literature for Blanchot. In the world but not of the world, literature will point to the insistence of an *arrière-monde*, "behind" the accomplishments which are brought to existence by power in the dimension of action. This world "behind the world" is the economy of proximity, in which totalization gives way to impossibility, and in which action is replaced by the contamination of the exigency.

LITERATURE AND THE EXIGENCY

Two fundamental propositions, elaborated for the most part in the years after the publication of his *Somme athéologique,* define Bataille's initial concept of literature. Firstly, the basic notion of transgression, considered as the institutionalized violation of an ineluctable law — with the many complex conditions applied to this moment in an economic sense — is privileged by Bataille in a distant past or in a context foreign to Western culture. In his eyes, the history of Christianity in its solidarity with capitalism represents a progressive movement of institutionalized values in the direction of utility, work, and a "primacy of the future" grounded in comprehension and conservation. These values describe for Bataille a "profane" world of activity which is not interrupted in Western society by a sacrificial or in other way transgressive behaviour. Instead, the exigency toward transgression which had a legitimate place in other societies is specifically condemned in the culture of Christianity and capitalism.[1] This condemnation of transgression is, for Bataille, a banishment of the sacred from the world of religion or a profanation of religion itself. The result of this profanation for the citizen of the Christian society is an unprecedented solitude. No longer may he share with his community a ritualized form of *dépense,* for it is ultimately *dépense* itself that is outlawed by the advent and influence of Calvin. Since prohibition and transgression are understood by Bataille as complements, equal and equally ineluctable moments of human comportment, the solitude of the Christian becomes absolute. In this context, the exigency of transgression will take a new form: *le mal.* "Evil [*le Mal*] is not transgression, it is transgression condemned. Evil is precisely sin [*péché*]."[2] Evil, in its initial and most systematic definition in Bataille's text, is a transgression attempted in solitude and silence, without the sanction of a common language or ritual. The exaggeration of this condemnation, in the context of the strangely profaned Christian sacraments and the capitalist world, is characteristically privileged by Bataille. The aggravated violence of Evil, whose spasmodic assault on limits is yet more constrained and less efficacious that that of the ancient sacrifice, is a contamination of the notion of "possible" transgression, and as such is admired by Bataille.

The second proposition which prepares an introduction of literature in Bataille's text is a concept of language as an institutionalized and essentially profane code. By virtue of its conventional definitions, language is subordinate to the logic of utility which regulates the "profane" world. Language is a code which establishes a code: a signification which is implicitly a prescription and a proscription. Language is for Bataille the form, *par excellence,* of the *interdit.* It is the tool of a profane world of activity: "We speak in diverse ways in order to convince and to find agreement. We wish to establish humble truths which will coördinate our attitudes and activity to those of others."[3] Language is a function of the "catalysis" through which, by virtue of the intensity of closure, communication becomes correlation. As such, it participates in the proscription of communication's dissymetry, alteration, and excess. In Bataille's thematic terms, language articulates a cultural condemnation which results from a perennial horror of transgresssion. Language is a code whose purpose is interdiction: the silencing of violence.

He who speaks is always civilized. Or more precisely, language being by definition the expression of the civilized man, violence is silent. This partiality of language has many consequences: (. . .) (C)ivilization and language were constituted as though violence were exterior, *foreign* not only to civilization but to man himself (man being the same thing as language). . . . If one wishes to extricate language from the impasse into which this difficulty forces it, it is thus necessary to say that violence, being the fact of humanity in general, has in principle remained without a voice, that thus all humanity lies by omission and that language itself is founded on this lie.[4]

Bataille's apparently superficial Nietzschian inspiration hides perhaps the most profound Nietzschian proposition regarding language: that is, its economic transformation of communication into correlation. Language is the modality of a counter-communication which controls and organizes the essentially excessive field of communication: prohibition. Violence, a term designating the entire context of transgression considered as an excess and an exigency which are integral to the definition of subjectivity itself, is hidden or silenced by language. The latter, however, is not merely a code. It is an economic event whose tumult ruptures the tranquillity of determined being: a furiously active, violently organized, totalitarian instance whose force proceeds from the very excess it tends to reduce. Language is a conventional code because it is first the event of the exigency: an intense excess and insufficiency (the economic possibility of the *parole* and of receptivity) which invest an intense closure or homogeneity. Rather than to claim that we cannot speak violence through language, Bataille suggests that the *parole* – a fundamentally violent alteration – cannot mobilize violence. This inability does not result from the referential function of language. Instead, it articulates the fact that the referentiality or transitivity of language, as of consciousness, implies a prohibition: a concentration of excess in the form of a discontinuity and a rapport. It is neither language nor consciousness that "reduces" violence in this intense manner: it is multiplicity itself, the very economy of the general economy. Language can be a noise, a disturbance of silence, only because it articulates the excess of the proximal *parole.* But language "reduces" violence, mobilizes the useless, and results in correlation, because it is an integral function of the intensity of difference.

One does not speak violence. Violence speaks, violence invests the *parole*. From the point of view of assertion or of discursive mobilization, violence is silent. (In Nietzschian terms, it is foreign and inaccessible to the "gregarious" world of correlation.) But violence produces the sound or noise of language – a noise which does not interrupt the movements of meaning, but which invests these movements. Nevertheless, Bataille retains the fascination with discursive mobilization that haunted his *Somme athéologique*. Thus he poses as the exigency of the modern world the giving of a voice to violence. The status of this imperative is to be defined by Bataille in characteristically hyperbolic terms which mask a developing interrogation. The aggressive agency which is to restore a voice to silent violence will be *"la littérature"*. This agency, posited in voluntaristic terms, will be the heir to the sacrifice. "Literature is situated in fact as a successor of the religions, of which it is the heir. The sacrifice is a novel, a story, illustrated in blood."[5] Literature's appearance in a profane modernity is described in the terms of irresponsibility and power: "Only literature could reveal [*mettre à nu*] the play [*jeu*] of the law's transgression – without which the law would have no purpose – *independently of an order to be created*... Literature is even, like transgression of the moral law, a danger. Being inorganic, it is irresponsible. Nothing depends on it. It can say anything."[6]

Literature is the heir to the sacrifice. Evil, in a world which specifically condemns transgression, is also the heir to the sacrifice. The proximity of these concepts, whose compatibility has not been defined but simply declared by Bataille, is the field of the meditation entitled *La Littérature et le mal*. "Literature is the essential, or is nothing. The Evil – an acute form of Evil – of which it is the expression, has for us, I believe, a sovereign value."[7] The sovereignty of literature is to be its irresponsible, efficacious transitivity – its expression of that which is powerless, silent, hidden.

The theoretical act which privileges literature as subversion is homologous to the literary act it describes. It intends to discover in its aggressivity a pertinence which would exceed a traditional, profane configuration of pertinence. Miming precisely a traditional linguistic activity, it will destroy the repressiveness of this activity. However, it is precisely this concept of linguistic subversion that Bataille has shown to be impossible. The self-contradiction which inaugurates the study of literature and Evil is troubling to Bataille's reader. The basis of this self-contradiction is clearly the notion of an "expression" which would share the aggressive transitivity of its opposite: a profane language. The solidarity of transitive expression and interdiction, of aggression and prohibition, is clearly established by Bataille's categories, and will not admit the notion of a literature which "can say anything."

The foundation of the profane world is power. Prohibition is a definition or organization of the real in terms of power. Any attempt to extricate literature or Evil from such a context must take the form of an interrogation of the notion of power itself, since alterity in Bataille consists precisely in an irreducibility to the correlation of powers that is the profane world. This is the movement by which Bataille's theory of literature places in question its own hyperbolic beginnings. Its axis is the application to literature of a specialized, problematic predicate which links the question of creation to that of communication. This predicate is failure. For each writer he considers, Bataille will develop a personalized concept of "le mal", considered as the exigency of transgression. This exigency will confront accepted moral values, on one hand, and the problem of textual inscription on the other. The creative writer will assault a moral constraint through a problematic inscription of excess within his text. A privileged failure will be the predicate of both the creative comportment and the textual expression.

In the first place, textual inscription of a violence which would exceed the reifying transitivity of a profane language will be described as a failure, on the grounds that reification — considered as a closure whose ultimate implications are yet to be defined — is an ineluctable result of inscription or expression. On Baudelaire, Bataille will write: "It is true that the effort is vain, that the poems in which this movement becomes petrified. . . have made *infinite* vice, hatred and freedom into the docile, tranquil, immutable forms we know."[8] The expression of excess — the attempt to seize what Bataille calls a *dessaisissement*[9] — is a reduction of excess. Like potlatch, it is a mobilization of the useless which restores the latter inevitably to the world of utility. The aggressivity which seeks to liberate violence by assuming a privileged position with regard to the latter and by unleashing it, constitutes a voluntarism which cannot but misunderstand the passivity of violence itself, and of the unicity which undergoes its approach. The movement of inscription is always a domestication or recuperation — *if* excess may be said to be foreign to inscription itself, considered as a movement or exigency. But this is precisely the question Bataille is approaching.

In the second place, the comportment which seeks to destroy the constraints of the linguistic code by inscribing violence within it, is seen to be trapped in a voluntaristic context which itself reduces violence. Bataille says of Sade: "We are conscious finally of a last difficulty. The violence *expressed* by Sade had changed violence into that which it is not, of which it is necessarily the opposite: a considered [*réfléchie*], rationalized will toward violence."[10] The will to inscribe violence in the text is a voluntaristic detour in the activity of the writer which is irreducible and which radically compromises any prospect of an accomplished subversion. The text, and with it the existential process of its creation, is the limit of the opposition between obstacle and subversion, between constraint and destruction. To the extent that this duality exhausts the notion of the exigency of writing, the text must always be a failure. It attempts to codify that which escapes codification. It seeks to render transitive and destructive that which exceeds all transitivity and all destruction. It fails because it codifies; but most importantly, it fails because it attempts. It fails to the extent that the sole dimension of its movement is the context of power. This failure does not, however, constitute a limit imposed upon the writer's power. On the contrary: the inadequation to violence does not describe the relation of a power to express with a superior power of escape. It describes instead a power which the Other is powerless to resist. "To change violence": this is Sade's power. Violence or excess is not a power which escapes our efforts to mobilize or to liberate it. It is rather a passivity, "here below", which cannot compete with our very spontaneity, and which troubles our will, not by its escape, but by its passive persistence. The disquiet of the will does not articulate a finitude of power, but announces instead the approach of another space: a space of heteronomy and dissymetry, of alteration, in which the powerless approach of alterity no longer unleashes itself, no longer liberates us, but fore-closes the very possibility of our exigent position and of our resolution. It is not the escape of the absolutely other that frustrates power within a world of powers. It is the approach of the powerless Other, "here below", that signals the contamination of the entire universe within which the opposition of reification and escape was ultimate. This contamination, this collapsing, prohibited yielding which weighs upon all action, will not accomplish itself in the form of a destruction of the profane world. Bataille's context is no longer reification, but rather alteration. The rapport of consciousness with violence is no longer a frustrated attempt to mobilize the latter. The rapport is other — and is violent in another manner.

The value of sovereignty accorded the literary text becomes, for Bataille, the paradoxical value of powerlessness and of a desire which knows no accomplishment. He says of Blake:

To speak of Enitharmon does not reveal the truth of Enitharmon, it is even to admit the absence of Enitharmon in a world to which poetry vainly calls her. The paradox of Blake is to have returned the essence of religion to that of poetry, but at the same time to have revealed, through powerlessness [impuissance], that in itself poetry cannot at the same time be free and have sovereign value. (. . .) It is doubtless sovereign, but as the desire, not as the possession of the object.[11]

It is important to stress the incompatibility of Bataille's concept of powerlessness with the classical critical context of reification and frustration that it appears to reproduce. The difference between Bataille and the critical tradition proceeds firstly from the notion that desire is a positive economic event irreducible to will; secondly, from the concept that desire is sovereign; and thirdly, that the heterogeneity of the Other does not consist in a power to limit consciousness. Enitharmon is real, but not actual. Her being is not an accomplishment, but a communication. Our effective access to her is desire: a communicational configuration whose lack of accomplishment does not signify a lack of reality or of positivity. Desire, here as elsewhere in Bataille's critical text, is privileged as the movement of an exigency whose being is to attempt the impossible and to fail. This does not mean: to "at least" attempt the impossible (through a laudible resolution) and to fail "in spite of" the attempt (by a negation of the possible) – but instead: to attempt positively that which lies outside the duality "possible/impossible", and to fail positively (according to a criterion other than accomplishment) to reduce this movement to simple effectivity. Failure is an affirmation. That is: not a resolute and modest affirmation of impossibility as a limit or negation, but rather a heteronomous affirmation of impossibility as alteration. This affirmation, where there is no negation, does not however represent a secondary adequation to Enitharmon which would compensate by its transcendent movement the frustration of the will to capture her. Desire is the modality of an exigency whose proper domain is not that of decision and failure, but rather a space for which the notion of power is no longer determining. This space, and with it the writer, is designated by what may be the most fundamental of all Bataillian terms: *l'impossible.*

From the concept of a literature which "can say anything", Bataille displaces his predications and conditions in the direction of a literature which always "must" express Evil ("the Evil... of which it is the expression"), and is never "able" to do so. This literature is no longer the accomplishment of an expression, but the exigency of a text. Failing to express, it communicates. Thus the concept of transgression, in the context of literature, is brought to the same domain in which Bataille situated the contaminated violence of the ancient sacrifice: the domain of impossibility. Here, the concept of the exigency assumes the full force of its Bataillian definition. Its failure of accomplishment is the condition of its affirmation. Its sovereignty does not consist in its having confronted a superior power, but in its having articulated by its very heteronomy the dissymetrical approach of a space without power. Writing is more or other than an action. Its intensity is not a power. Failure is one index of its excess over the "profane" world of accomplishment. At this level, the congruence of impossibility and affirmation in Bataille parallels the approach of the *oeuvre* in Blanchot: "[The *oeuvre*] is without power," writes Blanchot, "impotent [*impuissante*], not because it is the simple reverse of the various forms of possibility, but because it designates a region in which impossibility is not privation, but affirmation."[12] Since violence, the other of the profane world's negations, is not a quantity which allows itself to be mobilized, the text fails in its attempt at such a mobilization. But communication is an involvement with that which remains inaccessible. To the extent that the violence of the exigency is irreducible to negation, and always contaminates the univocal strategy of mobilization itself – to the extent that reification is always incomplete, as a function of its absolute closure – the text affirms. But the powerlessness of the text neither responds nor corresponds to that of alterity itself; nor does the text's reality signal an ultimate adequation to alterity in the form of powerlessness or impossibility itself. Bataille's discourse belongs to a universe which has nothing in common with that of Heidegger, in which consciousness "responds", underneath or beyond reification, to the Voice of Being, in accordance with its exigency of a "jump" or a "step backward", away from the world of representation into a domain "to which we are already admitted". The Being meditated by Heidegger describes the world of reification and of its vicissitudes; the general economy, on the contrary, describes reification and the approach of its Other. This dissymetrial approach uproots and dispossesses, but does not "admit" or "root" consciousness within being. Thus the approach of Enitharmon will change Blake, will force him from his position toward a "new origin" in which his desire or his intention will no longer be the same — in the manner of the *oeuvre's* approach to Proust's narrator, through the altering weight of Time. This approach is not an investiture, but is an intensity of alteration, an exigency. It is invoked by Zarathoustra through an apt paradox which describes the weight of an event without accomplishment: "You desire your loss and your decline (even through your ignominious impulses toward the correlations of the public square). Desire, then, your loss and your decline." Bataille's fidelity to the inspiration of Nietzsche, Proust, and Freud, informs his patient and exasperated description of a dimension in which adequation (were it an adequation vainly sought) is no longer ultimate: a dimension of plurality without correlation in which the price of all communication is an "impossibility" that is not negative, a radical impossibility.

As a process of creation or as a document, the text is the event of a communication. Within the context of this event, an exigency toward closure (here a seizure of that which escapes seizure; elsewhere, the multiple forms of the exigency in Bataille's text) is always solidary with an exigency toward excess. This solidarity demonstrates that excess is a factor which is always already incribed in the communicative comportment but never susceptible of inscription by the power to express. On a more general level in Bataille's system, the concept of the text — "communication as failure to express", "communication in impossibility" — may be said to function as a basic model for subjectivity itself and for intersubjectivity in proximity. The text is a problematic dimension of communication in which an uneliminable violence always exceeds the concept of an individual subject from whom communication would emanate or to whom communication would return. Nevertheless, such a dimension is the only possible field for a subject's fugitive self-coincidence. The effort of this self-coincidence, or the violence of its process, is the being of the exigency. Like the voluntaristic attempt to express, it accomplishes itself in the very moment of its exigency to abolish its own limits. As the scene of this paradoxical and ambivalent effort, the text is a field in which desire is the sole economic principle of individuation. In such a field, reification — the enclosure of the Other — always succeeds too well, and always fails, for reification itself is an excess and an insufficiency: an alteration. The exigent subject, whose closure is always excessively complete and yet *inachevée* or incomplete, occupies this space in the form of the Bataillian *glissement*: a unicity metamorphosed by the Other. Here, alterity is an instance which has not yet accomplished its entry into existence, and which nevertheless dominates utterly the possibility of communication. Alterity is the principle of subjectivity's necessary enclosure of itself as identity or ipseity, and its necessary failure to abolish, through excess, the eternal imminence of that enclosure. This is the "positive" existence of the Evil sought by Bataille, as of all violence or alterity that the ambivalent spontaneity of Western culture seeks to "liberate": an inactual and passive excess which nevertheless alters the aggressive gesture which wishes to actualize it. A strange excess, "capable of destroying everything", an absolute dispersion, which nevertheless requires an effort on the part of human consciousness or action in order to be awakened from its passivity, extricated from its buried impotence — and which passively resists our efforts to unleash it. The error of consciousness' approach to alterity consists in its interpretation of the latter as an action. The Other is not a glorious power of dispersion, but is a contaminated powerlessness which alters the closure it invests. Refusing to violently rupture the limits of existence, it weighs from outside. It is the approach of another space: the nocturnal, latent birth of the Same.

The text, organized economically by desire, is a central Bataillian model of proximity. The "approach of the literary space" in Bataille, as in Blanchot, is a radical definition of the literary space itself as an approach or proximity whose irreducibility to power is also its irreducibility to manifestation. This is the sense of the failure of expression and of the positivity of failure as affirmation ("as though," in Blanchot's words, "to renounce failure were far more grave than to renounce success"). Enitharmon has no efficiency and no actuality. Her only presence is, perhaps, the *à venir* of the fictional event in Blanchot. (See below.) But this irreality is her insistence in the general economy, as well as her subterranean investment of the creative comportment which desires to accomplish her and fails to do so. In her escape, she is an approach. The instance which creates, and the literary result of creation, insist in an *arrière-monde,* a world behind or underneath the possible, which is without power, which cannot become actual, but which can and cannot but approach.

*

For the Bataille of *L'Expérience intérieure,* the word "silence" is an example of a "mot glissant".* "Perverse", "poetic", it calls attention to the paradox of its enunciation. "It is already... the abolition of the sound that is the word... It is itself the promise of its death."[13] The enunciation of the word is a strangely excessive, violent alteration of the silence it would inscribe in the discourse. The function of the word as expression is essentially compromised by the paradox of its reference. "Silence is a word that is not a word, and breath [which enunciates] an object that is not an object."[14]

Bataille's fascination with the word "silence" indicates a subordination of the privilege of silence itself to that of a paradoxical inscription. The perfection of silence is contaminated by the sound of a word whose own transitivity is placed in

---

* The *glissement* is the metamorphosed unicity of an instance which "cannot avoid its limits, and cannot hold to its limits." This term describes the dispossession and ambiguity of a unicity which cannot coincide with itself. Thus a *mot glissant* is a word whose meaning cannot be univocal, and whose very status as a significative entity is compromised by the *glissement* it implies.

question by its very movement. The word is thus a perverse betrayal of both silence and the abolition of silence. This perversity is poetry, as *La littérature et le mal* demonstrates. Inscription is the perversity of a paradoxical movement between two instances which prevent each other from accomplishing their entry into existence: silence, and the communicable, transitive word. Silence cannot affirm itself. The word cannot affirm the sovereignty of silence. The sound of the word affirms its own contaminated reference to a powerless absence over which this reference has, nevertheless, no power.

The word is a sound which is its own abolition. But the axis of this abolition must be the word's own reference, and this reference is a betrayal of itself. The word is the promise and the imminence of its own death, the movement of its own elimination. But this elimination never comes to pass. Instead, in the field of inscription, the word persists, in the form of a stubbornly imminent closure whose finality or totalization is prevented by the fact that such a totalization would be the abolition of closure itself. Such a word, which affirms simultaneously its own closure and the excess of that closure, is a *glissement*.*

Bataille writes that the subject is "the same thing as language." Indeed, from the perspective of inscription, subjectivity is the exigency of an enunciation which can neither accomplish itself nor silence itself. Subjectivity is an excess, a *dépense*, a transgression, whose paradoxical mobilization is always a closure, a reification, a prohibition. Subjectivity is a silence in the form of a word; an exigency whose intensity is the impossibility of its totalization; an entry into being which is its own imminent abolition: "itself the promise of its death." The ambiguity of the *mot glissant* is not a double or multiple "meaning" — not the vicissitude of an intersubjective comprehension or correlation — but is a rapport of meaning itself with what Blanchot has called "the other of meaning [*l'autre du sens*]": the excess of proximal alteration, the contaminated subsistence of an instance which is "incapable of ceasing to be." Within a universe of affirmation — a universe without negation — the word is no longer bound by its apparent signifying function. It is a proximal event whose ontology may not be coherently described in terms of reference, of ambiguity etc. The *glissement* indicates a ramification of economic functions, irreducible to comprehension and to the vicissitudes of comprehension, whose common denominator is alteration. Words are movements, objects, events of metamorphosis, noises. "Words can hurt." The philosophers of difference and of proximity tend to consider the question of signification as a function of communication and alteration, rather than to examine the signifying entity with a view to its relative efficiency in the context of comprehension. In this tendency they rejoin two

---

* Excess is the principle of Bataillian irony. Like the irony of the sacrifice, which does not mean what it means because its violence is not a destruction, the irony of literary reification is its economy of excess and incompletion. The rows of ellipses which intervene in Bataille's fictional text are a comment on the paradox of a literature which cannot say what it says, and says what it cannot say — a literature whose impotence is not a negation, but an excess.

traditions which, alone among Western interrogations of language, have perceived its function as event: literature itself, and psychoanalysis.

The privilege of the word over silence in a fragment of *L'Expérience intérieure* is the aphoristic equivalent of Bataille's more painstaking approach to the question of literature. Both meditations lead to the affirmation of a new value, that of a word which does not express silence, does not give a sovereign voice to silence, but rather contaminates silence in the domain of impossibility, whose name is "*la communication*". Inscription is a communication among entities which can never accomplish their own closure, but whose very incompletion is a problematic, insistent exigency of closure which makes impossible the explosive negativity of transcendent excess. Through its irreducibility to the vicissitudes of expression (of mobilization) within the world of accomplishment, literature encounters the nocturnal intrigues of an inactual world: that of transgression and of "*expérience*". It is in this sense that we may understand the apparently casual metaphor: "the sacrifice is a novel." In its failure to destroy limits, the sacrifice finds itself to be a violation as *mise en jeu,* a contamination rather than an abolition. The empirical taking of life or destruction of goods is not the accomplishment of that which was attempted, but rather a proximity, at the "extreme of the possible," of transgression and the "flouted prohibition" which "survives" transgression. The *interdit* does not disappear with the victim, and this is why the victim is *la part maudite*: the remainder which survives itself. Transgression sacrifices that which cannot be sacrificed, as does literature. The word, in its way, is communication's *part maudite.* Its density is the only axis of the ceremony which would abolish it. The failure of abolition to take place is the inscription of transgression into the domain of impossible communication. The sacred or the sovereign is this communication whose reality and whose value require a criterion other than that of effectivity. As heir to the sacrifice, literature is the heir to a contamination. And this irreducibility to totalization and manifestation is the ontological principle of the sacrifice's tendency toward the fictionality and irreality of the imaginary. The experience of transgression, as Blanchot says so well in his readings of Bataille, is a moment which never "takes place" in a dialectical or ontological sense. The *expérience* does not "exist" as a phenomenon; it is rather an insistence within an economy of proximity whose differentiations are not negations, and whose positivity is always the irreality of fiction and the image — an irreality, in Blanchot's words, "of which 'reality' is merely the negation." Impossible to actualize, impossible to eliminate: there is no transgression, nor is there a lack of transgression. The concomitant failures of negation and totalization which replace the possibility of silence by the impossibility of the *mot glissant* in the general economy, make of that economy, in Levinas' phrase, "a world in which one speaks and of which one speaks." It is precisely the contamination of totalization by communication that replaces the immobility of contemplation in the universal by the uneliminable sound of a word. Literature is one basic instance of this involvement with the inactual, this persistence of excess, which cannot become substantial or "real", but which cannot be eliminated by negation, and therefore haunts the world of action as an unacceptable and anomalous passivity — a "simple inability to cease to be."

The explicit thematization of literature as an economic instance irreducible to manifestation is not to be found in the text of Bataille's literary criticism. His concepts and his interpretation of these concepts rarely allow him to articulate literature and the *expérience* ontologically, and this is one source of the tension which is so palpable in *La Littérature et le mal*. The difficulty of extricating literature from the context of manifestation and comprehension has always frustrated literary criticism, and continues to do so. The singular and perhaps unprecedented ability to coherently found and condition literature's communicational status and inadequation to power and manifestation was to be the province of Bataille's most important interlocutor, Maurice Blanchot.

On the manifest or declarative level of Bataille's text, the dilemma of reification and expression, of desire and frustration, and the text as inscription tends to be subsumed by the perennial problematic of literature in its relation to manifestation. On this level, the author's lack of control over his work may be understood in a traditional sense as the vicissitude of a larger comprehension and a larger accomplishment. Within the context of inspiration, the artist's passivity appears to result from the economy of the work itself, which may exceed the powers of its creator in the course of accomplishing itself. The sense of this accomplishment remains, however, utility. Similarly, criticism, in the various moments of its self-consciousness and modesty, will attest an involvement of the work with an alterity beyond totalization. The disturbing common denominator of these two tendencies is their assumption of consciousness as a univocally transitive, objectifying and reifying activity whose economy is exhausted by this univocity. The alterity of the work of art is its escape from this limited activity, either in creation or in interpretation. Its alterity is its absolution: its lack of involvement with consciousness' reifications. This perennial view of creativity describes a universe organized exclusively by the problematic of totalization and its frustration, that is, by totalization and its vicissitudes. In such a context, the alterity of art can only represent a superior power and truth, within a universe exhausted by the complementarity of power and truth. This recuperation of alterity results from an inability to thematize any of these basic moments — creation, inspiration, interpretation, alterity — in terms other than those of power.

To attest a limitation of comprehension by the escape of art's alterity is to thematize alterity precisely as an escape and a limit. For the critical tradition, alterity's escape from totalization has always been its only meaningful predicate. But this predicate is neither univocal nor innocent. It designates an escape which is an independence, and a self-sufficiency and totalization implied by this very independence. This "absoluteness" of alterity, and the implicit self-sufficiency and self-determination of its escape, are the latent predicates of comprehension itself. Comprehension is an autonomy. The false modesty of criticism is its view of itself as a limited comprehension trapped in the aporias of assertion: a discourse whose sole purpose is an adequation of itself to alterity, and whose perennial frustration is its inevitable attestation of alterity's escape. The independence of alterity from language or thought's power to seize it does not compromise these powers, but merely limits them. The Other which escapes, consecrates the voluntaristic domain of the gesture which vainly pursues the Other. The escape from totalization tends to assume the predicates of a superior comprehension or higher truth because it already possesses the most important of these predicates: power. Transcending control and totalization, the work in its alterity reproduces the ontology of these factors. The Other assumes the utopian predicates of an accomplished identity: autonomy and comprehension. It is for this reason that the esthetics dominated by philosophy unself-consciously defines the instance which escapes comprehension as a higher truth, and thus ascribes to the work of art the ambitions of philosophy. Thus the criticism of art attributes to the artist the same concern with comprehension and mobilization that characterizes criticism itself, and attributes to alterity itself the efficacy and autonomy which are the dreams of comprehension. In this context the work of art can only assume the function of an accomplishment, in spite of its excess, heterogeneity or transcendence. The universe in which the uncanny personality of the artist appears, and the alterity he approaches, remains a universe of comprehension. This is why the most virulently anti-intellectualistic of artists find themselves recuperated by esthetics as passionate intellectualists. Baudelaire will become the thinker of synesthetic comprehension, Rimbaud the seer, Proust the recapturer of lost time, Nietzsche the man of power. Criticism – a function, *par excellence*, of correlation (which Bataille called utility, and which Nietzsche called *ressentiment*) – fails consistently to imagine creation and interpretation according to criteria other than that of a *savoir-faire,* and to imagine alterity according to a criterion other than that of the ability to escape. For this reason a multiplicity of relations irreducible to that of action and its limits, comprehension and its frustration, implied by the event of art – escape the field of criticism's curiosity. To the extent that art signifies the approach of a world without action, without atonomy, in which both creation and interpretation must be thought in a context other than that of accomplishment – art is not the interest of criticism. Its interests are rather the relative comprehensibility of art, and the relative inaccessibility of alterity.

In the more self-conscious context of contemporary criticism, the literary text assumes the function of a signification irreducible to representation or to reference: a communication which is not governed by a terminal signified which would be anchored in the values of manifestation. But the lack of subordination to representation which describes the text "relating only itself", again signifies an autonomy and an interiority guaranteed by an inaccessibility to totalization – and reproduces the image of an accomplished totality. This autonomy necessarily implies a superior comprehension. It is for this reason that the permanent temptation of the non-referential text is the notion of auto-referentiality: a reflexive self-sufficiency outside representation. The text's interiority describes the same *a priori* subordination to manifestation that the problematic of textuality was intended to reduce. This is because the sole horizon of the critical interrogation is power: the frustrated power to comprehend, and the exalted power to escape comprehension.* The dialectic of limits and the escape from limits describes a universe exhausted by comprehension's power and the frustration of this power by a superior power. It is for this reason that the absolution of an alterity beyond language, enthusiastically invoked by criticism, remains an implicit dimension of manifestation — of communication defined as correlation — whose very absoluteness accredits criticism's confidence in its approximations. The principle of the Other's escape is not different from the principle of comprehension's pursuit. This is why criticism can attest with modesty and with admiration to the capacity of escape represented by alterity. The limited or frustrated autonomy of interrogation on one hand, and the transcendent or limiting autonomy of the instance which eludes interrogation on the other, dominate this universe in their correlation. Power and superior power are its only axes. From this point of view it is possible to perceive the continuity of inspiration which animates the history of criticism. The classical image of the artist who, under the constraint of inspiration, discovers a precious and superior truth, worthy of appropriation by a culture gratified by his accomplishment, does not differ from the contemporary image of the artist who, by virtue of his involvement with the impersonal alterity of communication, produces a work

---

* The dialectic of totalization and its frustration by the Other's escape is not appropriate to the basic concepts of the philosophy of difference, but appears as a temptation of certain themes associated with this philosophy. For instance, the first and most influential sense of Jacques Derrida's concept of "deconstruction" as a strategic "displacement of concepts" designed to reveal and describe the limits of a reductive metaphysics, invites appropriation by criticism's most intellectualist tendencies. Although the concept of deconstruction far exceeds this initial sense by its implications (see below, Chapter 7), it tends to accredit the notion of a comprehension defined univocally as the transitivity and voluntarism of an attempt to totalize, and the notion of alterity as a factor which escapes the "oppositions" which structure Western metaphysics. Derrida's repeated stipulations that the economy of difference "makes possible" these oppositions, are not in themselves sufficient to pre-empt the voluntaristic interpretation of "deconstruction" as an exclusively critical strategy which unmasks the presuppositions of metaphysics, in the self-conscious pursuit of an escaping alterity. The Heideggerian resonances of a deconstruction understood as the refined, more lucid form of an irreducibly limited comprehension, or as the progressive adjustment of metaphysical concepts toward a superior adequation to alterity's excess or heterogeneity, are the principle of this concept's vicissitudes in contemporary criticism. It is the apparent intellectualism of a deconstruction pursuing with modesty the escaping Other — the efficacious and autonomous Other which "escapes" oppositions while "making possible" these oppositions — that animates the prompt recuperation of this concept by criticism. As will be discussed below, the concepts of the philosophy of difference ultimately point to a view of critical interrogation in terms of passivity, affirmation, and metamorphosis, which has nothing in common with the duality of totalization and its frustration. This is the more basic sense of deconstruction, not as a "correction" of concepts or as a "refutation" of presuppositions, but as the "other" of both construction and destruction, in a universe without negation.

which by its very opacity contributes to his modernity's critique of totalization. In each case, the alteration which conditions the artistic event is subordinate to a metaphysics which ascribes to the artist its own desire to progressively refine comprehension so as to more effectively approach an absolute alterity and to celebrate the latter's excessive power. It is the ambivalence of this thirst for heterogeneity and inadequation, within intellectualism itself, that characterizes not only criticism but also the entire metaphysics from which it proceeds.

As mentioned above, Bataille's attestations of failure and impossibility invite a hasty reading in terms of reification and the escape of alterity. But this mode of interpretation, rooted in a subordination of alterity to power, reduces two important factors which are integral to Bataille's concepts: the involvement of alterity with consciousness, both in the creative comportment and in the interpretative comportment; and the heteronomy of the work of art. On one hand, alterity's escape from totalization is its intrication with and investment of the communicative comportment which envisages it. The inability to totalize does not exhaust the sense of this comportment.* As the philosophers of proximity insist, the subjectivity which fails to recuperate alterity, remains involved with the latter in another sense. Alterity's economy is not exhausted by its escape: this escape is an approach. On the other hand, the escape of alterity from totalization does not imply a power, but a radical heteronomy, a radical lack of independence, an irreducible involvement with closure. The literary text is not referential, but describes in its heteronomy the hyperbole of that dependence and passivity that the concept of auto-referentiality is intended to reduce. The absolutely Other is "here below". Its escape from totalization is its proximity. Its alterity is not a power, but is precisely a lack of power in a world exhausted by the notion of power. Its incumbence or domination, like that of the sirens meditated by Blanchot (see below), is not a power, but the approach of a reality without power. This incumbence is necessarily a vulnerability, when confronted by a power like that of Ulysses, which organizes reality under the totalitarian duality of being and nothingness or existence and inexistence. Ulysses' calculation "exterminates" the sirens with ease, because their approach is not a power. The approach of alterity in proximity "cannot be stopped" because it is the approach of another space, a reality without power. That the urgency of this approach "cannot compete with action in the terms of action," in Blanchot's words, is the very principle of its alterity. Criticism, in its voluntaristic intellectualism, never senses that the alterity of art is "other" without being "absolutely"

---

* The creative writer's pursuit of the "impossible" is not a limited comprehension, but is itself an involvement – without correlation or adequation – with alterity. Its failure to totalize is but one modality of its contamination and affirmation. Likewise, the critic, in his failure to achieve a totalization of the literary text, may describe in his own text an involvement with the Other. Critics are singularly insensitive to the proposition that criticism itself is communication, and not merely the relative success or relative sterility of an attempt to totalize. It is possible, however, that this mode of insensitivity or "ressentiment" describes, in an economic sense, the function or reality of criticism itself.

other — without being superior, efficacious, destructive, useful, without reproducing the image of the Same's ambitions for itself; that alterity does not elude
comprehension through a power of escape, but through a powerlessness which
contaminates; that creation is not an act, but is an alteration; that critical interrogation itself hides a radical passivity. Alterity in art is important without being
"serious" — and this is why the destiny of art has always been the ambivalence'
of recuperation and of a denigration of the frivolity of the fictive. Art is
nocturnal; but, in its irreducibility to manifestation, it does not reproduce
through absolution the spontaneity of the day. It "recedes into the light."
Escaping nothing, it alters.

Bataille's contribution to an extrication of communication from the context
of manifestation is to be found in other zones of his system than that of literature
and evil. Nevertheless, Bataille's meditation of impossibility in literary creation
allows him to thematize a contamination of power in the literary dimension
which recalls his most radical descriptions of proximity, and which anticipates
the posing of the Blanchotian questions. For instance, although fiction and the
imaginary are not Bataillian categories, the phrase: "the sacrifice is a novel"
indicates, as discussed above, a correlation between literature and transgression
which is based not only on the problematic of power, but also on the question
of manifestation. There is a paragraph in "L'apprenti sorcier" (1938)[15] which
compellingly states this correlation:

Most often, human destiny can only be lived in fiction. Now the man of fiction
suffers from not accomplishing himself the destiny he describes. . . . So he tries
to make the phantoms which haunt him enter into the real world. But as soon as
they belong to the world that action renders true, as soon as the author links
them to some particular truth, they lose the privilege they had of accomplishing
human existence to the end: they are now no more than the boring reflections
of a fragmentary world.[16]

In reading a passage like the above, one senses an echo of the theme in *L'Espace
littéraire* that "art cannot compete with action in the terms of action," and of
the multiple demonstrations in *Le Livre à venir* that fiction is a positive, though
inactual dimension of the general economy. One senses as well the Proustian
distinction between the writer as creator, who enters by metamorphosis a world
without action, and the writer as artisan, who attempts to appropriate this
experience to his intramundane identity and spontaneity — a distinction which is
integral to Blanchot's meditation of literature. Art describes a world underneath
the manifest, and more importantly a world behind the accomplished or possible.

Bataille's meditation on expression and inscription, and his subordination of
power to the exigency in literary communication, constitute his major contribution to the thematization of literature in the general economy, as well as a
basic contribution to literary criticism. His essay on Baudelaire, for instance,
demonstrates the pertinence of the concept of impossibility for the study of an

individual author. This concept permits Bataille to understand evil, infinity, and impossibility itself — the "anywhere out of the world" in Baudelaire — as authentic categories in the economy of proximity. Most importantly, Bataille is able to designate the necessary approach of poetry or of subjectivity to these dimensions of a proximal reality as desire, in the form of the "wish for the impossible". In this way, Bataille supplants the familiar notion of a "contra-dictory wish" or "frustrated wish" in Baudelaire, by the concept of an impossi-bility or an evil whose only mode of manifestation — of communication — is desire, rather than the relatively limited possibility of a totalization, a pos-session, etc. This communicational approach to alterity cannot but be an irreduc-ible ambivalence, as is the Bataillian exigency. In Baudelaire, subjectivity always "must" communicate (with the cat, with the reality of obsession, with the infinity of "Le gouffre" in which negation fails), and never "is able" to com-municate (with beauty, with woman, with others in "Le guignon" or "La cloche fêlée"). The other of location in the "anywhere out of the world" is not only inaccessible, but also inescapable. "All I can see outside the windows is infinity." In Baudelaire as in the philosophy of proximity, the alterity which escapes also concerns me, is incumbent upon me, or approaches. Subjectivity's irreducible intimacy with the Other is desire: a dispossession more intimate than any actuality or possession. It is this notion of desire as a metamorphosing intensity entirely irreducible to will or to intention, that allows Bataille to identify the most profound weakness of Sartre's reading of Baudelaire — that is, its volun-tarism — and to read "bad faith" in Baudelaire in a context which anticipates indecision in Blanchot. "Sartre is founded in assuring that [Baudelaire] *wanted* that which seems passive [*à vau-l'eau*]. He wanted it at least in the sense that it is inevitable to wish the *impossible,* that is, at the same time firmly, as such, and mendaciously, in the form of a chimera. Hence his complaining life as a dandy, avid for work, bitterly floundering in useless idleness."[17] The necessary congru-ence of resolve, passivity, and the chimerical, in a rapport with impossibility conceived as a dimension irreducible to power, is basic to the Baudelairian notion of evil, and has rarely been attested in Baudelaire criticism or discovered by criticism in general. Bataille's invocation of passivity in literary creation recalls his fundamental meditation of transgression as the violence of an event which is less than actual and less than accomplished. On this level, the Bataillian concept of transgression in literature is more proximate to the essential defi-nitions of *L'Espace littèraire* than any contemporary critical concept. Literary communication is not the accomplishment of that which was attempted, nor is it the univocity of this privileged failure. The literary text describes the excess and heteronomy of an involvement with the Other. Its strangeness proceeds from interiority's transgression of interiority in a reality without power — and this transgression is perhaps the ultimate sense of the Bataillian term "evil". When Baudelaire, in his explosive "Au lecteur", describes an impossibility of creative sincerity or authenticity which nevertheless articulates a dangerous liaison between himself and his "semblable", his "frère", he does not merely invoke a human frailty or an excess of art's alterity over language: he invokes an experience of subjectivity and of intersubjectivity whose context is no longer comprehension, power, or correlation, but rather alteration. In Baudelaire's indecision, as read by Bataille, the approach of the *oeuvre* may be felt, as well as Orpheus' first transgressive steps toward the night.

SILENCE AND ORPHEUS

"La préhension persécutrice" and "L'interminable, l'incessant" are subsections of *L'Espace littéraire*'s extremely important introductory chapter.[18] In this chapter, Blanchot introduces his reader to such basic concepts as impersonality, inspiration, repetition, the *oeuvre,* etc. – concepts whose irreducibility to negation, totalization, and power must be understood before the remainder of the text may become intelligible. As discussed above (Chapter 2), the notion of non-voluntary prehension proceeds from the concept of proximity as it informs the context of writing as "action". There is in "La préhension persécutrice" and "L'interminable, l'incessant" an additional Blanchotian interpretation of this "action" of writing which brings about a sudden displacement of context and a considerable difficulty for his reader. This is the problematic of the imposition of silence.

The concept of non-voluntary prehension permits Blanchot to describe a priority and an irreducibility of proximity and passivity over action in the context of writing. This is the priority of the *parole,* incessant or repetitive time, and absence of decision in the literary space. Yet, in Blanchot's words, it is always possible for the "unaffected" hand to intervene and arrest the non-voluntary movement of the "sick" hand in prehension. The possibility of this arresting intervention is the possibility of introducing a form of differentiation into the continuous and therefore undifferentiated tracings of the affected hand. It is the status of this intervention and this differentiation that is in question in Blanchot's text.

Silence is, in many ways, an impossibility in the general economy. Its contamination by the sound of the *parole* which is closure's excess – the word "silence" in Bataille, the *parole d'écriture* in Blanchot, the *parler* of separation and the *visage* in Levinas – is an important modality of differentiation as communication and proximity in the economy. The absence of silence as negativity, on one hand, or as determination and contemplation in manifestation, on the other, is a basic principle of communication in proximity. The overall context of Blanchot's first chapter accredits and stresses this principle in all its implications. Nevertheless, in discussing the intervention of the unaffected hand, Blanchot writes:

To write is to make oneself the echo of that which cannot stop speaking, – and, because of this, to become its echo, I must in a way impose silence upon it. I bring to this incessant word [*parole*] the decision, the authority of my own silence. I render *sensible,* by my silent mediation, the uninterrupted affirmation, the giant murmur on which language in opening itself becomes an image, becomes imaginary, a speaking depth [*profondeur parlante*], an indistinct plenitude that is empty. This silence has its source in the disappearance [*effacement*] to which he who writes is invited. Or, it is the resource of his mastery, this right to intervene that is retained by the hand which does not write, the part of himself which can always say no and, when necessary, appeals to time, restores the future.[19]

This statement of the possibility of silence appears two pages after Blanchot has written, in the context of his basic concepts, this clear disqualification of the same proposition:

That which is written [*s'écrit*: also "writes itself:] delivers him who must write to an affirmation over which he has no authority, which is itself without consistency, which affirms nothing, which is not the repose, the dignity of silence, for it is that which still speaks when all [*tout*] has been said, that which does not precede the *parole,* for it prevents it rather from being a *parole* which begins, as it withdraws from it the right and the power to be interrupted [*s'interrompre*].[20]

The clear contextual solidarity of Blanchot's contradictory assertions is striking. On one hand, "mastery", "authority", and a "right" of intervention are disqualified entirely as reductions of the incessance of the *parole,* as in the following sentence: "But this mastery only succeeds in placing him, in maintaining him, in contact with the fundamental passivity in which the word [*mot*], now only its appearance and the shadow of a word, can never be mastered or even seized, remains the *insaisissable,* the *indessaisissable,* the undecided moment of fascination."[21] On the other hand, the concept of mastery which has thus been disqualified, is posited and accredited, in the very same terms as its disqualification: mastery, authority, right. Blanchot's reader, who may be prepared to understand mastery as a conditioned moment of the larger economy of indecision or passivity, cannot be prepared to understand mastery as a factor which escapes or transcends that economy. Yet it is this interpretation that Blanchot univocally proposes.

The bulk of *L'Espace littéraire* describes the complementary notions of inspiration, *parole,* incessance, repetition, etc. considered as moments of a proximity irreducible to negation and to the possibility of an imposition of silence. However, this possibility of silence is invoked at intervals within the text, and reappears in *Le Livre à venir.*[22] Blanchot continues to characterize the creative writer as "mediator" of the incessant, as "hearer" and "interruptor" of the interminable.[23] The vocabulary and atmosphere of a sentence like the following, for example, are disturbingly foreign to Blanchot's overall context:

And he who writes is, also, he who has "heard" [*entendu:* also "understood"] the interminable and incessant, who has heard it as a *parole,* has entered into its meaning [*entente*], has stood [*s'est tenu*] within its exigency, has lost himself in it and yet, for having endured [*soutenue*] it correctly, has made it stop, in this intermittence has rendered it seizable [*saisissable*], has preferred it in assigning it this limit, has mastered it by measuring it.[24]

Each and every operation designated in this sentence has been clearly defined, not only by preceding sentences but by the whole of *L'Espace littéraire* and the whole of Blanchot's theoretical text, as an impossibility. If these possibilities are accepted by Blanchot's reader as an authentic interruption and mastery of communication, in a dialectical sense, then the very pertinence of communication as a dimension irreducible to totalization is reduced to the desirory, at the deepest level of its definition. And it is just such a dialectical interpretation that Blanchot proposes, in a formulation which shows some hesitation: "This silence has its source in the disappearance to which he who writes is invited. Or, it is the resource of his mastery, this right to intervene that is retained by the hand which does not write, the part of himself which can always say no. . .". On one hand, Blanchot simply declares that the priority of the incessant, and of the radical passivity of prehension, do not resist or condition the mastery of a phenomeno-logically defined negating consciousness. On the other hand, he grounds this "mediation" in a Hegelian interpretation of impersonality. Thus, the "efface-ment" of the personal self in impersonality is defined as a negation which may then be mobilized for the introduction of silence and the positivity of the "sensible" into the incessance of the impersonal. The result of the two gestures is the same. Whether defined empirically or dialectically, the notion of mastery is extricated from the context of writing as inspiration and proximity, and returns to dominate that context. And with its return, the personal author of literary history returns as well, firstly through the concept of tone:

Tone is not the voice of the writer, but the intimacy of the silence he imposes on the *parole,* which makes this silence still *his,* what remains of him in the discretion which places him aside [*à l'écart**] .[25]

and secondly through the concept of preservation:

Of the erased "I", [the writer] retains the authoritarian although silent affir-mation. Of creative time, of the instant, he retains the cutting edge, the violent rapidity. Thus he preserves himself within the *oeuvre,* he contains himself there where there is no longer any reserve [*retenue*].[26]

---

* The word *écart* in Blanchot's theoretical text indicates the incompletion and dispos-session of closure. It is not the "gap" of a negativity, but the lack of self-coincidence produced by the alteration or becoming-other of closure in proximity. Thus impersonality and the *parole,* as communicational factors, are correlative to the writer's *écart* — the alteration affecting his unicity — in a dimension without *retenue,* i.e. without totalization and adequate closure. In the passage cited above, tone in its relation to silence is defined by Blanchot as a limitation or domination of the *écart.*

As mentioned above, the dimension of communication and proximity characterized by the incessant and interminable as repetition, and by indecision and fascination as the heteronomous investment of interiority, may not be understood as a regional phenomenon subsumed by the dialectic of silence, without rendering incomprehensible the entire conceptual framework of *L'Espace littéraire*. The notion of a mastery which would be exempt from the non-voluntary dimension of writing designates a literary space defined as a dialectical totality, in which differentiation is subordinated to negation, and in which the problematic of fascination is subordinated to manifestation in the form of the "sensible". Within this totality, incessance, indecision, and communication in general would signify simple undifferentiation, and would require a negating silence to take the form of a dialectical differentiation. Yet Blanchot's reader knows that indecision is not an opposite of decision (negativity and power), but is its condition and its larger economy. Fascination and indecision — heteronomy and repetition — are the predicates of differentiation in the general economy. These terms indicate an entirely differentiated unicity which, however, lacks totalization. To articulate them with decision and silence defined as mastery and negation is to transform the economy into a dialectic without communication.

"La solitude essentielle", which includes the sections discussed here, was published originally in 1953.[27] The economy of Blanchot's developing concepts and of the Hegelian thematization of negativity was clearly stated in the brilliant "La littérature et le droit à la mort" (1948). In that essay, through an explicit communication with Levinas' notion of the *il y a,* Blanchot invoked and clearly defined a "reality without negation" which was to inform the subsequent development of his thought. It is thus doubly striking to find the problematic of mastery and negation intervening in so violent a manner in *L'Espace littéraire*. At the same time, this intervention is not a stable moment of Blanchot's theoretical text. The notion of imposed silence does not reappear in *L'Entretien infini,* where essays such as "L'absence de livre" (1969) and "La voix narrative" (1964) treat the same context as "La solitude essentielle". In these essays, new terms such as "distance", "discontinuity", "absence", and "*écriture*" are invoked, whose definitions overwhelmingly foreclose any problematic of negation.

The concept of silence as mastery in *L'Espace littéraire* is important for an additional reason. In an economy of communication which would be organized dialectically by silence, negativity and manifestation, the drama of Orpheus and his encounter with Eurydice in the night would have no interest. And Blanchot's prefatory statement that *L'Espace littéraire* consists of a progressive movement toward "Le regard d'Orphée" is not derisory, as the overall interplay of his concepts shows. Orpheus' transgression and failure are not accidental, and are integral to the constitution of the oeuvre. From the point of view of silence and mastery, however, the situation of Eurydice in the night would not be ultimate, and Orpheus' failure to extricate her from the depths would not be founded. The right and the power to impose silence upon the undifferentiation of a nocturnal dispersion would be sufficient to return Eurydice to the light of day.

Although the whole of *L'Espace littéraire* contradicts the problematic of silence, it is the proximity of Orpheus in particular that requires a situation of this problematic.

Several adjustments of the notion of silence in "L'interminable, l'incessant" are possible, although such adjustments would not entirely reduce the contradiction stated by Blanchot. For instance, as Bataille shows in the context of the exigency, and as Blanchot shows in the context of dissimulation, the general economy is not a proximity which absolutely forecloses negation. Instead, negation is founded and conditioned by proximity, in the form of dissimulation, solitude, the exigency, etc. The problematic of reification in *La Littérature et le mal* and in *non-savoir* describes the inevitability of a problematic "totalization" in the profane world, however deeply this closure may be conditioned by the intensity of the *glissement*. In the general economy, closure is an irreducible heteronomy, but is also an irreducible discontinuity. Proximal communication is a hyperbolic intimacy which retains and even exceeds the opacity associated with totalization and the alterity of the "in itself". Communication is not communion or transparence. Separation is irreducible. The Albertine of proximity concerns, invades, or dispossesses me as she escapes me. Her escape is communicational and repetitive, and is grounded not in her unknowable interiority, but in her lack of totalization and her concomitant proximity. But this inaccessibility is nevertheless a discontinuity and a difference. Within the regional dimension of negation and power, this difference will be interpreted as, and will even function as a totalization. It is in this context that Levinas invokes an *autrement qu'être* or communicational economy which "of course resonates withing Being" — that is, which invests the totality. For Bataille, Blanchot and Levinas, the general economy of proximity produces a negation and a totalization which are regional and conditioned. If Blanchot's invocation of silence as mediation may be said to indicate this configuration, then it must be read as an ironic gesture in the direction of Hegel. In this sense, as discussed earlier, Blanchot's many authentications of the positive existence of history, action, negation, etc. in the general economy, might be recalled. Blanchot never contests the reality or even the domination of this dimension of existence, in which "art is for us a thing of the past" and in which "art cannot complete with action in the terms of action." Instead, he stresses its regionality and ultimately, as discussed above, conditions it by an instance irreducible to negation. From this perspective, it would be possible to interpret silence and mastery as the existence in proximity of this conditioned possibility of mediation. Blanchot's irony would consist in the baldness and exaggeration of the Hegelian model of mastery he proposes, and in the violence of its contradiction of the surrounding context. The pertinence of this interpretation is limited, however, by the lack of qualifying remarks in "L'interminable, l'incessant" and by the unqualified invocation of silence and mastery at key moments in *L'Espace littéraire* and *Le Livre à venir*. If there is irony in the notion of mastery through silence, it is an irony that is alloyed with a genuine temptation by the Hegelian concepts.

Another, more compelling interpretation of silence proceeds from the notion of the exigency itself. The exigency is a closure or discontinuity whose modality is incompletion and the economic pressure exerted by alterity. Closure is a heteronomy that is dense and intense: a turgidity forced by the exterior. Every *dépense*, as Bataille shows, is a closure in the form of excess. Thus the extremity of transgression is the tension of an assault on a limit which is itself an excess. The form of closure in the general economy is the excess of the exigency. Although Blanchot tends to present the dimension of proximity in the context of the anomalous or extraordinary, he follows Bataille in further defining this dimension as a condition of possibility of the dialectical dimension of existence. The problematic of dissimulation is perhaps the most important instance of this gesture. From this perspective, it is evident that the world of decision and initiative which appears to be confronted by a punctual involvement with proximity, is actually conditioned by proximity as an economic pre-originarity. The implication of this priority for the context of non-voluntary prehension is extremely important. For within Blanchot's system, there would be no alternative to the intervention of the "unaffected" hand. This intervention is not only integral to the differentiations produced in the *parole* or *murmure* by writing. It is integral to the very possibility of movement or "action" in the general economy. The unaffected hand *must* intervene, but not simply to arrest an entirely undifferentiated movement of prehension. It must intervene because its own latent economy is indecision: the being of intentionality in proximity.*
As Blanchot's reading of *The Burrow* shows, the force of closure's apparent spontaneity is its hidden involvement with the Other. Power is a moment of communication, and not its dialectical other. The exigency is not merely a voluntaristic detour accidentally produced by differentiation in the economy. It is the pressure of this differentiation itself as it weighs upon interiority. Thus the voluntarism of closure is inextricable from its subjectivity or passivity. These inextricable moments describe the pressure of desire which produces closure as an intensity. Thus the unaffected hand does not intervene from a position of "power". It *must* intervene, and this "must" is the pressure of the exigency itself. It is not possible to read non-voluntary prehension in Blanchot as the dialectic of undifferentiation and a power of intervention. Instead, this moment, which describes literary creation in general, must be understood in its totality as an exigency. The intervention of the unaffected hand is not a power, but a desire. Thus neither hand is "unaffected". This is the subtlety of "La préhension persécutrice", and of all the invocations of the extraordinary in Blanchot's text.

---

* As mentioned earlier (Chapter 1), the narrator's approach to Albertine's increasingly fragmented face is not the frustration of a curiosity, but the frustration of a desire. In her escape from totalization, Albertine concerns and involves the narrator. She draws his face to hers. His need to totalize her is an intimacy with her loss. He does not contemplate her: he kisses her. The word *recherche* indicates desire, and a theoretical experience grounded in the exigency. Similarly, the alacrity of the intervening hand in Blanchot must be envisaged in its latent economy.

The unaffected hand cannot but arrest the affected hand; prohibition cannot but transgress; transgression cannot fail to find its movement trapped within the limit it exceeds. The "absolutely other" in proximity is never "absolutely" other, but always informs and invests a closure and a discontinuity which are conditioned but irreducible. These manifold impossibilities are produced by the fact that the economy of proximity is not a dialectic. The differentiations which distinguish Baudelaire from Proust, or *Jean Santeuil* from the *Recherche* — the differentiations which create the empirical economy of literary creation — proceed from proximity and the exigency. They do not require a negation and a positivity over and above the discontinuity of communication. The economy of incessance or impersonality on one hand, and empirical distinction or differentiation on the other, is not a dialectic. Proximity is not an undifferentiation which requires power for its economy: on the contrary, proximity is an economy irreducible to power. This economy produces, in its empirical or intramundane dimension, an intensity of closure which may be hastily interpreted as "power" or "determination", and a dense unicity which may be interpreted as "totalization" or "identity to self". These intensities are the effects of proximity, or what Blanchot calls "dissimulation". Their mobilization as power and negation creates a world, a totalitarian dimension of existence — but it does not exhaust the economy.

The notion of the two hands in non-voluntary prehension may be said to be misleading, because it tends to draw the notion of communication into a dialectical context. And since Blanchot uses the concept of silence to account for the empirical differentiations which distinguish words, authors, and books, it may be said that he momentarily mistakes the incessant and impersonal for a situation of undifferentiation, and turns to the concept of silence, in a truly Hegelian inspiration, in order to make of this undifferentiation an economy. His mistake is to have forgotten that it always was an economy. In this sense, Bataille's meditation of silence in *L'Expérience intérieure* is more radical than that of Blanchot. Bataille's situation of silence within the irreducible murmur of the word "silence" describes the contamination which is differentiation in the general economy. No silence is possible, in a dialectical sense, within this economy. But neither is the empirical, efficient transitivity of the word or the "sensible" a possibility. The insistence of silence in communication is a "word that is not a word", an "object that is not an object". In the same sense, there is no entirely independent "sick hand" in communication. The continuity of its movement is always produced in the proximity of an "unaffected hand", and is, ironically, its effect upon this intervening hand. The production of the exigency as an effective reality is the suspended contact of the two hands which, like continuity and discontinuity, prevent each other from being constituted as dialectical totalities. In the urgency and efficiency of the unaffected hand which reaches to control the uncontrollable, we perceive not power, but transgression. It is from this perspective — the perspective of a mastery which is not a mastery, but an exigency — that non-voluntary prehension may be said to prepare, along with the bulk of *L'Espace littéraire*, the appearance of Orpheus, who cannot but turn and look at Eurydice.*

As discussed above, the interest of the myth of Orpheus for the context of communication is contingent upon a view of alterity which is neither the heteronomy of simple dispersion nor a dialectic of power and undifferentiation. Were communication simply a dispersion which overwhelms closure, the night and its dispossession would be ultimate, and there would be no concept of an *oeuvre* — a problematic positivity — as a consequence and condition of Orpheus' descent. In the case of a dialectic, the night would be conditioned, and the return of Eurydice to manifestation would be inevitable. The pertinence of Orpheus to communication is the fact that his gesture is to be understood neither as simple loss nor as mastery, but as transgression.

Differentiation in the general economy is a heteronomy and an exigency. It is the movement of a closure whose excess is defined as desire. There is no dialectical alternative to closure in the economy, but closure is an excess and a *glissement*. In other words, closure is always a proximity. Communication is irreducible to negation and unity, but is always incarnated in an economy which produces closure. As the basic movement of *L'Espace littéraire* shows, the problematic ontological status of the *oeuvre* is related to its escape from a

---

* The problem of involuntary prehension, which tends by its very form to suggest a dialectic of impersonality and manifestation, may indicate a more profound difficulty in Blanchot's theoretical text. This would be a difficulty in articulating the economy of communication with the unicity of subjectivity. There is a tendency in Blanchot to posit alterity as undifferentiation, rather than as a principle and a modality of differentiation — and then to describe this alterity as an inaccessible other of unicity, rather than as an instance involved with and conditioning unicity. When this occurs in an intersubjective context, the image of two "poles" with an alterity "between" the poles will enter his text. He will situate the *oeuvre*'s alterity "between" writer and reader in *L'espace littéraire* — as though alterity could not be situated within unicity — and will correctly criticize his own "faulty image" of polarity.[28] But in *L'Entretien infini*, where the notion of an intersubjective presence is a major theme, the image of alterity as the *entretien* which "se tient entre" or "stands between" will intervene repeatedly. As will be discussed below, the name of Levinas and the Levinasian theme of non-reciprocity will haunt these discussions of intersubjectivity. This progression in Blanchot's thinking suggests that his difficulty in situating unicity within an economy of alterity causes him to posit alterity as undifferentiation or as an element strictly outside unicity, and that the image of two interlocutors in intersubjectivity aggravates this difficulty. Blanchot's enthusiasm for Levinasian dissymmetry and non-reciprocity suggests his awareness of this problem, and his involvement with Levinas in an attempt to reduce it. Yet the dissymmetry of Same and Other in intersubjectivity causes serious problems in Blanchot's readings of Levinas (although Blanchot has articulated this dissymmetry most coherently in other contexts, such as that of death's approach). Two instances — the panoramic image of an intersubjective presence, and the name of Emmanuel Levinas — are involved in this problematic moment of Blanchot's thought. See below, Chapter 6.

dialectic of identity, power, and manifestation. The fugitive appearance of the *oeuvre* is, however, a moment in an economy of communication, and as such is never the simple transcendence of the "absolutely other". The *oeuvre* is always "here below", as an interpersonal, communicational object. Its tendency to refuse or escape the dimension of manifestation is inextricably linked to its necessary status as what might be called a "public" object. The *oeuvre* is an alterity, but it does not have the privacy of the "tout autre" — the power of the inaccessible — because it is a communication. (When Blanchot wistfully suggests that the *oeuvre* might be "better off" forgotton by posterity — rather than to be recuperated as a useful object — he attests the fact that its escape from totalization is a passivity, and that its communicational status implies an invasion of the "privacy" of its alterity.[29]) The production of the *oeuvre*, conceived as a rapport with alterity which is always a public communication, and thus a contemination of both manifestation and of the "absolutely other", is the major theme of *L'Espace littéraire*, and this is why the myth of Orpheus is basic to the organization of Blanchot's text.

Blanchot interprets Orpheus' descent not simply as the desire to return Eurydice to the dimension of life, but as the twofold desire to encounter her within the night and to possess her as she would appear within the nocturnal dimension. It is the contamination of this wish that constitutes Orpheus' exigency, and the exigency of creative writing in general. The writer's dilemma is his approach to a dimension whose proximity is always a dispossession, and his concomitant, irreducible exigency to possess, mobilize, or make manifest this radical alterity. The gods' injunction is an articulation of this excess and this excessive closure. Eurydice is the deepest "point" of the night's obscurity, "the instant at which the essence of the night approaches as the *other* night."[30]

This "point", Orpheus' work [*oeuvre*] does not however consist in assuring its approach by descending toward the depths. His *oeuvre* is to bring it back to the day and to give it, in the day, form, figure and reality. Orpheus can do everything, except to look directly at this "point", except to look at the center of the night in the night. He can descend toward it, he can — a yet stronger power — draw it to him and, with himself, draw it upward, but while turning away [*s'en détournant*]. This detour is the only way to approach it: such is the sense of the dissimulation which reveals itself in the night.[31]

Blanchot's reader will remember that dissimulation is an economic principle which, although irreducible to power and manifestation, has two basic tendencies. In the world of power, dissimulation "tends to become negation." This is its foundation of that world. In the dimension of essential solitude or proximity, dissimulation "tends to appear." This appearance is a proximity: a presence of absence, the *il y a* of presence beyond negation. Although dissimulation produces both night and day, it is essentially obscured by daylight, in a Heideggerian sense, and its appearance in the night is correlative of manifestation's defection, and is thus not an "appearance" but an approach.

Orpheus' "power" operates in the dimension of dissimulation's tendency toward negation. In the other night, where dissimulation "tends to appear," power is not an organizing principle. The other night is the locus of fascination, indecision, and the "obsession of existence" — the locus of impersonality. Power may enter this dimension only in the form of the deliberate blindness of the *détour* which approaches Eurydice without looking at her, or in the form of Ulysses' cunning, which "hears" the sirens without having to experience their fascination. But this "turning away" of power's calculation is already the more fundamental *détour* of the intentional approach in proximity, already the passivity of *errance* in the desert. The approach and the power permitted by the gods are derisory, because Orpheus' calculation is already the heteronomy of desire. And Orpheus' desire for Eurydice is already the inevitability of looking at her. Desire is the communicational principle of subjectivity, and is thus already the inherence of alterity in closure. Orpheus has entered the other night before he takes a step in its direction. On the other hand, desire as a rapport with alterity is the modality and the pressure of closure itself. Thus Orpheus has been unfaithful to the dispersion and dispossession of the other night, and has turned to look at Eurydice (rather than to "lose himself in Eurydice"), lost her, and returned to the day — before he has taken a step in the direction of the night.

Day and other night are not dialectical opposites. Each is the other's impossibility. Subjectivity insists in the dimension of this impossibility. The events of Orpheus' adventure must be envisaged synchronically, or in the proximal simultaneity of repetition. The only possibility of a rapport with Eurydice, or of an intersubjective rapport in general, is the dissymmetry of the approach. Orpheus' power is his approach to a Eurydice which may be an "ever more initial rapport" or a seizing of her presence "toujours en deçà ou au-delà" — a dropping anchor too late or too soon. This is the approach defined as power. It is always an approach, and never an accomplishment, because it is conditioned by a desire which is correlative of the Other's escape from totalization. Its complement is the approach of alterity in the other night, whose modality is not approximation, but rather the intimacy, inconsistency and intrusion of proximity. In this sense the encounter with Eurydice resembles the encounter with death: "Even when I decide to go to it, by a virile and ideal resolution, is it not [death] still that comes to me, and when I think I seize it, [death] that seizes me, that disposseses [*dessaisit*] me, delivers me to the unseizable?"[32] This second approach is the pre-originary condition of power's approach to exteriority. It is the inherence or proximity of the exterior which makes possible this approach. Orpheus has already encountered Eurydice, is already in her proximity, before he takes a step toward the depths. This proximity is already her escape from him, and his desire. The detour which fails to contact a substantial Eurydice is already and always the "looking" which contacts her excessively and loses her. The duality of the detour and the look conceals a more basic contamination: subjectivity's involvement with the inaccessible. One cannot see Eurydice in the other night — nor can one take one's eyes off her. The proximity of the other is the escape of the other, its intimacy and its irreducible, infinite distance from interiority. To communicate with the other is to discover him within me and outside me, in a twofold moment of escape.

The gods' injuction, and the power granted Orpheus, give the myth the aspect of a dialectic of power and the nocturnal, which would be disturbed by Orpheus' transgression. But his transgression is constitutive of the myth itself. As mentioned above, the *détour* is the only modality of an approach to alterity in the economy. At the same time, the differentiation which creates Eurydice as an alterity is already a looking at her. The only modality of the approach to Eurydice is the proximity and loss of Eurydice. Her only manifestation is her disappearance, and her disappearance is always a "manifestation" — that is, a passivity and an involvement with Orpheus. The existence of Orpheus and of Eurydice is an approach, a transgression, and a loss. The form of this existence is the exigency, understood as an economic principle, and its context is the other night, understood as an irreducible dimension of the economy. The drama of Orpheus, in its synchrony, is the being of interiority and alterity in the general economy. The *oeuvre* is, in ontological terms, the form of this encounter as communication. In empirical terms, every *oeuvre* in its positivity masks an Orphic encounter.

It is from this structure that the multiple predicates of Orpheus' comportment proceed. For instance, Blanchot writes that Orpheus "necessarily forgets" his purpose in the night.[33] This *oubli* or forgetting has a dual meaning. In the first place, Orpheus forgets that Eurydice can only be extricated from the night by his not looking at her — and this forgetting is constitutive of his approach to her. He has already looked. In the second place, he forgets his duty to "save" her, as he enters the fascination of the other night — and this fascination is also constitutive of his movement toward the darkness. *Oubli* — the intrusion within subjectivity of that which should have been held at a distance (to be totalized, to be possessed) — is interiority's transgression of its own closure, and is thus one principle of the approach.

In another formulation, Blanchot defines the turning to look at Eurydice as an "impatience".[34] He opposes this impatience initially to a patience which would, like Ulysses' ruse, have succeeded in drawing Eurydice from the night. Then, thinking better of this opposition, Blanchot subordinates the notion of patience as ruse and power to "true patience" which "does not exclude impatience," which "is its intimacy, it is impatience suffered and endured endlessly."[35] This correction is capital. Impatience is the inevitable separation which is correlative to the approach to Eurydice, the impossibility of "dying in Eurydice." But patience is not the form of a ruse which might have suspended this impossibility. It is rather impossibility itself, as the modality of the approach. "Patience" is defined here, in a Levinasian inspiration, as that more fundamental passivity which is the basic economy of the exigency, even as it takes the apparent form of power. The myth of Orpheus is not a story of power, for Blanchot, though it may be such a story in the text of mythology. Within the context of communication, the myth is the story of an exigency. Orpheus does not willfully "attempt" to save Eurydice. The night, and the nocturnal Eurydice, draw him downward. The myth does not describe power and its frustration, but desire and transgression.

In a section entitled "Le don et le sacrifice"[36] in which the presence and inspiration of Bataille are most palpable, Blanchot associates impatience and *oubli* with the notion of the sacrifice, defined as an "insouciance". Orpheus' infidelity to the sacred gravity of the other night, in its ostensible independence from manifestation, is a dual transgression. Orpheus "betrays Eurydice in favor of the night" on one hand, and betrays the "unapproachable depth" of the night by looking at Eurydice, on the other.[37] The insouciance of this look, which destroys both the approach to Eurydice as power and the approach as fascination or pure dispossession, is a Bataillian transgression, *par excellence.* It is unfaithful to the putative limits of prohibition, and correlatively unfaithful to the explosive negativity which would destroy limits. It is the loss of all possibility, and the notion of an insouciance within its solemnity is an extremely pertinent predication.* Transgression is the innocence and levity of the impossible: an "attempt" made in the secret passivity of a reality without power. By its privileged failure, it "liberates the *oeuvre* from its *souci* [care, seriousness] "[38] and transforms the dialectic of power and other night into an economy of communication.

"Certainly, in turning toward Eurydice, Orpheus ruins the *oeuvre,* the *oeuvre* immediately falls to pieces, and Eurydice returns to the shadows; the essence of the night, under his look, reveals itself as the inessential. Thus he betrays the *oeuvre* and Eurydice and the night."[39] The name for the event in which the *oeuvre,* Eurydice, the night, and Orpheus himself are lost, is the *oeuvre.* The pertinence of the myth of Orpheus, for Blanchot, is the definition of the *oeuvre* as impossibility. From the point of view of the possible – of action – the *oeuvre* will always be inessential. Blanchot suggests that, from the point of view of day (the point of view of power), Orpheus is to be reproached for the excessiveness of his approach to Eurydice. If he had accepted his singing of Eurydice as his only power over her, the disaster would never have taken place. But, writes Blanchot, the song is itself the loss of Eurydice: "He loses Eurydice, because he desires her beyond the measured limits of the song, and he loses himself, but this desire and Eurydice lost and Orpheus dispersed are necessary to the song, as is necessary to the *oeuvre* the ordeal of eternal passivity [*désoeuvrement,* inaction] ."[40] The sacrifice – the passivity, excess, and loss of transgression – is the approach to the *oeuvre.* And the positive existence of the *oeuvre* attests the

---

* The proposition of "insouciance" as the predicate of an exigency whose passivity is inadequate to the notion of *souci* or "care" must be understood as an element in Blanchot's continuing refusal of the Heideggerian predicates for communication. In the present context, it is less the pre-comprehension implied by Heidegger's *Sorge* that Blanchot refuses than it is the logic of "resoluteness", the insensitivity to the communicational proposition of a radical passivity, that characterize both the early and the late Heidegger. See below, Chapter 4.

inessentiality and uselessness of the other night, which escapes totalization but persists in its public passivity, its "simple inability to cease to be." The *oeuvre* exists in a dimension for which neither mobilization and power nor the independence of alterity are determining concepts.

"Le regard d'Orphée" is a meditation upon desire, the approach, and transgression as the context of proximity in literary creation. It is also the ontological derivation of a most important Blanchotian context: the context in which "art cannot compete with action in the terms of action" and in which Blanchot quotes with satisfaction Hegel's dictum that "art for us is a thing of the past." The context of the *oeuvre* is impossibility, and therefore, from the perspective of the possible, failure. The inessentiality of the night, revealed by the *oeuvre*, is the irreducibility of both night and *oeuvre* to the notion of manifestation. The *oeuvre*, like transgression in Bataille, veers toward inexistence and fictionality – not because it is fiction in an intramundane sense, but because it is communication in an ontological sense. Like the imaginary in Blanchot, in which "each thing recedes into its image" economically, and without reference to perception or imagination, literature's irreality stems from its involvement in communication, and not from its common interpretation as "fiction". From the point of view of manifestation, this irreality is the impudence and insouciance of the inexistent. In this sense it resembles the sirens, who must disappear when forced by Ulysses into the alternative of being and nothingness. Do they exist or do they not? "Nothing," writes Levinas, "can arrest this triumphant question." Blanchot accredits this denunciation of art as inessentially, in its most radical sense. Art is not a higher form of being or a higher form of truth. Its only positivity is its tendency to escape truth and being.

Of inspiration, we sense only the failure, we recognize only the wandering [*égarée*: also "mad", "wild"] violence. But if inspiration describes the failure of Orpheus and Eurydice lost twice over, describes the insignificance and emptiness of the night, inspiration, toward this failure and this insignificance, turns and forces Orpheus by an irresistible movement, as though to renounce failure were far more grave than to renounce success, as though what we call the insignificant, the inessential, error, could, to him who accepts its risk and gives himself to it without reserve, reveal itself as the source of all authenticity.[41]

This paragraph does not subordinate action to an authenticity of art. Rather, it describes, in the appropriate mode of the *comme si*, the insistence within the general economy of a positive dimension whose essence is the inessential, whose only authenticity is error, failure, and insignificance. This dimension has no power and dominates nothing. It is Blanchot's genius to refuse it the predication of a higher or other power. The only positivity of the literary space is the strangeness of its approach. It does not exist, but its persistence in a reality without power is uneliminable. Blanchot's involvement with Levinas is attested by his suggestion that, if the notion of existence does not exhaust the reality of the general economy, then the notion of authenticity may not be exhausted by its definition in the terms of power. Authenticity may be a function of impossibility.

The function of inspiration in Blanchot, as in Levinas, is the indication of a rapport between action and impossibility. Inspiration defines artistic creation as an activity which takes place, like involuntary prehension, in a "scarcely human time": the time of the exigency, a dimension of proximity without negation and without power. The *oeuvre,* in this context, becomes less a creation or the artifact of an activity than the scene or dimension of an exigency whose definition is communicational. The priority of the exigency in creation will be the derivation of Blanchot's characterization of the *oeuvre* as less, or other, than a real object. (See below.)

As discussed earlier (Chaper 1), the classical concept of inspiration is of interest to Blanchot to the extent that it implies an event which exceeds the power of an interiority to engender an *oeuvre,* but its interest is limited by its thematization of a higher power which engenders through the medium of subjectivity. This thematization subordinates heteronomy to determination and power, and thus reproduces in its exaltation of art the logic of the technological dimension it would have art escape. Blanchot's meditation of inspiration consists of a systematic withdrawal of power from its multiple predicates. It is this disqualification of power as an economic principle that structures the paradoxes of his demonstration.

Inspiration, prior to its status as an engendering instance, is a situation of subjectivity in communication. It is a proximity and a heteronomy which may produce effects such as interiority, mastery, and the text or *oeuvre.* Conceived as a proximity, it has a problematic accessibility to the traditional notion of inspiration as a source or origin. Like the heteronomous circulation of difference or information, inspiration is a context of differentiation which makes possible notions such as causality or determination, without being itself accessible to such notions. Differentiation produces discontinuities which are not negations, but which may be mobilized as such by a logic of determination which subordinates communication to autonomy, in forms such as the origin.

Subjectivity in inspiration is a moment of differentiation whose economy is an intrication with exteriority. The basic effect of this inadequacy of closure is the *parole* (which comes to be called, in *L'Entretien infini,* "parole d'écriture"), and its context is impersonality, defined as the irreducibility of communication to the proposition of a self-coincident subjectivity. The *parole* is that excess which proceeds from closure's *écart* (its incompletion and alteration) and consequent rapport with the exterior. In inspiration and impersonality, subjectivity is "not alone". Its economic constitution makes of every *parole,* in the apt phrase which organizes Jacques Derrida's reading of Artaud,[42] a "parole soufflée": a word which is secretly inserted into subjectivity by the exterior, and stolen from subjectivity by the exterior in the moment of enunciation. Interiority's involvement with this *parole,* underneath its ostensible initiative and self-coincidence, is a dual dispossession. The *parole* is the form of interiority's excess and heteronomy. However — and this is perhaps the true economy of proximity and difference — the *parole* is the very possibility of subjectivity's separation. It is not only the excess of dispossession — it is also the pressure of closure. Subjectivity's conation is a withdrawal from the economy which is also a withdrawal into the economy: a turgid, exigent closure which is already a spasm toward the exterior. The *parole* proceeds from this paroxysm of closure's excess. The sound or noise of the *parole* in the economy is the impossibility of subjectivity's immobility and silence within the universal. This movement and resonance are correlative to heteronomy and the impossibility of closure, and also to differential alteration as a non-reciprocal or dissymetrical *sens unique* (a "one way" orientation or univocity) in being which inclines closure toward the exterior. This inclination or forcing of closure is incompatible with the notion of a systematic stability of entities whose differential equilibrium would substitute for their lost identity. The movement of the differential trace in proximity constitutes an interiority whose closure is always the *parler* and the *pour l'autre* of excess and heteronomy, rather than the relative stability of an informational nexus.

The possibility of the *parole* in the economy is the replacement of negative constitution by differential intrication. The absence of negativity in this economy is necessarily an absence of causality and of the possibility of a source or origin. Communication differentiates and individuates without totalizing. The "parole soufflée" of communication is not an instance which would proceed from alterity in the manner of a power, but is precisely the impossibility of such a separation of Other and Same, and the impossibility of power. The *parole* does not come from an external totality to invest a non-totalized interiority. It proceeds rather from the lack of totalization which characterizes the general economy as a whole. It is within this economic context that Blanchot discusses inspiration and the lack of inspiration. These two concepts are not posited by him in a relation of opposition, but in a necessary congruence:

In [the *parole*], the poem is close [*proche*] to the origin, for everything that is original stands the test of this pure impotence of repetition [*recommencement*], this sterile prolixity, the superabundance of that which can do nothing, of that which is never an *oeuvre* ["work", "action"], ruins the *oeuvre* and restores in it endless passivity [*désoeuvrement*]. Perhaps it is the source, but a source which in a certain way must be dried up in order to become a resource.[43]

The informational proximity of subjectivity's *parole* to a strategically invoked "source" or "origin" is the communicational constitution of closure as exigency and excess. It is the priority of communication that defines closure as "excessively closed and not closed enough." The excess of closure in the general economy is its breach and its *dépense*: an invasion by the exterior, a spasm toward the exterior, and a remainder left within the exterior. It is this excess that informs the definition of the *parole* as a production without power, and an excess or fragmentary remainder rather than an integral entity. Like the subjectivity which produces it, the *parole* is an excess and an insufficiency — a "sterile prolixity, the superabundance of that which can do nothing," or, in another formulation, a "satiety which has nothing."[44] The impossibility of closure of which the *parole* is the paradoxical positivity, is also necessarily the impossibility of a source or origin. In Levinasian terms, the *parole* is essentially a *bruit* or noise which proceeds from the impossibility of totalization within the economy. Were such a totalization possible, the entities of the economy would be capable of "remaining at their posts" within a system of determinations, and the *parole* as excess would be silenced.

The economy of the *parole* includes no source, and proceeds from the absence of a source. Inspiration — the heteronomy of closure — does not proceed from a totality, nor does it approach interiority as to a totality. It comes from within and without. It invests and dispossesses from an exterior with which heteronomous interiority is intricated. Therefore, the gesture of "returning to the source" in this economy discovers not a reservoir but a lack. The source, like all closure, is an excess and an insufficiency: an "empty plenitude", in Blanchot's words. Its engendering of information is precisely its lack, which is not produced by negativity, but which insists within negativity, making origination impossible. This coincidence of surfeit and lack, which is correlative to the impossibility of a location of origination, links inspiration with *erreur,* and the writer who turns to the source of inspiration with the *errant* or wandering exile: "as though the richness he plumbs, this superabundance of the source, were also an extreme poverty, were above all the superabundance of a refusal, made of him the man who does not produce, who wanders [*erre*] in an infinite inaction [*désoeuvrement*]."[45] The approach to the source is an *erreur* in the Blanchotian sense of a detour which cannot attain its object. But inspiration itself is the larger movement of *errance,* considered as exile and the *pour l'autre* which forces subjectivity toward the outside, requiring it to "desert its post" as a function of remaining at its post. The *parole* as a sound is also *errance* as movement. And in itself, in the public passivity of its circulation as the literary *oeuvre,* the *parole* is always a *parole errante,* "outside itself" by virtue of its fragmentary economy.[46]

On the basis of these economic definitions, Blanchot returns, in one of several such moments in *L'Espace littéraire,* to the empirical dimension of literary creation, and founds within his own logic the coincidence of richness and sterility in inspiration which has been attested by so many artists:

Common sense is thus wrong to believe that the state of aridity to which the most inspired artists are exposed signifies that inspiration — this gift which is given and withdrawn — suddenly fails them. It is necessary to say rather that there is a point at which inspiration and the lack of inspiration merge, an extreme point at which inspiration. . . takes the name or aridity, becomes this absence of power, this impossibility that the artist vainly interrogates, which is a nocturnal state. . . .[47]

Inspiration is not a gift or possession, but an impossibility whose form is the passivity of *dépense*: an excess which always has, from the point of view of possibility, the status of a privation. Ultimately, however, as artists also attest, inspiration is not a privation, but rather impossibility as "affirmation": a communication without negation and without power. As Levinas states so compellingly in the context of *jouissance* and the *il y a*, inspiration is the plenitude and fulfillment of an element which invests, and already the spasm of a rapport with alterity which dispossesses. The "pneumatism of proximity" for Levinas is a breathless *essoufflement* in which subjectivity's inspiration by the Other forces it to breathe out the *parole* without ever having the privilege of breathing in.[48] Inspiration is interiority's *pour l'autre*: the intensity of closure as a permanence of loss.

The word *désoeuvrement*, in the context of inspiration and the source, indicates not only *errance* and lack of location, but also the global sense of impossibility in the economy, which is inspiration's true context. The production of the *oeuvre* "makes the *oeuvre* impossible," writes Blanchot, because it is "that which never allows [us] to arrive at the *oeuvre*, the *en deçà** in which nothing is made of being, in which nothing accomplishes itself, the depth of being's *désoeuvrement*."[49] *Désoeuvrement* (inaction, confusion, passivity) is impossibility: the real without power. In *Le Livre à venir*, Blanchot articulates this impossibility with the negligence and insouciance characteristic of transgression,[50] and, in a formulation which echoes Levinasian responsibility, describes the contaminated structure of guilt and innocence by which inspiration is incumbent upon the writer:

There, certainly, there is no more fault, but no innocence, nothing that can bind [*lier*] me, free [*délier*] me, nothing for which "I" have to answer, for what can be asked of him who has left the possible behind? Nothing — except this which is the strangest exigency: that through him speaks that which is without power, that on this basis the *parole* appears itself as the absence of power, this nudity, the impotence, but also the impossibility, which is the primary movement of communication.[51]

---

* *En deçà* in French means the opposite of *au delà* ("beyond"): "on this side of". Its temporal resonance in Blanchot is the *à venir* of being which does not "yet" include totalization, and the tension (*attente, attention*) of the general economy's disturbance by the movements and emissions which proceed from totalization's failure.

The involvement of subjectivity with an instance which has no power creates the peculiar responsibility of impossibility – a responsibility for something over which one has no control, and by which one is not controlled. This will be Levinasian responsibility: the pure incumbence or gravity of the impossible, and the non-indifference of interiority toward alterity. Blanchot's perception of a solidarity between this gravity and the negligence of transgression not only describes his affinity with Levinas, but also what is perhaps the most intense point of the Bataille-Blanchot-Levinas proximity. For all three thinkers, the levity of excess is also and always the pressure – the approach – of the Other.

One basic logical condition of this responsibility for and to alterity, in both Blanchot and Levinas, is the repetitive temporality of the impossible, in its pre-originary moment. Inspiration for Levinas is a *récurrence*: an awakening of subjectivity which finds itself already involved in a drama for which it is responsible. For Blanchot, inspiration is Orpheus' adventure: a mobilization of possibility which, when Eurydice has been lost, realizes too late its essential rapport with impossibility, and realizes that its unwavering trajectory toward failure is its only "authenticity". Inspiration is a pre-voluntary and pre-originary pact made with impossibility, before the awakening of the possible within a world of totalities. The multiple invocations of repetition as indefinition, *ressassement* etc. in Blanchot's text must not be conceived as lacking the violent intensity of proximity. Instead, their relation to the immemorial disaster of Orpheus must be understood to be fundamental.

Writing begins with Orpheus' look, and this look is the movement of desire which breaks the destiny and the care [*souci*] of the song and, in this inspired and insouciant decision, attains the origin, consecrates the song. But, to descend toward this instant, Orpheus already needed the power [*puissance*] of art. This means: one writes only if one has reached this instant toward which one can only move, however, in the space opened by the movement of writing. To write, it is necessary already to write.[52]

This is the sense of the *parole's* repetitive pre-existence in Blanchot: "where speaking [*parler*] precedes, not this or that word [*parole*], but the possibility of the *parole*, where speaking always precedes itself."[53] The *parler* and the *écrire* pre-exist themselves, but not as possibilities. Their pre-existence points to the production of impossibility in being. This is the pre-originary moment of Blanchot's time "without beginning", "without decision", "without initiative". By thinking impossibility in time, Blanchot thinks, in his own way, the passive synthesis which has occupied Levinas for many years. Temporalization, for both thinkers, is a heteronomous communication which conditions the spontaneity of manifestation. And passivity is the one necessary and sufficient predicate which distinguishes subjectivity as an ontological instance from the thematics of manifestation in which it is traditionally embedded.

The writer's involvement with the impossible, prior to his "first steps toward the night" is, as shown in the context of Orpheus, an involvement with the inessential, the unavailable, the radically useless. Blanchot is attentive to creative writers' attestation of their work as the "must" and the "cannot" of the exigency in impossibility. But he is also attentive to the writer's feeling of control over "everyday words", his confidence in his own power of mobilization. This ambivalence of the inspired artist who is also the artisan is the necessary intensity of the exigency. "And because the writer thinks he can be both the one and the other – the man who has words at his disposal [*dispose des mots*] and this locus in which the unavailable [*indisponible*] that is language escapes all division, is pure indetermination, – he acquires the illusion that he has the unavailable at his disposal and, in this originary *parole,* say everything and give a voice and a *parole* to everything."[54] The initial hesitation and ultimate thematic movement of *La Littérature et le mal* are inscribed in this single sentence. The illusion of possibility is an essential vicissitude of creative writing's approach to the night. Blanchot's following sentence contains, in many ways, the force of his incalculable advance over literary criticism: "But is this an illusion?" On one hand, the confidence of the writer's installation within the possible is his very movement toward the night. His confidence is Orpheus' insouciance. Its failure or inadequacy is a function of transgression and impossibility, and far exceeds the universe of "illusion" and "reality". But beyond this optimistic attestation of a possibility on its way to impossibility, Blanchot's statement recalls that the night *is* the inessential, a dimension without truth and without authenticity – and that the writer's control is not an illusion, but the truth of the world of possibility. This truth is a positive ontological event. It is inadequate to the excess of the night, but this inadequacy is not to be compared to an attitude or comportment which would be appropriate to the nocturnal dimension. Transgression does not reproduce the ontology of totalization. It cannot compare to action in the terms of action. If illusion may be said to exist in the general economy, then illusion – the uselessness of inaction and impossibility – is a primary predicate of inspiration. Truth and its correlate, the power to accomplish what was attempted, have an effective existence within the "world" of the possible. Like Levinas, who accredits Husserl's subordination of the passive synthesis to intentionality, and Bataille who insists upon an intense reality of the profane world, Blanchot situates the positivity of action, rather than to overwhelm it by a metaphysics of dispersion and passivity. Totalization is a regional function of communication, and action is a function of transgression. These functions have effective existence. They are not subordinate to a proximity which has a higher value or a greater effectivity. If accomplishment exists within the general economy, it will be their province, their familiarity. The man who has left the possible behind accomplishes nothing.

"One must work for the day," writes Blanchot. "Yes, one must."[55] When the creative writer holds fast to this truth of his control over the indefinite, when he interprets his creations as his personal accomplishment and begins to repeat himself, ceasing to write inspired literature. Blanchot approves this failure as well. Similarly, he will approve the "inauthentic" public dimension of rumor, curiosity, and "impersonal avidity" in which the *oeuvre* circulates and is misunderstood.[56] If the question of inspiration and communication must be posed in terms of authenticity and inauthenticity, then Blanchot does not hesitate to inscribe not only the prudent retreat into the public dimension of fame and self-parody, but also the Orphic approach to the night, into the dimension of inauthenticity. In this he repeats and founds Bataille's fundamental reading of Baudelaire. The authenticity of accomplishment and comprehension belongs to a world that has renounced failure: the world of possibility. Inspiration draws the artist outside the world — "outside himself and perhaps outside everything." His comportment is no longer an action, his *oeuvre* no longer an accomplishment.

Inspiration is a heteronomy whose density is the only constitution of subjectivity in artistic creation. This is the situation of subjectivity within a general economy. Secondly, inspiration is a *parole* which results from the dissymmetry of subjectivity's rapport with exteriority. This is the *sens unique* of difference in the economy, and the murmur of proximity within the universal. Thirdly, inspiration proceeds from an exteriority that is not a source or origin — and this is the economy's irreducibility to negation and totalization. Fourthly, inspiration is impossibility and the exigency: subjectivity's involvement in a reality without power, and the paradoxical incumbence or force of this rapport. Concomitant to this incumbence is the irreducibility of inspiration to authenticity and inessentiality. In Blanchot as in Bataille, the *oeuvre* proceeds from *dépense,* and therefore from the enigma of the radically useless and unavailable, in a world of power. Finally, inspiration is a temporality of repetition as pre-originarity. It describes the latent insistence and passivity of the other night in Orpheus' decision to enter and frustrate the nocturnal.

In addition, Blanchot situates in the recent history of art a tendency of inspired artists to intuit the impossibility of inspiration as it applies to their activity. "The *oeuvre* is no longer innocent, it knows where it comes from." he writes.[57] The writer who becomes aware of impossibility in the *oeuvre,* "where possibility is in play," realizes that his activity leads him away from activity itself: "it is there that [the *oeuvre*] pushes the artist, far from it and far from its accomplishment."[58] In his renunciation of work after work, his tendency toward fragmentary works and his fascination with impossibility, the artist attests the approach of a new origin and a new comportment: "to make of the *oeuvre* a path toward inspiration. . . and not of inspiration a path toward the *oeuvre*."[59] Here, a new dimension of proximal time reveals itself: the *à venir* of the *oeuvre,* and the appearance of the imaginary in the song of the sirens.

APPROACH OF THE LITERARY SPACE

If *L'Espace littéraire* may be said to describe the rapport of the writer to the experience of proximity in literary creation, *Le Livre à venir* may be said to describe the rapport of fiction to the real in proximity. "Le Chant des sirènes"[60] is the inauguration of this problematic. In this essay, Blanchot designates in an economic sense the effective and positive insistence of fiction as an "irreality" within the real, and summarizes the necessary predicates and conditions of this insistence. His analysis consists of (1) a meditation of Ulysses' approach to the sirens, (2) a definition of the *récit* and the novel in terms of the approach of the fictional event (*événement*), and (3) a description, in terms of metamorphosis and temporality, of the production of irreality as proximity.

The sirens' song is a fascination and a "marvel", an unreal and mythological instance which lures sailors to their deaths by virtue of its "imaginary" status. Their error is to confuse the dimension of their power with the dimension of irreality. Blanchot notes that it is often supposed that the sirens are a "natural" instance which produces an illusory attraction, and that the fascination of their song is its uncanny reproduction of human song. This pragmatic supposition of a "natural" origin of the sirens' attraction is welcomed by Blanchot because it unwittingly situates the imaginary or fictive within the real as a problematic positivity, rather than to accredit its status as an entirely unreal or inexistent factor. The stangeness of their song, in its precise imitation of human song, contaminates the duality of reality and unreality, and makes the reality of human song suspect: "because the sirens. . . could sing the way men sing, they made the song so strange that they gave birth in him who heard it to the suspicion of the inhumanity of all human song."[61] The sirens, like involuntary prehension, reveal the implication of a "scarcely human time" in the positivity of human accomplishment. The strictly "natural" origin of their song describes an approach of the imaginary within the actual. This imaginary is not, however, a faculty of consciousness or a modification of intentionality. It is rather the "appearance" – the approach – of proximity as dissimulation, considered as an "extraordinary" event within the economy of reality. It is the time of fascination and proximal differentiation, "a time without negation, without decision, when here is truly nowhere, when each thing recedes into its image. . .".[62] The appearance of the image in dissimulation is the positive economic event upon which a philosophical definition of the imaginary may be founded – and not the reverse. The sirens are the nocturnality of the day, the appearance of dissimulation, and the latent economy of actuality in *espacement,* "when space becomes the approach of another space."[63] From this perspective, it is important to accredit the "real", "natural" aspect of the sirens" illusory call. They are not an absolute otherness, but rather the otherness of the "here below", the otherness of familiarity. "It is thus through despair that the men who were impassioned by their own song perished? By a despair very close to rapture. There was something marvelous in this real song, common, secret song, simple, everyday song. . .".[64] The sirens' song is the production of irreality within the real. It is space as the approach of alterity; it is intentionality become "passion", manifestation become the "obsession of being". It is communication's excess over manifestation. Its simplicity and everydayness are the familiarity of the uncanny, attested by Freud.

Ulysses' strategy is the strategy, or indeed the being, of power in the general economy. Lashed to the mast by his crew whose own ears are stopped with wax, Ulysses alone listens to the sirens; but, in a paradoxical ruse, by arresting his own power to approach them, he arrests the force of their fascination and attraction. Thus he mobilizes power to thwart desire. At the same time he constrains them to accomplish their existence within a dimension of power, and to produce theselves within the dimension of negation. Ulysses reduces the general economy to the duality of being and non-being, and this is his triumph — power's triumph — over the imaginary. "Ulysses' attitude, this astonishing deafness of the man who is deaf because he hears, suffices to communicate to the sirens a despair reserved until now for men, and to make of them, by this despair, beautiful real girls, for one moment real and worthy of their promise, and thus capable of disappearing in the truth and the depth of their song."[65] The sirens, like all manifestations of proximity, have no power. Power is not the dimension of their domination. Constrained either to "exist" or not "exist", they disappear. This is power's efficiency, superimposed over its rapport with proximity; and it is power's triumphant blindness. Ulysses is one of a very few cultural figures who elicit from Blanchot a note of true concept. "There has always been a less than noble effort by men to discredit the sirens by accusing them meanly of lying: liars when they sang, deceitful when they sighed, fictive when one touched them: in all, inexistent, of a puerile inexistence that Ulysses' good sense suffices to exterminate."[66] To question the existence of the sirens is to pose incorrectly the question of their reality; but, in Levinas' words, "nothing can arrest this triumphant question."[67] The reality of the sirens is the positivity of negation's remainder, the "presence of absence" which is the appearance of dissimulation. The rapport of power to this reality of the irreal is the blindness of its retreat into its own regionality — a retreat which is also, unknown to itself, an "organization" of proximity, a retreat into the general economy, like the Bataillian *interdit* which "organizes violence" rather than to abolish it. But the sirens, like art, "cannot compete with action in the terms of action," and must disappear when engulfed by the context of manifestation.

Every *récit**, in its accomplishment, reposes upon the priority of Orpheus' transgression. The purpose of "Le Chant des sirènes" is to designate a complementary, paradoxical futurity which conditions the presence of the *récit* in the general economy. Blanchot calls this futurity an *événement* or "event". It is, on one hand, the putative event whose narration is the purpose of the *récit*, and on the other hand, the event of the *récit's* production within the economy. On the level of its "pretention", the *récit* recounts an extraordinary event, "an exceptional event which escapes the forms of everyday time and the world of habitual

---

* The French word *récit* describes a recounting, telling, or reciting, and thus the communicational genre "story" or "narrative". Every novel or story is a *récit*, but the *récit* itself is a more general moment of communication, a pure "telling" of an event, whose economic implications Blanchot will meditate. In order to retain the sense of an irreducibility to literary genres, the word *récit* will not be translated for the present discussion.

truth," and, Blanchot adds, "perhaps of all truth."[68] This tendency of the exceptional to escape manifestation proceeds from the problematic economic status of the event, which is not only the object of the telling, but already the sole context or economy of the telling. "The *récit* is not the relating of the event, but the event itself, the approach of this event, the place where the latter is called to produce itself, an event still to come [*à venir*] and by whose attracting power the *récit* can hope to realize itself as well."[69] The sense of these striking definitions is that the production of the *récit* in the economy must pass through the positivity of the event within the economy. There can be no telling of a fiction without the effective economic reality of that fiction. This is why every *récit* has encountered the sirens, i.e. that point in the economy at which manifestation and power encounter proximity and the imaginary.

Blanchot's demonstration reposes upon the proposition of a positive existence of the fictive within the real; and this proposition reposes upon the definition of the real as proximity. The following passage from "L'infini littéraire: l'Aleph", describes this economic priority of proximity:

Literature is not a simple deception, it is the dangerous power to go toward that which is, through the infinite multiplicity of the imaginary. The difference between the real and the irreal, the inestimable privilege of the real, is that there is less reality in reality, which is merely irreality denied [*niée*], pushed away [*écartée*] by the energetic work of negation and by that negation that is work itself. It is this "less", a sort of reducing, of thinning of space, which allows us to go from one point to another, following the fortunate aspect of the straight line.[70]

It is in this sense of the positivity of irreality that Blanchot often says the *oeuvre* draws the writer outside himself, "outside the world," "outside everything". Literary creation draws subjectivity out of proximity's region of manifestation and totalization, and places it within the dimension in which dissimulation "appears" or approaches. Blanchot's gesture is entirely characteristic of the discursive procedure by which Bataille, Levinas and Blanchot himself establish, through the technical means of phenomenology's totalizations, the insistence of a domain "outside the totality" but within a general economy that is not a totality.

The *récit* produces an event, but the conditions of possibility of this production are not those of the world of negation. Both the event as object and the event as context including its telling, are constituted economically by proximity. The paradox which describes this economy is that the event as object or "happening" is a futurity to which the *récit* "calls", but must be at the same time a pre-originary condition of this calling. Both the happening and the relating which "calls" are proximal realities which cannot be totalized; and their rapport is itself a proximity which attests this foreclosing of totalization. This rapport, and the production of both its moments, appears in a proximal temporality in which the future is incumbent upon the putative "present".

This is a very delicate rapport, doubtless a sort of extravagance, but it is the secret law of the *récit*. The *récit* is a movement toward a point which is not only unknown, unsuspected, foreign, but such that it does not seem to have, in advance and outside this movement, any sort of reality, so imperious however that it is from it alone that the *récit* draws [*tire*] its attraction [*attrait*], in such a manner that it cannot even "begin" before having attained it, but it is only the *récit*, however, and the unforeseeable movement of the *récit* which furnish the space in which the point becomes real, powerful and attractive [*attirant*].[71]

In the duality of *récit* and event, Bataillian transgression, in which neither limit nor transgressive movement have any positive existence outside their violent congruence, may be perceived. This duality is a proximity and a communication whose positivity is the absence of that negation which would permit either entity to accomplish its existence. It is the same default of negativity that creates, as in all proximal situations, an instance whose inconsistency, indefiniteness, and evanescence are rigorously correlative to its urgency and incumbence. It is precisely the "irreality" of the event that compels or forces the *récit*, that weighs upon it from the future in the proximal temporality of imminence.

The *récit* exists only as the approach of an event. But this approach is not the groping *détour* of the search for inspiration's source. It is rather the more fundamental approach of alterity "from inside" in the *sens unique* of communication's dissymetry in the economy. Like the approach of the other beast in the burrow, it is indefinite and inactual, but infinitely compelling — more compelling and urgent than any presence — because its approach is its pre-originary involvement with interiority. In order for the *Odyssey* to be produced, it is necessary for Ulysses to have already encountered the sirens. In order that *Moby Dick* may be produced, Ahab must have encountered the whale. And this encounter has taken place: "already", but also "not yet", and "never" — if the encounter, like the sirens, is constrained to exist in an economy exhausted by manifestation. It is only within the impoverished logic of what Blanchot calls the "negation of irreality" that these moments, and their congruence, might lack the plenitude of existence. In the economy of proximity, the very incompletion of both event and encounter is the excess of their insistence. Their proximity is a "meeting so imposing, so excessive and so particular that it overflows all the levels on which it occurs, all the moments at which one would situate it."[72] Like the Blanchotian *parole* which "speaks when all has been said," the resonance of the event in the *récit* is "the resounding in advance of that which has not been said and never will be."[73] The effective being of its *à venir* is the "already" by which it conditions the appearance of the *récit*.

The event is a futurity and an immemorial past or trace. But the *récit*, by virtue of its communication with the event and by their mutual determination of the event as the totality of that communication, is also less than, or other than, an empirical object. "What would happen," writes Blanchot, "if Ulysses and Homer, rather than to be distinct persons sharing commodiously divided roles, were a single, same presence?"[74] Homer's "power" to recount, and his very existence as an author, are conditioned by the fictional existence of Ulysses and of Ulysses' adventure. Homer is the proximity of this congruence, by virtue of his entry into impersonality, on one hand, and of his entry into fiction, on the other. In a formulation which both anticipates and dismantles the aims of formalist literary criticisms, Blanchot writes: "This is one of the strangenesses, let us say one of the pretentions, of the *récit*. It 'relates' only itself, and this relating, at the same time that it accomplishes itself, produces what it relates, is only possible as a relating if it realizes what occurs in the relation. . . ".[75] The heteronomy of the *récit* in proximity, as in a differential economy, is both the privacy of the text of formalism, and the secondarity of the text's dependence on an exterior instance. This secondarity and dependence exceed the submissive aspect of the representational or referential text, and the Blanchotian "solitude" of the *récit* describes the very impossibility of an auto-referentiality. In proximity, the text is not alone. Its escape from totalization is its extreme passivity.

In a general formulation of repetition, Blanchot writes: "this evokes the quandary of the first man, if, to be created, he had needed to pronounce himself, in an entirely human manner, the divine *Fiat lux* capable of opening his eyes."[76] This statement of the *récit*'s heteronomy reflects the ambiguity of the *cogito* in Levinas, and of many figures in proximity which pre-exist themselves in a communicational duration. This pre-originarity describes the event as the object of the *récit*, but it also describes the overall insistence of the *récit* as an event in the economy. The *récit* is entirely futural — a *livre à venir* — in its very presence. And it is thus a repetition, like the time of its creation: the time without "decision" or "initiative" which nevertheless conditions the writer's activity. This lack of a philosophically defined punctuality or effectivity, based on the event's indifference to negation and manifestation, leads to a rare Blanchotian response to possible objections: "But is this not a naive madness? In a sense. This is why there is no *récit*, this is why there is no lack of a *récit*."[77] No formulation could better describe the irreducibility of the *récit*, and of Blanchot's discourse in its entirety, to traditional and contemporary theories of literature. The *récit* does not exist or fail to exist because it appears in, and attests, a reality without negation. Within the general economy in its excess over manifestation, Blanchot's statement is not contradictory. Yet this problematic insistence of the *récit* would be, from the point of view of possibility, a naiveté, and the frivolous madness of the inessential. And this strange levity of the impossible — "the frivolity of the eternal and the heaviness of the imaginary", in Blanchot's words — is in fact literature's enigmatic positivity.

The third context of the *récit*'s definition is that of passage and the metamorphosis. The *récit* is the event of the metamorphosis which links Homer and Ulysses, Melville and Ahab, the quotidian and imaginary, the navigation and the sirens. Its overall context in Blanchot is the metamorphosis constitutive of interiority in proximity, discussed earlier in the proposition of the *nouvelle origine*. In a most general sense, all effectivity or self-coincidence in the general economy is a metamorphosis, defined as an alteration or becoming-other of the Same, and its correlate, the non-indifference of the *pour l'autre.*

When navigation approaches the island of the sirens, it is already the sirens who are approaching the navigators. No one can attain and drop anchor at the Isle of Capri, writes Blanchot, "no one can steer for this island, and he who would have so decided would only proceed however by chance [*hasard*], a chance to which he is linked by an understanding [*entente,* accord] difficult to penetrate."[78] The approach to a destination is a detour, a chance or *hasard* which contaminates causality, and always a dropping of the anchor too late or too soon. But this frustrated approach is already the approach of the destination, of alterity, from its own dimension — the approach of another space — and it is this second approach that transforms navigation into indecision and *errance.* This is the sense of metamorphosis as the correlate of the approach. When we sail toward the exterior in the virility of resolution, it is already the approach of the exterior that changes us, that alters our resolution. In time, metamorphosis is one of several familiar notions whose structure confounds their intramundane context. Like all becoming, the moment of metamorphosis is a temporal ambiguity. "A" is already the imminence of "B", already the positive existence of "B", and already, in the instant, an immemorial intrication of "A" with the priority of "B". "A" is essentially the approach and the pre-originarity of "B". The only positivity of unicity is this becoming-other. The "not yet" of alterity in metamorphosis is both the urgency of its approach and the repetitive indefinition of its irreality.* Blanchot describes this proximal temporality in the phase, "peu à peu quoique aussitôt" — "little by little although already."[79] This phase is heavy with Blanchotian meanings. It describes the gravity of the "always-already" and the slowness and monotony of the *non-concernant;* the immemorial surprise of the unexpected, which is inadequate to anticipation, and the paradoxical sense in *oubli* that "there is nothing new under the sun"; and the enigma of repetition as a production of the new. Metamorphosis is the existence of the writer or the subject in communication, and it is also the problematic being of the event. The *livre à venir* is the literary space as the "approach of another space," the alteration of space "in which nothing happens [*se passe*] except this very passage."[80] It is a fundamental appearance of dissimulation — of communication — and of metamorphosis in being,[81] "when each thing recedes into its image," when "space is the vertigo of *espacement.*"

The dimension of which fiction is the approach, is proximity. Blanchot speaks of a "metaphysical" struggle between Ahab and the whale, between Ulysses and the sirens. His vocabulary echoes the perennial movement of desire in proximity: "Each one of these parts wants to be all [*tout*], wants to be the absolute world, which makes impossible its coexistence with the other absolute world, and each one however has no greater desire than this coexistence and this meeting."[82]

---

* "Always still to come, always already past, always present in a beginning so abrupt that it takes your breath away, and yet deploying itself as a return and an eternal beginning again (. . .), such is the event of which the *récit* is the approach."[83]

Each of these instances is the other's impossibility, and the impossibility of a dialectical relation of both. The priority of the one is that which forecloses the other's accomplishment of its existence. And yet the urgency of each entity, and the intensity of their encounter, is the paradoxically effective existence of both entities as impossibilities, "having no reality outside this encounter." The force of their "struggle" is the modality of desire in proximity: the very movement by which one instance, in order to complete itself, must force the other to take a "distance" approaching absence, and the correlative "come closer" of a desire to engulf the other within totalization. Because of the priority of the communicational alteration which renders each imminent totality inherent to the other, the desire to eliminate alterity is always the desire of the encounter itself. Desire is the turgid exigency of a closure involved with the Other. Separation in proximity is always this attraction or *attrait* and this *attente* or imminence in being, although not on the model of a gravitation. The center of gravity of the exigent totality is outside itself. What Blanchot calls a "struggle" between manifestation and fiction is precisely their proximity and their production of an economy. The immensity of this economic moment is impossibility in being, an impossibility which surrounds and conditions the poverty of the phenomenal world, and of which Blanchot says with ironic regret: "To unite in a single space Ahab and the whale, the Sirens and Ulysses, here is the secret wish that makes of Ulysses Homer and of Ahab Melville, and of the world which results from this union the greatest, most terrible and most beautiful of possible worlds, alas a book, nothing but a book."[84]

"Le chant des sirènes" is a meditation of the possibility of fiction's reality in the general economy, and a thematization through the temporality of the event, of fiction's problematic rapport with phenomenality and negation. As mentioned above, this demonstration is complementary to the problematic of impersonality in literary creation. The approach of the other night in *L'Espace littéraire* is correlative to the approach of the sirens and the fictional event in *Le Livre à venir*. Blanchot states this correlation within "Le chant des sirènes" by means of the phrase, "les puissances irréelles (inspirées)" — "irreal (inspired) powers".[85] In a later section entitled "La recherche du point zéro", he describes the context of this congruence, in answer to the question of language's metamorphosis into literature:

It is that the only world in which it is given to us to use things be first collapsed, that things first be infinitely separated [*éloignées*] from themselves, have become again the unavailable distance of the image; it is also that I no longer be myself and that I can no longer say "me". A redoubtable transformation. What I have through fiction, I have, but on the condition of being it, and the being through which I approach it is that which dispossesses me of myself and of all being, as it makes of language no longer that which speaks, but that which is, language become the passive [*désoeuvrée*] depth of being, the milieu in which the name becomes being, but neither signifies nor illuminates [*dévoile*].[86]

In order for language to become literature, both language and subjectivity itself must be defined as moments of communication rather than of manifestation. In the approach of the literary space, dispossession becomes the form of their unicity. Under the weight of this approach, passivity becomes the form of an *attente* in being which is the paradoxical effectivity of the literary space: not the efficiency of a totalization, but the incumbence of an approach. The escape of alterity from manifestation in Blanchot is not the privacy of the "absolutely other" whose very absolution consecrates the pertinence of the critical gesture which notates its escape and its unavailability to a metaphysics of presence, totalization or autonomy. Alterity in proximity is the hyperbole of an absence which is more immediate in its approach than any presence. And this may be the most fundamental irreducibility of proximity to the concept of difference in its contemporary vicissitudes — although not in its basic economic implications. The communicational trace in proximity, as in difference, indicates an escape, an unavailability, and a lack of terminus. As Blanchot writes, the encounter with the sirens "is always elsewhere [*à l'écart*] than the place and the moment at which it affirms itself, because it is this very *écart*."[87] This *écart* is not a negativity, but is negativity's deferral and impossibility. It is the *écart* of difference itself, as Bataille discovered it in the *glissement* — but not only as escape and indefinite circulation. It is the approach hidden within the non-reciprocity and the *sens unique* of differential alteration — an approach which extricates alterity from its absolution and inscribes it within the violence of the economy. The axes of this inscription in Blanchot are the "book to come" and the "approach of the literary space" as they constitute the ambiguity of the *oeuvre*.

THE OEUVRE

The term *"oeuvre"* in Blanchot refers to literary communication, defined as a paradoxically passive self-sufficiency which is independent from its creator on one hand, and from the dimension of manifestation and comprehension on the other. The *oeuvre* is not simply a document or artifact created by a writer, nor is it the totality of his published and unpublished "production". It is rather the overall communicational dimension of his creative activity, defined as the failure of that activity to engender a totality. This failure proceeds from the basic economy of closure in proximity. Closure is an intense incompletion which produces a fragmentary, irrecuperable remainder as a function of its very density. Against this background, the only autonomy or self-sufficiency of the *oeuvre* is the strange privacy of what Blanchot calls its "refusal" or "reserve" — that is, an "independence" from manifestation which is precisely the *oeuvre*'s failure of totalization, its *inachèvement* or incompletion. It is this radical incompletion, in its proximity to the writer, that engenders the problematic predicates of the rapport between writer and *oeuvre*. At the same time, writing is an essentially public comportment, and the *oeuvre* is a rapport to what Mallarmé calls the "approach of a reader." But this rapport is also structured by incompletion and communication; and it is this structure that draws literary communication from the reader's perspective into the realm of impersonality. Considered panoramically, the *oeuvre* is the context of literary creation as communication within the economy. It is the invasion of the writer's privacy by the public dimension, and the concomitant insistence within the public dimension of the *oeuvre*'s fragmentary, heteronomous privacy. The *oeuvre* is a communicational moment in the economy of being which takes the form of a public item or document. But its ontology is not defined by this documentary or objective aspect. Like the night, the desert, and the burrow, the *oeuvre* is an economic dimension which may invest an empirical form.

The *oeuvre* is the writer's heteronomous experience of communication and proximity, within the irreducible empirical context of the personal, decisive, and resolute activity of creation. Blanchot's discussion of this congruence in *L'Espace littéraire* is organized by predicates discussed earlier: the *nouvelle origine* or metamorphosis of subjectivity, involuntary prehension, and essential solitude, defined as instances of communication's approach – an approach which transforms action into indecision. Blanchot emphasizes this quasi-temporal approach of the writer to a dimension which engulfs his initiative within its own approach. This is the dimension of impersonality, indecision, incessance, neutrality, fascination, etc. Writing is an initiative, like the construction of the burrow, which discovers "in spite of itself" and within itself a new intimacy and a new origin in transgresssion. The *oeuvre* is the context or event of this preoriginary and repetitive passivity which overtakes the transitivity of the act of writing.

The *oeuvre* is an economic event which includes the production of an "objective" or intramundane remainder: the writer's "work". In the introductory pages of *L'Espace littéraire,* Blanchot describes the economy of this event and this remainder which cannot be totalized, by means of the duality of *oeuvre* and *livre* ("book"). "The writer belongs to the *oeuvre,* but what belongs to him is only a book, a mute accumulation of sterile words, the most insignificant thing in the world."[88] The word *livre* describes the manifest aspect of the *oeuvre* – that is, its failure of totalization, and the hapless, passive circulation of this failure within the dimension of manifestation. What is "readable" in the *oeuvre* – what is available to comprehension – is the *livre.* As will be discussed below, the book's insignificance is not an inferiority of manifestation to the "true" communication of proximity, but is paradoxically faithful to the *oeuvre*'s essential irreality and incompletion – its inadequation to a world of action. Every *oeuvre* has its origin in impersonality, and thus desires to become a *livre*: a mute item in the public domain. The writer may read his book. He may manipulate the unfamiliarity of its printed pages with baffled, inquiring fingers. But his rapport with the *oeuvre* is a different comportment: to write it. On one hand, Blanchot's distinction explains the writer's tendency to denigrate his past achievements and to hold that only "the next work" counts for him. More profoundly, however, it indicates the futurity of the *oeuvre* which can never enter the punctual realm of the manifest. It indicates the impersonality of the *oeuvre,* understood as its inadequation to the self-coincidence and integrity of the writer, which are correlative to his decision and his power. Yet it has always already escaped into the public dimension. It is an irreducible exteriority. The *oeuvre* which can never be read, but only written, is a basic instance of communication's non-reciprocity or *sens unique.* The writer cannot "read" his *oeuvre* because its escape from him does not constitute it as an independent object susceptible of contemplation. This escape is rather a function of closure's excess: an alteration of the possibility of interiority, and thus the production of a remainder which is not a totality. It is, in Blanchot's terms, a defection or alteration of the domain of possibility itself. Like *dépense* in Bataille, the *oeuvre* is an escape from closure which reveals closure's integrity as a regional or secondary moment in being. The *oeuvre* is "outside" subjectivity, although not at a phenomenal distance. It is rather the event by which "outside" and "inside" as dialectical functions of the Same are revealed as impossibilities, and by which a more radical exteriority approaches. The *oeuvre* is outside the Same, outside the totality. Its escape knows only one direction: *au dehors,* "outward". Its independence from its author results from its economic status as the *pour-l'autre* of interiority, the alteration of the Same. The Blanchotian verb *écrire,* "to write", always designates this univocity of closure's dispossession in the general economy. The sense, inclination or orientation of closure's excess is univocal: "toward the Other". Thus the author may not "read" his *oeuvre.* But this impossibility, as attested so often by Blanchot, is not a "negative" condition: firstly, because it is not lamentable or unfortunate, and secondly, because its context is not reducible to the notion of negativity. "This impossibility of reading is not however a purely negative movement, it is rather the only real approach [*approche*] that the author can have to what I call the *oeuvre.*"[89] This statement is the first incarnation in *L'Espace littéraire* of two essential moments: (1) an impossibility which is "no longer privation, but affirmation,"[90] and (2) an impossibility which is the problematic positivity of an approach. The approach of the *oeuvre* (and Blanchot's reader is constrained progressively to accept the ontological definition: "not the *oeuvre,* but the approach of the *oeuvre*") is, among other things, the impossibility for the author to read it.

As discussed earlier, Blanchot's career as a thinker in punctuated by a dialogue with Hegel. The moments of this dialogue include the important phenomenological inspiration of Blanchot's early critical texts, the many explicit refusals articulated in his mature works, and on occasion a true inextrication with regard to the Hegelian influence which haunts a number of Blanchot's most important concepts. The introductory moment of the *oeuvre*'s incompletion is one instance of a programmatic refusal of the Hegelian inspiration in Blanchot's text. Foreclosing the possibility that death might constitute the *oeuvre*'s only completion and effectivity, Blanchot writes: "Which is what is expressed when it is remarked that the artist, terminating his *oeuvre* only at the moment of his death, never knows it. It is perhaps necessary to reverse this remark, for isn't the writer dead as soon as the *oeuvre* exists, as he himself sometimes senses in his impression of a most strange passivity [*désoeuvrement*]?"[91] This "death" which would contain the possibility of the *oeuvre*'s production, is not the death of phenomenology which would, through its radical negativity, found a positivity of the *oeuvre* as an accomplishment. The writing of the *oeuvre* is not a "work" grounded in the destructive and productive power of the negative, as Blanchot explains in a footnote to his discussion.[92] Creation is involved rather with the "other death" of proximity: death as the "impossibility of dying", the "death without truth" which is the excessive economy of incompletion and the exigency. Rather than a negativity, this death is closure's excess over closure itself, in an economy whose communications proceed from the weakening or altering of negation. Against this background, the incompletion of the *oeuvre* is irreducible. The *oeuvre* is what Blanchot calls the essentially "fragmentary": a remainder which is an affirmation where there is no negation. This fragment cannot be differentiated and made manifest by the author's disappearance. His death is involved in its differentiation, but the latter is not a totalization.

The separation of the *oeuvre* from its creator is not only its escape from his initiative. It is "separation", in its most general sense, as differentiation or individuation within the economy. The escape of the *oeuvre* remains its intrication with the writer, and for this reason his inability to "read" it is correlative to his inability to take an adequate distance from it in any sense. Thus Blanchot calls the *oeuvre* a "solitude",[93] which both escapes the writer and weighs upon him, constituting his center of gravity outside himself. It is this concept that structures a series of predicates indicating an impossibility for the author to "abide in the proximity" of the *oeuvre*.

The impossibility of reading is this discovery that now, in the space opened by creation, there is no longer any room for creation — and, for the writer, no other possibility than always to write this *oeuvre*. No one who has written the *oeuvre* can live, can abide [*demeurer*] near it.[94]

There is no space in which to create; and this lack of space or interval, this proximity, is creation. The distance of the escaping *oeuvre* is its approach. It does not allow subjectivity the adequate and adequating interval of phenomenality or intentionality. The *oeuvre* is always "too close" and "too distant" for such an interval. It is a proximity, and it is proximity itself, as it produces itself in creation. The supplanting of the possibility of negativity by this economy creates the correlation of "not being able to read" and "not being able to stop writing."

The problematic of the *oeuvre*'s proximity to the writer, and of the *nouvelle origine* produced by this proximity, generates the contextual economy of *L'Espace littéraire* in its totality, and informs many concepts which describe the literary space without being entirely specific to it. These concepts designate events of proximity in a more general sense, and are therefore discussed in other sections of the present study. They include (1) fascination and "contact at a distance", defined as intentionality's remainder in proximity; (2) the pre-voluntary exigency as the context of the inability to stop writing (and its strategic illustration, involuntary prehension); (3) the image as the context of manifestation in proximity; (4) incessance, interminability, and repetition, defined as the temporality of differentiation in the general economy; (5) pre-originarity and the *nouvelle origine* as the being of the exigency in a "time without decision"; and (6) the negligence, passivity, and ultimate indecision of transgression, in the comparison of literary creation to suicide. If one Blanchotian figure may be said to have a "centrality" in his meditation of proximity, it is certainly the *oeuvre*. The predicates of literary communication in *L'Espace littéraire* are generalized economically in their initial definition, and further generalized in *Le Livre à venir*, *L'Entretien infini*, *Le Pas au-delà*, and all Blanchot's later books, both discursive and "fictional". The literary context loses its thematic primacy in these books, whose discussions of communication explore a variety of cultural dimensions. Nevertheless, the overall movement of Blanchot's thought retains the direction indicated by "La Littérature et le droit à la mort" and *L'Espace littériare*, and the notion of literature tends to reappear in Blanchot as a topic or as a comparison to another subject.

The writer's involvement with the *oeuvre* is a proximity which transforms intentionality by a withdrawal of negativity and power from its structure. Thus intentionality in creation tends to become indecision, fascination, and repetition. One common denominator of these moments is the basic notion of dispossession. This notion indicates the *oeuvre*'s loss as *dépense,* on one hand, and the writer's entry into impersonality on the other. It is with relation to this common denominator that Orpheus' transgression is most pertinent. For the writer, like Orpheus, conceives a fundamental "possibility" in his comportment: the dual possibility of encountering alterity "in the night" — that is, without reducing alterity — and of making manifest this encounter. This "illusion" of possibility, produced not only by consciousness' naive spontaneity but also by the more fundamental negligence of transgression, describes the classical exigency of "experience": the dispossession of a fidelity to the exterior, and the recuperation of this dispossession by thought's adequation to the exterior. The ambivalence of this stance characterizes creation in all its stages. Creation is not the accomplishment of that which was attempted — not is it, ultimately, an accomplishment at all. Creation is not an action, but an exigency. Faced with the frustration of this situation, the writer may abandon literature in favor of silence.[95] As a retreat into the world of possibility, he may begin to conceive his work in terms of his personal mastery, and thus to parody himself or to write uninspired works.[96] He may enter the public dimension as a savant, discoursing on matters of actuality such as politics.[97] These retreats from literature itself as a realm of inspiration and impossibility attest a more basic, and inevitable creative "illusion": the mistaking of a mastery over "everyday language" for an ability to order and control the dimension of indecision. "He acquires the illusion that he has the unavailable at his disposal, and, in this originary *parole*, can say everything and give a voice and a *parole* to everything."[98] The writer thus shares Orpheus' belief that his song may enchant the gods: that his song may be an action. On the other hand, the first steps of the writer toward the nocturnal conceal within their resolve the passivity and indecision of transgression's extremity. Because of this priority, the moment at which the *oeuvre*'s irreducible privacy or solitude tends toward a becoming-public may force the artist into violence, a wandering indecision, or the complement of literary violence, suicide.[99] But most initially, as Blanchot notes with some irony, the stubborn resistance of the *oeuvre* to totalization causes the writer to "go back to work" ("se remettre à l'oeuvre"[100]), without realizing that by this persistence and application he is entering the dimension of repetition and the interminable. The writer's resolve conceals the insouciance and negligence of transgression, and his approach to the *oeuvre* is already the *oeuvre*'s escape from him — an escape which is not accidental, but is rigorously correlative to his approach itself, as Eurydice's disappearance is implicit in Orpheus' first step toward the depths. The principle of certain artists' violent destinies is not different from that of others' prudent retreat into the possible. The writer whose communicational "suicide" takes the form of "seeing the *oeuvre* through to the end" has no privilege in Blanchot's eyes. No comportment is adequate to the dispossession of inspiration. The only approach to the *oeuvre* is transgression. Failure is integral to this approach. Transgression creates both the sacred and the profane worlds. On this level, the endurance of a Proust is not more praiseworthy than the withdrawal of a Rimbaud. To privilege the former is to appreciate the gift of a "larger" cultural contribution, to laud a certain creative resoluteness, but not to comprehend the proximity which links all creativity to failure and even to insignificance.

Impersonality is the form of ipseity's excess in communication. The information emitted in inspiration and creation belongs to "no one", because its escape from the writer is its escape from closure in general. Thus, the *oeuvre* is an "impersonal, anonymous affirmation."[101] On one hand, the writer in communication becomes the "someone" of suicide and essential solitude, because creation cannot proceed from "himself". On the other hand, as so many writers attest, the act of literary communication interrupts the possibility of an intersubjective relation. In a paragraph which anticipates the "interruption" and "rapport of the third type" of *L'Entretien infini,* Blanchot describes this rapport which forecloses relation:

To write is to break the link which unites the *parole* to myself, to break the rapport which, making me speak toward "you", gives me a *parole* in the understanding [*entente*] that this *parole* receives from you, for it summons you, it is the call that begins in me because it ends in you. To write is to break this link. It is, moreover, to withdraw language from the currency of the world, to dispossess it of that which makes it a power by which, if I speak, it is the world that speaks to itself, it is the day that erects itself through work, action and time.[102]

Impersonality is a proximity which contaminates (1) the rapport of the *parole* to the subject of its emission, (2) its relation to an interlocutor, (3) its rapport to manifestation, and (4) its rapport with power. The common denominator of these four predicates is the irreducibility of writing to an economy organized by the negative. Once again, Blanchot takes a distance from Hegel, by refusing the *parole* the negative status of an illuminating interval in being. The *parole* is rather a proximity in being: a remainder or fragment which troubles the silent contemplation of the totality. This is the sense of the proposition that the *parole* is not its effectivity, but its escape from negativity. The being of literary tation's remainders in "La littérature et le droit à la mort".[104] The "is" of the parole is not its effectivity, but its escape from negativity. The being of literary language is its escape from the duality of being and non-being. "Where it doesn't speak, already it speaks; when it ceases, it persists."[105] There is no *récit*, but there is no lack of a *récit*. The irreducibility of the *parole* to the oppositions of identity and non-contradiction or of dialectics is called by Blanchot its "neutrality". "What there is to hear [*entendre*: also "understand"], is this neutral *parole*, that which has always been already said, cannot stop being said and cannot be heard [*entendu*]."[106] The incessant, the interminable and the repetitive are predicates of impersonality itself, understood as a rapport without the possibility of relation. The *parole* is the context of impersonality: the scene of a dispossession. When considered in itself as an entity, it has the problematic ontological boundaries of the fragmentary remainder. It is "essentially errant, being always outside itself."[107] Its only "positive" existence is its contamination of the positivity of closure in general. But this contamination or alteration is the only condition for closure itself, when closure is communication. The *parole* and the *oeuvre* are impossibilities in being which reveal being as an economy of impossibility. Commenting the "fait, étant" of Mallarmé's *Livre*, Blanchot writes: "The evidence of the *Livre*, its manifest brilliance are thus such that one must say that it is, that it is present, since without it nothing would ever be present, but that it is however always lacking with regard to the conditions of real existence: being [*étant*], but impossible."[108] The *oeuvre* is the index of *désoeuvrement* (impossibility) in the general economy. This is its escape from manifestation and the éclat of its presence. Its language and its being are that of the image, defined as the appearance of absence or of that which cannot become manifest. (See below, Chapter 5) As Blanchot writes in one of his most striking formulas, "not a language that would contain images or that would put reality into figures, but that would be its own image, the image of a language, – and not a figurative [*imagé*] language –, or an imaginary language, a language that no one speaks, that is, which speaks on the basis of its own absence, as the image appears upon the absence of the thing. . . ."[109] It is not an escape from referentiality or representation that characterizes the *oeuvre*, but rather a far more fundamental escape from possibility itself, in the *oeuvre*'s failure to achieve effective existence.

In Blanchot's demonstrations, the writer is considered as an individual and an intentionality before his *nouvelle origine* in impersonality is derived and imposed. The introduction of the reader follows the opposite order. The reader is an instance within impersonality ("la lecture": "reading") whose predicates will condition the secondary definition of the empirical reader.

Reading in Blanchot is homologous, although opposite in meaning to a phenomenologically defined reading which would exhume a book from obscurity or from its place in the library, to participate with the author in rendering manifest the content of the book. On such a phenomenological model, the reader's act would not be the simple passivity of reception, but would be the intentional power to make manifest and to inaugurate a dialogue with the author, however problematic this latter instance might be. For Blanchot, the empirical aspect of reading may suggest a resurrection, but its more basic context is that impersonality which reading "completes".

The *oeuvre* is impersonal, in the sense that it escapes the self-coincidence and interiority of its author, while escaping, as impossibility, all interiority and all closure. The *oeuvre*, as communication, is an excess and a fragment which is irreducible to negation and unity. The author's difficult process of creation consists of his approach to the reality of this excess, which implies an impossibility of those traditional predicates of writing which are reducible to intentionality and its spontaneity. For Blanchot, the reader is the impersonal context which makes this process "complete", which extricates the *oeuvre*, in a movement of gaiety and insouciance, from the author's drama on one hand, and from all manifestation and personal dialogue on the other. In this sense, the reader is impersonality itself, considered as the dimension of the *oeuvre* in its excess over closure.

The section on reading in *L'Espace littéraire* begins with a contrast between writers' anguish and the fact that no one speaks of an "anguish" of reading. A second passage contrasts the unproblematic "ability" to read with the generally attested "talent" constitutive of a musical "ear" or an "eye" for painting. Reading is "the easiest thing in the world," a function "anyone" can perform.[110] The reader who is misled by the terminological similarity of Blanchot's text to familiar theories of literature expects this apparent ease of reading to be contested in favor of a more usual configuration prescribing resolute application and comprehension. Instead, Blanchot reaffirms with satisfaction that reading is in fact "easy", unproblematic, and not at all inauthentic in its facility.* The basis of this description is Blanchot's fundamental economic definition of the reader as

---

* Blanchot is not insensitive to the communicational proposition that a text might alter or "change" a reader. The text's escape from comprehension is not limited to its frustration of a "serious" reader's wish to totalize it. In a proximal sense, this escape from totalization may affect or involve the reader. But this communicational involvement will not be the result of an adequate or reduced comprehension. Thus the terms of its description in Blanchot's text are "desire", "anguish", and "the blitheness of a movement of passion."[115]

the moment in being which consecrates the *oeuvre*'s incompletion, assuring the absoluteness and permanence of this incompletion.

What is a book that no one reads? Something which is not yet written. Reading would thus be, not to write the book anew, but to make the book write itself or *be* written, — this time without the intermediary of the writer, without anyone writing it. The reader does not add himself to the book, but he tends first of all to relieve it of any author, and what is so prompt is his approach, this so vain shadow which passes over the pages and leaves them intact, all that gives reading the appearance of something superfluous, and even the paucity of attention, the paucity of interest, all the infinite blitheness of the reader affirms the new blitheness of the book, become a book without an author. . . .[111]

The reader's "prompt approach" is the approach of impersonality which engulfs the book economically and gives it the definitive status of a proximity. Reading is the definitive disappearance of the personal author — and of a personal reader. The *oeuvre* "needs the reader to affirm itself as a thing without an author and also without a reader."[112] Thus the reader is first of all "reading", not a person who reads. He is "fundamentally anonymous", "any reader at all."[113] He is the impersonality of proximity, as it manifests itself in the public dimension: "Not adding his name to the book (as our fathers did long ago), erasing rather any name from it, by his nameless presence, by this modest, passive, interchangeable, insignificant look, under whose slight pressure the book appears written, removed from [*à l'écart*] everything and from everyone."[114] The reader is implicit in the *écart* which produces author, *oeuvre* and reader in a universe without negation and totalization, and which inclines interiority toward the radical alterity of the *dehors* or exterior. Thus the reader's approach is not an eventuality, but a pre-originarity which is implicit in the writer's contaminated decision to write. As Baudelaire declared perhaps more compellingly than any other author of a prefatory statement, the reader is a function of the invasion of privacy inherent in writing — the public act of a solitude — and already implies by his presence the inaccessibility of literary communication to a world of accomplishment and authenticity. The reader as impersonality already forecloses the writer's ability to produce a valid document for contribution to a world of comprehension.

It is on the basis of the economic definition of reading that the predicates of "facility", "privilege" and "passivity" are applied to the reader. Reading "merely 'makes' the book become* an *oeuvre* beyond the man who produced it."[116] But this "makes" "does not indicate here a productive activity."[117] Reading is an economic function or instance, and not an action. Reading must

---

* "que le livre, l'oeuvre, devienne — devient — oeuvre par-delà l'homme" etc. Blanchot's replacement of the subjunctive by the indicative emphasizes that nothing depends upon reading as an activity. Reading is a function without being an effective action. The *oeuvre* "needs" the reader but does not depend upon his contribution.

"be there" in order that the *oeuvre* may become entirely impersonal. If reading may be said to have the function of a resurrection of what lies hidden in the unread book, then this resurrection, writes Blanchot, is "something vertiginous which resembles the unreasonable movement by which we wish to open to life the closed eyes of the dead."[118] "The fact is that here the stone and the tomb not only hide the cadaveric emptiness which we would animate, this stone and this tomb consitute the presence, dissimulated however, of that which must appear."[119] Reading's "resurrection" is the paradoxical consecration of a dissimulation, the ostentation of the non-manifest as this very inability to become manifest. Such a resurrection "illuminates" the nocturnality of the day. "Only that which is the more closed may open itself; only that which belongs to the greatest opacity may be transparent."[120]

As mentioned above, there is a temptation to read Blanchot's meditation on reading in the terms of the phenomenological tendencies of his time. This temptation results, on one hand, from the problematic of intimacy and proximity which structures *L'Espace littéraire* in its entirety. On the other hand, in a section like "Lire", the context and terminology of existentialism and phenomenology are confusingly present. Blanchot speaks of a "freedom" of reading and even of a "laisser être" or "letting be" as reading's reception or *accueil* of the *oeuvre*. The context of resurrection tends to force the superstructure of his thinking into a problematic of manifestation, and when he mentions a "generosity" of the *oeuvre*, it is difficult to avoid seeing "Lire" as part of the genealogy of *Qu'est-ce que la littérature*? rather than as a most radical response to the Sartrian concepts. When Blanchot writes, "Reading is situated beyond or on this side of comprehension,"[121] the reader is tempted to hear an echo of phenomenology's insistence upon the personal and subjective as opposed to the impersonally essential. But the "comprehension" to which Blanchot refers is precisely that of phenomenology, and his ironic presentation of the problematic of resurrection is his contestation of phenomenology's "illuminating" reader. The "freedom" of a reading which "welcomes" the *oeuvre*, "saying Yes" to its manifestation, is firstly an essential passivity which is the very context of power's defection in communication, and secondly the "Yes" of affirmation where there is no negation.[122] The following quotation from "Lire" indicates the terminological intrication of Blanchot's writing with a tradition he subverts from a somewhat subterranean angle: "Reading is, in this sense, more positive than creation, more creative, although producing nothing. It takes part in the decision, it has the latter's blitheness, irresponsibility and innocence. It does nothing and everything is accomplished."[123] The vocabulary of creation seems to link reading to the categories of French rationalism in the post-war years. And yet Blanchot is describing an impersonality which corresponds in every respect to both Sartrian and Heideggerian "inauthenticity", and is defining both the irreducibility of this impersonality and the regionality of the problematic of inauthenticity. The ontological status of reading is its lack of power, freedom, and illumination, and this is the sense of its "participation in creation." By its very presence, prior to its activity, reading allows the *oeuvre* itself to escape these phenomenological absolutes, and to become the hyperbole of the inauthentic and inessential. No matter what "stormy approaches" may involve the reader in the creative text as a result of the latter's problematic relation to an "intentional" reader, the most basic aspect of reading will always be a "tranquil and silent presence,"[124] the "bonheur" of an instance which is less its own effectivity than it is the anonymous context of the author's disappearance and the *oeuvre*'s *errance*.

Blanchot's meditation upon reading contains one important instance of the Hegelian inspiration which occasionally appears in his text, particularly in its dualistic moments. Here, it is the opposition between writing as impossibility and reading as facility or "power" that produces a Hegelian formulation which Blanchot is quick to pre-empt, although not able to eliminate.

Reading is thus not to obtain a communication of the *oeuvre*, it is to "make" the *oeuvre* communicate itself and, to use a faulty image, it is to be one of the two poles between which, by mutual attraction and repulsion, the illuminating violence of communication bursts forth, between which this event passes and that it constitutes by this very passage. But, of course, this comparison is faulty.[125]

The "faulty comparison" consists of a tendency to define reading and writing as "fixed poles", "following the crude schema of two powers" whose dialectical communication would be the positivity of literary manifestation.[126] Blanchot corrects this "faulty image", in the first place, by situating the struggle between power and impossibility within the creation of the *oeuvre* itself, prior to the approach of a reader and even to the familiar definition of a writer. Rather than the "stabilized exigencies" of writer and reader, there is a struggle of "more indistinct exigencies"[127] — power and impossibility — within creation. In the second place, Blanchot defines the "opposition" of these exigencies as that of transgression, in which there is no confrontation of opposites, but rather a chiasma or intrication of exigencies which have no existence outside this intrication. The insistence of each exigency is the impossibility of the other. They are "irreconcilable and inseparable moments."[128]

There is not power on one side, impossibility on the other; there is not the clash of these antagonisms; there is, in the event of the fact of writing, the tension which, through the intimacy in which writing joins them, demands [*exige*] of the opposites that which they are in their extreme opposition, but demands also that they come to themselves leaving themselves, retaining themselves together outside themselves in the unquiet unity of their common belonging [*appartenance*]. A power which is power only with regard to impossibility; an impossibility which affirms itself as a power.[129]

The "struggle" between power and impossibility takes place within impossibility itself, defined as the economy of proximity. Blanchot's Hegelian vocabulary conceals his arresting of the dialectic at its differential or proximal moment, where differentiation is not contradiction and is neither the origin of a power nor the effect of a power. But proximal alteration is not belonging. The presence of a Hegelian-Heideggerian inspiration in phrases such as "unité inquiète" and "commune appartenance" is not to be minimized in the section entitled "La Communication". Blanchot indeed seems haunted by a thematics of struggle, freedom, opposition and, in subsequent paragraphs, origin and beginning. At this point in *L'Espace littéraire* he is unable to define literature's escape from these themes without allowing them a confusing lexical supremacy in his own text. This proximity of a problematic from which he has not been able to entirely extricate his own concepts (in spite of their radicality of which he is certainly aware), may motivate the placement of the section entitled "La littérature et l'expérience originelle", with its explicit criticisms of both Hegel and Heidegger, immediately following "La Communication" in *L'Espace littéraire*.

In attesting both a terminological and conceptual temptation of phenomenology in "La Communication", it is important to recognize a most fundamental advance in this text that is not underlined by Blanchot himself. By concentrating the "struggle" between reading and writing within one instance, i.e. creation as impossibility, Blanchot designates the *oeuvre*'s escape as a function of the basic dissymmetry of communication in the general economy. Escaping the author, the *oeuvre* escapes the reader as well. It escapes everyone and everything. Its movement is the univocity of differential heteronomy in the economy: *au dehors*, "outward", *pour l'autre*, from Same toward Other. Blanchot's ambivalent. digression on struggle, polarity and belonging, obscures but does not compromise his understanding of the communicational force which inclines interiority toward an exterior which is not a totality. The *oeuvre* is always a priority of excess over interiority, always an escape from closure as a possibility — and from this perspective, in which reader and writer are subsumed by writing as impossibility, the structural opposition of these terms in a panoramic perspective is already foreclosed. The *oeuvre* is a repetitive, proximal moment: the *pour l'autre* and its remainder in being, which does not "exist" and which includes both writer and reader in its impersonal production. The approach of the *oeuvre* concerns the Same. It does not concern this writer in his correlation to others. This non-reciprocity of communicational contact with exteriority is implicit in all Blanchot's definitions. "When I approach it, is it not already it that is approaching me?" The exterior is the inaccessible with which interiority remains involved. The dialectical proposition of a polarity "between" whose terms alterity insists, is a repeated detour in Blanchot's formulations, and is perhaps the chief inequality in his theoretical text. (See below, Chapter 6)

*

The above discussion may be taken to describe reading as an economic instance involved in the creation of the *oeuvre*. Reading is the becoming-public of the *oeuvre* in its own ontology, prior to the approach of a "real" reader. Once the *oeuvre* has become an actual item in the public dimension, its irreducibility to manifestation and totalization takes on a new aspect. This is its refusal and its "réserve": an unavailability to comprehension which assumes the appearance of a self-sufficiency. "Reading is born in the moment at which the *oeuvre*'s distance with regard to itself changes its aspect, no longer indicates its incompletion, but its accomplishment, no longer signifies that it is not yet accomplished, but that it never had to be accomplished."[130] The *oeuvre*'s impossibility, its distance or *écart* with regard to the dimension of power, now takes the form of its "inhuman" accomplishment, its closure which excludes the human effort and work which was its history. At this point, the empirical reader is certainly "delighted with his happiness" in the ease of reading, but also senses his superfluity in impersonality. Someone is required for this book to be read, but not this reader, this person. He feels that he cannot "exhaust" the *oeuvre* by his reading, "that it remains entirely outside its most intimate approach."[131] This distance of the *oeuvre* in its independence and its "refusal" of totalization is its "proximity" to the reader.[132] Reading is now its secondary definition as intentionality and the exigency of manifestation. The oeuvre's "intimacy" — its failure of totalization and its fundamental passivity — is a frustration of this tendency. It is a public object, but not a manifestation. It cannot be totalized, but its refusal is not that of a thing in-itself. Its escape has the appearance of an effective closure or absolution, but proceeds from the passivity of incompletion. The *oeuvre* is not an accomplishment, and its behaviour is not an action. But within the region of manifestation, its proximal strangeness cannot but be interpreted as an effectivity whose absoluteness (whose totalization) frustrates knowledge. Now the *oeuvre*'s écart with regard to totalization gives it an opacity which makes reading difficult and, more fundamentally, "impossible".

The last pages of *L'Espace littéraire* offer a brilliant and in many ways overwhelming display of Blanchot's ability to articulate the economic derivation of the *oeuvre* with its empirical dimension. Here Blanchot derives, on the basis of the *oeuvre*'s irreducibility to manifestation, the manifold recuperations which are the rapport of the *oeuvre* to the public dimension of culture. These descriptions are remarkable not only for their ontological penetration, but for their fidelity to Heidegger's descriptions of a metaphysics which is "not without its own truth," and for Blanchot's consequent refusal to denigrate or lament their superfluity and inadequacy. These recuperations include the value judgment,[133] the interpretation of the *oeuvre* in terms of utility,[134] the literary critical interrogation of the technical conditions of the *oeuvre*'s production,[135] the "ideality" of the *oeuvre*'s self-sufficiency or reserve,[136] and the apearance of the *oeuvre* as the container of a cultural "content".[137] All these conditions are recuperations whch inscribe the *oeuvre*'s fundamental "distance" (its écart, incompletion and heteronomy) into a world of values subordinated to manifestation and power. For this world, the *oeuvre*'s distance must always be understood as the result of a superior power or a superior truth. Blanchot notes that these recuperations which apparently fill the "void" of the *oeuvre*'s distance are also mobilizing that distance in a formal way. Thus the *écart* of incompletion and *glissement* assumes the appearance of a negativity, in the work of art which "cannot" be totalized, and in the correlative cultural positivity of this privileged escape. In this way the passivity of the *oeuvre* becomes its excellence as a cultural object which escapes common truth in the name of higher truth and higher accomplishment. For Blanchot, the *oeuvre*'s heteronomy lends itself to this recuperative interpretation of it. "It takes part in public dialogue, it expresses, it refutes that which is said in general, it consoles, it diverts, it bores everyone, not by virtue of itself or by a rapport with the emptiness and the cutting edge of its being, but by the detour of its content. . . ."[138] The *oeuvre* is "at the mercy" of its public density, although not by an unfortunate accident, and not by comparison with a different dimension in which it might be "truly" comprehended and appreciated. As will be discussed below, the *oeuvre* is a public, impersonal instance in its basic economy. The heteronomy of its public circulation is integral to its ontology.

The *oeuvre* has the extreme density of closure in an economy whose communicational singularities are discontinuous. Thus there is an apparent perfection or accomplishment in its refusal and reserve. For this reason, it may be interpreted as a beautiful object – and this is, for Blanchot, the possibility of esthetics.[139] From the point of view of manifestation, beauty is understood as an efficacy correlative to transcendent power and truth; and this is why the writer assumes the status of a "genius": the active, magically gifted creator of an object whose perfection is a superiority over common totalization, whose truth is a superiority over common truth.[140] Genial subjectivity is a power, and the mystery of a less differentiated but more efficacious comprehension. The genial work of art may be celebrated for its hyperbolic efficacy as a representational entity, or for the magnificence and superiority of its alterity, which is not subordinate to the submissive referentiality or representationalism of common communication. These two gestures are the same. Manifestation celebrates an alterity whose escape is a power, and whose absolution mimics the form of a totality. Finally, the *écart* of becoming, repetition and futurity in the *oeuvre*'s incompletion becomes the negative temporal interval constitutive of history, and the *oeuvre*'s escape is recuperated by its situation within art history.[141] The indefinite and repetitive appearance of the *oeuvre* as dissimulation, in an actuality which it always renders inactual, becomes the future of history: the endless possibility of "another completion, accomodating all the metamorphoses which, linking it to history, seem to make of its own distance the promise of an unlimited future."[142] The *oeuvre*'s becoming is the principle of its vicissitudes in history, and the manifold totalizations which will incarnate and document them. History, in addition, must always regret its ignorance of the precise conditions and milieu of a work's first appearance, "the language it had at its birth,"[143] its precise meaning within the culture of its time – that is, its situation within an actuality, its historical totalization. This regret, and the optimism of a progressive historiographical future, is history itself as an understanding of temporality.

The *oeuvre* is a simulacrum of truth and beauty.[144] In other words, it is that dimension within the economy which escapes and engulfs truth, by its inability to equal the adequacy of the latter, and which may produce truth as a simulacrum of power whose public destiny is to be a recuperation by the logic of power. It is an inhuman sound, an "unnameable" instance, whose destiny is to be a circulating cornerstone of the humanism of power.

At one point in *L'Espace littéraire*, Blanchot suggests that the *oeuvre* might be better off forgotten, burned, or left to the obscurity of the library. Such an *écart* with regard to culture's concepts of utility, such a lack of recuperation, might "prolong its distance" or "correspond to the force of its withdrawal."[145] But this suggestion is not repeated, and for good reason. The *oeuvre* might be better off if it were safe from the contaminations of manifestation, but under this condition it would not be an *oeuvre*. The ruination of the *oeuvre*, correlative to the loss of Eurydice in the return to the light of day, is constitutive of the *oeuvre*. Its being is not the distance of the "absolutely" other, but rather the paradoxical and contaminated insistence of alterity "here below", where the *autrement qu'être* "certes s'entend dans l'être", deploys itself and resonates in Being. Like the sirens, the *oeuvre* becomes public in its very being, and must fall victim to the exigency of Ulysses' strategem. This is its "expiation of its authority," to paraphrase Blanchot. The *oeuvre* must approach the dualism of being and nothingness, power and determination, and find within this context its designation as inessentiality. This *oubli* or forgetting of the *oeuvre*'s communicational economy, and the powerlessness which is related to it, are the truly public dimension of its otherness, far more "effective" in a proximal sense than a literal escape from manifestation. In this sense, the last chapter of *Le Livre à venir* is a more acceptable formulation of the *oeuvre*'s destiny. Here, Blanchot meditates the publication of the *oeuvre* as an abandonment of it to the impersonality and formlessness of a dimension of incurious avidity, rumor, and "incessant prolixity"[146] in which everything has always been read and commented, without ever having been read. "That which is public does not precisely need to be read; it is always already known, in advance, in a knowledge that knows everything and does not wish to know anything."[147] Public interest, "insatiable", "yet always satisfied", the essence of what one calls "inauthenticity" in reading, "is a movement that one has been quite wrong in describing with a denigrating prejudice. We see here, in an admittedly lax and stabilized form, the same impersonal power which, as obstacle and resource, is at the origin of the literary effort."[148] On one hand, public impersonality, the secret inessentiality of the world of truth, simply corresponds to the impersonality for which the name *oeuvre* stands. The need to be published and to enter the inessentiality of the public dimension "belongs to the *oeuvre*."[149] Every *oeuvre* wants to become a *livre*. Its escape from its author precludes its glorious entry into a world in which it will be comprehended and appreciated. The essence – not the accident – of *Moby Dick,* in Blanchot's phrase, is that it is "a book, alas nothing but a book." On the other hand, according to the concept of reading described above, the public dimension is not strictly exterior to the realization of the *oeuvre*. The author who "publishes before he writes," the public which "forms and transmits what it does not understand," the critic who "judges and defines what he does not read,"[150] are not simply vicissitudes of the *oeuvre*'s innocence. They are involved in its creation as impersonality, and are hyperbolic manifestations of its stubborn, passive resistance to truth.

*

The repeated gesture which structures the last chapters of *L'Espace littéraire* is a situation of art with regard to action. Blanchot cites with satisfaction Hegel's statement that "art is for us a thing of the past."[151] "Art acts little and acts badly," writes Blanchot.[152] If Marx had written novels, he would have "enchanted" the world rather than to have "overthrown" it.[153] "One must therefore write *Capital* and not *War and Peace*."[154] Action is a mobilization and organization of proximity which, like dissimulation, "tends to become negation." Art is proximity's dissimulation which "tends to appear." As such, it is all that action abhors — with good reason, in Blanchot's eyes. "Art, as image, as word and as rhythm, indicates the menacing proximity of a vague and empty exterior [*dehors*], a neutral, null, limitless existence, a sordid absence, a suffocating condensation in which being ceaselessly persists underneath nothingness."[155] Art is proximity as the nocturnal nightmare of the day. It is the presence within manifestation of an instance — sometimes disturbing or terrifying (by virtue of its proximity), more often irksome and annoying (by virtue of its heteronomy) — whose economy is not a totalization. Art is an instance out of its element: the passivity of the impossible in a world of power. "Art is originally linked to this depth of impotence into which everything collapses when the possible becomes attenuated."[156] Hegel's statement was not an empirical notation, but rather the declaration that "from the day when the absolute consciously became the work of history, art is no longer capable of satisfying the need for the absolute."[157] Blanchot multiplies the modalities by which art's heteronomy, refusal, inessentiality and impossibility "cannot compete with action in the terms of action." As discussed above, his interest is not to guarantee for art a superior authenticity or truth. He recognizes that such a guarantee would simply place art in the service of the same manifestation whose regionality his entire theoretical effort is designed to show. Instead, it is this irreducible regionality of the totality, and the uneliminable remainder which troubles its margins, that produces the *écart* constitutive of art as proximity within the general economy. "As long as the world is not entirely the world, art can doubtless find its reserve within it."[158] It is the attestation of art's concomitant strangeness and inferiority in a world engulfed by action, that defines Blanchot's articulation of these concepts. The paradox of totalization in proximity is that it is capable of engulfing *everything*, while leaving outside a tiny remainder. This remainder, which lacks the power either to accomplish its entry into existence or to cease to exist, has no other positivity than its poverty and its inessentiality.

What would the *oeuvre* be within its own "real" element, safeguarded from the contaminating recuperations of the public dimension? A contamination, an impossibility. Blanchot's genius is his refusal to reconstruct for the general economy of proximity the principles of efficacy and comprehension which define the totality. The inessentiality of the *oeuvre* is not relative, but absolute.

While it is necessary to concede with Blanchot the triumphant totalizations of action in its constitution of a "world", and to perceive in proximity's impossibility a reality which can never be an effectivity, it nevertheless seems that he accords to a Hegelian-phenomenological model of action an excessive thematic supremacy. Although Blanchot discovers in essential solitude and the *il y a* a true impossibility of negation, he nevertheless allows totalization in an intramundane sense an unquestioned priority. Proximity in Blanchot becomes a marginal instance whose extrication from totalization (and most importantly from the logic of possibility) is his thematic concern. But in the contrast of totalization and its remainder, the theme of the absolutely other, and of art's traditional allergy to action, is retained. Blanchot's creativity discovers an incompletion which must contaminate totalization in all its moments, but the superstructure of his text attracts the Hegelian inspiration by its very opposition to that inspiration. This attraction may proceed from the domination of the political context at the time of Blanchot's maturation as a writer, and from the theme of art itself as the primary axis of his work. Thus Blanchot contrasts impersonality and action; but there is an impersonality (and a passivity) of action, and a production of proximity within the closure of the totality. The "investment" of totalization by proximity, and the philosophical consequences of this investment, were not to be meditated explicitly by Blanchot, but by his contemporary Emmanuel Levinas.

PROXIMITY AND PHILOSOPHY

SAVOIR AND NON-SAVOIR

Bataille's meditation of discontinuity in proximity, from his earliest essays, concentrates its attention upon differentiation and individuation rather than manifestation. One index of this concern is his consistent invocation of physical and biological categories for an elaboration of the event of interiority in being. At the same time, the thematic level of Bataille's text is faithful to the twentieth century's intellectualism (informed as it is by the apparent subjectivism of the philosophies of existence), in its concern with the irreducibility of closure as a moment of manifestation. On this thematic level, the proposition of the accessibility or "communicability" of closure's heteronomous *expérience* is a constant in Bataille, and has dominated many influential readings of his text.

As mentioned earlier, Bataille's description of closure has two characteristic moments, whose interplay motivates the many rejections and recuperations which are the public dimension of his thought. On one hand, Bataille invokes an instance irreducible to closure, such as heterogeneity, communication, continuity, etc., and positively values this instance. On the other hand, he attests a problematic irreducibility of closure, and punctuates this gesture with statements of exasperation as well as ironic displays of a certain satisfaction. The "mystical" Bataille of the 1940's, produced to some extent by the influence of Sartre's reading, is the Bataille of *extase,* atheology, and the priority of heterogeneity over the constraint of limits. The "transgressive" Bataille of the 1960's and 1970's is the Bataille whose description of a profane *savoir* or "knowledge" may be understood and recuperated by the contemporary intuition, in a Heideggerian inspiration, of a regionality and partiality of Occidental "metaphysics", and an alterity which is irrecuperable by the concepts of this metaphysics. These two hyperbolic interpretations concern the same Bataille: the thinker of the priority of abandon or loss, in the form of *dépense,* over the constraint of discursive limits. Each of these tendencies takes its force from the enthusiasm of the Bataillian text, and from the play of its concepts at a thematic level. However, both traditions tend to overlook the economic dimension of Bataille's thought, in which the struggle of limits and their destruction is subordinated to the concept of contamination which is Bataille's thinking of proximity.

There is a stable and important epistemological predication associated with Bataille's concept of communication. It takes the programmatic form of *non-*

savoir ("non-knowledge", an "other" of manifestation implicit in subjectivity's economy) and the "method of meditation" in *La Somme athéologique,* and in other works the form of Bataille's stipulation that the thinking of the *expérience* requires a "turning inside-out of thought."[1] The Bataille of *L'Erotisme* compares his theoretical activity to that of a "theologian" rather than that of a scientist.[2] This is because the *expérience* is itself in a proximity to the effort of its thematization which forecloses the scientific exigency of "defining its object" and examining the phenomenality of that object. The term *expérience,* in its ultimate definition as proximity itself (the subjectivity and non-indifference of closure in a heteronomous economy) designates not only an "object" of investigation, but the overall context of investigation, in a new understanding of this comportment. Bataille's "theologian" is closely analogous to Levinas' "metaphysician", whose rapport with proximity is not the philosopher's avidity for comprehension, but rather desire, in the communicational definition of this word. Both Bataille and Levinas are faithful to Nietzsche's concept of a compelling future, the incumbence of the eternal return, in which subjectivity will no longer "want" from the exterior the same configuration of pertinence it has historically wished. Passivity and affirmation, rather than determination and illumination, are the predicates of this proximal interrogation of the exterior. And the *expérience,* like recurrence and the idea of the infinite in Levinas, implies this interrogation and this affirmation as an integral moment of its economy. Bataille writes in *L'Erotisme*: "Of the continuity of being, I will say only that it is not in my opinion *knowable,* but, in aleatory forms, always partially contestable, the *experience* of it is given to us."[3] By this formulation of experience Bataille does not mean a reduced or limited consciousness which would not yet be clear and distinct; nor does he mean a more immediate form of knowledge. Experience, like the "expérience du dedans" or "interior experience" which is impersonal and does not require human consciousness, is a configuration of differentiation and communication, as discussed earlier in the context of the *glissement* and the *effort d'autonomie.* In other words, the term *expérience* in Bataille, like that of "subjectivity" in the philosophy of difference, is not derived from a prior concept of consciousness or intentionality, although it may condition any subsequent definition of these concepts. The modality of this conditioning is the originary implication of subjectivity, conceived as an aptitude to be affected by exteriority, in the definition of closure itself.

As discussed earlier (Chapter 2), the differentiation of discontinuity becomes consciousness in a moment which is correlative to prohibition. This production of a reduced "clear and distinct" consciousness on the basis of a reduction of proximity, is not in itself a moment defined as manifestation, but rather a catalysis or detour of interiority within the general economy. Thus, the priority of communication over illumination or manifestation is retained in Bataille's definition of prohibition. The banishing of the "worse than nothing" of the economy's excess over negation, and the concomitant institution of identity, utility, and the "primacy of the future" as coordinates of the profane world, are not vicissitudes of a consciousness. They are modalities of an exigency whose ontology is not reducible to an originary definition as interval or "disclosedness". The anti-intellectualism of this configuration is Bataille's proximity to the Hegel of "Force and Understanding", who subordinates consciousness to alteration and desire — and it is his immediate distance from Heidegger's appropriation of the Hegelian concepts in an intellectualist inspiration. (See below) *Expérience* is not consciousness, nor is it the originary comprehension of a *Dasein*. It is rather an alteration or contamination within being — a lapsing and collapsing of heteronomous closure — which produces subjectivity.

Within this general context, however, autonomy and consciousness are not indifferent concepts, but are authentic problems within the economy. In proximity, as in a differential economy, closure remains a discontinuity. Its rapport with exteriority is not mere invasion or dispersion, but difference. Subjectivity's intrication with alterity, having the form of the exigency, always encounters the detour of autonomy, in the *effort d'autonomie,* and this detour of interiority in being has the manifold correlates which create the "profane world". The question of an "access" of "consciousness" to the reality of the *expérience* arises on the basis of a communication whose catalysis produces the prohibition and the "necessity" of integrity. Subjectivity's exigency — its placing of proximity at a distance and its "interpretation" of the real in terms of closure and negativity — produces the dilemma of a consciousness which desires to see beyond the reifications which are constitutive of its spontaneity. It is this dilemma that creates the intense atmosphere of Bataille's aphoristic *Somme athéologique,* as well as its provocatively derivative thematic aspect. For the Heideggerian design of a subjectivity whose being as manifestation is strictly correlative to its obscuring of the Being it illuminates (and the endlessly transformed inadequation of Hegel's *Geist* in its failures to extend its illuminations to its own movement — which is the profound predecessor of *Sein und Zeit,* as will be discussed below), along with the climate of anguish which surrounds this subjectivity, are clearly perceptible in Bataille's pages.

The fugitive congruence of *expérience* and discontinuity as "consciousness" is given in the event of prohibition itself, which organizes violence by placing an intense limit upon the proximity of the "worse than nothing" of death and sexuality. "Consciousness" is a function of subjectivity's spasmodic conation as closure. In transgression, a similar communicational "revelation" takes place, although in an opposite sense. We can perceive the *interdit* and know that it is not imposed from outside, writes Bataille, only in transgression. "This appears to us in anguish, at the moment at which we *transgress* the prohibition, above all at the suspended moment at which it is still in play, and at which we nevertheless yield to the impulse it opposed."[4] Prohibition is closure's withdrawal from the economy. Transgression is the withdrawal into the economy implied by this movement. But transgression is not a consciousness. It is rather the hyperbole of the *expérience* itself, which Bataille calls the "extremity of the possible." Transgression is an economic event whose irreducibility to free will, power, and negation has been discussed above (Chapter 2). Transgression is not a dispersion or destruction of closure, but is a moment of differentiation. Thus it is the modality of an *expérience du dedans* or "experience of interiority". It is the extremity of an exigency, the violent excess which creates closure, and thus a moment in the economy of a subjectivity — that is, an incompletion or *inachèvement* whose susceptibility to exteriority is integral to its constitution.

To the extent that transgression's movement as a hyperbole or excess of closure's conation produces a "revelation" — to the extent that its violence gives rise to a theme of illumination — this movement will always veer toward the Bataillian concept *savoir* or "knowledge", in the sense of a reduction. This is the regionality of manifestation among Bataille's concepts. Any proximity which has the urgency of a revelation, in a human context, will always be the imminence of its interpretation by interiority's exigency of totalization under the sign of identity and utility. Transgression's excess is "given" to us in *expérience*, but not available to us as illumination. The classic theme of revelation and reification thus appears in Bataille's text. The secondary question of subjectivity's thematization of its *expérience* becomes primary. But this displacement is not accidental, as Bataille's basic description of subjectivity in prohibition demonstrates. The "interpretation" of *expérience* is integral to the differentiation of *expérience* as subjectivity. Closure in the economy is in itself an "interpretation" of the economy. It is important to emphasize the anti-intellectualism of this moment. On one hand, Bataille is faithful to Heidegger's Nietzchian proposition that *Homo sapiens* is essentially *Homo metaphysicum*, on the basis of consciousness' involvement with closure, autonomy and effectivity. But more profoundly, Bataille's inspiration is the Nietzchian and Freudian situation of this closure as a function of differentiation, rather than of manifestation. "Metaphysics" — an "interpretation" of the exterior as effectivity and autonomy — is not a vicissitude of comprehension, but of individuation. It is a moment of an economy whose principle is not illumination.

As Blanchot writes in his interpretation of *expérience*, "how, from such an attainment, could thought — supposing it had affirmed itself for an instant within [this attainment] — over return and bring back from it, if not a new knowledge [*savoir*], at least, at the distance of a memory, that which would be necessary to maintain itself under [the] guardianship [of the *expérience*]?"[5] Since the *expérience* is essentially inadequate to any thematization of it in terms of the categories inaugurated by prohibition, and since prohibition is correlative to any definition of consciousness, the revelation of the *expérience* must always be defined in the terms of reification. Blanchot answers his rhetorical question by mobilizing its own terms. What is retained, he writes, is the *parole* and *affirmation*. These instances, irreducible to comprehension, are also irreducible to the thematics of reification and the escape of the absolutely other. This correct formulation is suggested by his phrase, "thought, supposing it had affirmed itself for an instant within [the *expérience*]". If the unavoidable categories of the thematization of *expérience* produce a reification, thematization is nevertheless an incarnation of *expérience* itself. Thought is an affirmation. As such, its economy is irreducible to the discursive dimension of negativity and power which it creates. Through his own concepts, Bataille reproduces Hegel's subordination of consciousness' attitude to the "experience" which produces consciousness as an attitude. He also reproduces the most important sense of Heidegger's assertion that metaphysics has "its own truth". Knowledge as affirmation is not a univocally voluntaristic movement of comprehension which is frustrated by alterity's escape. Instead, knowledge's affirmation proceeds from its involvement with alterity. But the "truth" of this affirmation is not an approximation. It is the permanence of an involvement with the inaccessible. *Savoir* is communication. Its failure to comprehend exteriority does not exhaust its rapport with the latter. From this perspective, the primacy of reification is reduced, and the regionality of the profane world in an economy of proximity is delimited. Interiority's interpretation of the economy is revealed as a production of the economy itself, although not as a totalization. The Hegelian situation of consciousness within being is repeated, but without the predication of manifestation which is fundamental to both Hegel and Heidegger. The limitations of the profane world and of its epistemology do not reduce the economic constitution of that world in proximity. *Savoir*, in its own definitions, is indeed a reifying instance, but the context of its production as an affirmation and what Bataille will call *contestation*, is not exhausted by the logic of reification. We cannot "think" proximity's *expérience*, but it is proximity that "forces us to think." Thus the *autrement qu'être* which invests Being or what Levinas calls *essence*, and the other night which secretly invests the voluntarism of the day, are inscribed in Bataille's text, under the name *non-savoir*.

The principle of *non-savoir* — subjectivity's excess over comprehension — is the proposition that receptivity is not the predicate of an autonomy, but necessarily the result of a radical incompletion. The repeated theme of *L'Expérience intérieure* is a relatively autonomous ipseity which takes its autonomy for an absolute. "These two principles — a composition transcending the components, a relative autonomy of the components — govern the existence of each 'being'."[6] Within an economy of communication whose "links" transcend the autonomy of separation, Bataille defines autonomy in general as a fugitive instance invoked by subjectivity's exigency. "(S)ubject, object, are perspectives of being at the moment of inertia, (. . .) the object envisaged is the projection of the subject *ipse* desiring to become all [*tout*]."[7] "Suppression of the subject and the object, the only means to avoid ending up with the possession of the object by the subject, that is, to avoid the absurd rush of the *ipse* desiring to become all."[8] The notion of "composition" or communication reveals unicity as a proximity, a heteronomy, and a *mise en jeu*: a fugitive closure "in play", involved with the exterior in a sense irreducible to determination. "The sufficiency of each being is unceasingly contested by its neighbors [*proches*]."[9] The exigency of reducing this proximity is not primarily the project of a consciousness, but the economic being of closure itself. Discontinuity is the economy's detour, consecrated as autonomy in the categories of *savoir*.

The dialectical aspect of this inadequation of subjectivity to the communication constituting it, in which Hegel's "for us — not for consciousness" is perceptible, is not ultimate for Bataille. On one hand, the exigency of the object is already defined by him as a breach within autonomy — a function of differentiation and incompletion. "I will say this obscure thing: the object in the *expérience* is the projection of a dramatic loss of self."[10] The "necessity of an object" is "the necessity to take leave of the self."[11] The object proceeds from the exigency, and from closure's remainder within the exterior. In a sentence which recalls the Blanchotian proximity of the burrow, Bataille adds, "it is the image of the subject. The subject tries first of all to go to his fellow man."[12] The object is subjective, is an image, and is, as in Levinas, a heteronomous rapport to alterity in *autrui*. These communicational conditions, however, do not in themselves reduce the univocity of the "absurd rush of the *ipse*" for which the constituted object is primary and ultimate. To this extent, the dialectical framework of communication remains intact. On the other hand, however, the concept of *non-savoir* will contaminate, on the basis of communication, the possibility of an essentially transitive or intentional *savoir*. In this context, the inadequate or conditioned totalizations of ipseity will be secondary to an arresting of its spontaneity by the proximity of communication itself. The "idea of communication", like the idea of the infinite in Levinas, is not a concept, but a proximity:

I saw ultimately that the idea of communication itself leaves one naked, knowing nothing. Whatever it is, without a positive revelation present in the extreme within me, I can give it neither *raison d'être* nor ultimate sense. I remain in intolerable *non-savoir* . . . .[13]

The idea of communication is a proximity which develops the predicates of an encounter and a contamination. Its insistence is not exhausted by its escape from reification. Instead, reification itself is one correlate of communication's approach. *Non-savoir* is not only a failed totalization. "*Non-savoir* denudes."[14] Nudity, in this context as elsewhere in Bataille (see below, Chapter 5), is not a simple lack of attributes or a dispossession. It is the incompletion and vulnerability of a closed surface: the proximity of a surface to exteriority. Nudity is the subjection which is the principle of receptivity.

In a choice of words which must be described, historically, as most unfortunate, Bataille calls the experience of proximity in *non-savoir* "extase" and applies to it the predicate of "anguish". In spite of the derivative and confusing use of these words, Bataille sustains both the complexity of his context and its irreducibility to manifestation. *Extase* does not indicate a pre-comprehension correlative to existence in a phenomenological sense — this pre-comprehension being unavailable or inadequate to the reifications of intentionality. Instead, *extase* is nudity and communication,[15] defined precisely as that proximal intrication which forecloses the possibility of "ecstasy" or ekstasis as either immediacy or illumination. In other words, *extase* is closure itself, in its Bataillian definition as the excess of an exigency. Closure in *extase* is a nudity or basic susceptibility which cannot be understood as a simple opening to the exterior. "Anguish", in this context, does not function as a correlate of "disclosedness" in a Heideggerian sense. It is rather the modality of an interiority whose autonomy is compromised by the approach of an exterior which cannot become manifest. It is, in a Levinasian inspiration, the tension of a subjectivity whose disquiet is the overtaking of its spontaneity by its passivity or nudity. As Levinas will remark in his criticisms of Heidegger, the concept of anguish as the "possibility of impossibility" is a concept for which possibility remains the ultimate dimension. Heideggerian anguish is a moment of manifestation. For Bataille, anguish is not reducible to the idea of a "window on the exterior,"[16] but proceeds from a "breach" which is not the negativity of existence but rather a "rupture of every possible,"[17] the *écart* of proximity. Impossibility is the principle of a differentiation without negation and without manifestation.* This differentiation produces a closure whose excessive economic force is its nudity or vulnerability. The ambiguity of this incompletion whose exigency is its susceptibility, is "anguish".

Non-savoir is a proximity and a heteronomy of which *savoir* is an irreducible moment. Consciousness or intentionality, in its traditional definition, is the form of the exigency as closure. The following paragraph from *L'Expérience intérieure*, in its enthusiastic Hegelian inspiration, describes the communication of these concepts in a dialectic which becomes a proximity:

Anguish supposes the desire to communicate, that is to lose myself, but not entire resolution: anguish attests my fear of communicating, of losing myself. Anguish is given in the theme of knowledge itself: *ipse,* by knowledge, I would wish to be all, therefore to communicate, lose myself, remaining however *ipse.* For communication, before it takes place, the subject (self, *ipse*) and the object (partially undefined, as long as it is not entirely seized) are posed. The subject wishes to seize the object in order to possess it . . . . But he cannot but lose himself: the non-sense of the will to know supervenes, the non-sense of all

---

* It is significant that in the context of this extrication of *expérience* and *non-savoir* from manifestation, the proximity of Blanchot to Bataille's text becomes manifest — not only in the "conversation avec Blanchot" of page 67, in which *expérience*'s lack of "authority" is described, but also in the intervention of nocturnality on page 74: "rupture of every possible, violent kiss, rape, loss in the entire absence of the possible, in the opaque and dead night, light nevertheless, not less unknowable, blinding, than the bottom of the heart." Bataille correctly articulates nocturnality as a presence of absence and as a blinding light which exceeds manifestation. As will be discussed below, a lengthy quotation on nocturnality in *Thomas l'obscur* is to be found in *L'Expérience intérieure,* and describes Bataille's understanding, through his involvement with Blanchot, of the *il y a* of proximity's excess over negation.

possibility, revealing to the *ipse* that it is going to lose itself and knowledge with itself. As long as the *ipse* perseveres in its will to know and to be *ipse*, anguish continues, but if the *ipse* abandons itself and knowledge with itself, *ravissement* [rapture, ecstasy] begins.* In *ravissement*, my existence regains a meaning, but the meaning refers immediately to the *ipse*, becomes *my ravissement*, a *ravissement* that I *ipse* possess, giving satisfaction to my will to be all. As soon as I return to this point communication, the loss of myself, ceases, I have ceased abandoning myself, I remain there, but with a new knowledge.

The movement begins again from there . . . .[18]

Bataille's mimicry of the Hegelian dialectic of separation, communication and secondary separation, is not without irony, but also has the intensity of an effort to think communication in abstraction from the voluntaristic and intellectualistic aspects of the dialectic. As cited above, the object in proximity is always already in a differential rapport with subjectivity, and therefore implies the insistence of a *perte de soi* or "loss of self" within exteriority. The object, like all unicity in proximity, is a fragment or remainder, and its lack of totalization is also interiority's lack of self-coincidence. The object's escape from comprehension is its involvement with interiority. The vulnerability of the latter is precisely this incumbence of the exterior. Against this background, the desire for totalization and possession of the object is essentially ambivalent, and conceals what Bataille calls a *glissement*. "The uncertain opposition of autonomy to transcendence puts being in a slipping position [*position glissante*]: at the same time that it closes itself within autonomy, by this very fact each being *ipse* wishes to become the whole of transcendence, and firstly, the whole of the composition of which it is a part."[19] The desire of the object in proximity has two irreconcilable and inseparable modalities. In the first place, it tends to bring the object "close enough" to be engulfed by ipseity. This is totalization as communion and possession. As Bataille notes, the limit-case of this absorption would be ipseity as the totality of existence. But since such a totalization would leave nothing outside, and since ipseity is a heteronomous economy in itself, the result of this tendency would be the destruction of closure, and the elimination of the economy. To leave "nothing outside" is to foreclose discontinuity, and thus to produce simple dispersion. Therefore as the object approaches in desire, its exteriority is actually increased by this intimacy. Its proximity is the excess and incompletion — the desire — of the surface which attracts it. The object can "come closer", but it cannot be engulfed by interiority, because its existence and its approach are correlative to the impossibility of totalization which is interiority itself. On the other hand, desire is the tendency to place the object at a distance adequate to phenomenality, and to totalize it by severing the communicational trace (which Bataille calls a "link") which involves it with subjectivity. This is totalization

---

* The French word *ravissement*, like the English "rapture", indicates etymologically both rape and loss, i.e. both penetration and dispossession.

as correlation: the "far enough" which adequates subject and object within the Same. But again, the constitution of interiority is economic, and such an adequate distance would also abolish the economy by destroying closure. The retreat of the object would ultimately absorb interiority into the undifferentiation of a purely continuous exterior. Since closure in the economy is a function of difference and heteronomy, i.e. a function of the communicational trace, neither the approach nor the withdrawal of the object can be "adequate" without subsuming both subject and object within undifferentiation. Thus the object may "take a distance", and may even be infinitely distant, in the sense of its inadequation to intentionality — but this distance will always be what Blanchot calls "contact at a distance" or a "seeing which is touching", because distance is also proximity. The form and possibility of exteriority is its intrication with interiority. Thus, totalization in either sense would be the destruction of communication and therefore the destruction of separation. The desire for totalization always tends toward the "absolute loss" of undifferentiation or continuity at the same time, and this is the basic involvement of desire with death in Bataille.* The moment of closure which produces a discontinuity of subject and object is a proximity, and a function of desire as the principle of an economy without totalization. The intensity of this

---

* In his books *Logique du sens* (Paris: Minuit, 1969) and *L'Anti-Oedipe* (with F. Guattari; Paris: Minuit, 1972), Gilles Deleuze has mobilized the concept of a "body without organs" (*corps sans organes*), borrowed from his readings of Artaud, in order to describe the complex process through which the excess of difference invests a problematic closure whose interiority is precisely a dispersion or undifferentiation. The extreme importance of this concept of closure (which intervenes in the context of the radical impossibility of totalization, and which structures Deleuze's most basic arguments), consists in the fact that the body without organs does not represent a desire proceeding from a constituted interiority, but describes rather a differential exigency which invests all interiority precisely as an "impossible" intensity of closure within an economy of general heteronomy. Desire, defined as a principle of differentiation, always produces a body without organs, i.e. an inactual but uneliminable exigency, simultaneously dispersed and closed, which mobilizes in the form of closure the non-totalizable movements of difference. This is because differentiation produces an economy of unicity and of intensity, rather than a field of simple dispersion. Although the context of Deleuze's arguments intersects that of psychoanalysis, the body without organs cannot be understood as a function of desire or of the unconscious, in the psychoanalytic sense of these terms. The intense, undifferentiated closure of this fugitive instance proceeds not from the functions of the psychic organism, but from the intensity of difference or of multiplicity. This is why the body without organs appears within a real which is "produced" by desire, rather than envisaged by the latter: an impersonal field of communications which presupposes neither consciousness nor the psychic organism. The body without organs is an impossible, inactual unicity which nevertheless haunts the general economy and organizes desire, because it is, as exigency, a basic function of differential separation. Within the philosophy of proximity, it may be recognized in the series of moments through which alteration undergoes a "catalysis" producing local configurations such as identity, correlation, determination, etc. On the most general level, the concept of the "totality" itself, whose immobile undifferentiation is most clearly evoked by Levinas, describes a global ramification of the enigmatic closure meditated by Deleuze.

discontinuity, in the wish for totalization, is *savoir.* The animation and force of this intense discontinuity — the excess of closure which makes closure a reality — is *non-savoir.*

Non-savoir is knowledge's transgression of its own tendency toward comprehension as totalization. This transgression proceeds from the excessive economy of knowledge itself as a rapport with the exterior. Knowledge is not a contemplation or illumination, but a desire and an interrogation. The thematic regularity of Bataille's terms, in the context of *non-savoir,* consists of their rapport with the complementary notions of desire as ambivalence and desire as non-voluntary exigency. Such terms as *supplice, expérience, méditation, contestation,* and *rire* attest this congruence of desire and passivity in cognition. They describe an exigency which is always a contestation of its own movement toward closure, because closure is always the excess of its own *dépense.* The massively overdetermined concept of the *rire* ("laughter", "burst of laughter") describes the extremity of desire in proximity. It suggests the spasmodically visceral and the orgasm; it is essentially non-voluntary, while retaining the context of intentionality and cognition; it breaks the silence of contemplation; it is an excess within closure which recalls the problematic of nudity; and most importantly, it is the insouciance and blitheness of transgression in its irresponsibility and failure. The *rire* is the irony of the event which does not do what it does, and does not mean what it means. This event or moment may be the intensity of closure or the impossible destruction of transgression. The basic irony of melancholy and anguish, in their concatenation with outbursts of laughter, structures most of Bataille's fiction, and should be understood as the fundamental irony of the exigency in desire.

In spite of the dialectical atmosphere of the paragraph cited above, there are temporal indications of proximity within its progressive, circular terms. For instance, the subject in totalization "cannot but lose himself;" the excessive and impossible aspect of knowledge "supervenes"; the subject "is going to lose himself;" *ravissement* "begins". When Bataillian violence moves toward the extremity of the possible, a moment of imminence appears, which describes transgression. At this moment, both totalization and destruction are imminent, but never come to pass. Their imminence is the incumbence of exteriority upon the Same. Subjectivity in proximity is a rapport with a moment whose futurity is its non-actuality or lack of manifestation. But this non-actuality is an intrication with the "present" which has the paradoxical power to dominate or weigh upon it. This domination — a force which is not a power — is the approach of the Other, in interiority's uneliminable rapport with alterity. The future, in this time of inactuality, is already the pre-originarity of the immemorial past. The temporal ekstases have become temporal proximity. What has not yet come to pass, and will never come to pass (the manifestation of the Other to a constituted comprehension), has the urgency of that which "cannot be stopped", by virtue of this very inactuality. The Same has a rapport or "contact" with the radically exterior — and thus its wish for experience has always already been granted. But the exterior is not in the service or at the service of the Same. In its passivity, it refuses to deploy itself as a totalization offered to comprehension. The Other always approaches, and only approaches. Thus *ravissement* always "begins", loss is imminent and unavoidable, and the extremity of desire becomes a reality which "supervenes" or approaches. The *aussitôt* ("already", "immediately") of Bataille's demonstration ("mais le sens se réfère aussitôt à l'*ipse*") describes not only the inevitability of reification as communication makes the detour of closure, but also the larger pre-originarity and unforeseeability of communication's excess over closure. The *rire* is the ironic extremity of this approach and inherence of loss within totalization, and of interiority within the economy. Communication has always already made itself "my" communication, and thus ended; the loss of self has always already ended; the movement is always "beginning again." *Non-savoir,* considered as the overall context of the desire of the object, is, like the *oeuvre* in Blanchot, a moment in being which precedes itself and survives itself. *Non-savoir* is neither a circle nor a dialectical progression, but a repetition: the fugitive presence of manifestation's inactuality.

The exigency of totalization which proceeds from the constitution of subjectivity in the catalysis of closure in the general economy, is necessarily a communication whose effort is to reduce communication. *Inachèvement,* in its spasmodic violence and its repetitive temporality, is necessarily the imminence and the *aussitôt* of closure. This collapsing and passivity of temporal discontinuity, combined with its correlate, the intensity of temporal proximity, is the time of separation in the general economy. The persistence of closure within a situation of such violent excess recalls, as mentioned above, the Nietzschian situation of theoretical activity with regard to life and survival; but more importantly, it is a consequence of the irreducibly economic aspect of being. The limited and limiting movements of *savoir* in Bataille are basic correlates of differentiation in this economy. As such, these movements are always inextricably involved with the fugitive excess of *non-savoir,* although not in a simple configuration of reification and absolute alterity. Reification in Bataille, like closure, always succeeds too well, and not well enough, because it is essentially an excess and a communication. The vocabulary of voluntarism which haunts the *Somme athéologique* is interrupted with regularity by statements like the following: "Our existence is an exasperated attempt to complete [*achever*] being (completed being would be the *ipse* become all). But the effort is *undergone* [*subi*: suffered, endured] by us . . . ."[20] *Savoir* is neither a spontaneity nor a determined agency: it is an exigency. Bataille writes that a consciousness truly adequate to the incompletion of the economy would be "an immense architecture in demolition, in construction at the same time."[21] Such a configuration, whose construction is precisely its demolition, is separation itself in Bataille's definition. It is this coincidence and contamination that renders Bataille's concepts irreducible to the duality of reification and its other, and that allows Bataille to perceive in the very knowledge he contests, a problematic latency of affirmation and contestation:

Only philosophy takes on a strange dignity by the fact that it assumes infinite placing in question. It is not results that earn it a dubious prestige, but only that it answers to the aspiration of man demanding the placing in question of all that is . . . . Its entire value is in the absence of repose it maintains.[22]

In this formulation one hears the echo of Levinas' situation of proximity as the condition of theoretical consciousness. The only truly "critical" experience of subjectivity, for Levinas, is the desire and heteronomy of an involvement with the Other. Bataillian *non-savoir* describes the same priority, while articulating the gravity of proximity with the insouciance of the *rire* in transgression.

PROXIMITY AND ONTOLOGY

The general economy is a dimension of communications or differentiations which produces closure or separation. Closure is essentially subjective — even in the case of the inanimate "particle", as Bataille writes — by virtue of its heteronomy. This heteronomy is a passivity and a non-indifference. Closure is always a susceptibility to the exterior, and thus always a sensibility or capacity to receive an impression. It is perhaps the ambiguity of this word "capacity" (aptitude, tendency, ability, etc.) that renders most clearly the rapport of proximity with philosophy. For closure, regardless of its heteronomy and alteration, is always a discontinuity. The pressure or force of the exterior invests this discontinuity as a turgid, exigent density. The exigency or conation of closure is a tendency to oppose this exteriority with which it is intricated, and to create itself as the adequate autonomy of identity to self. Thus the "in reverse" or "inside out" of a conation whose force is its involvement with the exterior, always tends to present itself as a primordial integrity which subsequently enters into relation with existence. To recoil from the economy is to recoil into the economy, with a force or intensity invested by the economy. This moment, with its regional and even illusory sense of autonomy, is totalization as an economic event or "catalysis". Conceived in its fugitive and illusory integrity, interiority has the aspect of a spontaneous "ability" to receive information from without. Conceived in its latent economy as a radical heteronomy, interiority is a passivity, turned toward the exterior in its *pour l'autre*, which cannot but receive the force of exteriority as a function of its own closure. The enigma of receptivity is this irreducible passivity and alteration which assume the function of a power of comprehension. The interest of separation is closure, and a concept of the real in terms of closure. Separation, in a purely economic sense, is in itself an "interpretation" of the economy as a field of totalizations. When differentiated as a theoretical activity or as a discourse such as philosophy, this behavior of interiority retains its intensity and ambiguity. In philosophy or thought in general, subjectivity speaks of subjectivity. The Nietzschian inspiration of the philosophy of proximity is its consistent intuition that this *logos* of comprehension is an interested discourse, produced by beings whose interiority is an exigency and not an autonomy. The turgidity of the *effort d'autonomie,* defined as "survival" and conservation, and the latent excess of this turgidity, defined as "mortality", are the principal Nietzschian resonances within Bataille's meditation of theoretical consciousness, and are palpable indirectly in the texts of Blanchot and Levinas.

The ambivalence of an economically defined conation is the two-fold exigency of placing the Other at a distance and engulfing the Other within closure. This exigency is impossible in both of its senses, because it aims to eliminate the communicational involvement of interiority with alterity, and such an elimination would be the destruction of closure itself. If the altering trace of communication is eliminated, either by an ultimate distance of exteriority or by an ultimate incorporation which leaves nothing outside — if the difference which is closure is eliminated —, then absolute dispersion replaces separation, and the economy is no longer an economy. Yet this exigency of discretion and integrity is the necessary form of a closure which endures or "survives". The exigency is subjectivity's "must", its effort, and the economic investment of the exigency is subjectivity's "cannot", i.e. the grounding of its conation in impossibility. The term "desire" in Bataille, Blanchot and Levinas, describes this fundamental ambivalence of interiority's conation. In Bataille's "profane world", which Blanchot calls simply the "world" and Levinas calls the "totality", the two axes of the exigency are accredited as possibilities. In philosophy, considered in the generality of its aims and predications, they are accredited as givens, under the name "comprehension" or "knowledge". Comprehension describes the ontological moment at which the existent assumes an adequate interval with regard to consciousness, and at which this interval becomes the adequation and correlation of subject and object within a larger totalization. Negativity grounds this dual possibility, in its consecration of the distinction between interior and exterior and in its guarantee of the totalization which subsumes their opposition. At this level, the critical exigency of philosophy is at its most derisory: consciousness doubts its capacity to penetrate the opacity of the integral object. Doubt is a function of totalization. The object may trouble the gaze of comprehension, may have a "dark side", an unknowable "in itself" — but only by virtue of its inner adequacy, and thus of its basic adequation to comprehension. Totalization is less than complete, but the disturbance of this approximation is actually its familiarity and its complacency.

But thought is an exigency, informed economically by communication. The world of comprehension it produces is an image of the general economy, in terms of its "effects". Within this world, the entities or singularities which are effects of differentiation, play the role of totalities. The problematic intervals of differentiation play the role of negativity or contradiction. The communications which produce the differential incompletion of singularities play the role of determinations which consecrate the identity of terms. The heteronomy and passivity which produce the excessive and incomplete closure of the singularity, play the role of totalization itself, proceeding in a dimension of power from integral, causative terms. Finally, the dissymetry of the *pour l'autre* in the economy of communication, plays the role of a reciprocity of determination in the region of totalization. In these multiple transformations, the differentiations produced by the general economy are mobilized in terms of negation and totalization to form a world whose principle of coherence is power or possibility. Being, in this regional dimension, is existence: a power to stand in opposition to the real, an appearance or manifestation which is correlative to this power, and an ability to enter into the rectitude and reciprocity of relation and determination, on the basis of essentially solitary, immaculate existence. Levinas calls this dimension of totalization *essence*: the *esse* of being which is also an *interesse*, an economy in which unicity is always totalization and the solitude of totalization. Plurality, in this field of correlations, is what Levinas calls an "allergy of beings" (*allergie des étants*). Its principle is a totalization which forecloses the compromising involvements of communication by interpreting the interval of difference or discontinuity as a negativity. Within this world, nothing is affected in its being (its interior economy, its possibility) by another instance. Closure knows no Other of closure. Everything determines and is determined, in an immobility which consecrates both identity and possibility.

The Bataille of "La Structure psychologique du fascisme" derived, in his own terms, the essence of the Heideggerian critique of philosophy, through his notion of an intense homogeneity conditioned by the unassimilability of the heterogeneous ("The *heterogeneous* mode explicitly undergoes a profound contamination [*altération*], which results in the production of an intense *homogeneity* without the fundamental *heterogeneity* being reduced."[23]). The region of totalization is an interpretation of the real (and, in consequence, a genuine configuration or dimension of the real) in terms of discretion, negation, and power, which are made possible by the movements and effects of the general economy. The integrity and spontaneity of this dimension, whose power to change the real is beyond question, are nevertheless understandable as a most hyperbolic and spectacularly violent moment of the exigency, in the general economy.* The intensity of totalization — its conservative and destructive force — is its intrication with the Other of totalization, i.e. the economy which produces it. Philosophy, which is totalization's thematization and rationalization of itself, is a most intense, anguished, self-critical discipline. This is because its economy is in excess over its own interpretation of this economy. For Blanchot, this economy is a priority of dissimulation over the negation which is its tendency. For Levinas, it is the *autrement qu'être* in its priority over the *essence* or totality it informs. For Heidegger, it is a pre-comprehension in terms of "beings" (the *étant*, *Seiendes*) which takes its force from its rapport with Being (a rapport which is, however, itself conceived as comprehension), and has its

---

* One aspect of Bataille's genius was his interpretation of humanity as the greatest power of loss or *dépense* in the history of the planet, rather than as a new power of construction and conservation. Cf. *La Part maudite*.

own, contaminated modality of "truth". The "truth" of totalization, its response to "that which desires to be thought," is its excess: its rapport with a proximity which exceeds and conditions its spontaneity. Thus, prior to its own contestations of this spontaneity, which will be so significant to Bataille and Levinas, philosophy in its very position of totalization is the insatiability of a totalization which is never complete enough: an excessive totalization. This is philosophy's exigency, and its fundamental "fidelity" to proximity, regardless of its betrayals of the communication it desires to reduce.

Differentiation in the general economy produces separation as a passivity and a communication. In Bataille, individuation is an incarnation or animation, whose predicates are excess and incompletion. In Blanchot, individuation is essential solitude: a lack of solitude or integral interiority whose predicates are impersonality and neutrality. In Levinas, individuation is a communication of condition and conditioned in the passivity of *jouissance* and sensation, and in the "illusory" spontaneity of the *cogito*. For all three thinkers, separation is a communication or inextrication based on an irreducibility of differentiation to negation. Bataillian continuity, the presence of absence in Blanchot, and the *il y a* in Levinas are names given to the essential weakness or inefficiency of the negative in proximity. Communication in the general economy produces not totalities, but impossibilities: singularities whose closure is forced by a dimension without negation and without power. These singularities are subjectivities, in the sense that their interiority is, in its very intensity, a reception of exteriority. The force of their separation, and the density of their interiority, is a passivity: an intrication with an alterity which itself has no power or substantiality. This is why closure is a desire, or the "exigency of the Other": the alterity from which it is differentiated, participates or collaborates in this differentiation. This collaboration, and the ambivalence of the exigency, produce the most important aspects of proximity: the *pour l'autre*, the *parole*, and *errance*. The heteronomy of closure is its non-indifference toward exteriority. The univocity or dissymetry of being in proximity is the force of the exigency, which inclines or orients discontinuity from the inside out, toward the Other. Conation is always a conation inside-out, an interiority *au dehors* in the economy. This inside-out of closure's excess has two basic consequences, beyond the breach or incompletion which defines subjectivity. The first is the *parole*, a sound or noise which troubles the silence of contemplation within a universe of comprehension. The second is *errance*, a movement which disturbs the immobility and reciprocity of determination. *Errance* is the exile of beings in their difference and their non-indifference: the desertion of their posts which is the modality of their unicity, and thus the only possibility of their remaining at their posts. The *parole* is the escape of excess from a unicity which is inspired or "insufflée" by the Other. Both these concepts designate the *reste* or remainder in being which resists the operations of negation, and which haunts the interiority of closure, leaving an essential part of it outside (*parole*) and forcing it into an incessant displacement (*errance*). The exigency is an inclination which is always a dispossession: the *au dehors* and *pour l'autre* of a breathless unicity which is involved with alterity.

Jacques Derrida, in an apparently hyperbolic response to a question during a colloquium, stated an important theme of difference and proximity: "As to perception, I should say that once I recognized it as a necessary conservation. I was extremely conservative. Now I don't know what perception is and I don't believe that anything like perception exists."[24] Appearance and phenomenality are communicational terms which designate an "effect" of difference and proximity. In the philosophy or proximity, as in that of difference, manifestation is not a given, and has no privilege. This is perhaps the greatest opacity of these philosophies to surrounding tendencies in contemporary thought. The terms which describe difference and proximity imply no originary manifestation, but rather a fundamental communication which exceeds the manifest while conditioning its possibility. Subjectivity, the differential heteronomy of closure, conditions the possibility of a force or movement in being (*parole, errance*) which may have the name "consciousness" within a regional dimension of communication. Dissimulation, which tends to appear in the "other night" and tends to become negation in the "day", produces a proximity of exteriority to subjectivity which may be named "manifestation". Heteronomy in differentiation produces a passivity or subjection of interiority which may be interpreted as the power and spontaneity of "intentionality". In most general terms, proximity produces closure as an inextrication from exteriority which may be named "comprehension": a communication in the form of adequation and unification. In the same sense that Freud derived the moments of consciousness from a differentiation which did not itself presuppose consciousness or manifestation, the philosophy of proximity discovers the possibility of the *apparere* and the *experire* in communication. Thus, in Levinas, the sensible − the proximity of sensing and sensed in individuation − is "déjà dit", already spoken, already the *parole*; and the excess of the *parole* over closure is the economic moment from which manifestation must be derived. The approach of the Other in sensation and the *visage*, and the dispossession of interiority in recurrence and inspiration, are the differentiation and the interval which philosophy interprets as an illumination. All the basic moments of proximity in Bataille, Blanchot and Levinas, indicate intervals and communications which, when interpreted as negations and totalizations, assume the form of manifestation and the *logos* of comprehension. Manifestation is a vicissitude of communication, an image of proximity, a region of the general economy. It is perhaps Bataille, in his exuberance and unself-consciousness, who best designates the transformation of proximity into manifestation, when he thematizes intentionality and *savoir* as productions of the *interdit* or prohibition. Communication becomes totalization when the contaminations of proximity, the "worse than nothing" of being underneath negation, are outlawed by subjectivity's interest in closure. Bataille's genius, and his Nietzschian inspiration, is his willingness to undertake, in the problematic of survival and *dépense*, an explication of manifestation's origin in closure. As irresponsibly anthropological as it must necessarily seem to most tendencies in philosophy, this problematic is able to transcend the familiar thematization of a metaphysics of presence, identity, causality, etc. which is inherited and which informs our philosophical language, but whose aims and whose genealogy are beyond our interrogation. The notion of survival which is common to Bataille and Nietzsche describes communication's interpretation as illumination, and the regionality of this interpretation, in a single moment: the exigency of closure. The principle of the metaphysics whose moments include causality, determination, presence, etc., is autonomy, along with its correlate, power. And this is the principle of closure's interest in proximity: the ability to recoil from the economy.

Any concept of manifestation or representation requires the positing of an interval or discontinuity within being which would produce consciousness and phenomenality. The philosophy of proximity thematizes this discontinuity, and the "opening" of subjectivity which is its correlate, while insisting upon the excess of discontinuity over the possibility of closure or totalization. As discussed above, closure in the general economy is an ambivalent exigency and a dual impossibility. The totalization accredited by philosophy is thus an assumption of two impossibilities: the interval as negativity, and comprehension as adequation. It is Levinas who states this criticism most clearly and most often. In the first place, he points out that a correlation of subjectivity and exteriority within totalization requires a reduction of alterity to the dimensions of the Same, and therefore a dissolution of exteriority itself. Totalization is not a relation at all, but a reduction of exteriority in adequation and totalization. In order for manifestation to retain even the possibility of a subject-object relation, the alterity or pluralism of separation must be maintained. Manifestation cannot be a totalization, because totalization eliminates both subject and object. "The exteriority of being does not signify, in effect, that multiplicity is without rapport. But the rapport that links this multiplicity does not fill up the abyss of separation, it confirms the latter."[25] The totalization of interior and exterior within the Same reduces relation to an essentially undifferentiated homogeneity. Pluralism implies a rapport of interiority with an exterior which is not another Same, and not another moment of the Same. Relation requires exteriority. In the second place, consciousness implies a capacity of subjectivity to be affected by exteriority. The critical or theoretical moment of consciousness cannot be thematized without its subjective moment. Manifestation describes a consciousness which illuminates, gives meaning, and totalizes, without itself being affected by the exteriority which is subject to its spontaneity:

an exteriority surrendering to thought in illumination and without immodesty [*impudeur*] all its being, that is, totally present without anything, by right, shocking [*heurter**] thought, without thought ever feeling itself to be indiscreet.

* By the word *heurter* ("to shock", "to collide with"), Levinas indicates the incumbence, weight, or force of an alterity which is not a power or substantiality: not another Same.

Illumination is the disappearance of all that might shock. Intelligibility, the very fact of representation, is the possibility for the Other to be determined by the Same, without determining the Same, without introducing any alterity into the latter, the free exercise of the Same. The disappearance, in the Same, of the self opposed to the non-self.[26]

The privilege of consciousness in manifestation is its impersonal spontaneity. Whether defined as spirit, concept, understanding, or the care of *Dasein,* consciousness is primordially adequate to the exterior. The exterior may "determine" consciousness as spontaneity or as illumination, but, as Levinas insists, "the Other does not determine the Same here."[27] Object and subject are adequated within the Same, subsumed by the Same. The object "determines the thinking [*pensant*] . But it determines it without touching it, without weighing upon it."[28] Again, as in the first objection, no true interval or receptivity has been established. The totality is a correlation, but not a true manifestation. It is rather the undifferentiated interiority of a whole, within which the immobility of determination forecloses an encounter of interiority with another instance. It describes a truth without the possibility of truth and error, without the possibility of the question, of the behavior of consciousness. This is the lack of verisimilitude of Hegel's dialectic. The insufficiency of the Spirit's self-consciousness in the phrase "for us — not for consciousness" is absurd, in the terms of Hegel's argument. How can the absolute be "not absolute enough" — unless it is secretly affected by an incompletion, a properly communicational insufficiency which is correlative to closure itself? Levinas' argument is that manifestation and totalization, illumination and closure, cannot be thought in their own terms, but must be thought as effects of communication. Only differentiation and proximity can produce an interval in being and a receptivity of consciousness. Totalization — the dissolution of difference within correlation — is a homogeneity and an undifferentiation which are the impossibility of totalization itself.

The philosophy of proximity thematizes a critical or theoretical interval within being, and a receptivity of consciousness, which condition manifestation without themselves being reducible to moments of manifestation. In Bataille, this interval is discontinuity, and receptivity is the excess and incompletion of closure. In Blanchot, the interval is dissimulation or "interruption", and receptivity is impersonality and essential solitude. In Levinas, the interval is separation, and receptivity is the heteronomy of sensation, creation, and recurrence. For all three thinkers, the form of the interval is difference — a differentiation which individuates through the force of communication — and receptivity is proximity: the weight or incumbence upon interiority of an alterity which is "not in the same concept" as interiority. The critical "capacity" of subjectivity in proximity is desire, i.e. its non-indifference toward alterity. This capacity is a passivity which tends in philosophy to assume the form of a spontaneity. In a complementary moment, the heteronomy of subjectivity is the excess of the *parole*, which will tend in philosophy to assume the form of the transitive and illuminating *logos*. In proximity, the price of lucidity or manifestation — the price of interiority's rapport with the exterior — is an involvement which compromises and contaminates. Subjectivity is intricated with the exterior in a sense more "immediate", more "certain", than its rooting in being by phenomenology would indicate. But this rooting is an involvement, an incumbence, and a pressure of exteriority which "approaches from within," which is always too close, too distant, and too excessive to become manifest. The approach of the exterior does not leave consciousness untouched, as Hegel and Heidegger attest in spite of themselves in their denunciations of immediacy, fascination, and inauthenticity in all its forms. The Other's approach — a difference which is a non-indifference — "changes", "alters" the Same. Phenomenology's intuition of this alteration is its consistent claim that the "fascination" of consciousness' originary adequation to the exterior is not sufficient or not authentic, and must be supplanted by a comprehension which takes a more appropriate distance from the exterior — a distance correlative to domination and self-consciousness. The only "adequation" — the only proximity — of intellect and things is the heteronomy of desire, as phenomenology attests by its very allergy to this proximity. Exteriority escapes as it approaches, in the dissymetry of the *pour l'autre*. As in the approach to Eurydice, we can neither illuminate it nor take our eyes off it. This escape which approaches informs the most important terms of the philosophy of proximity, such as dissimulation, inactuality, *non-savoir*, fascination, and impossibility.

Every discourse, including that of philosophy, is a production of proximity, and therefore, in a sense, a description or manifestation of proximity. Every discourse proceeds from the *parole* of subjectivity's rapport with exteriority. At the same time, any discourse describes the detour of separation in being, and therefore the opacity of discontinuity. No discourse is adequate to proximity, but no discourse simply reifies proximity. Philosophy tends to mobilize communication in the direction of the manifest, the discrete, and the spontaneous. Its preferred logical and discursive element is negation. It is perhaps for this reason that philosophy's perennial style has been, not commentary or exegesis, but refutation and objection. The individual philosophical discourse tends to present itself and to be received as a unitary system of definitions. The univocity of its predications and conclusions tends to be the principle of its interpretation — although not of its influence or cultural resonances. In these resonances, the philosophical text has the same destiny as the literary text. The fecundity of its inequalities and the dissemination of its meanings exceed its enclosure among schools in the history of philosophy, and inform its displacements and importations within the text of its culture. In this communicational aspect, the philosophical text finds its animation in proximity. Thought is not the univocity of a frustrated or approximate comprehension, but is communication. Its own definitions of its efficiency or transitivity do not exhaust its economy. The concern or interest in totalization which defines philosophy in its desire for truth, is itself an insatiability of totalization which is animated by proximity. Levinas points out consistently that philosophy's critical moment proceeds from its origin in the heteronomy of communication, and thus from the "shame" of its spontaneity. The possibility of error proceeds from the larger intuition that totalization conceals another economy.

In its apparently facile paradoxes, philosophy is obsessed not with the inefficiency or approximate aspect of its definitions, but with their latent economy. In the ambivalence of experience, which desires to approach the Other without reducing its alterity, and yet to make of this approach an adequation, the alternative of idealism and realism defines philosophy as a preoccupation with a concerning or incumbent alterity. In its situation of consciousness within Being, rather than in simple opposition to an objective totality, philosophy describes the involvements of proximity, in spite of its desire to reduce their contaminations. At the same time, philosophy's obsession with reification and the escape of the Other (however anthropomorphic this escape may be, in its absolution and spontaneity) attests its intuition of an alterity which concerns us, in its inaccessibility. The "miracle" of an interiority "preoccupied by something other than itself" is, to paraphrase Levinas, an event of proximity and not of comprehension. The possibility of interrogation or curiosity is unthinkable within an economy of totalization, unless — as in phenomenology — subjectivity's pre-comprehension of the exterior is defined as a fascination, a heteronomy, or a desire. But this definition is precisely an attestation of proximity's excess over totalization.

Levinas returns with admiration to the theme of skepticism, "which is not afraid to affirm the impossibility of assertion while daring to *realize* this impossibility by the very assertion of this impossibility."[29] Skepticism's persistence when refuted by logic attests its sense of a *diachronie* or lack of conceptual adequation of its denial on one hand, and the truth it denies on the other. Skepticism, like philosophy in general, intuits the *diachronie* of Other and Same which are "not in the same concept." The critical tendency of philosophy is its involvement with communication: not its comprehension, but the excess which haunts this comprehension. Gilles Deleuze, in his *Différence et répétition,* correctly describes representation as the exigency of a "représentation orgique", an infinite and excessive discursive movement which nevertheless wishes to return to the form of the identical. In this definition, Deleuze repeats Bataille's notion that *savoir* is always a contestation of its own totalizations, and that the insistence of this contestation proceeds from the passivity of *non-savoir* in proximity. The best contemporary readings of the history of philosophy approach classic texts with an eye to the fecundity of this communicational tension, and with a calculated indifference to the conclusions which subsume it. The influence of Heidegger in this context cannot be gainsaid, although the attention and creativity he brings to his readings of philosophers are often compromised by his tendency to understand communication's excess as simple inequality or self-contradiction, and to subordinate philosophical texts to the "metaphysics" which dominates their movement. Heidegger's insistence upon the role of literature in the history of thought is also an important and influential moment of his philosophy, although his tendency is to privilege in the literary text a pertinence he refuses the philosophical text on the same basis, and to subordinate literature to manifestation. In general, Heidegger's superiority is his perception of philosophy as a communication whose animation or rapport with "that which desires to be thought" exceeds the apparent complacency of its definitions. Heidegger's appreciation of the "metaphysical" texts he rejects and often reduces, is not a pose, but is his perception of essentially contaminated forms of "truth" whose value attests his own intuition of proximity.

En route to his notion of contradiction and to the hyperbolic totalization of the Concept, Hegel thematizes a subjectivity which is involved with differentiation in being, and describes the passivity of this dialectical proximity to alterity. This is his influence, generally unacknowledged, upon Bataille, Blanchot, and Levinas. All three thinkers reject the Hegelian intellectualism which subordinates communication to totalization, but all three concede to totalization an effective reality and a regional status within the general economy — a gesture which itself attests Hegel's influence. Hegel's interpretation of difference as negativity, and proximity as contradiction, does not prevent him from positing a properly communicational moment in the dialectic. It is perhaps this intuition of communication that motivates Bataille's admiration for the Hegel who "thought he was going mad" in the elaboration of the system, and that informs the respect of the philosophy of proximity for Hegel's excessive, violent model of totalization. The philosopher whose rejection and denigration seem to be integral to proximity's elaboration, particularly in Blanchot and Levinas, is Heidegger. Blanchot punctuates his discourse, at relatively distant but regular intervals, with univocal rejections of Heidegger.[30] The career of Levinas, as is well known, consists of an early preference for Heidegger over Husserl, and a subsequent refusal of Heidegger which is so insistent, and intervenes so often in his text, that it may confuse his reader. Comprehension and totalization, in their servility, submission and violence, are inextricably linked with the name of Heidegger, in Blanchot and Levinas.

No modern philosophical text is more creatively contaminated than that of Heidegger. From *Sein und Zeit* to his last published works, Heidegger describes a proximity of subjectivity to exteriority which tends to exceed the concept of manifestation as totalization and appropriation. The *Sorge, Geworfenheit,* and *verfallen* of *Dasein,* ultimately correlative to its *Da,* describe an involvement of subjectivity in exteriority on the basis of differentiation. This involvement, despite its interpretation as disclosedness, pre-comprehension, possibility and potentiality, implies a latent heteronomy of spontaneity itself. It is this priority of involvement over the intervals of comprehension that produces, as mentioned above, Heidegger's lengthy critiques of *Dasein*'s loss of itself in the everyday, and that animates the description of being-toward-death. The latter is a rapport with the indefinition of alterity's approach, and with a "possibility of impossibility" that Blanchot and Levinas are not entirely justified in refusing as a subordination of impossibility to possibility.[31] Heidegger intuits impossibility, i.e. the reality of a dimension outside or underneath negation and power, although he posits this dimension as a function of spontaneity and comprehension. In this he is Hegel's student, throughout his career. For the situation of subjectivity in being as a comprehension, albeit an essentially insufficient comprehension, appropriated to Being in its very inadequation to Being, is the Hegelian gesture, *par excellence*. Heidegger's thinking of *Dasein*'s spontaneity in the alternative of inauthenticity and authenticity, his association of authenticity with *Dasein*'s potentiality for "being-a-whole" (*Ganzsein*), and his definition of an authentic Being-toward-death in "anticipatory resoluteness" (*vorlaufende Entschlossenheit*) in its essential appropriation to "disclosedness" (*Erschlossenheit*), serve to underline his overwhelming debt to Hegel. The subordination of subjectivity's passivity to its rooting in manifestation, and the consequent tendency to ground authenticity in spontaneity and resolution, are Heidegger's Hegelian inspiration. That Hegel's name and concept of temporalization intervene at the close of *Sein und Zeit*, and punctuate the permanent interruption of the book's development, is noteworthy. Heidegger's rejection of Hegel's grounding of temporalization in differentiation is most unconvincing, given the latter's compelling influence on *Sein und Zeit*'s discussion of time. The implication of repetition and of a proximal temporality of inactuality in the temporal ekstases of a subjectivity that "comes back to itself futurally"[32] indicates Heidegger's important contribution to the Hegelian analysis of comprehension's latent economy.

Heidegger's inextricable involvement with Hegel is his positing of metaphysics, inauthenticity, and pre-comprehension as the vicissitudes of a comprehension. While consistently revealing implicit and unfounded suppositions of presence, substantiality and punctuality in the philosophers he reads, Heidegger retains the context of comprehension as the ultimate dimension, the "last word" of *Dasein*'s communication with Being. Within the context of this disturbing insistence upon appropriation and spontaneity, however, Heidegger is able, in the many aphoristic moments of his later texts, to state the most important themes of both difference and proximity. In several of these texts, including *Vom Wesen des Grundes, Identität und Differenz,* and the later editions of *Was ist Metaphysik?*, Heidegger specifies that the *Sein/Seiendes* duality cannot be thought in abstraction from the concept of difference, and that the excess of Being over beings proceeds from this uneliminable ontological difference. The rapport of Being with beings, and of subjectivity with exteriority, is a differential and communicational rapport. That this rapport is defined by Heidegger in terms of appropriation, as in the following statement from *Identität und Differenz*, does not entirely reduce its radicality:

> The onto-theological constitution of metaphysics proceeds from the permanence of Difference, which holds separate and in a rapport with each other Being as ground, and beings as grounded and founded in reason.

What we thus name, refers our thinking to a realm for which the governing terms of metaphysics — Being and beings, ground and grounded — are no longer sufficient. For what these words name, what the way of thinking governed by them represents, proceeds from that which differs, as a function of Difference.[33]

The difference which grounds and exceeds the oppositions of metaphysics, is not exhausted conceptually by its escape from these oppositions. Difference involves and concerns subjectivity, because it produces subjectivity. Difference is "what must be thought", "that which desires to be thought": the exigency of thought. In Gilles Deleuze's excellent phrase from *Différence et répétition,* difference is that which "cannot be thought, and cannot but be thought." Difference forces subjectivity to think. It is subjectivity's inextrication from Being, beyond its problematic adequation to Being in comprehension. The escape of difference from comprehension is an incumbence. In this context, difference is linked to its own concealment or forgetting, not by virtue of an inauthenticity of thrown consciousness, but by virtue of its communicational excess over the possibility of manifestation. "Forgetting" (*Vergessenheit*) is not a moment of comprehension, but of communication, as Heidegger states in a cumbersome but compelling formulation: "Forgetting belongs to [*gehört zur*] Difference, because the latter belongs [*zugehört*] to the former. Forgetting does not happen to Difference only afterward, as a consequence of the forgetfulness of human thinking."[34] The surrounding context of Heidegger's intellectualism does not reduce the affinity of this configuration with Blanchotian *oubli,* i.e. the intrusion in subjectivity of a proximal exteriority which can never become actual, phenomenal, or manifest. *Oubli* and the incumbence of difference also inform the characteristic Heideggerian concept of the unthought or yet-to-be-thought: "an unthought [*Ungedachten*] from which what has been thought receives its essential space. But only the already thought prepares the still-unthought, which always enters anew into its abundance."[35] The unthought is the inactual element of thought, and the excess implicit in thought's economy. As such, it deploys itself as the immemorial and the forgotten which, in proximity, are involved with the *à venir*: a futurity of excess which never becomes punctual or present, but which compels from the future. The force or intensity of interiority's rapport with the exterior is this continuing and uneliminable involvement with the inaccessible.

By virtue of his concept of metaphysics, of a Difference beyond or underneath manifestation which conditions the possibility of metaphysics' totalizations, of the immemorial past of this difference, and of the indefinition characteristic of its effects,[36] Heidegger exerts a considerable influence on the philosophy of difference, and particularly on that of Jacques Derrida. The concepts of the *jeu* ("The essence of Being is the *Spiel* itself."[37]), the *trace* as a contamination of presence in a differential singularity,[38] and *différance* and *espacement* as experimental predicates for differentiation as a moment or process in Being, are all present in the aphoristic themes of *Identität und Differenz,* as well as in other essays of Heidegger's later career. On the other hand,

Heidegger's notion of the incumbence of difference upon subjectivity, the economic force which inclines subjectivity toward alterity,[39] points to the congruence of difference and proximity in the *parole*. *Was ist Metaphysik?* shows both Heidegger's intuition of proximity's excess and his exigency to reduce a proximal model of thought to spontaneity. On one hand, thought is

the human response to the *parole* [*Wort*] of the silent voice of Being. Thought's response is the origin of the human *parole,* a *parole* which alone gives birth to language as the manifestation of the *parole* in words.[40]

The *parole* is the form of exteriority's investment of subjectivity, and the excess of this investment over the possibility of manifestation. Thought is not an illumination, but rather a response (*Antwort*), a *parole* inspired by the *parole* of communication: the *pour l'autre* of interiority. In a formulation which recalls the complex temporality of proximity, particularly in Blanchot, Heidegger defines thought's "attention" as a reception of the approach of alterity, both immemorial and futural:

Essential thought is attentive to the slow [*langsamen*] signs of the Incalculable [*Unberechenbaren*] and recognizes in the latter the immemorial [*unvordenkliche*] approach [*Ankunft*] of the Ineluctable [*Unabwendbaren*].[41]

The unavoidable actuality of the ineluctable is an immemoriality, an imminence, and an "inhuman" slowness. This inactuality, in Blanchot's phrase, is its "domination". But Heidegger continues, "this thought is attentive to the truth of Being and serves the being of truth."[42] This submission and service, which so annoy Levinas and convince him of subjectivity's dissolution in Heideggerian comprehension, nevertheless indicate Heidegger's sense of a passivity of attention, and a receptivity of subjectivity which is irreducible to its spontaneous, illuminating function. That Heidegger cannot sustain this fleeting although recurrent sense of passivity is clear from the bulk of *Was ist Metaphysik?* Thought, for Heidegger, remains an "action"[43] and the vigilance of an appropriation to Being in which passivity is always secondary to *Sorge.*[44] Thought's "response" to Being's incumbence remains a moment of comprehension. Similarly, in *Identität und Differenz,* the approach of the exterior is subordinated to the *Ent-Fernung* which places the former at a distance both "far enough" and "near enough" so that proximity may become comprehension.[45] The involvements and contaminations of proximity are consistently subordinated to the notion of "belonging" in the key terms of *Identität und Differenz* (*Ge-Stell, Zusammengehörigkeit, Ereignis,* etc.), and in this sense, the continuity of Heidegger's thinking throughout his career is clear. Appropriation and adequation are the ultimate principles of Heidegger's concept of communication.

In general terms, Heidegger's notion of proximity and communication as foundations of an involvement of thought with Being, takes the form of a spontaneous comprehension, in care, resoluteness, service, guardianship, and the "letting be" of his later works. The limited or conditioned aspect of this spontaneity takes the form of pre-comprehension, forgetting, fascination, the everyday, etc. — concepts whose situation of inadequation within a larger appropriation recalls not only Hegel's Concept, but the history of philosophy in its generality. At the same time, in repeated aphoristic formulations, Heidegger attempts to designate an aspect of thinking which is other than a comprehension. One such formulation appears at the end of *Identität und Differenz*:

Our Western languages are languages of metaphysical thought, each in its own way. Whether the essence of Western languages is marked with the imprint of metaphysics, and thus marked permanently by onto-theology, or whether these languages offer other possibilities of speaking, including that of the non-saying which speaks [*sagenden Nichtsagens*], must be left an open question.[46]

Heidegger offers no explanation of what is meant by *sagenden Nichtsagens:* a *parole* prior to transitivity and comprehension, defined as a latent possibility of philosophical language, and described exclusively in the form of the question. The placement of this possibility in the margins of a text devoted to comprehension; its interrogative mode; and its lack of elaboration, are typical of the "last Heidegger". It is clear that, by the repetition of such moments, Heidegger's text compellingly describes the "shame" of spontaneity, and the communicational aspect of philosophy's self-criticism, which are so important to Levinas. The "letting be" in general, in spite of its ingenuousness and its rudimentary intuition of a passivity within comprehension, describes Heidegger's sense of spontaneity's limits. Although he is not able to thematize proximity explicitly, Heidegger in his later works seems to be the best critic of his own intellectualism.

None of these tendencies impress either Blanchot or Levinas. For the former, Heidegger remains the philosopher of comprehension ("the providential fact that being and the comprehension of being go together"[47]) who subordinates impossibility to possibility,[48] who subordinates the Other's approach to the appropriation of Other and Same within a manifestation defined as Unity,[49] and who subordinates the approach of death in indecision to the absurd resoluteness of a "being for death".[50] The later chapters of *L'Espace littéraire* contain numerous denunciations of Heidegger's subordination of art to manifestation.[51] In Blanchot, the phrase "neither dialectics nor ontology", which repeatedly punctuates a description of proximity in its excess over manifestation and power, is intended to evoke the names of Hegel and Heidegger. In Levinas, the flouted concept "dévoilement" ("illumination", "disclosing") refers directly to Heidegger, although the latter's name and concepts are the negative spring-board for nearly all of Levinas' most important themes.*

The common denominators of Levinas' manifold rejections of Heidegger are (1) Heidegger's descriptions of consciousness as an originary spontaneity; (2) his thematization of comprehension as an appropriation in which exteriority surrenders its alterity as it dissolves in the neutrality of the Same; (3) the im-plicit theme of a power over alterity which proceeds from this panoramic view of Other and Same; and (4) the untroubled spontaneity of a Same in mani-festation, upon which no alterity is incumbent. For Levinas, the primacy of comprehension in Heidegger subordinates the Other to manifestation in the same moment that it subordinates the Other to power. Heideggerian compre-hension, in its phenomenologically inspired rooting of consciousness in being, is the image of the totality: a distribution of beings in the immobility of their subordination to totalization, and in the *allergie* of their correlation. As dis-cussed earlier, Levinas considers the correlations of manifestation to be neither true communications (since beings in correlation have no weight or effect upon each other beyond the equilibrium of determination) nor a true production of separation (since the difference which defines unicity is dissolved within the undifferentiated neutrality of the totality). For Levinas, the univocity of Being in Heidegger is the image of the Peace of Reason: the spurious non-violence

* Although the rapport of Levinas to Heidegger would require a lengthy study on its own, the following list resumes Levinas's major criticisms of Heidegger's philosophy:
(1) The primacy of comprehension in Heidegger reduces the functions of both subjectivity and communication to that of manifestation (including contexts such as inauthenticity and *oubli*).[52]
(2) The sole context of comprehension in Heidegger is power, in consciousness' transitivity and in the "allergy" of beings implied by Heidegger's view of the general economy.[53]
(3) Heidegger's model of temporalization fails to account for the temporal dephasing which produces subjectivity, and for temporalization as a rapport with alterity.[54]
(4) In Heidegger's notion of comprehension, the Other's alterity surrenders itself to mani-festation, producing a spurious totalization without true relation.[55]
(5) Comprehension and the *Mitsein* reduce interiority's rapport with *Autrui* to manifest-ation and correlation.[56]
(6) Comprehension reduces the proximal incumbence of alterity and therefore fails to account for the *éthique* – without which theoretical consciousness is an impossibility.[57]
(7) Heidegger conceives subjectivity only as spontaneity, and thus fails to perceive the communicational constitution of interiority.[58]
(8) The primacy of spontaneity and comprehension in Heidegger reduces *Dasein* to the form and the economy of the Same.[59]
(9) Heidegger's dependence upon power as the economy of totalization forces him to reduce the notion of impossibility, especially in the concept of "being-toward-death".[60]
(10) Heidegger's panoramic view of communication as manifestation reduces the involve-ment of Same and Other to the undifferentiation of the Same, and fails to account for the dissymetry or non-reciprocity of communicational alteration.[61]
(11) The complicity of Heideggerian comprehension with power and negativity reduces the fundamental economic notion of the *il y a* in being.[62]
(12) The *Sein/Seiendes* duality in Heidegger cannot account for an incumbent instance outside manifestation, neither *voilé* nor *dévoilé*.[63]

of beings which cannot desert their posts within the universal — a non-violence which conceals the more fundamental violence of their *allergie,* i.e. the reduction of their difference and their communication by the totalitarian aspect of their correlation. *Esse* within the totality is always *interesse* for Levinas: the untroubled solitude of beings whose unicity involves no communication. Heidegger's perennial insistence upon a limitation of comprehension, a forgetting of Being in the spontaneity of *Dasein*'s enthusiasm for technological control of existence, does not reduce Levinas' rejection of the larger context of comprehension which defines both the forgetting and the originary contact of *Dasein* with Being. The "letting be" and the passivity which are Heidegger's most serious problematizations of the congruence of comprehension and power, are refused and even ridiculed by Levinas as indices of a submission to Being's definition as a totality.[64] In general, Heidegger's criticisms of the spontaneity of manifestation, which are a constant throughout his career, are considered by Levinas to be the derisory vicissitudes of a thinking for which comprehension must always be the ultimate dimension, the "last word" of communication.

It has been said that the creativity of the most radical thinkers depends to some extent on their narrowness. They follow the exigency of their *oeuvre* (or are drawn by it, in Blanchot's phrase, "outside themselves and perhaps outside everything") at the price of a certain incuriosity with regard to other texts in the surrounding culture whose proximity to their own creativity is extreme. Bataille's refusal of Genet is an example of this necessary narrowness. The proximity of certain interlocutors troubles the essential solitude of the creative writer — a solitude which is itself the hyperbole of proximity and of dispossession. The writer whose creativity is already an inextricable involvement with something outside himself, may have little curiosity regarding manifestly related texts in his vicinity. Such a configuration may describe Levinas' refusal to read in Heidegger a questioning of totalization which is in true sympathy with the radicality of *Totalité et infini.* On the other hand, the nearly obsessive invocation of the name of Heidegger at close intervals in Levinas' text indicates a more intimate involvement and an allergy beyond incuriosity. During a brief period in the 1930's, Levinas preferred Heidegger's existential situation of consciousness to what he then perceived as Husserl's intellectualism. At this moment in his career, the influence of Heidegger's denunciation of metaphysics in its innocent spontaneity (involved as it is with Husserl's criticism of the "naive natural attitude" of consciousness, and with the Hegelian genealogy of this phenomenological gesture) could not but affect the development of Levinas' concern with totalization as a region of the general economy. The rejections of Heidegger which punctuate Levinas' philosophy suggest a latent recognition of the former's collaboration in the thematization of an instance which passively resists totalization. On the other hand, Levinas' discovery of an instance which approaches as it escapes, and which concerns interiority from a dimension beyond power, is the true radicality of his rejection of Heidegger, and his exigency to "leave the atmosphere of (Heidegger's) philosophy."[65] In this context, Heidegger's remaining in Germany during the Hitlerian period is decisive. It represents, not a personal submission to totalitarianism or an involvement with anti-semitism, but the ultimate complicity of philosophy, in the very movement of its contestations and self-criticisms, with the essentially totalitarian congruence of manifestation and power. The Peace dreamt of by Reason, as Levinas was to show so compellingly in *Totalité et infini*, is the very image of war, and the "permanent possibility of war." The complicity of comprehension and power describes an allergy of beings and a reduction of alterity in totalization which reinstates the violence against which it protests "in the name of reason."

Ontology as a primary philosophy is a philosophy of power. It leads to the State and the non-violence of the totality, without taking precautions against the violence upon which this non-violence lives and which appears in the tyranny of the State. The truth which was intended to reconcile persons, exists anonymously here. Universality presents itself as impersonal and there is here another inhumanity.[66]

Philosophy's involvement with "injustice" is its indifference to an instance which would resist the spontaneity of comprehension while not representing in itself a superior power or superior truth. It is for this reason that, in Levinas' eyes, philosophy as the arm of manifestation will never be sensitive to the weight of the Other's alterity which characterizes both "justice" and the notion of communication. Philosophy will always desire to inaugurate a reign of peace by "making war on war." The futility and the persistence of its self-criticisms indicate its tendency, "in spite of itself," toward the dissymmetry and heteronomy of the *éthique*, in Levinas' definition of this term.[67] This secret heteronomy, the "shame of spontaneity", is the only possibility of a true theoretical consciousness. But a spontaneity which subordinates this latent economy to the triumph of its own power is, in Levinas' words, "the price paid for separation." Thus, despite his sympathy for its animation in communication, philosophy's inevitable recourse to a concept of non-violence rooted in totalization motivates Levinas' abandonment of its definitions.

A refusal to accredit philosophy's intuitions of proximity, on the grounds of its ultimate recourse to the notion of power as the final principle of Being's economy, amounts to a recognition in the spirit of Marx that metaphysics' self-criticisms are essentially internal. For Levinas, it matters little that Heidegger designates limits of comprehension, power, and spontaneity, or that he reshapes his prescriptions of resolution in terms of passivity and of a response to the Voice of Being. Since adequation and correlation remain the ultimate criteria of communication, the philosopher's critical exigency is always the same: to posit a limited comprehension, and to prescribe a superior comprehension; to posit a veiled or forgotten or contaminated adequation, and to prescribe a more vigilant consciousness of this adequation; to posit a primordial appropriation, and to prescribe a perfecting of this appropriation. Never does this critical exigency exceed its tendency toward a situation in which adequation subsumes all difference and all contact between interiority and the exterior. The modesty of thought remains false, as long as the entire field of communication is envisaged under the sign of comprehension and its vicissitudes. At this level, thought does not interrogate Being, but rather the availability of Being. To the extent that philosophy reduces itself to the question: "What can comprehension accomplish?", its categories must be abandoned. The need to take a distance from thought's thwarted questioning of its own spontaneity is common to Bataille, Blanchot, and Levinas, and underscores their fundamental involvement with the inspiration of Nietzsche and Proust. There is a sense of Levinasian *eschatologie* — a thinking "out of season", a thinking for a time and place outside the totality — in the texts of all three thinkers. Hence the futuristic aspect of titles such as *La Part maudite, Le Livre à venir,* and *Autrement qu'être ou au delà de l'essence.* There is a willful marginality in the philosophy of proximity, a refusal to share the epistemological horizons of its culture. The impressive independence of this stance conceals, however, a more fundamental solitude or separation: that of alteration itself. The concept of proximity implies a non-negative, intensive inadequation of thought and the exterior. This inadequation is not compensated by a belonging of the thinking being to alteration itself — proximal separation begins where appropriation ends — but opens instead a new rapport with the nocturnal paths of error: paths whose sign is no longer negative. This rapport not only imposes new criteria upon the action of thought, but also produces a change in the mind that contemplates the rapport: a solitary, latent birth of thought itself which, in proximal Time, "comes from the point toward which it goes" — *à venir, au dehors, pour l'autre.*

NEGATIVITY AND IL Y A IN PROXIMITY

The Hegel of "Force and Understanding" concludes his exposé by declaring a necessity of thinking plurality or opposition within the dialectic as an interior moment or a function of closure, rather than as an intramundane state of affairs. This communicational process describes not an indifferent multiplicity, but a plurality arising from the essential heteronomy of the Same. Rather than to reproduce "the sensible representation of a solidification of differences in a distinct element of subsistence," consciousness must "set forth and apprehend in its purity this absolute notion of difference as *interior* difference [*Als innerer Unterschied*]."[68] "What we must now think is pure change, opposition in itself, that is, *contradiction.*"[69] Hegel's entire exposé has been pursued with reference to the term "difference" (*Unterschied*) and has described, through the notions of "force", "law", and "infinity", a series of instances whose only positivity is their intrication with each other. The "equality" of each instance, by virtue of this inextrication, is always a "becoming-unequal". The term "contradiction" (*Widerspruch*) supervenes only at the end of this demonstration. Its appearance is correlative to Hegel's final definition of interior difference as a scission which creates contraries whose relation is not simple indifference and opposition, but an "animation toward one another"[70] whose force is the *Aufhebung*. Thus difference is not an intramundane notation of opposition, but rather the movement of the concept which creates a dynamic exteriority. "There are two different terms which subsist, they are in-themselves as opposites, that is, each is the opposite of itself, they have their other within themselves and are merely one single unity."[71] Each term has "its" other within "it", and the two terms are posed within a unity. The form of unification conditions all three moments of difference. Interior scission is a heteronomy and an alteration which is subsumed by the larger totalization which is its context.

"That the self-identical breaks asunder signifies that, as well as it supercedes itself *as* already sundered, it supercedes itself as being-other [*Anderssein*]. The unity one thinks of ordinarily when one says difference cannot come out of unity, is itself in fact merely one moment of the process of scission; it is the abstraction of simplicity, which stands in contrast to difference."[72] Thus Hegel criticises the common supremacy of unity. But, as in so many moments of the *Phenomenology*, it is also his own model of unification — which never unifies enough, and which thus engenders the manifold separations and mediations which structure the work — that is in question. This unity may itself be a "moment of the process of scission", a moment of communication, and an "abstraction", as the tradition of Hegelianism and its critics attests. The "idealism" of totalization in Hegel motivates his critics' insistence upon a return to the concrete and empirical; but his discovery of a comprehension more fundamental than the vicissitudes of certainty before the opacity of the object, remains his domination. European rationalism is not wrong in assigning Hegel a unique centrality in recent intellectual history. The arresting of the dialectic at one of its moments, be it contradiction, comprehension, intersubjective alterity, or unification, seems to characterize each major tendency of 19th and 20th century thought.

Like Saussure, who thematizes difference in order to subordinate it to distinction and "negative" constitution, Hegel describes a becoming-other which is subsumed by contradiction and *Aufhebung*. At the same time, however, a configuration of alterity which is irreducible to contradiction and negation makes a fugitive but regular appearance within his text. The following passage, when read with the intellectual atmosphere of proximity in mind, is such an appearance:

(I)n that difference which is an interior difference, the opposite is not only one of two factors — if it were it would be an existent and not an opposite — it is the opposite of an opposite, or the Other is immediately present in this opposite. No doubt I put the opposite here, and the other, of which it is the opposite, there; that is, I place the opposite on one side, taking it by itself without the other. Just on that account, however, since I have here the opposite in itself and for itself, it is the opposite of its *own* self, that is, it has in fact the Other immediately within itself.[73]

While placing opposites in a dialectical intrication which situates difference within each term and the univocity of opposition itself within a larger context, Hegel invites his reader to perceive this moment in a different sense. In the first place, the Other which haunts the Same may be taken not as a result of opposition or even of scission, but as an instance contaminating the solitude of the Same, prior to its destiny as opposition or contradiction. This instance is not the other in opposition, but the Other of opposition, a becoming-other which does not exhaust its insistence by its concentration as the other term of dialectical opposition. Alterity would not result from opposition, but would produce an excess over the possibility of the Same itself as unity. Opposition and multiplicity would be effects of this conditioning excess. Alterity would not describe the possibility of mediation, but its latent impossibility: the excess of the dialectical economy over totalization and correlation. In Blanchot's expression, the Other is not the other term of the *entretien* or rapport, but is the impossibility of closure which makes possible the *entretien.* "Cela se tient entre" — alterity "stands between". It is a becoming-other and a heteronomy which precedes and exceeds the correlation and unification of dialectical opposition. Alterity is the fact that a term is not alone, but also not in an *ensemble* or relation with its opposite. No situation within the universal or within the dialectic reduces this contamination of solitude. In the second place, since alterity is not reducible to the presence of a constituted or differentiated other, it is therefore an instance which cannot be thought on the basis of a communication in opposition. The panoramic view of two terms in a dialectical intrication is not sufficient to describe the more basic problem of the term which is "not alone", prior to its definition as a term in a system. This is why the Blanchot of *L'Espace littéraire* calls the concept of a proximity which insists "between two poles" a "faulty image". Alterity approaches and conditions not a term, but the Same. Communication is a proximity of Same and Other, and not an opposition of "this Same" to "that Same". The one term is not the Other of the other term: alterity is the Other of this correlation. Alterity is not another Same. It is the inactual Other of the Same which invests the latter as an alteration and a heteronomy, an intense unicity of proximity — prior to the approach of a constituted intramundane other, explicit or implicit. Opposition is not the principle of this heteronomy. In Levinas' phrase, the "orientation in being" from Same toward Other is irreversible and asymmetrical. Alterity is by definition a non-reciprocity. It may produce effects such as relation and multiplicity, but in itself it describes a pure contamination without terms or correlation. When Hegel writes, "the Other is immediately present in this opposite," he describes an alterity which is "in" the opposite without being reducible to the presence of the opposite. And when he writes, "it has in fact the Other already immediately within itself," he again describes not an inherence of the opposite, but of an alterity which makes possible the concretion of the opposite.

That difference is ultimately named contradiction by Hegel, and that the supremacy of negation inscribes difference into the unifications of the *Aufhebung,* does not eliminate the inspired moment in his text at which negativity becomes difference and difference becomes a rapport with the Other. Within this moment, the possibility of proximity appears, in the form of a rapport with alterity which is not only differential and non-reciprocal, but is also irreducible to the simple indefinition and escape from totalization which are the permanent temptation of the differential trace. The notion of an interiority which is "not alone" describes not only an incompletion and lack of presence, but also an alterity which is incumbent upon, or weighs upon, an interiority which is essentially, in Levinas' words, "non-indifferent" to alterity. Difference in proximity means non-indifference. The proximal entity can neither "desert its post" in the economy nor "remain at its post." Its unicity is an intensity forced by the Other, a turgidity which is also what Blanchot calls an "attraction in place" which contaminates the possibility of locus or position. This configuration is attested by the dynamism of most of Hegel's terms, although it tends to be obscured by the engulfing reciprocity of the master-slave correlation which immediately follows "Force and Understanding" in the *Phenomenology.* The "becoming-unequal of the equal" in Hegel, in spite of its immobilization within dialectical opposition, carries the force of proximity's fundamental dissymmetry and radical dispossession.

Every basic term in proximity — every important term in the massive textual involvement of Bataille, Blanchot, and Levinas — describes a weakness or defection of negativity whose remainder is not only the trace of differential alteration but also the violence of non-indifference and non-reciprocity. The withdrawal of negativity is also a withdrawal of Saussurian difference, which leaves terms at their places within a system of negative constitution. The collective informational pressure of difference within the economy of proximity produces interiority, but not as the equilibrium of a position. Instead, interiority is the *pour l'autre* of the exigency, whose only positivity is the exile of *errance,* the spasmodic dispossession of *dépense,* or the approach of the Other in the burrow. This lack of position or situation, this impossibility of the term *demeurer* (to "remain" or "abide") in proximity, is the reason why the terms of the approach and transgression intervene with such regularity in its thematization.

*

In the essay "Il y a"[74] Levinas proposes an irreducibility of the economy of being to negation. The concept *il y a* ("there is") describes an "event" or "experience" of being which is not conditioned by the negative, and which alters any philosophical definition of positivity or presence. "This impersonal, anonymous but inextinguishable "consuming" of being, which murmurs at the bottom of nothingness [*néant*] itself, we fix by the term *il y a.*"[75] At the "bottom" of the negative persists an uneliminable moment of existence, an impossibility of nothingness which implies an impossibility of the intervals which consecrate identity and non-contradiction. With the defection of the negative, the dualities of universal and singular, particular and general are contaminated. "Indetermination gives it its acuity. There is no determined being . . ."[76] The experience of the *il y a* is inadequate to the notion of consciousness, whose classical definition requires an interval adequate to illumination and phenomenality. Yet the *il y a* is that interval in being which is not negation. "One is exposed. All is opened upon us. Rather than to serve as our accession to being, the nocturnal space delivers us to being."[77] Levinas' theme throughout "Il y a" is the night: a dimension of communication without manifestation, an "obscure bottom of existence" in which things appear "through a night, like a monotonous presence which suffocates us in insomnia."[78] Presence in the *il y a* is exposition: an inability to see, and an inability to close the eyes. Subjectivity is an inability to experience that which it must experience: a presence without interval, without discretion. "To kill or to die is to seek an exit from being, to go where freedom and negation operate. Horror is the event of being which returns within the bowels of this negation, as though nothing had moved."[79] The "horror" of the *il y a* is not the anguish of negation in existence, not an anguish correlative to consciousness' negative constitution or spontaneity. Instead, it is the horror of negation's contamination. It proceeds from a passivity of subjectivity in a dimension without power.

The horror of the night, as the experience of the *il y a*, does not therefore reveal to us a danger of death, nor even a danger of pain. The essential point of this entire analysis. The pure nothingness [*néant*] of Heideggerian anguish does not constitute the *il y a*. A horror of being, as opposed to the anguish of nothingness; a fear of being, and not at all for being; a being a prey to, being delivered to something which is not a "something" ["*quelque chose*"].[80]

The *il y a* is an involvement with existence which forecloses the distinction between consciousness and object, without foreclosing their difference. Its experience is thus a passivity: the absence of power in an absence of totalization. It is both a dispersion (an intrication of interiority with the exterior, a slow inanimation of subjectivity) and a suffocating closeness (the intrusion of the exterior). It is a horror without danger, an insecurity which is not an eventuality of destruction. The experience of the *il y a* is both urgent and monotonous, both intimate and impersonal, because it describes an approach of alterity which is incumbent without being powerful.

The absence of perspective is not purely negative. It becomes insecurity. Not that the things covered by obscurity escape our prevision and that it becomes impossible to measure in advance their approach. The insecurity does not come from the things of the diurnal world that night hides, it proceeds precisely from the fact that nothing approaches, nothing comes, nothing menaces: this silence, this tranquillity, this lack of sensations constitute a muffled, indeterminate menace, absolutely.[81]

The exterior approaches, menaces, but nothing, no thing, no substantial and destructive reality — rendered positive by negation — approaches. Nothing approaches; but underneath negation, an exterior that is not a thing, approaches. The absence of substantial menace is an approach. Subjectivity in the *il y a* is the passivity of a communication prior to or beyond the spontaneity of consciousness: an inability to understand or not to understand, an involvement with the exterior.

Levinas' themes in "Il y a" are uncharacteristic: the night, horror, insecurity, contamination, monotony. His references are also uncharacteristic: Lévy-Bruhl, Shakespeare, Maupassant, Rimbaud, Racine. In his later books, whose concepts are all based upon a priority of differentiation over negation, but whose thematic context is considerably removed from that of "Il y a", Levinas nevertheless returns to the *il y a*, with its evocations of horror and nocturnality. It is as though this anomalous moment, at which Levinas speaks with Blanchot's voice without ceasing to describe an essentially Levinasian universe, expressed an aspect of proximity that the later Levinas does not wish to relinquish. A note near the end of "Il y a" invokes, without equivocation or even the hint of contrast, the name of Blanchot: "*Thomas l'obscur,* by Maurice Blanchot, opens with a description of the *il y a* (. . .). The presence of absence, the night, the dissolution of the subject in the night, the horror of being, the return of being within the bowels of all negative movements, the reality of irreality, are admirably spoken here."[82]

In "La Littérature et le droit à la mort" (1949), which is Blanchot's first explicit thematization of the presence of absence in a theoretical text, we read that literature is "the only expression of the obsession of existence, if the latter is the very impossibility of taking leave of existence, the being which is always thrown back to being, that which in the bottomless depth is already at the bottom, an abyss which is yet the ground of the abyss, a recourse against which there is no recourse."[83] In a note, Blanchot adds:

In his book *De l'existence à l'existant,* Emmanuel Levinas has "illuminated" under the name *Il y a* this anonymous and impersonal current of being which precedes all being, the being which is already present in the heart of disappearance, which at the bottom of annihilation returns again to being, being as the inevitability of being, nothingness [*néant*] as existence: when there is nothing, "there is" ["*il y a*"] being.[84]

As discussed earlier, "La Littérature et le droit à la mort" is the scene of Blanchot's extrication of his thinking from that of Hegel. It is in this text that the notion of literature is definitively detached from pehnomenology's concepts of authenticity, negation, and action. This detachment, and Blanchot's subsequent distance from the philosophical currents of his time, are produced by his meditation of proximity as an economy in which the negative is weakened or conditioned. This movement involves Levinas. As the dialogue of "Il y a" and "La Littérature et le droit à la mort" shows, the appearance of these texts indicates a fundamental inextrication of the thought of Blanchot and Levinas, which will be manifest in a series of references and essays that punctuate their careers.

The fourth part of Bataille's *L'Expérience intérieure* (1943), entitled "Postscriptum au supplice", begins with a lengthy quotation from *Thomas l'obscur*, accompanied by the comment, "Beyond the notes of this volume, I know only *Thomas l'obscur* where the questions of the new theology are insistent, although they remain hidden there."[85] The section of *Thomas l'obscur*'s second chapter quoted by Bataille describes the passivity and alteration produced by Thomas' experience of the night:

The night seemed to him far more somber, more terrible than any other night, as though it had truly issued from a wound of thought which no longer thought itself, of thought taken ironically as object by something other than thought. It was night itself. Images which constituted its obscurity inundated him . . . * He saw nothing, and, far from being distressed, he made this absence of vision the culmination of his sight. Useless for seeing, his eye took on extraordinary proportions, developed beyond measure, and, stretching out on the horizon, let the night penetrate its center in order to create for itself an iris. Through this void, it was the look and the object of the look which mingled together. Not only did this eye which saw nothing apprehend something, it apprehended the cause of its vision. It saw as an object, that which prevented it from seeing.[86]

This passage describes the ironic *cogito* of a subjectivity whose intrication with the exterior is both a thickening inanimation of interiority and an animation of the exterior. It also describes the impossibility of a reality without power, in which the inability to see does not exhaust the reality of seeing. Finally, it describes the dual predication of the *il y a* as urgency and monotony, danger and the *non-concernant,* which are integral to Blanchot's meditation of the rapport with alterity. Bataille's reader is struck by the thematic disparity of this passage with regard to the bulk of *L'Expérience intérieure* — but also by the massive intrication of its logical implications with those of Bataille's concepts. The menacing tranquillity of the *il y a* harmonizes poorly with the exasperated urgency of *L'Expérience intérieure*'s search for a "method" of communicating

---

* The additional phrase: "et le corps transformé en un esprit démoniaque cherchait à se les représenter" ("and his body, transformed into a demoniacal spirit, tried to imagine them") which completes this sentence, and is quoted by Bataille, is one of the many deletions from the "new version" of *Thomas l'obscur.*

sovereignty and transgression — and yet it is the *il y a* that Bataille chooses to cite as an example of the "new theology". This is because the *il y a* — the approach of the exterior in a reality without negation — describes interiority's transgression of interiority, as a function of its very closure.

The *entretien* which links *Thomas l'obscur,* "Il y a", *L'Expérience intérieure* and "La Littérature et le droit à la mort" is the extremity of the communication which involves Bataille, Blanchot, and Levinas in the discovery of proximity. For all three thinkers, the period of the mid-1940's is a critical juncture. There is a common denominator in the communication which launches their maturity: the positing of a differentiation in being which is not negation, and a notation of the enormous consequences produced by this "weakness" of the negative. In the texts cited above, many of the basic themes of proximity are palpable: a communication of subject and object which contaminates the relation of subject to object; the passivity of subjectivity in exposition; the supplanting of phenomenology's "anguish" by the urgency and repetition of a rapport with alterity; the persistence of a heteronomous but compelling remainder underneath negation; the rapport of communication with the "obscurity" of being's irreducibility to manifestation; and perhaps most importantly, the incumbence or approach of an exteriority which itself has no power, but against which consciousness has no power. Bataille's discovery of continuity, Levinas' thematization of the *infini,* and Blanchot's descriptions of neutrality and dissimulation, are pursued in isolation from each other, but not in isolation from the *il y a* which is the common detour of these thematically disparate texts. As mentioned above, the weighty inconsistency of the *il y a,* in which alterity approaches as it escapes manifestation, is perceptible in every important concept of the philosophy of proximity — not only in Bataille, Blanchot and Levinas, but also in Nietzsche, Freud, Proust, Artaud, and in the philosophy of difference. Again, the importance of Hegel in the background of this philosophy must be stressed. For it was Hegel who described the detour of difference and proximity in the constitution of contradiction and in the excessive moment of manifestation, and whose position of the *Aufhebung* in its virility and its implacable march toward totalization, paused at the fugitive moment of a passivity in being: the subjectivity of communication, and the heteronomy of the *pour l'autre* in separation.

*

Perhaps the single most triumphant common denominator in Western culture is its tendency to thematize the real in terms of limits and their destruction. Negativity, in this configuration, always tends to guarantee the adequate separation and correlation of terms in its economy, and at the same time to disappear entirely in the moment of their communion — only to reappear as the guarantee of this communion as unity. For Levinas, this "allergy of beings" or *interesse* of closure which is not eliminated, but in fact strengthened by the figure of communion, is not true separation. It is the artificiality of a correlation whose subordination of communication to totalization is essentially violent. In Levinas' phrase, this metaphysics of autonomy and correlation implies the "permanent possibility of war." There can be no "peace through reason" when reason is the image of destruction and exploitation. It is for this reason that Levinas uses the somewhat confusing term "non-violence" to describe communication in proximity. The Other does not "limit" my freedom in proximity, but rather "invests" it — although this investment is already a placing in question or "disarming" of spontaneity, and its *nouvelle origine* as the passivity of the exigency. The "violence" of totalization in Levinas is a violence heavily weighted by its accreditation in Western culture. War, exploitation, the institutionalization of poverty, etc., are forms of violence which are and are not perceived as violent by a culture in which they are "facts of life", correlative to and sanctioned by the logic of limits and the destruction of limits — that is, the logic of constraint and the liberation from constraint. Like the prohibition, these instances are perceived as accidental aberrations, "irrational" interruptions of a rational universe. This is because the prohibition does not abolish violence, but rather "organizes" violence, in Bataille's most pertinent phrase. The confused perception that violence is not in fact accidental but is produced and required by a cultural or more general configuration, motivates the great religious and political upheavals of Western history. The ambivalence of these movements, and their frustration, often results from their unwitting recourse to the very concepts which organize violence: their need to "make war on war," to "define" and "eliminate" an "ultimate cause" of injustice, to "perceive the totality" which produces violence, to sacrifice the egoism of human power in the name of a "higher power" or "higher wisdom". On the other hand, the "non-violence" of communication in proximity, meditated by Levinas, is the true figure of violence in the Western imagination: a withdrawal of power in the failure of a negativity which leaves behind it an uneliminable remainder. This violence, attested by art, myth, magic and religion, is the suffocating approach of an alterity whose lack of consistency and often of reality is precisely the fact that it "cannot be stopped." Although it may assume the guise of a malevolent power, this instance is fundamentally an escape from negativity and autonomy, and its very lack of power is its domination. Its approach renders impossible an encounter with it as power against power, and transforms resistance into passivity: the most consistent and compelling nightmare of the Western imagination. Levinas' interpretation of the duality "violence/non-violence" is a highly personal one, which contributes importantly to his marginality in contemporary thought, and to his recuperation by a theological tradition with which he has little affinity. As mentioned earlier, it is important to perceive the congruence of Levinasian non-violence, the disturbing predicates of nocturnality and the "presence of absence" in Blanchot, and the ironic extremities of erotism in Bataille, in a general configuration of proximity as an economy without negativity, and consequently without power or manifestation. Power, in this economy, is supplanted by the exigency; absence and negation are supplanted by the presence of the *il y a*; effectivity is supplanted by incompletion and the approach.

The thematic richness of Bataille, Blanchot and Levinas proceeds from the progressive discovery in their texts of discursive possibilities which have always appeared to be unproblematic in Western thought, and which are suddenly foreclosed or contaminated by the intuition of proximity. Chief among these are comprehension, non-contradiction, and power. As philosophy since Heidegger has attested with some discomfiture, the withdrawal of a single discursive possibility may overwhelm an entire philosophical language, placing many of its predications within the parentheses or erasure of a new indecision. In the case of Levinas this vigilance takes the form of the negative stipulation, "not A, not B, but C": "not a comprehension, not a limitation, but an approach," etc. In Blanchot, it takes the form of a situation from which the predicates of power and comprehension are progressively and enthusiastically stripped: a subject cannot stop walking, cannot close his eyes, cannot see, cannot understand, cannot but understand. In Bataille, the form of discursive vigilance is its apparent opposite. His text is an exuberant play of self-contradictions whose overall movement progressively forecloses the terminological and epistemological possibilities he appears to accredit. On a purely thematic level, the defection of negativity in Bataille may be said to take the form of excess and the irony of the exigency in transgression. In Blanchot, its form is the presence of absence in the night, and the passivity of an approach to alterity which is already an approach of alterity. In Levinas, its form is the awakening of intentionality which finds itself late for an assignation, and finds its spontaneity compromised by the pre-originarity of this involvement with the Other. For all three thinkers, a proximity which exceeds manifestation and totalization by virtue of its communicational economy, always has the fundamental effect of a contamination of power. As mentioned earlier, the tendency to meditate the economy of the real in terms of differentiation rather than manifestation roots the philosophy of proximity in the radicality of Western thought since Hegel. On the other hand, the tendency to derive on the basis of this meditation the concept of an alterity which does not limit or frustrate the wish for totalization, but rather constitutes in its own heteronomy the disarming approach of a reality without power, describes the more subterranean aspect of this philosophy, and its persistent marginality. The West welcomes with complaisance the notion of an alterity whose power to escape our grasp exceeds our power to grasp it, but is perennially allergic to the notion of an alterity which has no power, but against which we have no power. One term, perhaps more than any other, designates in the text of proximity this approach of an alterity which implies the approach of another dimension. This term is "impossibility". It describes the passivity of the exigency ("the savage *impossibility* I am, which can neither avoid its limits nor hold to them"[87]), the excess of closure over totalization ("Subjectivity realizes these impossible exigencies: the astonishing fact of containing more than it is possible to contain."[88]), and, most importantly, an irreducibility to accomplishment which is not itself a negative moment ("[the *oeuvre*] is without power, impotent, not because it is the simple reverse of the various forms of possibility, but because it designates a region in which impossibility is no longer privation, but affirmation."[89]). Impossibility, as Blanchot says so well in commenting Bataillian *expérience,* is a dimension without power and without manifestation, which does not however designate a simple heteronomy or a simple escape of exteriority from our desire to experience it. It is rather "that which escapes our very power to experience it, but whose experience we cannot escape."[90] Its unavailability to comprehension, and its lack of power, are correlative to the urgency of its approach. The interiority which experiences this approach is not the self-coincidence and spontaneity which philosophy dreams of, but neither is it the inert immobility of a determined heteronomy. Its positivity is its escape from a universe exhausted by negation, and this is, in many respects, the aptness of its name. Proximity, in the region of manifestation, is the impossible.

DESIRE AND THE QUESTION

The philosophy of proximity does not attest the limitations of a comprehension whose aims are frustrated by its inadequation to the exterior. Instead, it thematizes a general economy whose communications produce comprehension and totalization as positive ontological events. That these events are conditioned by an economic factor which cannot itself assume the form of a totality, and cannot be exhausted by its participation in comprehension, does not reduce their positivity. The detour of closure or discontinuity is an irreducible moment of the economy. On the basis of this detour, and of the intense and opaque unicity it produces, the region of totalization is erected. Within and for this region, autonomy and correlation, comprehension and reification, integrity and destruction, are ultimate logical and ontological principles. Their underlying common denominator is the notion of power, which itself is produced as a possibility by the intensity or force of communication. The altering force of communication's heteronomy becomes power (along with its correlates, action, determination, and causality) when closure becomes identity, and discontinuity becomes correlation, in the *diastase* or "catalysis" of the totality. That totalization is a regional event whose spontaneity is not "adequate" to the larger movements of the economy, is not a negative or limiting proposition. As mentioned earlier, the philosophers of proximity tend to meditate the articulation of Same and Other, of interior and exterior, from the point of view of differentiation rather than of manifestation. It must also be said that the possibility or impossibility of an adequation of these opposites, in comprehension or in experience, is a notion to which they are indifferent. These thinkers share with certain other tendencies in modern philosophy a striking incuriosity with regard to the question of "what can be known with certainty" or "how the alterity of the exterior may be reduced." Their interest, in a Hegelian and Nietzschian inspiration, is not comprehension's limitation by comparison with its claims for itself, but rather, in Hegel's words, comprehension's "experience" or latent economy. Thus they consistently attest the "escape" of an alterity to which comprehension is not "adequate", but they also describe the "approach" of an alterity which invests the spontaneity of comprehension, in a communicational context for which adequation is not a pertinent principle.

The purpose of a philosophy of proximity is not merely to notate a regionality of totalization, but to describe the communicational process by which totalization is invested as an economic event. Thus the Bataillian term *non-savoir,* and the term "dissimulation" in Blanchot, do not describe dialectical opposites of comprehension, or limitations of the latter. They describe a larger communicational element whose intervals and contaminations not only make possible but actually produce the intense, exigent world of comprehension. In Blanchot, it is the enigma of dissimulation's "tendency to become negation" that produces the illumination and industry of what he calls the "world". In Bataille, the definition of the exigency as a hyperbolic closure whose intensity proceeds from its latent heteronomy, describes in far greater detail the same catalytic moment. But it is Levinas above all who explicitly concerns himself with the precise modality by which comprehension or theoretical consciousness is invested and conditioned by the intense contaminations of proximity. His description of the *cogito* as an assumption, "perhaps vain and tardy," of a prior involvement with alterity, is one example of this investment of spontaneity by a heteronomous element. The analyses of sensation, intentionality, temporalization, and *jouissance* which punctuate Levinas' later works, are other examples of the same configuration. These later works clearly show that Levinas' ambition was always to ground the possibility of manifestation in proximity itself, rather than to invoke the latter as an exceptional element escaping comprehension and constituting a "beyond" in which the *éthique* would insist. For Levinas, the reality of proximity (and thus of the *éthique*) can be delimited only if manifestation itself is shown to be a "moment of proximity" — an illumination conditioned by communication. From this perspective, the chief inequality of such earlier studies as *Le Temps et l'autre* (1948) and "L'ontologie est-elle fondamentale?" (1951)[91] consists in their attempt to articulate Levinas' developing concept of a latent heteronomy of interiority with the notion of an *autrui* and an intersubjectivity which remain "exceptional" moments escaping manifestation.[92] The path from *De l'existence à l'existant (1947)* to Levinas' phenomenological essays of the 1950's describes a situation of proximity in the constitution of interiority, most notably through sensation and the *il y a*, which makes possible a successful return to the theme of *autrui* in "La philosophie et l'idée de l'infini" (1957). From the opening paragraphs of the latter essay, and throughout Levinas' later books, it is clear that subjectivity's involvement with alterity in the *visage* of *autrui* is no longer defined as an exceptional moment, but as the latent possibility and production of comprehension itself. The Other of which *autrui* is the hyperbole, is an instance which is the "principle of the phenomenon" no less than of the *visage*. Alterity is not limited to the existence of *autrui*, but is an element which collaborates in the conation of all closure within the general economy.

As discussed earlier, separation in Levinas is defined as an "independence" with regard to totalization. The paradox of this configuration is that the only possibility of true separation is an irreducibility to the determinations and relations which situate entities within the totality. Since these determinations define the autonomy of beings and their "allergy" in the *interesse* of correlation, separation's "independence" must proceed from its radical heteronomy — that is, its very lack of integrity. The totality, for Levinas, is a homogeneity which cannot produce true unicity or true relation. These possibilities must proceed from a rapport of the Same with an alterity which is not another Same. Therefore, the unicity of separation must be situated precisely in the heteronomy of subjection, in the *parole* of subjectivity's dispossession, in the *pour l'autre* which is the dissymmetry of this dispossession, and in desire, which is interiority's fundamentally "non-allergic" rapport with the exterior. Since totalization describes an essentially undifferentiated homogeneity of the Same, the only "independence" of separation must arise precisely from its difference — that is, the unicity of its incompletion.

In the early pages of *Totalité et infini*, Levinas suggests, in a radical though not explicit criticism of Hegel, that in an economy defined as manifestation no such thing as the "possibility of truth and error" could exist. If differentiation is subordinated to comprehension in its very definition, then neither the behavior of consciousness nor the incompleteness of the dialectic's manifold stages can be taken seriously. Both the separations and the dialectical communications which structure the *Phenomenology* are posed under the sign of unity. Totalization is the principle of multiplicity; the Same is the sole context of the articulation of Same and Other. Incompletion, and thus communication, are not possible in such an economy. Neither is the problematic of truth and error, since every rapport within the Same is a function of comprehension. For Levinas, this problematic appears only when (1) consciousness is extricated from its "rooting" in the totality, and is thus "independent" or "separate", and (2) when, by virtue of this irreducibility to totalization, consciousness can be defined as a radical heteronomy or incompletion — that is, an instance capable of being affected by the exterior.

The search for truth — the possibility of the question, for both Blanchot and Levinas — cannot describe the fulfilling of a need by a totality, because this moment would be a simple contradiction in terms. Instead, the possibility of interrogation or of a theoretical consciousness must proceed from an incompletion which is not the vicissitude of a totality. The principle of the general economy must be incompletion and proximity, in order that such a movement or disturbance as the search for truth might arise within it. "Truth supposes a being which is autonomous in separation — the search for a truth is precisely a relation which does not repose upon the privation of need. To seek and obtain truth, is to be in a rapport, not because one is defined by something other than oneself, but because, in a certain sense, one lacks nothing."[93] By distinguishing between the "definition" of causal or dialectical determination, which would simply be a totalization requiring no interrogation, and the more radical possibility of a search for truth which arises from a fundamental weakness or failure of totalization, Levinas derives the notion of interrogation as a desire which proceeds from an irreducible incompletion. Thus he echoes Blanchot's definition of Bataillian *expérience* as "the dissatisfaction of the man who is 'completely' ['*en tout*'] satisfied."[94] Interrogation can only proceed from subjectivity, which is the irreducible involvement of separation with the exterior: a unicity which is a receptivity, a non-indifference, and a desire. Levinas describes this intrication of theory with communication in the following terms:

But the search for truth is an event more fundamental than theory, although the theoretical search is a privileged mode of this relation to exteriority that is called truth. Because the separation of the separate being was not relative, was not a movement of distancing [*éloignement*] with regard to the Other, but was produced as *psychisme,* the relation to the Other does not consist in reproducing in an opposite sense the movement of distancing, but in going toward [the Other] through Desire, from which theory itself borrows the exteriority of its term.[95]

The possibility of interrogation is *psychisme*: a rapport with alterity which is a proximity and a desire. Only by the very impossibility of the *Ent-Fernung* which reduces proximity to comprehension, can the closure of interiority become a receptivity. Interrogation is a correlate of desire, and desire is the impossibility which haunts totalization. Interrogation is an approach to the Other which is already the approach of the Other in its investment of interiority. It is thus the non-indifference of a unicity which "goes toward" the Other in its very position as separation — a unicity which is a *pour l'autre.*

Truth and error in their duality are made possible by separation's "autonomy" with regard to the immobility and homogeneity of totalization. But the possibility of this possibility is separation's heteronomy: the differential and proximal constitution of interiority as a subjectivity or "subjection" to the exterior. This subjection, the vulnerability of incompletion, is also a *parole,* i.e. the excessive spasm of interiority's conation outward, toward the Other. And the *parole,* inspired or invested by the Other's approach, is the force of the question, as Blanchot states in his essay "La Question la plus profonde": "It is the *parole* as a detour."[96] This statement implies an involvement of the question with error and *errance* which points up the strategic aspect of Levinas' demonstration. The search for truth can be the behavior only of an interiority whose being is not exhausted by its determinations or its autonomy. Therefore this search is correlative of the dispossession outward, *pour l'autre,* which tears interiority from its place within the totality and forces it into the exile of a movement outward, into the exterior. Thus the search for truth is a moment of *errance,* the larger movement of closure's heteronomy in the general economy: a movement which is itself irreducible to the notion of truth as adequation or totalization. But the notions of *errance* and detour are not inconsistent with the proposition of a search for truth: they are its animation. As Levinas implies in the quotation above, the search for truth is not an event of comprehension, but of communication and proximity.

Closure in the general economy is always a question: an incompletion, a receptivity, and an exigent avidity for the exterior.* But it is not only interrogation that proceeds from this permanent, intense breach within totalization: it is subjectivity itself, and the possibility of experience. It is at the logical moment of incompletion and desire that Levinas derives, from the same communicational nexus, both theoretical consciousness and the idea of the infinite. The common denominator of these concepts is interiority's failure to constitute itself as a totality, and the violent capacity to receive the approach of the Other which proceeds from this failure. But this "capacity", this inclination toward the exterior — a non-indifference toward an alterity which "concerns" subjectivity, and the miracle of an interiority "preoccupied by something outside itself" — is itself the idea of the infinite, in its Levinasian definition: a placing in question of the Same by an Other which weighs upon it.[97] Like *savoir* which is an organization of *non-savoir,* and like the day which is a moment of a larger nocturnality, theoretical consciousness is a moment of the *éthique.* It is an illumination made possible by the only interval in being which could produce an interiority: subjectivity.

Theoretical consciousness in Levinas veers toward the *éthique*; that is, it desires to experience the alterity of the Other without reducing this alterity. This is because theoretical consciousness is grounded in interiority's involvement with the Other.

For the idea of exteriority which guides the search for truth, is possible only as the idea of the Infinite. The conversion of the soul to exteriority or the absolutely other or the Infinite is not deducible from the identity of this soul, because it is not proportionate to this soul. The idea of the Infinite does not proceed from Me [*Moi:* the self], nor from a need within the Self which precisely measures its gaps [*vides*]. In it the movement proceeds from the *pensé* [the thing thought] and not from the thinker.[98]

---

* The names of Proust and Proust's great reader, Gilles Deleuze, are central to the genealogy of this notion of closure. The possibilities of the *recherche,* the question, and the problem, proceed from the intensity of interiority's latent heteronomy — not only in the manifest moments of desire and interrogation, but also in the mute *jouissance* and complacency of Habit. For the Deleuze of *Proust et les signes* and *Différence et répétition,* exteriority invests closure as an intensity which is both a pleasure principle and the dispossession of the question.

The idea of the infinite — which is not an idea, but a communication, as Levinas often explains — is desire, and thus is not deducible from interiority as identity, but only from interiority as incompletion and heteronomy. It is on the basis of this an-archic or pre-originary involvement with exteriority that Levinas privileges the Cartesian notion of the idea of the infinite "placed in us." From the concept of an interiority rooted within the exterior, Levinas draws the conclusion that phenomenology was never able to draw. The rapport with the exterior "proceeds from outside" and cannot be assumed. Assumption and adequation are not the principles of its economy. When, in the *cogito* or in intentionality, this "illusory" assumption is accomplished, it will retain a para-doxical positivity: the positivity of its investment by a larger heteronomy.

The idea of the infinite is a communication and a proximity. Interiority's only "access" to this idea is desire. This is because interiority's only ontology is desire. Within the general economy, this configuration may invest the deter-minations of the totality, on one hand, and the fugitive, contaminated appear-ances of the *éthique* on the other. But the common denominator of these dimensions is that proximity which renders possible a communication with the exterior, irreducible to a situation within the totality. The *éthique* is thus the principle and the element of an opposition between totality and infinity.

Interiority is an incompletion which is susceptible to the Other's approach. It is a desire which brings alterity "closer" in the moment of its ambivalent, heteronomous conation. It is an exile within the exterior, by virtue of this heteronomy which forces it outward, outside itself, outside "everything". Finally, it is the paroxysm of a pre-originary approach to the Other, in its *pour l'autre* and in its *parole*. It is on the basis of this *parole,* inspired by al-terity's collaboration in the intense closure of the Same, that theoretical con-sciousness is involved with *autrui.* In Levinas, as in Bataille and Blanchot, the concept of subjectivity is already a concept of intersubjectivity — not because the interrogative or philosophical assertion is an implicit appeal to others, or because the existence of others is correlative to consciousness' illumination of a "world", but because closure is, in the ambiguity of this phrase, an "exi-gency of the Other." The intensity of closure is its involvement with an ex-terior that is not objective or phenomenal, but Other; and toward this Other, interiority cannot be indifferent. Alterity, in its escape from manifestation and adequation, is a dispossession of the Same which constitutes the Same. As it escapes, it approaches. Its distance is a contact. It concerns and weighs upon the Same because, in desire, in the *pour l'autre,* and in the *parole,* it invests the same. Yet it has no power, no substantiality, and it cannot assume the form of a totality. This is its subjectivity: a powerlessness, an incompletion, which concerns interiority, and over which interiority has no power. The sub-jectivity of the Other is, on one hand, its participation in the economy of in-teriority, as attested by Blanchot in the concept of essential solitude and by Bataille in the concept of the object as a dramatic loss of self. On the other hand, in a sense which is explicitly articulated by Levinas alone, the Other's subjectivity is the paradox of a vulnerability which compels or is incumbent upon interiority, in the impersonal moment of difference and non-indifference. The Other is *autrui*: a subjectivity in the exterior, a passivity which concerns me. When *autrui* becomes its common meaning as "others" or "the other person", it describes not the interiority or consciousness of the intersubjective other, but his exteriority. "The alterity of the Other . . . does not result from its identity, but constitutes it: the Other is *Autrui.*"[99] *Autrui* is not "others", but the alterity of the Other which is not another Same. To refer to *Autrui* we must say "it" and not "he" or "them". *Autrui* is the subjectivity of the exterior. Interiority is involved with *autrui* before it enters into relation with others. *Autrui* proceeds from the very subjectivity of the general economy, and from the intersubjectivity implied by the *parole* as interiority's excess.

Levinas' derivation of both the *éthique* and the theoretical on the basis of differentiation and non-reciprocity allows him to supplant his earlier arguments for an exceptional ontological status of intersubjectivity by the more radical concept that the only ontology of the general economy is subjectivity as proximity. The spontaneity and "egoism" of the Same, in the *cogito* or in intentionality, are invested by its latent subjectivity, which is an involvement with the Other. Closure is an exigency, an intensity inspired by the exterior. Thus, in the very moment of its untroubled "freedom", interiority is already compelled by alterity, already rooted in the heteronomy of the *éthique*.

I think that existence *for-self* [*pour soi*: for itself] is not the ultimate sense of knowledge, but the placing in question [again] of self, the return toward the before-oneself, in the presence of *Autrui*. The presence of *Autrui* — a privileged heteronomy — does not collide with freedom, but invests it. Shame for self, the presence and the desire of the Other, are not the negation of knowledge: knowledge is their very articulation.[100]

Consciousness' spontaneity is not possible without what Levinas calls the "shame" of spontaneity. This "shame", the placing in question or *mise en jeu* of freedom, is the presence of the Other in a consciousness which is already subjectivity and already intersubjectivity. Levinas refuses the concept of "negation" here, as elsewhere in the context of the Other's approach. This approach is not grounded in negation, but in the weakness and defection of negation. "The 'resistance' of the Other does not do violence to me, does not act negatively; it has a positive structure: *éthique.*"[101]

Interiority's contact with alterity forecloses the drama of a spontaneous intentionality and its determination in a causal universe. The logic which governs invested freedom is not that of determination, but of affirmation. In the Cartesian *cogito*, as discussed earlier, the process of negation arrives at the Other of *il y a* which says "Yes".[102] The presence of alterity is an affirmation which invests intentionality as an affirmation — as Bataille discovered in *non-savoir*. This affirmation is an-archic and repetitive, and is impersonal before it may become intersubjective in an intramundane sense. "In the indirect ways of illeity*, in the anarchic provocation which orders me to the other, the path appears which leads to thematization and to an awakening of consciousness."[103] The pre-originarity of this rapport with alterity repeats itself in the intersubjective context of action. The act (*oeuvre*), in an intramundane context, is not reducible to interiority's spontaneity, but is a "movement toward the unknown," a rapport with exteriority which conditions its intersubjective destiny. "The act is dedicated to this foreign *Sinngebung*, from the moment of its origin in me. It is important that this destination of the act dedicated to a situation that I cannot foresee − for I cannot see it − is inscribed in the very essence of my power and does not result from the contingent presence of other persons in my vicinity."[104] Action here has the passivity of Orpheus and of transgression in general, because it is involved with a proximal and an-archic future whose insistence arises precisely from the defection of power in the general economy.

For Levinas, intentionality's power to receive objective information implies a pre-originary rapport with alterity as the "critical" principle of subjectivity. Spontaneity requires the "shame" of spontaneity: a *mise en jeu* of consciousness and a preoccupation with the exterior. Therefore, consciousness is always already in a rapport with *autrui*: an exteriority whose incumbence exceeds its manifestation. Although *autrui* has neither power nor actuality, the incumbence of its approach (which Levinas calls *signifiance* or *signification*) concerns or involves subjectivity, because it invests the latter. Consciousness, like the day in Blanchot and the profane world in Bataille, is a relation which superimposes itself over this more basic rapport with alterity. Manifestation is a regional mobilization of proximity. Thus *autrui*, the powerless weight of the exterior, remains for Levinas "the principle of the phenomenon."[106] The priority and eventuality of the *visage* and the infinite are inherent in manifestation itself. Levinas' argument is incomprehensible if *autrui* is understood to mean "the other person" instead of alterity in its generality. *Autrui* arises from being's irreducibility to negation, the proximity and impersonality of the exterior − in the *il y a*, in illeity, in the accusative *se* of recurrence. Levinas' intention is not to subordinate objectivity to the intersubjective, in a humanist or phenomenological sense. These tendencies would be, in his eyes, the opposite of an understanding of intersubjectivity. Instead, his effort is to sustain, in the context of manifestation, the basic concept of the subjectivity of the economy itself. It is for this reason that Levinas' thematizations of the rapport with alterity tend toward impersonal formulations, and recall Blanchot's demonstrations in vocabulary as well as in inspiration. *Autrui* is exteriority. When *autrui* is an intersubjective other, it is the exteriority of this other, irreducible

* The term *illéité* describes the impersonality and neutrality of the Other in its excess over negation and manifestation. This excess escapes the dualities of self and other, immanence and transcendence, the particular and the general, etc., and describes the Other as an impersonal "profile" which cannot assume the form of a phenomenon or a totality. Cf. "La Trace de l'autre" (1963).[105]

to his own interiority, that is *autrui.** The intersubjectivity of proximity is not that of phenomenology, because it is entirely non-reciprocal and dissymetrical. *Autrui* is not another Same, but the Other of the Same. It influences consciousness not as "the other person", but as "someone": "Attention is attention to something, because it is attention to someone. The exteriority of its point of departure is essential to it, which is the very tension of the self."[107] The attention or interrogation of intentionality is unthinkable for Levinas without a priority of alterity and a consequent incompletion or tension of interiority. "To be attentive signifies a surplus of consciousness and supposes the call of the Other."[108] The Other is implicit in consciousness' excess — its subjectivity — in both a pre-originary and a futural sense. It retains its impersonality — its irreducibility to the concept or the presence of the other person — even as it becomes *autrui* and the *visage*. The *visage* is the incumbence and *"signifiance"* of exteriority, which we can neither see nor avoid seeing, which we cannot experience and cannot but experience. As such, it is "the evidence which renders possible evidence."[109]

"It is only in approaching *Autrui* that I meet myself," writes Levinas.[110] Interiority in proximity has, in Proust's phrase, a "rendezvous with itself" within the exterior. Alterity invests the closure which goes, tardily, to meet alterity in the rectitude of manifestation. The "rooting" of subjectivity in being by phenomenology becomes, in the philosophy of proximity, a dangerous and

---

* As mentioned above, Levinas' insistence upon the intensive dissymetry of the intersubjective presence underscores his proximity to Proust's inspiration. Another index of this proximity is the intensive inactuality of *Autrui* in both thinkers. Thus Swann, exhausted by the intellectual effort of his desire, reflects that Odette must after all be, in herself, a banal and interchangeable personality whose afternoons, even if spent in the arms of other men, represent the boring passage of intramundane hours. The narrator will reflect, in similar confusion, upon the fact that Albertine's tastes, intelligence, and habits have been altered by her liaison with himself. Love presents both men with the same enigma: that *Autrui* is not "others", and that the perspective in which the beloved appears as an actual being, homogeneously correlated with the lover, has no significance for the painful experience of the *recherche*. This is why the physical presence of the beloved — the mysterious warmth and intimacy surrounding her movements, clothing, habits, etc. — describes an indubitable, supporting actuality which nevertheless does not contradict the lover's indifference to the fact that she has gained weight, grown older, lost her beauty. The clothing, the body, the habits are actual, but *Autrui* is not actual — as Swann senses when he reflects that it is not the "person" of Odette that concerns him, and as the narrator realizes when he shows Albertine's photo to St. Loup. It is not the bourgeoise Albertine Simonet, entirely comprehensible in her choice of words or of clothing, or in her lies, who concerns the narrator: it is Albertine the fugitive, an inactual, altering presence which appeared within the economy of the real in order to modify himself only. Thus it remains possible to catch Odette or Albertine in a lie, through an empirical manipulation — as it remains possible to murder *Autrui* in Levinas. But the escape of the fugitive or of *Autrui* from manifestation is not affected by this act. "Others" are actual: *Autrui* is Other. To know the "hideousness" of Albertine means to know through desire her altering flight, rather than to suspect her intramundane infidelity, whose insignificance the lover senses through his justifiable credulity.

disarming involvement, predicated not on intervals and adequation but on inextrication and the weakening of the negative:

But this way the subject has of finding himself within the *essence** . . . is not a harmonious and inoffensive participation. It is precisely the incessant buzzing which fills each silence in which the subject detaches himself from the *essence* to pose himself as a subject over and against his objectivity. (. . .) The buzzing of the *il y a* − non-sense into which *essence* turns and into which turns also the justice which issues from *signification*.[111]

The *il y a* is alterity's excess over negation, and is thus *autrui*'s excess over the domain of power or possibility. "Justice", in its Levinasian sense, is not the peace of Reason, but proceeds from proximity's "non-sense" or excess over comprehension. Subjectivity's rooting in the economy of proximity is not a primordial adequation, but an exile, a dispossession, a "going toward the Other" which is the only principle of its unicity. "Justice" is the violence of this "non-allergic"· rapport with the Other − a rapport which invests freedom rather than to limit it, and is therefore the "source of unpunished crimes." But, writes Levinas, "this is the price of interiority, which is the price of separation."[112] The *éthique* does not proceed from, or limit, a world of power. This is why it is not an ethics.

In a section of *Totalité et infini* entitled "Metaphysics precedes ontology", Levinas articulates proximity and theoretical consciousness in an explanatory generality which recalls the Bataille of *non-savoir*:

The theoretical relation has not been the preferred schema of the metaphysical relation by accident. Knowledge or theory first signifies a relation with being such that the knowing being allows the known being to manifest itself while respecting its alterity and without marking it, in any way, by this relation of knowledge. In this sense, metaphysical desire would be the essence of theory. But theory also signifies intelligence − the *logos* of being − that is, a way of approaching the known being such that its alterity with regard to the knowing being disappears. The process of knowledge is indistinguishable at this stage from the freedom of the knowing being, which meets nothing that, other with regard to it, might be able to limit it.[113]

This formulation, which articulates the tendencies of idealism and realism in a consciousness which desires to respect alterity while never being affected or "limited" by it, describes the fundamental ambivalence of desire in proximity. Desire, an essential intrication with alterity whose paradoxical modality is its persuasion of its autonomy, is the exigency, the *non-savoir* that Levinas calls

---

* The totality: an economy of correlation and comprehension in which *esse* means *interesse*, and in which discontinuity is reduced to autonomy, the "allergy of beings".

a "metaphysical" relation with exteriority. Although the latent economy of desire describes the "non-allergic" involvement with the Other which is basic to "metaphysics" and to the *éthique*, its irreducible tendency or detour is toward the autonomy and correlation of totalization. Desire is a *métaphysique* which tends irrevocably to become ontology, as dissimulation tends to become negation, and as *non-savoir* tends "aussitôt" to become *savoir*. "This is the price of interiority, which is the price of separation." Ontology for Levinas is the fundamental ambivalence of the exigency in proximity. It is a communication which tends to abolish communication. But in ontology's self-critical tendency or search for truth, the latent heterogeneity of its economy is perceptible: "But theory as a respect for exteriority designates another essential structure of metaphysics. It has a critical concern in its intelligence of being — or ontology. It discovers the dogmatism and the naive arbitrariness of its spontaneity and places in question the freedom of the ontological exercise."[114] By its very critical tendency, and by its very insatiability for totalization, ontology articulates the "shame" of its spontaneity, the desire which animates it, and the approach of the Other which is its immemorial destiny or *nouvelle origine*. This priority of desire is not the "redeeming quality" of a knowledge whose complicity with violence has always accompanied its spontaneity. It is rather the precise modality of its insistence, and of its positivity, in an economy of communication. Knowledge is a *recherche* — a non-allergic liaison with alterity* — which, through an astonishing catalysis, becomes a self-interested movement toward the blind immobility of appropriation. This immobilization of difference recalls the naiveté of Swann who deplores the waste of his time on a woman who "was not his type", and that of the narrator who becomes bored with Albertine whenever he feels assured of her fidelity. Thus thought immures itself within its naive spontaneity and within the false modesty of its respect for the excess of alterity. Yet it is the Other that forces the "exaggerated sally", the "absurd rush" of the *ipse* into its tumultuous world of questions and researches. Hence the "strange dignity" of philosophy which, for Bataille, "assumes an infinite placing in question."[115] But the rapport of the *éthique* and of the profane world is not a dialectic. This is why the philosophers of proximity resist the temptation to deplore the egoism of consciousness and to celebrate its latent birth in an alteration which would compensate this egoism. Proximal alteration promises no secondary or ultimate adequation. Instead, it produces an "uncertainty concerning the future" which the philosopher of proximity may "love". Not through a wisdom, or through a modest philosophy of the future, but through a dangerous liaison born of chance and of desire. This uncertainty

---

* When Swann, standing in the dark street outside Odette's window, suddenly perceives a mysterious affinity between his jealous avidity for information and the disinterested intellectuality of the "search for truth", he has intuited the essence of this search: the non-indifferent avidity of an interiority whose identity has been compromised by its liaison with the Other.

marks each important text of this philosophy (the eternal return, Time, transgression, eschatology, the book to come) with the sign of space become the approach of another space. "There, nothing which could bind me, free me . . .". It is neither through a project nor through a modesty that the philosopher of proximity envisages his approach to the Other: it is through a metamorphosis.

THE EXIGENCY AS EXPERIENCE

CLOSURE AND NUDITY

"I think the way a girl takes off her dress," writes the Bataille of *L'Expérience intérieure*.[1] His irony and enthusiasm attest the importance and overdetermination of the theme of nudity in proximity. Within Bataille's discursive and fictional texts, nudity and denudation are constant presences which describe, on one hand, the excess of the exigency, and on the other hand, the communicational proposition of intersubjectivity. It is noteworthy that these themes are largely absent from Blanchot's text, and that they are a constant in Levinas. The latter's concept of nudity is a basic axis of his latent involvement with Bataille.

As mentioned earlier, the common concept of nudity is a contradiction in terms, when considered within the logic of correlation and comprehension, and designates a primary moment of proximity's appearance within the universe of what is called "common sense". Nudity describes a closed and integral surface which "lacks a covering." Yet such a surface, defined in terms of relation and determination, cannot lack a covering. Its very quiddity or identity is this covering. A "naked" surface is a lack where nothing is lacking: a pure vulnerability of closure which is the essence of closure, and not its accident. Nudity is a manifestation which is "too manifest", an appearance of that which should not have appeared — an impudicity which shocks, and a vulnerability which inspires a pity that becomes desire. Nudity is also the context of a caress which is a tenderness, a generosity, but also, already, an avidity. The caress is the great correlate of nudity in Levinas. This exigent gesture, at the frontier of action and passivity, is, from the point of view of manifestation, as uncanny and meaningless as the inhuman movement of the affected hand in involuntary prehension. It is an inexplicable excess over the concept of touch in perception and comprehension. It "searches when it has already found," in Levinas' phrase, and its intentionality cannot be situated. It signifies a touching which is not a knowing. Like nudity, it is a common concept whose self-contradiction is reduced by the notion of its merely subjective context, or by its appropriation to spontaneity and comprehension in a phenomenological inspiration.

The derivation of nudity in Bataille is the notion of excess in differentiation. Nudity is the inadequacy of a closure which is excessively complete and therefore not complete enough: a closure forced by, and involved with, the exterior. Thus nudity has two basic modalities. In the first place, it is a breach within the adequacy of closure which constitutes an exposition to exteriority. This breach, consistently associated by Bataille with the themes of the "wound" and *fêlure* ("splitting", "cracking"), is not an accident or attribute, but is a principle of closure's economic possibility. "Through what one might call incompletion, animal nudity, wound, diverse separate beings *communicate*, come to life losing themselves in a *communication* from one to the other."[2] *Inachèvement* as nudity and breach is the principle of closure which makes closure a possibility of experience, and of the privileged form of experience that is erotism in Bataille. "In human life ... sexual violence opens a wound."[3] "Profoundly, secretly, this *fêlure*, being the distinctive feature of human sensuality, is the principle [*ressort*] of pleasure."[4] The subjectivity of closure in incompletion is the approach of alterity that collaborates in the production of interiority. In a surprisingly Levinasian metaphor which attests the hyperbolic perfection of the closure which is affected by nudity, Bataille writes: "*Others* in sexuality ceaselessly offer a possibility of continuity, *others* ceaselessly menace, and propose a tear [*accroc*] in the seamless gown [*robe sans couture*] of individual discontinuity."[5] The proximity of alterity does not supervene to tear an immaculate surface. It is this tear and this surface, in their very proposition. The approach of the Other, in its compelling indefinition, is the force of closure's density or turgidity. Nudity tends to describe a statuesque integrity or plastic perfection as well as an exposition, because it is a hyperbole of closure as well as an incompletion. This hyperbole indicates the second sense of nudity in Bataille. The uneliminable breach which allows the exterior to approach and penetrate, is also an excess of interiority over its own closure. This is the manifestation of the "too manifest", the public or spectacular aspect of discontinuity, a catalysis of vulnerability and impudicity which both Levinas and Bataille call obscenity. "Obscenity signifies the excitement which upsets a state of bodies in conformity with self-possession, with the possession of a durable and positive individuality."[6] Nudity in obscenity is the excess of closure as what Bataille calls a *pléthore*. It is the spectacle of a closure which overwhelms its manifestation, contaminates its quiddity, approaches and attracts. In Bataille's general economy of "fermentation" and "decomposition", in which negation and totalization are not authentic possibilities, obscenity is not an anomaly but a basic predicate of discontinuity.

As the metaphor of the "accroc dans la robe sans couture" or "tear in the seamless gown" suggests, nudity is an excess of interiority which already indicates the approach of alterity and an approach to alterity. It is the proposition of exteriority, a proposition which is the essentially public nature of the surface in nudity. Like many of the figures of proximity, nudity describes a subjectivity whose excess is already an intersubjectivity. In *Sur Nietzsche*, there is a description of this approach to and of alterity which underlines the thematic congruence of proximity and obscenity in Bataille: "This wound does not exactly place life in question [*en jeu*], but only its integrity, its purity. It does not kill but it soils [*souille*]."[7] When exteriority approaches — when discontinuity becomes an approach rather than an interval — the perfection of the closed surface is soiled. That is, its closure has become its contact with the exterior — a contamination that does not destroy, but invests. The excess of the interior is also a contamination of negation and an alteration of the exterior. By virtue of this excess, in Levinas' phrase, "l'être s'altère." Being becomes an alteration. Its economic principle becomes, not negation, but desire. "Pretty, voluptuous nudity finally triumphs in the *mise en jeu* that *souillure* effects (in other cases, nudity fails, remains ugly, entirely at the level of the soiled)."[8] The congruence of ugliness and seduction in desire is proximity: the approach of an excess which should have remained at a phenomenal distance. The ambivalence of desire and repugnance in the properly economic context of *souillure* is the ambivalence of desire itself in proximity: the non-indifference of interiority toward a concerning, incumbent exterior. It is this configuration that informs the appearance of nudity as insolence, impudence and "folie" in Bataille's fictional text.

Nudity in Bataille describes an excess of closure which grounds the possibility of experience in heteronomy and contamination. In Levinas, the same basic configuration is mobilized to define an excess of communication over the possibility of manifestation. The nudity of closure in Levinas describes a receptivity which is not an intentionality, and an alterity which is not a phenomenality. For the Levinas of *Humanisme de l'autre homme* and *Autrement qu'être* . . . , sensibility or receptivity is unthinkable in terms of comprehension and totalization, and presupposes, like sensation in Husserl, a pre-originary heteronomy and passivity. The notion of an opening in subjectivity cannot be derived from its spontaneity in manifestation, which is subordinated to negation and unity, but must proceed from a "denudation", exposition, or subjection which is implicit in the economy of closure. "Vulnerability is an obsession by *autrui* or an approach of *autrui*. It is *pour autrui*, from behind the *other* of the excitant. An approach which can be reduced neither to the representation of *autrui* nor to a consciousness of [its] proximity."[9] The approach of *autrui* — the subjectivity of the exterior and the intersubjectivity of closure — is the principle of interiority, in an economic context which precedes the possibility of manifestation. Interiority's intense self-coincidence proceeds not only from its intrication with the Other, but from its *pour l'autre*, i.e. its dispossessing inclination toward exteriority. "Its closing [*recroquevillement*] is a turning inside-out. Its "toward the other" is this very turning inside-out. An inside-out without an inside [*envers sans endroit*]."[10] This excessive dispossession which produces an equally excessive density of closure is the modality of differentiation in an economy of impossibility: an economy without negation and without power. Here, the *esse* of Being in totalization becomes the *autrement qu'être* of Being in impossibility. Unicity in such a dimension "lacks" being as effectivity; and this lack is another sense of nudity. "*Is* it? Doesn't its being consist in a "taking off" of its being; not to die, but to become altered, to 'other-than-to-be' [*autrement qu'être*]?"[11] Subjectivity is the intensity of a rapport which forecloses the initiality of totalization and relation. Thus, like the sirens in Blanchot, it is inadequate to the being/non-being duality. This contamination of negativity and positivity is the "alteration of being" which Bataille discovers in *souillure*. The alterity of proximity is correlative not to negation, but to contamination.

The exterior in proximity is "too close" to become phenomenal. Its insistence, and its effect or incumbence upon interiority, always precede and condition its manifest aspect. For Levinas, this configuration is the condition of possibility for any model of receptivity or discontinuity which might be understood as illumination. In addition, the *pour l'autre* of interiority is a non-indifference to exteriority which cannot be understood as a contemplation or adequation. The Other's proximity is an inspiration and dispossession of the Same. This dispossession is the principle of the Levinasian terms *parole*, *signification*, and *dire* ("saying"). A subjectivity which enters existence already involved with the Other, is a subjectivity which already speaks or signifies on the basis of this heteronomous inspiration. The familiar concept of signification as the emitting of a message from within — as a social movement with an individual moment — presupposes proximity in the same sense that receptivity and illumination presuppose it. Signification proceeds from the fundamental inadequacy of closure in a communicational economy. Levinas asks: "Doesn't subjectivity signify precisely by its incapacity to enclose itself from within?" [12] Consciousness does not signify as a moment of manifestation. Closure signifies as a moment of its economy. The word "signification" in Levinas, as in the philosophy of difference, describes a modality of differentiation rather than of illumination. The same is true of the word *sens* ("sense", "meaning"), which describes not the "meaning" of comprehension, but the univocal or dissymetrical dispossession "outward" of closure in the general economy. "As though the *dire* has a sense [*sens*] prior to the truth it unveils; prior to the advent of the knowledge and the information it communicates . . .". [13] This "sense" of the *dire* is the *pour l'autre* of interiority. It is the single "direction" followed by communication's force in an economy of difference and non-indifference: outward, toward the Other. Every *conatus* in the general economy is a *conatus à l'envers*, the spasm "inside-out" of a closure which opens to the exterior. Every closure is vulnerable or "naked"; every closure signifies; every closure "speaks". The general economy is a "world in which and of which one speaks." And every *parole* in this economy is a *parole soufflée*, inspired by the Other and torn from interiority by the Other. But the Other is not a position to which signification would "return"; and interiority can never abide in its own time and position as the Other approaches. The movement of communication does not describe a polarity of Same and Other within the Same (that is, a polarity of Same and Other Same), but a rapport of Same and Other. Both the involvement with alterity and the approach to the Other in the *dire* or *parole* are "one-way" movements: *pour l'autre*. That which approaches me always escapes me; that which I approach always escapes me. This is the sense or orientation of heteronomy in the economy, and the fundamental non-reciprocity of signification in proximity. Thus Levinas says the pre-voluntary and pre-originary *dire* always "consents".[14] Its spasm outward is a nudity which yields and accepts — a heteronomy which is an affirmation where there is no negation.

When his context is receptivity and signification, Levinas invokes the concept of nudity as a correlate of closure's passivity. But the Other is also "naked", also passive, and the Other also "signifies", although in another concept or dimension. And Levinas is alone among the philosophers of proximity to thematize this powerlessness of alterity as a function of its incumbence. In Levinas' eyes, it is not sufficient to understand alterity's approach as a force which is not a power. It is necessary to understand the force as a direct result of the lack of power. It is the Other's powerlessness that concerns us or involves us. In this context, the "nudity" of the Other is defined by Levinas as its lack of attributes or lack of phenomenality. The Other is the Levinasian "trace": an essentially fragmentary remainder whose escape from totalization is also an excess over manifestation. The Other is that which cannot be present or "here", and which cannot be simply "gone" in a universe of negation. The alternative of presence and absence, being and non-being, is not the principle of its insistence. The trace — both a lack and a remainder, an absence and an indelibility — is the form of this insistence. When considered strategically as a presence or manifestation, the Other is both a nudity ("denuded of its own image"[15]) and an excess over the "finality" of phenomenality.[16] It "lacks" totalization, but it "exceeds" its own manifestation. It is thus the nudity of privation, and also the nudity of ostentation or impudicity. Like the alterity of fascination in Blanchot, it "dominates" its own manifestation. "*Autrui* which manifests itself in the *visage*, pierces in some sense its own plastic essence; like a being which would open the window upon which its figure was however already visible. Its presence consists in 'taking off' the form which however already manifested it. Its manifestation is a surplus over the inevitable paralysis of manifestation."[17] The Other's appearance conceals its approach and incumbence. The exteriority of the Other is already the fact that the Other "concerns" interiority. Its distance is a contact. The rapport with it is a contemplation which is already a desire. To approach it is to be dispossessed by it. Thus its impoverishment or "lack" of totalization is an excess which approaches and a breach which attracts or commands the approach to it. Subjectivity is "ordered" to the Other, or inclined toward the latter, by the non-indifference which is its uneliminable rapport with exteriority. In this Levinasian definition of separation, Bataille's concept of the dual valence of excess as lack and exorbitance is perceptible, although the theme of the Other's "independence" with regard to manifestation is not Bataille's concern. This theme in Levinas is somewhat confusing, because it correctly designates the incumbence or weight of the Other, while introducing however the temptation to interpret this incumbence as another power or another center of gravity. The proximity or *significance* of exteriority, which will take the forms of *hauteur*, *enseignement* and *visage* in the context of the *éthique*, is not a superior power, but is what Blanchot calls the "domination" of that which has no power. The approach of the Other does not take place in a phenomenological universe, in which consciousness would encounter another consciousness — but rather in a differential and proximal dimension, in which alterity's pure passivity is a factor which dispossesses interiority.* In Levinas, this radical passivity is attested by the theme of nudity which always accompanies that of incumbence or *hauteur*, but is sometimes obscured by the notion of independence, particularly when Levinas invokes Plato's *Phaedrus*, with its notion of answering for or supporting one's own signification, to describe the Other's "domination" of its own manifestation.[18]

Alterity is then a denudation, a "taking off" of both phenomenality and effectivity, and at the same time the excess of a "surplus inadequate to intentionality."[19] This excess over phenomenality will become the trace, conceived as an "indelibility" of being with regard to negation. Its evanescence or inconsistency is, like the Blanchotian image, an instance correlative to its involvement with interiority, and therefore constitutes its "contact" and its approach. At the same time, the trace indicates interiority's rapport with an irreducible "past" which was never present and cannot be recuperated, but which nevertheless (like the past of *oubli*, the *nouvelle origine*, and repetition in Blanchot) "concerns" interiority's actuality. In both these senses the inactuality of the Other's proximity is an incumbence and an approach. When the Other becomes *autrui* and the Levinasian *visage*, this *visage* will not be correlated to interiority as a term within a system, but will be "turned toward" interiority — not in the Sartrian sense, as another subjectivity, but in an impersonal, proximal sense. The Other's incumbence is my non-indifference toward an exterior in which my own center of gravity is located. The Other is not its own center of gravity, and this is its nudity. "The *visage* has turned toward me — and this is its very nudity. It *is* by itself and not at all by reference to a system."[20] The Other cannot assume the adequating distance of an actuality in correlation. This is its proximity. But the Other cannot "limit" interiority, as a substantiality, a power, or another consciousness. This is its nudity and its passivity. The Other is on one hand a lack of manifestation, an immemorial past, a poverty and powerlessness — and on the other hand an immemorial assignation, an incumbence, and a proximity which dispossesses. These two series of predicates structure the entirety of Levinas' discourse on the rapport with alterity in the *éthique*. The Other is a powerlessness against which I have no power: a nudity which disarms

---

* The Other's "lack" in proximity is a heteronomy essentially intricated with the economy of interiority. Thus the latter cannot but "fulfill" this lack — in the infinite and expanding dispossession of desire — as a function of its own separation. The latent logical solidarity of this properly economic configuration with the concepts of the philosophy of difference is extreme. For example, the concept of "supplementarity" in the work of Jacques Derrida, in spite of its strategically limited mobilizations, describes an irreducible, impersonal dispossession of closure "toward the Other" which is not only a principle of *errance* in Blanchot, but also of Levinas' *éthique*.

and exposes me. "My exposition to it, anterior to its *apparoir*, my tardiness with regard to it, my passivity [*subir*], denucleate that which is identity in me."[21]

The only approach to an alterity which cannot become present or phenomenal, and which concerns interiority by virtue of this very failure of totalization, is desire. Desire is the context of nudity's articulation with the caress in Levinas. The approach of an exterior which can neither become present nor absent, substantial nor inexistent, invests subjectivity as a non-indifference while "disarming" its intentionality. This approach which involves and contaminates, which invests and dispossesses, compels interiority outside itself. "To approach *Autrui* is to still pursue that which is already present, to still search for what one has found, not to be able to 'be quits' with the other [*prochain*]. Like caressing. The caress is the unity of proximity and the approach."[22] On one hand, the caress is an approach to that which cannot be touched, cannot be manifest in the sense of philosophy's sensations, subordinate to intuition. On the other hand, the caress is an exorbitant contact whose incessance (which Levinas does not comment, but which is a most Blanchotian moment of this problematic) results from the lack of negation which underlies its movement. The hand that caresses is not an intentionality, not itself a presence, but is an instance essentially intricated with the surface it touches. This lack of negation and distinction which is nevertheless a discontinuity, produces not only the other's inconsistency or evanescence, but also the incumbence or "attraction" of this evanescence, and the insatiability of the desire that approaches it. The caress is a self-contradiction in a universe exhausted by totalization and manifestation. "(I)n the caress, that which is there is sought as though it were not there, as though the skin were the trace of its own retreat, a languor seeking still, like an absence, that which however is, hyperbolically, there."[23]* But the movement of the hand is not simply this paradox of a misguided or errant intentional movement. It is the dispossession of the exigency, the conation "inside-out" of an interiority inspired or animated by the exterior, which conditions the possibility of consciousness as a rapport with existence.

The Other's escape from manifestation does not frustrate interiority's desire to seize it. It produces this desire, it is this desire. Its difference — the dis-. continuity which produces its radical opacity and inaccessibility — creates the non-indifference of interiority which "goes to it". And this escape is also a passivity, an inability to become substantial, which is the nudity and the impoverishment of the Other. The caress is a generosity and a desire: the *pour l'autre* of a subjectivity forced outward, toward alterity, by its very constitution in an economy of proximity — an economy whose intervals are "passions" or "obsessions". The caress is thus a touching which is not a knowing — an event which cannot take place in an economy of manifestation — and a movement which is not an action: an event which cannot take place in an economy of

---

* "ce qui, cependant est, on ne peut plus, là." In another essay, Levinas repeats this proposition with the following variation: "celui qui cependant est, on ne peut plus, proche [*close*]."[24]

totalization and determination. It is an incessance and a rapport with an immemorial past and an indefinite future — "searching still" — which could not take place in a temporality of actuality and punctuality. Its "languor" reproduces the inhuman "slowness" of the "affected" hand in involuntary prehension. That the one movement seeks an object which is "already" there, and that the other movement clutches an object which is "not" there, does not obscure the solidarity of these two economic moments. Both describe an alteration of the Same by the proximity of the Other. Interiority's movement no longer proceeds from within, but takes place "outside", within the exterior — and this dispossessing involvement is interiority itself as an ontological moment. The "denucleation" of subjectivity's identity by its rapport with alterity is the production of subjectivity's unicity.

In the proximity of the Other, interiority's center of gravity is outside itself. But the Other is not a center, not another Same. The Other is the exterior. Its nudity is its lack of phenomenality and substantiality. Interiority's nudity is an inability to remain unaffected or unchanged by this lack within the exterior. The Other's passivity is a lack of power. Interiority's passivity is an inability to dominate or oppose this lack. The Other's signification or *signifiance* is its excess over its manifestation or actuality. Interiority's signification is its inability not to be inspired or invested by this excess — its inability to silence the *parole* which is the excess of its own closure. The movement of excess in the general economy proceeds from, and returns to, the exterior, while investing the Same as a heteronomy. But the exterior is neither a source nor a terminal. It is the Other of the Same, and not another Same. It is the economy's excess over the possibility of totalization. The economy of proximity produces intervals or discontinuities, but not negations. It produces a dense and intense closure which is not a totality. Thus it produces an intentionality which is already a nudity, and an exteriority which is already an approach. The heteronomy of the Same, in its contamination by exteriority, is the principle of its unicity. This unicity is always already a caress ("the visible caresses the eye"[25]) — that is, an approach of the Other which invests and supports the interiority of *jouissance*, while already dispossessing and inclining "outward" the interiority of desire. "But the caress sleeps in all contact, and contact in all sensible experience."[26] The caress — the non-indifference of closure toward an exterior by which it is "concerned" or with which it is "involved" — is the principle of experience, because it is the principle of unicity itself. That the density or turgidity of this closure may produce a world of determination, illumination, and power, is but its regional destiny. Underneath this world, in a powerlessness which may not, perhaps, change the world, remains the avidity of the caress which is an inability to "be quits" with the Other (*ne pas pouvoir être quitte envers le prochain*). Levinas sees in this expanding sense of desire "toward the Other" the trace of an obligation and a gravity which will characterize the rapport with alterity in the *éthique*. Desire in non-indifference and the "*conatus* à l'envers" is a pouring-outward which, considered differentially and repetitively, defines the unicity of subjectivity. Consciousness in proximity is compelled toward that which has nothing: the Other. "I did not know I was so rich, but I no longer have the right to keep anything." The *cogito* of proximity is a fulfillment and a dispossession, an avidity and a generosity, whose sense is the same: *pour l'autre*. The nudity of closure in the general economy is the sense of its opening to, and unforeseeable movement into, the exterior. *Au dehors*, outward, is both the sense and the force of unicity in proximity.

SENSATION AND INTENTIONALITY

Levinas' early contact with Husserl's teachings was never an uncritical inspiration, as his *Théorie de l'intuition dans la phénoménologie de Husserl* (1930) attests, particularly in its conclusions. The studies of Husserl and Heidegger which constituted the initial stage of Levinas' philosophical career have in common an admiration for phenomenology's "rooting" of consciousness in the economy of being, but also share a suspicion of the "intellectualism" by which phenomenology tends to subordinate this economy to manifestation. The dominating presence of Hegel in the background of this rapport between phenomenology and the philosophy of proximity cannot be exaggerated. For Hegel's descriptions of an "experience" or latent economic modality of consciousness, and his subsequent refusal to discover in this economy an element irreducible to manifestation, remain the principles of phenomenology's ambivalence. Levinas' qualified enthusiasm for Husserl and then Heidegger, and his ultimate rejection of phenomenology's definitions, articulate his consistent interest in the economy of consciousness as a communicational event which cannot be thematized by a logic for which manifestation, totalization and spontaneity remain irreducible detours. Yet Hegel, Husserl and Heidegger share an inclination to describe a differential and heteronomous moment of consciousness' experience; and this inclination in Husserl is the topic of recurrent, enthusiastic discussions in Levinas' text.

In the second edition of *En découvrant l'existence avec Husserl et Heidegger* (1967), which is in so many ways a document of Levinas' entire intellectual itinerary, the reader has the opportunity to study Levinasian readings of Husserl from the 1950's and 1960's. These readings postdate the involvement with and rejection of Heidegger, and constitute not a "return to Husserl" but rather a brilliantly reasoned statement of the stratum of Husserl's thought which is of ultimate interest to Levinas. Within these essays, which surround the publication of *Totalité et infini* (1961) and anticipate important moments of *Autrement qu'être ou au delà de l'essence* (1974), the charge of intellectualism in Husserl has not disappeared, but has assumed a secondary position. Levinas' primary concern is the relation of intentionality to sensation and temporalization in the *Urimpression*, as elaborated particularly in the *Phenomenology of Internal Time Consciousness*. He attests the intellectualism which subordinates this problematic of sensation to manifestation, but enthusiastically resumes the ambiguous temporality and economy of sensation, in their anticipation of the subjectivity of the *éthique* and the *autrement qu'être*.

Husserl's position of the *Urimpression* as the ground for intentionality's fundamental, spontaneous "access" to an exteriority whose economy implies this very access, describes a passivity of reception which, in Husserl's text, may be said to "accompany" rather than truly to condition spontaneity. This ambiguous concatenation is noted by Levinas in his 1940 essay on Husserl: "The origin of all consciousness is the primary impression 'Urimpression'. But this originary passivity is at the same time an initial spontaneity. The primary intentionality in which it constitutes itself, is the present. The present is the very upsurge of consciousness, its presence to itself. A presence which does not paralyse it: the impression passes."[27] Although Levinas' context in 1940 is his attestation of Husserl's intellectualism and his preference for Heidegger's concept of a "worldhood" irreducible to intentionality, he nevertheless reads in the *Urimpression* Husserl's sense of a temporal "modification" which implies a
- contamination or alteration constitutive of subjectivity. Nearly twenty years later, when Levinas' refusal of the primacy of comprehension in Heidegger is in place, and "La Philosophie et l'idée de l'infini" (1957) has been published, he returns to the theme of the *Urimpression*, prepared now to read this concept in the terms of differentiation and heteronomy which he has developed during the intervening years. This reading will discover in the ambiguity of sensation not only passivity, but difference, Bataillian incarnation, the subjectivity of proximity in impersonality, proximal temporality, and the *parler* of separation within the general economy.

The priority of sensation or, in a more general economic sense, of a receptivity which precedes intentionality's manifestation and ontological
- constitution of what it receives, indicates an ambiguous moment at which condition and conditioned coincide. Manifestation proceeds from a moment of receptivity which is itself not yet manifestation, but rather differentiation. The *Urimpression* describes a moment of differentiation which becomes the distinction between reception and given. It thus constitutes both the interiority of reception and the exteriority of the given, but constitutes these terms in its own unitary and ambiguous moment. The *Urimpression* is thus an "individuation", "at the same time first subject and first object, giver and given."[28] This simultaneity, which describes a primacy of differentiation, remains homologous to the ambiguity of intentionality's access to being, and its chief importance is its problematization of the subject-object correlation and its tendency to subordinate manifestation to communication. "The world is not only constituted, but constituting. The subject is no longer a pure subject, the object is no longer a pure object. The phenomenon is at the same time that which is revealed and that which reveals, being and the access to being."[29] The concept of "impression" implies a pure vulnerability or susceptibility of closure in the economy of manifestation. It is for this reason, in Levinas' eyes, that

sensation retains a priority in Husserl, in spite of its simultaneity with constitution and illumination. "Sensible experience is privileged, because in it this ambiguity of constitution occurs [*se joue*], in which the noema conditions and shelters [*abrite*] the noesis which constitutes it."[30] This priority is not yet temporal, but insists nevertheless by virtue of its grounding of spontaneity in a differential moment irreducible to spontaneity and to the rooting of intentionality in manifestation.

At this point in Levinas' thinking, the importance of the *Urimpression* is twofold. In the first place, it inscribes the passivity of reception into the constituting spontaneity of the intention. In the second place, it describes the ambiguous moment of an existence of intentionality prior to the economy of manifestation in which it will participate — that is, a moment at which intentionality itself is not yet intuition or illumination. The congruence of passivity, which indicates an intrication with alterity in the "pressure" of the impression, and an escape from manifestation, is already the design of Levinasian separation in its escape from totalization, as the following paragraph declares:

It is to the extent that the concept of the subject is attached to sensibility, in which individuation coincides with the ambiguity of the Urimpression, in which activity and passivity are joined, in which the *now* is anterior to the historical ensemble it is to constitute — that phenomenology preserves the person. The latter does not dissolve into the product constituted or thought by it, but remains always transcendent, *en deçà.** And in this sense I think phenomenology situates itself in exact opposition to the position of Spinoza and Hegel in which the thought [*pensé*] absorbs the thinker, in which the thinker is dissolved in the eternity of the discourse.[31]

The ambiguity of the moment of differentiation or "individuation", and the passivity of impression or reception correlative to this moment, indicate an origin of intentionality in an economy without totalization and without comprehension. This latent origin, by virtue of its passivity (and not by virtue of its independence or integrity with regard to historical or objective time), is precisely Levinasian "subjectivity". The rapport of intentionality to being in sensation is essentially subjective because its passivity is not engulfed by its spontaneity or its adequation to the exterior. Differentiation itself produces this subjectivity — this heteronomy of closure under the force or pressure of the impression. The differential trace, defined as closure's inextrication from an exterior which alters, is the principle of receptivity. The "person" is this contamination of totalization at the root of manifestation. Thus, phenomenology "preserves the person" for Levinas in exactly the opposite sense that it preserves the person from its own perspective, i.e. as a subjectivity which is its own center of gravity and the autonomy of its being in the world. It is the hyperbole of facticity — the passivity of subjectivity in an element of

---

* "Not yet", "before": "on this side of" as opposed to "beyond".

differentiation which supports ("shelters") and dispossesses, that produces the "person" for Levinas. Thus he approvingly reads in Husserl a philosophical moment which phenomenology has always tended to reduce: the moment of differentiation as passivity. Thus, in 1959, already looking back on the idea of the infinite, Levinas writes, "the phenomenological self does not appear, ultimately, in the history it constitutes, but in consciousness. And thus it is extracted from the totality. And thus it can break with the past and is not, in the rupture with the past, a continuation in spite of itself of this past that a sociology or a psychoanalysis will rediscover. It can break and can consequently speak [*parler*]."[32] The escape of intentionality is its latent passivity and its involvement with alterity prior to the "history" which is correlative to its constitutions. It is not from the immobility of the in-itself that subjectivity escapes, but precisely from the manifestation and temporalization which are its ultimate context in phenomenology. Its escape proceeds from its very inability to participate in the economy of illumination without a contaminating involvement with alterity, at the heart of this economy. Its independence is its very dependence upon alterity, in a moment of differentiation – the impression and the *parole* – which precedes the ontological economy of manifestation and temporalization, by virtue of its priority over negation and the phenomenal interval. In this dependence or radical passivity beyond the passivity of philosophy's concept of receptivity, the outlines of the general economy are already perceptible: "in thought there is thus revealed a fundamental *passion* which no longer has anything in common with the passivity of sensation, of the given – from which empiricism and realism proceeded."[33] The passivity of sensation, become the passivity of difference, is already the obsession – the communication – of existence in the economy.

At this point in his reading of Husserl, at which temporalization is not yet the context of subjectivity, Levinas has subordinated consciousness' existence in its correlation to negation and illumination – an existence attested by phenomenology to be the problematic irreality of an interval – to a new ambiguity which is no longer that of negation, but of proximity. "And now the thought which is directed upon the object in all the sincerity of its intention, does not touch being in its naive sincerity," not because of the naiveté of its natural attitude, but because its fundamental ontology is already conditioned by differentiation and proximity. And thus it "thinks more than it thinks and otherwise than it thinks in its actuality and, in this sense, is not immanent to itself, even if, by its gaze, it captures 'in the flesh' the object it envisages!"[34] The rooting of consciousness in differentiation by phenomenology implies a heteronomy for which adequation, totalization and illumination are insufficient and excessive predicates, ascribing both an illegitimate homogeneity or undifferentiation and an insufficient intimacy or involvement to the rapport of consciousness with the exterior. This rapport is a hyperbolic intimacy of heteronomy and an irreducible opacity of difference which both exceed the logic of manifestation and totalization. Intentionality's rapport with alterity is a proximity, and therefore a subjectivity, and therefore a *parole*. "This life which gives sense is given perhaps in another way [*autrement*] and supposes for its revelation relations between the Same and the Other which are no longer objectivation but society [*société**]."[35] Alterity is extricated from its subordination to negation, and becomes the approach and pre-originarity of that which, in its primordial inadequation to manifestation, produces the latter: "the Other guides the transcendental movement without offering itself to vision."[36] In a surprising moment, Levinas notes Husserl's characteristic gesture which subordinates the ambiguity of differentiation to the spontaneity of the pure consciousness in reduction which "perceives" itself in this intrication with the concrete. In his posthumous notes on corporal kinestheses,[37] Husserl describes an ambiguity of movement and the sensation of movement, but does not stress the heteronomy implicit in this configuration. Instead, he describes consciousness as "taking itself" as or for a kinesthesis, thus grounding this kinesthesis in intentionality. Levinas enthusiastically approves this description, whose intellectualism he has been consistently criticizing in surrounding passages:

This *"taking for ..."*, is it the purely theoretical act of a disincarnated being? I think there is in the obsession of the Reduction, in this insurmountable temptation to seek, behind the intentionality of incarnation, the intention of a pure self — a positive possibility, constitutive of kinesthesis, *of the memory of its own origin in an interiority.* ... This possibility of searching for oneself, perhaps vainly and tardily [*après-coup*], belongs to the essence of the transcendence that sensibility accomplishes. Man integrally masters his destiny only in memory, in search of lost time [*à la recherche du temps perdu*].[38]

This unexpected accreditation of Husserl's gesture is not incomprehensible to Levinas' reader, because it describes a consciousness which assumes the past that conditions it — and this consciousness is the Levinasian *cogito*. The *cogito's* assumption of what precedes it, as discussed earlier, is an illusory, conditional, and impossible event by which heteronomy produces spontaneity — an event which has the positive ontological status of this very illusion, inactuality, or impossibility. It is the paradox of manifestation, the *comme si* or "as though" which produces consciousness as an interiority or "egoism", and which effectively introduces reversibility and repetition into historical time. In its spontaneity and confidence in its own constitutions, however, consciousness attests or articulates an involvement with alterity in the pre-originary form of the *il y a* and of the Other which interrupts the *cogito's* negations by its affirmative "Yes". Thus the *cogito*, like intentionality, hides the heteronomy of separation under its participation in manifestation. Levinas' approval of Husserl's interpretation of kinesthesis is his awareness that Husserl, within and because of his very intellectualism, articulates a basic moment of proximity which is the intellectualism of separation as egoism. This perhaps double-edged appreciation

---

* Communication: the "non-allergic" rapport described by inspiration and heteronomy in the *parole*, as opposed to adequation and correlation in an economy of manifestation.

of Husserl's very insensitivity to the uneliminable aspect of communication is characteristic of Levinas' nature rapport with his teacher.*

The notion of an intentionality which is involved with alterity in a temporal pre-originarity which conditions its spontaneity — "in search of lost time" — is the context of Levinas' 1965 essay "Intentionalité et sensation".[39] Here, Levinas interprets intentionality's temporal relation to sensation as it is elaborated in the *Vorlesungen zur Phaenomenologie des inneren Zeitbewusstsein*. Resuming Husserl's concept of intentionality's idealization of its sensations as *Abschattungen* or "raccourcis" ("abridgments", "abstracts", "shortcuts") in the *Erlebnis*, Levinas engages his own reading at the point of Husserl's situation of time within the moment of sensation. The "minimal distance"[40] implied by the *Urimpression's* presenting of itself to an intentionality which is produced by it, describes a temporal interval in sensation itself. Here the differentiation of "sensing" and "sensed" produces a minimal but irreducible *écart* or gap between impression and intention which is temporalization itself as a function of differentiation. Just as there is a differential *écart* — a gap and a heteronomous alteration — in the identity of "sensed" or "sensing", there is a temporal "lapse" in the punctuality of the *Urimpression* — a lapse which produces the linear aspect of time in the minimal "tardiness" or *après-coup* of the intention. The latter, which gives itself as a pure punctuality and actuality rooted in manifestation, retains the trace and the impression of an irrecuperable "past" — the priority of the *Urimpression* — because it is affected in its unicity by the alterity which produces this impression. The actuality of the intention is affected by an irrecuperable "before", because it is affected by an irrecuperable "other" to which its function as manifestation is not adequate. The "lapse" of temporal heteronomy or alteration is a product of the basic *écart* inherent in individuation itself, in a differential economy. Thus, the *Urimpression*, when considered in itself as a moment of differentiation and alteration, is an expanding, repetitive, inactual moment which produces the apparent punctuality of protention and retention as its "effects". "An accentuated, living, absolutely new instant — the proto-impression — already has a distance from this needle point at which it

---

* It is noteworthy that Levinas' essay ("Intentionalité et métaphysique", 1959) ends with a footnote on Maurice Blanchot, in which Levinas suggests that without the radical concept of intentionality as a proximity irreducible to manifestation, the modern philosophy of art and its "most remarkable manifestation, the critical work of Maurice Blanchot," would be incomprehensible. Blanchot, writes Levinas, conceives art as "the ultimate relation with being in an anticipation, quasi-impossible, of that which is no longer being."[41] To support this claim, Levinas cites the passage from "Le Chant des sirènes", noted more than once in this study, in which the *récit's* approach to its "event" is defined as the only reality of the event, and in which this futurity of the inactual is defined by Blanchot as its "imperiousness".[42] The name of Blanchot in Levinas' text is thus accompanied by a reference to proximity in the approach. This reference points up the pre-originarity of alterity in the constitution of an intentionality which will itself be an approach to the manifest. In both cases, the passivity of the approach is ultimate: "When I approach it, is it not already it that is approaching me?"

comes to a head absolutely *present*, and, by this gap [*écart*], *presents itself*, retained, *to* a new punctual present, sensed [*pressenti**] in a protention proceeding from the first protoimpression and embracing in this presentiment the imminence of its own retreat into the immediate past of retention."[43] Thus the punctuality of the *Urimpression* has the form of a metamorphosis, the pure *différer* of a difference which produces discontinuity without totalization, a moment which is in itself the *écart* by which it produces differences. It is already the sensation it is about to become, and already the pastness of the sensation it will have become. And it is the force of this imminence, and the escaping indefinition of this retention. It is an imminence, an "already" and an "always-already". It is a differential moment which produces temporal intervals themselves as differences rather than totalities. It is thus a proximal punctuality which stretches itself toward a future and a past which it creates by this stretching − a future and a past which are no longer protention and retention, but the proximal incumbence of alterity upon a "present" which will henceforth describe a temporal heteronomy or subjectivity. The *Urimpression* is a production of time through difference rather than negation: "this 'is no longer' is also a 'still there', that is, a 'presence for . . .', and this 'not yet' is an 'already there', that is, a 'presence for . . .'."[44] Differentiation produces not only discontinuity and intervals, but the very possibility that closure might be "affected" by exteriority, in the form of another moment or another entity. When Levinas writes "presence for . . ." he attests the fact that differentiation, because it produces closure as a heteronomy affected by an *écart*, produces the possibility of experience or consciousness in the same moment that it produces multiplicity. The possibility of time and of a time "consciousness" proceeds from differentiation, to the extent that differentiation produces unicity not as a totality, but as a communication, an alteration, and a heteronomy. But this "consciousness" of and in time is no longer consciousness: it is subjectivity. Levinas' meditation reproduces phenomenology's situation of temporalization within the economy of being, while insisting that this economy cannot be a manifestation produced by negation and totalization, but must be first a communication produced by differentiation and the *écart* of alteration. It is against this background that Levinas mobilizes Husserl's concept of "modification" to designate this economy of alteration and contamination. "Here, *aim* [*visée*: intention] *and event coincide*: intentionality is the production of this primordial state in existence which is called modification."[45] The possibility of a *visée*, i.e. an interval and a consciousness of discontinuity produced by this interval, is the *écart* which separates and the communicational *écart* or gap which renders unicity incomplete and vulnerable. Intentionality or consciousness, the product of the *écart* and the *écart* itself in the *Urimpression*, can only appear in an economy whose principle is not negation but difference. "A knowledge ·and an event which are a *modification* and not a negation. Consciousness is

* *Pressentir* means to sense as a foreseeing or presentiment.

not negativity, 'knowledge' does not let go of the event that time does not destroy."[46] Only through the inextrication and heteronomy of negation's "weakness" in the general economy can a "subjectivity" of time and eventually a "consciousness" of time appear.

Thus intentionality's temporal constitution, and the temporality of manifestation itself, are not deduced from the negations which produce time and space, punctuality and separation, but rather from a proximal differentiation which creates communications, in the form of imminence, pre-originarity, and repetition. The *Urimpression* in itself is a moment of difference and repetition. "One must admit here of a returning of time upon itself, a fundamental *iteration*."[47] The familiar notion of a present which disappears in the continuity of temporal flux is, for Levinas, understandable through the concept of flux as the differential alteration or modification which produces both temporal intervals and the subjectivity of these intervals. Flux is the "continuity" of time in proximity, and as such is not a simple undifferentiation, but the stretching and incumbence of differentiation itself. These predicates are correlates of the *écart* which is not negative, but proximal — an *écart* which produces intentionality as proximity rather than illumination. The only possibility of consciousness — subjectivity — is the very impossibility of manifestation and totalization as ultimate economic principles. Only the weakness of the negative and the *écart* contaminating the totality can produce receptivity: the heteronomy of closure.

The look that notates the *écart* is the *écart* itself. The consciousness of time is not a reflection upon time, but temporalization itself: the *après-coup* [delay] of the becoming-conscious is the very *après* [after] of time. Retention and protention are *the very manner* of flux: the retaining or the protending ("thought") and the "being-at-a-distance" (event) coincide. The consciousness-of . . . is here the flux.[48]

Retention and protention are both modalities of "impression": a differentiation producing remainders whose incompletion is an involvement with each other. Intentionality is born in the heteronomy of closure. Flux is the temporal differentiation which produces this heteronomy. The "event" of discontinuity can be a "consciousness" of discontinuity only when the interval is a contact and the difference is not a totalization.

The *après-coup* or "already", "always already" of closure's involvement with an alterity which both escapes and concerns, creates the "after" of time's linear aspect. The past of manifestation is an effect of the larger, irrecuperable past of interiority's involvement with the Other. The "not yet" which is both the indefinite future and the imminence of the Other's approach (the *à venir* and the incumbence of this *à venir* in the second sense of proximity's "already") describe interiority's involvement with an alterity that cannot become manifest or punctual, but approaches and compels from the very position of its inactuality. And this indefinite incumbence of exteriority is the "yet to come" of the future in time's linear aspect. Past, future, and the contaminated presence of flux, écart and alteration, are products of a proximal differentiation which creates subjectivity as an involvement with the inaccessible. In the "egoism" of spontaneity, these contaminated intervals become the ekstases of a consciousness adequated to a linear and progressive time of manifestation. But this very spontaneity is an effect of the modification and passivity by which temporal discontinuity becomes a lapsing, collapsing, and inextrication. The miracle of the *cogito* (or even of memory, as Levinas suggests in *Totalité et infini*[49]) — the "memory of its origin in an interiority" — is made possible by subjectivity's involvement with an "other" time: the time of the Other's approach and escape, which is a function of temporal differentiation. When temporal moments have the capacity to "concern" each other across temporal intervals, this is because the Other — the Other of closure — is involved in the creation of intervals. Subjectivity, with its paradoxical power to "assume" and dominate these discontinuities within totalization, appears in time by virtue of this insistence of the Other. When exteriority "weighs upon" closure as a function of an economy without totalization, consciousness becomes a possibility.

The *Urimpression* is a moment of differentiation which produces intervals and fragments or remainders, while exerting a pressure and leaving a trace or impression within any closure. The insistence of this uneliminable incompletion and contamination in closure is the possibility of consciousness. In *Autrement qu'être ou au delà de l'essence*, Levinas writes of this moment: "consciousness glimmers in the impression to the extent that the impression recedes [*s'écarte*] from itself: to wait for itself *still* or to recuperate itself *already*."[50] The *écart* of the impression is not only its difference — that is, its non-coincidence with itself, its expanding undecidability, or its production of multiplicity — but is also the latent principle of this difference: proximity. The *écart* of the impression exerts a pressure or produces a force which introduces into temporal plurality both the *à venir* ("yet to come": "approaching") and the "already" (both "gone" and "concerning"). Consciousness proceeds from difference ("There is consciousness to the extent that the sensible impression differs from itself without differing; it differs without differing, other within identity."[51]), although not as a "possibility". Difference forces subjectivity to think, to exist. Subjectivity is precisely this force which compels the differential or temporal fragment toward alterity. The fragment itself is time as the contamination of becoming and metamorphosis: a position or punctuality which is subject to the weight or incumbence of the Other: "*just* past, on the *point of arriving*."[52] The proximal instant produced by the *Urimpression* is an imminence and a disarming "already": modalities of force, incumbence, pressure or impression in time which are inadequate to protention and retention. At this point a basic adjustment of the notion of difference in consciousness appears in Levinas' text. The *Urimpression* "in itself" may appear to be a difference in the sense of simple undecidability, a becoming of multiplicity, or a production of fragmentary remainders whose unicity is their communication with each other. But intentionality, which is produced by the *écart* or lapse of sensation in the impression, is not itself in the indifferent or reciprocal position of these differential remainders. Intentionality is entirely "turned toward" this irrecuperable past. Its position is a non-indifference. It is "entirely passivity, receptivity of an 'other' penetrating the 'same', life and not 'thought'."[53] The concept of difference, viewed panoramically, reveals the absolute ambiguity of an alteration of the Same, a schismatic production of fragments which is the only unicity of the moment of differentiation. For subjectivity in proximity, this panoramic view is impossible. The movement of differential alteration is a *sens unique*, a "one-way" movement, which produces the communicational possibility of unicity — although not as an integrity or an indifference, but as a *pour l'autre*. The "loss" of the exterior experienced by subjectivity in the impossibility of "presence" or phenomenality implied by communication, is also the approach of the Other: an approach which is already the dispossession of subjectivity's approach to the Other. The difference which invests, also dispossesses, and forces interiority toward the exterior, into the exterior. Interiority or separation proceeds from this *sens unique* of differential alteration, this *pour l'autre* of a unicity "preoccupied" by exteriority. The force and dissymetry of the *pour l'autre* are irreducible predicates of a differentiation which produces singularities that are not totalities, but these predicates are not manifest in the panoramic view of difference as dispersion, dissemination, or loss of presence. The trace is not an indifferent circulation of information or an indefinite dispersion consequent to the impossibility of totalization. Differentiation produces a force, an incumbence, and a dissymetrical "inclination" within being. This inclination is proximity: the non-indifference of interiority to alterity. It is against this background that Levinas thematizes intentionality itself as an inclination and a passivity, rather than an ambiguity: "'Internal consciousness', it will become consciousness through the temporal modification of retention, designating, perhaps, the essence of all thought as the retaining of a plenitude that escapes. The mystery of intentionality lies in the gap [*écart de* . . .] or in the modification of temporal flux. Consciousness is a senescence and a search for lost time."[54] The rapport with the past — that is, with the Other's escape and incumbence — is not merely a loss or inadequation, but a *recherche*. This search, this desire, is subjectivity. Difference is not dispersion, but a compelling incumbence of that which has been lost. Levinas' invocation of Proust's title is also a description of the essence of Proustian subjectivity: a permanence of loss as the element of familiarity for a consciousness defined entirely as desire.[*]

---

[*] "A bit of time in its pure state" which reveals to the narrator of the *Recherche* the loss of the appropriation required by Habit, produces simultaneously a new indifference toward death. This singular moment corresponds precisely to "modification", as Levinas understands this concept: the production of the Same as metamorphosis within an altering

The principle of subjectivity in proximity is passivity. The *Urimpression* in its ambiguity is what Levinas calls a *déphasage* of time — a moment which is not in phase with itself. Intentionality as proximity is what he calls the *passage* of time: the Other which "a passé" ("has passed", "is gone"), a time which "se passe de moi" (does not need the self), the *passion* of temporal heteronomy, and the passivity (senescence, vulnerability) of unicity in a time of alteration and becoming. The passivity of intentionality is the inspiration of the Same by the Other,[55] and is therefore the permanent possibility of an instance irreducible to manifestation which nevertheless conditions manifestation. "Signification as one-for-the-other [*l'un-pour-l'autre*], without an assumption of the other by the one, in *passivity*, supposes the possibility of a pure non-sense invading and menacing signification."[56] This notion of a regionality of "meaning" as manifestation has often been attested by the philosophy of difference. What the panoramic view of a differential freeplay may obscure is the passivity of signification, and its dissymetrical movement. This movement is an impossibility of location or equilibrium, an extravagance of closure which is inadequate to the theme of circulation or dispersion. Levinas returns to Husserl's kinestheses in order to describe it:

Kinesthesis is not the psychic equivalent of corporal movement recorded or reflected by a subject, immobile in itself, (immobile in this idealist immobility that no empirical matter could equal) and which, in the Hegelian manner, ends up belonging to the world it thinks and participating in a structure with the things of the world. Kinesthesis in Husserl is the original mobility of the subject. *Movement and displacement* [*marche*] *are in the very subjectivity of the subject.*[57]

The contraction of the exigency which recoils from exteriority is already its inspired, heteronomous movement into the economy, as Blanchot's text shows

temporal element. In this latent birth of consciousness, this new origin, the loss of all retention opens a new rapport with the *à-venir*. It is this new, nocturnal rapport, which in its inactuality had conditioned the reality of Habit itself, that is sensed by the narrator, and that motivates his ultimate decision. But this decision does not represent a "leap", in Heideggerian terms, outside the actual toward a dimension to which we are "already admitted". The contaminated, suicidal joy of the narrator who leaves the world of habit and social life, proceeds from the intensity of affirmation which uproots and "tears" the separate being from the totality. Rather than to return to an element of appropriation, the narrator moves, through a transgressive modification, toward the future, toward the Time of alteration, *pour l'autre*. Thus, in Levinas' words, he "can break and can consequently speak (*parler*)," can begin to write his *oeuvre*. What the "vocation" of the artist has taught him is that the Same is an alteration: neither opposed to the Other nor related to the latter by adequation or inadequation, but rather involved with both the Other and *Autrui* through the non-allergy of metamorphosis. The narrator's apparently fearful calculations regarding his age and health do not contradict his indifference to death, but articulate a proximal duality: having welcomed death as alteration (a function of repetitive Time), he must concern himself with the intramundane possibility of death as negation (a function of historical time).

with unequalled intensity. The "position" of subjectivity in being is an *errance*, because this position is precisely a subjectivity: that is, a *pour l'autre*. The indecision of the exile described by *errance* and *erreur* is not a directionless indifference. It has a direction which is precisely the force of its displacement: toward the Other.

In his essay "Langage et proximité",[58] Levinas writes, "the immediacy of the sensible is an event of proximity and not of knowledge."[59] The priority of sensation in Husserl reveals, through the ambiguity of the *Urimpression* and, more importantly, through the secondarity of intentionality's spontaneity, the basic predicates of communication as proximity. Sensation represents for Levinas the differential moment of separation or individuation in the economy of being. This differentiation produces a unicity which is inspired by or involved with alterity, and whose "intentional" structure, in an etymological sense, is an inclination toward the Other. The insistence of this Other is an immemorial past and a compelling though indefinite future, a time beyond manifestation which weighs upon consciousness whose awakening is always too late. The rapport of intentionality with this time outside manifestation is a passivity and an impression which invests or conditions the possibility of its power to "act" intentionally. These predicates — passivity, inclination, involvement — are the definition of subjectivity as an effect of differentiation, and not differential predicates applied to a familiar notion of subjectivity. Differentiation, in the general economy, is precisely subjectivity: the non-indifference, non-allergy, or "society" which opens closure to alterity. The most basic form of this opening is the *parole* of inspiration, which resumes its predicates and grounds the possibility of intersubjectivity. "The sensible," in Levinas' crucial formulation, "is already spoken."[60] The possibility of receptivity is already a response to the Other's approach. The insistence with which Levinas returns so often to Husserl does not result from a desire to discover the non-manifest or non-idealizable underneath Husserl's categories, but from an intuition that within the differentiations attested by these categories, the proximity of the *parole* is concealed.

FASCINATION AND THE IMAGE

The problematic from which the themes of fascination, the "presence of absence" and the image emerge in Blanchot is the rapport of literature to negation in "La Littérature et le droit à la mort". In this essay Blanchot articulates the negating or distancing function of literary language with the insufficiency of this language by comparison with the negations of action, and with the materiality of the literary word as a residue which contaminates the function of negation. On the basis of this articulation, Blanchot designates literary language as an ambivalent tendency to approach the element which exceeds and conditions its own movement. This element is defined as a reality which precedes the economy of negation, totalization, and illumination. In the first radically Blanchotian gesture of this essay, the inaccessible alterity of this hidden reality is re-defined as a nocturnal and proximal dimension whose pure or absolute unavailability conceals its contaminating approach — an approach which links literature permanently to the economy of the residue and the *il y a*. The frustration of literature's attempts to mimic the active nagations of existential commitment ceases to be Blanchot's context. He now attests with enthusiasm the involvement of literature with proximity, and its consequent tendency toward the inessential and a reality without truth. The thematics of anguish and inefficiency are supplanted by the logic of passivity and impossibility. Literature "is not beyond the world, but it is not the world either: it is the presence of things before the *world* is, their perseverance after the world has disappeared. . . ."[61] As mentioned earlier, this moment of transition from the first section of "La Littérature et le droit à la mort", with its Hegelian definitions, to the second section, which introduces the theme of the presence of absence within an entirely communicational logic, is a basic moment in Blanchot's career as a thinker. The Hegelian inspiration which haunts *Faux Pas*, *La Part du feu*, and *Lautréamont et Sade* is supplanted by the discovery of proximity which is to inform the brilliant publications of the early 1950's, collected in *L'Espace littéraire* and *Le Livre à venir*. The "exceptional" moment of proximity, which already had an explicitly expanding resonance in Blanchot's novels of the 1940's, appears finally in his theoretical text as a statement of the regionality of manifestation. It is at this moment that the problematic of the image becomes possible in Blanchot, although the image does not become a theme until the publication of "Les deux versions de l'imaginaire" (1951).

The context of fascination and the image in *L'Espace littéraire* is the solitude of the writer in the approach to, and of, the *oeuvre*, and the exceptional or anomalous mode of receptivity which is correlative to this approach. Blanchot's reader may be tempted to understand the concept of fascination precisely as an anomaly and an affective or subjective impression proceeding from the pressure of artistic creation; and he is, in fact, invited to do so by Blanchot's manner of presenting this concept. As is the case with involuntary prehension and many other Blanchotian themes, however, the notions of fascination and the image exceed the context of writing, and tend toward a larger definition of receptivity or experience in proximity. Initially, the image is defined as the form of the imaginary or fictive in literary language's designation of a reality irreducible to manifestation. The writer's involvement with this reality forces him to "persevere in beginning again that which for him never begins, to belong to the shadow of events, not to their reality, to the image, not to the object, to that which makes words themselves become images, appearances — and not signs, values, a power of truth."[62] The literary word is a residue which is not eliminated by its function as designation and distancing. It is no longer a sign rooted in a universe of adequation, but an unelimable remainder proceeding from a dimension without negation and totalization. To deal with this word is to "work with" an instance which is not amenable to utility and intentionality, and thus to become involved with the image as language itself. The writer's activity becomes "the fundamental passivity in which the word, now only its appearance and the shadow of a word, can never be mastered or even seized, remains the *insaisissable*, the *indessaisissable*, the undecided moment of fascination."[63] The writer's attempt to manipulate the literary word, and the ironic moment at which he "goes back to work" (*se remet à l'oeuvre*) without realizing that his initiative has become repetition, is the overdetermined moment at which proximity and impossibility have become the *nouvelle origine* of his behavior. The writer has entered a dimension of the general economy which is no longer the "world": the dimension of affirmation "over which he has no authority;"[64] of the *parole* which is "that which still speaks when all has been said;"[65] of the time without "decision" or "initiative" which is incessance and repetition.[66] Within this dimension, as the concept of indecision indicates, the writer's spontaneity and intentionality have become a problematic remainder of intentionality in a reality without power. This remainder is the exigency. Blanchot invokes and defines it under the name "fascination". The exteriority it confronts is the image.

The image is an "appearance", or rather the possibility of appearance – of discontinuity and subjectivity – in an economy of communication. There is a virtually programmatic statement of this moment, and its constitution in the defection of negativity, in a section of *L'Espace littéraire* entitled "La fascination de l'absence de temps":

It is the time in which nothing begins, in which initiative is not possible, in which, before affirmation, there is already the return of affirmation. Rather than a purely negative mode, it is on the contrary a time without negation, without decision, when here is truly nowhere, when each thing recedes into its image and when the "I" that we are recognizes itself dissolving into the neutrality of a face-less "He". The time of the absence of time is without a present, without presence. This "without a present" does not refer however to a past.[67]

In this repetitive temporality whose principle is the affirmation which proceeds from negation's defection, that which appears is an instance which cannot become "present" or phenomenal, and is therefore a "presence of absence".[68] It is also an instance which cannot appear in a punctual present which would be extricated from the contaminations of temporal proximity, and is thus a presence of the "inactual".[69] This instance is the residue which the operation of negation has not eliminated: a contaminating instance which affects all discontinuity in an economy without totalization, "the being which is at the bottom of the absence of being."[70] Its persistence allows the punctual and present to be invaded by the indefinitely non-present: the inactual, the unsubstantial, the immemorial past and the eternally futural.[71] When negation is supplanted by communication, both spatial and temporal intervals become communications or alterations. The inactual is as present as any presence; the absent is as present as the present. The "here and now" has become the "nowhere" of a space without locus and a time without punctuality. The identical particularity of the "I" has become the proximal unicity of the "He" — that is, the intersubjectivity of solitude, which is a consequence of its intrication with alterity, prior to the possibility of an actual, constituted other.

In the thematic terms associated with the philosophy of difference, the time of time's absence is a time absolutely without presence. It includes no phenomenality and no actuality. But it is not a time of indifferent dispersion. It is a time that is not without an "appearance" — a difference, an incumbence, an approach — of alterity. This is because it is a dimension of differentiation which produces interiority in the very movement of its destruction of identity. This is the sense of the "remainder of intentionality" to which the image appears. In the absence of negation and correlation, difference produces a subjectivity which is no longer an intention, but a passivity. The image is the insistence and approach of an exteriority to which interiority is not indifferent — an alterity which, by the pre-originarity of its involvement with interiority, is incumbent upon the latter. Alterity's escape from presence, in the image, is also its approach and its penetration. The heteronomy perceived by Levinas in Husserl's concept of the *Urimpression* is reproduced in Blanchot, although its form is the violent and ironic figure of an intentional act without negation. The intentional object has suddenly become a proximity, and the act is no longer an act. "It is not, but returns, comes as already and always past, so that I do not know [*connais*] it, but recognize [*reconnais*] it, and this recognition ruins in me the power to know, the right to seize, makes of the unseizable the *indessaisissable* as well, that which I cannot take [*prendre*], but only take again [*reprendre*] — and never let go."[72] The object of consciousness' access, in Blanchot's irony, has become what he called in "La Littérature et le droit à la mort" an "impossibility of preventing oneself from understanding."[73] The proximity of the image is comprehension become impossibility and passivity. The inaccessible seizes consciousness. The complementary concepts which organize this moment are the *insaisissable* and the *indessaisissable*: the "unseizable" which we "cannot let go of." No phenomenal interval exists between subject and object. Intentionality is no longer an illuminating existence within the real, but has become a function of differential alteration within the inactual. Negation is now communication: the dispossession of the integral. The ethereality of the object is its lack of totalization and consequent tendency to melt into the surrounding exterior — which is not itself an existent, not an objective totality, and thus not a horizon or ground. The object cannot be seized because it is insufficiently differentiated. But this insufficient differentiation is difference or communication itself, and constitutes the only unicity of the object. On the other hand, this object is insufficiently differentiated from the subject that envisages it. It is a differentiated instance or "appearance" which is involved with subjectivity, although not as a phenomenon across an illuminating interval. It is "too close" to be totalized and held up for contemplation by a subjectivity rooted in manifestation. Its "presence" is not its phenomenality, but its intrication with a subjectivity whose own density or unicity is precisely its detour, its "conation in reverse", which involves this object and this surrounding exterior. The presence of the object is its economic or communicational involvement with the subject — which is already an inherence to the subject. Thus the object is more, or other, than an object, and the subject is less, or other, than a subject. The otherness of the object is precisely its forbidden collaboration in the economy of its correlate — its very lack of the "alterity" of philosophy, which merely escapes.

Since negation is not the condition of differentiation between subject and image, the logical interval requisite for causality, determination, or power, is also weakened or contaminated. This is the *indessaisissabilité* or incumbence of the object. To see it is to be unable to see it, and to be unable to close the eyes. To understand it is not to understand, but to be unable not to understand. The rapport with the object is entirely passive: a movement that is not an action, in a reality without power. At the same time, the object's own incumbence which "seizes" the eye is not itself a power, but proceeds from the very heteronomy of the object, i.e. its lack of totalization and substantiality. Its incumbence, like that of the sirens, is a passivity which compels and dominates: a force which proceeds from the excess of exteriority over the alternative of being and non-being.

But what happens when what one sees, although at a distance, seems to touch you by a gripping contact, when the manner of seeing is a sort of touching, when seeing is a *contact* at a distance? When that which is seen imposes itself upon the gaze, as though the gaze were seized, touched, placed in contact with the appearance?[74]

As this quotation shows, the transitivity of the "seizing" and "touching" of the image is not reversed — the image is not a power to touch me — but is differentiated insufficiently or ambiguously, and ultimately defined as a force which is not a power. Contact, on the other hand, is not simply the result of an intentional "access" or phenomenal presence which has become hyperbolic. It is not a result of intentionality's power, or of the immediacy of manifestation. It results from the fact that the image appears in a reality without power. As Blanchot notes in "Les deux versions de l'imaginaire",[75] this communicational production of subjectivity tends to create a subjective or intentional aspect of the inanimate exterior, and a concomitant "thickening" or "condensation" of interiority which becomes the object of this gaze from the exterior.* These

---

* In this context, Blanchot describes "magic" as the "methodical" interpretation of a proximal exterior in terms of power — a power transferred to the inanimate. The error of this interpretation is its retention of the term of power, which is a consequence of its exigency to mobilize the context of radical passivity. The example of magic attests a most stable tendency in Western thought to interpret the passivity of communication as a superior power — malevolent or divine — and to define alterity as the independence of this power, which may yet be dominated precisely because it is a power.[76]

apparently paradoxical predicates, invoked so often in the history of literature, do not describe an anomalous or exceptional moment of experience, but rather articulate the "exposition" or "subjection" which is integral to the production of subjectivity in proximity.

The object's ethereality or lack of consistency in fascination is complementary or even identical to the urgency of its contact with subjectivity. This is because the communication of these two instances is a separation, but not a distinction. Their differentiation is a difference, rather than a negation, and is thus an essentially inefficient differentiation which implies proximity. The rapport with the object is an alteration rather than a comtemplation. Although Blanchot speaks briefly of the "indeterminate milieu of fascination,"[77] his context clearly shows that he does not intend to describe a situation of dispersion or undifferentiation. The image is differentiated from the subject, although not in the regional and perhaps impossible configuration of identity and non-contradiction. Its escape is thus its approach. Its lack of manifestation is its appearance; its absence is its presence. The contamination of negation in the general economy produces an escape into absence, an infinite distance, which is always a hyperbolic presence, the urgency of the approach. In this dimension without spatial or logical locus, "here has dissolved into nowhere, but nowhere is however here."[78] Dispersion — the impossibility of closure — is not lacking in this proximal dimension, but its modality is not confined to undifferentiation. The *agora* of subjectivity is also its *claustrum*, as the following quotation, so fundamental to the thinking of both difference and proximity, demonstrates:

Where I am alone, the day [*jour*] is now the very loss of abode [*séjour*], an intimacy with the exterior without locus and without repose. The approach to this place makes him who comes belong to dispersion, to the fissure in which the exterior is an intrusion which suffocates, is nudity, is the cold in which one remains exposed, in which space is the vertigo of *espacement*. Then fascination reigns.[79]

The production of an interiority *au dehors* ("in the exterior") in proximity is correlative to a communicational production of space, time, and discontinuity, in *espacement*. Fascination is an awakening of subjectivity in this universe without determination, but not without differentiation. Dispersion is an exteriority to which interiority is integral, and *vice versa*. The dispersion of the "here" in "nowhere" does not eliminate the unicity of separation: it creates this unicity. The dispersion of "nowhere" is "here". The incumbence of its proximity creates a claustrated intensity which is infinitely more dense, more compelling, more "here", than the "here" of negation and actuality. It is noteworthy that the above quotation describes both the exile of *errance* and the vulnerability of the burrow. Blanchot's manifold themes, like those of Levinas and Bataille, tend to be linked by the notion of a proximity which creates location or position as an "inability to remain at one's post" which is also an "inability to desert one's post." The "non-lieu" of proximity is at the same time the pressure of an exterior which renders impossible the initiative of mobility, and an elimination of the integrity of location, which defines interiority as a wandering or exile. A penetrating Blanchotian expression of this configuration is the concept of the *attrait sur place* ("attraction in place"): a force which displaces while immobilizing. The coincidence of these predicates results from the fact that the apparent dispersion of *errance* has a more fundamental direction — *pour l'autre* — which is also that of the claustrated inability to move.

The same economy which defines space as a dispossessing fascination, defines time as a repetition. "In the absence of time, that which is new renews nothing; that which is present is inactual; that which is present presents nothing, re-presents itself, belongs already and always to the return."[80] In a time without negation or totalization, every instant pre-exists and succeeds itself, by virtue of its proximity to the indefinite generality of the time surrounding it in *espacement*. Similarly, the temporal actuality of any entity in proximity is its communication with a time preceding and succeeding it. As mentioned earlier, the forms of precedence and succession, "before" and "after" in proximity, both proceed from the notion of an involvement with an "other" time: the irrecuperable and incumbent time of the Other. Repetition is the form of a temporal discontinuity which is produced by this involvement wth alterity. Thus the *parole* is "that which speaks when all has been said": a remainder within totalization. Its repetitive insistence prevents it from being a "*parole* which begins": "before the *parole*, the *parole* still." Exteriority in fascination is an instance with which subjectivity is already involved, in an immemorial past, and also an instance which approaches, in the manner of the other beast. These two possibilities are temporal modalities of a communication irreducible to totalization. The other beast can never arrive and become manifest, because its approach is its very lack of manifestation. The past of the *parole*, the verb *écrire*, or the beginning of the sound of the other beast's digging, is beyond retention, because the involvement of subjectivity with alterity precedes the possibility of its awakening within manifestation. However, the "already" and the "yet to come" of repetition, in the inactuality of the present, are not simple escapes from actuality, but are approaches. The "already" is a shock; the "yet to come" is an imminence. The themes accompanying the notion of repetition in Blanchot and Levinas indicate an extreme violence. That which is irrecuperably past, in what Levinas calls a "passé absolument révolu", escapes retention while concerning or involving subjectivity. That which will never arrive to be confronted, gains momentum in its approach. The escape of these moments from the presence correlative to negation is their proximity: an inaccessibility which is an intimacy. When their congruence describes a repetition or return in "incessant" time, this repetition has the same interplay of predicates as the image. It is simultaneously the non-concerning monotony of that which cannot become punctual — a *ressassement* — and the urgency of an affirmation over which no decision can exercise a control. Repetition is the interminable and the incessant. Its only rapport is passivity: the *reconnaître* ("recognizing") which renders impossible the *connaître* ("knowing"), and which, in the context of *oubli,* unites the eternal surprise of that whose return cannot be awaited, and the paradoxical impression that one "always knew this was going to happen." In repetition, one recognizes what one never knew.

The appearance of the image, as mentioned above, is a somewhat ironic moment in Blanchot. This is because the image "held up" before consciousness is fascination is a proximity which is posed in the form of an intentional act. Ultimately, the appearance of the image is inadequate to the concept of vision. Blanchot speaks of a fascination "in which blindness is still vision, a vision which. is no longer the possibility of seeing, but the impossibility of not seeing, an impossibility which makes itself seen [*se fait voir*: also "makes itself a seeing"]."[81] The image is the impossibility produced by the general economy — the heteronomy of a dimension without power or negation — tending to become a contact or "presence". Thus dissimulation, in essential solitude — the context of fascination — "tends to appear." But that which fascinates, as the following formulation shows explicitly, is inadequate to the homology with intentionality. "That which fascinates us, takes away our power to give meaning [*donner un sens*], abandons its 'sensible' nature, abandons the world, recedes before [*en deçà*] the world and draws us with it, no longer reveals itself to us and yet affirms itself in a presence foreign to the present of time and to presence in space."[82] The "appearance" of the image has none of the predicates of manifestation, except the fugitive instance of a "regard" or "look" whose very possibility has become what Blanchot calls "the power that neutralizes it."[83] The "visibility" of alterity is precisely its invisibility, and the approach or incumbence of this invisibility — "the absence that one sees because it is blinding."[84] On one hand, Blanchot's use of vision in the sense of interval and illumination, is typical of his strategic discursivity, which tends to pose subjectivity as an intentional approach to an alterity which suddenly reveals the principle of this approach to be inadequate and even impossible. One approaches through vision an exterior which reveals itself to be invisible, but which produces in this very escape an "other" contact: the heteronomy of the impossible. This is the *nouvelle origine* of vision in impossibility. On the other hand, Blanchot's discussion tends to discover in the intramundane concept of vision and imagination a relation to alterity which exceeds the familiar and philosophical concepts of vision. In the manner of Levinas, Blanchot invokes a latent condition for phenomenality and retention, which is precisely fascination. The common sense of the image is subjectivity's ability to call back or make use of a thing in its absence. The image is the remainder which can be mobilized in this absence. For the Blanchot of "Les deux versions de l'imaginaire", this remainder, with its "resemblance" to the thing, is not a correlate of the imagination, but of the thing itself. "The *éloignement* [distancing, withdrawal] is here in the heart of the thing."[85] The thing's capacity to overwhelm its own self-coincidence or totalization, to recede from itself, is its capacity to involve consciousness, and is thus the principle of imagination. The "mental image" of which use is made, appears to be an inactual presence of the "original" which is available for totalization. But the confidence of intentionality's manipulation of the image, particularly in art, conceals the more profound unavailability and proximity of the thing whose very presence is inactual. The image is "not the same thing placed at a distance, but the thing as distancing."[86] This *éloignement* is correlative to a unicity of the thing whose modality is not negation and distinction, but communication. The inactual presence of the thing "within" consciousness proceeds from the thing's excess over negation and over the alternative of presence and absence. Imagination is not a capacity rooted in manifestation, but is "the formless weight of being present in absence."[87] Manifestation is that region of the economy in which this communicational dispersion or non-coincidence within the thing "tends to" be perceived in terms of negation and possibility. But the dispersion which is the thing's difference, is also its proximity. Its *éloignement* with regard to itself is its approach to a subjectivity which is not an illumination, but an exposition. "The passivity which is integral to it comes from this: a passivity which makes us suffer [*subir*] it, even when we call to it."[88] The image may be mobilized as an arm of manifestation because it is a function of closure. It is a "limit" imposed upon absolute undifferentiation. Yet the *écart*, the gap or distance produced by this limit, is not a phenomenal interval, but the *écart* of proximity. The image is a "thin limit, but which does not hold us separate [*à l'écart*] from things so much as it preserves us from the blind pressure of this interval [*écart*]."[89] The thing's *écart* or gap with regard to itself is its involvement with subjectivity: the pressure of its approach and subjectivity's inability to "let go of it." This inability is the latent birth of imagination: the inextrication of interior and exterior. This approach is the fundamental economic sense of the word "appearance". This word describes not an illumination, but an apparition. In manifestation, things do not truly appear: they are the indifference of their determined locations within the universal. Appearance requires the concomitant capacity of the thing to escape its self-coincidence and to involve interiority. Recalling Heidegger, Bataille, and Breton in "Les deux versions de l'imaginaire", Blanchot invokes the rupture of the relation of utility, and the object's tendency to "appear" when its disappearance into utensility is contaminated. The object, at this moment, becomes its own resemblance, its own double, its excess over its identity. It is its own reflection, its own image. This "receding" of actuality into the plurality of the image is the possibility of appearance. "Only that which is delivered to the image appears, and all that appears is, in this sense, imaginary."[90] The philosophy of manifestation is a hasty or impatient interpretation of this appearance as a phenomenality produced by negation. But phenomenality is not a true meaning of appearance. The common notion of the image conceals its origin in a proximity which allows the thing itself, in its very *éloignement*, to insist within consciousness — not as a representation, but as a proximal presence.

Blanchot's text describes a communicational economy whose production of entities which are in excess over their own closure — which can double them-

selves, resemble themselves, be their own images — founds the possibility of appearance as approach. The regional subordination of this approach to negation, in manifestation, is conditioned by the priority of its economic production in proximity. Thus the "possibility" of phenomenal appearance is conditioned by impossibility in being: the failure of negativity and power which produces both the thing's "retreat" into its image and the incumbence of this image upon a subjectivity which is the passivity of subjection. The image is not seen, but "undergone". Impossibility is a "scission",[91] a "dédoublement" which is correlative to all economic closure. In L'Entretien infini, Blanchot calls this configuration the "duplicity of revelation." "The image is an image in this duplicity, not the double of the object, but the initial doubling which then permits the thing to be figured: higher yet than doubling, it is the bending [ploiement], the twist of a turning, this 'version' always in the process of inverting itself and carrying in itself the 'this way, that way' of a divergence."[92] *
What this difficult sentence describes is the "perverse" glissement of a differentiation which cannot totalize — an individuation which produces unicity as an alteration. Discontinuity in communication is an excess which veers toward its other as a function of its closure. This veering and approach of alterity are the possibility of subjectivity in a field of differentiation. Like Levinas, Blanchot perceives in the metaphysics which privileges subjectivity as negation and illumination, a perennial inability to correctly thematize the economic movements (such as appearance, error, receptivity, impression) which are subjectivity's ontology. Manifestation cannot thematize appearance, but the appearance it does invoke is conditioned by appearance as apparition, i.e. as escape and incumbence. As mentioned above, Blanchot's irony and willful marginality consist in his positing of an "appearance" which entirely escapes the philosophical context of vision. The reader who is misled by the familiarity of Blanchot's terminology is invited to understand L'Espace littéraire as a derivative phenomenological exposé. When Blanchot's economic definitions of apparition and image contradict the common sense of these familiar terms, the reader is invited to understand his text as a derivative exposé which is also incoherently aphoristic. The likelihood is, however, that notwithstanding such terminological difficulties, Blanchot's concept of fascination and of literary communication would have remained marginal in any case. This is because his notion of a manifestation or appearance which is not overthrown by communication, but is rather invested by the latter, could not be accepted as pertinent by a culture preoccupied by the univocal alternative of manifestation and signification, in the transition from phenomenology to formalism. It is significant that the developing philosophy of difference, whose rapport with contemporaneous epistemological tendencies was so ambiguous and contaminated, enthusiastically attested its Blanchotian inspiration throughout 1950's and 1960's.

The image and its approach are moments of differentiation or communication

---

* "le tour du tournant, cette 'version' toujours en train de s'invertir et portant en elle le de-ci de-là d'une divergence."

which produce manifestation as a region of the general economy. It is not the passivity of fascination that is an anomalous economic moment. What is extraordinary and "miraculous" to both Blanchot and Levinas is the mobilization of this passivity in a region whose sole principle is power. The image is a moment of proximity which produces both the "immediacy" and the "distance" requisite for the concept of phenomenality: "whoever is fascinated, what he sees, he does not see it, strictly speaking, but it touches him in an immediate proximity, it seizes and captures him, even though it leaves him absolutely at a distance."[93] When alterity's incumbence and escape become immediacy and interval, as a function of their origin in differentiation, proximity becomes an adequation of intellect to things in a universe of possibility. The triumph of this "catalysis" of communication which produces proximity as power, which limits the world and changes the world in its irresistible totalizations, is not a power over passivity, but is a passivity whose violence tends to become what Levinas calls the "allergy of beings". Thus dissimulation "tends to become negation." If this tendency totalizes existence, in spite of its regionality and naiveté, and condemns passivity to the exile of its marginal and anomalous insistence, "this," in Levinas' phrase, "is the price of separation."

Fascination and the image describe the differentiating principle of the general economy — *impossibilité* or *désoeuvrement* — in the moment at which "impossibility makes of itself a seeing." The "appearance" of the image is possible only because differentiation creates heteronomy and non-indifference — subjectivity — as a basic consequence of its economy. Manifestation is possible only because the image "appears". These possibilities proceed from impossibility — that is, from a communication which exceeds both negation and correlation. For this reason Blanchot does not hesitate to define fascination, the "passion of the exterior", as experience itself: a rapport with alterity. "(I)mpossibility is nothing but the principle of what we so facilely call experience, for there is experience in the strict sense only when something radically *other* is in play."[94] This sentence, which describes not only a proximity of Levinas to Blanchot's text, but also an explicit homage to Levinas' teaching, defines experience as the passivity of closure's non-allergic rapport with the Other in communication. Implicit in this definition is the dissymetry or non-reciprocity of a communication in which alterity is not a constituted center of its own gravity, but precisely the other of such a constitution. As mentioned above, the image is not a power to fascinate me. It is a passivity which approaches in a universe without power. Its exteriority or separation is already my exposition to it. Its escape from totalization is already my reception of it — a reception which is not a seeing, but a *parole*. The contact by which it "seizes" me is the production of the "me" in proximity: a unicity inclined toward the Other. Alterity is not a center of gravity, but its incumbence places my center of gravity outside myself. To be the Same is to go to the Other. That this movement is inadequate to the theme of vision is attested by Blanchot in 1960 essay "La marche à l'écrevisse", reprinted in *L'Entretien infini* under the title "Parler, ce n'est pas voir".[95] Here the problematic of fascination and contact at a distance is defined as a function of the *parole*: "a *parole* such that to speak would no longer be to disclose by illumination."[96] Fascination is a *parole*, experience is a *parole*: the non-indifference of interiority to alterity, "when speaking is not seeing." The most compelling statement of this moment, cited more than once in the present study, appears in Blanchot's fundamental reading of Bataille:

(T)hat which no existent can attain in the primacy of its name, that which existence itself in the seduction of its fortuitous particularity, in the play of its slipping [*glissante*] universality, could not contain, that which thus decidedly escapes, the *parole* welcomes it, and not only does it retain it, but it is on the basis of this always foreign and always stolen affirmation, the impossible and the incommunicable, that it speaks, finding here its origin.[97]

EXPERIENCE IN BATAILLE AND BLANCHOT

The concept of experience indicates a receptivity with regard to alterity: a capacity to be affected by exteriority without reducing its alterity and, simultaneously and paradoxically, a receptivity which is adequate to the dimensions of alterity. This is the rooting of experience in the dilemma of idealism and realism. It is also the context of the controversy surrounding Bataillian *expérience* during the 1940's and 1950's. This controversy was animated by the coincidence in *La Somme athéologique* of the notions of *extase* and incommunicability. The interior experience is thematically characterized in Bataille's aphoristic trilogy as a hyperbolic dispossession or penetration by exteriority which is necessarily unavailable to a discursive mobilization. The "communicability" of the *expérience* is not that of thematization or exposition. It was Bataille's insistence on this proposition that motivated the charge of mystical "privacy" in Sartre's "Un nouveau mystique".[98] After Bataille's death, the vocabulary of ecstasy ceased to organize critical readings of his text, and was replaced by a concern with the irreducibility of the *expérience* and its context to philosophical models of totalization. At this point, the relevance of Bataille's categories to the figure of an anguished but spontaneous existential subject was supplanted by its relevance to an absolute alterity whose insistence implied the destruction of this spontaneous subject and the metaphysics in which it was rooted. As mentioned earlier, the heteronomy meditated by Bataille has not been easily assimilable to the viewpoint of either of these traditions, because it forecloses not only spontaneous interiority and mystical communion, but also destruction and the primacy of the absolutely other, in the singular moment of its contamination. The erotic and transgressive themes of the Bataillian text assure it a currency in contemporary thought, but fewer claims are made for its epistemological importance than during the period immediately following Bataille's death. It seems likely that the destiny of Bataille's theoretical text will be an obscurity correlative to its complementary placing in question of limits and the destruction of limits. The alternative of closure and the escape of alterity from closure is not the proper context of Bataillian experience. Neither the theme of *extase* nor that of an alterity exceeding discursive limits is adequate to this concept. The universe in which it appears is not that of constraint and the liberation from constraint.

As discussed earlier, the context of *expérience* is an economy of "compositions", in Bataille's words, which produces a "relative autonomy" of the singularities forming these compositions. Each of these singularities is a discontinuity, i.e. an irreducible detour of closure in the general economy. It is also the density of an exigency toward totalization – an exigency invested or animated by the "composition" which exceeds its closure. Its involvement with exteriority, particularly in the context of *non-savoir*, is a concomitant desire for separation and communion: the paradoxical ambivalence of desire in proximity. But prior to the thematization of consciousness as ipseity, there is a Bataillian concept of experience which is derived from the economic modality of closure itself.

But animalcules, like complex animals, have an experience of interiority [*expérience du dedans*] ; I cannot link to complexity, or to humanity, the passage from existence *in itself* to existence *for itself*. I accord even to the inert particle, beneath the animalcule, this existence *for itself*, which I prefer to name experience of interiority, interior experience, and of which the terms that designate it are never truly satisfactory.[99]

The "insufficiency of the terms" which describe the *expérience* is their tendency to situate the latter as an experience "proceeding from inside" or as a correlate of closure's primordial adequacy. Experience proceeds from an excess which forecloses this adequacy – yet experience is the principle of an irreducible discontinuity or unicity. Experience is not the transitivity of an interiority, but is nevertheless the foundation of the *dedans* or interiority. Its enigma is precisely its excess over the alternative of closure and escape from closure. The contradictions and reservations which structure *La Somme athéologique, L'Erotisme, La Part maudite*, and many other Bataillian texts, are largely concentrated upon this discursive moment. A statement like the following, from *L'Erotisme*, shows the ambiguity and the tendency toward negative formulations that characterize Bataille's description of experience: "the *interior experience* of man is given in the instant at which, breaking the chrysalis, he is conscious of tearing himself apart within himself, and not a resistance opposed to the exterior."[100] The exterior collaborates in the unicity of an interior which is a *fêlure* and an incompletion, as a function of its very intensity. The voluntaristic context of consciousness and negativity which frames this configuration obscures its logical economy without overwhelming it.

Every theoretical text must be read for the creativity of its self-contradictions as well as for its manifest definitions, but this generality is hyperbolically true of Bataille's text. It is the exasperation and irony of conflicting claims that organizes Bataillian discursivity. Bataille consistently posits a radical alterity which, on one hand, offers either consciousness or experience a mode of access in any of several privileged configurations of violence, and which, on the other hand, retreats from the voluntaristic and intellectualistic aspects of this access, retaining its alterity at the expense of the exasperated subject of experience. It is this ambivalence, in its multiple displacements of vocabulary and context, that traces Bataille's intuition of the passivity and heteronomy of *expérience*. The very title *Méthode de méditation* suggests the largely derivative, voluntaristic context in which this notion of heteronomy is posed. In *L'Expérience intérieure*, Bataille writes: "the principle of the interior experience: to leave by a project the domain of the project."[101] The project of "knowing" or "communicating" the *expérience* is a secondary moment, in spite of its violent persistence. When the latent animation of the project in the exigency is revealed, as in *non-savoir*, Bataille attests with satisfaction the failure and frustration of its voluntaristic moment. "I am happy, in any case, with the failure experienced. And I lose my seriousness myself, laughing. As though it were a relief to escape the concern for my self-sufficiency. I cannot, it is true, escape my concern permanently."[102] Concern ("souci") is a permanent element of an exigency toward closure. It is an irreducible detour. But its frustration is secondary to its latent animation in the heteronomy of experience itself. The *rire* is the consistent, recurring attestation of this secondarity in Bataille's text. "It is in the failure that is interrogation that we laugh."[103] The universe of experience and of the interrogation which is its correlate, is not exhausted by the alternative of adequation and the frustration of adequation. The irony of the *rire*, like that of transgression which is "survived" by the "flouted prohibition", is that neither the constraint of closure nor the liberating explosion of destruction are true possibilities in the general economy. Closure is more or other than a constraint, and transgression is less or other than a liberation from constraint. Closure and transgression are both exigencies, both the exigency, both contaminations and impossibilities. *Expérience* is one principle of this economy of impossibility. Failure and irony are thus permanent factors in its thematization. "Essentially, what the *rire* proceeds from is *communication*."[104] The passivity of the *rire*, and its reference to a context in which closure and destruction are intimates whose lack of possibility is their very intimacy, motivates its thematic supremacy in the *Somme athéologique*.

Expérience is the intense heteronomy of a closure which is not a totality, and which does not confront the exterior in an economy of negation. Closure is an excess and an incompletion. In its preferred Bataillian context, which is sexuality, closure is described as a "plethora", an excessive intensity which is grounded in the moment of differentiation Bataille calls a *glissement*. The tendency toward an ontological generality in Bataille's formulations is manifest in the following passage, in which the word "being" resonates beyond its sense as "this discontinuous creature" to indicate a global sense of differentiation:

At this moment, that which was not yet a' was continuous with a'', but the plethora placed the continuity in question [*en jeu*]. It is the plethora that begins a *glissement* in which [the] being divides, but it divides at that very moment, at the moment of the *glissement*, at the critical moment at which these beings, which will momentarily be opposed one to the other, are not yet opposed. The separating crisis is born of the plethora: it is not yet separation, it is ambiguity.[105]

The plethora is not only the excess which prepares scissiparity, but is the excess of all discontinuity in separation or differentiation: an excess which is the principle of communication and of experience. The "déchirement" or "tearing apart" that defines interiority as an incompletion, is the principle of its unicity. Sexual differentiation for Bataille is the production of an interiority which is a difference in the illusory form of a totality. In the following passage, the term "being" again takes on a global sense: "It is the crisis of [the] being: [the] being has the interior experience of being in the crisis which puts it to the test [*à l'épreuve**], it is the *mise en jeu*** of [the] being in a passage from continuity to discontinuity or from discontinuity to continuity."[106] The terms *mise en jeu* and *glissement* describe a failure of totalization which produces both an excess and a vulnerability of closure. The time of the latter's self-coincidence is that of the metamorphosis in becoming, called by Bataille a *passage*. Its "not yet" and its "already" are the proximal moments of its communication with alterity: a communication that is its only interiority. The paroxysm of conation in discontinuity is the turgidity of living being which is already the conation "in reverse" of its excessive movement toward alterity.

The plethora is an important predicate of closure in Bataille, because it indicates not an approach to alterity on the basis of closure, but an approach of alterity which is constituted by closure's excess. It is the Other's approach, in its pre-originarity, that inclines interiority "outward" in experience. The plethora is not an excessive tension produced by sexual excitation, but is a more primordial excess which signals the non-reciprocal approach of the Other, as Bataille suggests in the anti-Hegelian implication of the following formulation: "Each being contributes to the negation that the *other* makes of itself, but this negation leads not at all to the recognition [*reconnaissance*] of the partner. It is, it seems, less a similitude that is in play in the approach [*rapprochement*], than the *plethora* of the *other*."[107] Bataille's panoramic view of the approach in sexuality makes difficult but not impossible his thematization of a dissymmetry in "rapprochement". This dissymmetry results from the fact that the plethora is an excess and an exposition which designates any approach to another as the

---

* "épreuve" means "experience". The violence of excess, the *épreuve* of closure's inefficiency, is also the origin of experience in differentiation.

** "placing in question", also "placing in play". The lack of totalization which renders closure ambiguous is also an aleatory, communicational element in its differentiation which is specifically irreducible to determination.

approach of the Other — the impersonal Other of the Same — which animates interiority. Recognition and reciprocity have no place in this schema, as Bataille clearly states. The alterity of the intersubjective other is not his identity or subjectivity, but rather the plethora of his exteriority. Every discontinuity in Bataille's economy is the fugitive, ambivalent spasm of a "passage" whose communicational constitution implies both the pre-originarity of the Other and its imminence in the violence of *dépense*. The only "pour soi" or "for itself" of this interior experience is its *pour l'autre*. The plethora and the *glissement* incline subjectivity toward an exterior which is its only element — even as they produce an uneliminable discontinuity which will produce prohibition and the profane world of totalization as an irreducible detour in the economy.

The plethora is interiority's spasm into the exterior: an excessive closing which is an opening, invested by the force of the economy. The secret passivity of the exigency is the non-allergic rapport by which it receives the Other in its very separation from exteriority. The intensity and ambivalence of Bataille's aphoristic text always gravitate toward this moment of passivity. "I arrive at this position: the interior experience is the contrary of action. Nothing more."[108] The putative origin of the experience in the project and the method tends toward a *nouvelle origine*: the blithe heteronomy of transgression. Bataille's text moves from the intense anguish of the dialectics of possibility to the origin of the *rire* in impossibility. In his brilliant essay published on the occasion of Bataille's death,[109] Maurice Blanchot correctly situates the interior experience with regard to its production by affirmation, impossibility, and the exigency. After a curious introduction which defines Bataille's discursivity as a "passion of negativity" which places in question the very totalizations which are guaranteed by negation, Blanchot defines the *expérience* as a contamination of closure so radical that it no longer belongs to the realm of possibility. The concept of a "placing in question", in negative form, of a totality whose own constitution is the aggressivity of negation, is impossible.

And yet the interior experience requires this event which does not belong to possibility; it opens in accomplished [*achevé*] being an infinitesimal interstice through which all that is allows itself suddenly to be overflowed and dispossessed by an increase which escapes and exceeds. Strange surplus. What is this excess that makes accomplishment still and always incomplete [*inachevé*]?[110]

Although Blanchot's formulation mimics the voluntarism that haunts Bataille's own text, his invocation of excess and impossibility penetrates to the heart of the Bataillian inspiration, as the following definition of impossibility shows:

One must understand that possibility is not the only dimension of our existence and that it is perhaps given to us to "live" each event of ourselves in a double rapport, firstly as what we understand, seize, endure and master (if with difficulty and pain) while relating it to some good, some value, that is in the final analysis to Unity, and secondly as that which escapes all use and all finality, more yet that which escapes our very power to experience it, but whose experience we cannot escape: yes, as though impossibility, that in which we can no longer be able [*pouvoir*], awaited us behind all that we live, think and say. . . .[111]

Blanchot correctly states the regionality of totalization in the general economy. When he speaks, with considerable sympathy for the perplexity of his reader, of a "double rapport" and of a reality which "awaits" "behind" the actual and possible, he correctly describes the secret heteronomy of closure as a reality which cannot become manifest, cannot "compete with action in the terms of action." Impossibility is the latent approach of a reality without power which invests the spontaneity and effectivity of the actual. It is the proximity of this reality that makes closure an *expérience*. Consciousness does not "attain" this reality, as Bataille's ironic intensity so often attests. The exterior awaits, in an incumbence without substantiality. Blanchot stipulates that impossibility is "not only the negation of power,"[112] not a function of negation, but rather that affirmation which proceeds from the absence of negation in an economy of communication. *Expérience* is the force of this affirmation by which closure's excess becomes a rapport with exteriority.

The limit-experience represents for thought a sort of new origin. What it gives thought is the essential gift, the prodigality of affirmation, an affirmation which, for the first time, is not a product (the result of a double negation) and, thus, escapes all the movements, oppositions, and reversals of dialectical reason, which, having accomplished itself before [affirmation], can no longer reserve it a role within its realm.[113]

Affirmation is the economic modality of closure in Bataille: a closure whose "discontinuity" is precisely its involvement with alterity in a rapport which is not negative. Affirmation is closure's immemorial animation by the exterior — an animation which produces not only the excess of *dépense* and the plethora, but also the *pour l'autre* by which interiority bounds or veers toward the Other in the economy. Experience is the non-indifferent and non-allergic rapport by which interiority receives and goes to the Other — not as a relation of ipseity to a constituted exterior but, prior to this possibility, as a function of closure's own exigency. Thus Blanchot adds, in a paragraph composed of one phrase: "Experience of non-experience."[114] The *expérience* is not experience, in its familiar and philosophical definition, but precisely the impossibility of the latter. Bataillian experience, considered in a discursive universe organized by the primacy of manifestation, is the impossible. It is, in Blanchot's most apt phrase, "that which we cannot experience, but whose experience we cannot escape." This formulation describes a reality without power which "must" be experienced, although it "cannot" be experienced in the integral rectitude of the *experire*. Its inexistence or lack of substantiality is its compelling approach, and the fact that, while it cannot take place or come to pass, and because it will not arrive to be confronted as a power, it "cannot be stopped." Thus the experience, with transgression, describes the most basic Bataillian figure of proximity.

As discussed earlier, the voluntarism of transgression understood as an assault on constraining limits, leads in Bataille to the proximal concept of a subjectivity which always "must" transgress and never "is able" to transgress. This configuration is admirably described by Blanchot in the proposition: "the *interdit* marks the point where power ceases."[115] Transgression is this "must" and "cannot" whose intensity appears in a reality without power. The paradox of the exigency is a coherent logical consequence of an economy whose individuations are not totalities. The *parole* which, in Blanchot's words, "welcomes" and "retains" the force of impossibility in this economy, is a spasmodic emission that "speaks the ultimate exigency."[116] Blanchot's reading of Bataille progressively exceeds the pertinence of interpretation and becomes a true proximity to the Bataillian inspiration, not only by virtue of a similarity of vocabulary, but also by virtue of the intrication of these discourses in a common animation. The following sentence is a hyperbolic instance of this involvement:

The experience is this exigency, it exists only as an exigency and such that it never gives itself as accomplished, since no memory could confirm it, since it exceeds all memory and since only *oubli* is proportionate to it, the immense *oubli* that is carried by the *parole*.[117]

The interior experience is a heteronomy which is never simply a determination by exteriority. It is rather an inspiration by alterity and an approach of the Other which is made possible by the excess of the economy over closure or "accomplishment". The density or unicity of the *expérience* is this uneliminable involvement with an inaccessible alterity, and this is why its closure is never the silence of a correlation or illumination guaranteed by negativity, but rather the force of an exigency whose "cannot" is its "must", whose impossibility is its affirmation. This affirmation is the *parole*, an inclination toward alterity within being. Blanchot's introduction of the concept *oubli* describes the irreducibility of experience to manifestation, through the term which, more than any other in Blanchot's own theoretical and fictional text, is intended to designate an escape of communication from the manifest or actual. *Oubli* is the incumbence of that which was never known, cannot be known, but conditions the possibility of manifestation, when "dissimulation tends to appear." *Oubli*, like the interior experience, is interiority before intentionality, experience as passivity, subjectivity before illumination. By imposing his private, overdetermined concept upon the Bataillian text, Blanchot makes of it a Bataillian concept, and attests its own origin in an involvement with Bataille.

"The interior experience is a conquest and as such *pour autrui*," writes Bataille in *L'Expérience intérieure*.[118] The "crisis of being" which produces the experience as an economic event is a production of interiority as the excessive heteronomy of the *pour l'autre*. *Inachèvement* or incompletion is the principle of this economy, and interiority is what Levinas calls an "uneliminable surplus within the universal."[119] The *parole* is that principle of individuation which is also a principle of communication: subjectivity's reception of, and response to alterity. There is in *Autrement qu'être ou au delà de l'essence* a most Bataillian statement of closure's "animation" by alterity, and of the non-indifference produced by this animation. "Animation, the very *pneuma* of *psychisme*, alterity in identity, is the identity of a body exposing itself to the other, making itself *pour l'autre*: the possibility of *giving*. The non-assemblable duality of the elements of this trope is the dia-chrony of the one-for-the-other."[120] *Dépense*, the plethora, the *rire,* and transgression are all themes which imply a pre-originary generosity of closure, in its exigent recoiling from the economy which is also a recoiling into the economy. Although Bataille does not explicitly articulate alterity's investment of *autrui*, he repeats in a variety of formulations the basic sense of Levinas' *éthique.* Generosity, the dispossession of the Same which produces the Same, is the principle of reproduction, of experience, and of *non-savoir*.

I find in myself nothing which, more than myself, is not the property of my fellow man. And this movement of my thought which flees me, not only can I not avoid it, but there is no instant so secret that it does not animate me. Thus I speak, everything in me gives itself to others.[121]

The sense of *dépense* as loss in Bataille always tends to assume the predication of donation, correlative to animation. Bataillian "loss without profit" is an articulation of the *pour l'autre* as stable as any Levinasian description of this concept. Experience in the general economy is not a philosophical situation of subjectivity within a dialectical totality. It is rather a surplus or excess which fills the silence of manifestation with the sound of the *parole* — a sound which is correlative in Blanchot and Levinas to the *il y a*'s "incessant drone", and in Bataille to the violence of *dépense*. Proximity in Bataille is the modality of the "too much" — "All that is, is too much"[122] — which defines every interiority in the general economy as an excess in which the Other's approach is implicit.

COGITO AND TEMPORALITY IN PROXIMITY

The philosophy of proximity, from Hegel to Nietzsche, Proust, Freud, and Levinas, discovers the possibility of experience in communication. The heteronomy of a closure whose differentiation creates it as a reception of alterity and a veering toward alterity, produces the strange contamination of a proximal *cogito* in a universe without manifestation. In proximity, the economy of difference produces an alteration of the Same whose effects are not limited to indefinition, circulation, escape from totalization, and a mode of signification correlative to this escape. These effects also include passivity, desire, the incumbence or force of exteriority upon closure, and the *parole* which is interiority's inspiration and its *pour l'autre*. When closure's incompletion exceeds the context of escape, referral, and undecidability, and describes a weight of exteriority upon interiority, the Other's approach becomes a principle of differentiation itself, and the general economy of communication's alterations becomes an economy of subjectivity.

The general economy lacks negation and lacks power. It is an economy of impossibility. Since closure's heteronomy proceeds from this "weakening" of negation, it is possible to say, paraphrasing Blanchot, that in the general economy "impossibility makes of itself a *cogito*." Impossibility, for the philosophers of proximity, implies a reality and a modality of interiority. The philosophy of proximity is not an exigency to retain the term of interiority in its classical sense, although its concern with this term and refusal to abandon it, within the very context of totalization's impossibility, invites such an interpretation and contributes to the subterranean status of proximity. Instead, this philosophy discovers subjectivity in the very moment of communication's excess over manifestation, and discovers interiority or unicity in communication's excess over identity and determination. As mentioned earlier, the marginality of proximity in contemporary epistemology is its interruption of the duality which opposes a humanist or phenomenological subjectivity to a destruction of totalization which implies the abolition of such a subject. It is the alternative between a nostalgia for self-coincident interiority and an impatience for the permanent elimination of such an interiority, that the notion of proximity exceeds and troubles. This excess motivates a critical reaction to proximity which may be paradoxically described as both hyperbolically enthusiastic and without enthusiasm. The philosophy of proximity describes an absolute alterity and a reality without "truth" in a thematic context whose violence, particularly in Bataille and Blanchot, far exceeds that of the philosophy of difference. Yet the absolutely other is "here below" in proximity, and the heteronomy it produces is not understandable in terms of dispersion and escape from totalization. It is perhaps most fundamentally this failure of alterity to escape or liberate itself from constraint, in proximity, that motivates the ambivalent critical reception of this concept. In a proximal universe, nothing is destroyed, nothing is dispersed. All is invested and contaminated by an alterity which is itself a passivity. Rather than to denounce the closure of oppositions or concepts which are inadequate to alterity, and to celebrate the latter's escape from these concepts, the philosophers of proximity consistently evoke the paradoxical, contaminated approach of a powerless and yet incumbent instance which can and does "alter" the Same, without being capable of changing the world. To a tradition preoccupied with the alternative of consciousness' power to totalize and alterity's power to escape and to disperse, this heteronomous approach of alterity in proximity is not a congenial concept. It is for this reason that many influential readings of Bataille and Blanchot have attempted either to adequate these thinkers' concepts to a critical epistemology associated with the notion of revolution, or to denounce these concepts on the basis of their inadequacy to the same epistemology. That the thematic superstructure of the Bataillian and Blanchotian texts may appear both virulently revolutionary and violently reactionary at the same time, is a consequence of proximity's conceptual economy. Without totalization, there is no power. Yet action is a regional phenomenon that alterity's insistence cannot overthrow. The Other's approach is itself a passivity which "cannot compete with action in the terms of action." It is always Ulysses whose ruse triumphs over alterity. The Levinasian economy of the *éthique* produces separation and interiority, and is thus the source of "unpunished crimes". Rather than to change the world, proximity invests its very spontaneity. To a great extent, the marginality of proximity in contemporary epistemology is also that of the philosophy of difference. Both these philosophies tend to describe a form of communication which is irrelevant to the ambivalent alternative of totalization's correlations and totalization's destruction. This alternative contrasts a power to enclose and a power to escape; a power of correlation and a power of dispersal; a power of the Same and a power to change. The concepts of difference and proximity describe an element which invests both these tendencies while retaining its irreducibility to either.

Communication in the general economy produces differentiation as impossibility. This term describes not a "negation of possibility", in Blanchot's words, but a positivity which is not a power, not an accomplishment or effectivity. In his extremely important essay "Le grand refus",[123] Blanchot defines "possibility" as "more than reality: it is being, plus the power of being. Possibility establishes reality and founds it: one is what one is, only if one has the power to be it."[124] The common sense of the word "possibility" as "potentiality", which is also its basic sense in philosophy, attests this irreducibility of power in the spontaneity of existence. In a section of "Le grand refus" entitled "La pensée (de) l'impossible: l'*autre* rapport", Blanchot defines impossibility as "a measure other than that of power," "perhaps precisely the measure of the *other*, of the other as other, and no longer governed by the luminosity which appropriates it to the same."[125] Impossibility describes an economy without manifestation or totalization, but not without differentiation. This is why impossibility indicates a "rapport": a discontinuity and a communication. For Blanchot as for Levinas, the possibility of a rapport requires the possibility of alterity, and of a vulnerability of closure to this alterity. Thus the proposition of multiplicity and rapport requires the concept of subjectivity.

In "Le grand refus" Blanchot introduces the *cogito* or subjectivity of impossibility by mimicking the philosopher's need to situate his ontological categories in an exemplary intramundane moment. He invokes a consistent theme from his fictional and theoretical text: the theme of *souffrance* or (particularly physical) "suffering". The concept of suffering suggests an immobility and a radical passivity or withdrawal of initiative. The bedridden person who suffers becomes the subject of an entirely passive verb, deprived of its transitivity by suffering itself. Suffering is no longer the power to suffer, but signals the approach of another space. The predicates of this rapport do not describe a constituted subjectivity which "has the experience" of impossibility, but rather the production, within impossibility, of a subjectivity whose latent economy implies a radical heteronomy.

"Suffering is suffering," writes Blanchot, "when one can no longer suffer it and, because of this, in this non-power, one cannot cease suffering it."[126] Suffering is the pure *subir* or "undergoing" of subjectivity in a reality without power. There are two basic aspects of this moment of "non-power". In the first place, as Blanchot was to write in his reading of Bataillian *expérience*, the discretion which would distinguish interiority from the alterity it confronts, does not exist in this situation, and indeed is the reality of suffering. Its experience is the impossibility of experience: a receptivity without position and without the power to receive on the basis of this position. Suffering is *errance*, the forcing of unicity "into" the exterior. In the second place, this lack of a negative interval between experience and the subject of experience is also a lack of the punctuality and substantiality of such a subject. Suffering is impersonality: the dispersed unicity of an involvement with the exterior. "He who is exposed to it is deprived, precisely by suffering, of this 'I' which would make him suffer it."[127] Suffering, in its irreducibility to experience, is thus already other than suffering: "a suffering as though indifferent, and not suffered, and neutral."[128] The contact with exteriority in suffering is not a relation to a substantiality, but a vulnerability to an approach. The exterior is not a totality, and is therefore "neutral", non-concerning, and not to be "suffered", as a function of its very incumbence. It cannot be "experienced" as a function of totalization and relation; nor can it be eliminated by negation. It "cannot" be experienced, but it "must" be experienced. Its impossibility is the fact that it defines experience as a behavior that is not an action; a comportment which is not a power. "(T)he mark of such a movement is that, by the fact that we experience it, it escapes our power to experience it, and thus is not outside experience, but is that whose experience we can no longer escape."[129] The coincidence of these predicates – lack of interiority, lack of substantial exteriority, lack of relation, lack of power – in their description of a rapport without totalization, is the definition of impossibility. In its impersonality, this moment is the only *ergo sum* of proximity. Its suspended punctuality is the insistence in being of an interiority which is not yet a *cogito*, not yet a manifestation, but a pure "passivity of the exterior". Like Levinasian *jouissance*, the concept of suffering in "Le grand refus" is not the predicate of an originary disclosedness, on a phenomenological model, but is precisely the impossibility of such an interval and such a predicate.

Suffering is an experience outside manifestation – a contamination of the phenomenal rapport. Thus it is a strangeness and estrangement from actuality, but the strangeness of non-totalized exteriority is also an approach. For this reason, the terminology of proximity enters Blanchot's text. "An experience

which one will conceive as strange and even the experience of strangeness, but
if it is so, let us recognize that it is not so, because too distant: on the contrary
it is that which is so close that any retreat [*recul*] with regard to it is forbidden
us – strange in proximity itself."[130] Proximity is the approach of that which
cannot become present and thus "arrive" or "take place". That which
approaches always escapes as a function of this very approach, because its
exteriority is neither a distinction nor a phenomenality. The interval between
interior and exterior is no longer an adequating distinction of subject and object,
but is an involvement or intrication which forecloses this distinction. That which
approaches is exterior without being phenomenal; intimate without being
present. Subjectivity is susceptible to it, in the non-indifference of individuation
– but not capable of receiving or intending it, on the basis of a dialectical or
phenomenological correlation with it, guaranteed by negation and totalization.
Thus the infinite distance of exteriority in its alterity is also an infinite
proximity – a collaboration in the alteration of closure – which permits no
recul, no "step backward", no *Ent-Fernung*, with regard to it. The adequate and
adequating distance of experience is foreclosed. Separation is a rapport which
cannot become a relation. Distance is a contact. As Blanchot will write in *Le Pas
au-delà*, the meaning of the *proche* ("near", "close") is its escape, its lack of
presence, and its status as a function of the *lointain* ("far", "distant").[131] That
which is near is intimate without being available or accessible. It is "immediate"
without permitting the mediation and correlation implied by the concept of
immediacy in its common sense. It is "the immediate which excludes every
immediate, like all mediation", "the immediate which permits no mediation, the
absence of separation which is an absence of rapport and also an infinite
separation, because it does not reserve for us the distance and the future
necessary for us to have a relation to it, to arrive at it."[132] Proximity is the
rapport produced by the lack of relation, in an economy which produces both
radical discontinuity and radical involvement in a single moment. "The
immediate is presence to which one cannot be present, but from which one
cannot retreat [*s'écarter*], or again that which escapes by the very fact that it
cannot be escaped, the *unseizable* of which one *cannot let go*."[133] The
proximity of the exterior – its insufficient definition and consequent collaboration in the conation of the interior – produces experience without
spontaneity. Subjectivity is "seized" by the exterior. The eyes cannot close, the
hand cannot open, because the exterior is involved in their heteronomous
movement. In proximity, the only in-itself or for-itself of interiority is the
detour of alterity. The *s'écarter* or distancing requisite for illumination and
intentionality is impossible, because the proximity of the exterior is its own
écart: the gap in its totalization, and its non-coincidence with itself which is
already its intrication with interiority. Every "distance" in proximity is an *écart*:.
a discontinuity which is also an involvement. Every closure is its own *écart*: an
incompletion which is a heteronomy and a *liaison dangereuse*. What is missing
in this dimension is not differentiation or rapport, but negation and adequation:

the possibility of the rapport as relation. Impossibility is the inextrication produced by totalization's weakness, and is the heteronomy of closure which makes separation an experience. The economy of impossibility is an indetermination that is not a dispersion, but a differentiation. If the closure it produces is "dispersed" by virtue of its lack of totalization, it is also subject to what Blanchot calls an "infinite reversal of dispersion"[134] — a density and incumbence of indetermination which proceed from the same lack. That which escapes approaches. That which is dispersed is yet a unicity. The inaccessible is an intimacy. The gravity of the exterior in these impersonal definitions is the production of interiority precisely as an impersonality, in the general economy.

Throughout Blanchot's description of impossibility, the presence of Bataille is palpable, although never more so than in a vocabulary of excess which intervenes to situate the lack of distance in proximity. Impossibility becomes the "too close", "the too present which refuses access because it is always closer than any approach, and becomes absence, being then the too present which does not present itself."[135] The *trop* or "too much" in being (along with its complement, the "less than nothing, worse than nothing") is Bataillian closure's excess — an excess which reveals closure as a unicity produced by affirmation rather than negation. Impossibility's urgency is not the danger of the negative. Blanchot writes, "we perceive that, in impossibility, it is not only the negative character of the experience that would make it perilous, it is the 'excess of its affirmation' (that which, in this excess, is irreducible to the power to affirm)."[136] Alterity is the excess of interiority's involvement with the exterior: either as the loss or *dépense* which escapes the closed surface, or as the *fêlure* which is the incompletion of this surface,* or as the *reste* or remainder left in the exterior, which forces closure outside itself. This incompletion and this remainder are produced by a differentiation which is never adequate, never a distinction. In Bataille as in Blanchot, the separation which produces alterity is not the *écart* or interval of negation, but the *écart* of difference, which is closure's non-coincidence with itself, rather than its opposition to the exterior. Thus that which permits no interval or *recul* in proximity is yet an *écart*, "the *écart* of difference," "that which no longer allows itself to be eliminated and allows neither retreat nor withdrawal, without ceasing to be radically different."[137] This introduction of differentiation as difference, which is a frequent gesture in *L'Entretien infini*, leads Blanchot to invoke the notion of *espacement* from "La

---

* In his book *Logique du sens* (Paris: Minuit, 1969), Gilles Deleuze has developed the concept of the surface as locus of alteration, firstly by contrast with depth or *profondeur*, understood as an illusory interiority of separate beings or determined states of things, and secondly in correlation with *profondeur* in its second definition as the locus of alteration through penetration and contamination. This correlation, which distinguishes alteration as deployment or extension ("events", "quasi-causes", surface "effects") from alteration as a differentiating process ("mélange", "emboîtement", etc.), does not signify an opposition of difference and undifferentiation. Both surface and *profondeur* describe the intensity of differentiation without determination, or differentiation as a primordial alteration.

Solitude essentielle" (1951) — perhaps to remind himself and his reader that his own use of this term in its differential sense pre-dated its mobilization in the philosophy of difference by over a decade:

we perceive finally, here, the point at which time and space are joined in the original disjunction: "presence" is as much the intimacy of this instance as it is the dispersion of the Exterior [Dehors], more strictly, it is intimacy as Exterior, the exterior become an intrusion which suffocates and the reversal of the one and the other, what I have called "the vertigo of espacement."[138]

Espacement is a production of the space/time duality, and of spatial and temporal intervals, as proximities. It is a disjunction whose terms are differences or alterations, for which the consistent predicate in L'Entretien infini is "the essentially fragmentary." Impossibility has in common with difference its irreducibility to negation, and thus to the positivity of totalization: "impossibility, that which escapes every negative, does not cease exceeding, ruining, every positive."[139]

It is in "Le grand refus", as cited earlier, that Blanchot defines impossibility as the principle of experience, and reproduces the Levinasian definition of experience as an involvement with "something radically other."[140] If there is a presence of Bataille in "Le grand refus" (1959), the thematic and conceptual intrication of this essay with Totalité et infini (1961) is yet more impressive and undecidable. This involvement, which may be traced as well in Thomas l'obscur (1941), L'Arrêt de mort (1948) and De l'existence à l'existant (1948), concerns the theme of passivity. The Levinas of Totalité et infini invokes the theme of "souffrance" in precisely the same spirit as the Blanchot of "Le grand refus", applying to this term predicates such as the "extreme proximity of being," an "impossibility of retreat," and a "no way out" of "contact" for an interiority "cornered by being."[141] Suffering for Levinas describes a rapport with an exteriority which does not deploy itself before the spontaneity of consciousness, but rather "touches" the latter in the incumbence of its alterity. "Here, the merely future negation of will in fear, the imminence of that which refuses power, inserts itself in the present, here the other seizes me, the world affects, touches the will."[142] For Levinas as for Blanchot, the alterity of the exterior is an infinite distance without distance: an inaccessibility which is an involvement. There is no retreat from an exterior which invests as it escapes. Yet this inextrication is not an undifferentiation or dispersion, but a rapport. In another explicit homage to Levinas, Blanchot writes, "desire is precisely this rapport with impossibility, (. . .) it is impossibility which becomes a rapport, separation itself."[143] Impossibility alters unicity while creating unicity; and the latter is always a non-indifference toward the alterity with which it remains involved. This non-indifference is desire: the separation from the exterior which is also a veering into the exterior.

It is characteristic of Blanchot to pose impossibility and the force of non-indifference or non-reciprocity within a thematic context of passivity, indefinition, and neutrality. Yet he shares with Levinas the exigency to discover in impossibility's contamination of totalization its production of another unicity: a non-interchangeable, non-identical unicity of separation. The notion of a communicational interiority cannot be situated within the alternative of totalization and dispersion, or the alternative of a humanist subject and no subject at all. It must be derived from a definition of the totality itself as an undifferentiated homogeneity, and from a concept of separation or unicity as a non-allergic, heteronomous communication with closure's other. Desire is the principle of this derivation. It is desire and the force of the exigency that invest a closure which may subsequently produce the "catalysis" of identity and totalization within the general economy. The secret passivity of desire, inspiration, and the exigency, creates the density of a closure which may be the principle of a world of spontaneity and power, erected on the contaminated "underneath" of impossibility. A price is paid for separation. It is no longer possible to envisage a moment at which the reifications of closure will be eliminated. Proximity invests and alters, but it does not destroy. Closure is an *écart*, an inability to coincide with itself, and an impossibility, but it is not a liberation from closure. As mentioned earlier, it is far more difficult for Blanchot to articulate this configuration in his theoretical text than for Levinas. This is because there is a recurrent tendency in Blanchot to pose alterity as an undifferentiated approach (of which death is the prime example), and to pose interiority as an identity which becomes a dispersion. Yet Orpheus' rejection by the night, and his condemnation to separation within the day, attests Blanchot's understanding that the rapport with alterity produces unicity, rather than to eliminate it. The recurrence of propositions such as the "infinite reversal of dispersion" or the "nowhere that is however here" indicates Blanchot's concern with an irreducibility and a positivity of closure. In the discussion of "suffering" which links "Le grand refus" to *Totalité et infini*, the contrast between Blanchot's insistence upon passivity and Levinas' alacrity in situating passivity as a latent investment of power, is striking. Blanchot writes: "(I)mpossibility is the rapport with the Exterior and, since this rapport without rapport is the passion which does not allow itself to be mastered in patience, impossibility is the passion of the Exterior itself."[144] Although the principle of differentiation and rapport is retained by Blanchot, his emphasis is impossibility's excess over interiority. Yet impossibility is the production of discontinuity. On this basis, Levinas immediately draws a conclusion which Blanchot is rarely able to articulate: "This situation in which consciousness deprived of all freedom of movement, conserves a minimal distance with regard to the present; this ultimate passivity which, however, changes desperately into act and into hope – is *patience* – the passivity of the *subir* and, however, mastery itself."[145] The *écart* of discontinuity in differentiation exceeds while producing a universe of closure. The philosopher of proximity cannot evoke this excess without attesting this investment. In the passivity of inspiration and desire, the principle of the totality is perceptible. The larger sense of "patience" as heteronomy is the context of consciousness' exigent retreat into its own spontaneity – as Blanchot himself shows in his meditation of Orpheus' "impatience".[146] Yet the priority of this configuration is far more palpable in Levinas' text than in that of Blanchot. The notions of unicity, non-reciprocity, and "invested" spontaneity are integral to Blanchot's thinking of proximity, from *Thomas l'obscur* onward. However, these concepts are often obscured by the thematics of neutrality, excess, and dispersion which organize Blanchot's text. On the other hand, the presence of explicitly Levinasian definitions regarding separation, experience, and non-reciprocity, throughout *L'Entretien infini,* suggests that when communication's dissymetry and density becomes a theme in Blanchot's theoretical text, it requires a consistent detour: the name and the inspiration of Emmanuel Levinas.

*

There is a temporality which is specific to the passive *cogito* of proximity. This temporality consists of a collapse or incompletion of temporal differentiation, irreducible to the notion of a temporal ekstasis. It includes several moments, which must however be thought in a contaminated simultaneity, not only for the formal purpose of describing a punctual *cogito*, but because this simultaneity is the proximal collapse of moments whose separation is not a discretion or distinction.

In "Le grand refus", Blanchot describes the presence of proximity in suffering as a "present which does not pass":

Time here is as though arrested, confused with its interval. The present here is endless, separated from any other present by an inexhaustible and empty infinity, the very infinity of suffering, and also dispossessed of any future: a present without end and, however, impossible as a present; the presence of suffering is the abyss of the present, indefinitely hollowed and, in this hollowing, indefinitely stretched, radically exterior to the possibility that one might be present in it by the mastery of presence. What has happened? Suffering has simply lost time and made us lose it.[147]

This passage describes a punctuality which is no longer punctual, no longer a moment in a progressive or linear time. The pure "interval" of presence, separated from other moments whose arrival, or even whose memory, might delimit it, is indefinitely "deepened", in the manner of a solitude, and does not pass. This is the first paradox of proximal time: a present which is not punctual, but infinitely prolonged. The "hollowness" of this present is its inadequation to the presence of spontaneity and phenomenality, which requires a subject-object distinction and correlation as well as the rectitude of temporal ekstasis, correlative to negation and manifestation. The presence of this non-punctual moment has the same economy as the spatial presence of impossibility: the presence "to which one cannot be present," the immediacy of the *indessaisissable*. The term *gonflé* ("stretched") suggests the expansion of this moment, which is at the same time more absence than presence, in its hollowness, and yet more disturbingly punctual or immediate than any punctuality, in its immobility and lack of passage.

The stretching or distending of presence in proximity is not a simple extension of punctuality, but is, like essential solitude, an exceeding of punctuality — an impersonal moment whose very impersonality is the fact that it is "not alone". The unicity of the present is the approach of another time which invests and exceeds it. Presence is an involvement with the Other. For this reason, the present which does not pass is already its formal opposite: a pure passage without punctuality. "(N)othing happens [se passe] but this very passage."[148] Presence is an invasion of actuality by communication. It is a passage, a passivity of the temporal discontinuity, a "passion" of closure in proximal time, and the "patience" of subjectivity in its constitution by the passivity and incompletion of temporal differentiation. This lexical ramification of the concepts of passivity and desire informs Levinas' text from Le Temps et l'autre (1948) onward, and is one consistent index of the textual entretien which links Levinas to Blanchot. As discussed earlier, the proximal aspect of temporality in Levinas is its excess over the spontaneity and discretion of ekstasis in the lapse: "Temporalization as lapse — the loss of time — is precisely neither the initiative of a self, nor a movement toward whatever telos of action. The loss of time is the act of no subject."[149] Prior to manifestation, time is a lapsing and collapsing, an écart which cannot be assumed, but only subi or "suffered". And this subir of time's own subjectivity is the production in being of that impersonal unicity which will become the self: a self whose spontaneity will always be a tardiness, late for an assignation, involved in a moment of passivity which cannot be assumed. The accusative se of this subjectivity in assignation, not different from the "he" of Blanchotian impersonality or essential solitude, is consciousness' origin in the passivity of an involvement with alterity. The time of espacement "does not need the Self" (se passe de Moi), but produces the "me" of unicity, through the essential detour of impersonality. Espacement is the production of an interval which is the "essential solitude" of presence as time and presence as impersonality. Passivity is the economy of this separation, in the écart of proximity,and is the possibility of interiority.

Subjectivity awakes in the presence of the Other's approach and escape. Its latent birth is the pure passivity of the écart and the lapse in proximal time. This primordial moment, when envisaged thematically, is the suffocation of a presence which does not pass, and the irrectitude of a pure passage without actuality or punctuality. Time is a passivity, an element without "decision", without "initiative", an incessance without negation or power, in which intervals are compressed into a dizzying simultaneity of moments whose only unicity is their involvement with each other. The most disturbing and uncanny predicates of impossibility and proximity appear in this context. On one hand, the cogito is a rapport with moments whose only reality is their escape into infinite distance. These moments constitute the past as an immemorial spectrum without retention, a "past which was never present," a "passé entièrement révolu": the past of the Levinasian trace and of a subjectivity "in search of lost time." This past is forgotten in *oubli*, but it nevertheless concerns subjectivity in desire. Closure is an involvement with this past. The word "past" in proximity means "gone", "irrecuperable", "inaccessible". But that which is gone concerns us "now". The past weighs upon the present. F. Scott Fitzgerald's proposition: "boats against the current, borne back ceaselessly into the past" includes among its many resonances the figure of a spontaneity whose confronting of the future is already a bound into the past. The past awaits. Its inactuality is an urgency, the very animation of interiority. Similarly, the actuality of presence in proximity becomes the indetermination of the *à venir* or eternally futural. Time is the *événement* or "event" of proximity. Its presence or approach comes "from beyond the future" and "does not stop coming when it is there."[150] "An event: that which however does not arrive, the field of the unarrived and, at the same time, that which, arriving, arrives without assembling itself in some definite or determinable point — the unexpected arrival [*survenue*: also "approach"] of that which does not take place as a possibility."[151] Where the past escapes, the future approaches. But the future is "already" past, in the immediacy of its incumbence and in its escape from presence. The past awaits, like a future, in its own incumbence upon a desire "in search of lost time." The *à venir* and the immemorial past are the coördinates of an inactuality which is not entirely without the aspect of succession, not a simple dispersion or simultaneity, but a differentiation which produces the succession of escape and approach. Subjectivity's rapport with both these temporal movements is what Blanchot calls an "always more initial rapport"[152] — the "closer and closer" of a radically reduced form of possibility which is nevertheless a reality. It is the approach of the immemorial and inactual, and their urgency. Inactuality does not frustrate desire. It creates desire, in its incumbence.

The escape of temporal discontinuity from totalization, in the future, is a contact with the present: an imminence. "Always yet to come, always already past, always present in a beginning so abrupt that it takes your breath away, and yet deploying itself as return and eternal beginning again"[153] — these are the predicates of a proximal time which escapes and approaches. The density and "abrupt" character of the present results from the pressure of past and future which constitutes it. This inactuality is a jarring intensity. The terror of the other beast is not the eventuality of its arrival, but precisely the hyperbolic "arrival" which is its approach. The difference between future and present is not an interval, but an *écart*, the *écart* by which the present is already futural — not as a function of protention and disclosedness, but as a function of proximity. The interval is an involvement or immediacy foreclosing mediation. The future bears down upon the present because it is "already" present. The *à venir* inspires the present, as the Other inspires the Same. While its dispossessing incumbence "takes one's breath away," this incumbence is also the possibility of interiority's "respiration". It invests and dispossesses, in an *insufflement* which is also an *essoufflement* or "breathlessness". The detour of the Other is the source of this "breath" which is one's animation but which cannot be "caught". The approach of the future is the "little by little although already"[154] of metamorphosis: the alteration of the Same which is the production of the Same. The "already" of the future is not only the "now" of its hyperbolic presence, but also its immediate escape into a pre-originary past. The future is already "gone", already a function of *oubli*. It is intimate without being available or accessible. Like the murmur after the "death of the last writer" in *Le Livre à venir*, the futural event is "the resounding in advance of that which has not been said and never will be."[155] Its inactuality does not limit the violence of its incumbence. Nothing is more compelling, or has more paradoxical actuality, than that which will never "happen". The scratching of the other beast never began as a punctuality, but "awakened" the protagonist. And the beast will not arrive. The awakening of the *cogito* is its involvement with a pre-originarity beyond retention which is an approach beyond protention. Ahab's encounter with the whale has occurred "already", although "not yet" and "never". The other beast's approach is the murmur of an immemorial scratching which was the condition, and in a sense the only reality, of subjectivity's appearance in the burrow.

There is an additional temporal predicate of the suspended moment of imminence. That which can only approach, and never arrive, nevertheless "cannot be stopped," cannot be prevented or anticipated. It is too late to arrest this approach, this "already" of the future. This is the sense of Blanchotian *oubli* in its aritculation with *attente*. That which escapes manifestation is "on the point" of arriving in an economy which does not yet include totalization. Consciousness comes to itself in a moment of infinitesimal tardiness, like Kafka's "He", who is "never quite ready for any contingency." The "too late" of the *cogito* in proximity is its involvement with an alterity which collaborated in its awakening, and its reception of an alterity which cannot become actual. The "too late" does not describe a punctual moment which follows an earlier moment; it is the punctuality of a moment which is involved with an "other" moment. This "too late" is the time of Oedipus' discovery of a past and a future which concern him — a past and a future which cannot be influenced because they are in a "different concept" from that of spontaneity and action. The "too late" is also the *Nachträglichkeit* of psychoanalysis: the latent insistence of subjectivity in an inaccessible time which involves it and from which no distance can be taken. It is also the time of the uncanny, in which the unfamiliarity of that which was never "conscious" arises from the larger strangeness of that which could never become actual — a strangeness which is irreducibly familiar and not unexpected. Consciousness' differentiation, as Freud suggested, involves the inactual. The unconscious is psychoanalysis' discovery of proximity in its fundamental implication of an inactual and repetitive temporality. The supremacy of psychoanalysis as the twentieth century's thematization of proximity is its insistence upon a latent birth of consciousness in communication, and its sense of a behavior of subjectivity which is irrelevant to the context of manifestation. Psychoanalysis' problematic status among the sciences does not result from the novelty of its vocabulary, but from its involvement with a realm of the general economy whose principle is not power or accomplishment, but communication — a realm traditionally indicated in the violent definitions of literature, myth, religion, and in the unchronicled excesses of the everyday.

The overall context of the immemorial past, the *à venir*, the "already" and the "too late" of imminence is, as mentioned earlier, repetition. Repetition is the temporality in which every moment cannot but pre-exist itself and succeed itself, and in which subjectivity as an event must "pronounce its own *Fiat lux*" in a dimension transcending its spontaneity. The event in repetition is the return. This return does not succeed an initial punctuality, but is itself the principle of punctuality, when the event is an involvement with alterity. "(I)t never took place, never a first time, and yet it is beginning again."[156] Subjectivity in the desert of *errance* "returns without ever having left." The *cogito* is a repetition, in the immobility of a present which does not pass and thus invests closure, and in the *glissement* of a present which is entirely passage, and thus dispossesses closure. Repetition is a stretching of punctuality and a concomitant invasion or dispossession of punctuality by the proximity of other moments. The repetitive moment is an immobile and distended "now", forced in its unicity by temporal proximity, and at the same time an indefinite slipping of the "now" into inactuality — into another time, into the time of the Other. The pressure of temporal proximity creates the "now" as a gripping moment which cannot be escaped, and also as the monotonous, non-concerning inconsistency of *ressassement*. There is boredom in the passivity of suffering, beyond the terror of heteronomy. In the *écart* of incompletion, exteriority falls upon and grips the Same, while nevertheless, in its lack of self-coincidence, assuming the form of a weightless inconsistency. In this sense, repetition is the correlate of impersonality in Blanchot and Levinas: a loss of the self, and the neutral, non-concerning profile of the "he", which becomes however the excessive unicity of a subjectivity which is no longer a replaceable totality: me. In the same sense that impersonality makes possible the unicity of separation, repetition makes possible, in spite of its apparent monotony, the new: a moment which proceeds from alterity.

The various moments of proximal temporality must be thought, as suggested above, in a simultaneity which is not strategic but inevitable, in the context of the *cogito*. The synchrony of these moments is the differential and proximal unicity of subjectivity. It is their collapse upon each other, in their escape from totalization and correlation, that produces the disturbance of a passivity in being. It is on the basis of this contaminated mingling which remains a discontinuity, that separation and the eventuality of illumination can take place. Interiority is, in Blanchot's words, a "way time has of accomplishing itself." It is the manner of time and space in the general economy. This manner is the incumbence and weight of dispersion as a "reversal of dispersion." The gravity of differentiation — the passivity of closure — is subjectivity. The simultaneity of differentiated temporal moments describes what Levinas calls a "diachrony" in being: the two "times" of interiority and alterity which "are not in the same concept." The sense of the *cogito* as passivity is the strangeness of an alterity which cannot be assumed, which is always inadequate to the Same while involving and investing the Same. Passivity or impossibility in being is the general economy's differentiation of Other and Same — a movement which is always "à sens unique", a "one-way" movement. The Other's approach and escape are not effects of a power, but of an absence of power. No power can oppose these movements. Blanchot writes in *Le Pas au-delà*: "it withdraws [*s'éloigne*], but I never withdraw."[157] The economy of the Same is its proximity to the Other — and the Other is not another Same. The force which invests interiority comes from a "nowhere" which is already "here". The Other is outside and inside, but always exterior. When I approach it, it is already it that is approaching me. The sense of interiority's non-indifference, of its desire, of its *pour l'autre* and the *parole* is this dissymetrical inclination in being. The intensity of discontinuity in being is its approach to the Other, as a function of the Other's approach. The *parole*, a murmur or noise which haunts manifestation, is the sound of differentiated beings "deserting their posts" within the totality. The sense of this movement is univocal: toward the Other, into the exterior.

Impossibility is the general economy's excess over the region of power and manifestation — an excess which invests the closure of this region. The "catalysis" of identity and accomplishment is an event rooted in the excess and heteronomy of differentiation. In the last pages of "Le grand refus", Blanchot draws conclusions which are identical to those of Levinas. He writes: "it is not impossibility that would be non-power: it is the possible that is merely the power of the no. Must we therefore say: impossibility is being itself? Assuredly, we must!"[158] And, several lines later: "But must we not also say: impossibility, neither negation nor affirmation, indicates that which, in being, has always already *preceded* being and yields to no ontology? Assuredly, we must!"[159] Impossibility is the irreducibility of being to the power of being, and as such is the irreducibility of the general economy to the Being of ontology. This is the sense of the *parole* which draws subejctivity, in Blanchot's words, "outside itself and perhaps outside everything" — outside the totality, into the exterior. Ontology, in the eyes of both Blanchot and Levinas, recognizes no such region, no region outside the Same. The *cogito* of proximity is not an awakening, but a *parole*. This *parole* is the *autrement qu'être* which "resonates in being" ("s'entend dans l'être"). It is not a plenitude of being beyond negation or totalization, but the strange inactuality of being as affirmation, which lacks both the positivity of plenitude and the negativity of determination. This excess is the subjectivity or passivity of being, which is not a totality including consciousness, but a dimension whose subjectivity prevents its totalization. Impossiblity is being as an *autrement qu'être*, an actuality of alterity which implies a paradoxically positive inactuality of the economy's reality. By virtue of its differentiation, being is an alteration: "l'être s'altère."

VI. ALTERITY IN THE GENERAL ECONOMY: PAROLE

PAROLE AND ENTRETIEN

The *parole* in proximity is the existence of closure as an excess, inspired by the exterior and inclined toward the latter. The Bataillian terms which describe this inspiration are *inachèvement* or "incompletion" and *dépense*. These terms describe closure as an exigency: a recoiling from the general economy which is, by virtue of excess and incompletion, a recoiling into the economy. Closure is a transgression of closure: a unicity whose paroxysm forces it "outward", "into the exterior": *au dehors, pour l'autre*. The terms *rire, expérience, non-savoir,* etc. describe the unicity of beings which "come to life losing themselves in communication."[1] Bataillian incarnation is an inclination toward alterity which is produced by an inextrication from the latter in the process of individuation. Closure's exigency becomes, beyond its thematization in reproduction, a "transfer to the impersonality of life."[2] The "effort of autonomy" is always, in its latent economy, a *perte* or "loss" and, as such, describes a communicational situation in which autonomy has no privilege. Against this background, Bataille has little difficulty in subordinating the concept of an intersubjective encounter to this non-reciprocal model of communication. The latter's movement is always a *sens unique* or "one-way" movement in which the economy's excess forces interiority toward alterity. The intersubjective other of Bataille's fictional and theoretical text is always defined as a *pléthore* or a moment of the *pléthore* (the excess of alterity over interiority), before it is defined as a constituted subjectivity. When the *parole* becomes a primary predicate of differentiation and affirmation in Bataille, its dissymetry is immediately palpable: "And this movement of my thought which flees me, not only can I not avoid it, but there is no instant so secret that it does not animate me. Thus I speak, everything in me gives itself to others."[3] The affinity of Bataille with Levinas is not only the thematic proximity of *dépense* to fecundity, or of the sacrifice to Levinasian *liturgie, diaconie*, or responsibility, but is also the basic notion of non-reciprocity, defined as a rapport with the Other which will condition any rapport with others.

In Blanchot the relation of communication to intersubjectivity is more complex and unequal. In spite of the prominence of a dissymetrical model of intersubjectivity in his fiction, and in spite of his stable and repeated intuition that the *parole* is the force or incumbence of differentiation in the general economy, Blanchot has difficulty articulating the concept of non-reciprocity in an intersubjective context. In *L'Espace littéraire* and *Le Livre à venir*, this concept is not explicitly thematized, although the theme of the dissymetrical approach, as discussed above, is a fundamental incarnation of it. The Other is an incumbence produced by differentiation, toward which interiority cannot be indifferent. *Errance*, experience, the *oeuvre*, and Orpheus' transgression describe an inspired approach to the Other which is a function of the Other's approach. On a thematic level, however, Blanchot's elaboration of impersonality and impossibility shares what may be called the "temptation" of the differential trace: a tendency to reduce the notion of alterity to escape from totalization, indefinite circulation, and dispersion. Although Blanchot never explicitly subordinates proximity to this configuration, he tends to pose the proximal economy in a disturbingly dialectical structure, as in the two hands of involuntary prehension. The invitation to read this problematic as a duality of incessant undifferentiation on one hand, and of silence as differentiation on the other, obscures the notion of the exigency as the context of both hands' passivity. Many Blanchotian contexts, including the approach to the sirens, the approach to Eurydice, the fascination of the image, etc., lend themselves to a hasty dialectical reading which opposes the transitivity of consciousness or action to the escape of the absolutely other. That this other does not escape into dispersion, and that its approach does not reduce interiority to mere dispersion, are stipulations that are not always clear to Blanchot's reader. It is this dualistic tendency in Blanchot's discursivity that motivates his reluctance to entirely abandon the structural and thematic proximity of Hegel to his own theoretical text, despite the virulence of his critique of Hegel in the context of dissimulation and of the presence of absence. The tendency to subordinate the excess of differential alteration to dispersion, undifferentiation, and the secret common denominator of these terms, negativity, has an authentic although restricted presence in Blanchot's text. On this level, the inequality of this text parallels that of the philosophy of difference.

It is said that when a theoretical text assumes large empirical proportions, its size and length indicate an inability on the part of its author to control the interplay of his concepts and contexts. Reiteration indicates a hesitation and a sense that the problematic in question exceeds the boundaries of its treatment. There is some truth in this generality as it applies to *L'Entretien infini*, in spite of the overwhelming creativity of this basic Blanchotian text. *L'Entretien infini* returns incessantly to the theme of the *parole* and the intersubjective presence, and even takes the form of a dialogue in many of its divisions. Its title indicates this preoccupation, as will be discussed below. Although it contains many meditations of literary communication which continue the movement of earlier books, *L'Entretien infini* concentrates its attention upon a discussion of intersubjectivity which was not included in these earlier books, and suggests a change in thematic emphasis in Blanchot's thinking from the 1950's to the 1960's and 1970's. Most significantly, a name which appears frequently in *L'Entretien infini* as a subject, and in comparisons and notes, is that of Emmanuel Levinas. In addition, as mentioned earlier, a proliferation of Levinasian concepts – often acknowledged, often not – is palpable in this book. The concept of non-reciprocity, in particular, intervenes repeatedly as a predicate of the *parole*. But the frequency of this intervention is associated with a tension in its definition, and a tension in Blanchot's proximity to Levinas. This tension is nowhere more palpable – not unpredictably – than in Blanchot's reading of the *parole* in Bataille, entitled "Le jeu de la pensée".[4]

When strategically envisaged as a presence of two interlocutors, as in "Le jeu de la pensée", the *parole* is an instance which is essentially irreducible to the notion of dialogue as duality and correlation, comprehension and mutual transitivity. The *parole,* prior to its mobilization as such a transitivity or exchange of information, is a remainder or *reste* which is the very economy of the intersubjective presence. In Bataillian terms, the *parole* is the unicity of the interlocutors, defined as their incompletion. It is the existence of the interlocutors in a communicational economy. It is their communication as a function of their separation – without, however, describing a "common ground" of incompletion or communion. It is the dissymetrical heteronomy of the Same – in the dialogue. Thus it does not correlate and adequate the two interlocutors. It requires no emission by the one or comprehension by the other. Instead, it is their communicational presence in its economy. Irreducible to comprehension or to signification in its common sense, the excess of the *parole* will condition these possibilities. Blanchot's attestation of this economic situation, in the form of the terms *inconnu, entretien, proximité, différence, parole plurielle,* and *attention,* structures his essay and leads to his thematization of dissymetry.

The rapport indicated by the *parole* is not a relation, since it is correlative to the very lack of positivity of the terms differentiated by it. This rapport is not a link which would reduce an intersubjective distance. It is instead this very distance, in its irreducibility, defined already as a rapport: the rapport of inextrication, separation, and heteronomy. This moment, which will have the names "rapport of the third type" and "interruption" in *L'Entretien infini,*[5] is a proximity which proceeds from the excess and incompletion of the Same. The problematic unicity of each interlocutor is produced by its involvement with the economic pressure of the economy in its generality – and thus, in a secondary moment, by its involvement with the presence of the other interlocutor. The heteronomy of closure is therefore not a principle of correlation, but is, as the principle of differentiation, the only basis on which to speak of these two interlocutors "together" in their "presence". While it would not be correct to say that each interlocutor has no positivity outside his intrication with "the other" (since such a formulation would lend the systematic positivity of determination or distinction to both interlocutors), it would be correct to say that, in this intersubjective presence, the Same has no unicity outside its involvement with its Other. Thus the *parole* is not a mobilization of intersubjectivity toward comprehension or correlation, but is rather the impossibility of mobilization, transitivity, power or comprehension, implicit in such a presence. The *parole* is unavailable to the interlocutors as a dialectical assurance of communication's immediacy, or of the mediation which correlates on the basis of negation and totalization. It is thus, in the most impersonal economic sense, an *entretien*. "What is present in this presence of the *parole*, as soon as it affirms itself, is precisely that which never allows itself to be seen or attained: something is there, which is inaccessible (as much to him who says it as to him who hears it); it is between us, it stands between [*se tient entre*], and the *entretien** is the approach [*abord*] on the basis of this between, an irreducible distance. . .".[6] The *parole* is, thus the Blanchotian *neutre* in its sense of irreducibility to identity and distinction. The *parole* is the "neither-one-nor-the-other" which is involved in the positivity of the intersubjective presence. As such, it is the figure of alterity — the other of closure — which is always irreducible to the empirical or dialectical opposition of two subjects. Blanchot repeatedly refers to this alterity as the "unknown"[7] which conditions the possibility of comprehension in dialogue. He also stresses its involvement with *oubli,* which is the perennial form in Blanchot's text of a communication irreducible to comprehension or manifestation. "*Oubli* speaks in the intimacy of this *parole*, not only partial and limited forgetfulness, but the profound *oubli* on which all memory erects itself."[8] "*Oubli* is the master of the game [*jeu*: "play", "freeplay"]."[9] When the parole invests a transitive "content" or "message" — the *dit* (the "spoken", the "said") of the *parole* — this *dit* will always be conditioned by the differential excess of the *parole*. It will always be a Bataillian *glissement* — a differential alteration, an undecidability and a heteronomy — before it can function as a message or object in a universe of comprehension. In its production by incompletion, it is a failure of communication to be "communicable", and a failure to assert itself within the realm of the possible. The *dit* as object, content or message of the spoken or written word, is an event of communication's heteronomy. It is a discontinuity produced by heteronomy and alteration. That this discontinuity may be mobilized as an integrity or pertinence within the region of manifestation, does not obscure this priority of communication. Blanchot enunciates this contamination by returning to the concept of the *entretien:* "the thing said enters into a rapport with its difference, becomes more acute, more tragic, not more unified, but on the contrary suspended tragically between two poles of attraction."[10] Every "word" or enunciation, in its discontinuity, is a function of the *parole* of differentiation, and is thus neither a totality nor an arm of totalization or comprehension. The parole is a *différence*,[11] a *redoublement*,[12] and an *affirmation infinie* or *redoublée*[13] — that is, the economic positivity of a differentiation without negation (an affirmation) which separates without producing integrity or the possibility of adequation. The *parole* is on one hand the separation of the inter-

---

* The French *entretenir*, unlike the English "converse", has an intransitive resonance which suggests the pure impersonality of a subsistence "between", "supported" by two instances — a pure abiding — which is absent from the sense of exchange and activity in the word "conversation" (but which is one archaic resonance of this word).

locutors, and on the other hand a separation or scission, an essential lack of quiddity, in itself. It is a rapport, but it is the impossibility of a relation.

Because the *parole* is a difference, i.e. an economic principle and a differential instance, Blanchot suggests that the intersubjective presence be termed, not a dialogue, but a *parole plurielle*, in this dual sense. "Rather than a dialogue, it would be necessary to call it a plural *parole*, if the latter, in its simplicity, is the search for an affirmation which, although escaping all negation, does not unify and does not allow itself to be unified, always indicating [*renvoyant*] a difference always more tempted [*tentée*] to differ."[14] The *parole* is the economy, the proximity, and the only reality of the interlocutors: it is their difference. The hyperbolic proximity suggested by this impersonal presence is also a hyperbolic distance, the distance of essential inadequation. The dialogue is thus a "non-familiar", "non-personal intimacy",[15] a co-presence "without an ensemble", "without accord",[16] that is, an intimacy which forecloses both the separation and the unification presupposed by these terms. This intimacy is the production of subjectivity in being by differentiation. Differentiation is never complete or adequate, never "yet" complete, and this is one index of the proximal temporalization described by the Blanchotian term *attente*: the "not yet" of being without totalization, the tension of a dispossessing communication without adequation or determination. For the notion of proximity in the *parole plurielle*, the concept of *attente* becomes the term "attention": "an impersonal attention, in the sense that it is no one's attention, but the very *attente* [awaiting, imminence] of that which is in play, through the *parole*, between those who are there."[17] Blanchot's characteristic overdetermination of terms and meanings is manifest in the concept of a "difference always more tempted [*tentée*] to differ" as a correlate and *attente* and *attention*. The process of differentiation creates unicity and discontinuity in a stretching, distending, intense moment which produces not only ambiguity or undecidability, but also an excessive force and an excessive incompletion of closure which is the possibility of both time and subjectivity. "Attention is between the one and the other: the center of meeting, the sign of this between which brings together [*rapproche*: also "closer"] while separating."[18] Attention – the heteronomy and subjectivity of the economy – is the principle of discontinuity and thus of intersubjectivity. "(B)etween two men speaking, linked by the essential, the non-familiar intimacy of thought establishes a measureless distance and proximity."[19] The intersubjective rapport reproduces the consistent configuration of proximity: the infinite "distance" of inadequation and alterity, produced by a lack of totalization, and the intimate proximal heteronomy or inextrication which proceeds from the same lack. The rapport is a function of separation, which is an economic moment foreclosing communication in its common sense as relation and correlation, while it introduces the possibility of proximity as the very "impossibility" of this mode of communication. The *parole plurielle* is the impersonal tension of separation in being.

Thus Blanchot, in his strategic description of an *entretien* with Georges Bataille, interprets the possibility of the *entretien* in proximity. What is striking in this interpretation is the reappearance of what the Blanchot of *L'Espace littériare* called a "faulty image": the image of two constituted poles of attraction "between" which the *parole* appears. Having defined the *oeuvre* as such a suspension between the poles of reading and writing, Blanchot added: "this comparison is faulty" by virtue of its implication of "fixed poles responding to the crude schema of two powers."[20] The stipulation that the two poles have no reality outside the *parole* which is their difference the their *entretien*, is implicit and explicit in "Le jeu de la pensée", but does not reduce the puzzlement of Blanchot's reader at this reappearance, in the text and title of *L'Entretien infini*, of a configuration which responds in so grossly approximate a manner to the problem of communication's dissymetry.

On one hand, the very form of Blanchot's discussion of the dialogue is a panoramic view of proximity, and such a view, which is impossible in Levinas' eyes, obscures the rapport of Same and Other which is the sense of proximity. As mentioned above, the Same in the dialogue, as in any other situation, has no reality outside its intrication with alterity. The *parole* is the inspiration and incompletion of the Same. It does not stand "between". It stands "outside". When "this interlocutor" and "that interlocutor" are articulated in the concept of dialogue, it is not incorrect to say that the *parole* is a neutrality which stands "between"; but this formulation is a misleading modification of the global concept of alteration which creates unicity in proximity. It correlates two subjects, two moments of ipseity, and gives the incorrect impression that the notion of alterity may be derived from this correlation. The "crude schema" of two "powers", two totalities, and of an alterity created by the articulation of these totalities, is virtually unavoidable, because no stipulation is made that "two" are not necessary for the rapport with alterity to take place. Alterity, and with it the *parole*, cannot be understood on the basis of a correlation of "this Same" to "that Same". On the other hand, such concepts as the *neutre*, the *parole plurielle*, and the *entretien*, which are basic to Blanchot's text, imply in themselves a panoramic or synoptic point of view with regard to proximity. Although the suggestion seems disproportionate to the overdetermination of Blanchot's title, the reader is tempted to ask whether the notion of the *entretien* is the best possible expression of the alterity described by proximity — even if the preferred context of this thematization is intersubjectivity.

The question of alterity is the question of interiority's rapport with an Other of interiority, and requires the thematization of an inequality or dissymetry of these terms. In the last pages of his essay, Blanchot attempts, with a strikingly uncharacteristic confusion, to situate alterity within the intersubjective presence:

One might say that, of these two men speaking, one is necessarily the obscure "*Autrui*" — and who is "*Autrui*"? the unknown, the stranger, foreign to every visible and to every non-visible, and who however comes to "me" as a *parole*, when speaking is no longer seeing. One of the two is the Other, the one who, in the greatest human simplicity, is always close to that which cannot be close to "me": close to death, close to the night. But who is me? where is the Other?[21]

Blanchot is able to describe the Other as "unsituated, unsituable" in the dialogue, and yet present in the *parole* as a function of the "Difference" which is its economy ("the Other speaks in this presence of the *parole*, which is its only presence, a neutral *parole*, infinite. . ."[22]). He also explicitly notes that the *parole plurielle* "aims neither at equality nor at reciprocity,"[23] which are concepts implicit in the notion of dialogue. However, apparently discomfited by both the reciprocity of the panoramically viewed dialogue and the Levinasian proximity described by the word *Autrui,* he returns to the ambivalent formulation of a non-reciprocity which is yet reciprocal:

Certainly, the interlocutors would speak as equals, if they spoke to each other, but to the extent that they respond to this *Autrui* whose *parole* coincides now with that of the one now with that of the other, there is each time between them an infinite difference such that it may not be evaluated in terms of superiority or predominance. And, at the same time, let us not forget, this play of thought cannot be played alone, there must be two partners in the game, it is necessary that the same decision, the same frankness, the same rapport with what is at stake [*en jeu*] engage them to play.[24]

This passage represents a serious breakdown in Blanchot's understanding of intersubjective alterity, as well as a curiously furtive reference to Levinas. While the phrase "they are answering *Autrui*" is a correct description of interiority's inspiration by the exterior, in any context, the phrase "whose *parole* coincides now with that of the one now with that of the other" is a true renunciation of the attempt to articulate difference and non-reciprocity with the *entretien*. The expression "my *parole*" or "his *parole*" proceeds from a phenomenological universe of dialectical alteration and correlation, and is a virtual absurdity in the context of proximity. The *parole* never coincides with "what one says". No one must speak in order for the *parole* to appear. It is the very existence of one interlocutor, of both interlocutors, of interiority, of the Same. Similarly, *Autrui* is the exteriority which collaborates in the conation of interiority. Since *Autrui* is involved in all intersubjectivity as in all subjectivity, it is not entirely meaningless to say that *Autrui* invests "now the one, now the other" — but it is derisory, and quite beside the point, to say so. *Autrui* concerns the Same, and not "now this one, now that one." Sensing the Hegelian inspiration which is confusing his approach to Bataille, Blanchot stipulates that the *entretien* involves a difference which cannot be understood as transcendence and domination. But the foreclosing of these concepts proceeds directly from the configuration of non-reciprocity which informs the *parole*: a configuration Blanchot is unable to articulate. It is difficult for Blanchot's reader to avoid the sense of a veiled reference to Levinasian *hauteur* in this rejection of Hegel and phenomenology — particularly since "Le Jeu de la pensée" (1963) was written soon after a text entitled "Tenir parole" (1962) which explicitly and most ambivalently rejected this Levinasian concept (see below), and which precedes "Le Jeu de la pensée" in *L'Entretien infini*. The presence of *Totalité et infini* (1961) in the background of this discussion is another important contextual factor. When Blanchot concludes that "two partners" with the "same frankness" are required for the *jeu* to take place, he succeeds only in rooting his argument more deeply in the phenomenological tradition he aims to avoid. In proximity, no encounter with another subject is necessary for the approach of *Autrui* to take place. *Autrui* is the exteriority whose proximity is the creation of the Same. In refusing the Hegelian model of domination, Blanchot returns confusedly to the Hegelian model of reciprocity which ultimately governs the Master-Slave correlation. This ambivalent involvement with Hegel occurs in an essay whose fidelity to Bataille is, in many respects, admirable. But the notion of non-reciprocity is integral to the Bataillian economy of *dépense* and transgression, and for this reason the fact that the rubric of dialogue chosen by Blanchot for his essay leads to a confusing detour on difference and dissymetry, is significant. To write on Bataille is a project which implies, for the Blanchot of the early 1960's, an approach to Levinas. The panoramic notion of the *entretien*, with its stubborn inappropriateness to communication's dissymetry, leads to an implicit rejection of Levinas which rekindles the inspiration that haunts Blanchot more than any other: that of Hegel.

The hesitation shown by Blanchot in "Le Jeu de la pensée" is not unique, but characterizes all his discussions of the *parole* and of non-reciprocity in *L'Entretien infini*. These discussions, which are structured by such concepts as "interruption", "intermittence", the "rapport of the third type" (i.e. neither adequation nor communion), the *parole d'écriture*, the plural, and the fragmentary, all organize themselves around the figure of the *entretien* and the difference which "stands between." The predicates of the *parole* which were posed in "Le Jeu de la pensée" are repeated, with subtle displacements in context and emphasis, throughout Blanchot's text. The *entretien* emerges as an intimacy without relation, a situation of differentiation irreducible to negativity, a fragmentary *parole* whose temporality is repetition in the eternal return, a speaking of the Other or the Exterior in the ostensible dialogue, an irreducible distance and proximity, and, most generally, the form of plurality in being.[25] As is suggested by the proximity of the latter concept to Levinasian "pluralism", the notion of non-reciprocity returns with regularity to all these contexts. Its return is always accompanied by an explicit reference to Levinas or by the introduction of a Levinasian term. For instance, in "La Pensée et l'exigence de discontinuité",[26] speaking of a dissymetry correlative to the concept of *maîtrise* and *enseignement*, Blanchot defines non-reciprocity as a function irreducible to equality and inequality, predominance and subordination, "such that, between two *paroles*, a rapport of infinity is always implicated as the movement of signification itself."[27] Here the context and the terms are Levinasian, the figure of the *entre* is retained, and the question of dissymetry is deferred to later essays. In "L'Interruption",[28] alterity in the *parole* is defined as "the infinity between us,"[29] and the Other of intersubjectivity is defined as "neither another self, nor another existence, nor a modality or a moment of universal existence, nor a superexistence, god or non-god, but the unknown in its infinite distance."[30] In "Le Rapport du troisième genre",[31] the alterity which invests or produces *Autrui* is distinguished from the presence of the "other person" ("the Other man that is *"autrui"* also risks being always the Other of man, close to that which cannot to close to me: close to death, close to the night. . ."[32]), and is again defined as an "infinite relation".[33] It is noteworthy that the terms invoked for this distinction are death and the night. These themes are most familiar to Blanchot and function as points of reference for the notion of alterity; but they remain themes which tend to pose the latter as undifferentiation and dispersion. In this essay, Blanchot also stresses the grammatical neutrality of the word *autrui*, and correctly associates this concept with the *neutre* and the "He" of impersonality. Throughout these essays on intersubjectivity, which date from the early 1960's, the notion of non-reciprocity is introduced in a strict proximity to Levinas' concepts, which gives the text of *L'Entretien infini* an oddly derivative aspect. However, these Levinasian concepts are never appropriated without an attempt to adjust their meanings to the context of neutrality and the *entretien*, and this continuing adjustment produces repeated moments of tension and ambivalence in Blanchot's text.

In the course of Blanchot's meditation of dissymetry in communication, there are important corrections of certain inequalities in Levinas' text. For instance, in "Tenir parole", the term *face-à-face* ("face to face"), occasionally used by Levinas to describe intersubjective proximity, is correctly criticized as being "misleading". This is because it suggests both a reciprocal or symmetrical relation, and because it suggests a directness or univocity of the presence of alterity. Blanchot writes, "when *autrui* turns toward me, he who is essentially exterior is as though infinitely turned away [*détourné*] . . . , the presence turned toward me is still that of separation, of that which is presence to me, while I am separated, distanced and turned away from it."[34] When *Autrui* in the *visage* "turns toward me", in Levinas' phrase, this turning is the incumbence of an alterity which remains inaccessible. This incumbence may be correctly described as the Other's "detour", in the profile of impersonal illeity, or as a presence to which interiority's own approach must always be a "detour" as a result of the Other's escape from totalization. The priority of the detour over the "face to face" indicates alterity's lack of immediacy or manifest presence which is correlative to its weight or approach.

In "Le Rapport du troisième genre", Blanchot demonstrates his understanding of alterity's irreducibility to the presence of *autrui* as another person: "alone, then, he is the ex-centered; alone, escaping the circle of vision in which my perspective deploys itself, and this is not because he would constitute in his turn the center of another horizon, but because he is not turned toward me on the basis of a horizon which is his own. The Other: not only does he not fall within my horizon, he is himself without a horizon."[35] This formulation, which correctly invokes the impersonal alterity which is *autrui*, nevertheless poses this alterity in a "coincidence" with the intersubjective other. Following this definition, Blanchot attempts a direct articulation of non-reciprocity in the inter-subjective rapport:

— (. . .) if it is true that *autrui* is never a self for me, the same is true of me for *autrui*, that is, that the Other who appears before me. . . is *for himself* nothing but a self who would wish to be understood by the Other. . . .
— Here, in effect, is one of the traps which are set for us. (. . .) (T)his redoubling of irreciprocity — this reversal which apparently makes of me the other of the other — cannot, at the level we are placed at, be assumed by dialectics, because it does not tend to re-establish any equality; on the contrary, it signifies a double dissymetry, a double discontinuity, as though the void between the one and the other were not homogeneous, but polarized, as though it constituted a non-isomorphic field, carrying a double distortion.[36]

In spite of the apparent pertinence and decisiveness of this formulation, which projects dissymetry onto a synoptic figure, it is clear that Blanchot's difficulties in thematizing non-reciprocity have not been resolved. The configuration of a symmetry and an *entretien* remains his context. The elevated perspective from which the thinker envisages two interlocutors in a rapport, is simply a view of two interlocutors, and not a posing of the question of Same and Other. Despite his attempt to adjust this panoramic perspective, Blanchot retains as an authentic proposition the concept that "I must be an Other for the Other", while defining this moment as the effect of a "double dissymetry". In fact, both the reciprocity and the dissymetry are derisory attestations. The Other is not a person. Without encountering another person, we remain involved with *autrui*. The intersubjective rapport in proximity is not exceptional, and is not the foundation of non-reciprocity. The economy of the Same itself is this foundation. To suggest that "I must be an Other for the Other," even for the purpose of situating this concept within a "double dissymetry", is to unwittingly claim that "the Other must be another Same for whom I am an Other" — that is, to dissolve alterity within its "coincidence" with the Same. The implication of this claim is that alterity proceeds from an encounter of Same with Same. This is to unwittingly trivialize the reality of alterity and to invite its interpretation as a subjective "impression" which invests the intersubjective rapport. "I must be the Other for the Other, because, in himself, he is merely another Same." The notion that in the dialogue, as elsewhere, the Same is involved with alterity — which is Blanchot's intended argument — is obscured. Alterity does not concern "me" and "him", but concerns the Same. Alterity never "coincides" with "me" or "him". It concerns not a term in a system, but the system as a whole, or interiority in general.

Ultimately, Blanchot's thinking of non-reciprocity in his proximity to Levinas retains this panoramic articulation. For Blanchot, non-reciprocity remains this paradox: "one of the two is the other, who is neither the one nor the other."[37] The Other is neither one nor the other, is "between" the two, or is the rapport itself. "(T)his Other which is in play in the rapport of the third type, is no longer in one of the terms, it is neither in the one nor in the other, being nothing other than the rapport itself, a rapport of the one to the other which requires infinity."[38] "The other is at the same time the *rapport* of inaccessibility to the other, is the other that this inaccessible rapport institutes, is however the inaccessible presence of the other — the man without a horizon — which [who] makes itself [himself] a rapport and first of all in the very inaccessibility of its [his] approach."[39] The problematic inpersonality of the alterity Blanchot evokes ("il": the Other "it" or the Other "he"?) shows his indecision with regard to the economy of *autrui* and the "other person" or "other Same". In spite of their pertinence to the inaccessibility and incumbence of proximity, Blanchot's statements tend to reduce the approach of alterity to the principle of an *entretien*, an "entre-deux", and to retain the disqualified figure of a "face to face". On one level, it appears that a most simple discursive dilemma creates this difficulty. Rather than to speak exclusively of the Other in its effect upon Me, as does Levinas, Blanchot speaks of the Other which affects a "term" or "the one" interlocutor, this Other being irreducible to "the one" or "the other". The dissolution and reduction of alterity seem to result from a certain view of the situation. On the other hand, the persistence of this view, and its exasperation and reiteration, are themselves noteworthy.

As mentioned earlier, Levinas' invocations of Plato's *Phaedrus* in its description of a subjectivity which assists or upholds its own signification in the spoken word, as opposed to the written word, represent a confusing gesture. They add the predicate of independence to the Other's escape from manifestation and proximal incumbence. Levinas invites his reader to interpret alterity's escape from totalization as the movement of a pure interiority which withholds itself from totalization while dominating its own presence — rather than as the predicate of an instance which has no power and no presence. In his essay on Levinas entitled "Connaissance de l'inconnu",[40] Blanchot notes this problem, but also overestimates its resonance among Levinas' concepts. He suggests that the reference to Plato introduces an "équivoque" in Levinas' thought which is not accidental, but which in fact defines its "theological" stratum. Here the most intense and ambivalent moment of Blanchot's rapport with Levinas in *L'Entretien infini* begins. The purpose of the *Phaedrus* comparison in Levinas is to articulate the theme of *hauteur* ("height", "dominance") in the rapport of Other to Same. The *hauteur* of the Other is the dissymetry of its approach to the Same — an approach which proceeds from another dimension, another "concept". *Hauteur* describes the incumbence of this approach which is inadequate to the region of power and totalization, and therefore disproportionate to the prospect of interiority's own approach to the Other. Blanchot repeats the familiar gesture which prescribes a retaining of the theme of non-reciprocity without its "theological" context:

On one hand, language is the transcendental relation itself, manifesting that the space of communication is essentially non-symetrical, that there is as though a curving of this space which prevents reciprocity and produces an absolute difference of levels between the terms called to communicate: this is, I think, what is decisive in the affirmation we must understand and that we must maintain independently of the theological context in which this affirmation presents itself.[41]

Thus Blanchot accredits the concept of *hauteur* as non-reciprocity, or what Levinas calls the *diachronie* of Other and Same. Yet *hauteur*, the compelling approach of an alterity whose escape from totalization is not reduced to mere indefinition and dispersion, is the necessary and sufficient definition of the *éthique* itself. Recognizing the danger of his own procedure, Blanchot adds in a note: "'Context', as J. Derrida remarks well, is here a word that Levinas could only consider out of place, inappropriate, as well as the reference to a theology."[42] What is the sense of this disclaimer, and of its invocation of Jacques Derrida's 1963 essay on Levinas – an essay which itself approvingly invoked Blanchot's criticism of the Platonic comparison in Levinas? Is the context "theological", or is it not? Can non-reciprocity be extracted from this context, or is it this very context? Blanchot continues his argument:

But here is, I think, the equivocation: this *parole* of *hauteur,* which speaks to me from a great distance, from on high [*très haut*] (or from far below), the *parole* of someone who does not speak in equality to me and in which it is not possible for me to address myself to *autrui* as though he were another Myself, suddenly becomes again the tranquil humanist and Socratic *parole* which brings close to us the man who speaks, since it makes us know, in all familiarity, who he is and from what land he is, according to Socrates' wish.[43]

If Levinas' invocation of the *Phaedrus* for its implication of an alterity which exceeds its own manifestation (rather than to receive its signification from its place within totalization) is to be understood as an accreditation of the *Phaedrus'* valorization of the spoken word over the written word, then the configuration of non-reciprocity is dissolved by Plato's insistence on presence and comprehension. The spoken word carries an implication of reciprocity. "(T)his privilege of spoken language belongs *equally* to *Autrui* and to *Me* and thus renders them equals."[44] This "sudden" recuperation of Levinasian dissymetry by a metaphysics of comprehension and reciprocity* is possible only if, in the first place, the entirety of the *Phaedrus'* predications is attributed to Levinas himself, and if

---

* In his essay on Levinas entitled "Violence et métaphysique" (*Revue de Métaphysique et de Morale*, 1964, nos. 3 and 4; reprinted in *L'Ecriture et la différence* (Seuil, 1967), pp. 117–228), Jacques Derrida approvingly cites Blanchot's reference to the *Phaedrus* (p. 151), and also cites Blanchot's suggestion that Levinasian non-reciprocity be "retained" without its theological context (p. 152). Derrida's intention, however, is to suggest that non-reciprocity is rooted in a properly theological or "metaphysical" context whose positivity removes Levinas radically from the Blanchotian universe of neutrality and alteration. "The

in the second place the sense of the *parole* as differentiation and excess is entirely abandoned in this equation of it with the spoken word. Neither of these interpretations is possible. Levinas' reader knows that the *parole* is not the spoken word, not a word at all, and has no fundamental relation to the duality

affinity [between Blanchot and Levinas] ceases, it seems to me, at the moment when [Levinas'] eschatological positivity comes to illuminate in retrospect the common road, to reduce the finitude and pure negativity of the question, when the neutral determines itself." (p. 152) Blanchot's involvement with Derrida in his attempts to articulate the concept of non-reciprocity at the expense of Levinas is noteworthy, for Derrida's essay, certainly the most well known of Levinas studies, is a virulent attempt to reduce the pertinence and originality of all the Levinasian concepts, from a philosophical perspective which is surprisingly traditional. This essay dates from a period in the early 1960's in which Derrida published a number of essays whose logic and discursive strategies were foreign to the differential and communicational framework of his later works. Among these essays, "Violence et métaphysique" is perhaps the least worthy of publication, since the concepts mobilized against Levinas are in direct contradiction to those which were to inform Derrida's major works, and since the pertinence of these concepts to their subject is minimal. Derrida defines *autrui* as the constituted intersubjective other (pp. 146, 149 sq.), the *visage* as the face of this constituted other (p. 169), the rapport of interiority in the *visage* in the *parole* as immediacy and presence (pp. 148–57), the *éthique* as an ethics whose context is intersubjectivity (p. 164), the non-allergic rapport of Same and Other as a "respect" and a "non-violence" understood in contrast to the "violence" of mediation and differentiation (pp. 188, 193 sq.), the alterity of *autrui* as his subjectivity (pp. 183–4, 187–8), and *expérience* as presence and phenomenality (p. 225). On the basis of these largely incompetent definitions, Derrida is able to claim that, contrary to Levinas' assertions, both Husserl's notions of intentionality and intersubjectivity, and Heidegger's notions of comprehension and manifestation, successfully describe the "respect for alterity" prescribed by Levinas' *éthique*. He also argues that Levinas' concept of the rapport with alterity as an immediacy and "non-violence" is a classically metaphysical and humanist problematic which is foreclosed by the "violence" inherent in differentiation and mediation. These and the many other assertions made by Derrida proceed from a failure to understand that the "non-allergic" rapport with alterity, the *visage*, the *parole*, "non-violence", and the Levinasian concept of alterity itself, are rooted in the concept of differentiation and in its multiple predicates – predicates which will motivate and inform Derrida's own critiques of both Husserl and Heidegger in later works. Derrida's astonishing incomprehension of Levinas is noteworthy less for the ambiguity of its intention, which is a virtual constant in his theoretical practice, than for the extreme intimacy of the Levinasian text to those concepts (trace, *espacement*, supplementarity, temporal alteration in *différance*, etc.) which were to structure Derrida's own text. No conceptual apparatus could be better adjusted to an approach to Levinas than that of differential alteration, with its predicates of escape, incumbence, an alterity of communication and the non-reciprocity implied by closure's "non-allergic" inspiration by exteriority. On the other hand, the Heideggerian intellectualism which informs the later pages of "Violence et métaphysique" is itself a constant temptation in Derrida's theoretical text, and might perhaps have produced under any circumstances some difficulty in a Derridian reading of the *éthique*. It remains puzzling that Blanchot, whose own understanding of the Levinasian concepts infinitely exceeds that demonstrated in "Violence et métaphysique", associates his reading with this essay in a note added for *L'Entretien infini*. His reader suspects that the ambivalence surrounding the articulations of non-reciprocity in this book is so compelling that Blanchot chooses as his reference the single publication most clearly intended to reduce the importance of Levinas' concepts.

of speaking and writing. This *parole* is precisely the impossibility of the comprehension prescribed by Plato. To say, as Blanchot does, that the *parole* "suddenly becomes the tranquil humanist and Socratic *parole*," is to make a statement about the *Phaedrus* and to extend this predication to Levinas, in whose text the concept of the *parole* has quite the opposite function. And the context of this Blanchotian claim is the elucidation of a problematic — non-reciprocity — which is borrowed precisely from Levinas.

The function of the *Phaedrus* intervention in Blanchot's reading of Levinas is important and overdetermined. On one hand, the independence and presence suggested by the Other's assistance in his own signification tend, as discussed above, to give the Other the predicates of another Self or subject, another center of gravity — and this tendency reduces non-reciprocity to correlation and comprehension. On the other hand, the overall context of such a reduction would constitute an equation of the *éthique* with theology, in which alterity tends to be subordinated to communion. Blanchot's adoption of this view, although inadequate for a reading of Levinas, is significant as a gesture concerning his own proximity to the latter. It reaches its most important point in the essay "Tenir parole", which immediately follows "Connaissance de l'inconnu" in *L'Entretien infini*.[45] Here, Blanchot rejects both *hauteur* and the *éthique* as contexts of the *parole*, on most contradictory grounds. He writes: "Emmanuel Levinas would say that [the inequality of non-reciprocity] is of an ethical order, but I find in this word only derivative senses. That *Autrui* is superior to me, that his *parole* is a *parole* of *hauteur*, of eminence, these metaphors appease, by putting it in perspective, a difference so radical that it escapes any determination other than itself."[46] Thus, to speak of the *parole* as an *hauteur* (and of this *hauteur* as the factor of an *éthique*) is to impose a predication or "determination" upon an alterity too radical for any predication whatever (by virtue of its inadequation to comprehension and to the dimension of the Same), and thus to put this alterity in a "perspective" which reduces its radicality.

Levinas' reader knows that *hauteur* designates non-reciprocity, and that the word *éthique* describes a proximity defined as the inaccessibility and incumbence of non-reciprocity in the Other's approach. ("I call *éthique* a relation between terms in which the one and the other are united neither by a synthesis of understanding nor by the relation of subject to object and in which however one weighs upon or concerns or is significant to the other. . ."[47] "A placing in question of the Same — which cannot take place within the egoistic spontaneity of the Same — is produced by the Other. We call this placing in question of my spontaneity by the presence of Autrui, the *éthique*."[48]) The words *hauteur* and *éthique* describe the dissymmetry of a rapport of the Same with an alterity which (1) cannot be determined within the Same, and which (2) cannot be placed in a perspective by or within the Same. This is its alterity, and its proximity. The existence of alterity, and its inadequation to the dimensions of the Same, constitute the necessary and sufficient definition of the Levinasian *éthique*. To refuse the terms *hauteur* and *éthique* as reductive, panoramic predicates, in favor of a configuration which is the very sense of these terms, is to refuse the *éthique* in the name of the *éthique*, to refuse *hauteur* in the name of *hauteur*, and ultimately to refuse non-reciprocity in the name of non-reciprocity. The latter concept enters Blanchot's text by way of a detour, which is the text of Levinas. The meaning of Blanchot's gesture is a refusal of Levinas. It implies that the dissymmetry of the *entretien* has no need of the Levinasian concepts in order to accomplish itself discursively, and that these concepts, in their theological bias, reduce the alterity of the *parole* and subsume it in a reciprocal perspective. Thus the inability to thematize non-reciprocity without reducing it, which haunts Blanchot's thinking of both *parole* and *entretien*, is ascribed to Levinas.

*

Although it would not be true to say, in homage to Levinas' genius, that Blanchot cannot thematize communication's dissymmetry "without Levinas" (since, as discussed earlier, the dissymmetry of a rapport with alterity is required, implicitly and explicitly, by Blanchot's basic concepts, and most notably by the theme of the approach), it is nevertheless true, in a Proustian sense, there are compartments or zones of the Blanchotian text which do not communicate easily. The concept of non-reciprocity which is palpable in the approach to the fictional event, to Eurydice, to death, to the image, or to the exterior in *errance*, resists Blanchot's efforts to clarify it when the context is an intersubjective presence. In this context, the symmetrical figure of the *entretien* repeatedly confuses the notion of dissymmetry. As seen above, the proximity of Levinas to Blanchot's efforts to thematize the dissymetrical approach in intersubjectivity, leads to an ambivalent and contradictory attempt to eliminate this proximity. Such a gesture is most rare in Blanchot, whose independence from the intellectual currents of his time is so extreme, and whose discourse is so private. Its violence results from the importance of the encounter with Levinas, which concerns the entirety of *L'Entretien infini* in its title and its project, and also the overall movement of Blanchot's thinking in the 1960's, which tends to concentrate its energy upon the topic of the *parole* in intersubjectivity. In the privacy of his marginality in a phenomenological universe which became a formalist universe, Blanchot was not alone. In proximity to him was Emmanuel Levinas. When the Other in Blanchotian proximity became *Autrui.* the detour of Levinas became an inevitability.*

* In 1975 Blanchot published a lengthy and complex essay on Levinas entitled "Discours sur la patience" (*Le Nouveau Commerce,* nos. 30–31, printemps 1975, pp. 19–44; reprinted with revisions in *L'Ecriture du désastre,* Gallimard, 1980, pp. 28–58). This essay, which postdates the publication of *Autrement qu'être ou au delà de l'essence* and treats the concept of "passivity" which concerned Levinas in the late 1960's and early 1970's, is an attempt to articulate the Levinasian questions in a somewhat different spirit from that of the studies discussed above. It must be said that this attempt is unsuccessful, for several reasons. In the first place, Blanchot introduces Levinasian passivity (the heteronomy of the Same in the proximity of alterity) by means of terms familiar to him, such as neutrality (p. 25), *souffrance* (p. 25), death (*passim*), immediacy (p. 37), and the specialized term *désastre.* These terms have in common the implication of alterity as undifferentiation and dispersion. It is the latter term that Blanchot invokes as a predicate for subjectivity's heter-

ALTERITY AND ECONOMY IN LEVINAS

The principle of the *autrement qu'être*, the idea of the infinite, subjectivity, and manifestation, in Levinas, is communication. Differentiation or separation — the fact that being is what Levinas calls an "economy" — is an ontological event which presupposes alterity and alteration. The proposition of multiplicity and relation cannot be coherently derived from a view of exteriority as a homogeneous totality, but requires the concept of difference and differential heteronomy: the fact that closure becomes involved with an instance outside closure.

onomy in its assignation by the Other, throughout his essay. Blanchot correctly states that the subjectivity produced by assignation and responsibility is not an identity. It is a "temporary singularity" (p. 24), a "simulacrum of unity" (p. 33), "no longer me" (p. 30). However, Blanchot fails to understand that the approach of alterity which "denucleates" identity in Levinas, simultaneously produces subjectivity's *nouvelle origine* as the unicity of separation: a non-totalized, non-interchangeable unicity whose name is "responsibility" (i.e. an inspiration by alterity and a response to alterity). On the basis of this misunderstanding, Blanchot argues that a "dispersion" which is not an identity cannot be termed a "subjectivity", since this term signifies the integral spontaneity of a phenomenologically defined consciousness (p. 41), and cannot be termed a "responsibility", since this term presupposes an assumption of alterity on a Sartrian-Hegelian model (pp. 32, 34, 39). Again, as in his earlier readings of the term *éthique*, Blanchot simply refuses to read Levinas closely and to understand the sense of the latter's predications. And again, as in these earlier readings, the consequence of this refusal is an involuntary restoration of the theme of reciprocity. Blanchot argues that, since the approach of the Other reduces identity to dispersion, interiority itself is now other "in the same sense" that alterity is other: "since the Same substitutes itself for the Other, it is now in me. . . that the traits of transcendence (. . .) are marked. . . ." (p. 31) "(S)ubjectivity, as an exposition wounded, accused and persecuted, as a sensibility abandoned to difference, falls in its turn outside being, signifies the beyond-being, (. . .) is, in the same sense as *autrui* and the *visage*, the enigma which upsets the order and exceeds being. . . ." (pp. 36–7) Thus Blanchot misunderstands the non-reciprocity of proximal alteration. When the Same is altered by the Other's approach, the former does not become equal to the latter. (Its passivity is its lack of totalization and attribute; my passivity is an exposion to this lack which concerns. Its escape from totalization is a lack and an excess, a trace and an approach. My lack of totalization is the non-indifference and desire produced by this approach. It escapes: I desire. It approaches: I receive and, in inspiration, I respond. The movement of inspiration is a "one-way" movement. Etc.) The failure of totalization in proximity does not produce an interiority whose dispersion is "the same" as that of the Other, but is the very alterity which creates interiority as a discontinuity or unicity, and not as a dispersion. The aternative of identity and dispersion is inadequate to the concept of proximity, in Blanchot as well as in Levinas. Were alteration defined as dispersion, Same and Other would be adequated in the reciprocity and equality of a new element: a Same or an alterity defined as dispersion itself. The concept of alterity would be reduced — as it is indeed reduced in the least important of contemporary ideologies. In the context of this involuntary return to a configuration of reciprocity, Blanchot again defines *autrui* as the other subject. "(I)f I reverse the rapport, *Autrui* is related to me as though I were the Other." (p. 29) He then superimposes the spectrum of concrete intersubjective relations over the involvement of Same with Other, and argues that since, in Levinas' system, I must be responsible even for the Other who persecutes me, this situation resembles "sado-masochism" (p. 31). Thus, on the basis of a misunderstanding of differential unicity as dispersion, of *autrui* as "others" or "the other subject", and of inspiration and the *parole* as the "responsibility" of common sense, Blanchot again fails to account in his own terms for the Levinasian logic of proximity. And, again, the logical figure which signals this failure is reciprocity itself.

Correlation, the arm of totalization, *par excellence*, is itself a moment of being's alteration in the event of separation. Same and Other Same cannot be thought within the Same. Only the presence or approach of the Other can make possible this correlation. Multiplicity is unthinkable without exteriority. It is this argument, more than any other, that animates Levinas' mature philosophy. Differentiation produces *essence* (being defined as totalization) and eventually manifestation (discontinuity defined as illumination) – but it produces these possibilities on the basis of a more fundamental configuration: communication as alteration and heteronomy. Relation proceeds from what Levinas calls "pluralism": the communication of the Same with alterity, as a function of separation. *Essence*, the totalization or "catalysis" which grounds identity and non-contradiction, is a spectrum in which communication becomes distinction and correlation: an immobility of beings and the "allergy" of their separation. The principle of this spectrum is adequation: the spurious non-violence of a distribution of beings through an adequate and totalizing differentiation. The latent principle of this model of differentiation is power. Levinas would certainly agree with Bataille and Blanchot that *essence* or the "totality" must also be termed "the possible' : the region in which closure is a function of power. He would also agree that the distinctions and determinations of this region are supported and animated by the "underneath" of impossibility: the obscure dimension in which every conation is a contamination, every closure a heteronomy, every totality a communication. Impossibility, the principle of an economy without negation or power, is the latent birth of what Levinas calls the *esse* of being: an *esse* which is also an *interesse*, a spectrum of closure whose communication is exhausted by the alternative of autonomy and dependence upon another autonomy. Without the secret excess of an "other space" in which unicity is produced as a receptivity to exteriority – without an *autrement qu'être* haunting *essence* from within and without – this domain of autonomy and determination would be an impossibility. Only the "non-allergy" of beings can ground their allergy in totalization.

The *autrement qu'être* is this latent *desinteresse* of closure in impossibility. It is communication's production of a closure which is an excess and an incompletion. The words "excess" and "excession" intervene regularly in Levinas and, along with the notions of economy, loss, sacrifice, and *non-savoir,* describe his profound and unacknowledged proximity to Bataille. Excess is the economic principle of unicity in differentiation, and the principle of alterity. In the process of separation, interiority's excess produces its quiddity on the basis of a detour through an instance irreducible to quiddity: exteriority or alterity. The Same, in the general economy, is always "Même par l'Autre" – "same through the other." Levinasian separation is an incompletion whose hyperbolic density results from the pressure of alterity in differentiation. Exteriority is the "insufficiency" of closure in the economy, as Levinas writes in *Totalité et infini*,[49] but it is this insufficiency, this inadequation and impossibility, as a function of an "enormity" or "démesure". Closure is "more and more one to the point of explosion, fission, opening."[50] The Bataillian concept of affirmation or transgression, understood as a being without negation which produces a congruence of excess and insufficiency, is perceptible in all of Levinas' basic definitions.

Communication is a passivity in being: an inability of the existent to accomplish its entry into existence without the detour of an involvement with alterity. This involvement is a heteronomy, but not a determination. The pressure of alterity in differentiation is not a power, but the Other of power. Alterity is a lack of positivity or effectivity whose insistence defines being itself as such a lack, within the very hyperbole of its intensity or density. The turgidity of closure, the "reality" or actuality of existence, is a function of this excess and intensity of differentiation — and this intensity is always already a fundamental exposition, vulnerability, or subjection. It is in the moment of this exposition or passivity that, in Levinas' phrase, "l'être s'altère". Being is a contamination and an alteration. This is why, and how, being is an economy.

The alterity which produces closure, when considered in its own "quiddity", emerges as an instance without attributes or substantiality, and which, by virtue of this lack, approaches or concerns the Same. "Not the Other, but the trace of the Other" is the form of this alterity. Illeity, the perennial "profile" of that which may never be viewed directly as a presence, is the escape of alterity from manifestation. Its context is inextricable from that of neutrality and impersonality in Blanchot, and from the "il" of il y a in Blanchot and Levinas. The trace is the factor of an excess in being which escapes illumination or existence while conditioning these possibilities. As such, it haunts manifestation. "This way of passing while disturbing the present without allowing itself to be invested by the archè of consciousness, streaking with lines the clarity of the ostensible, I have called the trace."[51] Like the image in Blanchot, the trace is an instance whose ineliminable involvement with interiority designates it as an evanescence or "retreat", and also as an incumbence. Thus it is "an enormous presence and the retreat of this presence. The retreat is not a negation of the presence, nor its pure latency, which would be recuperable in memory or actualization."[52] The presence of alterity is what the philosophy of difference correctly terms an impossibility of presence. This is the sense of Levinas' distinction between the "retreat" and latency. The Other is not a presence, but the "excess of proximity."[53] Its excess is its lack or écart with regard to its own positivity, and its production of the écart which is closure's subjectivity. As it escapes, it creates the subjectivity that will pursue it — as Levinas showed so compellingly in his readings of phenomenology. "An excession of the here, as locus, and of the now, as hour, an excession of the contemporaneity of consciousness — which leaves a trace."[54] The Levinasian trace is the immemorial persistence of a difference, and this has been its influence in European thought. When considered in its approach or incumbence as well as in its escape, the trace — alterity's inadequation to manifestation — becomes the truly impersonal instance called the visage. Levinas often explains that this term does not describe a presence or manifestation of alterity in the intersubjective autrui, but indicates the excess of this alterity over the presence of such a subject. As discussed earlier, the proximal term *Autrui*, in its concatenation with illeity and the trace, cannot itself be defined as the "others" of intersubjectivity. *Autrui* is not a subject, and the *visage* is not a face. "It is in the trace of the Other that the *visage* glimmers: that which presents itself is absolving itself from my life and visits me as already absolute. Someone has already passed."[55] The approach of alterity in the *visage*, considered in its communicatonal intrication with interiority, is called the "idea of the infinite." This "idea" is not an idea, not an instance adequate to consciousness, but rather a communication or proximity, a "surplus inadequate to intentionality,"[56] an *ideatum* which "exceeds its idea,"[57] and the "impossible exigency" by which subjectivity "contains more than it is possible to contain"[58] or "thinks more than it thinks."[59]

"A thought which thinks more than it thinks is Desire."[60] Desire is the rapport of subjectivity to a proximity produced by differentiation and inadequate to intentionality. As discussed earlier, desire is not the attribute of a consituted subjectivity, but is the communicational constitution of subjectivity as a proximal moment in being. Thus desire is not the need of an unfulfilled totality, but is the fundamental incompletion of closure in a universe without the possibility of fullfillment (that is, of investment as adequation, as opposed to the "too much" and "not enough" of proximal investment). In other words, desire is the economy of totalization itself in proximity. The excess "measured" by desire, in Levinas' words, is also the excess which desire itself is. "The excess measured by Desire is a *visage*."[61] Desire, ascribed to interiority, and the *visage* ascribed to alterity, are correlated not by their appropriation to each other, but by the inadequation they describe. Their rapport "confirms" separation rather than to reduce it. The "measure" of alterity means "the very impossibility of measure."[62] Desire is thus the economic event by which, when I approach the Other, it is still the Other that is approaching me. Desire is the intensity and dispossession of an invested interiority. As mentioned earlier, Blanchot calls this configuration the "passion of the exterior" or the "obsession of existence" in impossibility. Interiority's desire, like its *parole*, is the Other's force or domination, and does not belong to interiority. When the Other approaches, it escapes. When it invests interiority as a pre-originarity, it also escapes. The Other's "apatridie" or "statelessness", its "étrangeté" or "foreignness", inadequate to punctuality and locus – its escape – "is incumbent upon me."[63] Exteriority is a difference to which interiority cannot be indifferent. By its very distance, it forces subjectivity outside itself. The Other, in its escape, produces desire through its approach.

Alterity is produced in the general economy by the failure of differentiation to equal the distinctions of negativity. This failure, this "weakening" of the negative, produces the lack and the remainder which are closure's Other. The presence or incumbence of this Other which dispossesses every proximal unicity, is the element and reality of the Same: a passivity within being. The impersonality of subjectivity as a modality of differentiation is an important aspect of Levinas' thinking. It designates both his lack of affinity with traditional valorizations of human subjectivity, which are actually valorizations of consciousness as manifestation (the larger "impersonality" of correlation within the totality), and his basic affinity to Blanchot's concept of communication as impersonality. Subjectivity is not consciousness, is not even human subjectivity, but is the modality of what Bataille called the *expérience du dedans* or interior experience of being. When subjectivity becomes consciousness or ipseity, the latter's economy must be conceived in terms of the larger economy of communication. Consciousness appears "upon the foundation of this primordial relation of obsession which no consciousness can annul — and of which consciousness itself is a modification."[64] The word "obsession" in Blanchot and Levinas describes the incumbence of alterity which creates interiority — an incumbence which is perhaps the ultimate sense of the enigma of "obsession" in its common usage (i.e. an idea which touches consciousness in an inextrication). For Levinas, this incumbence is a "gravity" in being: the "one-way" movement by which alterity, in the weakening of the negative, "falls upon" the Same to create the Same. "Ipseity 'takes upon itself,' in the absolute incapacity of escaping proximity, the *visage*, the poverty of this *visage*, where infinity is also absence. More exactly: the upsurge of ipseity is the very fact of this gravity in being."[65] Levinas' bracketing of the phrase "takes upon itself" accents the fact that subjectivity, in its basic economy, does not "assume" the gravity of alterity, but is itself the inaccessibility, excess, and proximity of alterity. Thus subjectivity is "the Other inside the Same", but not as an adequation or reduction of alterity, and thus not as a consciousness.[66] The reason Levinas sometimes refers to the general economy as a proximity is that its gravity indicates a movement or approach which is unthinkable in terms of totalization or determination, and which is the very economy of the economy. "Proximity is not a state, a repose, but precisely a disquiet, a *non-lieu* [a dimension without locus]."[67] In *Autrement qu'être ou au delà de l'essence*, Levinas defines proximity as an "ensemble broken by the difference between the terms in which however the difference is a non-indifference and the rupture — obsession."[68] The only "version" of determination in the general economy is that which forecloses determination and the quiddity of the economy's "terms": communication.

Alterity in Levinas is then an Other of closure which produces closure in differentiation, precisely as an alteration. Viewed in its escape, this alterity is a trace. Viewed in its incumbence, it is an approach, an inspiration, and a dispossession (an *insufflement* which creates an *essoufflement*). Viewed as an escape which approaches, it is the *visage*, the idea of the infinite, *Autrui*. Subjectivity in Levinas is the passivity of closure produced by alterity's incumbence. It is a conation in reverse, "in itself through the Other",[69] a conation whose effort or exigency is already the *subir* of passivity.[70] It is a primordial involvement with exteriority, and a "manner" the economy has of accomplishing itself — without, however, describing an adequation. The totalization of *essence* or the totality is a "modification" of this primordial production of subjectivity in the "alteration" of being. Levinas' debt to phenomenology, like that of Bataille or Blanchot, is this irony. Subjectivity is indeed rooted "within being", as is the consciousness of dialectics, but not as an interval and illumination guaranteed by negation. The form of its "participation" in differentiation and temporalization is precisely its susceptibility and inadequation to the disproportionate escape and approach of exteriority. The subjectivity of proximity experiences the intimacy and immediacy of disclosedness in the everyday, and the distance of exteriority's deployment — but not as an adequation, and not as a correlation. As mentioned earlier, proximal interiority "sleeps" in the fascination, immediacy and "naive natural attitude" denounced by phenomenology in all its stages. The latter's allergy to the quotidian, as attested brilliantly by Blanchot, is its discomfited intuition of impersonality in proximity. Subjectivity is the approach of alterity beyond or across negation, and the contamination of totalization which causes the *essence* as a whole to veer toward proximity and toward the *éthique*.

But this way the subject has of finding himself within *essence* — whose present and freedom *essence* itself, as a gathering together [*assemblée*], should have rendered possible — is not a harmonious and inoffensive participation. It is precisely the incessant buzzing that fills each silence in which the subject detaches himself from *essence* in order to pose himself as a subject over against his objectivity. A buzzing intolerable to a subject who liberates himself as subject, who assembles *essence* across from him as an object, but in which the extrication is unjustifiable in a continuous tissue, of absolute equity. The buzzing of the *il y a* — non-sense into which essence turns and into which, also, turns the justice which issues from *signification*. An ambiguity of sense and non-sense in being, sense turning into non-sense.[71]

Levinas' reader knows that the aggravated impersonality and apparent undifferentiation of the *il y a* which forecloses totalization and haunts manifestation as a "non-sens", is the principle of the *parole* in the economy. The buzzing, scratching, absolutely nonsensical noise of a presence beyond negation in being — a presence which cannot keep "still" in a dimension of correlation and illumination — is the *parole* itself: the unquiet displacement of a subjectivity which is no longer an illuminating interval in being, but the appearance of another sense or inclination, irreducible to presence or meaning: *pour l'autre*. The *il y a* is a haunting positivity of alterity which floods the intervals of comprehension. The *parole* is the latent *errance* of closure, nearly imperceptible within the totality, which is produced by this approach of the Other. The quotation above is an important articulation of the *il y a*, because it defines this moment not as an extremity reached by a constituted subjectivity in insomnia or even in the *cogito*, but as the only possible modality of a "rooting" of subjectivity in being. The noise is not an instance heard by subjectivity — it is subjectivity itself: the irreducibility of differentiation to negation, and of communication to closure.

The grounding of the *parole* in the excess of differentiation or separation is an impossibility on the part of subjectivity to extricate itself from alterity in order to illuminate it and render it objective. The region of the economy called *essence* or the totality, in which the *autrement qu'être* produces a conditioned totalization, appears on the foundation of this *parole* which exceeds and invests it. On one hand, this is why totalization "tends" toward the proximity with which it is already involved: toward transgression in Bataille, toward the night in Blanchot, and toward the *éthique* in Levinas. The *parole* makes possible the "opening" of illumination. "La pensée consiste à parler" — "thinking consists of speaking."[72] The *parole* "introduces the new into thought; the introduction of the new into a thought, the idea of the infinite — here is the very work of reason."[73] On the other hand, the *parole* of differentiation and communication must be distinguished from the comprehension it produces, and must be discovered as a disturbance haunting the margins and the intervals of the totality. Proximity is not only the condition of possibility, but also the *nouvelle origine*, the violent destiny, of comprehension. Outlawed by the "peace of reason", it is a harassing persistence of communication's *pour l'autre*. "(T)he *parole* proceeds from absolute difference."[74] It is an excess produced by a movement which proceeds from nowhere, which "begins with the Other,"[75] and inclines interiority toward alterity. The figure of this exterior toward which the totality veers in spite of itself is the *visage*. Exceeding its "plastic form", the *visage* "speaks".[76] In its lack of attributes the *visage* is an impoverishment or supplication, but in its incumbence and inspiration of interiority it is an *hauteur* which "tears" the *parole* from the latter. Its *parole* is already my *parole* which answers it. The conation of interiority, the very existence of the totality, is already a response or consent to this imperious proximity. This response is the *parole* which is interiority's only closure. To say that the *visage* speaks, and that subjectivity speaks in answer, is not to designate a correlation or reciprocity, but to indicate a force of inspiration which is a single movement and direction. The *parole* of the *visage* is the pressure of exteriority which inclines, forces and, in Levinas' words, "obliges" interiority toward the Other. The *parole* of the exterior animates and escapes interiority. It is neither a transitivity nor the correlate of a relation. It is rather the excess of communication over closure, and thus the principle of the economy. The Same, in its totality, veers toward the Other — whose very distance is an approach and a dispossession. The *pour l'autre* is the secret inclination of all autonomy. Levinas' perennial return to Husserl and sensation moves toward the point at which he can assert that "the sensible is already spoken."[77] The possibility of multiplicity is a possibility of receptivity, and the latter possibility implies a non-allergic response to the Other. This configuration underlines again the extreme proximity of Levinas to Bataille. Incarnation is already *dépense*, already the *rire*, already the sacrifice in transgression. "Animation, the very *pneuma* of *psychisme*, alterity in identity, is the identity of a body exposing itself to the Other, making itself "pour l'autre": the possibility of *giving*. The non-assemblable duality of the elements of this trope is the dia-chrony of the one-for-the-other."[78] Other and Same never constitute themselves as terms in a system. The Other never accomplishes itself as the "there" of an exterior presence — and thus it is the excess called *visage*. It is always "inside", always "already" inherent to closure, always the impersonal fact of closure's excess, from which and to which closure moves and speaks. This univocal movement of the exigency is the basis of non-reciprocity as the animation of interiority in the *parole*.

The last in a series of predicates which define subjectivity economically is its *cogito* and the egoism of its *Moi* or "self". The spontaneity of this regional and secondary moment at which the catalysis of identity organizes the totality, is invested by the Other. Although the totality will always function as a reduction of alterity and of proximity, it will also tend toward the "non-sense" of proximity and the *éthique*, because its investment by alterity is its latent incompletion and the force of its density. The "world", in Blanchot's phrase, is never entirely the "world", and this is why proximity retains the capacity to draw subjectivity "outside itself and perhaps outside everything." The *pour l'autre* and the *autrement qu'être* insist or "sleep" within the intervals of the totality, because these intervals are differences and therefore communications. As Levinas writes in his essay "Langage et proximité", manifestation does not proceed from the miracle of an illumination in being, but from the weight or gravity which are produced by being's alteration:

> It is not because, among beings, a thinking being structure as a Self exists, pursuing its ends, that being takes on a signification and becomes a world; it is because in the proximity of being the trace of an absence — or of the Infinite — inscribes itself, that there is impoverishment, gravity, responsibility, obsession, and the Self. The non-interchangeable *par excellence* — the I — is, in a world without play, in a permanent sacrifice, substitutes itself to others and transcends the world. But this is the source of speaking [*parler*], for it is the essence of communication.[79]

Being, for Levinas, is "a world in which one speaks and of which one speaks,"[80] before it can become a manifestation. "Society is the presence of being."[81] "Signification", in its common sense, proceeds from the "signification" of proximity, which is the *parole* and the *pour l'autre*. The real can have a meaning and a presence, because closure is not adequate to itself, but describes in its very closing the approach of the Other. Comprehension is first of all this approach and this communication, in the Levinasian term *société*: the non-allergy of Same and Other. Totalization proceeds from the proximity of being — but not as an adequation. The escape and approach of the Other, which invests while disarming the Same, produces a totality whose silence and immobility are the scene of communication's incessant and uneliminable noise: the *parole*.

SAME AND OTHER

FROM DIFFERENCE TO NON-INDIFFERENCE

The only positivity or unicity of entities within a dimension of differential free-play is their intrication with each other and with the element of their separation. The differential dimension is a field of general or absolute heteronomy: a heteronomy which does not describe the "dependence" of unicity upon an exterior autonomy. The closure of the differential entity is its communication with, and constitution by, the entire economy with which it is involved. But this overall or "general" economy, and the manifold differences or effects of difference which organize it, have no positivity beyond their indefinite and irreducible communications. In other words, this economy does not have the ontological positivity requisite for a determination of the differential entity. It is an economy which cannot produce totalization, and an economy which cannot itself be coherently postulated as a totality. It produces generality, but it is not a totality of this generality. Thus, its differences are not subordinated to distinction and the "negative" constitution which, in a system such as that posited by Saussure and structural linguistics, produces an operational or systematic positivity of the minimal or elementary differential "term". Without a negativity which would guarantee the totalization of the system, and a complementary negativity which would ground the positivity of a term in its "non-coincidence" with other terms, the system becomes a general economy, and the differential entity becomes an irreducible alteration. Every "term" within the economy is a heteronomous secondarity whose closure is its alteration by exteriority. The lack of distinction, self-coincidence or operational autonomy which characterizes the movements of this economy does not signify undifferentiation, but rather a differentiation without negativity and without totalization. Unicity and communication exist here, but not as totalization and opposition, or positivity and correlation. Thus the differential entity or singularity is, to paraphrase the Gilles Deleuze of *Différence et répétition*, entirely constituted, adequately and positively "differentiated", entirely individuated, and yet entirely "undetermined". Totalization, determination, non-contradiction and causality, are not the principles of its individuation. *Inachèvement* or incompletion, heteronomy, and alteration are these principles. In a differential economy, secondarity is a necessary and sufficient condition for unicity. No term is primary. Every term is "ex-centric", in the sense that it cannot receive or exchange information as a center or position.

The unicity of any term is its alteration — from "within" and "without" — by the element of its differentiation. Envisaged in its unicity, such a term has two basic aspects. On one hand, it describes, in its very closure, a referral or "renvoi" to the exterior "from which" it is differentiated. Its quiddity is its secondarity. The interrogation of this quiddity is immediately "referred" to a "beyond" or "outside" which is exterior to it without being distinct from it or non-coincident with it. The exterior is integral to this unicity. On the other hand, in its unicity, the differential singularity manifests its radical heteronomy: the fact that, in and by virtue of its closure, it is "affected" by the exterior. Jacques Derrida borrows from Lévinas the term *trace* for the description of closure as an alteration. This term indicates (1) the pre-originary involvement of unicity with another element which "has passed", which has escaped the substantiality of presence or manifestation, into an essentially immemorial past; (2) the contamination of an integrity which always "carries the trace" of the economy in which and from which it is differentiated; (3) the lack of substantiality or manifest presence of the differential entity, correlative to this communication (every entity is itself a trace, a pure alteration, before it may be envisaged as a unicity); and (4) the movement or instance of differential communication itself, in the global sense of difference as "movement of the trace."[1]

The *renvoi* or "referral" which affects unicity in the movement of the trace, is not a secondarity to a constituted and determining positivity, but is a heteronomy of every Same with regard to communication. Differentiation or individuation cannot be thought as articulations or correlations within an economy already understood as a totalized field. Differentiation involves all unicity with an element irreducible to unicity, an Other of closure which "affects" unicity as it produces the latter. The heteronomy of the Same is an intrication with the exterior, and the alterity of the exterior, rather than a dependence upon a transcendent effectivity which would be another Same. The *renvoi* refers "outward", toward other terms and immediately toward the Other of unicity, by virtue of its rooting in the alteration produced by the trace. The differential singularity is involved with an inactual and unsubstantial element, in the economy of its closure, and this involvement inclines this singularity "outward", not only as a function of interrogation, but also as a function of its very unicity. The trace indicates an inaccessibility with which unicity remains involved and, more importantly, an escaping alterity which contaminates or alters as it escapes. Thus the *renvoi* is a secondary moment proceeding from a primordial alteration. The interrogation of quiddity in difference is always referred "elsewhere" (in a configuration which mimics the movement of causal interrogation itself) — toward "this other term", "these others", "all these others", in a movement whose lack of termination or origin results from its involvement with the Other of closure. The referral "elsewhere" or "outside" directs interrogation into an economy without negation or totalization. The exterior — not a finite field of totalities — is the element of this referral. The philosophy of difference defines the term *signification* as this production of information on the basis of alteration. The differential singularity is a "sign" because it is an incompletion and a referral. And every singularity is a sign defined as a signifier, in a field without a transcendent or terminal signified, because no term in such a field is unaffected by the alteration which makes of every term a secondarity. The signifier exhausts the concept of differential unicity, since signification is a purely economic concept in an element without manifestation. The word "meaning" or "sense" in the philosophy of difference is derived from an economy of alteration in which the proposition of illumination or comprehension has no primordial pertinence. It is on this basis that the philosophers of difference criticize structural linguistics for its subordination of difference to distinction and opposition — a subordination which is rooted in a logic whose latent principle is manifestation.

Meaning or signification in a differential dimension proceeds not from the priority of manifestation and totalization, but from their impossibility. It is the disturbance created by alteration in a heteronomous economy, and the "sense" of this disturbance: "outward", *au dehors*. The sign is a unicity affected by exteriority, and inclined toward exteriority. The referral points to an instance which can only escape totalization. As mentioned earlier, the thematic congruence of escape, ambiguity and indefinition, describes difference as a movement without "truth" in the sense of substantiality and totalization, and has tended to constitute both the accessibility and the controversial aspect of the philosophy of difference in recent decades. The escape from totalization is difference's inaccessibility to what Jacques Derrida calls, in a Heideggerian inspiration, a "metaphysics" of presence, substantiality, and non-contradiction which dominates the West's thinking of communication. The notion of the irrecuperable escape, of the irreducibility of categories of presence and totalization in Western metaphysics, and of the need for an adjustment of Western concepts to the excess of difference over totalization, is the thematic horizon of Derrida's presentation of difference. As discussed earlier, this thematic spectrum proceeds from a thinking of communication in abstraction from the proposition or eventuality of manifestation, and from a confrontation of this interrogative mode with a surrounding epistemological culture whose consistent presupposition is manifestation as the element of communication. Against this background, one of Derrida's most important contributions to the philosophy of difference in his designation of "deconstruction" as a discursive strategy which must exceed the voluntaristic ambiguity of its name, and must problematize the epistemological aims or exigencies of the metaphysics whose concepts it necessarily repeats. Totalization is not simply an inherited conceptual orientation. It is rather, in a sense most clearly described by Bataille in his Nietzschian inspiration, a manner of thought in its relation to subjectivity as closure. Totalization is not only a proposition, but also an exigency. Thought's involvement with this exigency is not an inherited conceptual schema, and is not limited to occidental culture. Deconstruction is therefore not only a manipulation of concepts whose perennial implication is totalization and manifestation (an implication Derrida evokes under the name of "presence", but whose larger context is autonomy as a principle of communication). It is also an attempt to influence or "displace" a fundamental orientation of discursivity toward closure, in its own communicational constitution. Like Bataille's "method of meditation", deconstruction must "leave by a project the domain of the project" — and this movement entails a new discovery of passivity, rooted in the inspiration of Nietzsche. The philosopher of deconstruction, like Bataille's "theologian" and Levinas' "metaphysician", must allow his own exigency toward pertinence and knowledge, in a most problematic sense, to exceed its own tendency to concentrate itself in the immobility of the discursive assertion or *dit*. This process is not strictly voluntary or strategic, but implies a new passivity of thought, and an excess over the detachment and indifference correlative to pertinence in its perennial definition. Deconstruction describes a mobilization of thought's affirmative economy (in an element without negation) which exceeds the reifying tendency of thought's involvement with closure and autonomy — an involvement which proceeds from thought's rooting in the discontinuity produced by difference itself. Yet this passivity remains a mobilization. The "signification" or inspired heteronomy of thought remains an exigency. The ambivalence of this configuration is integral to the economy of signification, and is the very "history" of thought. It is not to be superceded or lamented, but to be studied for its own dynamics. Thus the philosophy of difference becomes an epistemology, within its very anti-intellectualism.

The passivity of deconstruction is also an impersonality. The concepts within a given discursive text, or the larger text of discursivity in general, are the locus of deconstruction — and not the critical philosopher who would read and "deconstruct" these texts. Deconstruction is a conceptual economy rather than a mere strategy. These two notions — passivity and impersonality — have been the least understood predicates of deconstruction, partially because Derrida tends to thematize this concept as a "patient", interminable strategy, a "calculated" affirmative excess. But when he speaks of a "patient" and "interminable" displacement of concepts, Derrida describes the excess of deconstruction over the voluntarism of the project. Deconstruction is ultimately a differential play and alteration of concepts, and not an adjustment of concepts by a critical reader.* This is its sense as "the other of a construction", rather than as a

---

* This altering communication of concepts is often attested by Derrida and his students as the ambivalence of a discursive personality who "deconstructs" — most often inadvertently — his own tendencies toward a safeguarding of totalization, presence, etc. as principles of communication. "Declaring" the supremacy of comprehension, such a subject will "describe", as though in spite of himself, the escape of alterity from comprehension. This attestation is pertinent to the concept of difference as a textual principle, although it is of limited value for the thematization of an impersonality of deconstruction. In addition, since it ascribes the ambivalence of the exigency to a Rousseau or a Saussure while implicitly absolving the critical reader from this ambivalence, this interpretative tendency returns in

modification of Heidegger's prescription of a "destruction" of metaphysics. The passivity of deconstruction inclines it toward a communicational universe which is not Heideggerian, but Nietzschian. (The ambivalence of Derrida's own theoretical text takes the form of a contradictory oscillation between these two names, and more basically between these two universes.) The "interminability" of deconstruction is its impossibility, in a Bataillian sense. Deconstruction does not belong to a universe of totalization and power. It appears in a differential dimension for which these concepts are not ultimate: a dimension of passivity, inspiration, and affirmation. Although within Derrida's text it tends to assume the form of a critical unmasking of presuppositions, deconstruction in a larger context is not a critical procedure, but a communicational rapport with difference itself, at the level of the concept.

The ambiguity of deconstruction attests a second and most basic character of difference as a model for communication. Although the freeplay and indefinition of differential singularities in the movement of the trace implies an escape and an "elsewhere", it also describes an orientation, inclination, or dissymetrical sense in being. Escape from totalization is correlative to a movement and a passivity in differentiation. The *renvoi* is a heteronomy of the differential entity which is also its rapport to an investing or inspiring exteriority. The trace is certainly a *non-sens*, an impossibility of meaning as totalization. But it is also a differential alteration as "signification" — that is, as a contemporaneity and communication of singularities in their heteronomy. The "sense" of this communication is univocal: "outward", "toward the Other", "into the exterior". The *renvoi*, produced by the altering inherence of the trace, is not a movement of the interrogative eye which envisages the singularity, but is an inclination of the singularity itself, as a function of its economy. The trace contaminates closure and quiddity by involving unicity with an Other of closure — but, by virtue of this contamination, it also forces this unicity "outside itself", "outside everything", toward exteriority. The "sense" of the trace, and the "signification" affecting closure, are the univocity of this "one-way" movement which creates closure as an alteration. When Derrida

---

spite of itself to the Heideggerian procedure which admires the audacity of a textual subject who nevertheless "remains rooted" in metaphysics' reductive values and predications. Although the critical reader may self-critically attest that his own interpretation remains trapped within the same spider's web of reification, that alterity exceeds language's power to attain it, etc., the affirmative economy of thought is obscured by the intellectualism of this attestation. The escape of alterity from a thought defined exclusively as the univocity and voluntarism of reification, is not an authentically communicational concept, but repeats philosophy's perrennial respect for the Other's power to escape our power to capture. The notion of difference implies an investment of thought by alterity in the configuration of inspiration and affirmation. The Heideggerian intellectualism with which many readers speak of a Rousseau, a Husserl, or even a Nietzsche or Freud "in spite of himself" implies a universe exhausted by the proposition of totalization and its frustration, of reification and escape from reification. This is a universe whose principle of coherence, as mentioned in earlier sections of the present study, is not difference but negativity.

writes, "the trace is in effect the absolute origin of meaning [*sens*] in general. Which is to say . . . that there is no absolute origin of meaning in general,"[2] he describes a lack of terminus and a lack of totalized or manifest "meaning" in difference. But he also describes the philosophy of difference's definition of the word *sens* as the altering movement of communication's heteronomy. *Sens* is the intensive dispossessing of closure which produces the possibility of communication in the economy of difference — and which thus produces the eventuality of the very "meaning" which will be recuperated as manifestation in Western metaphysics. *Sens* is the heteronomy of closure which allows the latter to be affected by something outside itself. Thus *sens*, the *pour l'autre* of closure, is the possibility of communication and of signification. The *renvoi* is always an escape, but always an *au dehors*, "outward", an inclination of closure toward the communication which constitutes and alters it. Derrida's interest in the notion of the "general economy" indicates this most Bataillian dimension of his thought. The singularity in the differential economy is always a *dépense*, a loss, a dispossession into the exterior, as a function of its closure. Thus it is not only the differential entity which escapes interrogation, into its heteronomous economy. It is also this entity which escapes and transgresses itself toward the Other, as a function of its primordial lack of self-coincidence, which proceeds from its pre-originary intrication with alterity. Closure is a becoming-other, a *glissement*, an invested dispossession, as the principle of its intense unicity. The trace is the animation of the *renvoi*; and both these concepts describe a univocal or dissymetrical excession of interiority toward the exterior. As in Levinas' complex descriptions of intersubjectivity, this movement of excession may appear to describe an involvement with "another" entity or with "other entities", but its true inclination is toward the "other of the entity", the exterior. (This is why Saussure, in spite of his explicit naming of the concept of difference, is not a serious inspiration in the philosophy of difference. The general economy is not a system.)

The *renvoi* is always an *au dehors*. Although it describes an escape of communication from closure, and a consequent escape of closure from totalization, the *renvoi* proceeds from the trace which invests closure. The economy of closure in differentiation is a passivity and a receptivity which is always immediately an escape and a loss: a capacity to be affected by alterity which is a "going to the Other". Derrida says very well that the "passivity" produced by the trace — the immemorial intrication of closure with a past that was never present — is also its "rapport à l'avenir,"[3] a rapport with a future that is also an *à venir*. Closure is an involvement in repetition with a futural element which is no less irrecuperable than the past of the trace. Temporal differentiation produces multiplicity as communication and alteration, rather than as distinction and correlation. The conditioned unicity of the differential singularity orients it toward an irrecuperable exteriority, in a time of alteration. The escaping past and future, which were not and will not become present, are the temporal element of a closure whose unicity is its involvement with the exterior. As such, they concern and invest closure. This is the non-indifference of unicity in a differential economy: an inextrication or implication with regard to alterity which is an impossibility of locus or position with regard to alterity. When Derrida, in a Levinasian-Blanchotian inspiration, derives the passivity of the *parole* from its differential economy, he relates this passivity to *espacement* (the differential constitution and consequent inextrication of space and time) and to the *temps mort* of being without presence or actuality.[4] This lack of presence is also a lack of position or integrity, which designates every Same as a becoming-other, and thus as a fundamental passivity. The *parole* as subjectivity is a rapport of interiority to its alteration in death — but not in the death produced by negativity.[5] Death describes an Other of interiority which conditions the latter in its excess over its own self-coincidence. Every subject is a rapport to his own disappearance, by virtue of the becoming-other which is unicity in the general economy. The "économie de la mort" which informs this alteration is the economy of what Blanchot calls "death without truth": a death which does not organize a totalized existent through a negating function, but which prevents this totalization through its differential function. The inclination of subjectivity toward exteriority in its primordial alteration is the *parole* which roots interiority in the larger economy of difference, which Derrida calls by various names, including *archi-écriture, économie, dissémination,* etc.

The detour by which a differential singularity accomplishes its conation "through the other" is also the detour by which interiority's quiddity is its *pour l'autre.* Differential interiority is always "au dehors" (within the exterior), i.e. produced in an economy without autonomy or totalization — and also "au dehors" ("toward the outside") in the sense of its conation "inside out", i.e. its passive exposition and its inspired heteronomy. The economy of difference produces an intense unicity inclined toward exteriority. For this reason, deconstruction can never be a panoramic overview of the general economy, but must understand itself to be an intrication with this economy and thus a passivity. The frustration of a metaphysics which cannot thematize its beyond, inherited by a transgressive comportment which must employ the concepts of this metaphysics in order to approach this beyond, is not the ultimate context of deconstruction, but rather its major temptation. Difference does not describe the absolutely other which escapes thematization. It is rather the powerless other which invests and contaminates thematization as it escapes totalization. The duality of totalization and its frustration is not adequate to the concept of difference, and this is why the notion of strategy is not adequate to the violence of deconstruction. The value of disorientation, loss of meaning, and lack of foundation associated with difference in Derrida's text, proceeds precisely from the passivity discovered in deconstruction as a communicational moment. Considered simply as a discursive strategy which explodes presuppositions in its discovery of new forms of pertinence, deconstruction would be indistinguishable from the perennial, iconoclastic aggressivity of philosophy, in its respect for the escape of the absolutely other, and its enthusiasm for its own approximations. Deconstruction is not a strategy, but rather a transgression, in the Bataillian sense of this word. Its violence is its excess over its own discursive or critical context — this excess being necessarily a passivity. Deconstruction does not "demolish the old structure": it is, instead, an experience of communication. Having attested the impossibility of totalization as a principle of communication, it does not reproduce the pertinence of totalization in a new and more forceful language. It is a new "manner" of thought, in a Nietzschian inspiration, and not the discovery of a new and superior efficiency of thought. It cannot compete with the "truth" of totalization which it so convincingly perceives as a conditioned pertinence. It is for this reason that the philosophy of difference is criticized for "taking truth away and giving us nothing in return." At the same time, the failure to perceive the passivity of deconstruction, and the enthusiastic tendency to recuperate this concept in a critical inspiration, has dominated the reception of Derrida's concepts in Western philosophy. This tendency may result from the ambiguity of the term "deconstruction" in its voluntaristic and Heideggerian aspect. It may also result from the regularities of Derrida's own theoretical practice, which tends to privilege the terms of metaphysics and escape and tends to pose the differential economy in a largely epistemological overview. From this panoramic perspective, the sense of the trace and the *renvoi* as escape, indefinition and ambiguity, and the sense of metaphysics as closure, appear to be ultimate, and obscure the economic implications of difference in its rapport with closure in general, and interiority in particular.

*

The rapport of difference with subjectivity is derived from the non-indifferent heteronomy of the communicational entity, and from the univocity of the differential alteration which produces this non-indifference. This rapport has been most clearly stated by Gilles Deleuze in his *Différence et répétition*. In a brilliant situation of difference with regard to philosophy and science, Deleuze defines differential communication not only as an indefinite intrication (described by the terms *implication, complication, enveloppement,* etc.), but also as a fundamental dissymetry or inequality which produces unicity or "individuation" as an inspired passivity. This inequality is correlative to the remainder or *reste* which haunts differential unicity and inclines or forces it toward the exterior. A regularity of Deleuze's exposition is the notion of difference as intensity and force, analogous to the incumbence of proximity, which always produces discontinuity as a non-indifference. "Contrary to extensive quantities, intensive quantities are thus defined by enveloping difference — the distances enveloped — and the unequal-in-itself which describes a natural 'remainder' as the material of a change in nature."[6] Differential discontinuity is an "extension" which is always already "intensive" and enveloping. Exteriority or plurality in a differential field is the intensity of alteration. Closure is an inequality "in itself": the dissymetry of an altering orientation toward the exterior. "Every individuality is intensive: therefore cascading, flooding, communicating, including [*comprenant*] and affirming in itself difference in the intensities which constitute it."[7] When thematized in terms of receptivity or consciousness, differential intensity describes a radical passivity which exceeds and conditions the possibility of action. The sense of this passivity, and often its context,[8] is identical to that of impossibility in proximity. "Intensity is simultaneously the insensible and that which cannot but be sensed."[9] In a Nietzschian sense, intensity is that which cannot be thought "transitively", but which forces us to think, and, in the logic of impossibility, forces us to think difference. Transitivity and comprehension are no longer the sole dimension of thought's economy. "Thought must think difference, this [factor which is] absolutely different from thought, which however gives food for thought [*donne à penser*], gives thought a thought."[10] "We are forced to feel and to think difference."[11] Difference is no longer an escape from totalization which frustrates the panoramic vision of the epistemologist in search of origin, presence or terminus. It is an economic dimension which comprehends and invests the comportment of the thinker. It does not merely "escape the oppositions" of metaphysics while "making possible" these oppositions, in its function as the possibility of discontinuity or plurality. Escaping totalization, it creates the desire which pursues it — and this desire is not univocally transitive or reductive, but is a positive economic event. Thus Deleuze, whose inspirations are Nietzsche and Proust, reproduces the Levinasian universe of desire. Difference is unthinkable, and yet it "cannot but be thought." Like the *expérience* of proximity, it cannot be experienced, but the experience of it cannot be avoided. Its approach to subjectivity is pre-originary and dissymetrical. It invests the intentionality that would approach it. "When difference is subordinated by the thinking subject to the identity of the concept (even were this identity synthetic), what disappears is difference within thought, the difference of thought from thought, this *genitality* of thinking, this profound *fêlure* of the I which leads it to think only as a function of thinking its own passion."[12] The thinking of difference, like that of *non-savoir* and the *autrement qu'être*, is a non-indifference and an altering "passion" whose heteronomous force proceeds from difference itself: the proximity of exteriority. The possibility of thought is its inspiration, its differential alteration, its "genitality". In a universe whose principle is not manifestation but communication, difference introduces the "new" into thought, and creates thought as the affirmation of something new — something unpredictable and irrecuperable — as a function of repetition itself. In the text of difference as in that of proximity, the excess of communication over negation produces a dissymetry and a passivity whose name is "affirmation": the forcing of unicity "outward" in an element without negation. "(C)omprehending the unequal in itself, being already difference in itself, intensity *affirms* difference."[13]

Deleuze, like Levinas, is concerned with the situation of subjectivity within the economy of difference, and thus attests the impossibility of a panoramic view of this economy. The univocity of differential intensity or alteration describes a rapport of Same and Other, and not a synoptic view of alterity's circulation within the Same. The most fundamental context of this configuration is the question of subjectivity as a product of difference, in the most impersonal sense. From "How must we think difference?", the question becomes: "How does difference produce subjectivity?". In the most compelling and difficult Chapter 2 of *Différence et répétition,* entitled "La répétition pour elle-même", Deleuze systematically elaborates this production. Beginning with a citation of Hume's concept that the difference between identities in repetition proceeds from a "change in the mind that contemplates" repetition, Deleuze defines this change as a "contraction" of the repetition of temporal instants. The mind which contemplates repetition retains repeated instants and expects the appearance of the next repetition. But this retention and expectation are not modalities of reflection or consciousness. They are the very "contraction" of repetition as a temporal synthesis. The difference between moments in repetition is "soutirée" ("drawn", as in the image of a pouring from one container into another) from repetition itself, in its contraction. Contraction indicates an intensive coexistence or contemporaneity of repetitive instants by which past and future, or simply exterior repetitions insist within the present by virtue of their communication with each other. This insistence correlative to contraction is the differential rapport of these instants, and is, more fundamentally, the differential and therefore repetitive insistence of the instant and the entity in general. Repetition is contraction in time. Contraction is the inextrication of closure from the economy which surrounds and produces it. In other words, contraction, understood as a differentiation producing intensive intrication, is the modality of exteriority's production in difference and repetition. This production of exteriority is already a production of subjectivity. When Deleuze speaks of a difference "that the mind *draws* [*soutire*] from repetition,"[14] he describes the impersonal moment at which repetition in its contraction — its pressure, its gravity — produces a difference which is already subjectivity. Contraction is separation. The locus of subjectivity in this configuration is the passivity of the repetitive instant in contraction, and the passivity or heteronomy of the differential unicity which is produced by contraction. Subjectivity is a "power of contraction,"[15] produced by or "drawn" from the intensity of repetition itself. In other words, subjectivity is a passivity in being, a collapsing and contracting — the passivity of the differential and repetitive economy.

This synthesis must, in all respects, be named: passive synthesis. Constitutive, it is not however active. It is not made by the mind, but accomplishes itself *in* the mind which contemplates, preceding all memory and all reflexion. Time is subjective, but this is the subjectivity of a passive subject.[16]

The contraction which accomplishes itself "in" the mind that contemplates, is actually a producing of the mind that contemplates, by contraction or as contraction. This is the sense of the impersonal and passive verb *soutirer*. The word *contemplation* describes a production of passivity and alteration in being by difference and repetition — this passivity being a *soutirer* and a *contracter* of difference. When differentiation produces discontinuity as a pre-originary tendency to be affected and altered by exteriority, discontinuity becomes the possibility of subjectivity. Difference and repetition are themselves a subjectivity or passivity, before a constituted subjectivity might contemplate these instances. Differentiation itself is a contemplation.

But, in the order of constitutive passivity, the perceptual syntheses reflect organic syntheses, and a primary sensibility that we *are*. We are water, earth, light and air contracted, not only before recognizing or representing them, but before sensing them. Every organism is, in its receptive and perceptual elements, but also in its viscera, a sum of contractions, of retentions and of expectations [*attentes*: imminences].[17]

Subjectivity is not derived from an analysis of receptivity as an empirical given or as an evidence of manifestation, but rather from difference itself, which is a differentiation that contracts. Subjectivity is a modality of differentiation as communication and alteration, and not simply a predicate of receptivity. This is why the viscera as well as the sense organs "contemplate". The heteronomy of the Same is a contemplation of the exterior, in the exterior. "The passive Self is not defined simply by receptivity, that is, by the capacity to experience sensations, but by the contracting contemplation which constitutes the organism itself before constituting its sensations."[18] "We do not contemplate ourselves by ourselves, but we exist only in contemplating, that is, in contracting that from which we proceed."[19] Individuation is a passivity of differentiation in being: a differentiation which cannot totalize. For this reason, closure is an inspired alteration or "contemplation". The basic terms which structure the bulk of Deleuze's essay, including *apprendre*, pleasure principle, unconscious, habit, and above all *Idée*, presuppose and articulate this production of subjectivity by differentiation.

The similarity of Deleuze's thematization of contemplation to the Bataillian interior experience, to Levinasian sensation or separation, and to the *cogito* in Levinas and Blanchot, proceeds from the insistence with which Deleuze thinks proximity in all the basic moments of difference and repetition. Contraction, and the subjectivity or passivity produced by it, are the precise figures of proximity in repetition. The two basic predicates of this proximity are passivity and non-reciprocity. The expressions *je fêlé, moi dissous, moi passif*, describe the origin of receptivity in closure's heteronomy. The "asymmetry" of the passive synthesis, and of repetition in its generality, describes non-reciprocity. "The passive synthesis, or contraction, is essentially asymmetrical: it goes from the past to the future in the present, thus from the particular to the general, and in this way orients the arrow of time."[20] This passive synthesis is differentiation's lack of totalization in its production of time: a lack which constitutes time as a production of closure which dispossesses closure. The two additional temporal syntheses meditated by Deleuze — a "pure past" as the passing and passivity of time,[21] and the "empty form" of time as the *à venir*[22] — describe the dissymmetrical passivity of a time which escapes as it approaches, and a proximal communication of differentiated instants which is nevertheless not a reversibility or recuperability of these instants.[23] The present is the event of contraction (the differential investment of punctuality); the past is the element of alterity's escape from totalization which makes possible this event of contraction; and the "empty form" of time, the *à venir* of the eternal return, is the repetitive element of contraction: the Other's approach as a function of its escape. Time as repetition is a production of discontinuity through the dispossession of closure (which Deleuze calls "disparation": multiplicity without correlation) and through the incumbence of exteriority. Closure, in this dimension, is the dispossession, alteration of "dissolution" of the *je fêlé*, and also its investment or inspiration by the pressure of the eternal return. The form of ipseity is inequality: the force of an inadequation to exteriority. And inequality, the forcing of closure by alterity, is the possibility of time's "passing" or movement. Subjectivity in repetitive time is the "unequal in itself", because discontinuity in such a time is this inequality.[24] The third synthesis or *à venir* is the ultimate dimension of repetition which includes the pure past and the present of contraction ("the present and the past are in their turn nothing but dimensions of the future"[25]). The dispossessing imminence of the eternal return is simultaneously the incumbence or approach of the Other as the element of repetition, and the eschatological *pour l'autre* of subjectivity in its involvement with a time exceeding its spontaneity and punctuality. This is the time of affirmation, of transgression, and of the word *oeuvre* in both Blanchot and Levinas. "The synthesis of time constitutes here a future which affirms simultaneously the unconditioned character of the product with regard to its condition, and the independence of the *oeuvre* with regard to its author or actor."[26] Time is the element of an irrecuperable passing and an imminence which alters. Subjectivity is a passivity in time and as time. The proximity of Levinasian sensation, senescence, *liturgie*, *diaconie*, and eschatology to Deleuze's meditation of temporality is so palpable that the absence of Levinas' name among the many references in *Différence et répétition* is most remarkable.

The basic terms which structure *Différence et répétition* articulate many common aspects of difference and proximity, such as irreducibility to manifestation,[27] contamination of negativity,[28] movement,[29] and the exigency.[30] All these terms imply or explicitly articulate passivity and non-reciprocity: the essential non-indifference of difference as inequality, "disparation", univocity, *sens*, force, and the eternal return of the Same (which is no longer a Same, but the dissymmetry of the "return" as described by Blanchot). The verb *répéter*, in its comportmental sense and in its relation to psychoanalysis, describes a differentially constituted subjectivity whose irreducibility to spontaneity, manifestation, and power is the passivity of a movement *au dehors*: toward the future, toward what Deleuze calls "generality", toward the Other. "I do not repeat because I repress. I repress because I repeat, I forget because I repeat. I repress because, in the first place, I can live certain things or certain experiences only in the mode of repetition."[31] Repetition is the "double rapport" of proximal experience described by Blanchot: an intramundane configuration of activity which alternates with, but secretly reposes upon, the dimension of impossibility, in a reality without power. Repetition is temporalization in this reality without power, as Nietzsche clearly stated, and as the profoundly Proustian inspiration in Deleuze attests. Passivity is Proustian Time. "Underneath the self which acts, there are little selves [petits moi] which contemplate, and which render possible action and the active subject.[32] The interior discontinuity of subjectivity, its dispersion which is its closure, is subjectivity's investment and dispossession by the discontinuous element of Time, in which the repetition of Combray is the "essence" of Combray, whose irrecuperability does not exhaust its approach.

"A philosophy of repetition," writes Deleuze, "passes through all the 'stages', condemned to repeat repetition itself."[33] The exigency of such a philosophy is not to extricate its own movement from the passivity of repetition, in a new indifference of illumination, but rather to "make of repetition, not that from which one 'draws' a difference, nor that which includes difference as a variant, but to make it thought and the production of the 'absolutely different' — to make repetition, for itself, be difference in itself."[34] The formulation of thought's exigency as a project is impossible, since the exigency is a passivity which moves, speaks, or thinks. Thought is no longer action. Thus Deleuze's formulation of a "purpose" of a philosophy of repetition reproduces the ambivalence of the concept of deconstruction: the Other of a construction which nevertheless thinks. Thought "must" make thought what it already is — a difference, a repetition, a communication — because thought is a desire and an exigency: a "question", a "problem", a recherche, and an apprendre or "learning". The eschatological aspect of the philosophy of difference is its attestation of a reality without "truth" as totalization or illumination, in which however there is something to be "learned", there is experience.

*

Proximity, in Levinas' phrase, is "an ensemble broken by the difference between the terms in which however the difference is non-indifference and the rupture — obsession."[35] The rupture of ensemble — of totalization and correlation — by difference, and the contaminations which result from this rupture — the redoubtable excess, the mad circulation of movement, the groundlessness — proceed from the non-indifference of difference. When alterity escapes our power to render it manifest, the frustration of consciousness' voluntarism is not yet a touching of consciousness. Power is merely frustrated by superior power, in a world exhausted by the concept of power. The inadequation described by the philosophy of difference is of another order. In the differential economy, subjectivity is produced and invested by the passivity of communication. The alterity which escapes, approaches in its own powerlessness. Its approach is subjectivity's *nouvelle origine*. Intentionality's action becomes a heteronomous inclination toward the exterior, a forcing of ipseity into the exterior — the wandering, breathless, strangely avid hebetude of the *pour l'autre*. Alterity is an escape which obsesses, concerns, approaches. Its distance is the "attraction in place" of an interiority which must always desert its post. When communication eludes and contaminates the intervals of phenomenality, relation, negation and adequation, and when, as a function of this approach, autonomy ceases to be the principle of rapport, the element of subjectivity's conation assumes terrifying aspects. The hectic buzzing, intrusive intimacy, and involuntary movement which force closure "outside itself, outside everything," the gripping approach of an instance from "nowhere" that is already "here", proceed from the fact that, in communication, subjectivity is for the first time "not alone". Its only privacy is its inspiration by the Other. The disappointment of a frustrated metaphysics or a transgressive modernity which must approach the absolutely other through the secondarity of its approximations, is not the violence which has rendered the philosophy of difference disturbing to the culture in which it has appeared. The withdrawal of truth's foundations and the refusal to replace the latter with new principles of pertinence is not the provocative aspect of this philosophy. The nightmare and the obsession of its culture, as mentioned earlier, is not the frustration of a totalization which cannot totalize "enough", cannot seize the absolutely other — but is rather the subterranean passivity which, in its approach to the Other, senses the approach of the Other as the unknown animation of this industrious movement. The theme of the Other's escape retains the allergic economy of Same and Other which has characterized the complacency of Western thought. It is the proposition of a non-allergic, inspired reception of the Other, in desire and in the terror of the approach, that invests the novelty and foreignness of the concept of difference in philosophy. The name of Emmanuel Levinas dominates the recent genealogy of this concept. The *éthique*, with its discovery of passivity in the gravity of non-reciprocity, is the dimension of difference, when difference becomes proximity.

SEPARATION IN PROXIMITY

The context of the Levinasian *éthique* is not intersubjectivity. This context is communication. The possibility of intersubjective communication and, on a more general level, of signification, meaning and manifestation, is separation in the economy of proximity. These possibilities have in common the requirement that the real be defined as an element which produces discontinuity. In Levinas' terms, communication proceeds from the fact that being is an "economy": a field of differentiations and rapports. As mentioned earlier, Levinas' career in philosophy is motivated by the exigency to think separation or multiplicity as factors which are not reduced or dissolved by their rooting in the homogeneity of the Same. Relation cannot constitute communication, for Levinas, if its only economy is totalization and correlation. Relation is possible only as a function of a separation proceeding from the impossibility of totalization. Such a separation must imply a problematic but positive reality of exteriority: a communicational element irreducible to closure. Since the homogeneous undifferentiation of the "totality" precludes true interiority and relation, closure in the general economy must itself be defined as a unicity irreducible to the form of the totality. Interiority must be, as a function of its very closure, a capacity to be affected by exteriority. It must be inclined toward the Other. The non-allergic rapport of Same and Other is the Levinasian principle, not of an "ethical" non-violence or of an "authentic" intersubjective relation, but of communication itself, in its most impersonal sense. The proposition of exteriority is the condition of possibility of a unicity which can communicate — which can become involved, in any sense, with something outside itself — even if this exterior instance be defined merely as "another" unicity, in correlation, determination, or intersubjectivity. The economy of negation and totalization produces entities which cannot be "touched" or "concerned" by each other. This is an economy in which nothing is changed by anything else. Correlation is its only principle: the immobility and interchangeability of terms or elements whose unicity or difference is dissolved by their homogeneous participation within the immobility of the Same. This situation does not merely describe a reification for Levinas. It describes an undifferentiation. Relation requires difference. Difference requires a mode of differentiation in which exteriority participates. Closure, in order to retain the capacity to enter into a rapport with the exterior, must be defined as such a rapport, in its very separation. Closure must be a difference — that is, an instance whose very quiddity is derived from its primordial or pre-originary alteration — in order that it may experience the "change" that is relation. The field of correlations that is the totality, can be seriously termed a field of discontinuity and relation only if its immobility reposes upon a prior involvement with the exterior, as the condition of possibility of its differentiations. Totalization is made possible by its latent involvement with the Other of totalization. The Same constitutes itself in the proximity of the Other. Without this proximity, the Same would be the pure undifferentiation of homogeneous dispersion — and not the violent, exigent, constructive and destructive dimension the philosophers of proximity recognize it to be. Just as dissimulation in Blanchot is the principle of negation, and transgression in Bataille is the latent animation of the world of activity and utility, the exterior in Levinas is the principle and element of manifestation and correlation.

The movements which characterize the region of manifestation and totalization are alterations whose passivity has been mobilized as spontaneity and power. This mobilization, the "catalysis" which crystallizes difference in a world of identity, is itself a moment of alteration. Causality, determination, non-contradiction, mediation, etc. are interpretations of communication as correlation. These moments of correlation can articulate different entities only because difference itself — the Same's rapport with exteriority — is the principle of the multiplicity they organize. The totalization which reduces difference to identity, and alteration to relation, in the economy of negativity, is an effect or regional modality of that communication which produces unicity as a capacity to enter into a rapport — in the absence or contaminated weakness of the negative, which is difference itself. Difference is the principle of plurality, when plurality is an economy rather than a totality. Totalization in its principle — an elimination of alteration which grounds relation — is an impossibility, since the elimination of alteration is also the elimination of difference, and since without difference multiplicity becomes dispersion. But totalization in its reality is a dimension of differentiations and communications, mobilized perhaps in the direction of power and correlation, but invested by the exterior and by the alterations of the general economy.

The condition of possibility of closure or of the Same is its inspiration by the Other. The philosophy of difference consistently articulates this configuration by defining closure as a moment of intensity, of inequality, of an altering freeplay, or of the "movement of the trace." That this situation of inspiration or heteronomy does not, however, signify dispersion or undifferentiation, is the second consistent attestation of this philosophy, and is its most palpable link to the philosophy of proximity. The exterior invests multiplicity in a differential field. Closure, in such a field, is a compromising and dispossessing alteration, but is nonetheless a unicity. Its becoming-other forecloses its identity, but does not eliminate its unicity. Its pre-originary rapport with the exterior founds and conditions its rapport with "other" elements within the differential field. In the proximity of the exterior, the differential singularity has a density or intense turgidity — forced by the pressure of difference itself — which far exceeds the mere self-coincidence of an identity in a dimension of non-contradiction. Similarly, the rapport of this singularity to an "other" singularity is a rapport of maximum discontinuity or difference and maximum opacity, since the presence of the other singularity is conditioned by its exteriority. When consciousness or interiority is envisaged within the differential field as a contemplation of exteriority, the opacity it envisages in the exterior "thing" far exceeds that attested by philosophy in its doubt before the thing "in itself". The maximal heteronomy of differential unicity is also a maximal discontinuity. The hyperbolic involvement which contaminates differential unicities is also a hyperbolic separation. Their difference is a rapport and an intense discontinuity. Their difference is not a totalization, and thus their communication is neither relation, correlation, determination nor comprehension. But this communication produces the extreme unicity, extreme separation, and extreme intimacy which are the possibility and the modality of such relations. In the field of difference, as in that of proximity, the exterior element escapes into indefinition as it approaches and contaminates. It escapes and approaches as a function of its differential unicity, and its rapport with an interiority which itself remains a unicity. Separation and rapport are the differential principles which thought, in its exigent "manner", may understand to be identity and relation. The genealogy which includes Hegel, Nietzsche, Proust, Deleuze, Bataille, Blanchot, and Levinas, constitutes a philosophy of difference as well as a philosophy of proximity, by virtue of its concept of a dispossessing communication which forecloses negation and identity while producing the density of separation.

The proposition of separation and unicity within a dimension of communication is perhaps the essence of the philosophies of difference and proximity, although it is neither the point of their greatest consistency or equality, nor the principle of their reception by philosophy. The alternative between totalization and dispersion, correlation and undifferentiation, Truth as comprehension and "nothing at all" remains the ambivalence of Occidental epistemology. The concept of communication, in a culture whose interest is comprehension and power, remains rooted in the duality of correlation and communion — which are, as discussed earlier, the two axes of subjectivity's exigency in proximity. Blanchot's interest in a "rapport of the third type" — a rapport which retains separation and communication while eluding this exigency of comprehension — describes the necessity of thematizing a rapport whose economy is not exhausted by the form of the Same: a rapport which is neither the correlation of two Sames nor the communion of a Same which eliminates multiplicity. The vicissitudes encountered by the concepts of difference and proximity in recent history have in common a reduction of difference to negation and dispersion, and a reduction of proximity to communion. Hegel, the philosopher of totalization; Nietzsche, the philosopher of power and the return of the Same; Proust, the recapturer of lost time; Bataille, the thinker of transcendent excess; Blanchot, the thinker of impersonal dispersion; and Levinas, the philosopher of ethical communion — are creations of this tendency. The chief obscurity of these thinkers, and often their chief inequality, is that they meditate an alteration which resembles dispersion without signifying the latter; that they describe a communication which resembles communion without signifying communion; that they describe an irreducibility to totalization and comprehension which resembles both nihilism and negative theology while signifying neither. It may be said, in a larger sense, that most major thinkers of communication in the West, and that all great literary creators in the West, share this obscurity and this inequality.

The importance of Levinas in the philosophy of communication is his insistence upon separation and unicity as principles of an economy which nevertheless forecloses identity. It is Levinas who describes with a superior clarity and consistency the notion of a closure which is dispossessed by the Other's approach in communication at the same time that its unicity is invested by this approach. It is only by refusing to attribute to alterity the power to destroy the Same that Levinas is able to maintain the concepts of difference and exteriority in proximity, and to avoid a characterization of the Other in the image of the Same. The Other is not another power, and this is its alterity. Concomitantly, it is only by refusing to accord the univocal predicates of totalization to the Same itself that Levinas is able to avoid the correlation of Same and Other which would reduce their inadequation. In order to thematize communication without reducing the latter to totalization, it is necessary in the first place to define interiority or closure as an irreducible separation; in the second place, to define this separation itself as an escape from totalization; and in the third place, to define alterity as a powerless instance which invests closure without "limiting" the latter. The immediate consequence of this discursive exigency is a contaminating communication of Levinas' own terms, which continually confuses the integrity of their opposition and respective value, and, far more importantly, a foreclosing of the proposition that alterity in the *éthique* might compete with power, within the latter's own concept, and "change the world." Levinas repeatedly accords an ontological or communicational positivity, and consequently a dignity, to the terms he apparently denounces: totality, egoism, spontaneity, comprehension. At the same time, he repeatedly stipulates that the *éthique* or the *autrement qu'être* which invests and conditions these possibilities — albeit in a larger economy of impossibility — cannot eliminate their excess. In this he forecloses an enthusiastic reception of his text by its surrounding culture. But his marginality does not proceed from the "theological" context in which the *éthique* would prescribe an impossible non-violence. It proceeds rather from the same theory of communication which produced a less palpable but equally important marginality in the destinies of the Nietzschian and Proustian texts, i.e. the extraordinary incomprehension which was a function of their fame.

Separation in Levinas is always an inspired heteronomy, the *parole* of excess, and the *pour l'autre* of a pre-originary involvement with alterity. Yet alterity always invests separation as a "point of departure" in the rapport with the Other. The "sense" of alteration in the economy is a *sens unique*. It proceeds from "nowhere", approaching the unicity it creates, to incline it outward, toward alterity. This creation and this inclination define separation itself. The non-indifference of closure is its unicity. The dissymmetrical *sens* of alteration in being invests closure as the possibility of signification and eventually of manifestation. But the totality which will erect itself upon the foundation of separation will never constitute itself as a pure totality in opposition to alterity. It will never be, in Blanchot's phrase, "entirely the world." It will be a Same whose latent economy is its non-allergic inclination toward the Other. It is this proximal investment of the Same in its totality that the texts of Bataille, Blanchot and Levinas describe in a virtual thematic unanimity. The separation of the Same — its industry, its totalitarian immobility, its homogeneity — proceeds from its rapport with the Other. The very familiarity and intimacy of closure — its apparent complacency and allergy to alterity — are invested by its prior inclination toward exteriority. This inclination is its animation, its primordial transgression of its own closure, and the principle not only of its spontaneity, but also of its apparently exceptional or anomalous excess. Bataille's genius, and his irreplace-

ability among modern thinkers, consisted in his attention to an element traditionally spurned by philosophy and formal discourse in general – the everyday – and
in his intuition of an "other world" whose approach could be perceived in the
spasmodic episodes of violence which haunt the world of totalization.

The economy in which separation – a unicity inspired by alterity and retaining
its difference with regard to alterity – is possible, is called by Levinas *éthique*.

Atheistic separation is *required* by the idea of the Infinite which does not however dialectically produce the separate being. The idea of the infinite – the
relation between the Same and the Other – does not annul separation. This is
attested in transcendence. In effect, the Same can rejoin the Other only in the
aleas and risks of the search for truth rather than to repose upon it in all security.
Without separation, there would not have been truth, there would only have
been being.[36]

The "atheistic" separation which is produced and altered by alterity without
being converted to the dimensions of the Other, is the principle of the *éthique*.
"Transcendence" is the irreducible inadequation of Same and Other which is
precisely their difference. The Levinasian "metaphysician" who approaches the
Other in thought, is always and essentially an "atheist". (Thus Levinas, in his
own thinking of the rapport with alterity as *expérience*, brings an important
correction to Bataille's notion of the "theologian" of experience.) The rapport
with alterity in the *visage* does not eliminate the "egoism" of separation – in
sensation, in the *cogito*, in *jouissance* – but conditions and confirms it. Inspiration or alteration is not communion. "Separation and interiority, truth and
language – constitute the categories of the idea of the infinite or *métaphysique*."[37] The infinite is not a totality, not a transcendent, superceding
dimension of superior truth or authenticity; and this is why it "allows a being
outside itself which it does not engulf."[38] The *éthique* is a dimension of communication, and therefore of separation and inadequation. Levinas' distaste for
"positive" religions proceeds from their tendency to dissolve interiority and
exteriority within a superior or "sacred" dimension whose principle is the same
correlation that characterizes totalization. Within such a dimension, communication is again foreclosed by a communion which is an undifferentiation.
Perhaps the greatest difficulty of Levinas' thought for a reader whose formation
is philosophical or scientific, is the configuration in which alterity conditions
closure while not superceding it. The "transcendence" of the infinite is its
powerlessness to compete with totalization. Levinas' thought is not a metaphysics
of alterity, but a theory of communication. The separation which is inspired by
and inclined toward alterity in desire, is not on this basis adequated to an
alterity which would be a new Same. "But the Desire of the Other, above happiness, requires [*exige*] this happiness, this autonomy of the sensible in the world,
even if this separation can be deduced neither analytically nor dialectically from
the Other."[39] The desire or inspiration which involves Same with Other without

reducing this involvement to a correlation or communion, is the production of the Same as true separation, and is the possibility of multiplicity within the Same as well as within the general economy. Only when separation is "absolute" rather than "relative" to a system or totality, can plurality and relation become possible. The extraordinary or miraculous moment produced by the ethical or metaphysical relation is not a non-violence or authenticity, but the fact, in the absence of totalization or communion, of an interiority "preoccupied by another being."[40]

As discussed earlier, Levinas' mature writings may be distinguished from his earlier publications by their refusal to characterize the ethical rapport as an exceptional moment, in comparison with the norms of totalization and comprehension. His consistent concern is to show that the principles of the totality, such as multiplicity, relation, and spontaneity, must themselves be economically derived from a latent investment of the Same by the Other. Closure is already inspiration. On the other hand, when the most intense moments of the ethical rapport are thematized by Levinas, he always stipulates a maintaining of separation within these moments. The ethical rapport with the Other is never a simple correlation ordained by a higher power or comprehended by an ethical order of being. Subjectivity in the rapport with alterity does not play a pre-determined role in a drama organized by God. Instead, it retains its separation, invested by the Other. Levinas' contact with Judaism is perhaps resumed in this moment at which heteronomy does not limit the fact that subjectivity "knows what is happening to it."

The ethical relation is defined, against all relation with the sacred, by excluding any signification that it would assume *unknown* to him who entertains it. When I entertain an ethical relation, I refuse to recognize the role that I would play in a drama of which I would not be the author.[41]

Interiority's non-allergic rapport with the Other is the principle of its separation, and not of a participation in an "order" of being. Separation is produced by its own lack of totalization, its own "breaking of participation," as Levinas wrote on Husserl. Individuation is an uprooting rather than a rooting within being or within manifestation. But this uprooting is no more an entry into communion than an entry into dispersion. "Signification, proximity, *dire*, separation, I do not merge [*me confonds*] with anything."[42]

As mentioned above, the *éthique* is not an ethics of intersubjectivity, but a description of separation and the possibility of multiplicity. The panoramic view of an intersubjective rapport is not Levinas' primary interest, although it is the thematic context of many of his terms. Each time Levinas speaks of intersubjectivity, he describes a rapport of Same and Other before a rapport of Same to other Same. And in this rapport of Same to Other, he articulates separation. The first and third divisions of *Totalité et infini* consist in large part in a derivation of highly private terms which describe (a) the production of separation in proximity or inspiration, (b) the rapport with alterity on the basis of this separation, and (c) the implicit condition for manifestation or intersubjective rapport which is based upon the prior configuration of separation. These terms include: *langage* ("a rapport such that the terms are not limitrophe in this rapport, that the Other, in spite of the rapport with the Same, remains transcendent to the Same"[43]); *discours* ("Discourse is not simply a modification of intuition (or of thought), but an original relation with exterior being. (...) It is the production of sense."[44]); *sens* ("a presence more direct than visible manifestation and a distant presence – that of the other"[45]); *expression* ("To approach *Autrui* in discourse is to receive its expression in which at every instant it overflows the idea a thought would have of it."[46]); *religion* ("a relation between being here below and transcendent being which leads to no community of concept and no totality – a relation without relation"[47]); *absolution* ("The terms remain absolute despite the relation in which they find themselves"[48]); and, most generally, *pluralisme*: "Separation opens between terms which are absolute and however in relation, which absolve themselves of the relation they entertain, which do not abdicate in it to the profit of a totality that this relation would describe. Thus the metaphysical relation realizes a multiple existing, pluralism."[49] All these terms indicate the same basic configuration, which is in the first place an involvement without communion or dispersion, in the second place a separation without correlation, and in the third place a dissymetrical incumbence of alterity upon the Same. This dissymetrical rapport will condition the economy of intersubjectivity, but is not derived from a meditation of the intersubjective relation. It is a rapport of Same to Other, and is thus, as Levinas often stipulates, "invisible to a third party." It cannot be viewed panoramically as a relation of Same to Other within a larger element or ethical order. Were this view possible, the rapport would become a new correlation of Same to other Same.

Every basic term which describes a rapport or relation, in Levinas' philosophy, describes the production of separation by the alteration of being: an alteration which makes being an economy by introducing discontinuity and relation into undifferentiation. The heteronomous inspiration of the Same is basic to this process, but so also is its "absolute" separation. The collaboration of exteriority in the conation of the Same does not annihilate difference, but produces closure as a difference. The ethical rapport with alterity remains an absolute discontinuity. "The exteriority of being does not signify, in effect, that multiplicity is without rapport. But the rapport which links this multiplicity does not fill up the abyss of separation, it confirms the latter."[50] Within every relation, intersubjective or other, that organizes multiplicity within totalization, the latent rapport of Same to Other will insist as its possibility. "The rapport between separate beings does not totalize them...."[51] The possibility of relation is already the impossibility of totalization: the investment of the Same as an alteration and an inclination toward exteriority. The intensity of closure – the eventuality of totalization, power, and the "unpunished crimes" of freedom – is produced by the approach of the Other. The name of the economy in which communication produces neither totalization, communion, nor dispersion, but separation, is "proximity". "It is necessary to show in the *Dire* — as approach — the de-position or de-situation of the subject which remains however an irreplaceable unicity. . . ."[52] Proximity, as cited earlier, describes a separation which is an "obsession" or involvement. But it is necessary to stress its primary definition as "an ensemble broken by the difference between the terms, in which however the difference is a non-indifference."[53] The *éthique* describes an economy of proximity in which the approach of the exterior produces the non-totalized, non-interchangeable unicity of closure — a unicity which is not a term, and whose rapport with alterity is not a mere location or situation within the Same. Proximity is the *des-interesse* or alteration of being which produces, in the weakening of negation, the difference that is unicity and the non-indifference that is the force of this unicity.[54] Closure's non-allergic involvement with an inspiring alterity is the modality of multiplicity in this differential economy. This involvement will make possible the manifold variations of power and illumination which organize the totality — movements which will not describe a reified world in mere opposition to the *éthique*, but which will be in themselves "events of proximity."[55] The non-allergy of totality and infinity which underlies their thematic opposition in Levinas' text results from the fact that proximity is not only the possibility of subjectivity and of intersubjectivity, but is also the possibility of communication itself.

RECURRENCE

The concepts developed by Levinas through his readings of phenomenology, and through his progressive discovery of an alterity and a communicational economy which were inadequate to the universe of phenomenology's predications, led in the late 1950's to the appearance and dominance of the *éthique* in his text. To the reader of *En découvrant l'existence avec Husserl et Heidegger* (1967), in which Levinas' entire itinerary is visible in compressed form, the appearance of the *éthique* may seem sudden and brutal, as well as logically distant from Levinas' earlier work. This impression has both a thematic and conceptual basis. On one hand, such publications as "L'ontologie est-elle fondamentale?" (1951) and *Le Temps et l'autre* (1948), whose concern with *Autrui* and with an "ethical" order anticipated the discovery of the *éthique*, showed a provocative and somewhat aggressive aspect which was never entirely eliminated from Levinas' subsequent writings. These texts posed *Autrui* and the concept of an "absolute" alterity as exceptional moments in the economy of being which were unassimilable by the otherwise effective categories of phenomenology and philosophy in general. The anti-Heideggerian, anti-intellectualist moment of Levinas' thought dominated hs publications of the 1940's and early 1950's. On the other hand, with the explicit thematization of the *éthique* in "La philosophie et l'idée de l'infini" (1957) and *Totalité et infini* (1961), the logical basis underlying Levinas' themes had changed. His interest in *Autrui* as an exceptional moment escaping totalization was supplanted by an interest in a communicational alterity which invests or conditions the possibility of totalization and comprehension, by virtue of the very economy of its escape. At this point, the provocative element in Levinas' criticisms of phenomenology did not disappear, but assumed a secondary position. The project of revealing an incapacity of the philosophical discourse to account for the anomaly of *Autrui* and for communication's excess over comprehension, became a project of discovering in philosophy's predications a latent attestation of this very excess. And ultimately, as discussed earlier, Levinas' concepts would situate the very possibility of philosophy – of comprehension and manifestation – as a moment of the *éthique*. Levinas' renewed interest in Husserl, documented in *En découvrant l'existence avec Husserl et Heidegger*, proceeded from the self-confidence of his independence from phenomenology, and from the economic definition of alterity and proximity which now informed all his concepts. Thus, all nine essays added to the second edition of *En découvrant l'existence* – not only the "Raccourcis" which introduce the *éthique*, but also the essays on Husserl and phenomenology – presuppose the *éthique* as their conceptual basis. The reader's surprise in the face of the private and difficult vocabulary of the "Raccourcis" conceals the fact that the preceding essays (the "Commentaires nouveaux") were themselves written from a point of view which was no longer that of phenomenology, but of communication. Levinas' readings of sensation, manifestation and temporalization in Husserl are deliberate and inspired notations of phenomenology's tendency to veer in the direction of the *éthique* through its analyses of the concept of receptivity.

In his discussions of *jouissance* and the *cogito* as well as in his interpretations of intentionality, Levinas invokes a latent communicational element in the economy of subjectivity while stressing consciousness' ability to "assume" and mobilize this element as a function of spontaneity and illumination. Though this "assumption" may not eliminate the priority and irreducibility of this heteronomous moment, it remains a positive if problematic ontological moment in itself. The "tardiness" and "illusion" of intentionality which constitutes its own condition; the "egoism" of *jouissance* which recuperates the element in which it "bathes"; and the spontaneity of the *cogito* in its assumption of an affirmation proceeding from the Other, are events of proximal differentiation which consecrate manifestation. They are able to do so because difference in proximity produces a density of closure which may be interpreted as autonomy, and a distance and intimacy of exteriority which may be interpreted as adequation or illumination. This "interpretation", which is not a consciousness or comprehension, but an impersonal economic event, is interiority itself in the general economy: the exigency of closure. Its assumption of its own spontaneity is a moment with paradoxical or "impossible" predicates, such as the reversal of historical time, the conditioning of condition by conditioned, etc., because this very assumption is a proximal event outside totalization. The "egoism", "atheism", or "naive" spontaneity of consciousness is not a given which will be opposed to the anomaly of intersubjectivity, but is itself a communicational event, grounded in the subjectivity of differentiation. Levinas' attitude toward this event, in his mature philosophy, is univocally admiring. Memory, the *cogito*, intentionality, etc. – the "memory of its origin in an interiority" – are onto-logical moments whose constitution of a totality or of a reductive dimension of correlation does not exhaust their economy. These moments describe a produc-tion of interiority in the proximity of alterity – a proximity which is already the subjectivity and the inspired *parole* of closure. Thus intentionality, by virtue of its very assumption of its heteronomy – as assumption which is a refusal – "can break [with the totality] and can consequently speak."[56] In its very conse-cration of manifestation, subjectivity is a rapport with exteriority which is not comprehension but *société*. Proximity – the impossibility of totali-zation – founds manifestation. The heteronomy of inspiration is the origin of power.

This configuration of inspired or conditioned autonomy is correlative to a second basic change in Levinas' concepts: the fact that *Autrui* is no longer "others", but is the Other. Sensation is "already spoken", the *cogito* has "already received *Autrui*", because *Autrui* is not the constituted other of intersubjectivity, but is the subjectivity – the escape and incumbence – of the exterior. Concomi-tant to the notion of a totalization whose latent economy is proximity, is the notion of an impersonal *Autrui* whose exceptional escape from totalization does not exhaust the sense of its approach. *Autrui* as the Other is the principle of totalization and manifestation, because it is the principle of closure and rapport. The *éthique* is not the principle of intersubjective relations, but of separation. The totality, for the mature Levinas, is a moment of the *éthique*.

As discussed earlier, the differentiation which makes possible both illumination and totalization as functions of separation, is correlative to a passive temporal synthesis. The principles of this synthesis are impression, lapse, and a proximal repetition which produces temporal intervals as functions of closure's rapport with alterity. Subjectivity's appearance in time results from an inextrication and incumbence of temporal differences whose heteronomy articulates a "pressure" of differentiation. This appearance is inadequate to the concept of punctuality or spontaneity, and describes subjectivity as a pure susceptibility to the Other's escape and approach in an irrecuperable and concerning or incumbent past and future. Subjectivity's intensity or exigency, produced by this pressure of alterity in time, may assume the form of a constituting spontaneity, but this assumption will always be an *après-coup* or tardiness with regard to its economic investment. The temporal *cogito*, in its punctuality, reposes upon subjectivity's more funda-mental configuration as a pure alteration or "senescence", and as the inspired desire of a "search for lost time". It is the notion of a pre-originarity or *an-archie* conditioning interiority's conation, and the passivity of this immemorial involve-ment, that informs the rapport of interiority to proximity in Levinas' later books. In these books, however, it is not the assumption of exteriority in consciousness that is stressed, but rather the communicational "impossibility" underlying this assumption. The focus of Levinas' attention, and of the terms associated with the *éthique*, is the moment of primary and irreducible passivity which produces subjectivity in the proximity of the Other. Although Levinas will consistently characterize this proximity as "non-assumable", it is important to perceive the continuity of his inspiration. The "invested freedom" or "accused" unicity of the *éthique* is not an eventuality which supervenes to alter the structure of interiority. It is rather a *nouvelle origine* of interiority whose configuration is already perceptible in the economy of the *cogito*, of *jouissance*, or of intentionality. *Autrui*, the *visage*, and the event of "substitution" are involved in the very differentiation of subjectivity. Thus the *cogito* is not merely an intrication with impersonal alterity in anticipation of *Autrui*'s approach, but is in itself a "receiving of *Autrui*". And, as will be discussed below, the configuration of responsibility in the approach of the *visage* is not unassimilable to the logic of "assumption" which characterizes interiority's "egoism". The *éthique* is the dimension of subjectivity's uneliminable passivity: a passivity which can never be superceded by a spontaneity, but which may itself invest the possibility of spontaneity's "assumptions" of the exterior. The difficulty of Levinas' text parallels that of Blanchot, in the sense that it describes a proximal "event" which supervenes to interiority after having already collaborated in the creation of the latter. The proximity of the *visage*, "non-assumable", is not logically distinct from the impersonal alterity "assumed" by subjectivity in its *cogito*. The *éthique* is not a vicissitude of consciousness, but rather its only possibility and its only economy. Although the dramatic formulations of *Totalité et infini* and *Autrement qu'être ou au delà de l'essence* may suggest the contrary, it remains true that the *visage* and responsibility do not punctually confront a previously untroubled spontaneity. They constitute this spontaneity.

The word *psychisme* in Levinas describes the subjectivity of interiority, i.e. its pre-originary involvement with alterity. This involvement reaches a point of extreme urgency and passivity in the approach of the *visage*, after having invested interiority's familiarity in sensation and *jouissance*. The repetitive and proximal temporality of this "increase" of alterity's pressure is that of transgression. Like the beast which approaches in the burrow, the *visage* began its approach at the moment of subjectivity's differentiation. Although its appearance is, in Levinas' words, "unforeseeable", and although its incumbence will always take subjectivity "by surprise", its approach is not entirely unexpected. In the pure differentiation of *jouissance*, subjectivity's immersion in a supporting element was already an involvement with the *il y a* — that is, with communication's excess over negation. In the "il" of *il y a* the "third person" of illeity — the Other, in its excess over the alternative of immanence and transcendence, being and non-being — resonates. And in the "trace" of illeity, the *visage* approaches. Although subjectivity's irreducible delay or tardiness with regard to alterity's incumbence prevents it from anticipating this approach, the collaboration of alterity in its conation forces upon it another modality of "understanding". This is the "inability not to understand" of subjectivity in impossibility: a comprehension that is no longer transitive, not a function of interval and illumination, but a moment of proximity. To become separate in differentiation is to "know" the Other's approach: in the *attente* of closure's inspired intensity, and in the *oubli* produced by the Other's investing proximity. The sound of the approach "wakes" subjectivity from its sleep — that is, it participates in the *cogito* of interiority. It is present now, as a trace: a concerning rapport with the immemorial. And when the *visage* approaches, it will not arrive as a phenomenon. It will weigh, compel, or signify from its *à venir* which is its "already". The approach of the *visage* is implicit in the forced, distended punctuality of a subjectivity which is involved with an "other" time. Since it is a function and a principle of separation, this inactual approach cannot be stopped. It takes place in what Levinas calls a "dimension without contradiction."[57] The "weakening" of negation in proximity — the fact that differentiation bypasses or contaminates negation — is the economic principle of the approach; and this is why, in the most private dimension of Levinas' thought, the Blanchotian predicates of communication are palpable. The Other approaches after having always already approached. Subjectivity returns to itself — without ever having left — from the detour of its involvement with alterity. This detour and this contaminated, repetitive punctuality are the element of *psychisme*: "a *psychisme* which does not come to graft itself onto a substance, but which alters the substantiality of this substance to the extent that this substance undergoes [*supporte*] all things: which alters it by an alteration in which identity is accused [*s'accuse*] ."[58]

There are several meanings to the phrase "où s'accuse l'identité" in the above passage. In the first place, interiority's very closure or intensity — the force or "catalysis" which Levinas often describes as an "exaggeration" — is *accusée*, "highlighted", "hyperbolically accented", by its involvement with alterity. The excessive aspect of closure is this involvement. In the second place, the word *accuser* means "to manifest", "to show" and, in its reflexive form, implies "recognition". *Psychisme* is identity's appearance in being and the principle of its *cogito* or experience of itself. In the third place, the reflexive *se* of *s'accuser* is first the pronominal *se* of passivity. Identity "is accused", "is produced" in its intensity. Its conation is a passivity. In the fourth place, this pronominal *se* implies the *il* of interiority's impersonality which conditions the personal identity of the "I" or *Moi*. In the fifth place, the pronominal *se* is also an accusative *se*. By virtue of its primordial involvement with another instance, subjectivity is implicitly "envisaged" by this instance. It is first an object — an instance that is not alone in its *cogito* — and only then the solitude of consciousness. The pronominal *se* and the accusative *se* describe an interiority which is involved with and concerned by alterity, and already other than a totality — in the becoming-other of impersonality, and in the problematic intersubjectivity of the accusative. The rapport with alterity in closure's conation is already a *société*, a primary non-allergy or lack of distinction. The reflexive moment of solitude implies this detour through alterity. The *cogito* identifies itself and contemplates its own spontaneity, the certainty of its ipseity, in the "essential solitude" of a proximity to the Other. In the sixth place, consciousness is "accused" — that is, envisaged in a concerning and compromising way, by alterity in the *cogito*. The "too late" of its spontaneous punctuality implies a prior involvement for which, in some sense, interiority must answer. The answer is impossible, since the element of conation is immemorial, but the exigency of the answer is interiority itself, in its closure which is forced by alterity. Identity is not a spontaneous abiding, but is the force of an exigency, excessively closed and not closed enough. The word *accuser* suggests this unquiet tension of a self which, in its primary appearance, should not have been "already" disturbed. (It is for this reason, among others, that Descartes' doubting, preoccupied *cogito*, whose rooting in exteriority implies an exigency, is the object of Levinas' admiration.) And finally, the accusative case of identity becomes its reflexive mode. Its innocent, naive spontaneity is already an accusing of itself. Because it is involved in an immemorial situation which concerns as it escapes, interiority accuses itself as it recognizes itself. This accusation is inspired by the Other. The origin of spontaneity — the possibility of comprehension and manifestation — is already the "shame" of spontaneity. This self-critical "shame", and not the originary rooting of the *cogito* in a differentiation defined as illumination, is the principle of comprehension itself. Subjectivity's curiosity and search for truth will proceed from its desire of the Other: a desire inspired by the Other in separation, a non-indifference and passivity which make possible any rapport of the interior with exteriority. To be "accused", to be "not alone", to be "one" as a function of an involvement with and an avidity toward alterity, is the definition of consciousness.

Separation is a proximity and an obsession, a heteronomy and an inspired desire. The phenomenological "rooting" of subjectivity in being becomes, in proximity, a primordial "uprooting", a tearing of interiority from its self-coincidence and an inclination of it toward alterity, in the moment of differentiation. By virtue of the irreducibility of difference to negation and of interiority to autonomy, separation is already an approach to the Other in the approach of the Other. The *il y a* of exteriority's approach is a basic modality of this latent economy, and it is perhaps for this reason that this concept retains a centrality in Levinas' later books. "But this way the subject has of finding himself within *essence*. . . is not a harmonious and inoffensive participation. It is precisely the incessant buzzing that fills each silence in which the subject detaches himself from *essence* in order to pose himself as a subject over against his objectivity. (. . .) The buzzing of the *il y a*. . . ."[59] The *il y a* in its uneliminable noise is the "signification" — the differential heteronomy — which bypasses negation and creates interiority as a non-indifferent *pour l'autre*. From this signification, "justice" issues, because opposition and correlation are already impossibilities. Subjectivity's rapport with alterity is already a non-allergy, a *société*. The Other is already *Autrui*, in the obsession and inspiration which individuate. This obsession is thought's "experience", in Hegel's words, regardless of the direction it may take in interiority's mobilization of its experience. Because closure is "not alone" in its conation, and because separation is a non-indifference, the process of differentiation in being must be defined as the event of the *éthique*. The first critical or theoretical experience of thought is its obsession in the proximity of the Other, the "shame" of its spontaneity in its inspired reception of alterity. As mentioned earlier, the logical province of the *éthique* is not intersubjectivity, not an exceptional dimension of experience, but the derivation of experience itself from the economy of difference. The thematic distinction between Levinas' discussions of spontaneity's "assumptions" of its origin, on one hand, and its "non-assumable" involvement with alterity, on the other hand, reposes on the proposition that the non-indifference of interiority's conation may be directed toward autonomy and comprehension, but may not be eliminated. And the "directing" of inspiration toward autonomy will itself be an event of proximity's *sens unique*, a modality of inspiration itself. The *éthique* insists in the production of closure and rapport, and therefore secretly invests the manifold vicissitudes of closure. That the "price of separation" may be totalization and the eventuality of "unpunished crimes", does not imply an elimination of the non-allergic *société* that is separation itself. The principle of the totality is "infinity".

The moment at which subjectivity appears and discovers itself to be concerned by an instance beyond its spontaneity, is called *récurrence*. In the solitude of its *cogito*, subjectivity is not alone. An Other instance has collaborated in its creation. From this Other there can be no extrication, and toward it, no indifference. Alterity's collaboration in the production of interiority is already its proximity: an intimacy and an inaccessibility which are both inadequate to comprehension. The only rapport with this proximity is the passivity implicit in the differentiation that produced it. In *Autrement qu'être ou au delà de l'essence*, the differential aspect of this moment is stressed far more than in earlier works. Subjectivity's "unity" is already a differential "singularity": "A unity in its form and in its content, the self [*soi-même*] is a singularity, prior to the distinction of the particular and the universal. A rapport, if one wishes, but without a disjunction of the terms which are in the rapport."[60] This rapport as a function of individuation is the "contraction" of interiority in the impersonality of differentiation: its *soi-même* before its personal identity.[61] "It is on the basis of subjectivity understood as *soi* — on the basis of *excidence* and dispossession, of the contraction in which the *Moi* does not appear to itself, but immolates itself — that the relation with the other can be communication and transcendence and not always another way of seeking certainty or self-coincidence."[62] Contraction is a difference which creates subjectivity as a dispossession or fission, even as it invests subjectivity as a unicity. Unicity is the other of identity: "already an implication of the one in the other."[63] * The *soi* is the impersonality

---

* The form and context of this predication show that, when Levinas uses the expression "the one", he means "unicity" itself — and not "the one unicity" or "the one term". The apparently panoramic intersubjective notion of *l'un-pour-l'autre*, "the one for (toward) the other", must be translated as "unicity toward the Other". It is not a synoptic view of two persons in intersubjectivity, but is a statement about unicity in the general economy — which is always inclined toward alterity by the intensity of difference.

and the economy of this moment at which ipseity loses its self-coincidence[64] and at which the *infini* of communication appears in the *soi*'s distance from itself – a distance which is not a negativity, but a proximity of alterity.[65] The "one" of unicity in the *soi* is the impersonality of essential solitude. To be "one" means "not to be alone", to be involved with the exterior. Subjectivity is no longer its own arbiter, but is the object or captive of another instance which cannot be deduced from the concept of solitude: *Autrui*, the passive and incumbent subjectivity of the exterior. "(C)alled without the possibility of escape to be someone [*quelqu'un*]."[66] When identity is lost – when exteriority is no longer the element of opposition and correlation – separation is produced. The event which concerns subjectivity in this moment is not a determination in a world of action, not the accident or vicissitude of a totality, but is the uneliminable heteronomy which invests the unicity of the Same. Thus, when the integrity of the Self (*Moi*) is foreclosed in the altering impersonality of "someone" (*soi*), the proposition of true unicity (*moi*, "me") becomes possible. This unicity is "non-interchangeable" because it is not a totality. Its experience of alterity is not a relation to another totality, but is an investing rapport with the exterior. The event of this rapport is "unforeseeable" and irrecuperable because it is not a correlation within the Same. It is rather the difference that produces the possibility of the Same in communication, and thus produces the possibility of relation. True unicity proceeds from a non-allergic inextrication with regard to alterity because, without this communication, the manifold relations of the totality would be impossible. This unicity of what Levinas calls "election" or "assignation" is the impersonal heteronomy of closure which is the necessary and sufficient economy of the *Moi* – of ipseity in general. Only by its uprooting and *errance* within the exterior can interiority be coherently "rooted" within being as a unicity. Closure must be a difference before it may behave as an identity. It must be a rapport with alterity before it may enter into relations with the elements of the exterior. When the Self of *jouissance*, of the *cogito* and of intentionality experiences and clings to the intimacy of its interiority, it unknowingly attests the supporting participation of alterity in this intimacy. Integrity is a function, an effect, of essential solitude. The ambivalence of allergy and desire which will dominate the comportments of interiority's relations with the exterior – in intersubjectivity, in the search for truth, in generosity, in war – is produced by the non-allergic non-indifference which creates interiority in another "sense": the *sens unique* of inspiration. In an economy understood as a totality of correlations, nothing could "happen" to a self-identical unicity. Experience would be an absurdity, as would unicity itself. Closure would be reduced to the undifferentiated homogeneity or dispersion of the Same. But because unicity is produced by communication in the absence of negation and totalization, the secondary moment of identity and relation becomes possible. The exuberance, spontaneity, and power of totalization, the hubbub of the totality, its "personal" self in the humanism of philanthropy and exploitation, its metaphysics, the violent ambivalence of its search for a peace of reason and its bellicose desire to "make war on war" — these eventualities are, in Bataille's phrase, humanity's "organization of violence". They are positive ontological events grounded in the inspired, heteronomous moment of unicity. Levinas' protestations against the impersonal signification thematized by contemporary formalisms, particularly in *Humanisme de l'autre homme* (1972), should not be understood as a nostalgia for the "personal" unicity of humanism. This unicity, as attested by the philosophies of difference and proximity, is the replaceability and abstraction of closure as totalization. "Each" person, "every" person is unique, in a derisory uniformity. Levinas' solidarity with the philosophy of difference is his thematization of an impersonal, communicational unicity whose reality bypasses the alternative of closure and dispersion, and his suspicion of the formalisms' notions of a dispersed, indefinitely circulating signification which mimics the configuration of correlation itself. As Gilles Deleuze states in his *Différence et répétition*,[67] the concept of difference invites the hasty interpretation of the "belle âme" that "everything is different, everything is unique." This is an interpretation of difference as identity. The unicity of difference and proximity is of another order. It is the dispossessing and investing heteronomy which prevents closure from becoming a totality, and which produces the inspired unicity that the *belle âme*, and Western metaphysics in its generality, will interpret as the valued privacy of identity in correlation. In his maturity, Levinas will no longer condemn as a reification this spurious privacy and independence of the humanist or phenomenological subject. Its identity, and its participation in a totality, are "miraculous" economic eventualities produced by the essentially proximal, essentially communicational moment that is unicity. Levinas rejoins the Bataille who admires the "intense" homogeneity of the profane world, and the Blanchot who refuses to condemn the inauthentic world of rumor in which the *oeuvre* "wishes" to circulate. The dualistic superstructure of these three theoretical texts is superceded by their thematization of a general economy whose movements produce not only the strangeness of proximity, but also a familiar element whose own latent principle is communication. Like Proust's narrator, who discovers that Habit is a function of desire and that "lost time" is the element of subjectivity's inspired, discontinuous insistence in Time, the philosophers of proximity discover that communication is not an excellence and an anomaly, but is the experience of the everyday — an experience that is not to be comprehended, in a Hegelian or Heideggerian inspiration, but that admits of no position toward it, even as it inspires the exigency to comprehend it.

Interiority in the accusative *se* is a unicity produced by difference, and therefore the heteronomy of a non-indifference. Its alteration by exteriority is the intensity of its closure; its primordial *errance*, outside the totality, is the possibility of its identity. It is pre-originarily

the *soi-même* which refuses the annexations of *essence*. *Moi* as unicity, outside comparison, because outside community, genus and form, finding however no repose in itself, un-quiet, not coinciding with itself. A unicity whose "outside itself", whose difference with regard to itself — is non-indifference itself and the extraordinary recurrence of the pronomial or reflexive.[68]

As a constituted or invested spontaneity, the *soi* is already the *mise en jeu* of this spontaneity, already its *glissement* and its transgression of its own interiority. This transgression is a *dépense*, a conation toward the Other: "a *soi* in spite of itself, in incarnation as the very possibility of giving."[69] The "generosity" attributable to closure's excess is not a "giving" which proceeds from autonomy, but is the destitution of closure, forced by the Other. "It is an exigency coming from the other, beyond the activity of my powers, to open a limitless 'deficit' in which, without calculating, freely, the *Soi* expends itself [*se dépense*]."[70] Unicity is the loss of integrity in closure, as a consequence of closure's excess. This excess is the principle of interiority's non-indifference. The conation by which subjectivity asserts its "for-itself" is already an unquiet preoccupation with alterity, which is implicit in *jouissance* and the *cogito*, and urgently explicit in recurrence. In a repeated formulation which articulates Blanchot's *nouvelle origine*, Levinas describes recurrence as the paradoxical punctuality of a conation which "returns to a point prior to its point of departure" ("recule en deçà de son point de départ").[71] This subjectivity "borne back ceaselessly into the past" is the unicity of a repetitive time whose principle is the violent pressure of proximity: "a recurrence to self [*soi*] through the irrecusable exigency of the other."[72] The temporal *déphasage* or "dephasing" of subjectivity in its difference with regard to itself, is not a mere undecidability, but is the trace and the approach of the Other.

The temporal lapse which characterized sensation and the production of subjectivity in Levinas' readings of Husserl, remains the underlying configuration of recurrence. Subjectivity proceeds from the "difference of the identical" in a temporal unicity "out of phase with itself."[73] Interiority is a modification, an alteration of discontinuity, produced by temporalization as proximity. "(T)he Same rejoins the Same modified: this is consciousness."[74] The subjectivity of the subject is the *écart* separating the instant from itself in repetition — an *écart* which is the possibility of a pressure and impression in time. This pressure or incumbence of exteriority is not only the subjectivity of time, but also its very discontinuity or extension. The unicity of temporal difference is an infinitely distended and infinitely compact closure, forced by the pressure of exteriority. In the escape of the Other which is time's passing, subjectivity is on one hand the "recherche du temps perdu" of desire and senescence, and on the other hand the "preoccupation by the Other" of the trace in recurrence. Both these predicates articulate a rapport with passing or past time which is the more basic *diachronie* of interiority's rapport with an Other that is "not in the same concept." "(I)t is necessary that in recuperable temporalization, without lost time, without time to lose and in which the being of substance appears [*se passe*] — an irrecuperable lapse of time, a diachrony refractory to synchronization, a transcendent diachrony, be distinguished."[75] Senescence or temporal alteration — the "permanence of a loss of self"[76] — is the passivity of a temporal difference which produces the irrecuperable past, a past which conceals an involvement with the Other. This involvement concerns the present. "Preoccupied by the irrecuperable": this proposition, in its overdetermination, is one definition of proximal subjectivity. To the conation *à l'envers* of a subjectivity in exposition to alterity (*envers sans endroit*, an "inside-out without an inside") is related the conation *à rebours* or "backward" of a subjectivity whose presence is an involvement with the irrecuperable past. This conation "in reverse"[77] is an inescapable rapport with pre-history, and a true reversal of time, in repetition, which conditions the secondary reversals of intentionality and the *cogito*. The past which was never a presence is rigorously contemporaneous with any present, because it is the "passing" of time, the differential element of temporalization. Recurrence is the passive and repetitive insistence of subjectivity in this element. Subjectivity is time's *an-archie*: the repetition and proximity which articulate time's failure to totalize its discontinuity — as Levinas states in a striking passage from *Humanisme de l'autre homme*:

Interiority is the fact that in being the beginning is preceded but that which precedes does not present itself to the free gaze which would assume it, does not make itself a present or a representation; something has already passed "over the head" of the present, has not passed through consciousness' cordon and does not allow itself to be recuperated; something which precedes the beginning and the principle, which is, an-archically, *in spite of* being, which inverts or precedes being.[78]

The trace of the Other which "has passed" in an "entirely accomplished past", is the *sens* of time: the differential "signification" of temporal alteration, and the *sens unique* of a dissymmetrical contamination which invests or inspires spontaneity in the one-way movement of its escaping approach.

The trace is the escape and incumbence of the Other in time. It is the alteration that is time's economy. When it is strategically posed as a presence, its proximity or approach becomes the principle of this presence. Levinas shares with Blanchot the tendency to mimic phenomenology's situation of intentionality in a moment of primordial adequation, and then to strip the predicates of adequation from this moment. When he does so, the concepts which defined the Blanchotian "image" are reproduced in his text. These concepts are excess and lack, escape and incumbence, passivity and dispossession. The trace is a reality which "lacks" presence or existence, and is thus always and essentially "past" or, more properly, "gone": "the presence of that which, strictly speaking, was never there, of that which is always past."[79] It is the "sign" of a passivity, an alterity without power or substantiality, the "signification" of an instance which had no "intention" of leaving a sign of its passing.[80] And the trace is a remainder: the excess of communication over negation and totalization. "The trace would be the very indelibility of being, its domination over all negativity, its immensity, incapable of enclosing itself and in some way too great for discretion, for interiority, for a Self [*Soi*]."[81] Like the image, the trace "recedes" into inexistence while not ceasing to be an excessive reality. This reality concerns the punctuality of consciousness by altering this punctuality. It implies the approach of another space and of another time. "An excession of the here, as locus, and of the now, as hour, an excession of contemporaneity and consciousness — which leaves a trace."[82] It is a *non-lieu* — a radical lack of self-coincidence, which strips consciousness of its own locus and punctuality.[83] This is because in its escape, the trace is an approach: an immemorial and unsubstantial element which concerns subjectivity, because it collaborated in the latter's constitution. Its escape produces the insatiable desire which pursues it, and its approach is its inspiration of this desire. The weakening of the negative is the principle of this progression. The "lack" in the trace is not a negativity, but an *écart* whose excess dispossesses the subjectivity in its proximity: "not a 'less than being',," but rather "all the enormity, all the excess, all the Infinity of the absolutely Other, escaping ontology."[84] The trace is the escaping incumbence of the Other in time. Like the pressure of the *Urimpression*, it dispossesses the interiority it creates. "(T)he trace does not place us in relation to that which would be less than being, but (. . .) obliges with regard to the Infinite, the absolutely Other."[85] The trace is a remainder, as is the *il y a*. And, like the *il y a*, it is a residue which contaminates all closure. Its escape is a contact, its unseizability also an *indessaisissabilité*. Its indefinition grips interiority, forcing it outward, toward the Other. Its presence is thus an "ob-sessing proximity", "bypassing consciousness: not by lack, but by excess, by the 'excession' of the approach."[86] Considered thus as the drama or vicissitude of an intentionality, the trace is a proximity which "disarms the intentionality that envisages it."[87] But the trace is not such a vicissitude. It is not an exterior instance encountered by consciousness, but is the very exteriority that creates subjectivity. The only rapport with the trace is passivity and desire, because the primordial ontology of interiority is passivity and desire. Consciousness is possible only as a modality of this proximity. Thus the escape or pastness of the trace is "an absolute past which unites all times"[88] — a passing and passivity of time which creates subjectivity. No intentionality encounters the trace — all intentionality is produced in the trace of the Other. Its predicates, like those of the Blanchotian image, proceed from a concept of differentiation which produces subjectivity in the collapsing of totalization — in space or in time. The trace and the image are not perceptual or intentional moments, but properly economic moments in a communicational reality.

The true common denominator which links the predicates of the image in Blanchot and the trace in Levinas is communication's excess over negation and correlation: an excess which creates subjectivity as an "inability not to understand" the signification of alterity's approach, which forces the interior to "go to the Other", which "obliges" toward alterity. Not the escape of the Other, but subjectivity's non-allergic *société* or communication with this Other, is the principle of the Blanchotian-Levinasian inspiration. This communication implies subjectivity's involvement with an exterior element irreducible to the form of a totality — the *il y a* of negation's remainder — and the alteration of interiority by this approaching excess, which is called impersonality. By virtue of its investment and contamination by the "third person" of alterity, the *ille* of illeity which escapes the alternative of immanence and transcendence, interiority is no longer identity, but is the *soi* of impersonality. And to this communicational unicity which is henceforth an inspired involvement with alterity, the subjectivity of the exterior — *Autrui* and the *visage* can now appear.

Beyond Being is a third person which is not defined by the "itself", by ipseity. It is the possibility of this third direction of radical irrectitude which escapes the bipolar play of immanence and transcendence, proper to being, in which immanence wins at every stroke over transcendence. The profile the irreversible past takes, through the trace, is the profile of the *Il*. The *beyond* from which the *visage* comes is the third person.[89]

The theme of the trace in Levinas describes the alterity of the exterior while stressing its irrecuperability, as a function of temporal alteration. The theme of the *visage* describes the same alterity while stressing its immediacy and its subjectivity. Like Blanchot's "nowhere" which is nevertheless "here", the Other is essentially "gone" while retaining a hyperbolic presence, in the proximity of the *visage*. The latter term describes the hyperbolic and overwhelmingly concerning passivity of alterity. The *visage* is *Autrui*: a powerless alterity toward which the heteronomy of inspiration "obliges" interiority. *Autrui* is the exterior in its difference, as a function of subjectivity's non-indifference toward this exterior.

When, in recurrence, the spontaneity of consciousness no longer has the "last word", and the passivity of subjectivity is revealed as the latent birth of this spontaneity, the temporal predicate of "pastness" associated with the trace becomes that of "tardiness" in the proximal *cogito*. Where the trace escapes into irrecuperability, the *visage* grips consciousness, as though on the basis of this forgotten but concerning past. "(I)n the trace of illeity,"[90] the *visage* is "invisible"[91] — that is, neither present nor substantial — and thus shares the "goneness" or *abscondité* of the trace, in its excess over manifestation. As mentioned earlier, this lack of presence is also the excess by which the *visage* dominates or overwhelms its manifest aspect. It is not an object, but rather an approach and a "signification" or "significance" of alterity. "It *is* by itself and not at all by reference to a system."[92] Its lack of attributes, of presence or phenomenality — its nudity — is also its incumbence. It is the form of an alterity with which subjectivity is "already" involved, and it approaches on the basis of this "already" which compromises. The *visage* is an instance which one does not recognize, but its significance is a commanding sense that one "knows" the *visage*. In other words, the *visage* is the *sens,* and the inspiring *sens unique,* of an alterity which invested interiority prior to its spontaneous moment, and which now grips interiority, on the basis of its uneliminable but forgotten reality. It is the immemorial past with which spontaneity remains involved: the unassumable element hidden within assumption. Subjectivity in its *cogito* is "late for an assignation." It has not arrived in time to assume a situation in which it is nevertheless concerned. "My exposition to it, anterior to its appearance, my lateness with regard to it, my passivity [*subir*], denuncleate that which is identity in me."[93] The subjection or exposition of subjectivity is its involvement with the irrecuperable. Called by various names, including election, assignation, and creation, in Levinas, this moment describes interiority's production in the proximity of the Other, and the latent non-indifference of constituted interiority toward this moment which precedes its retentions. The incumbence of the *visage* describes the secret moment in all consciousness at which its subjectivity is a "receding to a point prior to its point of departure" — a moment Blanchot has described in the concepts of *oubli* and the *nouvelle origine*. A past which was not "my" past, a past in which something penetrated consciousness within having the power to become manifest, now concerns me. And consciousness now is inadequate to the violence of this approach. "No movement of freedom could appropriate the *visage* or appear to 'constitute' it. The *visage* was already there when one antici- pated or constituted it — it collaborated in [this constitution], it spoke."[94] The *visage* "speaks" because it inspires the *parole* of interiority's heteronomy. It is not a totality which can be articulated with ipseity within the system of the Same. It is rather the investing alterity which produces closure, and toward which the passivity of the *pour l'autre* is the only attitude or "position". "(N)ot correlation, but *irrectitude* itself" is the rapport with the *visage*.[95] Its exteriority dispossesses and alters interiority. The "already" of alterity in the *visage* is that moment in subjectivity's conation in which it is "not alone", and in which this invasion of privacy which is essential solitude compromises the "egoism" of consciousness: a pre-originary and inactual moment whose resonances haunt the universe of manifestation.

The *visage* is an *écart* within the exterior — a collapsing, passive subjec- tivity — which is now, already, the *écart* of interiority itself, that is, its lack of self-coincidence which describes an intrication with alterity. Thus the inactuality of the *visage* compels from an intruding exterior. That interiority is now already outside itself, within this exterior, is the sense of the Levinasian term "substi- tution". Unicity is in the place of the Other — that is, nowhere, *au dehors, pour l'autre*. The approach of the *visage* is "immediate",[96] "unforeseeable",[97] and infinitely "urgent",[98] because its pre-originary involvement or preoccupation of subjectivity is the latter's very conation. Levinas stresses the inadequation of this approach to the concept of consciousness and phenomenality, because he is con- cerned to show in the proximity of assignation the latent birth of consciousness itself. "The extreme urgency of the assignation upsets the 'presence of mind' necessary for the reception of a given and for the identification of the diverse in which, noema of a noesis, the phenomenon appears. Extreme urgency — the modality of obsession (which is known but is not a knowledge): I do not have the time to face it."[99] The future in assignation, as in all proximity, is the immediacy of imminence, because, in differentiation and in repetition, it is "already" in the present, as it is "already" in the immemorial past. The inactual "concerns" subjectivity, in the immediate future, far more compellingly than an object or moment which would be merely actual. The lack of a temporal interval adequate to intentionality, and the insistence of a pressing temporal intrication, proceed from time's own irreducibility to manifestation. There is "no time" between the future and now; no time between assignation and the response to assignation. Both Blanchot and Levinas call this collapsing contamination of historical time by an *écart* which is not an interval, *temps mort*, "dead time".[100] This is the time of being's passivity in differentiation: a time in which discontinuity does not mean distinction or correlation. Here, the Other's approach fills every interval, because here subjectivity is created by communication. On the basis of this primary moment, the proposition of a future which concerns subjectivity from the past, and of a past which involves a subject who was not present when something happened, can have meaning. Within the totality, this proposition will be prohibited and neglected, but will retain a jarring currency and familiarity, in art, in religion, and in the communicational events of the everyday. With the advent of psychoanalysis, and in the most remote horizons of scientific interrogation and political activism, it will enter formal discourse while retaining its prohibited aspect. The proximity described by the *visage* is an inactuality which concerns the present. It is inexistent, but not unreal. To Ulysses' question of alterity's existence or inexistence, Levinas responds: "nothing could arrest this triumphant question. How transparent it is, in effect, the shadow which troubles the clarity of the coherent discourse!"[101] Of communication's alterity, one must say with Gilles Deleuze, "it no longer exists, it does not exist, but it insists, it consists, it *is*."[102] Its unsubstantiality does not exhaust its reality. Its lack of power, in a world of action, does not reduce the urgency of its approach.

The production of spontaneity, for Levinas, is the contamination or "shame" of spontaneity: its preoccupation with and by the Other, which is based on its intrication with the Other. This communicational moment is the production of interiority, and of an exterior which weighs upon interiority, in the dimension called the *éthique*. This dimension, by virtue of the heteronomy and incompletion it introduces into closure, is the possibility of manifestation, of relation and totalization. In its inability to extricate itself from the insistence of alterity, and in the inclination toward alterity which is its conation, subjectivity has its first "critical" or "theoretical" experience. And in this experience of separation, the possibility of negation and of a spontaneity which may "act" upon the exterior is grounded. But negation is first difference, and the totality is first a moment of the *éthique*. Spontaneity is first what Levinas calls "responsibility". In the economic and heteronomous movement of its closure, subjectivity already "responds", in an entirely passive or pre-voluntary manner, to the assignation that creates it. Conation, the "effort toward autonomy" which is always a *dépense* and a desire, is this response. "To the idea of the Infinite there can only be an extra-vagant response"[103] — that is, a response which dispossesses as it invests. The response is the *pour l'autre* and the *au dehors*, the pouring outward, which is the very intensity of closure. It is not an assumption by a spontaneity, but is precisely the impossibility of such an assumption, for a subjectivity whose being is no longer exhausted by the correlation of action and reaction in a world of power. The density of interiority is its inspiration by communication, and the heteronomy of its desire. "In this movement, my freedom does not have the last word, I never recover my solitude, or, if one wishes, moral consciousness is essentially unsatisfying, or if one wishes, always Desire."[104] The repeated Levinasian phrase "a passivity never passive enough" describes the inadequation inherent in subjectivity's inspired desire of alterity. Interiority's radical dispossession by the Other's approach does not constitute an adequation to this proximity, or a rejoining of the Other in a utopian element — as Levinas' hasty readers, including Blanchot, have concluded. Inspiration invests separation while producing transcendence: the escape and approach of alterity. The concept of desire — closure's inspired affirmation in a world without negation — is central to this configuration. In the proximity of alterity, closure is an exigency: an excessive closing which is a paroxysm toward the Other. Responsibility is an "increase of exigencies"[105] because increase is the only ontology of desire. "The more I face up to my responsibility, the more I am responsible."[106] The fact that responsibility cannot be assumed is the definition of responsibility. "(A) responsibility I have assumed at no moment, in no present. Nothing is more passive than this implication anterior to my freedom."[107] Subjectivity is a "responsibility before being an intentionality"[108] — a consciousness produced by communication. Responsibility is the affirmation of an interiority which is involved with alterity, which responds to alterity, and whose inability not to respond is its very positivity. This situation proceeds from the definition of closure in the general economy as a *parole*, a desire, and a *pour l'autre*. The common denominator of these predications is affirmation: the impossibility which is not negative.[109]

The *visage* is a passivity within the exterior over which interiority has no power. This moment can have reality because the general economy individuates without totalizing. Closure is an uprooting which "goes to" the Other without refusing, because refusal is not the primary moment of its ontology. Inspiration is this moment. And, as discussed earlier, the *sens* or movement of inspiration is univocal and dissymetrical: *pour l'autre*. Closure's turgidity is a *dépense*, a destitution or sacrifice, toward the exterior. Thus the poverty of *Autrui* in the *visage* is a lack within the exterior which interiority "must" fulfill and is "already" fulfilling, as a function of its closure. Dissymetry or non-reciprocity is the principle of closure's investing dispossession, in affirmation, inspiration and desire. The poverty and passivity of the *visage* — its lack of totalization and consequent incumbence — "empty" the subjectivity in its proximity. This is subjectivity's primordial economy. "But this supplication is an exigency. The humility in it is united with *hauteur*."[110] The theme of *hauteur*, a passivity in the exterior which touches and dispossesses interiority across the interval of separation, articulates the irreducible dissymetry and heteronomy of all communication, when communication is not totalization. "The dimension of *hauteur* in which *Autrui* is placed, is as though the primary curving [*courbure*] of being from which *Autrui* receives its privilege, the de-levelling [*dénivellement*] of transendence."[111] The "curving" of being's economy is its *sens unique*: the inclination and dispossession of the Same toward alterity, which proceeds from the fact that the Same is not a totality, and cannot be correlated dialectically or ontologically with the Other. Communication is a non-reciprocity, because closure itself is a "radical irrectitude." The impossibility of correlation or reciprocity in this situation is its necessary and sufficient condition, and is the Levinasian definition of the term "éthique".

Negativity is incapable of transcendence. The latter designates a relation with a reality infinitely distant from mine, without this distance destroying on this basis this relation, and without this relation destroying this distance, as would occur in the relations interior to the Same; without this relation becoming an implantation in the Other and a confusion with it, without the relation violating the very identity of the Same or its ipseity. . . .[112]

The contaminating investment of closure by a powerless alterity which is not itself another Same, and cannot annihilate closure within dispersion, is the "ethical" aspect of the general economy. This differential economy produces separation as a non-indifference — an inspiration which may subsequently assume the form of a relation — and not as an identity which may enter into the reciprocity of relation on the basis of its self-coincidence.

The concentration of the *éthique* in "responsibility" must be understood in its irreducibility to negation, assumption, and power. The "response" is not ordained by a power or value, and is not dictated by the prescriptions or exigencies of a practical reason. Entirely outside truth — a *sens* or "signification" which is a *non-sens* — it is not a higher truth. The assignation is not organized by God: it is the economy of separation. Perhaps the best expression of responsibility's production in proximity is its irreducibility to the concept of "right", i.e. to a value which would be correlative to truth. The *éthique* is a dissymetrical force in being which produces communication as separation. As such, it invests freedom and produces the eventuality of "unpunished crimes". This eventuality is the essence of the *éthique*, and not its accident. It is what Levinas calls the "price of separation". The atheism of the *éthique*, by comparison with what Levinas calls "positive religions", is its excess over the concatenation of manifestation, power, and correlation which is sacred communion. "Against all relation to the sacred,"[113] the *éthique* produces separation. The totality is an "ethical" economy — "a world in which and of which one speaks [*parle*] " — because the *parole* of separation is its ontological principle. The totalitarian movements of *essence*, the *esse* of being which is an *interesse*, will obscure their communicational foundation; and this obscuring is not an event which can be "opposed" by the *éthique*. Bataille and Blanchot intuited this configuration in their enthusiastic agreement that the *expérience* has no "authority" or "expiates" its authority. Communication does not compete with action, but invests the latter. Although the Levinasian metaphysician is always an "atheist", and although the *éthique* itself is an atheism in the common sense of this term, its description of proximity has an important common denominator with religion. This is the latter's intuition, in many forms and in an endlessly repeated configuration, of an alterity which has no power, but which nevertheless involves or compels subjectivity, because power is not the ultimate dimension of subjectivity's appearance in being. Although most religions, in their "positivity", tend to subordinate the incumbence of this alterity to the governing context of a divinity which is itself a higher power or higher truth, they nevertheless discover a fugitive moment at which incumbence is neither power nor determination. The allergy of philosophical and political activity to religion proceeds from the nonsensical aspect of this "powerless domination" from an ontological point of view. The cooperation or complicity of religion and Western metaphysics, on a more profound level, is their tendency to subordinate proximity to the correlations of a higher power or truth, which Levinas calls the "peace of reason": a peace which is the image of war. The notion of an incumbence without power is perhaps the sole point of contact between Levinas and religion, but it is an important contact. Religion, like psychoanalysis, literature, and myth, is a context in which the theme of an approach from beyond manifestation intervenes with regularity. The common denominator of these contexts is their rapport with an instance without truth, and their rejection as irrationality by Western culture in its concern with totalization. This rejection often takes the form of a cumbersome recuperation, which has been best described by Blanchot in the context of art and literature. Its basis may be either the correlations of humanism or the aggressive iconoclasm which exalts dispersion in favor of closure. The familiar figure of Levinas as a "theologian" who thematizes communication as though in spite of himself, is reminiscent of Freud's familiar characterization as a stern, orthodox father who also thematizes communicational alteration as though in spite of himself. These prodigal sons of Western epistemology are pictured as purveyors of a spurious non-violence (the "non-violence" of non-allergic communication in Levinas, the psychic determinism and sexism attributed to Freud) because the contaminations they evoke describe the single face of violence to which the Western imagination is most allergic: passivity.

Levinas often speaks with feigned embarrassment of his "recourse" to a vocabulary of ethics and transcendence for the description of a rapport of Same and Other within the general economy. Although it is true that the Levinasian concepts of invested interiority and the approach of the exterior have little affinity with traditional ethical discourse, and that these concepts cannot be deduced from the synoptic view of intersubjectivity which is their apparent context, Levinas' choice of the *éthique* as his thematic context is most compelling. If the history of formal discourse on intersubjectivity has taken the form of an overwhelming exigency toward correlation and reciprocity, the actual "history" of intersubjectivity within the everyday describes a spectrum of contaminations to which the definitions of this discourse are virtually irrelevant. Attested with discomfiture and avidity by rumor and journalism — themselves moments of impersonality — these contaminations consistently imply an involvement of Same with Other. The public discourse whose perennial purpose has been the description of this involvement, and which has on this basis the greatest affinity with Levinas' *éthique*, is literature. And literature's exigency has always been the invocation of subjectivity's concerning, non-allergic rapport with an instance that is important without being "essential", that is compelling without having the form of a "truth", that must be attested and experienced, although not through action or comprehension.* The anomaly of literature among discourses — the "frivolity of the eternal and the weightiness of the imaginary" which are, in Blanchot's words, its province — is this veering toward an instance which approaches from outside the Same, and which "concerns" both subjectivity and intersubjectivity from the very distance of its inactuality. This instance is the Other of closure: an inaccessibility whose escape from comprehension or experience is not the only sense of its reality. As it escapes, it approaches. In its inessentiality, it concerns. Subjectivity's separation is its non-allergic involvement with this alterity. The only "position" which may be assumed toward it is the passivity of desire and inspiration. The Other's approach is our exigency. The violent avidity, the ambivalence and non-reciprocity of intersubjective relations proceed from the fact that separation is their principle. Separation is always an "essential solitude", in the Blanchotian sense of this expression: an invasion of privacy and an impossibility of correlation with or totalization of the instance which intrudes. Separation in intersubjectivity — the preferred topic of nearly all literary texts — describes, in Blanchot's profound terms, a "non-familiar intimacy" without adequation, a dispossession without communion, and a discontinuity or distance without correlation: a "presence without ensemble". In intersubjective communication, as in all communication, the principle of separation is the exigency. As psychoanalysis was to attest — less, perhaps, in its theoretical discourse than in the economic event of its own therapeutic communications, founded on the principle of non-reciprocity — the intersubjective rapport is an ambivalence and an avidity without correlation. In the intersubjective presence, the Same desires the Other on the basis of its immemorial and constituting inclination toward the exterior. The contamination produced by desire in the exigency invests not only the allergic and violent moment of intersubjective communication, which the metaphysics of totalization must always understand as a persistent accident susceptible of correction by a

---

* Common sense is not wrong in ascribing to the strange gravity of literature a moral or ethical value. Its mistake lies in interpreting as an intramundane ethics designed to reconcile persons through correlation, what is rather, in Batille's term, an *hypermorale*, or in Blanchot's expression, an "authenticity" without action or truth: that is, the Levinasian *éthique* itself, which haunts nearly all literary communication.

more subtly adjusted form of correlation. It also produces the continuing involvement of the Same with its Other that is the true face of communication. In the
paradoxical avidity of the caress, which "still seeks what it has already found,"
Levinas perceives subjectivity's latent birth as an "inability to be quits with the
other" (*ne pas pouvoir être quitte envers le prochain*[114]). Subjectivity remains
involved with the inaccessible — the Same remains involved with its Other — in
intersubjectivity. This involvement is the "price of separation", when separation
is proximity. The Levinasian *éthique* is the dimension of this proximity which
allows and forces interiority to be "concerned" by the exterior and by the
exterior person, by virtue of the fact that, in separation, interiority is not alone.

BATAILLE, BLANCHOT, AND LEVINAS

Transgression, essential solitude, and inspiration are the three principles of the
Levinasian *éthique*. The general economy produces closure as an excess and an
insufficiency whose exigency is its intrication with the exterior. Closure is a
transgression of closure. The "sense" of this transgression is univocal: into the
exterior, toward the Other. By virtue of closure's excessive exigency in an
economy which cannot produce totalization, closure is an essential solitude.
"Where I am alone, I am not alone." "Where I am alone, I am not there." "Where
I am alone, someone is there." Closure's density proceeds from the proximity of
the exterior: a proximity which creates unicity as it forecloses identity. Closure
is Someone, in the proximity of Someone. The exterior is a subjectivity and a
passivity: a powerless and unsubstantial proximity which invests unicity as it
dispossesses the latter. The exterior is not only an element. It is Someone: the
Other and *Autrui*. The exteriority of this alterity collaborates in the conation of
a Same which is an irreducible heteronomy. The Same is not a totality, but a
difference. And by virtue of its differential economy, the Same is a subjectivity
which cannot be indifferent toward alterity. Its intense closure is an *errance*: a
heteronomy forced into the exterior. The force of this *pour l'autre* of closure is
inspiration. The univocal sense of investment and alteration, the "curving", dissymmetrical *sens unique* of communication in proximity, proceeds from the fact
that the general economy's principle is not totalization and correlation, but
incompletion and inspiration. The process of differentiation in being produces
closure through the detour of an element irreducible to closure: exteriority or
alterity. Unicity is not determined by another unicity, in a universe of autonomy
and correlation, but is invested by the exterior. This investing exterior is not
another Same, not a totality which determines. It is a passivity which inspires.
The inspiration of unicity is its transgression, its essential solitude, and its non-
allergic rapport with this passivity of alterity. The powerlessness or subjectivity
of the exterior is an approach which compels or concerns interiority. This is
because interiority, in the intensity of its solitude, remains involved with this
inaccessible exterior. Inspiration is the turgidity of a closure which goes to the

338

Other as a function of its own closing. In the configuration of difference and non-indifference, interiority's conation moves "backward", inside-out", "in reverse": toward the Other. The only rapport with alterity in proximity is the passivity of inspired desire. When I approach, it escapes. When it approaches me, it escapes. When I withdraw into my privacy, the intimacy of this privacy is already the presence of the Other. But most basically, when I abide, it approaches. Unicity is the exigency of the Other. Because closure is inspired by alterity, the only economy of its fugitive self-coincidence is the Other's approach. By virtue of the fact that exteriority "concerns" inspired unicity, rather than to be correlated with the latter — by virtue of the fact that unicity is "not alone" in its closure, but is a desire — relation and totalization are possible in the general economy. But these factors are events of communication, articulations of a non-allergic rapport of Same and Other. They are moments of the *éthique*.

The economic constitution of the *réponse* of responsibility in recurrence is desire: an irreducible excess and incompletion which contaminates closure as it produces closure. Responsibility is unicity's primordial inclination or veering toward the exterior: an apparently punctual invasion of subjectivity's spontaneity by an approach, the *visage*, which paralyzes this spontaneity. Yet this approach is not an occurrence. It is a recurrence: the repetitive and proximal "event", in the Blanchotian sense of this word, that is separation in being. For this reason, the paralysis of spontaneity does not exhaust or disperse the unicity of interiority. The latter retains, in the proximity of the Other, its *quant à soi*, its closure, and a sense of what is happening which is "known" without being a "knowledge". In this ambiguous moment, Bataillian *expérience, non-savoir*, and the "resolute passivity" of transgression are perceptible, as are Blanchotian indecision, fascination, and Orpheus' exigency. The common denominator of these experiences of proximity is separation: an absolute heteronomy and passivity which is nevertheless the economic investment of subjectivity and the possibility of consciousness. In an impossible congruence brought about by negation's "weakness" in proximity, the "effort of autonomy" and its own *dépense* — closure and the excess of closure — coexist in the moment Bataille called the *glissement*. The notion of separation in proximity describes an involvement of two "opposite" moments, interiority and alterity, whose distinction is not a contradiction, and whose rapport is not a dialectical transcending of opposition. These moments are not correlated in an economy of totalization which would itself be defined as a totality or system. They describe the production of the Same as an alteration, in a "general" economy which is not a totality and which cannot totalize its elements. In such an economy, both unicity and rapport must be understood as the "radical irrectitude" of contamination and differential intensity. Multiplicity and relation are functions of the Same's alteration in proximity.

This alteration is first an excess: a *dépense* and a *parole*, a "response" to the exterior which inspires by its approach. What Bataille called closure's "transfer" of its discontinuity "to the impersonality of life" is the configuration of substitution and responsibility. When Levinas speaks of an "exigency coming from the other" to open a "limitless 'deficit' in which the *Soi* expends itself [*se dépense*],"[115] he speaks in Bataille's voice. For Levinas, interiority is a "gravity" in being, a susceptibility to alterity's pressure or incumbence — and this gravity is an "effort toward autonomy" which is always primordially a *dépense*.

This self we have seen appear in *jouissance* as a separate being having apart, in itself, the center around which its existence gravitates — confirms itself in its singularity by emptying itself of this gravitation, which does not cease emptying itself and which confirms itself precisely in this incessant effort to empty itself. I call this *bonté*.[116]

Interiority is a *dépense* informed or invested by the proximity of alterity, and which, by the very force of its loss or "emptying", is a closure. This inspired destitution is subjectivity's "response" to the approach of the Other. The fulfilling element in which the subjectivity of *jouissance* bathes, is also the dispossession which forces interiority toward the Other. The time of *jouissance* is also the Proustian Time of a supporting *habitude* or Habit which is also desire and alteration: a time of change and metamorphosis which Levinas calls "senescence" and then recurrence. In time as in separation, interiority is desire and loss: not a capacity for generosity, but a dispossession toward the Other which proceeds from the ontology of "incarnation".[117] Closure is not totalization, but communication. "To be in-itself is to express oneself, that is, already to serve *Autrui*. The foundation of expression is *bonté*."[118] The experience of thought was, for Bataille, "my thought which flees me." And this excessive heteronomy of thinking is for Bataille a function of closure's *parole*: "thus I speak, everything in me gives itself to others."[119] Interiority's investment by the exterior is a fulfillment which is the force of a destitution. Levinas' proposition, "I did not know I was so rich, but I no longer have the right to keep anything,"[120] is a most Bataillian *cogito*, in its description of a concupiscence and excess which are closure's transgression toward the Other.

Recurrence is interiority's *nouvelle origine* as inspiration and substitution. Interiority is "already" involved with *Autrui* within the exterior. This is its "rendezvous with itself" in essential solitude. Inspiration is on one hand the Other's approach within the Burrow — an exteriority which concerns — and on the other hand the *errance* of closure which is forced into the exterior by communication. In his descriptions of responsibility, Levinas reproduces the Blanchotian predicates of consciousness' awakening in *Thomas l'obscur*. "The *Moi* in relation with the Infinite is an impossibility of arresting its forward movement;"[121] responsibility is an "impossibility to stop speaking."[122] The common denominator which links these formulations is impossibility itself: the production of inspired unicity in an economy without negation, totalization, or power. Interiority's self-coincidence is the "must" of the exigency which forces it toward the Other on the basis of its prior involvement with the Other. Levinas repeatedly identifies "inspiration" as the principle of substitution[123] — an inspiration in which unicity is "in itself through the other"[124] and in which this contamination confirms separation. "Without ceasing to be other," the Other invests the Same "without alienating the Same."[125] In the inspired *parole* of non-indifference, the Other "commands by my own voice"[126] because the proximity of the Other is "the very *pneuma* of *psychisme*."[127] Yet dispersion or communion is not the principle of this heteronomy. Difference or separation is this principle. The inspired *parole* belongs to interiority, when interiority is communication. Responsibility makes me "the author of that which has been insufflated in me without my knowledge."[128] The *parole* is an inability not to answer which articulates the very positivity of closure, in an economy without power or spontaneity. The paradoxes of the *éthique* trouble common sense from the same point of departure as the paradoxes of difference: inspiration, and its economy of radical or general heteronomy. In the "pneumatism of proximity," the "insufflation" or inspiration of interiority is the breathlessness of *essoufflement*: the excess of "the spirit which breathes out without ever breathing in."[129] Heteronomy is the *sens unique* or univocity of inspiration, and the *sens* or signification which creates movement in the general economy. The approach of the Other divests as it invests. It never approaches interiority as to a center or point, but creates interiority in recurrence as the *non-lieu* of *errance*. Subjectivity is *au dehors*, outside itself and outside everything, as a function of its unicity. The intense and violent self-coincidence of closure is what Blanchot calls its *attrait sur place* or "attraction in place": its immobilization by the very inspiration which forces it to move. Interiority in substitution is the *ôtage*, the captive, of alterity.

Interiority is a captive which is also a fugitive: it is the forced immobility of exile. This intense and excessive moment is the unicity of interiority, when unicity is not totalization. Closure is a "response to an assignation which identifies me as the unique, not at all in restoring me to myself, but in stripping me of all identical quiddity and, consequently, of all form, of all investiture. . . ."[130] The enigma of a unicity which is forced by the Other, which is not independent — not alone — is the enigma of difference, in its contamination of the alternative of totalization and dispersion. Unicity is a heteronomy without determination or correlation, but not a destruction. It appears in an economy of impossibility, in which closure can be thought without the predicate of power. "The unicity of the chosen [*élu*] or called who is not an elector, a passivity not converting itself into spontaneity. A unicity which is not assumed, sub-sumed, traumatic. . . .".[131] This unicity is unique and non-interchangeable because it is not a term, not a totality and, in the vocabulary of the philosophy of difference, it does not "resemble" the other elements in its proximity. It insists in a universe without correlation. Its lack of power is a necessary consequence or necessary condition of this impossibility of correlation. Closure's non-allergic rapport with the exterior — a radical heteronomy — is its unicity. "The unicity of the self is the fact that no one may answer in my place."[132] The terror of proximity, in the burrow, in the night, in the approach of death, is this non-interchangeability of the captive whose destiny is his own, while proceeding from outside himself — from another time, from the Other. And election is not determination. Beckett's repeated proposition in *Fin de partie*, "quelque chose suit son cours" — "something is following its course" — is inadequate to the heteronomy of proximity. The captive in proximity "knows what is happening to him" — in a knowing which is not a knowledge — but this experience is a passivity unrelated to an exterior autonomy. Closure has no "investiture". It is for this reason that the *éthique* is as estranged from religion as it is estranged from philosophy. Nothing determines the closure of assignation. But this closure cannot become a dispersion. This destruction would be the action of a power. Western thought, in its aggressive haste to eliminate the closure of totalization, betrays its commitment to the latter by always meditating heteronomy as a return to autonomy. "Able to be unique"; "able to be absolutely heteronomous"; "able to transgress all limits": these concepts and their analogues are the West's dreams of a subjectivity which "goes beyond" the totality, into an element of dispersion free from constraint. The public destinies of Nietzsche and Bataille are implicit in this ambivalent concept of an alterity which destroys and disperses on the basis of its ability to destroy and disperse. In another sense, it is this commitment to the alternative of autonomy and destruction that motivates most misreadings of the Levinasian text. The proposition of a heteronomous Same that is not a dispersed Same (not dispersed within alterity) and which nevertheless has a rapport with an Other that is not another Same, is entirely nonsensical in a discursive universe exhausted by the duality of totalization and dispersion. In such a universe, "I must be an Other for the Other"; "the Other must be another Same for himself"; "if I am dispersed I cannot be responsible"; "the Other must be within being and therefore cannot be Other." The economy of proximity begins where correlation ends — and, to paraphrase Blanchot, proximity "marks the point at which power ceases." This "point" is the moment of separation. Unicity in proximity is "one" — but "not alone" in its unicity. From the point of view of manifestation and correlation, a communication which does not proceed from an identity is impossible. It is significant and appropriate that for Bataille, Blanchot, and Levinas, "impossibility" is the principle of the general economy. The Blanchot of "Le grand refus" says very well that the Being of ontology is "being, plus the power of being." The opacity of proximity, and of the philosophy of difference informed by the concept of proximity, to surrounding tendencies in traditional and modern thought, is its description of a reality without power, and of a unicity which is not immediately conceived as an extrication from the exterior which might then enter into relations with the latter. The notion of a unicity which proceeds from a powerless exteriority with which it remains however inextricably involved in the configuration of non-indifference, is the ultimate radicality of the philosophies of proximity and difference. Their critical descriptions of the closure which characterizes philosophy's interest in totalization (presence, determination, phenomenality, illumination) are the superstructure of the more basic moment at which the concepts placed in question are autonomy and power. Although the Levinasian text apparently suffers most from contemporary misreadings of its context and intention ("How can I be responsible?" "How can the unsubstantial concern me?"), its obscurity and marginality are shared by all Occidental texts which have articulated the theme of difference — when difference is non-indifference.

The text of proximity is anomalous because it evokes the proposition of passivity. It is Bataille above all, in his Nietzschian inspiration, who defines autonomy as the interest or exigency of closure. His genius consists in part of his discovery that the very force of this exigent closure proceeds from its non-allergic rapport with the exterior. The exigency is the insatiability of exteriority, the "passion", the "obsession" of being. Closure is an inspiration and a communication. Thus it is capable of impossible comportments: a knowing that is not a knowledge, a movement that is not an action, a signification that is not an illumination. The passivity of closure is the principle of these and the many other excessive, heterogeneous movements which haunt the everyday. These movements are events of impossibility and of inactuality which lie "underneath" the possible, which surround and invade the universe of the spontaneous and effective, and which are attested by the impersonality of rumor and common sense far more often than by formal discourse. They cannot compete with action and actuality, and they cannot change the world — although they point to the communicational factor which defines the world as change and alteration — but they "insist" and "consist". They are uneliminable, because they approach from an "other" space. They are the nocturnal, transgressive, and ethical element which haunts the familiarity of the Same. Thus Levinas writes of responsibility: "Will is free to assume this responsibility in the sense it wishes; it is not free not to know the sensible [sensé] world into which the visage of Autrui has introduced it."[133] The sense of assumption and the sense of the sensible are the sens unique of closure's inspired passivity, and are the "signification" which is its latent birth in communication. Inaccessible but concerning, unsubstantial but uneliminable: these terms describe the reality of proximity which is not an existence. That this reality cannot become effective, cannot compete with action in the terms of action — that its only reality is the autrement qu'être and the irreality of the approach — cannot foreclose or eliminate the uncanny sense that it invests both the violence and the non-violence of the totality, on the very basis of its passivity.

The Bataille of La Somme athéologique speaks of a "moral" exigency toward Autrui which is implicit in the concept of expérience. In his essay on Emily Brontë, he speaks of an "hypermorale" required by the concept of transgression.[134] In L'Erotisme, he speaks of his own theoretical position toward proximity as that of a "theologian". At two points in L'Espace littéraire,[135] Blanchot speaks with some ambivalence of an "authenticity" which might be conditioned by the failure and passivity of transgression in proximity. The second of these passages is cited erroneously by Emmanuel Levinas as the sole factor which extricates Blanchot's discourse from its "Heideggerian" inspiration.[136] This passage reads:

the more the world affirms itself as the future and the bright daylight of truth in which all will have value, in which all will have meaning, in which all will be accomplished under the mastery of man and for his use, the more it seems that art must descend toward that point at which nothing yet has meaning, the more it is important that it maintain the movement, the insecurity and the misfortune of that which escapes all seizing and all ends. The artist and the poet have as though received the mission of recalling us obstinately to error, of turning us toward the space in which all that we propose for ourselves, all that we have acquired, all that we are, all that which opens upon the earth and in the sky, returns to the insignificant, in which that which approaches is the non-serious and the non-true, as though perhaps burst forth here the source of all authen-ticity.[137]

Although Levinas, in his 1956 essay on Blanchot, vainly attempts to appropriate the Blanchotian universe of impersonality to the economy of the *éthique* on the basis of this exceptional use of the word "authenticity", he correctly reads in this passage the essence of proximity's "reality". This reality is an approach, and only an approach. It invests and contaminates the "light of day", the "profane world", the "totality" or *essence* from the position of its inactuality and pass-ivity. Although it cannot become actual or effective, it produces the totality itself as an inspiration. Totalization is possible only because identity, relation, comprehension and action are the moments of an insatiability in being: the exigency of the Other. The punctuality and spontaneity of the day, and the progressive history of action, are moments of recurrence: the *nouvelle origine* of unicity in a repetitive time which is concerning and proximal. The time of the Same is its eternal return and its metamorphosis: a time in which the Same is never entirely the Same, the "world" is never entirely the "world", because Time is the element of the Other's approach. Although no mention of au-thenticity or of moral exigencies is required for a situation of the *éthique* in the texts of Blanchot and Bataille — since every important concept in these texts articulates the passivity and non-indifference which are the essence of the *éthique* — it remains true that, by virtue of its non-allergic and forever obscure response to this approach of the Other, the totality can be a dimension "pre-occupied" by the impossible realities of authenticity or generosity. It can be so preoccupied because its most totalitarian moments presuppose its immemorial preoccupation with this approach. Underneath the immobility of its correlations and the violent ambivalence of its actions, the Same is an economy of inspiration and desire in which the proposition of an exterior element which concerns in spite of its passivity, is never entirely nonsensical. In the recurrence of the Same — its eternal return in the proximity of the Other, which Levinas calls *eschatologie* — the Same is the alteration of Desire. It is only in this Time of alteration and non-indifference that the Same can be what it is, and never be entirely what it is: separation as exigency, in the approach of the Other.

NOTES

References to *L'Erotisme, La Part maudite, La Littérature et le mal, L'Espace littéraire,* and *Le Livre à venir* initially indicate the pagination of the more widely circulated paperback editions. The pagination of the original editions is given in parentheses.

All quotations have been translated for this volume. For the convenience of the English-speaking reader, the pagination of *Totalité et infini, De l'existence à l'existant, L'Erotisme,* and *La Littérature et le mal* in their English translations is given in parentheses with the notation "tr.".

The following abbreviations are used:

Books by Georges Bataille:

O.C.:   *Oeuvres complètes*, 8 vol. Paris: Gallimard, 1970–7.
E.:   *L'Erotisme*. Paris: Minuit, 1957.
                Paris: U.G.E. "10/18", 1970
                Death and Sensuality (tr. Mary Dalwood). New York: Walker, 1962.
P.M.:   *La Part maudite*. Paris: Minuit, 1949.
                Paris: Minuit "Points", 1967.
Ex.I.:   *L'Expérience intérieure* (Paris: Gallimard, 1943). O.C., Vol. 5, 1973.
C.:   *Le Coupable* (Paris: Gallimard, 1944). O.C., Vol. 5, 1973.
S.N.:   *Sur Nietzsche* (Paris: Gallimard, 1945). O.C., Vol. 6, 1973.
L.M.:   *La Littérature et le mal*. Paris: Gallimard, 1957.
                Paris: Gallimard "Idées", 1970.
                Literature and Evil (tr. A. Hamilton). London: Calder & Boyars, 1973.

Books by Maurice Blanchot:

E.L.:   *L'Espace littéraire*. Paris: Gallimard, 1955.
                Paris: Gallimard "Idées", 1968.
L.V.:   *Le Livre à venir*. Paris: Gallimard, 1959.
                Paris: Gallimard "Idées", 1971.
E.I.:   *L'Entretien infini*. Paris: Gallimard, 1969.
P.F.:   *La Part du feu*. Paris: Gallimard, 1949.
P.A.:   *Le Pas au-delà*. Paris: Gallimard, 1973.

Books by Emmanuel Levinas:

T.I.:   *Totalité et infini*. The Hague: Nijhoff, 1961.
         Totality and Infinity (tr. A. Lingis). Pittsburgh: Duquesne, 1969.
A.E.:   *Autrement qu'être ou au delà de l'essence*. The Hague: Nijhoff, 1974.
         Otherwise than Being (tr. A. Lingis). The Hague: Nijhoff, 1981.
E.D.E: *En découvrant l'existence avec Husserl et Heidegger* (2nd ed.) Paris:
         Vrin, 1967.
E.E.:   *De l'existence à l'existant*. Paris: Fontaine, 1947.
         Existence and Existents (tr. A. Lingis). The Hague: Nijhoff, 1978.
H.H.:   *Humanisme de l'autre homme*. Montpellier: Fata Morgana, 1972.
T.A.:   *Le Temps et l'autre* in *Le Choix, le monde, l'existence*. Paris: Arthaud,
         1948.

Chapter 1: Separation and the General Economy

1. Most of these essays are collected in O.C. I.
2. Originally published in *La Critique sociale*, no. 7, janvier 1933, pp. 7–15. Reprinted in O.C. I, pp. 302–20.
3. O.C. I, p. 305.
4. *Documents*, no. 6, novembre 1929, pp. 297–302. Reprinted in O.C. I, pp. 200–4.
5. O.C. I, p. 203.
6. *La Critique sociale*, no. 10, novembre 1933, pp. 159–65, and no. 11, mars 1934, pp. 205–11. Reprinted in O.C. I, pp. 339–71.
7. O.C. I, pp. 302–3.
8. *Ibid.*, p. 346.
9. *Ibid.*, p. 340.
10. *Ibid.*, p. 347.
11. *Ibid.*, p. 344.
12. *Ibid.*, p. 345.
13. *Ibid.*
14. *Ibid.*, p. 361.
15. *Ibid.*, p. 363.
16. *Ibid.*, p. 359.
17. *Ibid.*, p. 347.
18. *Ibid.*, p. 302.
19. O.C. V, pp. 110–11.
20. E., p. 17 (18–19) (tr. 12).
21. *Ibid.* (19) (tr. 13).
22. *Ibid.*, p. 18 (20) (tr. 14).
23. *Ibid.*, p. 19 (20) (tr. 14).
24. *Ibid.*, p. 62 (62) (tr. 55).
25. *Ibid.*
26. P.M., p. 75 (87)
27. E., p. 105 (106) (tr. 96).
28. P.M., pp. 75–6 (87).
29. E., p. 111 (111) (tr. 101).
30. Ex.I., p. 111.
31. E., p. 24 (26) (tr. 19).
32. P.M., p. 62 (72–3).
33. Ex.I., p. 100.
34. E., p. 108 (109) (tr. 98).
35. Ex.I., p. 111.
36. C., p. 376.
37. *Ibid.*, p. 263.
38. *Ibid.*, p. 261.
39. *Méthode de méditation* (Fontaine, 1947; reprinted with Ex.I. by Gallimard, 1954) in O.C. V, p. 228.
40. E., p. 44 (45) (tr. 39).
41. *Ibid.*, pp. 114–15 (115) (tr. 104–5).
42. *Ibid.*, p. 115 (116) (tr. 105).
43. Ex.I., p. 67. Cf. below, Chapter 5.
44. E.L., p. 114 (95).
45. E., p. 51 (52) (tr. 45).
46. *Ibid.*, p. 46 (46) (tr. 40).
47. *Ibid.*, p. 112 (113) (tr. 102).
48. *Ibid.*, p. 113 (114) (tr. 102–3).
49. *Ibid.*, p. 109 (110) (tr. 99).
50. *Ibid.*, p. 28 (30) (tr. 23).
51. *Ibid.*, p. 16 (18) (tr. 12).
52. Cf. esp. "Proust" in L.M., pp. 151–69 (139–57) (tr. 109–24); "Marcel Proust et le mère profanée (*Critique*, no. 4, décembre 1947, pp. 601–11); "Digression sur la poésie et Marcel Proust" in Ex.I., pp. 156–75.
53. E., p. 106 (107) (tr. 96).
54. *Ibid.*, pp. 111–12 (112) (tr. 101).
55. Cf. Hegel, *Phenomenology of Mind*,

esp. "Preface" Parts I and II; "Perception" Part III; "Force and Understanding".

56. E.L., p. 22 (20–1).
57. A.E., p.19.
58. L.V., p. 142 (119)
59. T.I., p. 6 (tr. 36).
60. *Ibid*., p. 25 (tr. 54).
61. *Ibid*.
62. *Ibid*., p. 24 (tr. 54).
63. Cf. "Intériorité et économie" in T.I., esp. pp. 81–125 (tr. 109–51).
64. T.I., p. 102 (tr. 129).
65. Cf. *Ibid.*, pp. 115–16 (tr. 140–2).
66. *Ibid*., p. 115 (tr. 141).
67. *Ibid*., p. 65 (tr. 93).
68. *Ibid*., p. 66 (tr. 93).
69. A.E., p. 46.
70. T.I., p. 66 (tr. 93).
71. E.L., p. 229 (180).
72. *Ibid*., pp. 341–2 (263).
73. *Critique*, no. 20, janvier 1948, pp. 30–47. Expanded for P.F., pp. 324–45.
74. E.L., pp. 341–4 (263–5).
75. NRF, 82, octobre 1959; combined with "Comment découvrir l'obscur?" (NRF, 83, novembre 1959) as "Le grand refus" in E.I., pp. 46–69.
76. E.L., p. 285 (222).
77. *Ibid*., p. 342 (264).
78. *Ibid*.
79. *Ibid*., p. 24 (22).
80. *Ibid*.
81. *Ibid*., p. 343 (264–5).
82. *Ibid*.
83. *Ibid*.
84. *Ibid*., p. 341 (263).
85. E.I., p. 441n.
86. E.L., pp. 343–4 (265).

Chapter 2: From Decision to the Exigency
1. E., p. 50 (51) (tr. 44).
2. *Ibid.*, p. 63 (64) (tr. 57).
3. *Cahiers de la Pléiade*, XII, printemps-été 1951, pp. 115–125. Reprinted in E.L., pp. 345–59 (266–77).
4. E.L., p. 351 (270).
5. *Ibid.*, p. 349 (269).
6. E., p. 71 (71–2) (tr. 63–4).
7. *Ibid.*, p. 42 (43–4) (tr. 37).
8. *Ibid.*, p. 65 (66) (tr. 59).
9. *Ibid.*, p. 76 (77) (tr. 69).
10. L.M., p. 21 (20) (tr. 9)

11. *Ibid*.
12. E., p. 71 (72) (tr. 64).
13. "Le matérialisme dualiste de Georges Bataille", *Tel Quel* 25, printemps 1966 (pp. 41–54), p. 48.
14. "L'Expérience-limite", NRF 118, octobre 1962, pp. 577–592. Reprinted as "L'affirmation et la passion de la pensée négative" in E.I. (pp. 300–13). P. 305.
15. *Ibid.*, p. 304.
16. *Ibid.*, pp. 305-6.
17. E., p. 75 (76) (tr. 67–8).
18. Cf. E., pp. 45–6 (46–7) (tr. 40); S.N., p. 54.
19. Cf. E., p. 72 (72–3) (tr. 64).
20. *Ibid.*, p. 54 (55) (tr. 48).
21. P.M., p. 105 (118).
22. *Ibid.*, p. 106 (119).
23. *Ibid*.
24. E., p. 115 (116) (tr. 105).
25. *Ibid*.
26. *Ibid.*, p. 46 (46) (tr. 40).
27. E.I., p. 308n.
28. E., p. 95 (96) (tr. 86).
29. *Ibid.*, p. 24 (26–7) (tr. 19).
30. E.I., pp. 305–6.
31. Préface à la transgression", p. 753.
32. *Ibid.*, pp. 754–5.
33. *Ibid.*, p. 755.
34. *Ibid*.
35. *Ibid*.
36. E.I., pp. 311–12.
37. E., p. 41n. (42n.) (tr. 36n.)
38. P.F., pp. 305–345. The second half of this essay was first published under the same title in *Critique*, no. 20, janvier 1948, pp. 30–47.
39. P.F., p. 330.
40. *Ibid.*, p. 331.
41. *Ibid*.
42. *Ibid.*, p. 333.
43. *Ibid.*, p. 339.
44. *Ibid.*, p. 334n.
45. E.I., p. 310.
46. *Ibid.*, p. 225.
47. E.L., p. 126 (104–5).
48. *Ibid.*, p. 113 (94).
49. *Ibid.*, p. 114 (94–95).
50. *Ibid.*, p. 107 (89).
51. *Ibid.*, p. 140 (113).
52. *Ibid.*, p. 118 (98).
53. *Ibid.*, pp. 101–31 (85–107). Originally

published in *Critique*, no. 66, novembre 1952, pp. 915–33.
54. *Ibid.*, p. 128 (105).
55. *Ibid.*, p. 124 (102).
56. *Ibid.*, p. 128 (105).
57. *Ibid.*, p. 124 (102).
58. *Ibid.*, p. 118 (98).
59. *Ibid.*, p. 127 (104).
60. *Ibid.*, p. 129 (106).
61. *Ibid.*, p. 110 (92).
62. Ex.I., p. 174.
63. E.L., p. 131 (107).
64. *Ibid.*, p. 125 (103).
65. L.V., p. 132 (110).
66. *Ibid.*, p. 131 (109).
67. *Ibid.*
68. *Ibid.*, p. 118 (98–9).
69. *Ibid.*, p. 158 (132).
70. *Ibid.*, p. 119 (100).
71. E.L., p. 331 (255–6).
72. E.I., p. 275.
73. E.D.E., p. 196.
74. E.L., p. 23 (22), 331 (255–6).
75. L.V., p. 140 (117).
76. E.I., p. 45.
77. L.V., p. 292 (243).
78. *Ibid.*, p. 313 (260).
79. E.L., p. 22 (20).
80. Ibid., p. 300 (232).
81. *Ibid.*, p. 22 (20).
82. L.V., p. 140 (117).
83. *Ibid.*, p. 119 (100).
84. E.L., p. 331 (255–6).
85. *Ibid.*, p. 51 (45).
86. *Thomas l'obscur* (nouvelle version). Paris: Gallimard, 1950, p. 15. *Thomas the Obscure* (tr. R. Lamberton). New York: David Lewis, 1973, p. 13.
87. Cf. E.I., pp. 497, 563n.
88. E.L., p. 231 (182).
89. E., p. 112 (113) (tr. 102).
90. *Ibid.*, p. 16 (18) (tr. 12).
91. E.I., p. 304.
92. *Ibid.*, p. 67.
93. *Ibid.*
94. T.I., p. 282 (tr. 305).
95. *Ibid.*, p. 154 (tr. 179).
96. *Ibid.*, p. xv (tr. 27).
97. A.E., p. 161.
98. T.I., p. 282 (tr. 305).
99. A.E., p. 81.
100. *Ibid.*, p. 86.
101. *Ibid.*, p. 46.

102. E.D.E., p. 175.
103. *Ibid.*, p. 176.
104. T.I., p. 4 (tr. 34).
105. E.I., p. 76.
106. E.D.E., p. 193.
107. E.I., pp. 305–6.
108. H.H., p. 51.
109. E.L., p. 221 (174).
110. *Ibid.*, p. 222 (174).
111. *Ibid.*, p. 221 (174).
112. *Ibid.*, p. 225 (176–7).
113. P.F., p. 331.
114. *Ibid.*, p. 333.
115. *Ibid.*, pp. 333–4.
116. *Ibid.*, p. 333.
117. E.L., p. 223 (175).
118. *Ibid.*
119. *Ibid.*, p. 225 (177).
120. *Ibid.*, p. 223 (175).
121. *Ibid.*, p. 224 (176).
122. *Ibid.*
123. *Ibid.*
124. Cf. T.I., p. 13 (tr.43), E.D.E., p. 225.
125. E.L., pp. 14–15 (15).
126. *Ibid.*
127. *Ibid.*
128. *Ibid.*
129. *Ibid.*
130. *Ibid.*, p. 23 (21).
131. *Ibid.*, p. 22 (20–1).
132. *Ibid.*, p. 23 (21).
133. *Ibid.*
134. *Ibid.*, pp. 16–17 (16).
135. *Ibid.*, p. 284 (221).

Chapter 3: Literature and the Exigency

1. Cf. P.M. esp. Chapter 4; E.; L.M.
2. E., p. 140 (141) (tr. 127).
3. L.M., p. 236 (219) (tr. 170).
4. E., p. 206 (207) (tr. 186).
5. *Ibid.*, p. 97 (98) (tr. 87).
6. L.M., pp. 25–6 (24) (tr. 12).
7. *Ibid.*, p. 8 (7–8) (tr.n.pag.).
8. *Ibid.*, p. 53 (49) (tr. 32).
9. *Ibid.*, p. 50 (46) (tr. 30).
10. E., pp. 211–12 (213) (tr. 191).
11. L.M., pp. 98–9 (92) (tr. 66).
12. E.L., p. 300 (232).
13. Ex.I., p. 28.
14. *Ibid.*, p. 29.
15. In "Pour un Collège de sociologie", NRF no. 298, l^e juillet 1938, pp. 8–25. Reprinted in O.C. I, pp. 523–37.

16. O.C. I, p. 527.
17. L.M., p. 53 (49) (tr. 32).
18. E.L., pp. 14–20 (15–19).
19. *Ibid.*, p. 18 (17–18).
20. *Ibid.*, pp. 16–17 (16).
21. *Ibid.*, p. 15 (15).
22. Cf. E.L., pp. 31–2, 52, 245–6, 248 (29, 45, 192–4); L.V., pp. 318–21 (266–8).
23. E.L., p. 31 (29).
24. *Ibid.*, p. 32 (29).
25. *Ibid.*, p. 18 (18).
26. *Ibid.*, p. 19 (18).
27. NRF, 1, janvier 1953, pp. 75–90.
28. E.L., p. 266 (208).
29. *Ibid.*, pp. 270–1 (211).
30. *Ibid.*, p. 227 (179).
31. *Ibid.*
32. *Ibid.*, p. 118 (98).
33. *Ibid.*, pp. 227–8 (179).
34. *Ibid.*, pp. 229–30 (181).
35. *Ibid.*, p. 230 (181).
36. *Ibid.*, pp. 232–4 (183–4).
37. *Ibid.*, p. 233 (183).
38. *Ibid.*
39. *Ibid.*, p. 228 (180).
40. *Ibid.*, p. 230 (181).
41. *Ibid.*, p. 231 (182).
42. "La Parole soufflée", *Tel Quel* 20, hiver 1965. Reprinted with revisions in *L'Ecriture et la différence* (Paris: Seuil, 1967), pp. 253–292.
43. E.L., p. 31 (29).
44. *Ibid.*, p. 223 (175).
45. *Ibid.*, p. 243 (191).
46. *Ibid.*, p. 52 (46).
47. *Ibid.*, p. 243 (191).
48. Cf. A.E., pp. 227–9.
49. E.L., p. 45 (39).
50. Cf. L.V., p. 47 (40).
51. L.V., p. 50 (43).
52. E.L., p. 234 (184).
53. *Ibid.*, p. 241 (190).
54. *Ibid.*, p. 242 (190).
55. *Ibid.*, p. 225 (176–7).
56. Cf. L.V., pp. 365–7 (302–4).
57. E.L., p. 248 (195).
58. *Ibid.*
59. *Ibid.*
60. NRF, 19, juillet 1954, pp. 95–104. Reprinted as "La rencontre de l'imaginaire" in L.V., pp. 9–19 (9–17).
61. L.V., p. 10 (10).
62. E.L., p. 22 (20–1).
63. L.V., p. 131 (110), 348 (288).
64. *Ibid.*, p. 10 (10).
65. *Ibid.*, p. 11 (11).
66. *Ibid.*
67. E.D.E., p. 213.
68. L.V., p. 14 (13).
69. *Ibid.*
70. *Ibid.*, pp. 142–3 (119).
71. *Ibid.*, p. 14 (13).
72. *Ibid.*, p. 16 (14).
73. *Ibid.*, p. 319 (266).
74. *Ibid.*, p. 15 (13).
75. *Ibid.*
76. *Ibid.*
77. *Ibid.*
78. *Ibid.*, p. 13 (12).
79. *Ibid.*, p. 17 (15).
80. *Ibid.*
81. Cf. *Ibid.*, pp. 135–6 (112–13).
82. *Ibid.*, p. 16 (14–15).
83. *Ibid.*, p. 19 (17).
84. *Ibid.*, p. 16 (15).
85. *Ibid.*, p. 12 (11).
86. *Ibid.*, pp. 304-5 (253).
87. *Ibid.*, p. 18 (16).
88. E.L., p. 12 (13).
89. *Ibid.*, p. 13 (14).
90. *Ibid.*, p. 300 (232).
91. *Ibid.*, p. 12 (13).
92. *Ibid.*, p. 12n. (13n.).
93. *Ibid.*, p. 11 (12).
94. *Ibid.*, p. 13 (14).
95. *Ibid.*, p. 16 (16).
96. *Ibid.*, p. 14 (14–15).
97. L.V., p. 365 (302–4).
98. E.L., p. 242 (190).
99. Cf. *Ibid.*, p. 248 (196).
100. *Ibid.*, p. 16 (16).
101. *Ibid.*, p. 12 (13).
102. *Ibid.*, p. 17 (16–17).
103. *Ibid.*, p. 31 (29).
104. Cf. P.F., pp. 328, 343.
105. E.L., p. 51 (45).
106. *Ibid.*, p. 52 (45–6).
107. *Ibid.*
108. L.V., p. 336 (279).
109. E.L., p. 28n. (25n.).
110. *Ibid.*, p. 261 (205).
111. *Ibid.*, p. 256 (201).
112. *Ibid.*, p. 257 (202).
113. *Ibid.*, p. 256 (202).
114. *Ibid.*, p. 257 (202).

115. *Ibid.*, p. 272 (212).
116. *Ibid.*, p. 257 (202).
117. *Ibid.*
118. *Ibid.*, p. 259 (203–4).
119. *Ibid.*
120. *Ibid.*, p. 260 (204).
121. *Ibid.*, p. 261 (205).
122. *Ibid.*
123. *Ibid.*, p. 262 (205).
124. *Ibid.*, p. 261 (205).
125. *Ibid.*, p. 266 (207–8).
126. *Ibid.*
127. *Ibid.*
128. *Ibid.*
129. *Ibid.*, p. 267 (209).
130. *Ibid.*, p. 269 (210).
131. *Ibid.*
132. *Ibid.*
133. *Ibid.*, p. 270 (211).
134. *Ibid.*
135. *Ibid.*, p. 272 (212).
136. *Ibid.*
137. *Ibid.*, p. 276 (215).
138. *Ibid.*
139. *Ibid.*, p. 282 (220).
140. *Ibid.*, p. 287 (223).
141. *Ibid.*, p. 274 (214).
142. *Ibid.*, p. 275 (214).
143. *Ibid.*, p. 277 (216).
144. *Ibid.*, p. 310 (240).
145. *Ibid.*, pp. 270–1 (211).
146. L.V., p. 366 (303).
147. *Ibid.*, p. 361 (299).
148. *Ibid.*
149. *Ibid.*, p. 362 (300).
150. *Ibid.*, p. 367 (304).
151. E.L., p. 286 (223).
152. *Ibid.*, p. 284 (221).
153. *Ibid.*
154. *Ibid.*
155. *Ibid.*, p. 330 (255).
156. *Ibid.*
157. *Ibid.*, p. 286 (223).
158. *Ibid.*, p. 285 (222).

Chapter 4: Proximity and Philosophy

1. P.M., p. 65 (76); cf. also E., "Avant-propos", "Conclusion", "Etude VII".
2. E., pp. 36–40 (38–42) (tr. 31–5).
3. *Ibid*., p. 28 (30) (tr. 23).
4. *Ibid*., p. 43 (45) (tr. 38).
5. E.I., p. 312.
6. Ex.I., p. 101.
7. *Ibid*., p. 68.
8. *Ibid*., p. 67.
9. *Ibid*., p. 97.
10. *Ibid*., p. 137.
11. *Ibid*.
12. *Ibid*.
13. *Ibid*., pp. 24–5.
14. *Ibid*., p. 66.
15. *Ibid*.
16. *Ibid*., p. 69.
17. *Ibid*., p. 74.
18. *Ibid*., p. 67.
19. *Ibid*., p. 101.
20. *Ibid*., p. 105.
21. C., p. 279.
22. *Ibid*., pp. 374–5.
23. O.C. I, p. 359.
24. *The Structuralist Controversy* (eds. R. Macksey, E. Donato). Baltimore: Johns Hopkins, 1970, 1972, p. 272.
25. T.I., p. 271 (tr. 295).
26. *Ibid*., pp. 96–7 (tr. 124).
27. *Ibid.*, p. 97 (124).
28. *Ibid*.
29. A.E., p. 9.
30. Cf. below notes 47–51.
31. Cf. E.L., pp. 325–8 (251–4); T.I., pp. 170, 252 (tr. 196, 275); T.A., p. 165.
32. *Being and Time* (trs. J. Macquarrie, E. Robinson). New York: Harper & Row, 1962, p. 374.
33. Cf. *Identity and Difference* (tr. J. Stambaugh). New York: Harper & Row, 1969, pp. 71, 139–40; Fr. tr. in *Questions* I (tr. A. Préau). Paris: Gallimard, 1968, pp. 305–6.
34. *Ibid*., pp. 50, 117; Fr. tr. p. 285.
35. *Ibid*., pp. 48, 114; Fr. tr. p. 283.
36. Cf. *Ibid.,* pp. 62–3; Fr. tr. p. 297.
37. *Ibid*., pp. 66, 134; Fr. tr. p. 300.
38. Cf. *Ibid*., pp. 38, 69; Fr. tr. pp. 272, 297, 304.
39. Cf. *Ibid*., pp. 64, 65; Fr. tr. pp. 298–9.
40. *Was ist Metaphysik?* (Frankfurt A.M.: V. Klostermann, 1949), p. 45. Fr. tr. in *Questions* I (tr. H. Corbin, R. Munier), pp. 81–2.
41. *Ibid*; Fr. tr. pp. 82–3.
42. *Ibid*; Fr. tr. p. 83.
43. *Ibid*; Fr. tr. p. 82.
44. *Ibid*., p. 46; Fr. tr. p. 83.

45. *Identity and Difference*, p. 64; Fr. tr. p. 298.
46. *Ibid.*, pp. 72, 142; Fr. tr. pp. 307–8.
47. E.I., p. 441n.
48. Cf. E.L., pp. 325–8 (251–4).
49. Cf. E.I., pp. 32–4.
50. E.L., p. 205 (161).
51. Cf. esp. "La statue glorifie le marbre", E.L., pp. 300–1 (232–3); E.L. Chapter 7, "La littérature et l'expérience originelle", pp. 279–338 (217–60).
52. Cf. E.D.E., pp. 101–2, 169, 188; T.I., pp. 15–17 (tr. 45–7); A.E., pp. 20–3, 81–6; T.A., pp. 158–9; E.E., p. 74 (tr. 47–8); "L'Ontologie est-elle fondamentale?" in *Revue de Métaphysique et de Morale*, janvier-mars 1951, p. 91.
53. Cf. E.D.E., p. 89; E.E., p. 36 (tr. 27); T.I., pp. 15–17 (tr. 45–7). For a rapport of power and negation, cf. E.D.E., p. 89; E.E., p. 20 (tr. 19–20).
54. Cf. E.E., pp. 160–1 (tr. 94); A.E., pp. 11, 37–8; T.A., pp. 166–79.
55. Cf. E.D.E., pp. 186–8; T.I., p. 61 (tr. 89).
56. Cf. T.I., p. 39 (tr. 67); A.E., pp. 54–5, 83; T.A., pp. 127–8; E.E., p. 162 (tr. 94–5); "L'Ontologie est-elle fondamentale?", pp. 91–6.
57. Cf. E.D.E., pp. 170–1; T.I., pp. 15–17 (tr. 45–7); A.E., p. 22; "L'Ontologie est-elle fondamentale?", pp. 96–8.
58. Cf. E.D.E., pp. 170, 189; T.I., pp. 67 (tr. 94), 85 (tr. 112–13), 108 (tr. 134); T.A., p. 155; E.E., pp. 65 (tr. 43), 69 (tr. 45), 139 (tr. 81), 152 (tr. 89).
59. Cf. H.H., pp. 89–90, 96; E.D.E., p. 169; T.I., pp. 108 (tr. 134), 193 (tr. 218), 274–5 (tr. 298–9); A.E., p. 21; E.E., pp. 172–3 (tr. 100–1).
60. Cf. T.I., pp. 170 (tr. 196), 27 (tr. 56–7); T.A., p. 165.
61. Cf. T.I., p. 270 (tr. 294).
62. Cf. T.A., pp. 132–4; E.E., pp. 20 (tr. 19–20), 102 (tr. 62–3).
63. Cf. H.H., p. 74; E.D.E., pp. 200–1; A.E., p. 29.
64. Cf. T.I., p. 17 (tr. 46–7).
65. E.E., p. 19 (tr. 19).
66. T.I., p. 16 (tr. 46).
67. Cf. T.I., p. 13 (tr. 43); E.D.E., p. 225.
68. Hegel, *Phenomenology of the Spirit*. English. tr. by J.B. Baillie. New York: Harper & Row, 1967, p. 206. French tr. by Jean Hippolyte. Paris: Aubier Montaigne, 1939–41, p. 135.
69. *Ibid.*, Eng. tr. p. 206, Fr. tr. p. 135.
70. *Ibid.*, Eng. tr. p. 207, Fr. tr. p. 136.
71. *Ibid.*, Eng. tr. p. 208, Fr. tr. p. 136.
72. *Ibid.*, Eng., tr. p. 209, Fr. tr. p. 137.
73. *Ibid.*, Eng. tr. pp. 206–7, Fr. tr. p. 135.
74. *Deucalion* I, 1946. Revised in E.E., pp. 93–105 (tr. 57–64).
75. E.E., pp. 93–4 (tr. 57).
76. *Ibid.*, p. 96 (tr. 59).
77. *Ibid.*
78. *Ibid.*, p. 98 (tr. 60).
79. *Ibid.*, p. 100 (tr. 61).
80. *Ibid.*, p. 102 (tr. 62).
81. *Ibid.*, p. 96 (tr. 59).
82. *Ibid.*, p. 103n. (tr. 63n.).
83. P.F., p. 334.
84. *Ibid.*, p. 334n.
85. Ex.I., p. 120.
86. *Thomas l'obscur*, pp. 17–18 (tr. 14–15). Cited in Ex.I., pp. 119–20.
87. C., p. 261.
88. T.I., p. xv (tr. 27).
89. E.L., p. 300 (232).
90. E.I., p. 308.
91. "L'Ontologie est-elle fondamentale?", pp. 88–98.
92. Cf. *Ibid.*, p. 92: "Sauf pour autrui."
93. T.I., p. 32 (tr. 61).
94. E.I., p. 304.
95. T.I., pp. 32–3 (tr. 61).
96. E.I., p. 28.
97. Cf. T.I., p. 13 (tr. 43); E.D.E., p. 225.
98. T.I., p. 33 (tr. 61).
99. *Ibid.*, p. 229 (tr. 251).
100. *Ibid.*, p. 60 (tr. 88).
101. *Ibid.*, p. 171 (tr. 197).
102. Cf. *Ibid.*, p. 65–6 (tr. 93).
103. A.E., pp. 19–20.
104. T.I., p. 203 (tr. 227).
105. *Tijdschrift voor Filosofie*, no. 3, 1963; reprinted in E.D.E., pp. 187–202. Cf. esp. pp. 199–202.
106. T.I., p. 65 (tr. 92).
107. *Ibid.*, p. 73 (tr. 99).
108. *Ibid.*, p. 153 (tr. 178).
109. *Ibid.*, p. 179 (tr. 204).
110. *Ibid.*, p. 153 (tr. 178).
111. A.E., p. 208.
112. T.I., p. 32 (tr. 61).
113. *Ibid.*, p. 12 (tr. 42).

114. *Ibid.*, p. 13 (tr. 43).
115. C., pp. 374–5.

Chapter 5: The Exigency as Experience

1. Ex.I., p. 200.
2. C., p. 263.
3. E., p. 114 (115) (tr. 104).
4. *Ibid.*, p. 115 (116) (tr. 105).
5. *Ibid.*, p. 112 (113) (tr. 102).
6. *Ibid.*, p. 22 (24) (tr. 17–18).
7. S.N., p. 46.
8. *Ibid.*
9. H.H., p. 93.
10. A.E., p. 63.
11. H.H., p. 93.
12. *Ibid.*, p. 92.
13. *Ibid.*, p. 94.
14. *Ibid.*
15. *Ibid.*, p. 48.
16. T.I., p. 46 (tr. 74).
17. H.H., p. 48.
18. Cf. E.D.E, p. 173; T.I., p. 37 (tr. 66).
19. H.H., p. 50.
20. T.I., p. 47 (tr. 75).
21. A.E., p. 113.
22. E.D.E., p. 230.
23. A.E., p. 114.
24. E.D.E., p. 230.
25. *Ibid.*, p. 228.
26. A.E., p. 96n.
27. "L'Oeuvre d'Edmond Husserl" (*Revue Philosophique*, janvier-février 1940. Reprinted in E.D.E., pp. 7–52). E.D.E., p. 41.
28. "La Ruine de la représentation" (*Edmund Husserl*, Nijhoff, 1959. Reprinted in E.D.E., pp. 125–35.) E.D.E., p. 132.
29. *Ibid.*, p. 133.
30. *Ibid.*, p. 134.
31. "Réflexions sur la 'technique' phénoménologique" (*Husserl*. Cahiers de Royaumont, Minuit, 1959. Reprinted in E.D.E., pp. 111–123). E.D.E., p. 120.
32. *Ibid.*, pp. 120–1.
33. "La Ruine de la représentation", E.D.E., p. 131.
34. *Ibid.*, p. 135.
35. *Ibid.*
36. "Intentionalité et métaphysique" (*Revue Philosophique de la France et de l'étranger*, P.U.F., 1959. Reprinted in E.D.E., pp. 137–44.) E.D.E., p. 138.
37. *Philosophy and Phenomenological Research* (A. Scheutz, ed.), Vol. I. Buffalo, 1940, pp. 21–37, 217–26.
38. E.D.E., p. 143.
39. *Revue Internationale de Philosophie*, Bruxelles, 1965, fascicules 1–2. E.D.E., pp. 145–62.
40. E.D.E., p. 153.
41. *Ibid.*, p. 144n.
42. L.V., p. 14 (13).
43. E.D.E., p. 153.
44. *Ibid.*
45. *Ibid.*
46. *Ibid.*
47. *Ibid.*
48. *Ibid.*, p. 154.
49. Cf. T.I., pp. 26–7 (tr. 56).
50. A.E., p. 41.
51. *Ibid.*
52. *Ibid.*
53. E.D.E., p. 156.
54. *Ibid.*
55. Cf. A.E., p. 81.
56. *Ibid.*, p. 64.
57. E.D.E., p. 159.
58. *Ibid.*, pp. 217–36.
59. *Ibid.*, p. 225.
60. A.E., p. 46.
61. P.F., p. 330.
62. E.L., p. 14 (15).
63. *Ibid.*, p. 15 (15).
64. *Ibid.*, p. 16 (16).
65. *Ibid.*
66. *Ibid.*
67. *Ibid.*, p. 22 (20–1).
68. *Ibid.*, pp. 22–3 (21).
69. *Ibid.*, p. 23 (21).
70. *Ibid.*, p. 23 (21).
71. *Ibid.*
72. *Ibid.*, p. 23 (21).
73. P.F., p. 333.
74. E.L., p. 25 (23).
75. *Ibid.*, p. 357 (275).
76. *Ibid.*
77. *Ibid.*, p. 26 (23).
78. *Ibid.*, p. 23 (22).
79. *Ibid.*, p. 24 (22).
80. *Ibid.*, p. 23 (21).
81. *Ibid.*, p. 26 (23).
82. *Ibid.*, p. 25 (23).
83. *Ibid.*
84. *Ibid.*, p. 27 (24).
85. *Ibid.*, p. 347 (268).
86. *Ibid.*

87. *Ibid.*, p. 351 (270).
88. *Ibid.*, p. 346 (267).
89. *Ibid.*
90. *Ibid.*, p. 352 (271).
91, *Ibid., p. 25 (23).*
92. E.I., p. 42.
93. E.L., p. 27 (23).
94. E.I., p. 66.
95. "La marche à l'écrevisse", NRF, 91, juillet 1960, pp. 90–9. "Parler, ce n'est pas voir", E.I., pp. 35–45.
96. E.I., p. 41.
97. *Ibid.*, p. 312.
98. *Cahiers du Sud*, no. 260, octobre 1943, pp. 783–90; no. 261, nov. 1943, pp. 866–86; no. 262, déc. 1943, pp. 988–94. Reprinted in *Situations* I. Paris: Gallimard, 1947, pp. 143–88.
99. E., p. 109 (110) (tr. 99).
100. *Ibid.*, p. 44 (45) (tr. 39).
101. Ex.I., p. 60.
102. *Ibid.*, p. 106.
103. S.N., p. 63.
104. C., p. 390.
105. E., p. 106 (107) (tr. 96).
106. *Ibid.*, pp. 111–12 (112) (tr. 101).
107. *Ibid.*, p. 113 (113–14) (tr. 102–3).
108. Ex.I., p. 59.
109. "L'Expérience-limite". Cf. above, Chapter 2, n. 14.
110. E.I., p. 307.
111. *Ibid.*, pp. 307–8.
112. *Ibid.*, p. 310.
113. *Ibid.*,
114. *Ibid.*, p. 311.
115. *Ibid.*, p. 308n.
116. *Ibid.*, p. 312.
117. *Ibid.*, p. 313.
118. Ex.I., p. 76.
119. T.I., p. 220 (tr. 245).
120. A.E., p. 87.
121. Ex.I., p. 149.
122. *Ibid.*, p. 228.
123. NRF, 82, octobre 1959; reprinted with "Comment découvrir l'obscur (NRF, 83, nov. 1959) as "Le grand refus" in E.I., pp. 46–69.
124. E.I., p. 59.
125. *Ibid.,* p. 62.
126. *Ibid.*, p. 63.
127. *Ibid.*
128. *Ibid.*
129. *Ibid.*
130. *Ibid.*, pp. 63–4.
131. Cf. P.A., pp. 98–100.
132. E.I., p. 64.
133. *Ibid.*, p. 65.
134. *Ibid.*
135. *Ibid.*
136. *Ibid.*
137. *Ibid.*
138. *Ibid.*, pp. 65–6. Cf. E.L., p. 24 (22).
139. *Ibid.*, p. 66.
140. *Ibid.*
141. T.I., p. 215 (tr. 238).
142. *Ibid.*
143. E.I., p. 67.
144. *Ibid.*, p. 66.
145. T.I., pp. 215–16 (tr. 238–9).
146. Cf. E.L., p. 234 (184).
147. E.I., p. 63.
148. L.V., p. 17 (16).
149. A.E., p. 66.
150. L.V., p. 351 (291).
151. E.I., p. xix.
152. L.V., p. 313 (260).
153. *Ibid.*, p. 19 (17).
154. *Ibid.*, p. 17 (15).
155. *Ibid.*, p. 319 (266).
156. E.L., p. 22 (21).
157. P.A., p. 100.
158. E.I., p. 66.
159. *Ibid.*

Chapter 6: Alterity in the General Economy: Parole

1. C., p. 263.
2. P.M., p. 75 (87).
3. Ex.I., p. 149.
4. *Critique*, 195–6, août-sept. 1963, pp. 734–41. Reprinted as Part 2 of "L'Expérience-limite" in E.I., pp. 313–22.
5. Cf. the essays under these titles: E.I., pp. 94–112.
6. E.I., p. 315.
7. *Ibid.*, pp. 315, 317, 320.
8. *Ibid.*, p. 317.
9. *Ibid.*
10. *Ibid.*, p. 318.
11. *Ibid.*, pp. 318, 319, 320.
12. *Ibid.*, pp. 318, 319, 321.
13. *Ibid.*, pp. 317–21.
14. *Ibid.*, p. 319.
15. *Ibid.*, p. 322.

16. *Ibid.*, p. 319.
17. *Ibid.*, p. 316.
18. *Ibid.*
19. *Ibid.*, pp. 321–2.
20. E.L., p. 266 (208).
21. E.I., p. 320.
22. *Ibid.*
23. *Ibid.*
24. *Ibid.*, pp. 320–1.
25. Cf. E.I., pp. 47–50, 108–11, 228–32, 237–39, 252–4, 500–1, 564–5 and *passim.*
26. First published as "La pensée et sa forme" (NRF, 123, mars 1963, pp. 492–6; NRF, 124, avril 1963, pp. 684–8). E.I., pp. 1–11.
27. E.I., p. 9.
28. NRF, 137, mai 1964, pp. 869–81. E.I., pp. 106–12.
29. E.I., p. 109.
30. *Ibid.*
31. E.I., pp. 94–105.
32. *Ibid.*, p. 103.
33. *Ibid.*
34. *Ibid.*, p. 89.
35. *Ibid.*, p. 98.
36. *Ibid.*, pp. 100–1.
37. *Ibid.*, p. 591.
38. *Ibid.*, p. 105.
39. *Ibid.*
40. NRF, 108, déc. 1961, pp. 1081–95. E.I., pp. 70–83.
41. E.I., p. 80.
42. *Ibid.*, p. 80n.
43. *Ibid.*, p. 81.
44. *Ibid.*
45. NRF, 110, février 1962, pp. 290–8. E.I., pp. 84–93.
46. E.I., pp. 89–90.
47. E.D.E., p. 225n.
48. T.I., p. 13 (tr. 43).
49. *Ibid.*, p. 154 (tr. 179).
50. A.E., p. 136.
51. *Ibid.*, p. 127.
52. *Ibid.*, p. 114.
53. *Ibid.*
54. *Ibid.*, p. 115.n.
55. E.D.E., p. 202.
56. *Ibid.*, p. 196.
57. *Ibid.*, p. 172.
58. T.I., p. xv (tr. 27).
59. E.D.E., p. 174.
60. *Ibid.*

61. T.I., p. 33 (tr. 62).
62. *Ibid.*
63. A.E., p. 116.
64. *Ibid.*, p. 110.
65. E.D.E., p. 233.
66. A.E., pp. 31–2.
67. *Ibid.*, p. 103.
68. *Ibid.*, p. 105.
69. *Ibid.*, p. 143.
70. *Ibid.*, p. 69.
71. *Ibid.*, p. 208.
72. T.I., p. 10 (tr. 40).
73. *Ibid.*, p. 194 (tr. 219).
74. *Ibid.*, p. 168 (tr. 194).
75. *Ibid.*, p. 170 (tr. 196).
76. E.D.E., p. 194.
77. A.E., p. 46.
78. *Ibid.*, p. 87.
79. E.D.E., p. 234.
80. T.I., p. 156 (tr. 181).
81. *Ibid.*

Chapter 7: Same and Other

1. *De la grammatologie* (Paris: Minuit, 1967), pp. 68–70, 88–99, 102–3.
2. *Ibid.*, p. 95.
3. *Ibid.*, p. 97.
4. *Ibid.*, p. 99.
5. *Ibid.*, pp. 99–101.
6. *Différence et répétition* (Paris: P.U.F., 1968), p. 306.
7. *Ibid.*, p. 317.
8. Cf. *Ibid.*, esp. pp. 116–19, 140–5, 195–8, 299–312, 330–3.
9. *Ibid.*, p. 297.
10. *Ibid.*, p. 292.
11. *Ibid.*, p. 293.
12. *Ibid.*, p. 342.
13. *Ibid.*, p. 301.
14. *Ibid.*, p. 96.
15. *Ibid.*
16. *Ibid.*, p. 97.
17. *Ibid.*, p. 99.
18. *Ibid.*, p. 107.
19. *Ibid.*, p. 101.
20. *Ibid.*, p. 97.
21. Cf. *Ibid.*, pp. 108–14.
22. Cf. *Ibid.*, pp. 118–23.
23. Cf. *Ibid.*, p. 113.
24. Cf. *Ibid.*, pp. 120–1.
25. *Ibid.*, p. 125.
26. *Ibid.*

354

27. Cf. *Ibid.*, p. 103.
28. Cf. *Ibid.*, pp. 71–82.
29. Cf. *Ibid.*, pp. 78–9.
30. Cf. *Ibid.*, pp. 257–9.
31. *Ibid.*, p. 29.
32. *Ibid.*, p. 103.
33. *Ibid.*, p. 125.
34. *Ibid.*, p. 126.
35. A.E., p. 105.
36. T.I., p. 31 (tr. 60).
37. *Ibid.*, p. 33 (tr. 62).
38. *Ibid.*, p. 76 (tr. 104).
39. *Ibid.*, p. 34 (tr. 62).
40. *Ibid*.
41. *Ibid.*, p. 52 (tr. 79).
42. A.E., p. 17.
43. T.I., p. 9 (tr. 39).
44. *Ibid.*, p. 38 (tr. 66).
45. *Ibid*.
46. *Ibid.*, p. 22 (tr. 51).
47. *Ibid.*, p. 52 (tr. 80).
48. *Ibid.*, p. 156 (tr. 180).
49. *Ibid.*, p. 195 (tr. 220).
50. *Ibid.*, p. 271 (tr. 295).
51. *Ibid*.
52. A.E., p. 61.
53. *Ibid.*, p. 105.
54. Cf. *Ibid.*, pp. 176–7.
55. E.D.E., pp. 225, 227–8.
56. *Ibid.*, p. 120–1.
57. T.I., p. 175 (tr. 201).
58. A.E., p. 185.
59. *Ibid.*, p. 208.
60. *Ibid.*, p. 137.
61. *Ibid.*, p. 138.
62. *Ibid.*, p. 151.
63. *Ibid.*, 175.
64. Cf. E.D.E., p. 195.
65. Cf. T.I., p. 146 (tr. 172).
66. A.E., p. 68.
67. Cf. *Différence et répétition*, "Avant-propos", p. 2.
68. A.E., pp. 9–10.
69. *Ibid.*, p. 65.
70. *Ibid.*, p. 161.
71. Cf. *Ibid.*, pp. 139, 145, 147; T.I., p. 232 (tr. 254).
72. A.E., p. 139.
73. Cf. *Ibid.*, pp. 10–11.
74. *Ibid.*, p. 47.
75. *Ibid.*, p. 11.
76. *Ibid.*, p. 136.
77. *Ibid.*, p. 69.

78. H.H., p. 75.
79. E.D.E., p. 201.
80. *Ibid.*, p. 199.
81. *Ibid.*, p. 200.
82. A.E., p. 115n.
83. *Ibid.*, p. 103. Cf. E.D.E., pp. 230–1.
84. E.D.E., p. 199.
85. *Ibid.*, p. 200.
86. *Ibid.*, p. 229.
87. *Ibid.*, p. 195.
88. *Ibid.*, p. 201.
89. *Ibid.*, p. 199.
90. *Ibid.*, p. 215.
91. T.I., p. 4 (tr. 34).
92. *Ibid.*, p. 47 (tr. 75).
93. A.E., p. 113.
94. E.D.E., p. 177.
95. *Ibid.*, p. 198.
96. *Ibid.*, p. 229.
97. T.I., p. 173 (tr. 199).
98. *Ibid.*, p. 187 (tr. 212).
99. A.E., p. 111.
100. Cf. T.I., p. 29 (tr. 58); E.L., p. 23 (22).
101. E.D.E., p. 213.
102. *Différence et répétition*, p. 111.
103. E.D.E., p. 215.
104. *Ibid.*, pp. 176–7.
105. *Ibid.*, p. 176.
106. *Ibid.*, p. 197.
107. H.H., p. 94.
108. *Ibid.*, p. 75.
109. Cf. T.I., p. 196 (tr. 221).
110. E.D.E., p. 195.
111. T.I., p. 59 (tr. 86).
112. *Ibid.*, p. 12 (tr. 41–2).
113. *Ibid.*, p. 52 (tr. 79).
114. E.D.E., p. 230.
115. A.E., p. 161.
116. T.I., p. 222 (tr. 244–5).
117. A.E., p. 65.
118. T.I., p. 158 (tr. 183).
119. Ex.I., p. 149.
120. E.D.E., p. 193.
121. *Ibid.*, p. 196.
122. A.E., p. 182.
123. *Ibid.*, pp. 142, 180.
124. *Ibid.*, p. 143.
125. *Ibid*.
126. *Ibid.*, p. 187.
127. *Ibid.*, p. 160.
128. *Ibid.*, p. 189.
129. *Ibid.*, p. 17.
130. *Ibid.*, p. 63.

131. *Ibid.*, p. 73.
132. E.D.E., p. 196.
133. T.I., p. 194 (tr. 218–19).
134. Cf. L.M., p. 22 (21) (tr 10).
135. E.L., pp. 231 (182), 337 (260).

136. "Le regard du poète", *Monde nouveau*, no. 98, 1956. Reprinted in *Sur Maurice Blanchot* (Montpellier: Fata Morgana, 1975), pp. 7–26. Cf. esp. pp. 20–4.
137. E.L., p. 337 (260).